Gathering to His Name

The Story of Open Brethren in Britain and Ireland

Gathering to His Name

The Story of Open Brethren in Britain and Ireland

Tim Grass

Foreword by David Bebbington

First published 2006 by Paternoster

Paternoster is an imprint of Authentic Media
9 Holdom Avenue, Bletchley, Milton Keynes, MK1 1QR, UK
and
PO Box 1047, Waynesboro, GA 30830–2047, USA

12 11 10 09 08 07 06   7 6 5 4 3 2 1

Typeset by A.R. Cross
Printed and bound in Great Britain
for Paternoster
by Bell & Bain Ltd, Glasgow

Contents

Part 1: 1825–1849: A United Testimony

Part 2: 1850–1914: A Maturing Movement

Chapter 6
Evangelism and Expansion

Chapter 7
The Development of Open Brethren Identity

16.2.3 The Impact on Assemblies 335
16.2.4 Planning and Questioning 340

Chapter 17
Overseas Mission and Home Identity **342**
17.1 The Growth of the Work 342
17.2 Maintaining Interest 343
17.3 Missionary Study Classes 344
17.4 The Fear of Centralisation 345
17.5 Involvement with Other Missions 349

Part 4: 1945 Onwards: Change—and Decay?

Chapter 18
Responding to Social Change **353**
18.1 The Fast-changing Social Context 353
18.2 The Growth of Social Concern and Involvement among
Open Brethren 353
18.3 The Burning Issues 356
18.3.1 Politics and Trades Unions 356
18.3.2 Care of the Needy 359
18.3.3 Fiction and Football 361

Chapter 19
Open Brethren and the Religious World **364**
19.1 Open Brethren Involvement in Interdenominational
Evangelicalism 364
19.1.1 The Impact of Billy Graham 364
19.1.2 Para-church Agencies 367
19.1.3 Biblical Scholarship 370
19.2 The Impact of Wider Evangelicalism on Open Brethren 376
19.2.1 The Reformed Resurgence of the 1950s and 1960s 376
19.2.2 Longing for Revival 381
19.2.3 The Charismatic and Restoration Movements 385
19.2.4 Changing Thinking on Ecumenism 394

Chapter 20
Re-inventing Open Brethren Identity **399**
20.1 Open Brethren Agencies 399
20.1.1 Publishers and Periodicals 399
20.1.2 Conferences 406
20.2 The Various Strands of Contemporary Open Brethren 414
20.2.1 Increasing Polarisation 414
20.2.2 Conservatives 418
20.2.3 Progressives 420
20.2.4 What's in a Name? 425
20.3 The Open Brethren Identity Crisis 431
20.4 Exclusive Brethren and the Churches of God since 1914 434
20.4.1 Exclusive Developments 434
20.4.2 The Churches of God 438

Chapter 21

Chapter 22

Chapter 23

Part 5: Conclusion

Chapter 24

Appendix 1

Appendix 2

Appendix 3

List of Illustrations

List of Tables

Foreword

On 30 March 1851, the only occasion on which there was an official census of Christian worshippers in Britain, it was discovered that at Teignmouth, a fishing village on the south Devon coast, there was a chapel with some 400 seats where fifty-five people attended in the morning, fifty in the afternoon and forty in the evening. In addition there were twenty-five at the afternoon Sunday school. The census taker recorded, probably with some bemusement, the refusal of the members of the congregation to adopt a distinctive label. 'They are often called Plymouth Brethren by others', he explained, 'but they do not themselves use this name, but object to it. They use such names as are given in the New Testament to all believers, from whom they do not desire to be distinguished by denominational names.'[1] This was a congregation, or (as the members usually preferred to call it) 'assembly', of the body whose history is recounted in this volume. Its members were frequently described as 'Plymouth Brethren' by outsiders because they had some of their roots in the seaport just along the coast to the west of Teignmouth, but on principle they repudiated being associated with any particular place or being given any non-biblical designation whatsoever. They might, if pressed, be willing to be called simply 'Brethren', but they were essentially people who met in the name of Jesus Christ alone. They had gathered, as they liked to put it, to the name of the Lord.

The movement, beginning around 1830, aspired to recreate the pattern and atmosphere of the first Christian churches as depicted in the New Testament. In reproducing the pattern, the Brethren showed similarities to older Christian bodies that had separated from the Church of England because they wished to imitate biblical precedent. Like the Congregationalists, the members agreed that each local congregation was autonomous; and like the Baptists, they adopted the practice of believer's baptism. It is important, however, that the Brethren were eager to reproduce the atmosphere of primitive Christianity as well as the pattern. Although they wished to follow the example and instructions of the apostles, they usually avoided, at least in the early days, an unduly legalistic temper because they equally wanted to emulate the qualities of Christian fellowship described in the pages of the Bible. Above all, they wanted to generate a spiritual tone of worship that would, if possible, anticipate the delights of heaven. Accordingly they assembled in their weekly morning meeting to break bread, so remembering the sacrificial death of Christ on the cross that had purchased their salvation. Any brother (though not any sister) was permitted to contribute a prayer, a hymn or a word of exhortation, for the distinction between clergy and laity was abolished. These practices—weekly observance of the Lord's Supper and full male participation in leading worship—set them apart from earlier Nonconformists.

In addition the Brethren became known for other characteristics. They usually espoused a particular doctrine of the last things. They were almost always premillennialists, believing that the second coming of Jesus was imminent, and were often dispensationalists, holding the version of premillennial belief expounded by J.N. Darby. This teaching gave them a strong tendency to withdraw from aspects of contemporary life that they expected soon to pass away, whether worldly entertainments or political parties. Brethren were also commonly champions of the faith principle, the conviction that Christian mission should be conducted in complete reliance on the

---

[1] Michael J.L. Wickes (ed.), *Devon in the Religious Census of 1851: A Transcript of the Devon section of the 1851 Church Census* ([Appledore]: the author, 1990), 46.

support of the Almighty. George Müller ran an immense orphanage at Bristol on these lines and Hudson Taylor founded the China Inland Mission on the same basis. Overseas missionary work, in fact, became a field in which Brethren were disproportionately prominent. Their zeal for the spread of the gospel made them leading figures in interdenominational evangelistic work in the twentieth century. Since they had no denominational structures to support, they were free to share in activities that straddled confessional boundaries; and since they had no ministers to pay, they had the resources to give to joint efforts. Brethren were particularly significant participants in the conservative Evangelical coalition that stiffened the Christian presence in twentieth-century Britain.

Tim Grass has compiled the first complete history of the Brethren in Britain and Ireland. The Irish dimension is crucial, since the origins of the movement lay partly in Dublin Evangelicalism, and Scotland, as the book shows, generated some of its most virile expressions. England and Wales, however, were together home to most of the assemblies, though their coverage was very uneven, with Devon long retaining the highest density. The book is a study of the Open Brethren, the most numerous branch of the movement, though it also pays attention to the Exclusives, the followers of Darby in a split of 1848, many of whom maintained links with the Open section down the decades. In terms of chronology, this account covers the whole span from the beginnings of the movement down to the twenty-first century; in terms of content, it examines doctrinal convictions as well as social trends, and individuals as well as organisations. It relates the development of the Brethren to changes in the broader environment, both religious and secular. This comprehensive and carefully structured analysis is as sympathetic as it is scholarly. It sets out clearly the parameters of a movement in modern Britain whose significance always exceeded its numbers.

David Bebbington
2005

Acknowledgements

It is only right that I should acknowledge with gratitude my debt to Harold Rowdon and Roy Coad. It will be evident that at many points I have leaned on their work, especially in surveying the first half-century of Brethren history, and the present work is not intended to replace theirs. Both have been most helpful, and I have drawn considerably on their published and unpublished research. Jeremy Mudditt of Paternoster first suggested that I undertake this project, and I am grateful for his constant encouragement and practical advice. The Laing Trust made research possible by their generous funding; assistance with the cost of publication was provided by the Drummond Trust. Among those who have read all or part of the manuscript are Anthony R. Cross, Rob Dann, Neil Dickson, Roy Hill, Harold Rowdon, Timothy Stunt, Neil Summerton, and members of the Taylor Brethren. Their comments have improved the book significantly.

Among others who have assisted, particular thanks are due to the custodians of two archives: Edwin Cross of Chapter Two, and David Brady and Graham Johnson of the Christian Brethren Archive; their hospitality, practical help, and constant willingness to answer my queries have all made the writing process more straightforward than it might otherwise have been. I am also grateful for the ready assistance provided by the staff at Counties and Echoes of Service. Thanks are also due to those with whom I have corresponded, some of them repeatedly, or who have loaned or donated material. I am sorry that it has not been possible to mention them all in the bibliography, but their interest has been a real encouragement in a lonely task.

Approaching this task as an outsider, I have sought to build relationships with Brethren of various groups, and to attend their meetings. The welcome I have received has been much appreciated. A number of individuals have also shared their memories and perceptions with me in conversation; as some wished to remain anonymous, I have felt it better not to disclose the identities of any.

I am grateful to the following for permission to quote from copyright material: the Bible and Gospel Trust, Hounslow; the Christian Brethren Archive; Elmfield Church, North Harrow; Partnership UK; and *Precious Seed* magazine. Illustrations have been reproduced with permission from the following: Chapter Two (pp. 30, 64, 127, 173, 203, 213 and 265), the Christian Brethren Archive (pp. 310 and 464 [2nd]), Counties (pp. 139, 145 and 403), Echoes of Service (pp. 157, 183, 249, 263, 269, 271 and 487), Editions Bibles et Littérature Chrétienne (p. 70), the Evangelical Library (pp. 138 and 248), the George Müller Foundation (pp. 47 and 245), John Ritchie Ltd (pp. 372, 380 and 403 [2nd]), the London School of Theology (p. 301), Professor John Rendle Short (p. 257), Scripture Union (p. 361), and Wymondham Town Archive (p. 55). The photographs on pp. 458, 464 (1st) and 527 (2nd) were taken by the late A.W. Bain of Douglas, Lanarkshire, and are reproduced by permission of his daughter, Ruth McKee. The graph on p. 491 was prepared by Dr Neil Summerton. My thanks to them all for permission to use these items. Every attempt has been made to trace copyright holders of written and photographic material; omissions will gladly be rectified in subsequent printings.

My greatest debt is to my wife, Ann, who has made it possible for me to spend so much time on this project, and my parents John and Jean, who have shared my interest. To them this work is dedicated.

Abbreviations

A	*Aware*
AC	'Answers to Correspondents'
AQ	'Answers to Questions'
ASQ	'Answers to Special Questions'
AT	*Assembly Testimony*
BAHNR	*Brethren Archivists and Historians' Network Review*
BCC	British Council of Churches
BDCM	Gerald H. Anderson (ed.), *Biographical Dictionary of Christian Missions*
BDE	Timothy Larsen (ed.), *Biographical Dictionary of Evangelicals*
BDEB	Donald M. Lewis (ed.), *Blackwell's Dictionary of Evangelical Biography*
BGT	Bible and Gospel Trust, Hounslow
BM	*The Believer's Magazine*
BP	*The Believer's Pathway*
BQ	*Baptist Quarterly*
BQB	'Believer's Question Box'
BT	*The Bible Treasury*
CBA	Christian Brethren Archive, John Rylands University Library, Manchester
CBJI	*The Christian Brethren's Journal and Investigator*
CBR	*Christian Brethren Review*
CBRF	Christian Brethren Research Fellowship
CE	*Christian Examiner*
CH	*Church History*
CIM	China Inland Mission
CO	*Christian Observer*
CW	*The Collected Writings of J.N. Darby*
CWit	*Christian Witness*
CWo	*Christian Worker*
DBB	David J. Jeremy (ed.), *Dictionary of Business Biography*
DNB	Sir Leslie Stephen and Sir Sidney Lee (eds.), *Dictionary of National Biography*
DSCHT	Nigel M. de S. Cameron (ed.), *Dictionary of Scottish Church History and Theology*
EA	Evangelical Alliance
EH	*Eleventh Hour*
EOS	*Echoes of Service*
EQ	*Evangelical Quarterly*
EQR	*Echoes Quarterly Review*
ER	*The Eclectic Review*
FEC	'From the Editorial Chair'
GG	*Gospel Graphic*
GL	*Golden Lamp*
GS	*The Gospel Standard*
H	*The Harvester*

I	*The Inquirer*
IML	'Intelligence from Many Lands'
IPP	*International Partnership Perspectives*
JCBRF	*Journal of the Christian Brethren Research Fellowship*
JEH	*Journal of Ecclesiastical History*
LF	'Look on the Fields'
LMA	London Metropolitan Archive
LOH	*Links of Help*
ME	*Missionary Echo*
MR	*Missionary Reporter*
MS	manuscript
NA	*Northern Assemblies* (*The Assemblies* from March 1874)
n.d.	no date
NEI	*Northern Evangelistic Intelligencer*
NI	*Northern Evangelist*
n.p.	no publisher given
n.pl.	no place (of publication) given
n.s.	new series
NTr	*Needed Truth*
NW	*The Northern Witness*
ODNB	H.C.G. Matthew and Brian Harrison (eds.), *Oxford Dictionary of National Biography*
OM	Operation Mobilisation
PN	*Partnership Newsletter*
PP	*Partnership Perspectives*
PRO	Public Record Office, Kew
PS	*Precious Seed*
QA	'Question(s) and Answer(s)'
QB	'Question Box'
QJP	*Quarterly Journal of Prophecy*
SKI	Scriptural Knowledge Institution
TLWW	'(Tidings from some of) the Lord's Work and Workers'
VE	*Vox Evangelica*
W	*The Witness*
WCC	World Council of Churches
WML	'Witnessing in Many Lands'
WW	'Witness Watchtower', later known as 'The Watchtower'
YBQB	'Young Believer's Question Box'

Quotations are given as they appeared in the original: punctuation (including italics, underlining and abbreviations) is that of the original writers.

NB: unless otherwise identified, authors of 'AC', 'ASQ', 'BQB', 'FEC', 'IML', 'LF', QA', 'QB', 'TLWW', 'WML', 'WW', and 'YBQB' were the editors of the magazines in which these appeared.

CHAPTER 1

Introduction

Some years ago, when as a pastor I was thinking about undertaking postgraduate research, I contacted Dr Harold Rowdon to ask his advice. His response was that I would have to consider whether it could be justified in strategic terms as something which would contribute to the extension of God's kingdom. I did undertake the research, and the Brethren were one of the groups I studied. But in what sense could such study be described as strategic? After all, one of the most famous Brethren, Anthony Norris Groves, asserted that church history 'is to prove what *was* done, not what *ought* to be done'.[1] As a result, some Brethren have seen little point in studying the history of their movement. But such an attitude is, I believe, short-sighted. Many years ago, the independently-minded Open brother G.H. Lang observed that:

> The present generation troubles little about past history; partly because the Satanic rush and strain of modern life leave little leisure, energy or taste for serious reading; partly from the self-sufficiency, natural to youth, which breeds independence of mind and confidence that the present can be well ordered by ourselves; partly, perhaps, by a perverse use of the truth that the Word of God is enough, and there is little need to learn from our predecessors. By such neglect of the danger boards of history we may easily miss the road at the same point as our fathers, and fall into the same bog.[2]

Lang could never be described as traditionalist in his thinking, which makes his affirmation of the value of historical awareness all the more significant. It corroborates the assertion of the Brethren movement's first serious historian, William Blair Neatby, that in this story 'there are few of the tendencies of universal church history that have not been illustrated, and not many of its movements that have not been re-enacted in little'. Neatby put this down to the attempt of Brethren to start from Scripture alone in their understanding of church life, and to set aside the lessons to be learned from church history or Christian experience through the centuries.[3] I share the belief in the value and necessity of an understanding of history for an understanding of our own position in church life today. I am also convinced that the wider church has much to learn from this movement.

I hope that the book will also prove a serviceable introduction for historians. The impossibility of contacting every assembly in Britain and Ireland to gain access to their records means that I have relied heavily on the evidence provided by periodicals and other material accessible in archives and libraries, and in these respects some parts of the British Isles are much better covered than others. Nevertheless, I believe that this work does break fresh ground, not least in its use of evidence drawn from databases in which I

---

[1] A.N. Groves, *On the Liberty of Ministry in the Church of Christ* (Sidmouth: J. Harvey, 1835), 3.

[2] G.H. Lang, *The Local Assembly: Some Essential Differences between Open and Exclusive Brethren considered Scripturally and Historically* (Wimborne: the author, 1955[5]), 7.

[3] William Blair Neatby, *A History of the Plymouth Brethren* (London: Hodder & Stoughton, 1901), 3.

have listed every known assembly in England, Ireland and Wales.[4] In addition, the British movement's twentieth-century history has not hitherto been presented as a whole. In attempting this, I have been indebted to the work of other scholars. Research into aspects of Brethren history and practice has become something of a growth industry during the last forty years, and this work presents some of the fruits of that research to a wider audience. In the final chapter, I offer some suggestions for further research, which could be followed up by those who wish to take their interest further.

Although I have tried to be as objective as possible, I should state briefly my own perspective, since that has affected my interpretation of events, and indeed the selection of what to write about. I am an Evangelical believer, and for most of my Christian life I have attended Baptist churches, although I am now an Anglican. My father was converted to Christ during the 1950s through the outreach of an Essex Open Brethren assembly to which my mother at that time belonged, and several members of my mother's family were in fellowship with Open Brethren for a period.

My personal perspective also includes a particular understanding of how divine activity in history is related to human. These two aspects cannot be separated, but neither should they be confused. It used to be commonplace to speak of the Brethren movement primarily as a work of the Holy Spirit in which, independently of one another, groups of believers in various parts of the country began to meet along 'Brethren' lines. For example, the Carlisle Brethren historian David Beattie (1881-1964) assured his readers that 'the Lord's hand was independently at work designing to revive a testimony here, and another there, in the midst of His own children'.[5] Such an approach has a long history within the movement,[6] but it tends to minimise the importance of the human agents and socio-cultural factors in the story (with the result that histories written from this perspective are often frustratingly thin in detail). It also flattens out the distinctive aspects of the development of the work in different parts of the country, and makes analysis more difficult. Whilst more recent historians have not generally adopted this approach, it has persisted at a popular level. By contrast, non-Brethren writers have tended to portray the movement purely in human terms, as an example of nineteenth-century sectarian religion, an approach which reduces the Brethren to an intriguing bypath in religious history. This book attempts to strike a balance between the two extremes. As a historian, I wish to do justice to the contexts in which, and the agents through whom, the movement arose, developed, and (to some extent) declined; as a believer, I wish to acknowledge that the Spirit was at work within the movement and that there are things which today's church can learn from this story. But to learn those lessons, we must avoid reading back our own convictions and attitudes into earlier generations: Brethren must be allowed to speak for themselves before they can be interpreted.

---

[4] For Scotland, I have drawn on Neil Dickson, *Brethren in Scotland 1838-2000: A Social Study of an Evangelical Movement* (Carlisle: Paternoster, 2002), Appendix 3, which lists all known Scottish assemblies.

[5] David J. Beattie, *Brethren: The Story of a Great Recovery* (Kilmarnock: John Ritchie, 1940), 4-5. Dickson comments that Beattie's book was 'in effect, an exposition of the autonomy of Brethren assemblies' (*Brethren in Scotland*, 11).

[6] Cf. the recollections of several pioneers in Anon., *Interesting Reminiscences of the Early History of "Brethren:" with Letter from J.G. Bellett to J.N. Darby* (Weston-super-Mare and London: Walter Scott and Alfred Holness, [c.1884]), 10, 11-12, 18.

At this point, I want to raise the question, who are the Brethren? This has been answered in print many times, especially by writers wishing to commend to Christians in various denominations the distinctive approach to church life adopted by Brethren. It is the more difficult to answer because one of the distinguishing characteristics of Brethren is their dislike of distinctive labels; most Brethren accept the label only as a convenient form of shorthand, and as implying nothing about themselves which is not true of all believers. Unease at being labelled reflects the concern of many to stress that they do not regard Brethren as one denomination among many. Writers of past generations would occasionally register a protest against the use of such terms as 'our assemblies' or 'Brethren' in a manner which implied the existence of a distinct and more or less exclusive circle of fellowship. In the light of the insistence of many Open writers that Brethren are not a denomination, how can their history be written without implying that this claim is untrue? My response is that, whilst Brethren have lacked certain denominational attributes such as a central headquarters and a distinctive confession of faith, they can be regarded as a denomination in certain other ways: they are a body of local congregations which have tended to associate with one another, to be marked by certain distinctive beliefs and practices, to read the output of certain publishers, and to express their missionary obligation through certain agencies.

Very briefly, I have taken the designation 'Brethren' as referring to an Evangelical movement of spiritual renewal which began in Dublin and the South-West of England around 1827-31 (hence the term 'Plymouth Brethren'), and which had as one of its main concerns the realisation of a fellowship in which all true believers in Christ might find a welcome. The pioneers sought to be open to the illumination of the Holy Spirit concerning the teaching of Scripture, placing no credal or tradition-based restrictions upon where obedience to God might lead. The movement divided during the late 1840s, giving rise to two streams known since as 'Open' and 'Exclusive' Brethren. In view of the frequent misunderstanding of these terms, it is well to state here that the difference relates to the reception of believers from assemblies or other congregations where false teaching was believed to be condoned. Open Brethren usually contended for the right to receive any believer who was sound in faith and godly in life, but Exclusive Brethren insisted upon the necessity of examining such, especially if they came from congregations (such as Brethren assemblies) which should have a greater degree of understanding of the truth, to see whether they were linked in fellowship with teachers of erroneous doctrine. Open Brethren have sometimes been described as 'Independent' Brethren because they usually insisted upon the direct responsibility to Christ of each local assembly. By contrast, Exclusive Brethren have sometimes been described as 'Connexional' Brethren because of their belief that it should be possible to recognise those assemblies with which full intercommunion was possible, and that such assemblies should act together in matters of fellowship and discipline. However, it is incorrect to assert that Exclusives only welcomed members of their own circle of meetings to break bread with them: during the nineteenth century they generally received believers from one or other of the denominations, although some groups gradually became more introverted and defensive.

At this point, I must tender my apologies for the constant use in this book of the upper-case 'Brethren', which some will feel is a sectarian term; I assure readers that no slur is intended. The same is true of the term 'Exclusive': it merely denotes the particular viewpoint of those assemblies descended from those who sided with Darby, and is not intended to carry any negative connotations. Exclusive Brethren divided on several occasions from 1880 onwards, many of the resulting subgroups being known by the name of their *de facto* leader.[7] I have followed this convention when referring to particular subgroups, but use 'Exclusive' as a generic term to refer to them all. When the term 'Brethren' appears without any qualifying label, it should be obvious from the context whether I am referring to Open Brethren or to all Brethren; I felt that continual repetition of 'Open Brethren' would be clumsy and risked impeding the flow of the narrative.

My focus on Open Brethren contrasts with Neatby, who considered Open Brethren a modified species of Darbyism, and Darbyism the most powerful and typical form of Brethrenism.[8] Whilst he had reason for taking the approach he did, in view of the literary and evangelistic vigour shown by nineteenth-century Exclusive Brethren, hindsight, resulting from the passing of a century of history and the subsequent development of both streams, has given more modern writers cause to question his approach. On the other hand, Lang erred in the opposite direction in asserting that Darbyism (as he called it) should not form part of Brethren history because Darbyites rejected most of the fundamental principles which guided the movement's early development.[9] This may or may not be true in theological terms, and scholars debate it continually, but the fact is that in practice Open and Exclusive streams were linked in several ways. Aspects of Exclusive Brethren history are therefore discussed briefly here,[10] partly because Exclusivism sprang from the same roots as did Open Brethren, but also because there continued to be a considerable amount of interaction between the two: Exclusive writers such as Kelly, Mackintosh, and Darby were widely read among Open Brethren (and even published by them), and there was a continual trickle of individuals and assemblies moving from one to the other. More recently, negative media coverage of the Taylorite movement during the 1960s and 1970s has been a factor in the unwillingness of many Open assemblies to be known any longer as 'Brethren'; in that sense alone, it could be said that one branch of Exclusivism has shaped Open Brethren thinking by reaction.

My objective in this book is simply to tell the story of the growth and development of Open Brethren – 'how assemblies got to be the way they are', if you like. The story is divided into four periods, each representing what I believe to be a distinct phase of Brethren history. Within each one, I have allocated chapters to what emerged from my research as significant themes or issues. There is less statistical evidence available than might be desired, databases notwithstanding. For that reason and also because of my own interests I have focused on the ideas and personalities, and tried to bring them to life. I want readers to get a feel for what it was (and is) like to belong to one of the congregations here described. So much material has come to hand that it has not been possible to deal with Brethren in other countries; even discussion of the extensive missionary interest of assemblies has had to be confined to the 'home' side of things. Other important topics which I have not been able to discuss include that of the social class of Brethren: apart from the difficulty of defining this concept, and my own unfamiliarity with this area, much of the evidence for Brethren is anecdotal or impressionistic in nature. Here, then, is a story which, although unfinished, has

---

[7] A family tree of Brethren subdivisions appears as Appendix II.

[8] Neatby, *History*, 185.

[9] G.H. Lang, *Anthony Norris Groves: Saint and Pioneer: A Combined Study of a Man of God and of the Original Principles and Practices of the Brethren with Application to Present Conditions* (London: Paternoster, 1949[2]), 241-6.

[10] Briefer comment is also included on developments among the Churches of God, a group of assemblies which separated from Open Brethren in the early 1890s.

fascinated and moved me throughout the period of research and writing. I hope that something of that will come across in the chapters which follow.

PART 1

1825–1849:
A United Testimony

CHAPTER 2

The Earliest Days

All Christian movements take something of their shape and direction from the times in which they come to birth. In order to understand the movement which became known as the Brethren, therefore, we need to understand the context in which it arose.

2.1 Background

The French Revolution, which began in 1789, had an epochal effect on many aspects of British life and thought, both directly and indirectly. The decades which followed were marked by political, social, and ecclesiastical turbulence which contrasted sharply with the previous relative tranquillity. Probably the most prominent emotion evident in British reaction to events on the Continent was fear. The welcome initially given to the news, as indicating the downfall of a feudal and despotic regime, soon turned to horror as Britons learned of the 'Reign of Terror' and the execution of Louis XVI. War with France was to drag on from 1793 until the Battle of Waterloo in 1815, and at the turn of the century Napoleon controlled much of mainland Europe. Widespread renewal of interest in biblical prophecy led many to interpret current events in eschatological terms. The upper classes at home feared for themselves as potential targets of any uprising, and a larger segment of society feared any hint of social dislocation. This fear bred a rigid conservatism which was unable or unwilling to distinguish between reform and incipient revolution; the Government clamped down upon manifestations of discontent, and calls for reform along democratic lines were regarded with grave suspicion. The existing social order was defended as a divinely-ordained hierarchy, legitimated by the Established Church.[1]

Nevertheless, significant political and constitutional change was under way when Brethren first appeared on the scene. The Test and Corporation Acts were repealed in 1828, opening the way for Dissenters to play a full part in local and national government. Roman Catholic emancipation was seen as the logical next step, and as a means of quieting the restive Irish populace, George IV reluctantly signing the Emancipation Act in 1829 which enabled Catholics to stand for Parliament and hold most public offices. This was widely denounced as undermining the British constitution's Protestant nature.[2] The following year, a Whig government came to power in Britain, pledged to parliamentary reform. When a bill aimed at achieving this failed in 1831 through episcopal opposition, violent unrest ensued. The Reform Act was eventually passed in 1832, amid sustained clamour for ecclesiastical as well as political reform.[3] The

---

[1] Asa Briggs, *The Age of Improvement 1783-1867* (London: Longmans, 2000[2]), ch. 3; David L. Edwards, *Christian England* (revised ed.; London: Fount, 1989), 3.101; A.R. Vidler, *The Church in an Age of Revolution: 1789 to the present day* (Harmondsworth, Middlesex: Pelican, 1974), 33.

[2] Briggs, *Age of Improvement*, 200; Owen Chadwick, *The Victorian Church. Part I: 1829-1859* (London: SCM, 1971[3]), 7-8.

[3] Chadwick, *Victorian Church I*, 24-47.

Dissenters' campaign for disestablishment of the Church of England now began to gather momentum.

Such change was all the more inevitable because of the major socio-economic changes affecting much of Britain. By the 1820s, the Industrial Revolution had been in full swing for more than half a century. Rapid urbanisation resulted from the migration of the masses to new sources of work, and thus there was considerable social dislocation, with all its attendant problems. The landscape bore visible witness to the changes, criss-crossed by canals and (from this decade) railways, and dotted with townships, mines, and factories. In spite of rural decline in some areas, between 1801 and 1831 the population of England and Wales increased from 8.9 million to 13.9 million; that of Scotland from 1.6 million to 2.4 million; that of Ireland from 5.2 million to 7.8 million.[4] Britain was also an increasingly youthful society: in 1841, 45% of the population of England and Wales were aged under twenty.[5]

Evangelicalism was a movement with a message uniquely suited to such unsettled times.[6] This, coupled with its pragmatic flexibility and evangelistic vision, enabled it to reach many who would not have been touched by more conventional expressions of religion. As a result, it gained massively in terms of numerical strength and denominational influence, and by 1850 between two and three million people in England would regard themselves as Evangelicals, including the great majority of Dissenters.[7] In Scotland, Evangelicals were a majority in the Church of Scotland's General Assembly by 1833.[8]

The eighteenth century had been the age of the Enlightenment, a movement of thought which had affected much of Western Europe. Reason rather than authority was seen as the source of truth, and the movement offered an optimistic view of human ability to acquire knowledge and live in harmony with nature – in short, to progress. Rationality was a virtue highly prized, and reason and experience began to replace the traditional authorities in such fields as religion and science. To some extent, the Evangelical movement was itself an expression of the Enlightenment mentality, with its stress on the authoritative status of personal experience and its widespread assumption (which helped to fuel the flame of early British missionary concern) that human history would be a story of progress leading up to the reign of Christ.[9] By the end of that century, however, a reaction was setting in. The Romantic movement stressed the limitations of reason and human perception: mystery, emotion, and imagination assumed a much more prominent place than hitherto. In Britain, Blake, Shelley, and Wordsworth gave poetic expression to the new mood, while thinkers such as Coleridge tried to recast Christianity in Romantic terms. Since Evangelicalism had been shaped by the Enlightenment, Romantic reaction against Enlightenment values was bound to affect it. Three noteworthy features of Romanticism-influenced Evangelicalism were the normative status accorded to the

---

[4] Chris Cook and John Stevenson, *The Longman Handbook of Modern British History 1714-1987* (Harlow: Longman, 1988[2]), 110.

[5] J.F.C. Harrison, *Early Victorian Britain, 1832-51* (Glasgow: Fontana, 1988), 17.

[6] Ian Bradley, *The Call to Seriousness: The Evangelical Impact on the Victorians* (London: Jonathan Cape, 1976), 54; Briggs, *Age of Improvement*, 151.

[7] Bradley, *Call to Seriousness*, 52.

[8] T.C. Smout, *A History of the Scottish People 1560-1830* (London: Fontana, 1985), 218-19.

[9] This interpretation is worked out in detail in D.W. Bebbington, *Evangelicalism in Modern Britain: A History from the 1730s to the 1980s* (London: Unwin Hyman, 1989), ch. 2.

practice of the apostolic churches, a heightened stress on inward spiritual experience (which led to the accusation of tending to downplay the importance of right conduct), and the belief that God's working was to be looked for in supernatural events, rather than in the regular providential ordering of things (which gave rise to widespread prayer for the outpouring of the Spirit, stimulated by James Haldane Stewart's 1821 work, *Thoughts on the Importance of Special Prayer for the General Outpouring of the Holy Spirit*). All three would be evident in the early development of the Brethren mentality.

Brethren were just one of a number of such movements which emerged in early-nineteenth century Evangelicalism, dissatisfied with it and yet a fruit of its success. Their founders believed that Evangelicalism had lost something in the process of growth, having become formalised in its expressions of spiritual experience, and conformed to the world in its methods. Thus their most famous representative, the Scottish preacher Edward Irving (1792-1834), alleged that Evangelicalism by and large was rationalistic, guilty of compromise with the world, complacent and self-confident, and marked by reliance upon human effort rather than dependence on the Spirit's power.[10] Strength was given to this reaction by the disappointment felt by many that their hopes for revival, which had run so high during the decades of the 1790s and 1800s when the great missionary societies were formed, had only been partially fulfilled.[11]

The spirit of pan-Evangelical co-operation which had found expression in missionary enterprise such as the formation of the British and Foreign Bible Society in 1804, and in the promotion of 'experimental' religion, stressing the reality of a personal relationship with God worked out in a disciplined lifestyle, declined in the face of increasing tension between different outlooks within the movement. By the 1820s, relationships between Dissenters and Anglicans were being strained by Dissenting calls for disestablishment (along with campaigning for removal of the disadvantages under which they laboured in public life) and a certain amount of residual Anglican suspicion of Dissenters as potential revolutionaries. Evangelicalism was also riven by controversy regarding the nature of the church. Whereas more moderate Evangelicals saw an Established Church (i.e. one upheld by the state as the officially-sanctioned form of the Christian religion) as acceptable if under sound and godly leadership, many radicals moved towards a rejection of establishment in principle, which they expressed through secession. In their view, establishment resulted in the confusion of the church with the world, and a consequent inability to practise biblical church discipline. Unease among radicals regarding the interpretation of such parts of the Anglican *Book of Common Prayer* as the baptismal service, which appeared to assert that those baptised were thus made regenerate, or the burial service, which obliged them to treat the dead person as a true Christian, also

---

[10] Edward Irving, *For Missionaries after the Apostolical School* (London: Hamilton, Adams, 1825), xiv-xix, 22, 39-40. Irving was a Church of Scotland minister who came under suspicion of heresy because of his teaching that Christ inherited *fallen* human nature; he also came to believe that the supernatural gifts of the Spirit had been restored, and fostered their exercise in his London congregation. He was deposed from the Presbyterian ministry and locked out of his church, and founded in 1832 a new congregation, which developed under the rule of Apostles and Prophets. The 'Irvingite' movement was later to become known as the Catholic Apostolic Church.

[11] Harold H. Rowdon, 'The Problem of Brethren Identity in Historical Perspective', in Lorenzo Georgi and Massimo Rubboli (eds.), *Piero Guicciardini 1808-1886. Un Riformatore Religioso nell'europa dell'ottocento. Atti del Convegno di Studie, Firenze, 11-12 Aprile 1986* (Firenze: Leo S. Olschki, 1988), 165.

provoked secession. The radicals were themselves prone to further division over issues such as the reformulation of Calvinist doctrine in line with Romantic emphases, and claims to a restoration of spiritual gifts. Some radical groups provided striking parallels to Brethren practice in the areas of leadership and worship, but evidence of direct dependence is rarely available. Similar ferment was occurring in Switzerland in the aftermath of the Genevan *Réveil*, which began in 1817; we shall see later what happened when these groups came into contact with British Brethren.[12]

2.2 Beginnings in Ireland

It has been asserted by some that the pioneers of the Brethren movement were principled seceders who regarded the existing churches as having failed irremediably in their task, and by others that they were embryonic ecumenists who sought to overleap the denominational barriers which divided true believers. The evidence indicates that these two attitudes to mainstream Christianity co-existed in the earliest years of Brethren history, and that the balance was liable to shift from one emphasis to the other. The tension between them was one major factor which made for volatility in the movement. On occasion, both could be found within the same individual, a case in point being Anthony Norris Groves (1795-1853).[13] Although we must neither overestimate nor underestimate Groves' role in the movement's origins (Open Brethren writers tend to do the former, and Exclusive Brethren the latter), he had significant contact with most of the early leaders and centres, exercising considerable influence, especially in the area of personal lifestyle. Furthermore, his life and thought epitomise much that was distinctive about early Brethrenism.

Groves was born at Newton Valence, near Alton in Hampshire, and brought up in the Church of England. He trained as a dentist, and set up his own practice at Plymouth in 1814, experiencing an Evangelical conversion soon afterwards. Before marrying his cousin in 1816, he had offered himself to the Church Missionary Society as a missionary, but shelved this plan after marriage because of his wife's strong opposition. Spiritual unrest meant that he began a serious study of the Bible in 1822, as a result of which he and his wife agreed to give away a tenth of their income to the needy; they later increased the proportion to a quarter, finally deciding to keep back only enough to provide for their immediate needs. During the mid-1820s, Groves (who now lived in Exeter) became friendly with a lady by the name of Bessie Paget (c.1783-1863). Bessie, who had a Quaker background,[14] influenced him away from his early Arminianism, and also challenged his

---

[12] For thorough coverage of events in Switzerland and the interaction between Swiss and English radical Evangelicals, see Timothy C.F. Stunt, *From Awakening to Secession: Radical Evangelicals in Switzerland and Britain 1815-35* (Edinburgh: T. & T. Clark, 2000).

[13] On Groves, see *BDEB*; Robert Bernard Dann, 'Anthony Norris Groves (1795-1853): a radical influence on nineteenth-century Protestant church and mission' (forthcoming PhD thesis, Liverpool University); idem, *Father of Faith Missions: The Life and Times of Anthony Norris Groves (1795-1853)* (Waynesboro, GA: Authentic Media, 2004); Mrs. Anthony Norris Groves, *Memoir of Anthony Norris Groves (containing extracts from his letters and journals)* (London: J. Nisbet, 1856; reprinted, Sumneytown, PA: Sentinel, 2002); *ODNB*. Lang, *Groves*, is highly tendentious but contains some useful material.

[14] Edward Kennaway Groves, *George Müller and his successors* (Bristol: the author, 1906), 370; T.C.F. Stunt, *Early Brethren and the Society of Friends* (CBRF Occasional Paper No. 3, Pinner,

High Church prejudices by inviting him to preach in a mission room at Poltimore, just outside the city, for which she was responsible.

In 1825, Groves published a pamphlet, *Christian Devotedness*, which typified the radicalism of a number of early Brethren. It caused a furore because, unlike most Evangelical writing of the time, it offered an implicit challenge to the existing socio-economic divisions which Evangelicals tended to uphold as divinely-ordained.[15] A revised edition appeared in 1829.[16] Responding to the lack of impact made by Christianity in spite of so many centuries of mission, Groves called on Christians to dedicate themselves and their property to God, and to stop laying up treasure on earth, trusting instead to God's promises to provide for those who give up all for him. Such dedication was, Groves asserted, required by Christ's example as well as by his commands, which were all too often explained away instead of being obeyed. In this manifesto we see the germ of the concept of 'living by faith' which was to become so significant for Brethren missiological thinking.

Anthony Norris Groves

However, the settled opposition to missionary societies which characterised much radical Evangelicalism was not evident in Groves' writing. Indeed, around 1825 he had renewed his approach to the Church Missionary Society, and was accepted for service in Baghdad. Until this body opened its own training college at Islington in London, it used to send candidates to Trinity College, Dublin, for examination purposes,[17] and so Groves began to make periodic visits to Dublin. Eventually he came to the conclusion that he should not seek ordination: for one thing, he could not accept that it was legitimate for Christians to bear arms, as asserted in the Thirty-Nine Articles. For another, his growing doubts about the appropriateness of an academic preparation for missionary service were confirmed when a burglar broke into his house and stole a sum of money set aside for the next trip to Dublin. He therefore withdrew from the course in the summer of 1827. The

---

Middlesex: Christian Brethren Research Fellowship, 1970), 9n. On Bessie Paget, see *BDEB*; Stunt, *Awakening*, 119, 121, 175-6, 286-7.

[15] F. Roy Coad, *A History of the Brethren Movement* (Exeter: Paternoster Press, 1976[2]), 17.

[16] The second edition is reproduced as Lang, *Groves*, ch. 5, and as an Addendum to the reprint of Mrs. Groves, *Memoir*.

[17] Alan R. Acheson, *A History of the Church of Ireland 1691-1996* (Blackrock and Dublin: Columba Press and APCK, 1997), 149.

Society told him that unless he was ordained he would not be allowed to celebrate the Lord's Supper, but the perplexity which this caused was resolved by the dawning awareness that 'ordination of any kind to preach the gospel is no requirement of Scripture'.[18]

It was in Ireland that much of Groves' radical thinking about the church received its first public expression, and the Irish context did much to shape the concerns and outlook of early Brethren. Centuries-old tension between the Roman Catholic majority and their Protestant rulers had exploded in rioting during 1798-9 which was brutally suppressed amid fears of a French-style revolution. This unrest precipitated the Union of the Parliaments of Great Britain and Ireland in 1800, and the union of the Church of Ireland with the Church of England at the same time. By the 1820s, the Church of Ireland had begun to experience a considerable degree of reform, both administrative and spiritual. Furthermore, Evangelicals were enjoying more influence than ever before; William Magee (1766-1831), Archbishop of Dublin from 1822, worked to integrate them into the Establishment instead of attempting to marginalise or exclude them.[19] As the most recent historian of the Irish Church comments, 'the majority of early Brethren had come to faith in the Church of Ireland, and ... they seceded at a time when the vitality of the Evangelical revival in the church was most marked, and its evangelistic zeal at its most effective'.[20] Indeed, it was estimated that by 1840 as many as half the Anglican clergy in Ireland were Evangelicals. There was also a flowering of High Church theology and practice, rooted in indigenous tradition, stressing the primitive and catholic aspects of the Church's heritage and strongly anti-Roman Catholic.[21] The negative estimate of the state of the Church of Ireland which has been popular among Brethren should not, therefore, be accepted without significant qualification, and we should guard against the impression that the secession of the early Brethren was simply a response to its spiritual deadness; in some ways, it came about because of the life which was manifest and which was (to some extent) the result of its ministrations, and which sought new channels for its expression. All the same, it remains true that Evangelicals of a more radical cast of mind tended to have a negative perception of the Church of Ireland; whether or not they were correct, their perception undoubtedly did much to shape their attitudes and dictate their actions.

In spite of the growth of Irish Evangelicalism, Protestants remained a minority of the population in most areas. Anglicanism was seen as the religion of the Anglo-Irish landlord class, the so-called 'Protestant ascendancy'; whilst established by law, it was in a precarious position, since in large areas it could only command the allegiance of about 10% of the people.[22] Catholicism had been seen as a spent force after the French Revolution resulted in the temporary dethroning of the Pope, but a change in Irish Protestant perceptions occurred during the 1820s.[23] Apprehension regarding Rome's ultimate intentions was heightened by the pastoral and political resurgence of Irish

---

[18] Mrs. Groves, *Memoir*, 33.

[19] Acheson, *History*, 155, 157.

[20] *Ibid.*, 156.

[21] *Ibid.*, 153-6.

[22] In 1834, it was estimated that out of a total Irish population of almost 8 million, 853,000 were Anglican, 643,000 Presbyterian, and 22,000 belonged to other Protestant groups. The rest were Roman Catholic (*ibid.*, 19). Protestants would have been concentrated in the Ulster counties of Antrim and Down, and (to a lesser extent) the areas around Dublin and Cork.

[23] Bebbington, *Evangelicalism*, 101.

Catholicism during the decade, and galvanised Protestants into a wave of activity known as the 'New Reformation'. Its beginning may be dated to 1822 when Magee issued a charge upon his enthronement as Archbishop, encouraging his clergy to committed pastoral ministry which would include the evangelisation of non-Anglicans, whether Presbyterian or Catholic, in order to unite and thus stabilise the population. Evangelicals promptly redoubled their efforts for the conversion of Catholics, not without vigorous opposition. The stakes were high, and some warned that the price of failure would be Catholic emancipation and the possible dissolution of the United Kingdom. Heavily supported by English Evangelicals, and making triumphalist claims for its impact, the 'New Reformation' nevertheless won relatively few converts, probably because it was too closely associated with the civil authorities. A wave of conversions did occur in 1826-7, and many thought then that the anticipated harvest had begun.[24] But the movement was doomed after Magee, in another charge to his clergy in October 1826, represented church and state as two aspects of the same Christian community, portraying the clergy in their temporal capacity as instruments of state. He saw no place for a system which maintained a spiritual supremacy independent of the state, especially if that supremacy was foreign.[25] Strong Catholic opposition ensued, and on 1 February 1827 the Irish Anglican clergy drew up a petition claiming state protection against Roman aggression.[26] Magee responded by imposing the Oaths of Supremacy and Allegiance upon prospective converts, and since the movement was also losing momentum in the face of articulate Catholic resistance, the flow of converts virtually ceased.[27]

One man who was deeply troubled by these events, and whose spiritual pilgrimage during these years deserves fuller treatment because of his significance in the movement's development, was John Nelson Darby (1800-82).[28] Darby was the son of a prosperous merchant who had Irish family connections and inherited Leap Castle, Offaly, in 1819. After attending Westminster School, he graduated from Trinity College, Dublin, in 1819, intending to become a barrister. Conversion to Christ shortly afterwards was to change that.[29] Little is known of the spiritual crisis which provoked this change, except that it involved 'deep repentance and self-sacrifice', and although Darby always regarded it as the

---

[24] Acheson, *History*, 121, 160; Stewart J. Brown, *The National Churches of England, Ireland, and Scotland 1801-1846* (Oxford: Oxford University Press, 2001), 94-6, 122-6; for fuller coverage of anti-Catholic efforts, see Desmond Bowen, *The Protestant Crusade in Ireland 1800-70* (Dublin: Gill & Macmillan, 1978).

[25] W. Magee, *A Charge Delivered at His Triennial and Metropolitan Visitation in St. Patrick's Cathedral, on Tuesday the 10th of October 1826* (Dublin: R. Graisberry, 1827), 5, 27, 30.

[26] The petition is reproduced in Max S. Weremchuk, *John Nelson Darby* (Neptune, NJ: Loizeaux, 1992), 212-13.

[27] The Oath of Supremacy involved acknowledging the monarch as head of the realm in spiritual as well as temporal affairs (and thus rejecting all papal claims to jurisdiction). It supplemented the Oath of Allegiance, which was an expression of loyalty to the sovereign.

[28] On Darby, see *BDE*; *BDEB*; Jonathan D. Burnham, *A Story of Conflict: The Controversial Relationship between Benjamin Wills Newton and John Nelson Darby* (Carlisle: Paternoster, 2004); *ODNB*; Timothy C.F. Stunt, 'Influences in the Early Development of J.N. Darby', in Crawford Gribben and Timothy C.F. Stunt (eds), *Prisoners of Hope? Aspects of Evangelical Millennialism in Britain and Ireland, 1800-1880* (Carlisle: Paternoster, 2005), 44-68; Weremchuk, *Darby*.

[29] In a marginal note next to 2 Timothy 3 in his Greek New Testament, Darby dated his conversion to 'June or July 1820, or 21' (Weremchuk, *Darby*, 204).

point at which he was converted, for some years following his views were decidedly High Church in nature. According to William Kelly, who edited Darby's *Collected Writings*, 'Mr. Darby was converted when a barrister, and saw enough of a Christian's calling to throw it up for Christ's sake. Therefore he sought orders, knowing no better ...'[30] Darby himself recollected having been aware that Christ had given all for him and having felt that he therefore owed all to Christ, although he could not then testify to an assurance of personal salvation.[31]

Ordained deacon on 7 August 1825 and priest on 19 February 1826, Darby took a curacy in the parish of Powerscourt, south of Dublin, under the influential and well-connected Evangelical Robert Daly (1783-1872). Powerscourt had a high concentration of Protestant gentry, among whom Evangelicalism had made considerable headway; according to Daly, 'there was no place in the world where there was so much religion'.[32] He recruited a succession of able curates, and with his Evangelical cousin William Cleaver (son of Magee's predecessor as Archbishop), who ministered in the neighbouring parish of Delgany, he founded the perpetual curacy of Calary, a remote locality in the hills between the two places, whose Catholic inhabitants lived in great poverty. Darby's older brother Christopher had been a curate at Delgany, and his sister Susannah and her husband, Edward Pennefather, had a house there. It is not surprising, then, that Magee planned to assign him there. Calary became Darby's responsibility.[33]

In an *Analysis of Dr. Newman's Apologia pro Vita Sua*, published in 1866, Darby describes his religious practice during this period:

> I fasted in Lent so as to be weak in body at the end of it; ate no meat on week days – nothing till evening on Wednesdays, Fridays, and Saturdays, then a little bread or nothing; observed strictly the weekly fasts, too. I went to my clergyman always if I wished to take the sacrament, that he might judge of the matter. I held apostolic succession fully, and the channels of grace to be there only. I held thus Luther and Calvin and their followers to be outside. I was not their judge, but I left them to the uncovenanted mercies of God. I searched with earnest diligence into the evidences of apostolic succession in England, and just saved their validity for myself and my conscience. The union of church and state I held to be Babylonish, that the church ought to govern itself, and that she was in bondage but was the church.[34]

The outlook expressed in that last sentence meant that Darby was deeply concerned about Archbishop Magee's actions early in 1827. Looking back in 1865, Darby recalled with pardonable exaggeration: 'his course was ruinous – really stopped the deliverance from popery of masses, perhaps of all in Ireland; they were leaving from seven to eight hundred a week. He required the oath of supremacy and abjuration: it stopped as by a shot.'[35] In response, he circulated a paper entitled *Considerations Addressed to the Archbishop of*

---

[30] W. Kelly to P., 22 June 1899 (Chapter Two archive).

[31] J.N. Darby, *Letters of J.N.D.* (Kingston-on-Thames: Stow Hill Bible and Tract Depot, n.d.), 3.297 (185-[*sic*]).

[32] Stunt, *Awakening*, 163, quoting Mrs. Hamilton Madden, *Memoir of the late Right Rev. Robert Daly, D.D., Lord Bishop of Cashel* (London: James Nisbet, 1875), 170.

[33] Acheson, *History*, 129-30; W. Magee to T.P. Magee, 2 August 1825 (CBA Box 154(1(c)); Stunt, *Awakening*, 164-5; Weremchuk, *Darby*, 234n; Max Weremchuk to the author, 4 May 2003.

[34] Darby, *CW*, 18.156; cf. 1.37.

[35] Darby, *Letters*, 1.397 (1865).

Dublin and the Clergy who Signed the Petition to the House of Commons for Protection, which he had originally written after Magee delivered his charge the previous summer.[36] A note added by Darby in 1865 asserted that its importance lay in its representing 'the first germing of truth which has since developed itself in the Church of God'.[37] In it, he defined the church as:

> a congregation of souls redeemed out of 'this naughty world' by God manifest in the flesh, a people purified to Himself by Christ, purified in the heart by faith, knit together, by the bond of this common faith in Him, to Him their Head sitting at the right hand of the Father, having consequently their conversation (*commonwealth*) in heaven, from whence they look for the Saviour, the Lord of glory; Phil.3:20. As a body, therefore, they belong to heaven; ... On earth they are, as a people ... nothing and nobody ... They are delivered in spirit out of this present evil world, and become heavenly, spiritual, in their connections, interests, thoughts, and prospects ...[38]

The burden of his objection to the Archbishop's charge was that it was grounded in the erroneous view that the civil ruler is in a position to choose the best religion for his subjects and to establish it, its ministers thus becoming instruments of the state. Given British opposition to papal claims to temporal jurisdiction, this was fighting fire with fire; all that Magee was doing was to substitute the sovereign for the pope. Christian ministers served a Christ whose kingdom was not of this world, and so it was impossible for them to claim state support and still retain their independence as servants of Christ. Civil rulers might oppose the papacy's temporal claims; ministers of Christ were to fight its spiritual claims, and only by spiritual means – the winning of souls to Christ – could Roman Catholicism be overcome. It is important to notice that at this point Darby was still thinking along High Church lines. As Neatby recognised, Darby took 'his stand at the point where extreme Evangelicalism and extreme High Churchmanship join hands in the intensity of their common anti-Erastianism'.[39] Such opposition to the subservience of church to state, and insistence upon the church's independence as a divinely-founded institution, was to be a fundamental aspect of the ecclesiological thinking of the Tractarians (later known as the Oxford Movement), evident in John Keble's famous Assize Sermon of 14 July 1833 as much as in Darby's protest to the Archbishop.[40]

However, Darby's Christian understanding and experience were about to change radically. In October 1827, he was forced to lay aside his duties following a riding accident which left him severely injured. As he convalesced he experienced what he later described as his 'deliverance'.[41] In a brief account of his early pilgrimage, he stated

---

[36] Darby, *CW*, 1.1-19.

[37] *Ibid.*, 1.1.

[38] *Ibid.*, 1.5.

[39] Neatby, *History*, 14.

[40] The movements are compared by T.C.F. Stunt, 'Two Nineteenth-Century Movements', *EQ* 37 (1965), 221-31; see also his *Awakening*, ch. 8.

[41] The dating of Darby's deliverance has been debated, but he himself referred explicitly to 1827-8 (*Letters*, 1.185 (received 25 February 1851); cf. H.H. Rowdon, *The Origins of the Brethren, 1825-1850* (London: Pickering & Inglis, 1967), 45-6; Stunt, *Awakening*, 171; Weremchuk, *Darby*, 33, 62). He also stated that he remained at Calary for two years and three months (*Letters*, 3.297 [185-][*sic*]), which takes us from August 1825 to November 1827.

simply that 'much exercise of soul had the effect of causing the scriptures to gain complete ascendancy over me'.[42] Circumstances faced him with a question: 'Would I rest the faith of my soul as a living man on the Word of God?' As he did so, he experienced an increasing sense of the authority of the Scriptures as God's perfect revelation of himself in Christ. Only since that point, he recalled, had Scripture spoken to him 'as altogether Divine and self-sufficient'.[43] Given the pull which he had been feeling toward the concept of a divinely-instituted authority in the form of the visible church, it seems that Darby had now come to rest in the sole and sufficient authority of Scripture. 'Did heaven and earth, the visible church, and man himself, crumble into nonentity, I should, through grace, since that epoch, hold to the word as an unbreakable link between my soul and God.'[44] Coupled with his new way of reading Scripture was a new sense of God's love for him in Christ. His 'deliverance' was the culmination of this change, bringing a new sense of freedom and security arising out of an awareness of his being united with Christ. Whilst he had been converted six or seven years previously, he now knew peace for the first time, 'by finding my oneness with Christ, ... I was in Christ, accepted in the Beloved, and sitting in heavenly places in Him'.[45]

Following this, Darby returned to Calary in order to share with his flock his new understanding and experience of the liberty of the gospel: 'I had preached that sin had created a great gulf between us and God, and that Christ alone was able to bridge it over; now, I preached that He *had* already finished His work.'[46] However, he did not remain for long; as he later interpreted events, his deliverance made it impossible to continue as a minister of the Establishment because of his belief that ministry was to be founded upon the Spirit's gifting rather than upon human ordination. Since he could neither accept the union of the church with the world which characterised the Church of Ireland as established, nor the union arising from shared belief in denominational distinctives which characterised Dissenting communions, where could he go? The answer, he concluded, lay in Matthew 18.20: 'Where two or three are gathered in my name, there am I in the midst of them', and so he began to break bread with four others similarly exercised. The same truth which had brought him peace (his union with Christ in heavenly places) brought him out of the Establishment, because he realised that the church was composed of those so united with Christ.[47]

In practice, Darby's withdrawal from the Church of Ireland was a rather more gradual process. Huebner, who writes as an apologist for separatist Brethrenism, asserts that Darby resigned his curacy,[48] but this is going beyond the available evidence; an affectionate testimonial signed by thirteen of his parishioners and dated 28 March 1829 expressed warm appreciation of his ministry and the hope that he would return to them,

---

[42] Darby, *Letters*, 3.298 [185-].

[43] Weremchuk, *Darby*, 205 (marginal note next to 2 Timothy 3 in Darby's Greek New Testament).

[44] Darby, *CW*, 6.5; cf. idem, *Letters*, 1.344 (10 February 1863). Elsewhere he asserts that this was what stopped him from converting to Rome (*CW*, 1.38).

[45] Darby, *Letters*, 1.515 (1868).

[46] *Ibid.*, 3.299 [185-].

[47] Darby, *CW*, 1.36.

[48] R.A. Huebner, *Precious Truths Revived and Defended through J.N. Darby. Volume One: Revival of Truth, 1826-1845* (Morganville, NJ: Present Truth, 1991), 35.

which implies that at this point he had not submitted any formal resignation.[49] We should probably take Darby's statements about 'going outside the camp'[50] and leaving the Establishment because he 'did not think it the church of God'[51] as reading back his developed convictions into earlier events. As late as April 1833, he could write: 'I am no enemy to episcopacy abstractedly, if it be real and done from the Lord',[52] and it has been suggested that his final break with the Church of Ireland did not come until as late as 1834, his close friend John Gifford Bellett (1795-1864) describing him as 'all but detached' from the Established Church that year.[53] Until that point, he continued to tour Ireland, preaching and visiting small groups meeting along similar lines to those in Dublin and often working with the Home Mission of the Church of Ireland until the hierarchy clamped down on its allegedly irregular activities (such as the encouragement of lay preaching) in 1833.

Darby's itinerant ministry made him a marked man. On 2 February 1829, a death threat was sent him, warning him to leave the place where he was 'Seducing the people ... by [his] Bible business', Corofin in County Clare, a county which was a focal point for Catholic political activism.[54] The letter was sent by a member of the 'Rockites', one of a number of protest groups which flourished in Ireland during the 1820s. The combination of the passing of the Emancipation Act in 1829, unrest at the perceived injustice of the requirement to pay tithes to the clergy of the Established Church (which found expression in the 'Tithe Wars' of 1832), and resentment at Protestant evangelistic efforts, made Darby's work as an evangelistic preacher potentially very dangerous indeed.

His developing doctrine of the church found expression in *Considerations on the Nature and Unity of the Church of Christ*.[55] The work exists in two editions, the first (dating from 1828) in his *Collected Writings* and the second in the first number of the Brethren periodical, *The Christian Witness*, dated January 1834. The former is indefinite in its suggestions for action, rejecting all available options: co-operation, secession, and union of existing denominations; Neatby notes its lack of clear analysis of the problem and clear statement of the remedy.[56] The latter is more negative in its estimate of the churches and the world, clearly stressing the duty of separation from the world, and from churches mixed up with the world, and cautioning against any attempt to create new churches. The pamphlet was founded upon a belief that the visible unity of believers represented an aspect of God's purpose, because through it the world might see and believe. Such unity must be produced by the Holy Spirit. Whilst recognising the germ of

---

[49] The testimonial is reproduced in Weremchuk, *Darby*, 217-18. Significantly, Darby was addressed as 'Rev'd'.

[50] Darby, *Letters*, 2.379 (21 September 1876).

[51] Darby, *CW*, 20.288 (1869).

[52] Darby, *Letters*, 1.17 (received 30 April 1833).

[53] Anon., *Interesting Reminiscences*, 8; cf. Burnham, *Story of Conflict*, 129. Burnham notes that no evidence is extant in diocesan records which would help us determine the date of Darby's secession. Darby's father died in 1834, and his refusal to attend the funeral (Darby, *Letters*, 3.479 (1881)) may indicate that by then he was no longer an Anglican.

[54] Max Weremchuk to the author, 11 March 2003; cf. Gary Lynn Nebeker, 'The Hope of Heavenly Glory in John Nelson Darby (1800-1882)' (PhD dissertation, Dallas Theological Seminary, 1997), 139-40. A copy of the letter is in the Christian Brethren Archive (CBA 5540(188)).

[55] Darby, *CW*, 1.20-35.

[56] Neatby, *History*, 31.

true unity in such examples of interdenominational co-operation as the Bible Society and missionary outreach, Darby insisted that the outward union of existing Christian bodies was not the answer. Each believer must seek God's interests rather than their own, and hold fast to the hope of Christ's return; division had begun when they failed to do these things. Seeking God's interests entailed a life conformed to Christ's death in self-giving. The Lord's Supper was the outward symbol and instrument of true unity because in it believers proclaimed Christ's death, by which they were gathered into one body.

Darby was not the first to withdraw from the Irish Establishment. Two clergy in particular foreshadowed aspects of Brethren practice, although direct influence upon Darby or other Brethren cannot be proved. Thomas Kelly (1769-1855) had seceded in 1803 after the Archbishop of Dublin had inhibited him from preaching in the city's churches because of his doctrinal views and his irregularity in preaching in other parishes without the necessary permission. Kelly held that the Established Church could never be modified along New Testament lines. He rejected ordination, and practised baptism on profession of faith. A number of Kellyite congregations were established in Ireland, but the movement did not long survive his death. John Walker (1768-1833), a fellow of Trinity College, was inhibited at the same time as Kelly; he seceded in 1804 and set up meetings marked by extreme Calvinism, rejection of ordination, separation from other Christians except for purposes of proselytising, and a very closely restricted communion. Walker left for London in 1819, but in 1821 his congregation numbered 130, including twelve former clergy, and celebrated the Lord's Supper as its main weekly meeting. The Walkerite movement was introverted and exclusive and thus lacked any real desire to establish new congregations; however, the Dublin one lasted well into the twentieth century.[57]

Another precedent for Brethren-style meetings was provided by the erstwhile Presbyterian James Buchanan. Buchanan was influenced by the Scots James and Robert Haldane who had founded churches characterised by plural leadership and weekly observance of the Lord's Supper.[58] Contact with the Haldanes led Buchanan to read the Scriptures in a new way. In 1807, he and a few others formed a church at Camowen Green, near Omagh in County Tyrone, adopting the principle that 'we should not attend to any act of worship unless we saw it clearly ordered and practised by the first churches in the New Testament'.[59] In this body, brothers took it in turns to preside, calling on members to take part as gifted; the Lord's Supper was observed each week and eventually believer's baptism was practised. Buchanan became British Consul in New York from 1815, and the church which he had helped to form became a Baptist church, a secession in 1860 leading to the formation of a Brethren assembly.[60] In 1820, Buchanan issued *The First Part of an Epistolary Correspondence between Christian Churches in America and Europe* in which the church life of over twenty congregations in Britain and America was described in their

---

[57] For more on these movements, see Grayson Carter, *Anglican Evangelicals: Protestant Secessions from the* Via Media, *c.1800-1850* (Oxford: Oxford University Press, 2001), ch. 3; C.P. Martin, 'Recollections of the Walkerite or so-called Separatist Meeting in Dublin', *JCBRF* 21 (1971), 4, 9-10; Harold H. Rowdon, 'Secession from the Established Church in the Nineteenth Century', *VE* 3 (1964), 77-8.

[58] On the Haldanes, see BDE; BDEB; Alexander Haldane, *The Lives of Robert Haldane of Airthrey, and of his Brother, James Alexander Haldane* (London: Hamilton, Adams, 1852^2).

[59] James Quinn (ed.), *The Religious Belief of James Buchanan* (Omagh: n.p., 1955), 9.

[60] Rowdon, *Origins*, 24.

own words. Although it is virtually impossible to determine whether any of them developed into Brethren assemblies, the work demonstrates that many of the fundamental convictions and practices of the early Brethren were shared by others (it is noteworthy that the work was reprinted in 1889 by a Brethren publisher, Pickering & Inglis under the title, *Letters concerning their Principles and Order from Assemblies of Believers in 1818-1820*). Most of these congregations saw Scripture as providing a detailed pattern for church order, and the practice which resulted was remarkably consistent from one church to the next: weekly observance of the Lord's Supper, plural (non-ordained) ministry, and regular gospel preaching. They also abstained from political involvement. However, there was some diversity of opinion on such matters as whether baptism was a prerequisite for admission to communion, and the extent to which they should keep separate from other Christians. A number of these congregations were 'Scotch Baptist' churches,[61] but thirteen were located in Ireland, including two in Dublin. Some may have joined the 'Churches of Christ', another movement with a similar approach to the authority of Scripture and church order, though it developed a higher view of baptism than most of these churches or the Brethren.

A recent historian of Scottish Brethren, Neil Dickson, has argued that such groups established a vocabulary which passed into the religious setting from which Brethren would emerge.[62] Brethren themselves looked to these groups as forerunners: Stunt notes that as early as 1840 such a claim was made in *The Inquirer,* a periodical associated with those Quakers who joined the Brethren during the late 1830s.[63] Since none of these groups has survived, however, we must ask why the Brethren movement took root in a way that they did not. One factor may be that from the beginning the Brethren had the advantage of a strong sense of family unity arising principally from a close network of well-known leaders, which owed much to intermarriage, especially among former Quakers.[64] This phenomenon reflected the movement's origins among the aristocracy and gentry, and the developing links can be seen as we trace the origins of three groups of believers who began meeting in Dublin during the late 1820s.[65]

The first centred on Edward Cronin (1801-82), a Roman Catholic from Cork who, after an Evangelical conversion, had settled with the Independents.[66] Moving to Dublin in 1826, he was told that he might take communion at an Independent chapel as a visitor but could not continue to do so without joining a local church. Believing that participation at the Lord's Table expressed membership of Christ's universal body rather than of a particular congregation, Cronin refused; his growing disapproval of 'one-man ministry'

---

[61] The 'Scotch Baptists' appeared in the eighteenth century, and practised weekly communion and plural eldership. They were marked by a distinctive view of faith, which was conceived as mental assent to the truths of the gospel.

[62] Neil T.R. Dickson, '"The church itself is God's clergy": the principles and practices of the Brethren', in Deryck W. Lovegrove (ed.), *The Rise of the Laity in Evangelical Protestantism* (London: Routledge, 2002), 219.

[63] T.C.F. Stunt, 'The Origins of the Brethren', *W* 98 (1968), 147, citing *I* 3 (1840), 68-71.

[64] Peter L. Embley, 'The Early Development of the Plymouth Brethren', in Bryan Wilson (ed.), *Patterns of Sectarianism: Organisation and Ideology in Social and Religious Movements* (London: Heinemann, 1967), 216-17. Another factor, the movement's passionate commitment to evangelism, was not so evident in early years as it later became.

[65] For this division of the three groups, see Rowdon, *Origins*, 42.

[66] On Cronin, see *BDEB*. Independents were later known as Congregationalists.

led him to cease attending, and he began to break bread privately with a few friends. Denying the necessity of 'special membership' (i.e. of one church to the exclusion of others), they were seen as 'Evangelical malcontents'.[67]

A second group included Anglicans and Dissenters: it began in 1825 'with three friends who were closely associated in Christian work on weekdays, but who separated on Sundays. They included a baptist and a paedobaptist', and sought a congregation in which they could share fellowship together.[68] 'At one time they seemed to have found it, yet, at the last moment, in conference with the elders of that community, conditions were required which would defeat the object they had in view.'[69] As they saw no need of a consecrated place or an ordained minister, the three began breaking bread together to express their unity. Among those involved was John Parnell, later Lord Congleton (1805-83).[70] A wealthy member of the Protestant ascendancy, Parnell had been converted as a student at Edinburgh through reading Paul's Letter to the Romans.

Several Anglican Evangelicals, including Bellett, began meeting in a similar manner, forming the third group. When visiting Dublin, Groves preached and met with other Evangelicals for Bible study, staying at Bellett's home. Bellett had been converted in 1817, while studying at Trinity College. Graduating in 1819, he continued his legal studies in London, returning to Dublin in 1821. However, it is unlikely that he ever practised much as a barrister. For one thing, he possessed independent financial means; for another, he was much more interested in spiritual matters.[71] In later years, he became a saintly and spiritual writer loved and respected by all sections of the Brethren movement.

In the face of the prevalence of Roman Catholicism, denominational barriers seemed irrelevant and, by Spring 1827, the third group had concluded, under Groves's guidance, that they were free to break bread each Lord's day. Bessie Paget recollected Bellett saying to her:

> Groves has just been telling me, that it appeared to him from Scripture, that believers, meeting together as disciples of Christ, were free to break bread together as their Lord had admonished them; and that, in as far as the practice of the apostles could be a guide, every Lord's day should be set aside for thus remembering the Lord's death, and obeying his parting command …[72]

Late in 1828, Groves visited Dublin again, although he had by now withdrawn from Trinity College. In conversation with Bellett, he expressed the conviction that 'this, I doubt not, is the mind of God concerning us, that we should come together in all simplicity as disciples, not waiting on any pulpit or minister, but trusting that the Lord would edify us together, by ministering as He pleased and saw good from the midst of ourselves'.[73] It was not long, however, before several members left on a missionary expedition. On 12 June 1829, Groves and his party sailed for St Petersburg in a boat

---

[67] Anon., *Interesting Reminiscences*, 16-17.

[68] Rowdon, *Origins*, 42.

[69] W. Collingwood, *'The Brethren': A Historical Sketch* (Glasgow: Pickering & Inglis, [1899]), 6. According to Rowdon, the group in question may have been Walkerite (*Origins*, 42).

[70] On Congleton, see *BDEB*; H. Groves, *"Not of the World": Memoir of Lord Congleton* (London: John F. Shaw, 1884).

[71] Rowdon, *Origins*, 39. On Bellett, see *BDEB*.

[72] Mrs. Groves, *Memoir*, 39.

[73] Anon., *Interesting Reminiscences*, 5.

provided by Parnell (who accompanied them), as the first stage in their journey to Baghdad.

For the historian, the problems multiply once we try to establish how the three groups came together and who played the more significant parts. Darby related how four friends came to him and he proposed breaking bread together on the following Sunday.[74] In 1864, he reminded the dying Bellett that, with Cronin and Hutchinson, they were the first four to break bread in Dublin.[75] However, Cronin insisted that neither Darby nor Bellett were part of the movement's embryonic stage, and that they were initially reluctant to secede.[76] Bellett recollected being introduced by Darby to Francis Hutchinson (1802-33), son of the Archdeacon of Killala and cousin of John and Edward Synge (of whom more below). In November 1829, Hutchinson offered a room in his house in Fitzwilliam Square for breaking bread at a different time from local church services, initially with a prescribed pattern of worship. All who loved the Lord were welcome, and it appears that Cronin's group were involved from this point.[77] On his return from taking Groves and his missionary party as far as St Petersburg, Parnell joined with them and proposed moving to a room in Aungier Street. This they did in May 1830, though some were apprehensive, feeling that it implied the setting up of a separate church. Bellett and Hutchinson were reluctant, and Darby absent; the motivating spirit appears to have been Parnell. Various explanations have been offered for the move: Bellett attributed it to Parnell's wish that their celebration of the Lord's Supper would be more of a public witness, while Cronin thought that it was a less intimidating venue for poorer believers.[78] More recently, Carter has followed Embley in suggesting that the move sprang from a desire to consolidate the smaller meetings and to raise the movement's public profile, as well as a concern to put the poor at ease.[79]

In September 1830, a second party set out to join Groves in Baghdad, which included Parnell, Cronin, his mother and his sister, and F.W. Newman, brother of John Henry Newman. Darby was spending increasing amounts of time itinerating in England, Scotland, and France, while Hutchinson died in 1833. Thus many of the group's original leaders dispersed or died during the 1830s. Beattie asserts that it soon ceased to meet,[80] but this is open to question: Bellett remained active in Dublin for some while and another Brethren leader, R.C. Chapman, found two or three hundred meeting in a room in Brunswick Street to break bread when visiting the city in April 1848.[81] It seems that this meeting divided in the wake of the general division which affected the movement that year. Although Brunswick Street was apparently still in existence as late as 1858 and

---

[74] *Ibid.*, 14; Darby, *Letters*, 3.301 [185-].

[75] Darby, *Letters*, 1.383 (September 1864); for the identification of Bellett as the recipient of this letter, see Napoleon Noel, *A History of the Brethren* (ed. William F. Knapp; London: Chapter Two, 1993 [1936]), 1.48.

[76] Anon., *Interesting Reminiscences*, 17, 19.

[77] *Ibid.*, 3, 5-6, 14.

[78] *Ibid.*, 6, 17.

[79] Carter, *Anglican Evangelicals*, 199-200, following Peter L. Embley, 'The Origins and Early Development of the Plymouth Brethren' (PhD thesis, St Paul's College, Cheltenham, 1966), 59.

[80] Beattie, *Brethren*, 300.

[81] J.H. Hake (ed.), *Letters of the late Robert Cleaver Chapman* (London and Glasgow: Echoes of Service and Pickering & Inglis, [1903]), 147.

(according to Bellett) included some who had been members since the 1830s,[82] the assembly at Merrion Hall, which was to become one of the largest Open assemblies during the late nineteenth century, appears to have been started independently in 1863.

As for the rest of Ireland, in spite of Buchanan's pioneering work near Omagh, there appear to have been very few assemblies in Ulster before 1859; Beattie knew of none before the one founded in 1840 at The Clare, near Banbridge in County Down.[83] Elsewhere, apart from groups recorded at Limerick[84] and Ennis,[85] an assembly began to meet at Bandon, County Cork, during the 1830s; Bellett's brother George was curate there from 1830-40, and several who had been converted under his ministry decided to take things further than he did, withdrawing from the Establishment.[86] In Cork itself, an assembly appears to have commenced very early on: G.V. Wigram, who was to play a crucial role in the emergence of the assembly at Plymouth, spent a long time there before leaving Ireland for Devon in 1831.[87] Yet by 1850, there may have been no more than a dozen assemblies throughout Ireland.[88] One factor in the movement's failure to grow significantly in much of the country has been highlighted by Coad, who suggests that its progress was largely among the Protestant Anglo-Irish community; he lists a number of gentry and clergy who joined, noting that in time many emigrated to England.[89] This would have weakened the leadership base. Catholics would also have been suspicious of attempts to convert them by members of the Protestant ascendancy.

However, the movement was to provide at least one *cause celèbre,* in the area around Westport in County Mayo.[90] This was one of several meetings in whose formation Darby played a leading role in localities where clergy had recently seceded. The Church of Ireland in Westport was unfortunate in the relatively brief tenures of office of many of its clergy. The first of note was a curate, Edward Hardman, who moved to Ballincholla in 1831. Whilst heavily influenced by Darby and others, he refused to secede, but on adopting Irvingite views in 1834 (which he published in a pamphlet on 1 Corinthians 12-14) the Evangelical Archbishop Trench of Tuam suspended his licence. Hardman became Angel (bishop of a local congregation) of the Irvingite church in Dublin, and appears to have targeted the group at Aungier Street as a potential source of converts.[91]

---

[82] Anon., *Interesting Reminiscences*, 9.

[83] Beattie, *Brethren*, 280, 283.

[84] Coad, *History*, 83; Rowdon, *Origins*, 95-6.

[85] A Brethren-style meeting for the Breaking of Bread is said to have existed in Ennis during the late 1820s; Cronin visited it, possibly in 1828 (Rowdon, *Origins*, 104-5, following Anon., *Interesting Reminiscences*, 9-10). However, this may be a case of later understandings of assembly practice being read back into recollections of earlier events; this is especially likely in Ireland, given the existence there of various precursors of the Brethren. It could have been such a gathering that Cronin visited.

[86] Beattie, *Brethren*, 300-1.

[87] Anon., *Interesting Reminiscences*, 11, 15.

[88] Carter, *Anglican Evangelicals*, 63, following W. Urwick, *Brief Sketch of the Religious State of Ireland* (Dublin, 1852), 16.

[89] Coad, *History*, 84.

[90] See Rowdon, *Origins*, 100-4; Joseph D'Arcy Sirr, *A Memoir of the Honorable and Most Reverend Power le Poer Trench, last Archbishop of Tuam* (Dublin: William Curry, Jun., 1845), 338-45, 421-6.

[91] Anon., 'Irvingism in Ireland', *CE* n.s. 4 (1835), 521.

Also resident in the parish of Westport was the rector of the neighbouring parish of Kilmena, Charles Hargrove (1792-1870). Having already been in trouble with Archbishop Trench on account of his itinerant evangelistic activities, he seceded in 1835 to join the Brethren, as did his curate, J.M. Code, the following year.[92] Hargrove produced an apologia for his secession which focused on two issues. One was the worldliness of the religious Establishment: the confusion of the church and the world in it meant that the church lost its distinctive character; Christians could not stand out from the world, and others were lulled into a false sense of security by virtue of belonging to such a body; by contrast, the heavenly calling of believers entailed a clear separation from the world. The other issue was the doctrinal error found in the Prayer Book: baptismal regeneration, and the application of the liturgy to non-Christians, as in the Lord's Supper and the burial service.[93] Hargrove's secession created a furore, and in 1836 the rector of Kilcoleman, D'Arcy Sirr, published *A Dissuasive from Separation*, criticising Brethren views on separatism, ministry, and ordination; he also produced testy responses to Hargrove and later to Code.[94] The whole episode generated considerable ill-feeling and did much to polarise opinion on both sides.

Apart from its perceived divisive impact, another reason for the widespread suspicion of the new movement was its allegedly extremist views on eschatological subjects. The prevalent sense of unrest and apprehension contributed to an interest in prophecy which was evident across the Irish religious spectrum. Trinity College, Dublin, which trained men for the ministry of the Church of Ireland, had tutors on its faculty who wrote on the subject. There was widespread interest in it among Evangelicals, and there is some evidence of millenarian speculation within Catholicism as well. One person who fostered this interest was Theodosia Wingfield, Countess Powerscourt (1800-36).[95] She was an example of the close-knit nature of the Irish Evangelical network: her sister married Parnell's uncle and a daughter of theirs became Wigram's second wife. Wigram was also connected with Lady Powerscourt through his first wife, Fanny Bligh. Lady Powerscourt had experienced an Evangelical conversion through the ministry of Daly as her rector, and had been widowed in her early twenties.[96] Darby had thoughts of marrying her, although he was apparently advised that it would be better for his work if he remained single.[97]

Residential conferences played a significant role in other contemporary movements; an example is the series of conferences for prophetic study held annually at Albury, Surrey, from 1826 to 1830. These attracted clergy and laity from all over the British Isles

---

[92] On Hargrove and Code, see *BDEB*.

[93] Charles Hargrove, *Reasons for Retiring from the Established Church* (London: Tract Depot, 1838).

[94] Joseph D'Arcy Sirr, *Reasons for Abiding in the Established Church: a letter to the Rev. Charles Hargrove, A.B.* (Dublin: R.M. Tims, 1836); idem., *Westport Darbyism Exposed* (Dublin: Wm. Curry, Jun., 1843).

[95] On Lady Powerscourt, see *BDEB*; Lady Powerscourt, *The Letters & Papers of Lady Powerscourt* (London: Chapter Two, 2004 (first published 1838)).

[96] T.C.F. Stunt to F.R. Coad, 6 September 1966 (CBA Box 164); T.C.F. Stunt to the author, 28 November 2003.

[97] G.H. Lang, 'Inquire of the Former Age (II)', *The Disciple*, 1.2 (October 1953), 16.

and were dominated by Edward Irving and the host, the banker Henry Drummond.[98] They were a major factor in the development of a network which later assumed a more churchly form as the Catholic Apostolic Church. In Ireland, the Evangelical cleric Edward Synge had hosted a residential meeting for prophetic study at Kilkerran, near Galway, soon after moving there in 1829.[99] This, and memories of one of the Albury conferences, doubtless influenced Lady Powerscourt to arrange and host a week's meeting for prophetic study in 1830 for invited clergy from England, Scotland, and Ireland, to be chaired by Daly.[100] Among the topics on the agenda were the restoration of the Jews, the covenants in Scripture, present and future distinctions between Jews and Christians, and the present position and duties of Christians. The conference became an annual event, and an anonymous pamphlet published in 1838 lists the topics discussed, *Questions for Eight Weeks' Consideration, Addressed to the Church of God*.[101] This sheds considerable light on the issues which concerned the Brethren during this period. The 1831 conference was to discuss the gifts of the Spirit, the state of the world and the church at the Second Coming, and the 1,260 days of Daniel and Revelation: were these days or years, literal or symbolic? Early attenders had an opportunity to discuss the gifts of the Spirit, doubtless in the light of claims that tongues, prophecy, and healing had been restored in the west of Scotland in 1830.

The first two Powerscourt conferences had provided occasions for fellowship between Evangelicals from various denominations, but their unity was to be fractured by events at the 1832 conference. Topics discussed included the following:

> Wednesday 'Should we expect a personal Antichrist? ... Is there any uniform sense for the word *Saint* in the Prophetic, or New Testament scripture? By what covenant did the Jews, and shall the Jews, hold the land?' And on Friday 'Is there a prospect of a revival of Apostolic churches before the coming of Christ? What are the duties arising out of present events?'[102]

Darby reported that the division between Brethren participants and those from the established churches had caused great tension.[103] A report alleged that vital eschatological questions were 'assumed, rather than proposed as debatable; and the discussions, of course, turned upon the deductions from these *assumed* facts, and the doctrines supposed to be connected with them'. The critic also considered it unseemly for women and young people to be present during discussions on such issues.[104]

---

[98] For a fairly full account of these conferences and their significance which distances them from Darbyite dispensationalism, see Columba Graham Flegg, *'Gathered under Apostles', A Study of the Catholic Apostolic Church* (Oxford: Clarendon, 1992), 34-41.

[99] Sirr, *Trench*, 198.

[100] Although scholars have debated this, it does appear that Lady Powerscourt attended one of the Albury conferences on prophecy, held annually from 1826-30: in 1826, she wrote to Daly, 'I am going to the prophets' meeting at Mr. Drummond's' (Mrs. Madden, *Daly*, 149-50). Lady Powerscourt was already hosting monthly meetings for prophetic study by 1830, but these were not residential.

[101] Reproduced as an appendix to the reprint of Lady Powerscourt, *Letters*. Information from this pamphlet about dates and locations of conferences is tabulated in Appendix I.

[102] Darby, *Letters*, 1.7n.

[103] *Ibid.*, 1.16 [1833].

[104] *CE* n.s. 1 (1832), 790-1.

Apart from the likelihood of controversy arising out of any expression of dispensational thinking, there was the issue of charismatic gifts. Rowdon notes that

> ... the question of the supernatural gifts loomed large. In his account of this conference, Darby said no more than that 'there was marked and universal (I may say almost) reference to the Spirit',[105] but an evangelical clergyman who was present noted in his diary that at the conference 'the duty of seeking for miraculous gifts was strongly insisted upon!'[106]

A third controversial topic concerned the relation of the believer to the existing churches. Although Darby appears to have been reluctant to leave the Church of Ireland, he had become increasingly pessimistic about its future, especially after getting embroiled in a controversy over religious education in which he saw a new and threatening development – an alliance between infidelity and Romanism. Magee had been succeeded as Archbishop of Dublin in October 1831 by Richard Whately. Whately inherited a government proposing to restrict the teaching of Scripture in Irish schools, in deference to Roman Catholic objections, and began to promote it.[107] Darby had protested against such a course, attacking not only Whately's policy but also his personal beliefs.[108] If the Church of Ireland could not discipline such a man, he asserted, it must be ripe for judgement.[109] The Establishment was no longer an effective barrier against Romanism or infidelity, and henceforward he began to call for separation from apostasy, in the expectation of imminent eschatological judgement. With reference to Powerscourt, Rowdon asserts that 'It seems quite clear that Darby had been arguing that one of "the duties arising out of ... present events" was to withdraw from existing churches, and that another was to meet together in Brethren fashion.'[110] This, in fact, is what Lady Powerscourt would do, and her secession encouraged other Evangelical families to do likewise.[111] Small wonder, then, that at the conclusion Daly voiced his strong sense of impending evil.[112] He participated in no further conferences, and Anglicans gradually withdrew because of the preoccupation with prophetic study at the expense of evangelism.

The 1833 conference was therefore chaired by John Synge (1788-1845), who was sympathetic to the separatists, although he never seceded himself.[113] Among the questions discussed were the relationship between the Jewish and Christian 'churches', the analogy between the close of this dispensation and the close of the previous one, and

---

[105] Darby, *Letters*, 1.7 (15 October 1832).

[106] Rowdon, *Origins*, 80. For Darby's account, see *CH* 3 (1832), 290-2, reproduced in Darby, *Letters,* 1.5-7n.

[107] Stunt, *Awakening*, 272.

[108] Darby, 'A Letter on a Serious Question connected with the Irish Education Measures of 1832', *CW*, 32.306-14. He asserted that Whately was a Sabellian; Sabellius was a third-century heretic who had asserted that Father, Son, and Holy Spirit were simply different modes of God's self-revelation in the history of redemption.

[109] Darby, *CW*, 32.297; cf. Rowdon, *Origins*, 91.

[110] Rowdon, *Origins*, 94.

[111] Carter, *Anglican Evangelicals*, 208, following Walter Alison Philips, *History of the Church of Ireland* (Oxford: Oxford University Press, 1934), 3.352.

[112] Mrs. Madden, *Daly*, 154.

[113] John was Edward Synge's brother and an educationalist. See *BDEB*; Stunt, *Awakening*, passim; idem, 'John Synge and the Early Brethren', *JCBRF* 28 (1976), 39-62.

whether the call to come out of Babylon referred only to a particular period in history or represented a perpetual obligation. A future Exclusive Brethren leader, J.B. Stoney (1814-97), recalled that some Irvingites were present, although subsequently, as Darby's separatist note became increasingly insistent, those influenced by Irvingism 'gradually drew away from us and their society was avoided'.[114] Seven of the participants broke bread together away from the rest, an event which symbolised the emergence of the Brethren as a separate group of churches.[115]

In old age, Benjamin Wills Newton (1807-99), whose leadership at Plymouth would precipitate a devastating disagreement with Darby from 1845, asserted that Darby and Lady Powerscourt had set up these conferences to establish some kind of unity among Brethren.[116] He recalled that early Brethren relied wholly on private judgement; Darby and Lady Powerscourt recognised that, 'and so annual meetings were organised which should direct & control that individual judgment'.[117] Darby was thus using the conferences to establish his interpretation of prophecy as the normative one for the new movement.[118] Newton's recollections have a touch of paranoia about them because of his later antipathy towards Darby, but they do point to the importance of these conferences in providing a measure of cohesion for the rapidly-spreading movement.

After Lady Powerscourt moved out of the main property on the estate, the Irish conferences were held in Dublin from 1834.[119] That year, participants considered the church's divided condition, and pondered when the world had been given up to Satan. The views expressed seem to have been increasingly extreme; as one attender recalled, 'many wild and unsatisfactory opinions were started – so much so, that sober-minded people would not attend.'[120] Some within the Brethren movement also disapproved of Darby's views: the gap between Newton's views and Darby's was widening, as Newton's opposition to anything resembling Irvingite teaching led him to oppose Darby's developing belief in a rapture of believers to heaven before the Great Tribulation. Accordingly, Newton convened a meeting at Plymouth in 1834 at the same time as the Irish conference and considering the same questions. His action angered Darby, who saw it as proof of his isolationism, although the advertisement described the meeting as being for those prevented from visiting Ireland.[121]

The questions considered in 1835 took things a stage further, asking what separation from the world was involved in the present position of believers. 'Does each dispensation

---

[114] Anon., *Interesting Reminiscences*, 20-1. On Stoney, see H[enr]y Pickering (ed.), *Chief Men among the Brethren* (London: Pickering & Inglis, [1931]²), 88-9.

[115] W. Elfe Tayler, *Passages from the Diary and Letters of Henry Craik, of Bristol* (London: J.F. Shaw, [1866]), 168-9. The seven were Darby, Bellett, Percy Hall, George Müller, Henry Craik, B.W. Newton, and Lady Powerscourt.

[116] On Newton, see *BDE*; *BDEB*; Burnham, *Conflict*; *ODNB*.

[117] Fry Collection, 'Small Notebook 8', f. 63b (CBA 7062).

[118] Rowdon, *Origins*, 96, following 'Fry MS Book', 283 (CBA 7049).

[119] A.M. Stoney, *An account of early days* (London: Chapter Two, 1995), 3.

[120] Dora Pennefather to Mrs. C, 14 March 1835 (Robert Braithwaite, *The Life and Letters of Rev. William Pennefather, B.A.* (London: John F. Shaw, n.d.)).

[121] For a summary of Newton's views on the subjects discussed, see [B.W. Newton and H. Borlase], *Answers to the questions considered at a meeting held at Plymouth on September 15, 1834, and the following Days; chiefly compiled from Notes taken at the Meeting* (Plymouth: Tract Depot, 1847²).

end in apostasy only – or is the dispensation revived in a remnant, the rejection of which consummates the apostasy?' What light was shed by the historical portions of Scripture upon the characteristics of the close of the present dispensation?[122] Such questions show how some, at least, of the Brethren saw themselves and their movement as part of an eschatological remnant, perhaps paralleling the remnant who returned from exile in Babylon during the Old Testament era. The *Christian Herald,* which had been founded in 1830 to provide an Irish outlet for Evangelical prophetic interest, distanced itself from the views now being expressed by the Powerscourt circle, before ceasing publication in 1835 because of the editor's conviction that the prophetic movement had been taken over by extremists.[123]

The dispensational theme was continued in 1836, the syllabus including such questions as: 'What contrast and what resemblance may be discerned in design, workings, and end, between the dispensations revealed in Scripture? How many may there be? ... When is Scripture to be taken spiritually, when literally? ... How do the faithful from an Apostasy differ in character and testimony from the opening of a Dispensation?'[124] The third question was to be a bone of contention between Darby and Newton during the 1840s with reference to the interpretation of prophecy, but at Powerscourt it was raised with primary reference to such injunctions as those in the Sermon on the Mount regarding the use of oaths and not resisting evil, matters which were of vital interest to early Brethren as they worked out their relation to the civil order. The conference also discussed how to preserve unity in the treatment of brethren in error, an issue which was becoming somewhat pressing in view of Newman's increasing unorthodoxy. Further conferences were held in England, and we shall explore their significance later.

2.3 Radical Evangelicals at Oxford

A number of future Brethren leaders were students at Oxford during the 1820s, a period when Evangelicalism in the university was characterised by volatility and conflict.[125] Among them was Newton, one of the ablest minds among nineteenth-century Brethren. Of Quaker extraction, he was influenced as a schoolboy to adopt Anglican views by the former Quaker Thomas Byrth, who combined schoolmastering with the charge of the parish of Diptford, near Plymouth. However, it was not until Newton was a student at Exeter College that he experienced an Evangelical conversion, in 1827. Already recognised as a brilliant scholar, he had become a fellow of the college before graduating; he explained his success as due to the fact that the total concentration required for his work provided his only relief from despair under conviction of sin. On conversion, he experienced a strong reaction against his Quaker upbringing, informing his mother that 'Friends, as a society, have not the knowledge of God.'[126] This reaction would colour his thinking on matters of spirituality and church order and bring him into conflict with

---

[122] Anon., *Questions for Eight Weeks' Consideration*, 10-11.

[123] E.N. Hoare, 'The Conclusion of the Christian Herald', *Christian Herald* 5 (1835), 216-21.

[124] Anon., *Questions for Eight Weeks' Consideration*, 12-13.

[125] For fuller accounts, see Carter, *Anglican Evangelicals*, ch. 7; J.S. Reynolds, *The Evangelicals at Oxford 1735-1871: a record of an unchronicled movement, with the record extended to 1905* (Appleford, Oxon.: Marcham Manor Press, 1975); Stunt, *Awakening*, 183-219, 251-9.

[126] 'Fry MS', 126 (Newton to his mother, 30 December 1827).

Darby and others, but at this stage his intent was to proceed to ordination in the Church of England.

A second member of the network was Henry Bellenden Bulteel (1805-66), also a fellow of Exeter, and curate at St Ebbe's.[127] Bulteel had been converted in 1825-6 and had become a Calvinist some months later. He was to provoke a heated religious controversy by a sermon which he preached before the university on 6 February 1831.[128] Making a vigorous defence of the Calvinist doctrine of the Thirty-Nine Articles, Bulteel condemned the shortcomings of contemporary Anglicanism, such as the ordination of those manifestly unfitted for the office, the exercise of power in the church by the monarch, and the opposition of the clergy to its fundamental teachings. Unless repentance was evident, destruction would follow. Not only the Establishment, but also moderate Evangelicals, condemned the sermon, but Darby issued a vigorous defence.[129] Within six months, Bulteel had been ejected from his charge by the Bishop of Oxford after undertaking a preaching tour to the West Country with another cleric on the verge of secession, William Tiptaft.[130] Coad suggests that these and other secessions at Oxford appear to have incited considerable official disapproval of Darby, and may have reinforced his increasingly negative attitude towards the Establishment.[131]

George Vicesimus Wigram

A third notable individual was George Vicesimus Wigram (1805-79), a wealthy student at Queen's, who had been converted in 1824.[132] Bulteel introduced Newton to Wigram in Autumn 1827, and Newton appears to have found him more congenial company than many Oxford Evangelicals, describing him as 'more intellectual' and having a 'broader mind'.[133] Nevertheless, with memories soured by Wigram's inflammatory role in the

---

[127] On Bulteel, see *BDEB*; Carter, *Anglican Evangelicals*, 253-83; *ODNB*.

[128] H.B. Bulteel, *A Sermon on I Corinthians II.12 Preached before the University of Oxford, at St. Mary's on Sunday, February 6, 1831* (Oxford: W. Baxter, 1831).

[129] Darby, 'The Doctrine of the Church of England, at the time of the Reformation, of the Reformation itself, of Scripture, and of the Church of Rome, briefly compared with the Remarks of the Regius Professor of Divinity', *CW*, 3.1-43.

[130] Tiptaft was to become a Strict Baptist.

[131] Coad, *History*, 82, following Anon., *Interesting Reminiscences*, 21.

[132] On Wigram, see *BDEB*; *ODNB*; Stunt, *Awakening*.

[133] 'Fry MS', 262.

divisions of the 1840s, Newton later noted the contrast between Wigram's shabby clothes and his expensive horses[134] and alleged that he 'virtually killed his first wife by asceticism'.[135] Wigram provided finance for various early Brethren ventures, and lived at Powerscourt from September 1830 to March 1831, while working on a project (which he was funding) to produce a concordance to the Greek New Testament for use by those who knew only English.[136]

F.W. Newman (1805-97), brother of John Henry, is the fourth Oxford radical whom we must introduce.[137] Converted to Evangelical faith while at school, Newman graduated from Worcester College in 1826 and was then elected a fellow of Balliol. He went to Dublin during Autumn 1827 as a private tutor in the household of Darby's brother-in-law; there he came under the spell of the convalescent Darby, and was impressed by his other-worldliness and commitment to one book – the Bible.[138] Darby's developing views on the last things made a deep impression on Newman, who began meetings for prophetic study on his return to Oxford in April 1828.[139] Newton (to whom he was a private tutor and in whose rooms the meetings took place) was captivated. He had been dissatisfied (as was Wigram) with the dullness and narrowness of Oxford Evangelicalism and that '<u>F.W. Newman introduced to me Prophetic Truth & it turned the whole current of my life</u>.'[140] Newman persuaded Darby to visit Oxford in the early summer of 1830, introducing him to Newton, who was immediately won over: '<u>Darby</u> was the only person I knew then, who saw that separation from the world was necessarily involved in prophetic truth.'[141] This perspective would govern his ecclesiastical relationships for the rest of his life.

At some point during Spring 1830, news reached Oxford and London of an outbreak of charismatic manifestations in the west of Scotland.[142] Darby visited the scene: 'The sense he had of the want and power of the Holy Ghost in the Church made him willing to hear and see.'[143] However, he was not convinced of the divine origin of the manifestations, as Newton recalled: '[Darby] returned saying he had carefully watched everything, and one thing he noticed decidedly – that was that they denied the application of prophetic

---

[134] *Ibid.*, 303.

[135] *Ibid.*, 30.

[136] An account of the project appears in George V. Wigram, *The Englishman's Greek Concordance of the New Testament*, which has often been reprinted.

[137] On F.W. Newman, see *BDEB*; F.W. Newman, *Phases of Faith; or, passages from the history of my creed* (London: John Chapman, 1850); *ODNB*.

[138] Newman's predecessor in the post had been Philpot, on whom Darby had made a similar impression ('Editors' Review. *The Christian Witness*', *GS* 8 (1842), 78). Darby asserted that he had been instrumental in Philpot's conversion (*Letters*, 3.167 (27 July 1881)), though Philpot nowhere confirms this; Stunt points out that at that stage Darby's 'deliverance' had not yet occurred (*Awakening*, 205).

[139] 'Fry MS', 62-5 (Newman to Newton, 17 April 1828); Stunt, *Awakening*, 210-11.

[140] 'Fry MS', 79.

[141] *Ibid.*, 184, cf. 60-1.

[142] For details, see J.B. Cardale, 'On the Extraordinary Manifestations at Port Glasgow', *Morning Watch* 2 (1830), 869-73; Edward Irving, *Narrative of Facts connected with recent manifestations of Spiritual Gifts*, reprinted from *Fraser's Magazine* (London: James Fraser, 1832). These have been summarised ably by Gordon Strachan, *The Pentecostal Theology of Edward Irving* (London: Darton, Longman & Todd, 1973), chs. 6-7.

[143] Darby, *CW*, 6.284 [1853].

Scriptures & promises to Israel._ In a moment that decided me._ It convinced me unhesitatingly that the work was not of God, furnishing – [*sic*] one with a clear proof.'[144]

Running through Newton's rejection of Irvingism, of Darby's later 'mystical' or 'impulsive' view of ministry, and of the Quaker aspect of his own background, was an antipathy towards mysticism in any form. This undoubtedly helped to sour his later relations with Darby. Soon after his conversion, he had contrasted the silent Quaker meetings (in which he had never heard the gospel) with what he saw as Bulteel's anointed ministry.[145] He was therefore distressed to find on returning to Oxford from Plymouth in October 1831 that Bulteel had become an Irvingite, although the latter recanted his belief after a nervous breakdown in 1833.[146]

As for Newman, whilst he had been impressed by news of the manifestations, he eventually rejected both them and the Pauline teaching concerning such phenomena.[147] In 1830 he joined the party which went out to relieve Groves at Baghdad, returning late in 1832. Looking back, he considered that this time away from Darby's influence allowed his mind freedom to develop, and he read the New Testament without the accumulated baggage of centuries of church history.[148] This was something of which other Brethren would have approved, but they did not approve of its results in Newman's case: gradually he came to reject the traditional understanding of the deity of Christ, and the supernatural aspects of Christianity. For a while there was no unanimity in his treatment by Brethren: in a letter to Darby he contrasted his warm reception at Plymouth with the attitude towards him of Brethren at Bethesda, Bristol.[149] However, Darby eventually declared that he could no longer have fellowship either with Newman or with anyone who received him.[150] Newman claimed that Darby warned certain persons that if they did not break off all intercourse with Newman 'they should, as far as his influence went, themselves everywhere be cut off from Christian communion and recognition',[151] the first instance of an approach which he later adopted in dealing with Newton and Plymouth.

2.4 'The Brethren from Plymouth': Beginnings in the South-West

Brethren history in Devon owed much to John Synge, who belonged to Groves' circle of Dublin contacts but was resident in Devon from 1827 to 1832. In 1828 he invited a young Scotsman, Henry Craik (1805-66), to his home near Teignmouth to become tutor to his

---

[144] 'Fry MS', 234, cf. 207-8.

[145] *Ibid.*, 125 (Newton to his mother, 30 December 1827).

[146] For fuller coverage of this episode, see Tim Grass, '"The Restoration of a Congregation of Baptists": Baptists and Irvingism in Oxfordshire', *BQ* 37 (1998), 283-97.

[147] 'Fry MS', 234, 244; Newman, *Phases of Faith*, 177-8.

[148] Newman, *Phases of Faith*, 46.

[149] Darby, *CW*, 6.318. Rowdon asserts that Newman was still orthodox in his beliefs when baptised at Broadmead Baptist Church in Bristol during 1836, and therefore suggests that there was some non-doctrinal factor at the heart of Darby's attitude towards him (*Origins*, 194-5). However, Darby implies that Newman was becoming unorthodox as early as 1833 (*CW*, 6.315-20). Newman himself alleged that an encounter with a Muslim carpenter on the way to Baghdad in 1832 had played a role in his change of views (*BDEB*), and Newton put Newman's error down to 'that mistaken and disastrous missionary enterprise' ('Fry MS', 60-1).

[150] Darby, *CW*, 6.320.

[151] Newman, *Phases of Faith*, 58-9, cited in Rowdon, *Origins*, 194-5.

two sons.[152] Craik had been converted as a divinity student at St Andrew's in 1826, and had become tutor to Groves and his family that autumn. It was from Groves that he learned to 'live by faith' and practice fellowship with all Christian believers.[153] Groves' impending departure for Baghdad meant that Craik needed to find another situation, and so he joined the Synge household. Craik was already interested in mission, and had been invited to join the group accompanying Groves to Baghdad, but his father was not in good health and he felt obliged to decline. However, he was about to embark on an equally significant pilgrimage, in partnership with George Müller (1805-98).[154]

Müller had been converted during a prayer meeting at Halle in Germany in 1825, while preparing to become a Lutheran pastor. A desire to serve as a missionary brought him to London in March 1829, intending to train with the London Society for Promoting Christianity among the Jews (LSPCJ). Experiencing a physical breakdown shortly after his arrival, he came to convalesce at Teignmouth, a few miles from where Craik was living. Using the time to undertake some serious Bible study, and spending some days with a preacher who had impressed him, he came to a belief in the doctrines of election, particular redemption (the belief that Christ died specifically for the elect), the perseverance of the saints, the premillennial return of Christ, the final authority of the Bible, the Holy Spirit's role as teacher in divine things, and the need for a higher standard of devotedness – beliefs which were to be typical of the early Brethren in Devon. These changes had such an impact on him that he described them as like a second conversion. Müller and Craik came into contact, discovered they had much in common, and warmed to one another immediately.

Henry Craik   George Müller, aged 90

Like Groves, Müller had come to reject the establishment of religion and the need of ordination for preaching the gospel, and in January 1830 he severed his connection with the LSPCJ; he felt called to an itinerant ministry, not restricted to Jews, and wished to be

---

[152] On Craik, see *BDEB*; Tayler, *Craik*.

[153] Dann, *Father of Faith Missions*, 38n, quoting H. Groves, *Darbyism: Its Rise, Progress, and Development, and a review of 'the Bethesda question'* (London: James E. Hawkins, n.d.[3]), 26.

[154] On Müller, see *BDE*; *BDEB*; George Müller (ed. G. Fred. Bergin), *Autobiography of George Müller, or a million and a half in answer to prayer* (London and Bristol: J. Nisbet and The Bible and Tract Warehouse, 1906[2], a one-volume edition of *A Narrative of some of the Lord's Dealings with George Müller*); *ODNB*.

free to follow the Spirit's leading rather than be subject to human direction. He became pastor of a Nonconformist chapel in Teignmouth, and in October 1830 married Groves' sister Mary, whom he had met at Poltimore. Craik came to reject infant baptism, and in April 1831 he concluded his engagement with Synge in order to take the oversight of a Baptist chapel in the nearby village of Shaldon, where he baptised Müller as a believer. Müller soon began to celebrate the Lord's Supper each Sunday, allowing time in the service for open ministry. Influenced by Groves' tract on *Christian Devotedness*, he and his wife renounced a regular salary (which had been financed largely by the customary practice of renting out pews in the chapel to regular worshippers)[155] and decided to dispose of much of their property, as Groves and his wife had done.

Further west, Plymouth was to prove fertile soil for the new movement. The ground here had been prepared by the ministry of the Anglican high Calvinist Robert Hawker (1753-1827).[156] Many early members of the Brethren at Plymouth came from what had been Hawker's congregation, which experienced an unsettled period after his death: Newton recalled that it used periodically 'to swarm off like bees, and form a meeting'.[157] Darby first visited Plymouth in August 1830 or thereabouts, by invitation from Newton, apparently 'to preach in the Churches'.[158] At that stage, Newton was still hoping for the reformation of the Church of England, but he was shaken by three events: the decision of Bulteel and another Oxford radical, W.G. Lambert, to secede; reading a tract entitled *Reasons for leaving the Church of England* while travelling to Oxford to take his final examination for holy orders; and Bulteel's sermon and the resulting controversy.[159] In Summer 1831, Bulteel (who came from a distinguished Plymouth family) and Tiptaft visited Plymouth during their preaching tour, preparing the ground for Brethrenism and Irvingism by their bold denunciation of the Established Church. At some point in 1831, possibly in the early Spring, Newton had also invited Wigram (who had been refused ordination by the Bishop of London, probably on the grounds that he was not a graduate[160]) to Plymouth with the promise of introducing him to clergy who would welcome his ministry. Wigram was active in introducing Brethren ideas there and in

[155] According to Stephen Holthaus, Müller had begun to 'live by faith' as early as 1827 ('George Müller in Germany', paper delivered at the BAHN Conference, Wiedenest, Germany, 3 July 2005).

[156] For a critique of Hawker's views and practice, see Joseph Cottle, *Strictures on the Plymouth Antinomians* (London: T. Cadell, 1823). 'High Calvinism' was a version of Calvinism which minimised human activity in connection with salvation, and which often denied that the Law of God was to be regarded as the believer's rule of life (the latter belief was also known as Antinomianism). Many high Calvinists refused to persuade unbelievers to come to Christ on the grounds that this implied that their hearers possessed a natural ability to do so, and confined themselves to factual declarations of the way of salvation. 'Hyper-Calvinism' went beyond this in refusing to preach the gospel, even in a high Calvinist form, to all indiscriminately.

[157] Fry Collection, 'Reminiscences 1', 145 (CBA 7067). On Anglican Evangelicalism in Plymouth, see Stunt, *Awakening*, 288-9.

[158] 'Fry MS', 336 (Darby to Newton, April 1845).

[159] *Ibid.*, 100, 254-5; Fry Collection, 'Small Notebook 4' (CBA 7059), 118.

[160] Stunt, *Awakening*, 279. Newton was thus incorrect in attributing the Bishop's refusal to dislike of Wigram's extreme Evangelicalism ('Small Notebook 4', 114).

December 1831 he obtained a chapel in Raleigh Street, 'Providence', where prophetic subjects could be preached on.[161]

At this stage, the separatist impulse which would mark the assembly at Plymouth was barely evident. Local clergy attended the meetings, which were arranged to avoid clashing with church services; Darby recalled that: 'More than once, even with ministers of the national church, we have broken bread on Monday evening after meetings for christian edification, where each was free to read, to speak, to pray, or to give out a hymn.' But he went on: 'Some months afterwards we began to do so on Sunday morning, making use of the same liberty, only adding the Lord's supper...'[162] Newton and Darby were apparently taken by surprise in January 1832 when the Lord's Supper, which at Wigram's suggestion had already been observed semi-privately in the vestry, was first publicly celebrated (apparently also at Wigram's instigation); the clergy also stopped attending at this point.[163] As in Dublin, it was the taking of a more public stance which incurred disapproval. Newton asserted that 'no one knew what to do, for the moment, but they just drifted into acquiescence'.[164] I think he overstated the case, and that Darby and others would have seen this action as expressing something of their half-conscious aspirations, but it is important to realise that the developed pattern of assembly life did not emerge all at once.

Neither was there an agreed doctrinal understanding. A clash of prophetic views occurred between the strong-minded Wigram and Percy Francis Hall (1801-84).[165] Hall, whose father had been Regius Professor of Divinity and then Dean of Christ Church, Oxford, was said to have commanded the coastguards at Plymouth, although there is no evidence for this in Navy records.[166] On adopting pacifist views, he published a pamphlet entitled *Discipleship; or, Reasons for resigning his naval rank and pay*. Like several other early leaders, Hall sold his possessions and adopted a simple lifestyle. A persuasive preacher who could draw large congregations, Hall began to advocate the doctrine of the secret rapture, the belief that the saints will be caught up *secretly* to heaven and so escape the Great Tribulation which precedes Christ's visible return to earth. Although Wigram denounced it, Hall's view appears to have 'swept the board'.[167] Hall also insisted on making the doctrine of the immediate Second Coming (i.e. the belief that there were no biblical prophecies whose fulfilment was to be expected before the Lord's Return) a test of

---

[161] Rowdon, *Origins*, 76, following 'Fry MS', 254-5; C.E. Welch, 'The First Plymouth Brethren Chapel', *Devon and Cornwall Notes & Queries* 29 (1962-4), 9.

[162] Darby, *Letters*, 3.301-2 [185-]. Newton recalled that initially 'we only met on Monday mornings, and had clergymen attending, & we had the Lord's Supper and discussed subjects' (Fry Collection, 'Small Notebook 7', 145a (CBA 7061).

[163] Wigram had begun doing this privately every Sunday while at Oxford (Anon., *Interesting Reminiscences*, 15). There is reason to believe that he had witnessed similar gatherings at Geneva in 1824, immediately after his conversion; probably his thinking on such matters both influenced Newton and predisposed the group at Plymouth to contact with brethren from Switzerland (Stunt, *Awakening*, 199, 300).

[164] 'Fry MS', 300.

[165] On Hall, see *BDEB*. For the date of Hall's birth, I am indebted to Michael Schneider, '"The extravagant side of Brethrenism": Studies in the life of Percy Francis Hall (1801-84)', paper delivered at the BAHN Conference, Wiedenest, Germany, 4 July 2005.

[166] Schneider, 'Hall'.

[167] 'Fry MS', 238.

preachers at Plymouth. As if this were not enough, Newton recalled hearing Hall 'pray that the same gifts that were working in London might be given to' the believers there.[168] Newton must have been considerably disturbed, since he had left Oxford because of Bulteel's Irvingite extravagances; he later alleged that Wigram left Plymouth for London over the rapture issue.[169] However, Darby was frequently in Plymouth from 1830 to 1832, and he helped Newton sort things out. As part of this, Newton recalled being nominated by Darby as the presiding elder, whose function in meetings was to restrain the ungifted from participating.[170] Hall was soon cured of some of his enthusiasm: breakfasting with Irving in London soon after the publication of *Discipleship*, he defended the position he had taken. Irving told him in no uncertain terms that he was wrong to have resigned from the Navy as he had, as he should have sought to serve Christ in the world.

In spite of the confusion, Darby's testimony was that in Plymouth, rather than in Dublin, he had found his ideals realised: 'Plymouth ... has altered the face of Christianity to me, from finding brethren, and they acting together.'[171] Stressing the need to avoid sectarianism, he wrote to one member at Plymouth: 'I feel daily more the importance of the Christians at P., and I do trust that you will keep infinitely far from sectarianism. ... You are nothing, nobody, but Christians, and the moment you cease to be an available mount for communion for any consistent Christian, you will go to pieces or help the evil.'[172]

However, a more negative note soon began to be heard at Plymouth, especially after the accession of two local clergy. The first was Henry Borlase (1806-35), curate of St Keyne, Cornwall, who seceded late in 1832.[173] He produced two explanations of his actions: *Reasons for withdrawing from the ministry of the Church of England* (1833) and 'Separation from Apostasy not Schism'.[174] Borlase maintained that the Established Church was a hopeless mixture of the world and the church, whereas believers were to be a called-out minority in the world; consequently, it was impossible to practise church discipline. The Establishment was forced to treat as Christians all who were within its jurisdiction, while true believers were frequently excluded because they could not assent to the Thirty-Nine Articles. He viewed such a condition as apostasy, and rejected the idea of a coming time of glory for the church and adopting the belief that the end of the dispensation would be a time of spiritual darkness. The Church of England was schismatic because it was guilty of insisting on 'things indifferent' in its rites and ceremonies, of laying down inappropriate requirements for ordination to its ministry, of excluding laymen from speaking, and of hindering the freedom of the Spirit in worship; separation from such a body was always right. Newton, who became a thoroughgoing separatist, testified that he and Borlase saw eye to eye on everything except baptism (Borlase continued to hold paedobaptist views).[175] In Stunt's opinion, Borlase's secession

---

[168] *Ibid.*, 252-3. However, Newton also stated that Hall had urged that preaching should focus on the gospel rather than on doctrine or prophecy (*ibid.*, 78). Perhaps this refers to an earlier phase of his ministry.

[169] *Ibid.*, 238.

[170] Coad, *History*, 63; 'Fry MS', 301.

[171] Darby, *Letters*, 3.230 (13 April 1832).

[172] *Ibid.*, 1.18 (received 30 April 1833).

[173] For Borlase, see *BDEB*; *ODNB*.

[174] *CWit* 1 (1834), 332-57.

[175] 'Fry MS', 289. A useful summary of Borlase's views appears in Coad, *History*, 64-6.

stimulated the movement to develop a more principled and thoroughgoing separatist stance.[176] With Newton, he established a school as a source of income, and he also served as the first editor of the *Christian Witness*. However, early in 1834 he suffered a ruptured blood vessel, which led to his death the following year.

The second clerical seceder was Bulteel's cousin James Lampen Harris (1793-1877), perpetual curate of Plymstock.[177] Harris resigned his curacy in 1832, explaining his decision (arising from concerns similar to those expressed by Borlase) in an *Address to the Parishioners of Plymstock* and more fully in *What is a Church? or Reasons for withdrawing from the ministry of the Establishment*. Fundamental to his criticisms of the Anglican liturgy and its use in mixed congregations in which church and world were not, and could not be, separated, was his conviction that 'the law of the land compels me, as a Minister of the Church of England, to do that which it is unlawful for me to do as a Minister of Christ'.[178] Like Borlase, he appears to have remained a paedobaptist.[179] Harris, a cousin of Bulteel, had met Newton and Wigram at Oxford, and soon became a leader at Plymouth. He succeeded Borlase as editor of the *Christian Witness* until its demise early in 1841, and for many years he conducted weekly Bible readings, attended by many from outside the Brethren, and alternated with Newton in ministering on Sundays.

Other clerical accessions included a Mr Moseley, who later shared in oversight at Plymouth and at some point was instrumental in commencing the assembly at Galmpton in South Devon.[180] Richard Hill (1799-1880), who had been curate of West Alvington and South Milton, near Kingsbridge, was another.[181] A local Independent minister by the name of William Morris also joined, with about fifty of his members, and was described by Newton as 'a better preacher than any of us, a most acceptable preacher'.[182] He was to be excommunicated for annihilationist teaching,[183] taking a number with him to another chapel in Princess Street, opened in 1848.[184] Better known, although a layman, was James G. Deck (1807-84): influenced by Groves, he resigned his commission as a military officer in India in 1835 and returned to England intending to seek ordination, but instead associated with Brethren and began working in the villages of Devon. The hymns of devotion written by Deck became much valued by Brethren and others.[185]

---

[176] Stunt, *Awakening*, 293.

[177] On Harris, see *BDEB*.

[178] J.L. Harris, *Address to the Parishioners of Plymstock* (Plymouth: Rowe, 1832), 8.

[179] Cf. R. Cox, *Secession Considered: in a letter to the Rev. J.L. Harris, M.A., late fellow of Exeter College, Oxford, and Perpetual Curate of Plymstock; in Reply to an address to his parishioners, on seceding from the Church of England* (London: Hatchard, 1832), 4.

[180] *H* 3 (1926), 136.

[181] On Hill, see *BDEB*.

[182] 'Small Notebook 4', 125.

[183] Annihilationism, also known as conditional immortality, is the belief that the soul is not naturally immortal, and that after the Last Judgement the wicked are annihilated rather than enduring eternal conscious punishment. It was popularised by the Congregationalist Edward White (see section 3.2).

[184] John Bowes, *The Autobiography or History of the Life of John Bowes* (Glasgow: G. Gallie, 1872), 230-1; A.N. Harris, 'The Plymouth Brethren: reminiscences of over Fifty years ago', 5 (CBA Box 13/29); Michael J.L. Wickes (ed.), *Devon in the Religious Census of 1851: A Transcript of the Devon section of the 1851 Church Census*, ([Appledore]: the author, 1990), return no. 575 (PRO HO129/287).

[185] On Deck, see *BDEB*; David J. Beattie, 'Hymns and their Writers', *BM* n.s. 31 (1930), 141-3.

However, the most significant figure to join the Brethren at Plymouth, at least in terms of his impact on the wider church, was Samuel Prideaux Tregelles (1813-75).[186] Tregelles had a Quaker family background and his cousin had married Newton. Having become interested in biblical prophecy through visiting Newton, he was converted as a result of hearing him preach, and joined the Brethren. Tregelles soon began to devote himself to critical study of the text of Scripture. Assisting Wigram in the production of his concordance to the Greek New Testament, he also undertook much of the work on a similar concordance to the Hebrew Old Testament: when the work done by its original editor, Dr Bialloblotzky (a converted Jew),[187] was discovered to be inadequate, Newton requested Wigram to employ Tregelles, who did much to ensure the work's satisfactory completion. Until the movement divided, Brethren gave an annual sum of money to support Tregelles in his work. From 1845, he began to travel abroad to examine important biblical manuscripts. A fruit of his researches was his critical edition of the Greek New Testament, which appeared in parts from 1857 to widespread acclaim.[188]

Another leading figure at Plymouth was the barrister H.W. Soltau (1805-75), whose sister married Richard Hill.[189] Although he had attended the 1833 Powerscourt conference with Newton, he was only converted in 1837, through Hall's preaching. Soon after his conversion, Soltau decided to give himself full-time to studying the Scriptures and caring for the flock at Plymouth. He became known for his work on *The Tabernacle, the Priesthood and the Offerings*, one of the earliest and most influential Brethren books on Old Testament typology. With a retired judge from India by the name of Clulow, Soltau opened a tract shop at Plymouth, the first of many Brethren publishing and bookselling concerns.[190]

During the 1830s the group in Plymouth began to grow significantly, and the number in fellowship may have reached as many as 1,000, including members from the nearby communities of Devonport and Stonehouse. In 1840, therefore, a larger chapel was built in Ebrington Street, which seated about 800. The new chapel followed a design which gave visible expression to their conception of corporate worship:

> The centre front of the chapel was occupied by the communion table, and it was the custom of speakers to address the congregation from that point. To this end, the seating was arranged in gradually ascending tiers. In the large building at Plymouth, these tiers were arranged in three blocks, each centring on the communion table in an approximate semicircle ...[191]

There were always plenty of spectators in the three outer rows, the Breaking of Bread being 'one of the Sunday sights of Plymouth'.[192]

---

[186] On Tregelles, see *BDEB*; George H. Fromow, *B.W. Newton and Dr. S.P. Tregelles: Teachers of the Faith and the* Future (London: Sovereign Grace Advent Testimony, 1969[2]); *ODNB*.

[187] On Bialloblotzky, see Nicholas M. Railton, *Transnational Evangelicalism: the case of Friedrich Bialloblotzky (1799-1869)* (Arbeiten zur Geschichte des Pietismus, Band 41, Göttingen: Vandenhoeck & Ruprecht, 2002).

[188] 'Fry MS', 26, 29-30; Rowdon, *Origins*, 159-60.

[189] On Soltau, see *BDEB*.

[190] Rowdon, *Origins*, 160-1, following H.W. Soltau, *The Tabernacle, the Priesthood and the Offerings* (London, n.d.), v-vi.

[191] Coad, *History*, 66.

[192] A.N. Harris, 'Reminiscences', 3.

The quality of fellowship was as impressive as the numerical growth; although Newton later expressed disapproval of its disruptive effects upon family life, many in the assembly were given to practising sacrificial hospitality.[193] A simple lifestyle was the norm, even among those who were better off. A member during those days, W.H. Cole, recalled how

> distinctions between rich and poor were lessened by holy, loving fellowship and unity which characterized their intercourse. Their social meetings, where rich and poor were alike the welcomed guests, were for the study of the word, and religious converse. The homes of the wealthy were plainly furnished, presenting an air of unworldliness and making them more homely for their poorer brethren and sisters. Their dress was plain, their habits simple, and their walk distinguished by separation from the world.[194]

Newton was the principal teacher in the assembly; his focus was on prophecy, though he displayed a grasp of the whole of biblical revelation. Other leaders each had their particular emphases. Harris, as a pastor, was 'a very powerful exponent of the doctrines of grace, of the nature of worship, and the revealed counsels of God; an enthusiastic teacher of the Gospel, and an earnest exhorter of believers as to their daily walk'. Soltau focused on typological teaching. Not surprisingly, believers from elsewhere came to live in Plymouth to take advantage of what was available.[195]

In North Devon, a Particular Baptist church at Barnstaple was gradually transformed into a Brethren assembly, through the work of Robert Cleaver Chapman (1803-1902).[196] Chapman, whose long and devoted life was to give him a unique position of influence among Brethren, was a London solicitor who was converted in 1823 through the ministry of James Harington Evans (1785-1849).[197] Evans, who had left the Church of England as part of the 'Western Schism',[198] was minister of a chapel in John Street, London, which had been built for him in 1818 by Henry Drummond. Although it cannot be proved, it seems probable that Evans shaped Chapman's thinking in a number of significant areas, including acceptance of Scripture as the sole authority for faith and practice, refusal to make believers' baptism a test of church fellowship (Chapman taught it as an obligation upon converts but did not insist on it for believers seceding from other churches), weekly observance of the Lord's Supper, the importance of providing opportunity for those with spiritual gifts to exercise them in the church, and a longing for the visible union of true believers.

---

[193] 'Fry MS', 305-6, 315.

[194] W.H. Cole, 'Reminiscences of the Plymouth Meeting of "Brethren"', in Lang, *Groves*, 325.

[195] *Ibid.*, 326-8.

[196] On Chapman, see *BDEB*; Frank Holmes, *Brother Indeed: The Life of Robert Cleaver Chapman, "Barnstaple Patriarch"* (Kilmarnock: John Ritchie, 1988[2]); Robert L Peterson., *Robert Chapman: A Biography* (Neptune, NJ: Loizeaux Brothers, 1995).

[197] On Evans, see *BDEB*; James Joyce Evans, *Memoir and Remains of the Rev. James Harington Evans, late minister of John-Street Chapel* (London: James Nisbet, 1852).

[198] The 'Western Schism' was the name given to the secession from the Church of England of a number of extreme high Calvinist clergy around 1815. They adopted believer's baptism and some espoused unorthodox views of the Trinity. A parallel role to that of Lady Powerscourt was played by Mrs. Harriet Wall, who hosted meetings in the same house at Albury which would later be the venue for Drummond's prophetic conferences. See Carter, *Anglican Evangelicals*, ch. 4.

Struggling with the ethical dilemmas thrown up by his work as a solicitor, Chapman decided to resign, give away his possessions, and engage in full-time Christian work. In 1832, he was called to Barnstaple as pastor of a divided congregation which had had three pastors within the space of eighteen months.[199] Making it a condition of acceptance that he should be free to teach the whole of biblical truth, he nevertheless sought unanimity before introducing the radical change of opening communion to all believers. Even so, a minority of the membership refused to accept the practice of open ministry at the Lord's Table and withdrew, later asking him to vacate the chapel; a new one was built for the Brethren in the early 1840s.

Chapman was of a different temperament from Newton. In 1893, he recalled having been blamed by 'men of much grace' because he waited for unanimity among his flock before moving to set up an assembly; he stated that his critics were seeking to establish a joint testimony to the truth in South Devon.[200] This is probably a reference to the leaders at Plymouth. If so, it is corroborative evidence both of early contact between Plymouth and Barnstaple, and of the existence at Plymouth of a tendency to narrowness and sectarianism: one observer alleged that 'Robert Chapman, who in the deep things of God seems to know more than many, they deem uninstructed'.[201] Chapman's patience, however, was vindicated by the strength of the assembly he founded, which long had as many as 400 members.[202] One of the crucial factors in its growth was his extreme yet attractive simplicity of lifestyle, evident in his decision to live in a part of the town where the poor would not feel too intimidated to visit him. He influenced Christian workers far beyond North Devon, welcoming them to stay with him free of charge for as long as they wished, and he looked to God to provide the funds for such hospitality, believing that God's provision could serve as a lesson for his guests.

Robert Cleaver Chapman

---

[199] This church has been described as 'Strict Baptist', but it did not belong to that movement. A list of churches in *The Baptist Magazine* 27 (1835), 551, included it, naming Chapman as its pastor, and recorded it as belonging to the Western Association, which confirms Chapman's description of the transition to a Brethren assembly as gradual. The description of it as Strict Baptist most likely referred to the practice of restricting participation in the Lord's Supper to believers baptised by immersion (Kenneth Dix to the author, 6 September 2005).

[200] Hake (ed.), *Letters of Chapman*, 64-5 (Chapman to R.F.I., 20 June 1893).

[201] Bowes, *Autobiography*, 236.

[202] Beattie, *Brethren*, 54.

A work also flourished in the hamlets around Tawstock, near Barnstaple, which owed much to a draper by the name of Robert Gribble.[203] Spiritually awakened in 1815, Gribble began conducting Sunday schools in local villages, and progressed through reading sermons to evangelistic preaching, opening several chapels. At one of these, a cousin of Chapman's by marriage settled as pastor in 1829. Müller preached at the opening of another in 1830. Not surprisingly, therefore, the work became associated with Chapman once he moved to the area. Gribble himself went bankrupt and spent a period of time elsewhere, during which he was introduced to the Barnstaple Brethren through William Hake of Exeter, who encouraged him to examine his views in the light of the teaching of Scripture.[204] Returning to Barnstaple to evangelise, Gribble, like Chapman, began to 'live by faith', trusting God to supply his needs apart from any regular human means of material support. Recognising his ministry to be that of an itinerant evangelist, he moved on to plant assemblies elsewhere in Devon and Somerset. Yet he appears to have been a man with little outward evidence of gift:

> Darby is said to have remarked to Wigram, 'How is it, Wigram, that although you and I preach the Gospel more clearly than many, we see so few results, yet they tell us, that in North Devon, this Mr. Gribble in his meetings, only repeats a few Gospel texts and makes a few simple remarks, and souls are saved and assemblies formed'.[205]

In South Devon, assemblies soon began to be planted as a result of vigorous outreach from Plymouth. The first was at Salcombe, and this meeting provides a remarkable instance of Irvingite influence on early Brethren. Thomas Dowglass (1806-57) was a local squire who had been converted through the Calvinist preacher César Malan while visiting Switzerland.[206] He began preaching in Salcombe, and was greatly respected by the Plymouth meeting, with whom his group had close links as they met along similar lines. Hall christened Dowglass's fourth child on 22 January 1834,[207] Newton and others went to preach for Dowglass, and at some unspecified point the group began to break bread; Dowglass was also on the platform at Newton's 1834 conference in Plymouth. However, that summer he learned of the Irvingite movement through his sister, who had challenged his right to preach without an endowment of the Holy Spirit. An Irvingite source states that he embraced the work after an interview with Irving and was later advised to return to Devon and preach the universal love of God (by contrast with traditional Calvinist belief in limited atonement), for which he was allegedly 'cast out' by the Brethren.[208] In 1835 he issued a pamphlet entitled *Man's Responsibility for the gift of a Saviour, and the responsibility of the church for the gift of the Holy Ghost*, outlining

---

[203] On Gribble, see *BDEB*; Robert Gribble, *Recollections of an Evangelist: or, incidents connected with village ministry* (London: William Yapp, 1858²); Rowdon, *Origins*, 147-53.

[204] Peterson, *Chapman*, 36.

[205] F.W. Surridge, *The Finest of the Wheat* (Bridford Mills, Devon: n.p., 1950), 24, quoted in Rowdon, *Origins*, 152-3.

[206] On Dowglass, see Rowdon, *Origins*, 77-8.

[207] Devon Record Office, 57/4/2f. The entry was extracted from the baptismal register of what became the Salcombe Catholic Apostolic Church, which indicates that this had its roots in Dowglass's Brethren group.

[208] Edward Trimen, 'The Rise and Progress of the Work of the Lord' (typescript, 1904), Lecture 11; cf. 'Fry MS', 142, 267.

his new understanding of the gospel: reconciliation with God had already been effected, and nobody was now under condemnation because of their sin, but simply for failure to believe the Spirit's testimony concerning this in the gospel. Darby wrote to Dowglass but failed to reclaim him;[209] Newton preached against Irvingism throughout Devon and Cornwall, and later claimed that his *Christian Witness* article on Irvingism[210] saved two-thirds of the Salcombe Brethren from defecting.[211] Dowglass's defection would have strengthened Newton's growing isolationism and his concern to counter anything which he regarded as false doctrine – including aspects of Darby's eschatological and dispensational teaching.

Further along the coast, the resort of Torquay saw an assembly begin as early as October 1834, the nucleus of which was formed by a clerical seceder from Anglicanism, John Vivian, and some of his congregation.[212] Another Torquay assembly had its beginnings in a chapel opened for evangelistic preaching by Leonard Strong (1797-1874), an Anglican clergyman in Demerara (later known as British Guiana), who had seceded in 1837 on adopting Brethren-type views, returning to England in 1848/9 after planting a large assembly in Georgetown.[213] In 1837 or 1838, shortly after returning from India, Parnell settled at Teignmouth and founded an assembly there (Müller's congregation there does not appear to have developed into a Brethren assembly).[214] In 1842 he moved to London, and was created Lord Congleton, by which name he is better known.

In Exeter, Brethren were meeting by 1839 or 1840, when Providence Chapel was erected by Sir Alexander Campbell in Northernhay Street; the internal layout was based on that of the Ebrington Street chapel.[215] Since Newton lectured in Exeter on occasion, it is likely that this was a fruit of outreach from Plymouth. A split had resulted in there being two assemblies in the city by 1839, a strongly-Calvinist minority seceding from the existing gathering.[216] The controversialist and itinerant preacher John Bowes (1804-

[209] Undated letter, in Christian Brethren Archive (CBA5540(406)).

[210] [B.W. Newton], 'The Doctrines of the Church in Newman Street Considered', *CWit* 2 (1835), 111-28.

[211] 'Fry MS', 142.

[212] Beattie, *Brethren*, 64.

[213] On Strong, see Anon., 'Secession from the Establishment of Leonard Strong, late Rector of St Matthew's Parish, Demerara', *I* 2 (1839), 282-7; *BDE*; *BDEB*; Timothy C.F. Stunt, 'Leonard Strong: the Motives and Experiences of Early Missionary Work in British Guiana', *CBR* 34 (1983), 95-105. In 1909, the visiting Scottish evangelist Alex Marshall found that Strong had seceded in order to be free to minister to the slaves on the plantations, whose owners resented his interference with their chattels (John Hawthorn, *Alexander Marshall: Evangelist, Author and Pioneer* (London: Pickering & Inglis, n.d.), 83). If this is true, then it adds a significant dimension to our understanding of the motives for clerical secession.

[214] H. Groves, *Congleton*, 62.

[215] Allan Brockett, *Nonconformity in Exeter 1650-1875* (Manchester: Manchester University Press, 1962), 200, 228. On Campbell, see *BDEB*.

[216] Unsigned review of Brethren writings, *ER* 5 (January-June 1839), 587n. According to Bowes, the group seceded because a Mr Cann was not allowed to minister at Exeter or Plymouth, and objected to brethren from elsewhere being called in to adjudicate (Bowes, *Autobiography*, 231). Bowes may have made more of this issue than the facts warranted, given that he too was not permitted to minister at Plymouth.

74),[217] a former Wesleyan and Primitive Methodist who by this time could be described as a 'fellow-traveller' with Brethren, visited Exeter at the end of the year. He recounted that he had been about to speak at the Lord's Supper but was stopped, and alleged that there was no liberty of ministry because each part of the service was followed too quickly by the next. He liked the Brethren less here than anywhere else he had visited. At Exeter and Plymouth, Bowes felt that the Brethren were guilty of sectarianism in standing aloof from other believers, in refusing ministry from any who did not share their premillennial views (Bowes was a postmillennialist who at this time expected the world's conversion to precede Christ's return, and he was not allowed to minister at either place), and in the confident dogmatism with which they maintained their views.[218] Nevertheless, Brethren in Exeter continued to grow; in 1840, the minister of Bartholomew Street Baptist Chapel, John Offord, resigned his pastorate and joined the Brethren, accompanied by several of his members; he would later move to Plymouth.[219] By 1845, there were twenty-four assemblies in Devon, mostly in the south of the county or along the road between Exeter and Barnstaple. It was to become the county in England with the highest concentration of Brethren assemblies, a fact which remains true today.

2.5 The Partnership of Craik and Müller at Bristol[220]

We have seen that a close relationship was developing between Craik and Müller in Devon, but in March 1832 Craik was invited to minister to a group of seceders in Bristol, where there was a flourishing work in Gideon Chapel. This had been built in 1810 and occupied by a succession of seceding groups (including one influenced by Hawker, and then one aligned with the Western Schism, who also occupied Bethesda).[221] Craik's visit was a success, and he was invited to return permanently. He did so from May 1832, accompanied by Müller, on the understanding that they would not be the 'pastors' in any formal sense, pew rents would be abolished and their support given by means of an offertory box placed in the chapel (as in Devon), and they would be free to preach whatever Scripture taught without any reference to existing church rules. Since Bethesda was now empty, and was offered for their work, they had two rather different congregations in their care, one with an existing tradition, and one which was effectively started from scratch along what Craik and Müller considered biblical lines. After a few weeks' instruction, they commenced an open meeting at Bethesda: on 13 August, 'one brother and four sisters united with brother Craik and me in church fellowship at Bethesda, *without any rules, desiring only to act as the Lord shall be pleased to give us light*

---

[217] On Bowes, see Bowes, *Autobiography*; Dickson, *Brethren in Scotland*, 29-41; *DNB*; *ODNB*.

[218] Bowes, *Autobiography*, 230-2, 235-7.

[219] Brockett, *Nonconformity*, 221, cf. Carter, *Anglican Evangelicals*, 121. Bartholomew Street originated as a secession from South Street Baptist Chapel in 1817, and was associated with the Western Schism (Brockett, *Nonconformity*, 162; Carter, *Anglican Evangelicals*, 116-20).

[220] On Bethesda, Bristol, see [E.T. Davies and D.D. Chrystal], *Bethesda Church, Great George Street, Bristol. A brief account of its formation, history and practice, particularly in relation to pastoral oversight* ([Bristol: Bible & Tract Depôt, 1917]); K. Linton and A.H. Linton, *'I Will Build my Church'. 150 Years of local church work in Bristol* (Bristol: the authors, 1982). On Gideon, see Louis P. Nott, *Gideon 1810 to 1910: The Vicissitudes of a City Chapel* (Bristol: n.p., 1909).

[221] Carter, *Anglican Evangelicals*, 132.

through His Word'.[222] The work grew rapidly, and the pair therefore rejected an invitation in January 1833 to join Groves in Baghdad, feeling that their presence was required in Bristol.

Bethesda, Bristol

A major influence upon them was Robert Chapman. Since Chapman was concerned to promote Christian unity, it seems likely that he influenced Bethesda away from an early narrowness of communion of which Darby complained following a visit to Bristol: 'The Lord is doing a very marked work there, in which I hope our dear brothers M. and C. may be abundantly blessed, but I should wish a little more principle of largeness of communion. I dread narrowness of heart more than anything for the church of Christ, *especially now.'*[223] It was the practice of believer's baptism which precipitated the broadening which Darby desired. This was a condition of membership at Bethesda, but not at Gideon.[224] In August 1836, Chapman, who enjoined it on converts but not on seceders from other churches,[225] pointed out to Müller, in application of 2 Thessalonians 3.6, that if a believer was walking 'disorderly' in regard to the scriptural teaching concerning baptism (i.e. refusing to submit to it), then fellowship should be withdrawn in all settings. Given the variety of opinions concerning the practice of baptism, however, it could not be assumed that unbaptised believers were walking in conscious disobedience to Scripture, and therefore they could not be classed as 'disorderly'. Müller concluded that they should be accepted as those who were already accepted by Christ (Romans 15.7), and in 1837 Craik and Müller ceased requiring believer's baptism as a condition of membership at Bethesda (a requirement which presumably lay behind Darby's earlier

---

[222] Müller, *Autobiography*, 60.

[223] Darby, *Letters*, 1.8 (15 October 1832).

[224] Rowdon, *Origins*, 122.

[225] Peterson, *Chapman*, 52.

complaint, and which would effectively have excluded him as a lifelong paedobaptist[226]),
though still teaching it as the duty of every Christian. During these early years,
membership climbed rapidly to 181 at Gideon and 168 at Bethesda, and in November
1837 the two memberships were incorporated into one in order to reduce the number of
meetings and allow Craik and Müller more time for pastoral visiting. Müller now had
additional commitments (of which more below), and they hoped that others would share
the burden of pastoral work.

In February 1839, Craik and Müller spent two weeks in retreat studying the Scriptures
on the subject of church order. Rowdon summarises their conclusions, and the Scripture
passages to which they appealed:

I. Eldership
1. There should be elders (Matt. 24.45; Luke 12.42; Acts 14.23, 20.17; Titus 1.5; 1 Pet. 5.1).
2. Elders come into office by the appointment of the Holy Ghost (Acts 20.28).
3. Their appointment is made known to them by the secret call of the Spirit (1 Tim. 3.1); but it
is confirmed by possession of the requisite qualifications (1 Tim. 3.2-7; Titus 1.6-9) and by
the blessing of God resting upon their labours (1 Cor. 9.2).
4. Saints should acknowledge such and submit to them in the Lord (1 Cor. 16.15, 16; 1 Thess.
5.12, 13; Heb. 13.7, 17; 1 Tim. 5.17).
II. Discipline
1. Matters of church discipline should be finally settled in the presence of the assembled
church (Matt. 18.17; 1 Cor. 5.4, 5; 2 Cor. 2.6-8; 1 Tim. 5.20).
2. They are to be regarded as acts of the whole body (Matt.18.17, 18; 1 Cor. 5.4, 5, 7, 12, 13;
2 Cor. 2.6-8). We are bound to receive all who make a credible profession of faith (Rom.
15.7), as an act of the elders and of the whole church.
III. Church Meetings for Discipline
Though in the past these have been held on week-nights, matters of discipline should be
decided on Sunday mornings at the meeting for the breaking of bread for the following
reasons:
1. To prevent delays.
2. A greater attendance can be expected on Sunday mornings.
3. It will show that 'the individual who is admitted to the Lord's table is therewith also
received to all the privileges, trials and responsibilities of Church membership'.
4. It is singularly appropriate for such matters to be dealt with in conjunction with the
ordinance which is a demonstration of fellowship.
IV. The Lord's Supper
1. No command has been given in Scripture as to frequency of celebration, but the example
of the apostles and early Christians suggests every Sunday (Acts 20.7).
2. As to the character of the meeting at which the Lord's Supper is celebrated, since it is
symbolic of common participation in the benefits of our Lord's death and our union to Him
and to each other (1 Cor. 10. 16, 17), opportunity should be given for the exercise of gifts of
teaching or exhortation and communion in prayer and praise (Rom. 12.4-8; Eph. 4.11-16).
Though the meeting should not normally be in the hands of a single man, those who have gifts
of teaching or exhortation should feel their responsibility to edify the church.

[226] At a later point, Darby became an advocate of the practice of household baptism, according to
which all members of a household may be baptised on the grounds of the faith exercised by its head.
This includes newborn infants, but also servants and adult family members.

3. It seems preferable for each individual to break the bread for himself rather than that one of the elders should. This course is favoured by the letter of Scripture ('The bread which we break', 1 Cor. 10.16, 17); it gives expression to the fact that all, by their sins, have broken the body of our Lord; and it shows more clearly that the ordinance is 'an act of social worship and obedience' which does not require to be administered by 'some particular individual, possessed of what is called a ministerial character'.[227]

Some at Gideon had always found it difficult to accept the direction in which things had been moving; there was unease when open ministry at the Lord's Table was introduced there, and disagreement with the principles of church order enunciated by Craik and Müller after their retreat. According to E.K. Groves, the union of the two churches had brought differences to the surface.[228] There were practical problems, too: in spite of the amalgamation, the continuing need to double up meant that gifted brethren were divided into two groups, church discipline was made more difficult and contact reduced; furthermore, it was discovered that some of the pews were still looked upon by their occupants as private property. In April 1840, therefore, Gideon was given up, and almost all the 250-strong congregation moved to Bethesda. Soon after, another chapel, Salem, was occupied, and in due course it became possible to begin breaking bread there in the same way as had been done at Bethesda; this time, there was no discordant element and no trust deeds to offer any hindrance. The church continued to grow: membership after Gideon was given up rose to around 500, and attendance at the Lord's Supper during 1841 averaged between 550 and 600. Although Craik and Müller moved in the local community of Nonconformist ministers, they were careful to avoid the suggestion that they should be regarded as 'the ministers' at Bethesda to the exclusion of other brethren gifted in ruling or teaching. In 1841, therefore, they took down the boxes in the chapel in which donations for their support had been placed, lest these should give rise to such misunderstanding.

Some years earlier, Müller had founded the Scriptural Knowledge Society, which soon became the Scriptural Knowledge Institution (SKI). He and Craik had been trusting God to supply their material needs, and made a point of not disclosing these to anybody. Believing that their prayers had been answered, he

decided, after much prayer, to finance a new and much wider enterprise by the same method. Müller noted in his journal for 21 February, 1834, that he had that morning formed 'A plan for establishing upon scriptural principles, an Institution for the spread of the gospel at home and abroad'. Later he set down the reasons why he felt that existing societies were not conducted on Scriptural lines. They had as their object the conversion of the world, an object which Müller had not been able to find in Scripture; they included unbelievers as members if they subscribed to the funds, and as committee members or patrons if they were men of wealth and influence; and they appealed to unbelievers for money and did not scruple to contract debts. Müller determined to pray for money to be given by believers (free-will offerings by unbelievers would

---

[227] Rowdon, *Origins*, 125-6, cf. Müller, *Narrative*, 1.276-81 (Rowdon used the eighth edition, published in 1881).

[228] E.K. Groves, *Conversations on 'Bethesda' Family Matters* (London: W.B. Horner, [1885]), 15-16.

not be refused, on the ground of Acts 28.2-10, but unbelievers would not be permitted to assist in carrying out the work of the institution).[229]

The society focused initially on the support of day schools and Sunday Schools and missionaries whose work was conducted along scriptural lines, and the provision of Bibles and gospel literature, but it was not long before Müller began seriously to consider the idea of starting an orphanage. (While a divinity student, he had lived for two months in lodgings at an orphanage in Halle which had been founded by the Pietist A.H. Francke in 1696, and he revisited it in April 1835.) His primary motivation in undertaking such an enterprise was not so much philanthropic as apologetic. It was to be

> a testimonial to the faithfulness of God in answering prayer. He felt that he had a particular gift *'in being able to take God at His word and to rely upon it'* and that if he 'a poor man, simply by prayer and faith, obtained, *without asking any individual*, the means for establishing and carrying on an Orphan House: there would be something which, with the Lord's blessing, might be instrumental in strengthening the faith of the children of God, besides being a testimony to the consciences of the unconverted, of the reality of the things of God'.[230]

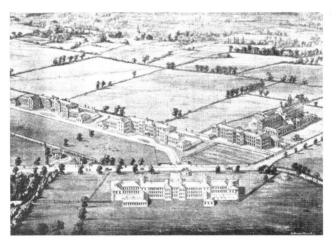

The Orphan Houses on Ashley Down were in a rural setting when first built

The finances were to be prayed in, as had been the case with Francke's institution, no appeals being made for funds. He published detailed annual reports, including accounts of how all needs had been met in answer to prayer, listing gifts meticulously, along with any singular circumstances which indicated that they arrived in answer to prayer. His stated aim was to edify and not to raise funds, though doubtless many readers were inspired to contribute by what they read. These reports formed the backbone of the famous *Narrative of Some of the Lord's Dealings with George Müller*. The first home was opened in 1836 in rented accommodation. Growth meant that the institution needed to move into its own

---

[229] Rowdon, *Origins*, 129-30, cf. Müller, *Autobiography*, 64-5.

[230] Rowdon, *Origins*, 131, quoting Müller, *Narrative*, 1.146 (20 November 1835).

premises, and five orphan houses were opened on Ashley Down between 1849 and 1870. No fire insurance was ever taken out, as Müller trusted God to protect the buildings if it was his will to do so.[231] Although 'living by faith' himself, and running the orphanage on those lines, it is noteworthy that Müller did not impose this on his helpers but provided them with a regular salary.

By the mid-1830s, then, the Brethren movement was firmly rooted in several locations, but it would be a mistake to confine our examination of its early development to these areas. In the next chapter, we shall see that it spread rapidly to many parts of England, and established a presence in the Lowlands of Scotland.

---

[231] [C. Russell Hurditch], 'In Memoriam. George Müller', *FT* 17 (1899), 115; G. Fred[erick] Bergin, *Ten Years After: a sequel to The Autobiography of George Müller* (London: J. Nisbet, 1911[2]), 189.

CHAPTER 3

The Movement Spreads

The rapidity with which Brethren spread throughout much of England and beyond calls for some investigation. This chapter looks at the areas where they established a significant presence during the 1830s and 1840s. Assemblies did emerge elsewhere during these decades, but little is known of their origins. However, from an examination of the areas discussed here, three recurring themes appear.

Firstly, this period was one in which the concept of denominational allegiance was still developing; central bodies such as the Baptist Union of Great Britain and the Congregational Union were only now appearing as a major force in the life of the churches. This fluidity was all the more evident in radical Evangelicalism (and beyond it); thus individuals could form churches which looked similar to Brethren but which were not actually associated with Brethren to any real extent; they could move into (or out of) Brethren circles; and, since the biblicism of many radical groupings meant that many traditional doctrines were subject to intense scrutiny in the light of Scripture, they could undergo quite far-reaching changes of belief. We must, therefore, guard against the tendency to view Brethren history as being that of a movement which was marked from the start by well-defined organisational or doctrinal boundaries. The practice of refusing any distinctive 'denominational' label makes it all the more difficult for modern researchers to distinguish Brethren assemblies from others which shared many of the same emphases.

A prime example would be those associated with John Bowes. At some point around 1830, Bowes seceded from the Primitive Methodists, rejecting all denominational affiliations. He became a vigorous controversialist and public debater with a passion for Evangelical religion, Christian unity, and social justice. Moving from Scotland to Liverpool in 1837, he was baptised as a believer by the Baptist minister C.M. Birrell in 1839, and that summer made contact with Brethren. The congregations founded by Bowes appear to have adopted a similar mode of worship to that of the Brethren, but he was reluctant to be too closely identified with Brethren, displaying more readiness to work with ministers of other denominations and to speak out on social and political issues. He also rejected as a hindrance to unity the idea that no bishops or elders could receive formal recognition once the apostles had passed away, an idea which was becoming increasingly popular among Brethren as a result of Darby's influence. Nevertheless, he continued to associate with, and occasionally preach for, Brethren in various places, including Craik at Bristol and Trotter at Otley in West Yorkshire. We shall notice below some of his assemblies which later passed into the Brethren orbit.

Secondly, the movement's spread owed a great deal to influential individuals who settled in particular localities. One such appears to have been the Rev. Sir Lancelot C.L. Brenton (c.1807-62), who seceded from the Church of England in 1831, and moved to Ryde on the Isle of Wight at some point in the 1840s.[1] From about 1845 he published a

---

[1] On Brenton, see *BDEB*. In the intervening period, Brenton had settled at Bath, where he sided with Darby in the division of 1848 between Open and Exclusive. For his residence in Ryde, see the return for the assembly at Albert Street, opened in 1847 (PRO HO129/299/3, in John A. Vickers (ed.),

series of tracts addressed to local believers setting forth a Brethren position on such matters as sectarianism, fellowship and church government. By the time of the 1851 Religious Census, a cluster of assemblies existed on the island. Other examples of what we might now call 'church planters' include Hall at Hereford, W.G. Rhind at Ross-on-Wye, and W.H. Dorman at Stafford. Apart from these, there were also men who exercised a vital pastoral or teaching ministry in their assembly or in a wider area: we have already seen such a ministry being exercised by Chapman at Barnstaple, and another example would be William Trotter in Yorkshire.

Thirdly, whilst many assemblies owed their foundation to the church planters mentioned above, it is nevertheless the case that a number of the churches so planted were composed largely of seceders rather than converts, at least in their earliest years. Beattie is not far off the mark in asserting that 'in the majority of cases ... those early gatherings were for the most part composed of Christians who had formerly been staunch Church members, but had left the denominations because of spiritual convictions as to what should be the true attitude of the child of God in relation to the Scriptural meaning of baptism and the Lord's Supper'.[2] However, two exceptions to this thesis call for its qualification. The first is Suffolk, where a number of assemblies sprang up which appear to have owed much to vigorous evangelism and were composed mainly of new converts; the movement's success in this rural context parallels that already evident in Devon. The second is another rural county, Herefordshire: whilst the assembly at Hereford was formed as the result of secessions rather than conversions, it soon became marked by evangelistic activism which resulted in the formation of a number of assemblies in the surrounding villages and small towns. It appears that during this period the more urban assemblies tended to be formed as a result of secession, and the more rural ones as a result of evangelism. This was to change later in the century.

3.1 Wiltshire and Bath

In North Wiltshire, as in the Plymouth area, several radical Evangelical movements aroused interest and attracted clerical seceders; some of these joined the Brethren, while others became Strict Baptists or Catholic Apostolics, and a regional study might turn up interconnections between the movements. The assembly at Corshamside began around 1832, with the secession of a local clergyman, John Methuen. It is not clear exactly when the assembly at Bath came into being, although two seceders from the Anglican ministry, Brenton and William Morshead (1805-74), were active in the area in the early 1830s, establishing an independent congregation in 1832 which later affiliated with the Brethren, apparently by 1837.[3] Another seceder, W.G. Lambert of Devizes, issued one of the earliest Brethren ecclesiological writings, *A Call to the Converted*, in 1831. He argued that the Spirit's role in forming, gifting and directing a pure church rendered detailed instructions unnecessary, and in their absence believers were to depend on the Spirit to guide them. However, Lambert did not plant any churches, and Newton recalled visiting him at Bath and finding that he had given up his Brethren views.[4] Bath was to

---

The Religious Census of Hampshire 1851 (Hampshire Record Series, Winchester: Hampshire County Council, 1993).

[2] Beattie, *Brethren*, 187.

[3] Carter, *Anglican Evangelicals*, 296; Stunt, *Awakening*, 296-8.

[4] 'Small Notebook 7', 20a; Stunt, *Awakening*, 256-8.

become a major centre for the movement; even today, the offices of 'Echoes of Service', the largest service agency for British Open Brethren mission, are located there. The assembly was strengthened by the resort's popularity with the wealthier classes, and among those who settled there were such leaders as Code of Westport, who arrived in 1840, and Bellett for a period later in the 1840s.[5]

3.2 Hereford

Dissatisfaction was an important factor in the beginnings of the assembly at Hereford.[6] The Anglican Rector, Henry Gipps, had attracted a large following, and his ministry was marked by a stress on prayer for the outpouring of the Holy Spirit. Gipps died in 1832, but his daughter would later marry William Kelly, editor of Darby's works and one of the most scholarly Exclusive Brethren. His successor from 1835, John Venn, was an Evangelical who belonged to a distinguished Evangelical clerical family, but his ministry was compared unfavourably with that of his predecessor; it was perceived as too Arminian, and one member of his congregation, impressed by what she had seen on a visit to Plymouth, invited Hall to preach in Hereford. His ministry proved to be most acceptable, and he was invited to make his home there, which he did in 1837. Venn preached and wrote against the Brethren, but at least a hundred of the most zealous of his congregation, attracted by the spiritual quality of Hall's teaching, seceded, apparently in response to this attack. Hall also asked Newton to go there and minister for a while, which he did. Newton's assessment of the situation at Hereford was coloured by his belief that 'the Evangelicals brought Christians to a certain point in Christian teaching but couldn't lead them farther being unwilling to go themselves. So when a development of those very principles, which they held, was set before persons those who were rightminded followed it.'[7]

The assembly included some men of wealth and social standing, who found opportunities of service which had not been open to them previously. They used their resources to engage in vigorous outreach and church-planting throughout the area, and the assembly grew rapidly, reaching a size of three or four hundred. Among them were Captain W.H.G. Wellesley (1806-75), a nephew of the Duke of Wellington who renounced his commission on joining the Brethren,[8] and Captain W.G. Rhind (1794-1863), a retired naval officer.[9] For a few years, Rhind had engaged in evangelistic work among sailors at Plymouth, before becoming secretary of the British Society for Promoting the Principles of the Reformation. In 1832, he was invited by John Synge, who had inherited Glanmore Castle in County Wicklow, to undertake religious and philanthropic work among the local populace. It was at nearby Powerscourt that Rhind met Hall, and thus came to

---

[5] Beattie, *Brethren*, 153-6; Anon., *The 120th Anniversary of the Bath Assembly of Christian Brethren And The 70th Anniversary of Manvers Hall* (n.pl.: n.p., [1957]).

[6] On Hereford, see Beattie, *Brethren*, ch. 7; C.B[rewer]., *Early Days in Herefordshire* (n.pl.: n.p., 1893); A.W. Langford, *An Account of Brethren in Hereford* ([Hereford]: n.p., [1958]); Rowdon, *Origins*, 164-72. Rowdon paints a vivid picture of life in the Hereford assembly, based on a detailed examination of the records, to which this section is particularly indebted.

[7] 'Small Notebook 4', 106-7.

[8] Pickering (ed.), *Chief Men*, 40.

[9] On Rhind, see *BDEB*; [J.B. Isbell], *'Faithful unto Death'. A Memoir of William Graeme Rhind, R.N., who fell asleep in Jesus, March 17, 1863* (London: William Yapp, [1863]).

Hereford in 1838. Within a few years, he moved to Ross-on-Wye, where he pioneered another assembly.

From the beginning of the Hereford assembly, records were well kept. They include details of the meetings of overseeing brethren every Friday morning. As well as dealing with applications for membership and pastoral problems, these brethren nominated one of their number to 'break bread', which probably involved giving thanks for the elements and handing them out for distribution. Assembly life revolved around the Breaking of Bread, which lasted from 10.30 until nearly one o'clock each Sunday; the length was because ministry formed a part of the service, for the benefit of those who lived at a distance and who could not attend at other times. The far-flung nature of the membership meant that the assembly at Hereford maintained a number of preaching stations as far afield as Ludlow, Worcester, and Ross-on-Wye, some of which developed into independent assemblies during the 1840s and after; to serve these, during the early years they kept several horses and a gig. The overseeing brethren also arranged other meetings, such as lectures on the Scriptures, special days of fasting and prayer, and occasional Sunday evening evangelistic services (held monthly from 1841).

The children were not neglected; apart from the provision of instruction for the children of believers on Sunday afternoons, the balance sheets refer to an 'Orphan Asylum' (perhaps in imitation of Müller's work at Bristol) and an 'Infant School'. The assembly's provision for its members also included a graveyard. During this period, Dissenters could not be buried in public burial grounds by their own ministers, and so the assembly at Hereford had its own burial ground, purchased by William Yapp in 1840; burials during the early years usually took place on Sunday afternoons.[10]

The oversight minutes reveal something of the fluidity of religious belief and allegiance in more radical groupings; during 1841, there were four cases of members embracing Mormon beliefs and having to be excommunicated. Mormons had mounted a spectacularly successful mission to Herefordshire in 1840, gaining a thousand converts in a year, including virtually the entire membership of a local Wesleyan schism, the United Brethren.[11] In another case, that of a couple put out of fellowship in 1842, the husband not only developed contacts with Irvingism, which the overseeing brethren deemed 'erroneous & heretical', but also had been in contact with an astrologer and was denying the eternal punishment of the wicked.[12] The last charge is of interest because an early advocate of annihilationism was the local Independent minister from 1842-51, Edward White. He may not have been responsible for this man's beliefs, but he did have some amicable contact with the Brethren while ministering there, being baptised as a believer and adopting premillennial views.[13] It was during his ministry in Hereford that he wrote

---

[10] Rowdon has made a statistical analysis of the social composition of the assembly, based on occupational details of those listed in the burial register (*Origins*, 169-70). During this period, other burial grounds are known to have been provided for Brethren at Tottenham, Abney Park Cemetery in North London, and Woolpit in Suffolk.

[11] For details of this mission, see V. Ben Bloxham, James R. Moss and Larry C. Porter (eds.), *Truth Will Prevail: The Rise of the Church of Jesus Christ of Latter-day Saints in the British Isles 1837-1987* (Cambridge: Church of Jesus Christ of Latter-day Saints, 1987), 135-7, 155, 249.

[12] Hereford records, 'Friday meeting minutes 1839-42' (photocopy, CBA 5625(1)), unpaginated.

[13] Frederick Ash Freer, *Edward White: His Life and Work* (London: Elliot Stock, 1902), 32; Geoffrey Rowell, *Hell and the Victorians: A study of the nineteenth-century theological controversies concerning eternal punishment and the future life* (Oxford: Clarendon, 1974), 187.

an exposition of his views on conditional immortality, *Life in Christ* (first published in 1845). Such teaching was to cause recurrent problems among Open Brethren.

3.3 London

Wigram seems to have begun the work in central London and to have taken a leading role.[14] However, he was not present at one of the earliest gatherings there, apparently in 1833, which was memorable for a confrontation on its second Sunday of meeting between Newton and Bialloblotzky who was then assisting Wigram in his work on the concordance. Newton, who was replacing the sick Wigram, had assumed that the meeting would be conducted on the same lines as those at Plymouth and was therefore controlling what happened in the meeting. Bialloblotzky objected to this, arguing that it was 'not a teaching meeting but a searching or Berean meeting', for which he had come equipped with lexicons for the purpose of contributing to the discussion.[15] The group survived this inauspicious start, and appears to have migrated to Orchard Street (near Portman Square), and later to Welbeck Street. Other assemblies soon began to appear in and around the capital: Tottenham (1838), Rawstorne Street in Clerkenwell (1839), Hackney (1841), Kennington (by 1842), Kensington (by 1844), Woolwich (by 1845), and Stepney (by the late 1840s). Further afield, assemblies began at Chadwell Heath (1835) and Barking (circa 1840) in Essex, both started by members of the Glenny family, who were local brewers. A dual-purpose meeting room and schoolroom was built at the former in 1844, the school apparently continuing until the end of the First World War.[16]

The initiator of the Tottenham assembly was John Eliot Howard (1807-83), son of the Quaker meteorologist Luke Howard.[17] Careful study of Quaker writings from an Evangelical perspective had convinced John that they were unsound, not least in the failure to observe baptism and the Lord's Supper. In June, he and his wife had several conversations with B.W. Newton and his wife, who were visiting the locality. He was baptised in July 1836 and resigned from the Quakers that October. In 1837 Howard began evangelistic meetings (initially at Wood Green). The following year, he came into contact with Brethren, and in June attended a prophetic conference at Clifton, near Bristol, which may have influenced him to adopt Brethren views.[18] In November, he held the first Brethren-style Breaking of Bread in Tottenham. A chapel was built for the growing assembly in Brook Street in 1839, and the assembly was to make important contributions to Brethren mission: Groves had links with it and Hudson Taylor was later a member.[19]

---

[14] London beginnings are outlined in Gerald T. West, 'The first Brethren Assemblies in London', *CBR* 41 (1990), 67-76.

[15] 'Small Notebook 4', 115; 'Small Notebook 6', 51b; 'Small Notebook 7', 51.

[16] Eric Dinnes to David Brady, 19 December 1983 (CBA 7343).

[17] On John, who became a distinguished quinologist, see *BDEB*; [Maria Howard], *Memorials of John Eliot Howard of Lord's Meade, Tottenham* (n.pl.: n.p., 1885); Gerald T. West, 'From Friend to Brother: The spiritual migration of Luke Howard & his family, and the meetings of Friends and Brethren at Tottenham' (typescript, July 2003). Luke also receives an entry in *ODNB*.

[18] This was one in the series of conferences which began at Powerscourt; see Appendix I.

[19] Luke Howard's name also appears on the first list of Tottenham assembly members (Michael Howard and Raymond Lloyd, 'Howard and other family connections in 19th century Tottenham', 4 (typescript, 1989; CBA Box 212)).

Another notable accession to the Brethren was the minister since 1835 of a respectable Independent chapel in Islington, William H. Dorman (1802-78).[20] Since his settlement in London, he had tried to remodel the church along the lines advocated by Brethren, but was hindered by the existing order. Visiting Bristol to preach, he appears to have attended the Clifton conference in June 1838, and then returned via Stafford, where a secession had recently taken place. When he finally reached London, he found the pulpit denied to him as a result of alarming reports of his preaching at Bristol which had filtered back to the deacons. For some months, therefore, he preached in a vacant chapel in Chadwell Street near the Angel, Islington, before the new assembly took over a chapel in Rawstorne Street nearby. The most prominent Dissenting minister to make this move, he published an apologia for his secession, *Principles of Truth*.[21] His chief allegation was that the Holy Ghost was not acknowledged as present and active in the church. Another object of his criticism was the influence of the world, evident in the way that Dissenting churches were run.

It was in London that what became 'the semi-connexional system of the Exclusive Brethren'[22] had its origins. Contemplating the formation of new assemblies in the city, Wigram asked in October 1838: '*How are meetings for communion of saints in these parts to be regulated*; would it be for the glory of the Lord and the increase of testimony to have *one central meeting*, the common responsibility of all within reach, *and as many meetings subordinate to it*, as grace might vouchsafe – or to hold it to be better to allow the *meetings to grow up as they may without connection and dependent upon the energy of individuals only?*'[23] The assemblies which were founded in various parts of the city were linked by means of a weekly meeting known as the 'Saturday Meeting', at which responsible brethren from each assembly reported local decisions on cases of discipline and applications for fellowship 'that they may be known; and brethren can consult in any matter that arises'.[24] Such a gathering promoted unity in judgment and action among the meetings. One of the meetings took a leading role, that at Rawstorne Street. This was probably because Wigram, Darby, and Dorman all associated with it when in London. After the movement split into Open and Exclusive, the 'London Bridge Meeting' continued to exercise a similar role among Exclusive gatherings.

3.4 East Anglia

The earliest evidence of Brethren activity in this area may be the secession (probably in 1839) of George Jeckell, curate at Wymondham Abbey in Norfolk.[25] A Brethren meeting

---

[20] On Dorman, see *BDEB*.

[21] W.H. Dorman, *Principles of Truth; or, Reasons for Retiring from The Independent or Congregational Body, and from Islington Chapel* (London: W.H. Broom and Rouse, n.d.[3]).

[22] Rowdon, *Origins*, 163.

[23] Groves, *Darbyism*, 11.

[24] Darby, *CW*, 20.82.

[25] Susan Weber Soros and Catherine Arbuthnott, *Thomas Jeckyll: architect and designer* (New Haven and London: Yale University Press for the Bard Center for Studies in the Decorative Arts, Design, and Culture, 2003), 54n; Rosamunde Codling to the author, 30 April 2005. Soros and Arbuthnott speculate that the 'Swing Riots' of 1834, during which Jeckell received a note threatening the burning of the Abbey as a demonstration of anti-clerical feeling, may have influenced him towards secession (*ibid.*, 23).

was commenced here, definitely by 1848 and possibly considerably earlier than that. Also associated with it was the town's Independent minister, Obadiah Atkins, who seceded in 1843 on adopting Brethren views.[26] In the meeting's return for the 1851 Census of Religious Worship, Jeckell recorded that 'A few but of various denominations left their denominations and met simply as Christians', most of whom belonged to the poorer classes.[27]

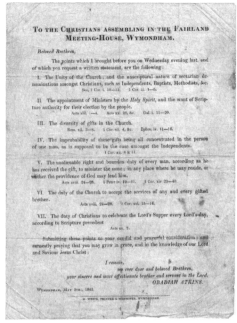

Obadiah Atkins issued this broadsheet explaining why he had resigned his pastorate; it is unique in its brevity

It was not long before Brethren established a fairly strong presence in West Suffolk.[28] As in other rural areas, we find a cluster of assemblies emerging around a centre, as a result of its outreach. Early in 1839, meetings began in the village of Tostock, near Bury St Edmunds, where a local landowner, Mrs. Brown, had a house with a barn and granary licensed for Dissenting worship, although one source suggests that the intent was to invite Anglican clergy and others to preach there.[29] However, by the summer these meetings had taken on a more clearly Brethren character; a local Baptist minister, Cornelius Elven, wrote to one of his flock who had left to attend these meetings, warning

---

[26] Rosamunde Codling to the author, 3 January 2005.

[27] J. Ede and N. Virgoe (eds.), *Religious Worship in Norfolk: The 1851 Census of Accommodation and Attendance at Worship* (Norfolk Record Society 62, n.pl.: Norfolk Record Society, 1998), no. 494 (PRO HO129/235/52).

[28] 'Archives from the Open Brethren Assembly at Woolpit, Suffolk' (CBA Boxes 102-3); Beattie, *Brethren*, ch. 24.

[29] 'Home Echoes and World-Wide Record of Work', *CG*, May 1923, 72.

them against what he called 'the most out & out <u>Dissenters</u> in the Kingdom'.[30] Numbers of hearers came from several surrounding villages, and when some were converted though the preaching of a Captain Towers, they were baptised in a slate tank in the neighbouring churchyard. A hall was built at the neighbouring village of Woolpit in 1841 and an assembly formed. Local tradition has it that Darby and Wigram conducted Bible readings at Woolpit; this is not improbable, as a letter in April 1841 was redirected to Darby at Tostock,[31] and he wrote a letter from Bury St Edmunds on 2 August.[32] Among other assemblies resulting from this work were those at Stowmarket, Pakenham,[33] and Rougham. In turn, the infant assembly at Stowmarket began outreach in the hamlet of Moat's Tye in 1843, followed by Bible readings, an assembly being established there in 1855.

Another location which may possibly have seen a Brethren assembly formed as early as the 1830s was the area around Steeple Bumpstead, Helions Bumpstead, and Birdbrook, near Haverhill, just over the border in Essex. According to one writer in 1936, just over a century earlier three believers studying the Scriptures together decided to follow the pattern of meeting which they found in the New Testament, and so began breaking bread in dependence upon the leading of the Holy Spirit, unaware of the existence of other such meetings. The account is somewhat stereotyped, but may point to the early existence of an assembly in this area.[34]

3.5 The Midlands

The meeting at Stafford, which was formed in 1839, was unusual because it owed its existence to the labours of three clerical seceders, each from a different denomination. In a letter apparently written following the conference at Clifton in June 1838,[35] Darby refers to a Presbyterian and an Independent minister as having been present and as having since seceded. It is reasonable to identify them with Alexander Stewart (d.1875) of Stafford and Dorman of London, since both of them seceded that year. After Dorman's resignation from the church at Islington, he returned to Stafford, which he had visited briefly on his return from Clifton and where he had ministered from 1829-35, and his influence now drew many to form the initial nucleus of an assembly. Stewart, who was apparently influenced by Dorman, was deposed from the Presbyterian ministry for imbibing Plymouthist heresies, and a room was built for him and his followers.[36] Later a third minister associated with the assembly, the Rev. J. Markham, an Anglican.[37] Once again, Darby was involved at an early stage, visiting the assembly at the beginning of 1839.[38]

---

[30] Letter of 18 July 1839 (West Suffolk Record Office 739/92, photocopy).

[31] See the envelope in CBA Box 154 (1(i)).

[32] Darby, *Letters*, 1.31.

[33] Beattie gives the location as Fakenham; although there was a nearby village called Fakenham Magna, it was Pakenham which appeared in later assembly lists.

[34] H. Germany, 'Beginnings of Assembly Life in East Anglia', *H* 13 (1936), 90.

[35] Darby, *Letters*, 3.234 (undated). Dickson dates the letter to 1838 (*Brethren in Scotland*, 27-8).

[36] After clashing with Darby and other Exclusive leaders from 1860 regarding the administration of discipline in the movement, Stewart returned to Presbyterian ministry on Guernsey in 1865.

[37] For Stafford, see Anon., 'Trustees of Church Lane Meeting Room, Stafford, 1839-1920' (typescript, n.d.; CBA 5635 (1)); George J. Venables, *Down Memory Lane with the Christian*

Birmingham, which was to be a dissenting stronghold during much of the nineteenth century, was another locality where Quakers were involved in Brethren beginnings. Samuel Lloyd (1768-1849), of the banking family, seceded in 1838 and commenced an assembly; his son Sampson (1808-74) followed him in 1840.[39] Samuel's daughter Rachel was married to Robert Howard, brother of John Eliot Howard, so here we may well have another example of the way that Brethren ideas spread via the Quaker marriage network.[40] However, further input came from the movement associated with John Bowes: one of his associates, Peter Anderson (1810-1907), joining the assembly late in 1839.[41] Other Bowesite meetings were founded in the West Midlands at Wednesbury (1848) and Walsall (1853), both of which would later appear on Open Brethren assembly address lists. It is also at Birmingham that we first find the former Anglican, R.M. Beverley (1796-1868), whose robust critiques of the Establishment achieved a brief notoriety, associating with Brethren in 1839; in a letter to Robert Howard, he requested help from Brethren in London towards the cost of providing lodgings for Hargrove and his family, on the basis that the opening available in the city (in which Dissent was strong throughout the nineteenth century) presented an opportunity to set up a beacon which would be visible far and wide.[42]

3.6 Northern England

In the North-West, the stimulus for the establishment of a Brethren presence was a division among the Quakers in 1835-6 regarding the relative authority of Scripture and the 'inner light', known as the 'Beacon Controversy'.[43] The name was derived from a tract by Isaac Crewdson (1780-1844) entitled *A Beacon to the Society of Friends*, which called for the movement's doctrinal renewal along biblical and Evangelical lines.[44] Several hundred Evangelical Quakers in the region withdrew; nationally, as many as 3,000 may have resigned or been disowned. Some started their own meetings, as did Crewdson in Manchester, but many settled eventually with the Brethren, whose church practice they would have found congenial: it included the observance of baptism and the Lord's Supper, the lack of which they saw as a deficiency in Quaker meetings, but rejected the necessity of an ordained ministry, as they did. In spite of his allergic reaction to Quaker mysticism, Newton had kept up his connections with Quaker family members, and his first major published work, *A Remonstrance to the Society of Friends* (1835), was called forth by the

---

Brethren of Church Lane Meeting Room, Stafford 1838-1982 ([Stafford]: n.p., [1982]); idem, *The Meeting Room, Church Lane, Stafford* ([Stafford]: n.p., [c.1984]).

[38] Cf. Darby, *Letters*, 1.30 (31 January 1839), written from Stafford.

[39] See the entries for both men in *BDEB*.

[40] For a survey of the links, see Stunt, *Brethren and Friends*.

[41] It is said that Anderson commenced a second assembly (Leonard G. Barton, *Bearwood Chapel: One Hundred Years of Witness 1879-1979* ([Halesowen]: n.p., [1979]), 7; Dickson, *Brethren in Scotland*, 35n), but a letter from him to John Bowes dated 14 December 1839 (Bowes, *Autobiography*, 228-9) indicates that he had made his way to the already-existing meeting.

[42] Beverley to Howard, 9 July 1839 (LMA Acc.1017/1525). On Beverley, see *BDEB*.

[43] For more details, see David Brady and Fred J. Evans, *Christian Brethren in Manchester and District: A History* (London: Heritage Publications, 1997), 10-17; Elizabeth Isichei, *Victorian Quakers* (Oxford: Oxford University Press, 1970), 9, 44-50; Stunt, *Brethren and Friends*.

[44] On Crewdson, see *BDEB*; *ODNB*.

controversy.[45] It was an Evangelical critique of the teaching of Quaker thinkers such as William Penn and Robert Barclay, with their stress on the 'inner light' of God within each person as the ultimate authority in religious matters. Darby joined in the debate, issuing *Remarks on Light and Conscience* in 1836.[46] For him, the root issue was the doctrine of the Holy Spirit, but it is significant that Darby's developed thinking on the Spirit's role in worship would show clear parallels with that of the Quakers.[47]

Among those elsewhere who joined the Brethren at this time were Richard Ball of Taunton, who had supported Isaac Crewdson in print, and J.I. Wright, father of James Wright who would become Müller's assistant in the Scriptural Knowledge Institution. Ball was baptised at a Baptist church in Exeter by Newton in August 1837; his wife, Wright, and Wright's two daughters were baptised at Bethesda, Bristol, by 'Rev.' [*sic*] Henry Craik that October.[48] The Howard family of Tottenham also came from the Quakers, and John Eliot Howard's wife was Isaac Crewdson's niece. Such accessions were faithfully recorded in *The Inquirer*, a Beaconite journal edited by Howard which gave considerable space to defending Brethren against their critics.

The Quaker practice of intermarriage continued among those who joined the Brethren, as Stunt and others have documented. This provided a network for the rapid dissemination of Brethren ideas over a large part of England. Thus Newton, though based at Plymouth, could play a part in the commencement of a Brethren meeting at Kendal in Westmorland during 1837. Quakerism in Kendal had a tradition of Evangelical views, and this meeting displayed clear evidence of its Beaconite roots, as a recent dissertation has documented.[49] The Kendal meeting also exemplified another characteristic aspect of much early Brethrenism, its social delicacy: differences in social class meant that the seceders did not seek a home in Methodism, which might have been perceived as socially inappropriate because of the lower social standing of Methodists, but formed their own gathering. Such sensitivity was evident on the Methodist side as well: when in 1844 a group seceded from the Inghamites (a small group of churches in the Methodist tradition) in Kendal, they set up their own assembly; only in 1857 did they join the earlier gathering.

Another group of meetings came into the Brethren orbit in the North-West as the result of a schism in the Methodist New Connexion during 1841. This group was led by William Trotter (1818-65)[50] and Joseph Barker (1806-75), who were expelled by the denomination's Conference;[51] Barker had refused to baptise infants, and both were apparently suspected of Quaker sympathies because of the biblical literalism which led Barker in particular to refuse to swear oaths, to advocate pacifism, and to oppose the

[45] Burnham, *Conflict*, 88; Coad, *History*, 78-9.

[46] Darby, *CW*, 3.57-72.

[47] Stunt, *Brethren and Friends*, 14.

[48] *I* 1 (1838), 64.

[49] John Cartmell, 'Friends and Brethren in Kendal: A Critical analysis of the Emergence of the Brethren Church in Kendal from the Quaker Meeting Between 1835 and 1858' (honours dissertation, International Christian College, Glasgow, 1999).

[50] On Trotter, who produced some influential works on prophecy as an Exclusive brother, see Pickering (ed.), *Chief Men*, 31-2.

[51] See W. Trotter, *The Justice and Forbearance of the Methodist New Connexion Conference Conference as they were illustrated in the case of W. Trotter, giving a complete account of his trial before the Halifax Conference, containing a full answer to sundry tracts or pamphlets published by J.H. Robinson and T. Allin, etc* (London: R. Groombridge, 1841).

concept of a paid ministry. Trotter criticised the ecclesiasticism and clericalism of the Connexion's Conference, and challenged the denomination's accumulation of wealth (used for purposes such as the provision of pensions for ministers). The congregations which followed them out were known as 'Barkerites' or, confusingly, 'Christian Brethren', and were concentrated in the West Midlands, the Potteries, Cheshire, Manchester, West Yorkshire, and Newcastle. Estimates of the movement's strength vary, but Barker and Trotter themselves put the number of churches formed at about eighty.[52] Barker later drifted into Unitarian and Chartist views, before returning to Methodism late in life, and most sources overlook his temporary Brethren sympathies.[53]

At first, Trotter continued as the recognised pastor of the group's Bradford circuit. He began meeting with Brethren in West Yorkshire early in 1843, and may have parted from Barker at the same time, although it appears that for the year 1843 they co-operated in editing a monthly magazine, *The Christian Brethren's Journal and Investigator*. Bowes or his colleagues were mentioned occasionally, indicating that there were some links between the two groups. Barker and Trotter expressed their approval of many Brethren emphases in two articles on the movement,[54] which included this description of a Brethren Bible reading:

> the plan generally adopted is this. Each has his Bible, and when any particular portion has been fixed upon for consideration, they read round, verse by verse, somewhat after the manner of a Bible class. When the portion fixed upon has been read through, a solemn pause ensues, during which all silently lift their hearts to God for the guidance of his Spirit; and then if anyone has a question to ask respecting the portion of Scripture that has been read, he asks it, and it is considered; and if any one present has light on the subject, it is answered. If any one of the brethren present have received enlarged views of truth from the Scripture that has been read, they state those views for the edification of the rest. They often read regularly through a book or a series of books in the Bible, commencing each time where they left off at the previous meeting…[55]

They were also moving towards acceptance of a distinctively Brethren approach to worship and ministry, advocating 'the adoption of the Lord's own plan – to meet weekly to break bread, and waiting on God alone, thankfully receive instruction and exhortation from any whom he may raise up or send to teach his children'.[56] Nevertheless, whilst they commended the movement warmly, they made it clear that at that stage they did not subscribe to certain Brethren views,[57] and they criticised Brethren for over-harshness

---

[52] *CBJI*, 47. It has been suggested that as many as 200 chapels were involved, and that they were incorporated *en bloc* into the Brethren movement (cf. Valentine Cunningham, *Everywhere Spoken Against: Dissent in the Victorian Novel* (Oxford: Clarendon, 1975), 27, 29). By contrast, Methodist sources give figures of twenty-nine chapels and 4,348 members (W.J. Townsend, H.B. Workman and George Eayrs (eds.), *A New History of Methodism* (London: Hodder and Stoughton, 1909), 1.525, followed by *BDEB*). Not all of these would have linked up with Brethren.

[53] For a reliable account of this group, see Brady and Evans, *Brethren*, 17-20.

[54] [J. Barker and W. Trotter], 'Some particulars respecting a number of Christian Brethren who meet simply as such in various parts of this and other countries', *CBJI*, 77-9, 94-6.

[55] *Ibid.*, 94.

[56] Editors' note, *CBJI*, 125n.

[57] [J. Barker and W. Trotter], 'The Present Aspect of the Religious World', *CBJI*, 45-6.

towards other denominations and a tendency to obscurity in explaining their views to believers.[58]

Although Bowes had moved to Liverpool in 1837, and was the stimulus for the formation of a number of meetings in Lancashire, there is no conclusive evidence of links between his congregations and later Brethren meetings. Brethren met for conference in Liverpool in 1843,[59] but the first assembly was not founded there until the following year, by William Collingwood (1819-1903), who would lead it for forty years. Collingwood was a noted water-colourist and a friend of John Ruskin, and came from a well-known Oxford Dissenting family.[60] Other centres saw their first Brethren meetings during the 1840s: Thomas Maunsell, who was one of the early members at Limerick and later moved to Hereford, referred in 1842 to small groups meeting in Lancaster, Manchester (which was not in a healthy state) and Sheffield. He had also visited the Isle of Man, where a few had just left their churches, and it seems that an assembly existed in Douglas by the middle of the century.[61]

In urban Yorkshire, several meetings sprang up, the first in 1840 at Ackworth, near Wakefield, where Luke Howard had a house. About the same time a meeting commenced in Sheffield. Trotter was in fellowship with meetings at Halifax and then Otley. On the coast, a meeting at Scarborough appears to have existed by the mid-1840s, when Beverley either began it or associated himself with it.[62] A curate in Hull, Andrew Jukes (1815-1901), was suspended by 1844 because of his inability to accept aspects of the Prayer Book services, was baptised as a believer, and founded an independent congregation.[63] Jukes associated for some while with Brethren, and produced two standard works on typology, *The Law of the Offerings* and *The types of Genesis*, which were widely used in the movement. Gradually, he reverted to his earlier Anglicanism, and when he opened a new church in the mid-1860s, some of the services were conducted according to the Prayer Book. In 1867 he issued *The Second Death and the Restitution of all Things*, in which he denied the doctrine of eternal punishment. In later life he became a combination of mystic and High Churchman, returning to the Anglican ministry.

3.7 Scotland

The earliest extant evidence of Brethren activity in Scotland is Darby's references to his having visited Edinburgh, where a group of three dozen was already meeting. In a letter which appears to have been written in 1838, he referred to a fragment of a flock, already

---

[58] *Ibid.*; [Barker and Trotter], 'Some particulars', 94-6.

[59] Darby, *Letters*, 1.66 (November 1843). The proceedings are recorded in Anon., 'Notes in unknown hand of Bible Readings Nov.2nd-8th. 1843 & Meetings at Freemasons Hall April 7-9. 1846 re:- Plymouth Division' (CBA Box 161(2)).

[60] On William Collingwood, see *BDEB*; [W.G. Collingwood], 'William Collingwood R.W.S. (1819-1903)' (typescript, n.d.; CBA Box 164(335)). His grandfather, Samuel Collingwood, who was Printer to the University of Oxford, left New Road Baptist Church around 1832 to help found a Congregational church in the city. His son, W.G. Collingwood, was John Ruskin's biographer, and his grandson, R.G. Collingwood, a noted philosopher.

[61] T. Maunsell to J.N. Darby, 16 July 1842 (CBA 5540 (164)).

[62] Rowdon, *Origins*, 174.

[63] On Jukes, see Coad, *History*, 79-80; Herbert H. Jeaffreson (ed.), *Letters of Andrew Jukes* (London: Longmans, Green, 1903); Rowdon, *Origins*, 174.

depleted by two secessions.[64] Another letter gives further details. Apparently, he was invited to the city by 'a small flock which was crumbling away for want of' observing the principle of complete dependence on the Spirit in worship. A split had occurred many years earlier, and another more recently because most were only willing to receive 'Baptists' (presumably those baptised as believers) 'and were denying entirely the action of the Holy Spirit, even in the conversion of the sinner', a comment which may indicate Scotch Baptist influence. There was, Darby considered, 'not a place where I could have had less hope than here', and yet blessing resulted from his ministry.[65]

Other meetings soon began to appear; there is a reference to small groups meeting in Glasgow, Paisley, and Kilmarnock by 1842.[66] During the 1840s, a new denomination adhering to revivalist principles and practice as advocated by the American preacher Charles Finney (1792-1875), and reacting against traditional Calvinist theology, appeared, the 'Evangelical Union'. Like other movements of the time, these churches proclaimed the Bible as their sole authority in doctrinal matters, and refused to be fettered by subscription to a creed. It is not surprising, therefore, that within a few years several Brethren assemblies had been formed as groups seceded from it.[67] Other denominations also saw secessions, as dissatisfied individuals were attracted to such practices as open worship and lay administration of baptism and the Lord's Supper as being more scriptural than their previous practice. Bowes, whose Wesleyan theology would have accorded with that of the Evangelical Union's founders, was partly responsible for this development, which at first took place independently of the Brethren movement. From 1849, Bowes's magazine *The Truth Promoter* linked his meetings in Scotland, which were located in the Lowlands and the urban areas along the East coast, but many died out during the 1850s, due to a variety of causes including local antagonism, division, and emigration. Bowes' coolness towards aspects of Brethrenism as a movement makes it difficult to identify his meetings *tout simple* with Brethren assemblies, although that at Wishaw (1847) did survive to become associated with Brethren. Brethren in Scotland were very largely the product of the 1859 Revival and subsequent evangelistic campaigns by Moody and others, a fact which has tended to make them shy of over-close association with earlier Brethrenism, and in particular with the English quarrels.[68] The strength of adherence to Presbyterianism in many parts of Scotland was another important factor retarding Brethren development; we shall see in a later chapter that Brethren experienced ferocious opposition in such areas.

In 1840, A.N. Groves noted that there were nearly 200 assemblies in England and Ireland, made up of believers from all classes in society.[69] By the end of the decade, the movement had established a fairly wide distribution of gatherings in much of England, and a significant presence in various parts of Ireland, especially those in which

---

[64] Darby, *Letters*, 3.234.

[65] Letter of 6 October 1838 (BGT folder 1, f.3).

[66] T. Maunsell to J.N. Darby, 16 July 1842. These were all locations of groups described in Anon., *Letters concerning their Principles and Order*, but it is not possible to tell whether the later meetings had their roots in the earlier ones.

[67] For further detail on developments mentioned in this paragraph, see Dickson, *Brethren in Scotland*, 41-58.

[68] See, for example, F.F. Bruce's Foreword to Coad, *History*, 13.

[69] A.N. Groves, *Remarks on a Pamphlet, entitled "The Perpetuity of the Moral Law"* (Madras: J.B. Pharoah, 1840), 133.

Protestantism was strongest. The existence of networks of marriage relationships and personal friendships seems to have provided the most significant initial impetus for the commencement of new gatherings, although once an assembly was established in a new area it often engaged in church-planting activity locally. This was frequently undertaken by an influential member with a vision for it, who was well-enough off to be able to devote all or most of his time to such work. Secessions were another factor, sometimes as the result of contacts via the networks just mentioned.

There were as yet few meetings in Scotland and it is unclear whether the movement had yet taken root in Wales, but the movement was establishing a presence overseas, although it is not possible to explore this further here.[70] At this stage, the leadership of most assemblies was in the hands of well-educated middle-class men (many of them former clergy). Whilst many assemblies fairly soon had a high proportion of working-class members, few leaders emerged from their ranks until later in the century. Brethrenism was not a democratic religion in the way that Methodism had been during the early part of the century, with its high proportion of working-class lay preachers and class leaders.[71]

However, a major hindrance to further expansion at home and abroad, because it absorbed so much of the movement's energy, was to be the controversy which resulted in the division of the movement into what became known as Open and Exclusive streams; the next chapter traces that part of the story.

---

[70] Accessible summaries of the movement's early expansion overseas are found in Rowdon, *Origins*, ch. 8, and W.T. Stunt et al, *Turning the World Upside Down* (Bath: Echoes of Service, 1972[2]).

[71] During the first half of the century, the various branches of Methodism were affected by controversy over alleged tendencies to clericalism and centralisation, and some schisms resulted, but this does not affect my point.

CHAPTER 4

The Parting of Brethren

One of the saddest aspects of British Brethren history is the division into Open and Exclusive streams which resulted from events at Plymouth and Bristol between 1845 and 1848. These events are confusing to follow, but there were three phases to the conflict. In the first, Darby clashed with Newton at Plymouth and the meeting there divided, the main issues of contention being prophecy and church order; in the second, aspects of Newton's teaching regarding the sufferings of Christ were condemned by virtually all leading Brethren; in the third, the movement as a whole divided over the reception of believers from meetings deemed to be infected with doctrinal error. A clear grasp of what took place during these years is vital for an understanding not only of subsequent relationships between Open and Exclusive Brethren but also of the theological development of each stream. However, before outlining what happened, we need to examine the background to the divergence, and especially the way in which differing approaches to questions of fellowship and church order were becoming apparent.

4.1 Light or Life?

The grounds on which believers were to unite in fellowship formed a constant topic of Brethren writing and discussion. Many who seceded from Anglicanism had condemned it as being too broad and yet also too narrow in its terms of communion – too broad because it allowed worldly people to take the Lord's Supper, and too narrow because it excluded believers who were conscientious Dissenters. Initially, Groves and Darby agreed in regarding fellowship as based on shared possession of life in Christ. Darby encouraged the assemblies to welcome all believers, and expressed concern if any placed further restrictions on fellowship: 'I could not recognise an assembly that does not receive all the children of God, because I know that Christ receives them. ... I would rather remain alone and isolated, ... than to restrict the limits of the church of Christ to some brethren, even though they may be more correct in their thoughts than others'.[1]

However, things were otherwise at Plymouth. Earlier we noted the separatist tone of some of the early leaders there, particularly Borlase; the initial openness to receive all believers was fairly rapidly replaced by an aggressive approach towards other churches which emphasised the call to separate from Babylon in the face of coming judgment. Since the visible church was doomed, according to Brethren eschatological thinking, separation was the only course open to the believer. As Coad explains, 'Much of the teaching and testimony of the church was based on prophetic interpretation, and upon the apocalyptic expectations of apostasy and judgment which that study generated. Its devotion and ardour were admirable and real, yet much derived from appeals for separation from corruption and apostasy in others.'[2] This is confirmed by examination of the contents of *The Christian Witness*: articles on prophecy formed a significant part of the contents and the call to separation was frequently sounded. When Groves visited them in

---

[1] Darby, *Letters*, 1.35 (2 January 1840).

[2] Coad, *History*, 68.

1836, he concluded that they had shifted position from union in the truth to union in testimony against all other views,[3] a position which was to prove disastrously inadequate as a basis for well-balanced church life.

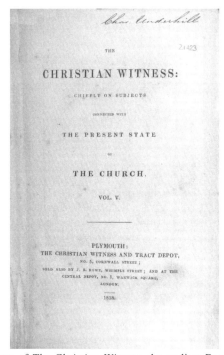

Title-page of a volume of *The Christian Witness*, the earliest Brethren periodical

Darby, too, was developing an emphasis on separation which at first sight appears contradictory to his earlier concern for unity and fellowship.[4] The precipitating factor was undoubtedly his disillusionment with the Church of Ireland's inability to exclude clerical teachers of error (as seen in Whately's appointment as Archbishop of Dublin) or recognise the ministry of laymen who preached the truth (as seen in the clampdown on the activities of the Home Mission during 1833). In Dublin, he had made a deep impression on J.B. Stoney in June 1834, when he preached from Joshua 7 that God cannot be with believers until they separate from evil; Stoney applied this to the question of secession, although Darby cautioned that he was not yet absolutely sure of the rightness of his views.[5] However, these were to be the lines along which his thought developed. At some point around 1836, Darby explained his new emphasis in *Separation from Evil God's Principle of Unity*.[6] Unity was not to be made an end in itself, since this could result in being united with evil; rather, true unity must always have God as its centre. The goal of

---

[3] Mrs. Groves, *Memoir*, 342.

[4] He reconciled the two by insisting that separation from evil to Christ was itself the divinely-sanctioned basis for unity.

[5] Anon., *Interesting Reminiscences*, 20.

[6] Darby, *CW*, 1.353-65.

God's work in the world was to unite all things under Christ, which of necessity involved dealing with evil, since God could have no union with evil. The Fall was an attempt at independence of God, and apostasy in its final manifestation would be characterised by unity in subjection to what was independent of God, a Satanic counterpart to true unity. Although there would be an eschatological judicial separation, by the Spirit God was now separating those whom he had called from evil to Christ, the church's heavenly Head and 'the separating power of attraction'.[7] Acknowledging that evil was bound to infect the body, Darby called for its agents to be excommunicated. If the church refused to do so, the believer must secede, since this amounted to a denial of God's holy nature. The believer could thus maintain the principles of unity in his conscience, even if alone, since he was united with Christ by the Spirit, an assertion which explains the apparent paradox of Darby's insistence on the principle of unity with his frequent involvement in controversy and his practice of separation. Neatby described the pamphlet somewhat tartly as 'a bold attempt to reconcile his principle of universal communion with his practice of universal schism'.[8]

On 10 March 1836, Groves wrote a strongly-worded letter to Darby occasioned by the latter's treatment of Newman and Plymouth.[9] Groves expressed a fear that Darby was returning to the sectarian position from which he had set out, by making doctrinal light rather than spiritual life the term of communion and by emphasising negatives (such as separation) rather than positives (such as unity and fellowship). Separation, for Groves, related to the believer's walk with God rather than his testimony to others, and he pointed out that when Darby had seceded (separating from much that was good because of evil which was present) he had lost much of his influence. Groves was convinced that Darby was being influenced by narrower minds. As far as he was concerned, one could only describe a church as apostate if Christ had withdrawn from it, and he was convinced that in fact Christ had not done so but was still at work in many traditional churches.[10] Writing in the summer of 1837, Groves developed this conviction further:

> I as fully admit as you can desire, that *in my own person,* it is my *bounden* duty to depart from *every* evil thing; but the judgment of *others,* and consequent separation from them, I am daily more satisfied is *not of God.* The blessing of God rests on those who are separated *by others* from their company, and it is a mark of apostacy to be of those who "separate themselves" from God's own redeemed ones; moreover, if ever there was a witness for God on earth, that witness was Jesus, and He never separated Himself from the synagogues; and this, if it proves nothing more, proves that *separation* is not the *only* way of witness, and yet, He was emphatically, 'separate from sinners,' not from their *persons,* nor *assemblies,* but *separate from their sins.*[11]

Another witness to attitudes at Plymouth was John Bowes, who noted in January 1840 that many there considered Groves too catholic in his sympathies and so refused to

---

[7] *Ibid.,* 1.359. Newton likewise described separation as the believer's first duty (*Catholicity, in a dispensation of failure, a sure token of apostasy* (London and Ryde: Houlston and Sons and Arthur Andrews, 1892[3]), 65).

[8] Neatby, *History,* 296.

[9] The text of his letter is given in Coad, *History,* 291-5.

[10] Burnham, *Conflict,* 98; Coad, *History,* 119-20.

[11] Mrs. Groves, *Memoir,* 359-60.

support his work.[12] Although Bowes had adopted Brethren views on many issues, he always denied belonging to the movement, possibly because of his desire to avoid being associated with what he saw as the sectarian spirit of the Plymouth assembly. Such was his disapproval of their attitude that 'for the first time, I pointed out the wrong of those who have abandoned a Sectarian name, but retain a Sectarian spirit'.[13]

If we look at the prophetic conferences which took place from 1838, we can see that such concerns were among the issues beginning to test the movement's unity.[14] In June that year, a conference was convened at Clifton, near Bristol. By now, these gatherings were considering matters of church order. The syllabus included such questions as:

> How may brethren meet for profit? [The work of the Holy Spirit in the believer] The distinctive character of the dispensation between the first and second coming of Christ. Christian Priesthood; Christian Ministry; how and to what extent is it to be recognized? The authority of the Church, and wherein lodged? Has she any, and what power of legislation? What Scripture authority for the distinction between the true and professing Church? What is the removal of the candlestick? What is the Scripture testimony as to the state of the Church at the close of the dispensation? What measure of the original blessing of the dispensation may a faithful remnant hope to recover? Would such be warranted in applying to themselves Mal.iii.6-7. How may such most effectually witness for the Lord?[15]

Prophetic issues for discussion included the prospects for Jew and Gentile in this dispensation and scriptural references to the earth, the nations and the two Jerusalems (heavenly and earthly) during the Millennium. Ominously, in view of the coming division, participants would also discuss the working of Satan, the character of heresy, and 'The source of division among those who love the Lord – What do we learn from the Word as to the means of union?'[16] This meeting appears to have been open to non-Brethren, as Darby stated that over a hundred were present from England and Ireland, including some whom he described as 'our enemies' and also, apparently, some from the Church of England.[17]

Prophecy again formed a major part of the discussion at the June 1839 conference in Leamington. J.E. Howard described it as a spiritual feast, but Newton was somewhat less positive about it. It seems that the two schemes of interpretation championed by Darby and Newton respectively were under review, and the delegates from Plymouth were somewhat shaken by the views expressed, although they eventually came round to Newton's way of seeing things.[18]

The last conference of which we have any details was at Liverpool in November 1843; Darby sensed an increased measure of blessing, and referred to individuals being linked up

[12] Bowes, *Autobiography*, 236.

[13] *Ibid.*, 233.

[14] No conference took place in 1837: Lady Powerscourt had died the previous year, and Darby left for Switzerland at the end of August.

[15] Anon., *Questions for Eight Weeks' Consideration*, 14-15.

[16] *Ibid.*, 15-16.

[17] Darby, *Letters*, 3.232-4 [1838].

[18] [Maria Howard], *Memorials*, 117 (letter of 13 June 1839); Fry Collection, 'Small Notebook 2', 58r (photocopy in CBA Box 13(30)); 'Small Notebook 6', 53b.

with Brethren and new localities opened up for work.[19] Clearly the failure to reach doctrinal unanimity had not stopped the conferences from serving as a 'shop window' for the movement. It is not clear why they ceased to be held, although it seems likely that the reason was something to do with the division affecting the movement from 1845. Large meetings lasting several days were convened at London in 1846 and Bath in 1848 and 1849 to deal with Newton's teaching and the resulting division, and it may be that it was not considered wise to attempt to hold other large gatherings, whether for practical reasons or for fear that increasing dissension might wreck them.

4.2 Darby and Switzerland

In attempting to provide a context for the emergence of Brethrenism and the development of Darby's thought, we should also note the Swiss influence on radical Evangelicalism in Britain. Many British radicals looked to Switzerland for a model: biblicist, Calvinistic, suffering, faithful, and assured, leaders such as Malan attracted much attention when they toured the country on preaching trips during the 1820s. Conversely, the Swiss Evangelical movement owed a great deal to foreign input at crucial moments.[20] Robert Haldane's lectures on Romans in Geneva during 1817 were a factor in the emergence of the *Réveil,* which represented not only a movement of personal renewal but also a reappropriation of Calvin's theology.[21] Henry Drummond, in founding the 'Continental Society for the Diffusion of Religious Knowledge' in 1819, was realising a dream of Haldane's, and the Society supported extensive work in Switzerland and France. Further revival followed a revolution in 1830, but relationships between the Established Church and the Evangelicals became increasingly hostile during the following decade. This would confirm Darby's negative estimate of religious establishments.

Darby visited Switzerland in 1835, and was invited to return late in 1837.[22] Although things were by then becoming difficult at Plymouth as differences with Newton were becoming evident on the question of ministry, he insisted that 'It was in no way any particular opposition that led me to Switzerland in 1837, but a report of a brother who had been there, and stated that there were meetings like ours.'[23] When he arrived in Geneva, he found things in turmoil as a result of Irvingite attempts to take over the assembly in the Bourg-de-Four, which had been founded in 1817 after awakened believers found it impossible to remain in the state church. Once more, foreign intervention was to shape the course of Swiss Evangelicalism. Darby became involved in the controversy, establishing a positive relationship with its pastors, seeking to reconcile the parties

---

[19] Darby, *Letters,* 1.66 (November 1843). The proceedings were recorded in Anon., 'Notes in unknown hand'.

[20] Important sources for this section include A. Christopher Smith, 'British non-Conformists and the Swiss "Ancienne dissidence". The Role of Foreign Evangelicals and J.N. Darby in The Rise and Fall of the "Ancienne Dissidence" in French-Speaking Switzerland: 1810-1850' (BD treatise, International Baptist Theological Seminary, Rüschlikon, Switzerland, 1979); idem, 'J.N. Darby in Switzerland at the Crossroads of Brethren History and European Evangelism', *CBR* 34 (1983), 53-94; and (for the period to 1835) Stunt, *Awakening,* chs. 2-5.

[21] Stunt, *Awakening,* 33-4.

[22] *Ibid.,* 301-4.

[23] Darby, *Letters,* 1.515 (Memorandum, 1868). However, he went on to say that in reality these assemblies were nothing more than dissenting churches.

concerned and using his idea of the church as ruined to this end.[24] Further afield, the dissidents in the canton of Vaud were united by what they opposed, rather than by common ecclesiological principles. This had given rise in earlier decades to tensions; it had also created a leadership vacuum, and he won their respect as a leader on his next visit from Autumn 1839 (which was by invitation) by his handling of an outbreak of Wesleyan perfectionist views.

However, his relationship with local leaders began to deteriorate. Experience of a chronically divided assembly, coupled with the hostility of the State Church, undoubtedly reinforced his developing conviction that the church on earth was irreparably ruined and that it was impossible to set up any kind of replacement as the dissidents were trying to do. By the end of 1840, therefore, he had broken with the *Ancienne Dissidence*; he was blamed for a division which occurred at Bourg-de-Four in March 1842; and he (along with a pamphlet he had written on the ruin of the church in 1840, *On the Formation of Churches*[25]) was denounced at a conference called by the movement's leaders on 6 September to consider the question of the apostasy of the present dispensation.[26] This last had formed the basis from which Darby had queried the position of the pastors in the Swiss movement and advanced his own, more radically congregational, views.[27] From this point he would work independently in Switzerland.

4.3 Division at Plymouth

It is difficult to know quite where to place Plymouth in the spectrum of Brethren views running from open to exclusive.[28] As Coad explains,

> In major matters the leaders at Plymouth were in agreement against both Groves and Bristol. Newton and Darby shared similar convictions concerning the ruined condition of the professing Churches, and the "apostasy" (as they termed it) of the Christian dispensation. They were united in their call to Christians to separate from existing systems and to meet in simple gatherings. Both were united in the central place they gave to the apocalyptic Scriptures, and in making eschatological views the central point of their systems. Only in matters of church government would Newton later find himself nearer to Bristol than to Darby.

> Yet, beneath this outward agreement there lay a difference of opinion, arising from their respective prophetic systems. The tragedy of Bulteel at Oxford had sealed for Newton (if, indeed, it was not its cause) a violent antipathy to Irvingism, and with Irvingism everything that

---

[24] Darby, *CW*, 4.188; Robert Henry Krapohl, 'A search for purity: The controversial life of John Nelson Darby' (PhD dissertation, Baylor University, 1988), 171.

[25] Darby, *CW*, 1.138-55. Its first English title, significantly, was *Reflections on the Ruined Condition of the Church; and on the efforts making [sic] by Churchmen and Dissenters to Restore it to its Primitive Order*. Its argument is summarised in section 5.2.4.

[26] Darby, *Letters*, 1.54-5 (21 January 1843); cf. Coad, *History*, 126; Smith, 'Darby in Switzerland', 68, 71-3.

[27] Burnham, *Conflict*, 158, following Smith, 'British non-conformists', 124-5.

[28] For more detailed accounts of events covered in this section, to which it is indebted, see Burnham, *Conflict*, 149-88; Coad, *History*, 139-48; Embley, 'Origins and Early Development', ch. 4; Neatby, *History*, ch. 6; Rowdon, *Origins*, chs. 9-10.

was connected with it. Notably, this rejection included a feature of prophetic interpretation which Darby had adopted, the doctrine of "the secret rapture of the saints."[29]

As well as prophecy, there were other serious issues at stake between Newton and Darby, one being Newton's leadership style. A growing church demanded strong leadership, which Newton sought to provide. The basis for his conduct had been laid years before at Oxford: his exclusivism, his passion for prophetic study, and his brushes with Irvingism, both at Oxford and in the South-West. He also appears to have had a growing conviction that Brethren 'open' meetings were uniquely prone to disorder. That this was a potential problem is evident from his experience at Wigram's meeting in London. To maintain order at the meetings and restrain ungifted contributors, therefore, Newton was appointed as presiding elder.[30] According to him, such a practice was followed by the other local Brethren meetings.[31] In 1846, he described how this had affected the assembly's worship practice:

> Every Lord's Day morning we meet for communion at the Lord's Table. It is a meeting open to the ministry of any whom God may have gifted for such service: there are generally three or four Brethren present, who are known either to speak or to pray to edification in the congregation; and although we do not know beforehand which of them may pray or speak, nor in what order, yet we always expect that some or all of them will take part in the meeting. We believe it to be their duty to stir up the gift that is in them. But whilst we thus expect the regular ministry of some, pauses are allowed to occur, which afford the opportunity for rising gifts, if such there be, to be developed and proved. If any speak, and after the trial their speaking *is not found to edification*, the Brethren who are regarded as addicted to the ministry of the Saints here (of whom there are at present three or four), after consulting others of spiritual weight, wait on the individual and advise him, or if the case needs, *request him not to minister*. We have not had occasion to act thus more than four or five times during fourteen years, but when we have been obliged to adopt this course, *we have never found it to fail.*[32]

However, it was not long before Newton resigned this office. His version of events was that at an unspecified point he was replaced by Harris, being no longer cordially supported by all,[33] but Tregelles stated that Newton laid down his office because he no longer believed such appointments to be scriptural, and that Darby left Plymouth in 1836 because the standing of overseers was insufficiently recognised.[34] Newton was seriously ill during that year, and (as he later recalled) his colleagues 'said to me that they would undertake the visiting in the mornings & afternoons, so that I might live a little way out of Plymouth & there write. _ They said that I ought to write; that was what I was best capable of. So they arranged it.'[35] His illness could have provided his colleagues with an

---

[29] Coad, *History*, 129.

[30] Ibid., 63; cf. S.P. Tregelles, *Three Letters to the Author of 'A Retrospect of Events that have taken place amongst the Brethren'* (London: Houlston, 1894² [1849]), 6-7.

[31] 'Fry MS', 301.

[32] Anon., *A Retrospect of Events that Have Taken Place Among the Brethren* (London: B.L. Green, 1849), 4.

[33] 'Fry MS', 301.

[34] Tregelles, *Three Letters*, 7n, 8.

[35] 'Fry MS', 305.

opportunity of suggesting that he lay down his office, a suggestion which his developing views might predispose him to accept. All the same, he continued to exercise rigid control over affairs by virtue of his bearing much of the responsibility for public ministry, as well as by his autocratic way of relating to others. This is borne out by Beverley's description of his political views as those of 'the antique ultra-Tory of the closing days of the House of Stuart'.[36] If Newton was the tragic hero of the Brethren movement, autocracy was the fatal flaw which led to his downfall.[37] His conduct continued to give rise to discontent in the church, which was to surface through Darby.

John Nelson Darby, aged 40   Benjamin Wills Newton

Darby had initially encouraged Newton in his handling of the assembly, advising him in 1839 to stop those who spoke error and warn those speaking 'in the flesh'; the vital thing, Darby asserted, was to be able to sense the feelings of the meeting about the profitability or otherwise of the speaker.[38] However, as he became more anti-clerical he became increasingly concerned about developments at Plymouth.[39] At the same time as Darby's personal ascendancy over many assemblies was increasing, he was retreating from belief in the need for elders (fearing the growth of a new clerical caste), and promulgating his doctrine of the church's ruin. Having approved of Newton's appointment as elder, he now held that a Spirit-led assembly would recognise God-given leaders without the need for formal appointment to office. He appears to have been developing a contrast between what was of God (which, in worship, was informal, spontaneous, and heavenly) and what was of man (which was formal, pre-arranged, and earthly). In the light of this and the desire for unity of testimony, Newton's control of affairs at Plymouth could not have been more unwelcome. To complicate things, Darby's espousal of an 'impulsive' concept of ministry, dependent on the Spirit's immediate inspiration, must have brought back unpleasant memories for Newton of his Quaker upbringing and of Bulteel's attempts at Oxford to preach 'in the power'.

Both men had apparently given up the idea that New Testament church offices were still to be recognised, which left them without a given structure for church order, defined

---

[36] [R.M. Beverley], *Analysis, by a Student of Prophecy, of "Thoughts on the Apocalypse" by B.W. Newton, of Plymouth* (London: Longmans, Brown, Green, and Longmans, 1845), 18.

[37] Cf. Anon., *Retrospect of Events*, 17.

[38] Darby, *Letters*, 1.29-30 (31 January 1839).

[39] Coad, *History*, 125, 139-40.

expectations of leaders, or checks upon them. The importance of personal relationships was thus all the greater in view of the lack of structures to hold things together. Both functioned virtually at will, and a collision was inevitable when they sought to lead and influence the same assembly. From the beginning, Darby had felt a sense of apostolic parenthood towards the company at Plymouth, where, as we have noted, he felt that he had seen a demonstration of what true Christian fellowship should be like. This, and the influence which he believed he had there, meant that he would not take kindly to any apparent attempts to marginalise him or his theology. Probably during 1839, a conference at Exeter provided the setting for a clash between Newton and Darby over the content of *The Christian Witness*. Darby accused Newton of controlling it to suit his views (Newton had been seeking to develop a dispensational system consonant with Reformed theology, which stressed the continuity of God's dealings with humanity under the Old and New Covenants), to which Newton responded by asserting that the magazine grieved him as it did Darby. 'I saw then that the difference between us was so radical, so vital, that I said to Tregelles that I would go back to Plymouth the next morning and arrange to leave Plymouth entirely._And I ought to have done so. It would have spared all that sorrow afterwards'.[40] Perhaps hindsight coloured his recollection, but it does demonstrate the way that tension was building up.

From about 1840, Newton circulated five letters indicating events which he believed must precede the Second Coming and expressing his belief that Darby's views contained a principle which could destroy Christianity (presumably a hermeneutical approach which gave rise to the implication that there could be more than one way of salvation, which would be especially abhorrent to someone of Newton's Reformed convictions). In another letter he pointed out that 'the almost invariable effect of the Jewish principle of interpretation on the mind of the Church generally, is to throw them into such a state of perplexity as to incapacitate them for interpreting the Scriptures for themselves'.[41] If such people did not fall prey to religious scepticism, despairing of ever being able to understand the Scriptures, they would defer implicitly to their teachers: 'It would be as if the Spirit of God resided only in the teachers ... one of the worst forms of Popish evil' (scepticism and Popery were the two great doctrinal evils of the age, for Newton as well as Darby).[42] It is ironic that Newton's opposition was based on his perception of Darby's approach as likely to lead to the interposition of a teacher between the individual and God, and yet this was precisely what Darby would allege was going on at Plymouth. Newton isolated himself from other Brethren, deciding to walk 'peacefully, but separately', seeing his views and Darby's as diametrically opposed.

> The great hindrance to any approximation of judgment appears to me to be this: that we have severally adopted as axioms two principles which are entirely counterparts one of another._ I believe that it is essential to the existence of prophecy about the Church that there should be intervening events foretold. You on the contrary say there can be no intervening events for the

---

[40] 'Fry MS', 319.

[41] B.W. Newton, *Letter to a Friend* (Plymouth: Tract Depot, n.d.), 21. The 'Jewish principle of interpretation', which was an outworking of Darby's dispensational views, was a description of the division of the New Testament (most notably the Gospels) by some interpreters into passages which applied to God's earthly people, the Jews, and those which applied to God's heavenly people, Christian believers.

[42] *Ibid.*, 22.

Church's expectation and refuse to receive any thought from Scripture inconsistent with this main principle.[43]

Newton believed that the church was a subject of prophecy, and that certain events were to be expected before the Parousia, and he rejected Darby's understanding of the rapture and its separation from the Second Coming. Darby, for his part, held that Newton's views involved denial of the church's unique privileges as a heavenly entity: as such, it was not the subject of prophecy, which strictly speaking was concerned with God's dealings with Israel, his earthly people.[44] Coad explains the consequences of Darby's approach to prophetic interpretation:

> [Darby] distinguished sharply between the Old Testament economy and the New. In his view the faithful of the Old Testament were not comprised in the Church, and the two dispensations were utterly distinct. Following out this distinction, he taught that the faithful remnant of the tribulation under Antichrist would be, in effect, a restoration of the Old Testament economy: they would be a remnant of Jews remaining faithful to God in the fires of persecution. In the millennial reign of Christ, all the Old Testament promises to the Jewish people would have a literal fulfilment, while the church, the "saints" of the dispensation of grace, would have no part in that "earthly" reign. In contrast to these "earthly" hopes of the Jewish remnant, the promises to the Church were essentially "heavenly" in character.

> To Newton, this teaching ... implied two distinct schemes of salvation ...[45]

An exchange of letters failed to produce any reconciliation, and Darby claimed that in an unpleasant interview Newton had declared their friendship ended; Darby had had to work to pacify him.[46] Later, Newton declared that he had long suppressed his disagreement with Darby in order to avoid controversy. Although Darby later alleged that those who taught an interpretation differing from Newton's were kept away from Plymouth,[47] at the time he sought to minimise the differences, though not without a sense of lurking evil: 'If it were a foundation truth for the soul, no peace could be held with error: mistake in the interpretation of Revelation, one may exercise much patience with. These things are always the sign of some other evil; but God will turn it to good. Perhaps knowledge has been too much attended to at Plymouth.'[48] In time, however, Darby was to find ample evidence of 'some other evil' and this, rather than prophetic matters, would precipitate division.

Darby was of the opinion that the whole atmosphere had changed at Plymouth. Whereas the 'power of union and brotherly love, the Philadelphian spirit' had presented a powerful demonstration to outsiders of the Spirit's presence in the church,

---

[43] 'Small Notebook 2', 58v-59r (Newton to Darby, undated).

[44] Darby, *Letters*, 3.240-3 (14 November 1844).

[45] Coad, *History*, 130-1.

[46] Darby, *CW*, 20.19.

[47] *Ibid.*, 20.17-18; cf. idem, *Letters*, 1.90 (20 January 1846).

[48] Darby, *Letters*, 1.46 (3 February 1841). Coad remarks on the repeated sense of foreboding evident in Darby's letters at this time (*History*, 111).

this has, if not absolutely, all as one disappeared; a hard and rigid dogmatism of view has entirely replaced it: nor am I aware of any one place where the views adopted at Plymouth have been the means of gathering the saints, though they have been propagated in many gatherings ... If a strange Christian or brother from another place were to go there, the consequence would be, not that he would find the testimony of the power of love in union and the truth delighted in and sought out, but that he would be instantly subjected to a process of imbruing his mind with certain views.[49]

Plymouth was now a meeting gathered round particular opinions, like any other sectarian body (and we should note Darby's aside that in his experience such opinions had never served to gather the saints together). Furthermore, he alleged that Newton's teaching resulted in the loss of the doctrine of the church.[50]

Tension was to increase dramatically when revolution necessitated Darby's departure from Switzerland, and he acted upon a suggestion made by Harris a few months earlier that he should visit Plymouth. He arrived in March 1845, expecting trouble ('I felt that conflict and trial awaited me'[51]). His arrival came as a surprise to Newton,[52] who recorded his perception of what happened:

Mr. Darby had not been in Plymouth two days before he commenced on the gathering generally but principally on me, an attack of the most violent character you can well conceive. I soon became its chief object – chiefly on account of my "Thoughts on the Apocalypse" – The violence of the attack and its exceeding bitterness would be almost inconceivable by one who did not witness it ... Yet no discipline was employed. ... Private admonition was the utmost that was employed, and here I think was the first decided failure on the part of the brethren; and we are now suffering the results.[53]

On 30 March Newton requested his colleagues (Harris, Batten, and Soltau) to intervene against what he saw as Darby's divisive activity and unorthodox teaching.[54] An exchange of letters followed, in which Darby launched an attack which avoided doctrinal differences and concentrated on Newton's weak spot - his high-handed attitude to others. Further letters followed, in which Darby refused to make specific accusations, feeling that he need not give details of what had gone on publicly for six years, but charged Newton with systematic and sectarian exclusivism. Newton laid this charge before his colleagues and when the two protagonists met before them he vehemently asserted his desire for a clear testimony in Plymouth and the South-West against the errors taught by other Brethren, as well as his opposition to Darby's theological views.[55] Nevertheless, Darby could still

---

[49] *Ibid.*, 3.237-8 [1844]. This perception does not appear to have been unique to Darby: the anonymous author of *A Retrospect of Events* claimed that Brethren felt that Newton's prophetic system was indeed different from that generally accepted among them, and that his possession of a firm base at Plymouth had enabled him to adopt a more aggressive attitude towards other viewpoints (*Retrospect of Events*, 7).

[50] Darby, *Letters*, 3.239 [1844].

[51] Darby, *CW*, 20.20.

[52] 'Fry MS', 331.

[53] *Ibid.*, 356-7 (undated letter of Newton). *Thoughts on the Apocalypse* had appeared in 1843.

[54] For the letter, see *ibid.*, 329.

[55] Darby, *CW*, 20.29-30; idem, *Letters*, 1.88 (20 January 1846); 'Fry MS', 328-37.

express the hope that Newton would give up his objective and their relationships continue unhindered.[56]

During the summer, Darby itinerated in Devon and Somerset, later claiming that he found abundant evidence of meetings in which the authority of teachers was emphasised in such a way as to endanger the practice of open worship.[57] This, of course, was precisely the kind of clericalism from which Darby had sought to break away by seceding; for him, Newton's control of meetings amounted to usurping the Holy Spirit's rights in the assembly. Newton's high-handed attitude was now losing him the confidence of others, and on 8 October Harris withdrew from leadership (and subsequently from communion), insisting that an act of humiliation was required and opposing Newton's sudden suspension of the Friday elders' meeting, an objection also raised by Darby on the ground that the meeting's suspension meant that pastoral matters were dealt with by Newton's immediate circle of supporters.[58] This was not merely an issue of personalities or power, but one of principle: Darby held that gifting entitled an individual to serve in any local gathering, as part of a unified visible body – something which Newton believed could no longer exist – whereas Newton asserted that while teachers could teach in any meeting, those gifted as elders could only function in their local congregation.[59] On this understanding, Darby could visit Plymouth as a teacher, but not exercise any authority as an elder – hence his apparent feeling that he was denied any opportunity of influencing what went on at Plymouth.

Returning to Plymouth on 18 October, Darby influenced Harris to join in calling a meeting for humiliation and prayer, a call which Newton (then in London) rejected. Eight days later, Darby withdrew from communion, alleging that the principles on which Brethren met were being subverted at Plymouth by the changes introduced by Newton, that evil was going unconfessed and unjudged, and that the Friday meeting was set aside.[60] At a public meeting in November, Darby explained his reasons for leaving, focusing on Newton's allegedly false account of the stormy April meeting in his *Letter to Clulow* and the alterations made to the published version of his *Five Letters*. Before being published, the *Five Letters* had circulated in manuscript form; Darby's allegation was that the published version was substantially different (the effect of the alterations being to reverse the flow of argument concerning the authority of teachers in the church) and that in some copies Newton had suppressed two of the letters and replaced them with an appendix. Miss Jeremie, who had copied the lectures into two notebooks, explained that she was responsible for the appendix, which included some statements of Newton's which in her

---

[56] Darby, *Letters*, 1.79 (21 April 1845).

[57] Darby, *CW*, 20.31-3.

[58] 'Fry MS', 343-5 (Harris to Newton, 8 October 1845). Newton's later recollection was that 'at an early period of our gathering, a meeting was formed of six or seven brethren, for purposes of general oversight or rule, before any of them had really proved their qualifications for such a position; the result was that several soon shewed they had no qualification for such a service, and the meeting, after lingering out an unprofitable existence for many years, was at last dissolved by the consent & desire of the majority who composed it, but not without leaving in the bosom of one or two an unhealed wound which has operated most banefully ...' (Fry Collection, 'Small Notebook 11', 123-4 (CBA 7065)).

[59] Burnham, *Conflict*, 160-1, 170.

[60] Darby, *CW*, 20.74; idem, *Letters*, 1.84-6 (12 November 1845), 1.88-91 (20 January 1846), 3.243-4 (10 November 1845).

opinion clarified his earlier teaching, and that the last two letters had not been suppressed but had been copied in a second notebook.[61]

Leading Brethren from elsewhere came down to investigate the affair from 5-8 December, attempting to convene a private meeting between the protagonists, but without success; Darby insisted (as he had earlier) that the matter was a public one and should be brought before the church, although his attempts to do so were unavailing.[62] Further meetings exonerated Newton of any intent to deceive. Wigram came from London to support Darby, convening prayer meetings on 7 and 14 December to which believers from the assembly in Ebrington Street were invited. He also demanded the return of Providence Chapel in Raleigh Street, where the assembly had met until Ebrington Street was opened, and which it still used. Darby's request for a church meeting having been refused, on 28 December he set up another assembly, the Lord's Supper being observed in homes, thus implying that Ebrington Street was no longer a meeting according to Brethren principles.

The dispute could not remain confined to Plymouth. On 11 January 1846, at the Rawstorne Street assembly in London, Congleton accused Wigram of helping Darby to make the schism at Plymouth; the assembly refused to investigate the charge. During April, a meeting was convened in London to discuss what had happened. An account of what was said enables us to glimpse how leading brothers were reacting to it.[63] According to Chapman, the evil at Plymouth was symptomatic of a disease affecting the whole body of Brethren: they had left their first love and their prime need was to return to God. In his view, a meeting for humiliation (such meetings were now being convened) had been needed six years previously. Bellett agreed but stressed the need to examine biblical principles to see how far Brethren had failed to act according to them. Dorman thought the problem was that worldliness had infected the movement, confessing: 'I am not the same crucified man I was nine years ago.' Congleton appears to have shocked the assembled company by asserting that he was present under protest because he could not keep company with Wigram or Darby. Hargrove, who had been moving away from aspects of Brethren thinking on such matters as ministry and spiritual gifting, considered the division at Plymouth unwarranted, and he too had difficulty in meeting Darby and Wigram. Darby appears to have brushed off criticism with the assertion that 'not any one of the Brethren ever had the sense [?] of the ruin of the church of God which I had'. No conclusions were offered, and the focus of the meeting was very much on self-judgment and the need for humiliation. Newton, when invited to attend such a meeting, had refused on the basis that he expected it to assume a judicial character and he could not be sure of there being impartial judges to oversee the proceedings. He also refused repeated requests that he should meet Darby at a meeting in Rawstorne Street, claiming that he had already been exonerated and the meeting was therefore unnecessary.

Newton's wife died on 18 May and there were no further developments until, in September, Darby published a *Narrative of the Facts, connected with the Separation of the Writer from the Congregation meeting in Ebrington Street*.[64] His attack concentrated on the 'system' which Newton had allegedly been seeking to inculcate. Characteristically, he

---

[61] 'Fry MS', 364 (Miss Jeremie to Newton, 19 January [1846]).

[62] [Lord Congleton], *Reasons for Leaving Rawstorne-Street Meeting*, *London* ([Brighton: J.F. Eyles, 1847]), 13-14.

[63] Anon., 'Notes of Bible Readings'.

[64] Darby, *CW*, 20.1-72.

viewed its reception as a complete entity as a mark of Satan's work, since the teacher was thereby set up as an authority between the individual and God. He charged that Newton refused to allow ordinary members to attend reading meetings as they would hear the authority of the teachers questioned, and dealt at length with the growth of clericalism at Plymouth and the stifling of open ministry.[65]

In November, Newton visited London, meeting certain Brethren privately in order to answer questions but again refusing to attend a meeting at Rawstorne Street. The result was that the assembly excommunicated him early in December. Among the protests from Newton's sympathisers was one from Tregelles which condemned the assembly's action as tantamount to an assertion of metropolitan jurisdiction. Probably as a result of this action, Congleton withdrew, refusing to side with Newton or Darby, but charging that the assembly had received Darby without investigation and yet excommunicated Newton without hearing why he refused to respond to their summons to a meeting.[66]

Differing views regarding the issues at stake may have been rooted in differing understandings of religious truth: for Darby, it was the moral power of truth which had always weighed most with him,[67] and he viewed Plymouth as a moral issue. By this he seems to have meant that he focused on how Newton had disseminated his views, rather than on which doctrine was closer to Scripture.[68] Since this made a difference to the kind of procedures deemed appropriate, it was impossible to resolve the conflict in a manner acceptable to both sides. The moral and doctrinal aspects were related, however: of Newton's prophetic views, he wrote: 'I believe the identification of the church and the kingdom to be of the very worst moral effect to the saint'.[69]

Tregelles saw disagreement over prophecy as the root of the problem: 'Had he [Newton] accorded with Mr. Darby on Prophecy, we should never have heard his voice raised against him as to Ministry or Church Order.'[70] In that connection, it is not without significance that the summer of 1845 had seen Darby going into print in response to Newton's *Thoughts on the Apocalypse*, even though it had been published two years earlier. A vigorous exchange of pamphlets followed in which Darby expressed opposition to Newton's attempt to formulate a theological system which could encompass all the biblical data. However, Darby himself denied that divergent prophetic views had caused him to act as he did,[71] and overall the conflict seems to have been precipitated primarily by divergent leadership styles and a personality clash.

There were other aspects to Darby's perception of what was going on: he appears to have considered Newton guilty of intellectual elitism; some years earlier, he had advised Newton that unrefined speakers were not to be silenced on that ground alone; he also alleged that it was openly taught at Plymouth that God did not now use uneducated fishermen such as Peter, but educated teachers such as Paul.[72] It is also likely that Darby

[65] *Ibid.*, 20.3, 13, 22-3.

[66] [Congleton], *Reasons*, 11.

[67] This is attested by Newman, *Phases of Faith*, 42-3.

[68] Cf. Darby, *CW*, 20.30.

[69] *Ibid.*, 8.322 (from 'Answer to "A Letter to the Brethren and Sisters who meet for Communion in Ebrington Street"').

[70] Tregelles, *Three Letters*, 71.

[71] Darby, *CW*, 20.195-6 ('To the Brethren at Rawstorne Street').

[72] Darby, *Letters*, 1.89 (20 January 1846), cf. 1.29-30 (31 January 1839). A.N. Harris thought that the assembly's collapse began when an uneducated fisherman, whose ministry was well received by

felt that the preaching of the gospel was receiving less emphasis than it should, as a result of Newton's sectarian emphasis on his distinctive views. A winsome and passionate evangelistic preacher himself, as the sermons and other pieces in his *Collected Writings* show,[73] Darby noted that the gospel meetings had been moved from Ebrington Street to the much smaller Providence Chapel.[74]

Darby's actions, like much of his writing, were not strategically planned but represented responses to specific circumstances. What remained constant was not his strategy but his jealousy for the church as constituted by the Holy Ghost, which led him to oppose anything which he saw as impugning that. It was his motivation, rather than his strategy, which remained consistent.

A feature of the controversy at Plymouth which has continued to play a prominent role in the polemic of some Brethren writers is what has been called its 'satanology' – the tendency to see an opponent's words and actions as satanically inspired – and a consequence of this was a tendency to dualistic explanations of events which left out relevant human factors such as personality clashes. Thus Darby could say: 'I have no doubt a direct power and delusion of the enemy was there, from which we have been rescued by the Lord's goodness'.[75] It would have been well if Brethren then and since had heeded the words of the perceptive author of *A Retrospect of Events*: 'It is quite possible to explain all the phenomena by the usual operations of religious antipathy, and by the well-known weaknesses of the human mind, without going to the bottomless pit for the solution.' As the same author pointed out, once developments are viewed in terms of satanic activity, the inevitable consequence is suspicion of every action of an opponent, because he is regarded as bent on evil.[76] Opponents were also liable to be treated as less than responsible human agents, since they were the dupes of Satan. Reconciliation in such circumstances was rendered all but impossible, as events were to demonstrate.

4.4 Controversy over the Sufferings of Christ

Early in 1847, notes of an address by Newton on Psalm 6, which he interpreted as describing the sufferings of Christ, were circulating at Exeter.[77] Newton's exposition represented an attempt to respond to Irvingite complaints that his 1835 *Christian Witness* article on the movement did not do justice to the reality of Christ's humanity.[78] The question of Christ's sufferings was not a new topic of debate; it had formed part of the agenda for the 1836 prophetic conference, when participants were due to consider whether Christ experienced the sufferings of both the Jewish (literal, bearing in mind Darby's hermeneutical distinction between literal Jewish and spiritual Christian) and the 'spiritual' remnants.[79]

---

the poor but unacceptable to the learned, was silenced as not being led by the Spirit to speak, and many left ('Reminiscences', 4).

[73] See Darby, *CW*, volumes 12 and 21.

[74] *Ibid.*, 20.18.

[75] Darby, *Letters*, 1.90 (20 January 1846).

[76] Anon., *Retrospect of Events*, 8, 10.

[77] For this section, see further Burnham, *Conflict*, 188-204; Coad, *History*, 148-53; Neatby, *History*, ch. 7; Rowdon, *Origins*, 258-61.

[78] Harold H. Rowdon, 'A Nineteenth-Century Nestorius', *VE* 1 (1962), 63.

[79] Anon., *Questions for Eight Weeks' Consideration*, 13.

The notes of Newton's lecture were taken by his cousin Amy Toulmin and she lent them to J.L. Harris's wife, who showed them to her husband. He was disturbed by the possible implications of what he read, and Coad explains what these implications were:

> ... Newton, in developing the truth of the Incarnation, seemed to have passed acceptable limits of doctrine. He was teaching that some of the sufferings of Christ arose to Him because, in his identification with mankind and with Israel, He had Himself become subject to the wrath of God and to the penalties laid on Israel, but not by direct voluntary submission to judgment, but as the necessary result of the relationship to God which He had assumed. Newton insisted upon the absolute sinlessness of Christ, but went on to suggest that, as a result of the relation to God which He had undertaken in His identification with men, it became necessary for Him to emerge from His condition of liability to judgment, by His own obedience. The teaching hardly touched orthodox doctrine concerning Christ's Person, but it was considered by many to have dangerous results in relation to the doctrine of the atonement, while its implications could be deeply offensive to men with a warm devotion to Christ. Müller later summed up this point of view, by remarking that the teaching implied that Christ Himself needed a saviour.[80]

In other words, some of Christ's sufferings were endured not because he was acting as a substitute for sinners, nor because he was sinful himself, but because he had entered voluntarily into relationship with sinners as a member of Israel. He did not deserve to suffer, but he had entered into relationship with those who did.

Instead of checking with Newton that the notes were an accurate summary of what he had said, Harris sent them to McAdam, a supporter of Darby's in Exeter. With them he included a letter of criticism, and he gave McAdam permission to print the notes and the letter. They appeared in July 1847 as *The Sufferings of Christ as set forth in a lecture on Psalm vi*. An exchange of tracts followed in which Darby alleged, among other things, that Newton got his doctrine from Satan in a manner analogous to the Irvingites.[81] Finally, on 26 November, Newton issued a *Statement and Acknowledgement respecting certain Doctrinal Errors*, admitting errors and withdrawing two tracts for 'reconsideration'.[82] In his recollections, Newton explained that this statement related only to expressions in his article against Irvingism which stated that Christ came under the imputation, rather than the consequences, of Adam's sin. The two tracts which he wrote in reply to Harris's critique of his lecture were withdrawn in order to restate his views, which he did in several subsequent writings. Tregelles feared that Newton's opponents would make capital of the statement, and Newton's second wife Maria, whom he married in 1849, thought that he should not have written it, but Newton's punctiliousness in such matters dictated that he must correct that which was wrong in his public statements.[83] As well as clarifying the relationship between Adam and Christ, Newton explained that Christ's human body was mortal in character because he took mortality upon himself in becoming incarnate rather than because he inherited mortality

---

[80] Coad, *History*, 148.

[81] Darby, *CW*, 15.109n. Similarly, Dorman saw in Newton's Christology 'as distinct a power of delusion and falsehood as that which, it is well known, accompanied Irvingism; of which, in its first introduction by Mr. N., it appears to have been an offshoot' (W.H. Dorman, *A Review of Certain Evils & Questions that have arisen amongst Brethren* (London: J.K. Campbell, 1849[2]), 5).

[82] The text appears in Coad, *History*, 296-300, and Lang, *Local Assembly*, 48-53.

[83] 'Reminiscences 1', 21-3.

as a result of coming under the federal headship of Adam. Darby rejected Newton's statement as worthless, seeing his orthodox expressions as there simply to hide his errors. As Coad explains,

> ... Newton read his remarks in the light of his own intentions, and to him they therefore clarified his earlier misunderstandings, and remained on the orthodox side of the fatal boundary. Others read them in the light of the conclusions which had been drawn from them, and to them they seemed to be mere repetitions, though in guarded form, of the error.[84]

On 8 December 1847 Newton left Plymouth,[85] and on 13 December the other Ebrington Street leaders held a meeting for members at which they explained and renounced the implications of their erroneous teaching which they (with Newton) had held and withdrew from the assembly. Dyer reflected on the condition of the assembly, expressing the belief that his greatest sin lay in the condition of soul which had made it possible for him to receive the error without detecting it, and confessing that the leaders had been guilty of devoting themselves to defending the truth rather than shepherding the flock.[86] On 10 January 1848 Ebrington Street issued a statement (probably drafted by Tregelles, who had stepped into the leadership vacuum left in December) rejecting Newton's errors and the deductions which might be drawn from them but affirming that they would continue to receive him if he visited Plymouth.[87] Darby rejected this as still giving opportunity for Newton's doctrines to be deceitfully propagated. The local meetings associated with Newton appeared to Darby to have collapsed as a result of the controversy; he recorded that seventy members had recently returned to 'us' (presumably Raleigh Street and the meetings in fellowship with it).[88] In the summer of 1848 the Ebrington Street assembly, now much reduced in size, moved to Compton Street, its chapel being taken over by Bulteel as a Calvinist cause. By the 1851 Religious Census, only 280 were present in the morning and 320 in the evening; the figures for Raleigh Street (Providence) were 116 and 154, and for Bulteel's congregation 343 and 426.[89] Newton, supported by Tregelles, continued to have a devoted following of prophetic students and ministered until about 1872 in a chapel in Bayswater, London.[90]

4.5 The 'Bethesda Question'

The dispute now entered its most damaging phase, in which division affected the entire movement.[91] The question at issue concerned the degree of culpability involved in

---

[84] Coad, *History*, 151.

[85] His later explanation of this was that although he had been requested to remain, the leaders wished to adopt a less separatist position, which would have been unacceptable to him ('Small Notebook 6', 2a).

[86] W.B. Dyer, *A Confession of Doctrinal and Practical Errors* ([Bristol]: n.p., [1848]), 4-5, 14.

[87] Anon., *A Statement from Christians assembling in the name of the Lord, in Ebrington Street, Plymouth* ([Plymouth]: n.p., [1848]), 3.

[88] Darby to P[ierre] S[chlumberger], 5 July 1848 (BGT folder 5, f.11).

[89] Wickes (ed.), *Devon*, nos. 593, 592, and 573 respectively (all PRO HO129/287).

[90] For Newton's later career, see Burnham, *Conflict*, ch. 7.

[91] For this section, see further Coad, *History*, ch. 10; Neatby, *History*, ch. 8; Rowdon, *Origins*, 261-4.

associating with those who shared fellowship with teachers of error. The different approaches to it would demonstrate radically different understandings of what was meant by the unity of the body of Christ, so much so that it was impossible for those holding different views to continue to walk together.

The chain of events which led to the wider division was set in motion when two of Newton's supporters (the Woodfalls) were admitted to communion at Bethesda in April 1848 after being cleared of personally holding his errors, not without some objections from existing members. Shortly after, Müller invited Darby to preach; Darby declined amicably, having a previous engagement, but later announced that he would never go to Bethesda again because it received followers of Newton. He demanded that it should, as a body, investigate and condemn Newton's errors. Müller and Craik refused, on the ground that they did not wish to risk irreverence by making Christology the subject of controversy. A meeting at Bath on 10 May brought together a hundred leading Brethren from all over the country, who rejected Newton's views, to discuss what had happened; however, it was not conclusive. Chapman, who had been working to avert a breach, criticised Darby for acting hastily; Darby felt that the meeting had become sidetracked on the matter of the extent to which he was to blame for what had happened.[92]

In June, one of Darby's supporters seceded from Bethesda, giving the errors which could arise there as his reasons. Bethesda held a church meeting on 29 June at which its leaders, in a document known as the 'Letter of the Ten', condemned Newton's errors but again refused a corporate investigation and stated their desire to be aligned with neither party. The sixth clause of this document asserted that even if Newton were heretical, it would not be right to refuse communion to those who had been sitting under his ministry unless they themselves had imbibed unsound opinions.[93]

On 26 August Darby issued the 'Bethesda Circular'[94] from Leeds, where he had received information (probably from Trotter) that many Yorkshire assemblies were taking Bethesda's side. He accused Bethesda of 'acting in the fullest and most decided way as the supporter of Mr. Newton, and the evil associated with him, and in the way in which the enemy of souls most desires it should be done'.[95] Jukes testified that Yorkshire assemblies were united in condemning Newton's views, but presumably the fact that Jukes determined to adopt the same attitude as Bethesda towards receiving individuals from Newton's meeting in Plymouth, and that other local assemblies looked like following his lead, meant that Darby could regard them as taking its side.[96] Darby also claimed in his circular that because the leaders refused a public investigation, Newton's errors could not be kept out of Bethesda. He therefore urged assemblies neither to receive individuals from Bethesda to communion, nor to receive individuals from assemblies which were in communion with Bethesda; Darby's emphasis on universal visible unity made the latter a

---

[92] Darby, *Letters*, 1.133 (31 May 1848).

[93] The letter is reproduced in Coad, *History*, 301-4, and elsewhere.

[94] Darby, *CW*, 15.164-7.

[95] *Ibid.*, 15.164.

[96] Andrew Jukes, 'Second Letter to the Gatherings of Brethren at Leeds and Otley, in reference to a Circular lately put forth by them', <http://mikevision.home.mindspring.com/fellowshipletter.html>, accessed 22 July 2003; W. Trotter, *The Origin of (so-called) Open-Brethrenism. A Letter by W. Trotter giving the Whole Case of Plymouth and Bethesda* (Lancing, Sussex: Kingston Bible Trust, [1987]), 35. First published in 1849 as *The Whole Case of Plymouth and Bethesda*, Trotter's work offers an authoritative Exclusive account of events.

natural step. Although he issued the circular in his own name, the fact that very many gatherings followed this course of action indicates the esteem in which his leadership was held. Trotter noted that some had hoped that a general meeting would have been called to sort things out, and explained that the urgency of the situation was due to the fact that Bethesda had links with virtually every assembly in the country through their support for Müller's orphan homes.[97]

Things were complicated by the fact that in October Wigram charged Craik with heretical statements concerning the person of Christ in his *Pastoral Letters*, published in 1835. Craik had affirmed that Christ's human body was mortal, like that of every human being; moreover, Christ was holy because he was preserved from taint, an interpretation which bore some resemblance to the controversial Christology of Edward Irving.[98] Responding to Wigram's attack, Craik pointed out that although Wigram was living nearby at the time of writing his tract, he had never checked the accuracy of his charges. Wigram's response, which well illustrates the 'satanology' at work in this dispute, was that Craik was the subject of spiritual delusion, and to have asked him for clarification would only have tempted him to further evasion and deception.[99] In a later tract, Wigram also set out the principle that an individual member of an assembly was responsible for the error taught there, even if personally dissenting from it.[100] The logical implication was, of course, not only secession from any assembly where unsound doctrine was tolerated but also refusal to accept into fellowship anyone coming from such an assembly unless they disavowed all connection with it and renounced its errors. The relevance of this was that Wigram saw the whole of Bethesda as committed to Craik's errors as sanctioned by the 'Letter of the Ten'. Whilst Darby did not offer any support to Wigram, and indeed asserted in 1852 that he threw Wigram's tracts on the matter into the fire unread, neither did he publicly dissociate himself from the latter's extremism.

Until 1847 Bethesda had accepted those on both sides of the division at Plymouth; thereafter they examined individuals for soundness. Now, however, they found it necessary to reject Newton's views publicly as a body, because of Darby's action in issuing the 'Bethesda Circular' and Newton's republication of some of the tracts in question during the summer. Matters were complicated by the fact that Newton's cousin Amy Toulmin sought to break bread at Bethesda in November 1848. After a lengthy cross-examination by Müller and Craik, her views were deemed sound, but she was warned that some were likely to withdraw because she 'upheld and defended' Newton's tracts. In a letter delivering their judgement, Craik appears to have passed the buck by abstaining from advising her which course to take, merely stating the facts and expressing a desire for

---

[97] Trotter, *Origin*, 34-5.

[98] The Exclusive leader William Kelly claimed that what Brethren rejected was the idea that Christ was doomed to die, rather than that he was capable of dying (marginal annotation to Neatby, *History*, 147, Chapter Two archive). However, this does not square either with Craik's own words or with Darby's understanding of them (for which see his letter to P[ierre].S[chlumberger]., May 1858 (BGT folder 10, f.8)).

[99] [G.V. Wigram], *An Appeal to saints that remain still in Bethesda and Salem, as to certain bad doctrine* (London: J.K. Campbell, 1848), 5-6, 8.

[100] G.V. Wigram, *The Present Question; 1848-1849* (London: J.K. Campbell, [1849]), 8.

further light.[101] Müller stated that they had been hoping that Newton's withdrawal of his tracts would be followed by a recantation; however, when the fruits of his promised reconsideration were discovered to amount to a defence of the writings in question, Müller felt obliged to change his approach and bring the matter to the church.[102] Bethesda held seven church meetings between 27 November and 11 December, as a result of which they decided not to receive anyone 'defending, maintaining, or upholding' Newton's views or his tracts. Cole asserted that on a visit to Bethesda Darby expressed his approval of their action. All that now needed to be done, in his opinion, was for them to withdraw the 'Letter of the Ten', and publish and circulate a statement explaining their reasons and their recent action regarding Newton's doctrine. They refused, on the ground that it was not their practice to publish anything (the 'Letter' had been published without their consent), although Darby was welcome to publish their more recent statement.[103]

The rift spread rapidly through the movement. Groves, who was in England from March 1848 until June 1849,[104] spent much time in Bristol, participating in the series of church meetings held by Bethesda late in 1848, and also in Tottenham. The result of the latter was that Dorman, speaking for Rawstorne Street, declared Tottenham out of communion with them because Groves was identified with Bethesda and thus chargeable with their error.[105] Elsewhere, those siding with Bethesda included Chapman, Congleton, ex-Quakers such as the Howards of Tottenham, former leaders at Plymouth (Harris, Soltau, Batten, and Dyer), and Code and Hargrove. Those siding with Darby included Trotter (who was one of those responsible for a circular distributed among Yorkshire assemblies in November 1848), Hall (though not until 1850, and not followed by most of the Hereford assembly), Bellett, Cronin, Stewart, and Stoney. Many assemblies in England followed Darby, although historians are probably inaccurate in asserting that the majority did so. Few among the small number of assemblies in Scotland became Exclusive.[106] The division received symbolic expression when in July 1849 Darby called on Müller, declaring separation unnecessary in view of Bethesda's action and seeking renewed fellowship. Müller refused without hesitation, considering that Darby's conduct in the whole affair required investigation.[107]

For several years, attempts were made to heal the breach by convening united meetings for humiliation and prayer, but these achieved little. Darby appears to have convened some of these himself, selecting those who were to be invited. At one in Bristol in 1852 he announced that he was withdrawing the 'Bethesda Circular'. The motivation for his action is not easy to establish, but it appears to have been precipitated by expressions of

---

[101] Amy Toulmin to Henry Groves, 4 March 1867, in [John Cox, Jr], *An Earnest Expostulation. A Letter addressed to the Author of "High Church Claims of the Exclusive Brethren"* (London: Houlston & Wright, [1869]), 10-12.

[102] Müller to J.G. Deck, 12 December 1848, in Noel, *History*, 151-2.

[103] Cole, 'Reminiscences', in Lang, *Groves*, 329.

[104] Mrs. Groves, *Memoir*, 466, 470.

[105] [Lord Congleton], *The Bristol Case; and divisions in other places connected therewith* ([London: J.K. Campbell, 1849]), 6.

[106] Dickson, *Brethren in Scotland*, 48.

[107] Lang discusses the evidence for and against the occurrence of such a meeting (*Groves*, 333-41; cf. idem, *Local Assembly*, 92-103). Some Exclusive writers offered a different interpretation of events which treated Darby's visit as a well-meant mistake, and denied that Darby had felt that Bethesda had cleared itself adequately (e.g. Anon., 'J.N.D. and Bethesda', *BT* n.s. 5 (1905), 368).

concern that the circular represented a stumbling block to reconciliation. It appears to have caused consternation and misunderstanding among his followers, and he found it necessary to stress repeatedly that his perception of the principles involved remained unchanged; he simply wished to start afresh, cutting his links with the old order among Brethren, although on the same basis which was expressed in the circular.[108]

Darby's later judgement was that Bethesda had acted on the principle of 'indifference as to the Person of Christ'.[109] Bethesda's actions against Newton's teaching were seen as motivated by external pressure rather than by a concern for sound doctrine; 'indifference' was to remain a fundamental charge of Exclusives against Open Brethren, and would give rise to protracted debate from 1890 onwards when moves were afoot to restore fellowship between Open Brethren and some Exclusive streams.

It is pertinent to stress in conclusion that the term 'Exclusive', often used to describe those Brethren who followed Darby, relates not to their reception of sound and godly believers from the 'sects' (as they often described the denominations), but to the reception of believers from meetings in fellowship with Bethesda, because such gatherings were thereby deemed guilty of knowingly condoning doctrinal error: Open meetings, having more light on Scripture and claiming to receive only believers, should have known better and been more discriminating than the sects. But other believers not infrequently received a warm welcome among Exclusives (perhaps partly because it was hoped that they might leave their denominations and settle among Brethren), and we shall discover that later in the century many Open assemblies were more exclusive in their attitude towards such individuals than many Exclusive ones.

---

[108] Several letters relating to these meetings appear in Darby, *Letters*, 1.210-25, including the invitation to the Taunton meeting.

[109] *Ibid.*, 1.202 (6 October 1851).

CHAPTER 5

Distinctive Principles of the Early Brethren

At this point, it is worth pausing briefly to review the main convictions which motivated the early leaders, because the Brethren movement was to change somewhat in later decades. Whilst there was no official body to issue any definitive statement of Brethren thought, and a variety of views were evident on some topics, the movement achieved a fair measure of doctrinal coherence; the networks of relationships which owed much to the itinerant ministry of leaders such as Darby, and the opportunities for debate afforded by the residential conferences, contributed significantly to this. Space does not allow a full exposition of doctrines considered fundamental by Brethren; instead, I have chosen to focus on aspects of their thought which came to be regarded as distinctive and thus as hallmarks of Brethren theology, or which received a distinctive outworking in church life.

Many scholars have attempted to isolate a central conviction which could be seen as underlying Brethren theology. The authority of Scripture was undoubtedly a fundamental principle, and has remained so; in some ways, everything discussed below followed from the recognition of this. We have seen the way in which Darby's 'deliverance' was linked with a new attitude towards the supreme authority of Scripture; indeed, for most Brethren Scripture was not merely the supreme authority, but the sole authority. Thus, Newton excepted, they rarely accorded authority to creeds and confessions, and sat lightly to the Protestant tradition of biblical interpretation. (In time, however, they developed their own interpretative tradition, as those who questioned standard teaching on such matters as the pretribulation rapture were to discover.) For Rowdon, the Brethren movement represented a radical return to the principle of the authority of Scripture in all matters of faith and practice. Callahan has fine-tuned this approach, pointing out that other groups shared such a commitment but Brethren were unique in applying their understanding of the authority and sufficiency of Scripture to church order.[1] However, his claim, like Rowdon's, does not account on its own for the particular form taken by the Brethren movement; other groups did the same thing without necessarily constructing a congregational structure which matched that devised by Brethren. Within the British Reformed tradition, for instance, the 'regulative principle' dictated that church worship and polity should not depart from what was explicitly sanctioned by Scripture; this would have been operative among more conservative Presbyterians and Particular Baptists. What made Brethren unique was a combination of factors: the sole authority of Scripture, certainly, but also a hermeneutic which stressed the discontinuity between Old and New Testaments, the social class from which many early leaders were drawn, and the influence of Romanticism, with its heightened sense of the supernatural.

Callahan sees the central principle of Brethren thinking as what he calls 'primitivism', the belief that normative Christianity was that of the apostolic church, with a consequent negative estimate of contemporary Christianity. He distinguishes this from restorationism, which attempts to restore apostolic church order, and asserts that

---

[1] James Patrick Callahan, *Primitivist Piety: The Ecclesiology of the Early Plymouth Brethren* (Lanham, MD: Scarecrow Press, 1996), 21, 33, 42; Rowdon, 'Brethren Identity', 174.

most early Brethren were primitivist but not restorationist.[2] This makes sense when we realise the pervasive influence of Darby's belief, discussed below, that the church was irreparably ruined and therefore believers should not attempt to restore it. In Callahan's view, it was interest in the primitive church which led to interest in prophecy: 'the first generation of Brethren ... used the subject of prophecy to serve the ends of ecclesiology'.[3] Other writers take a similar view. Ironside denies that prophetic study formed part of the initial motivation, as do Lang and Veitch.[4] Crutchfield points out that Darby's disaffection with the Church of Ireland did not spring initially from the study of prophecy.[5] Sandeen holds that ecclesiology was for Darby 'the catalytic agent for the rest of his beliefs'[6] and Elmore that Darby's eschatology was rooted in his ecclesiology.[7] More particularly, both Huebner, as an apologist for Darby's teaching, and Bass, as a stern critic, see his view of the rapture as arising from his recovery of church truth (including the idea of the church as heavenly).[8] This is interesting in view of the widespread tendency, particularly in North America, to accept Darby's teaching on the rapture but not his teaching on the church. Somewhat differently, Ward sees both eschatology and ecclesiology in Darby as rooted in his dispensational thinking,[9] and Bruce understands Darby's eschatology and ecclesiology as 'interdependent elements in a carefully constructed system', asserting the impossibility of retaining the former and rejecting the latter.[10] Whatever the primary doctrinal motivation, however, one consequence was widely apparent – separation from all that was deemed to belong to 'the world'.[11]

5.1 Separation from the World

There was clearly a strong ascetic strain in the make-up of early Brethren, separation from all things worldly being enjoined on members. In part, this was derived from their conviction that the existing world order was heading towards inevitable judgement, but it

---

[2] Callahan, *Primitivist Piety*, xiv, 33.

[3] *Ibid.*, ix, cf. xiv.

[4] H.A. Ironside, *A Historical Sketch of the Brethren Movement* (Grand Rapids, MI: Zondervan, 1942), 16; Lang, *Groves*, 289-90; Thomas Stewart Veitch, *The Story of the Brethren Movement* (London: Pickering & Inglis, [1933]), 17.

[5] Larry V. Crutchfield, *The Origins of Dispensationalism: The Darby Factor* (Lanham, MD: University Press of America, 1992), 5.

[6] E.R. Sandeen, *The Roots of Fundamentalism: British and American Millenarianism 1800-1930* (Chicago: University of Chicago Press, 1970), 66-7.

[7] Floyd Saunders Elmore, 'A critical examination of the doctrine of the two peoples of God in John Nelson Darby' (ThD dissertation, Dallas Theological Seminary, 1991), 21.

[8] R.A. Huebner, *The Truth of the Pre-Tribulation Rapture Recovered* (Morganville, NJ: Present Truth Publishers, 1982), 25, 40; Clarence B. Bass, *Backgrounds to Dispensationalism: its historical genesis and ecclesiastical implications* (Grand Rapids, MI: Baker Book House, 1977), 39.

[9] John Percy Ward, 'The Eschatology of John Nelson Darby' (PhD thesis, University of London, 1976), abstract.

[10] F.F. Bruce, in Rowdon, *Origins*, xi-xii.

[11] The few pre-1860 Scottish assemblies form something of an exception to this; Dickson characterises them as 'pre-sectarian', having withdrawn from the churches but continuing to engage with the world and its problems (*Brethren in Scotland*, 58).

also represented an outworking of their belief in the church's heavenly nature and the need for it to be clearly separate from the world. Unworldliness was evident in such matters as dress and household furnishing, in which Brethren denied themselves in order to release funds for the Lord's work. But things could be taken further: belief in the necessity of separation from the world risked producing an asceticism in which the material realm was seen as evil in itself. Thus in 1829 Groves asked:

> Why spend our thoughts and praises on that which is the great instrument of Satan in deluding and enslaving our fallen race, and which, being under the curse, is to be burnt up; instead of on the beauties of Christ, and of His world, moral and spiritual, which shall endure for ever. Let the natural man dwell with delight on natural objects; let the spiritual dwell with delight on spiritual, that his spiritual life may be manifested, and let him use natural things merely as illustrations to those who, being natural, can only understand natural things.[12]

Such an attitude meant that Brethren, while often well-educated themselves, sometimes appeared to disparage the value of education. All it could do was to fit for life in a world which was heading to destruction because of its rejection of Christ. Borlase, in a *Christian Witness* article, 'On Conformity to the World',[13] asserted that Christ came to deliver us from the world, and issued a particular warning against worldly use of the intellect in improvement which was not directed to God's service.

5.1.1 The Social Make-up and Social Teaching of Early Brethren

Such world-denying attitudes did not transform the Brethren into political or social radicals; far from it. Early Brethren in England and Ireland were perceived as genteel, even well-heeled. For all the radicalism evident at Plymouth, Brethren were intensely conservative in their social attitudes. Thus, although the use of titles was questioned at an early stage, these were justified on the basis of the injunction in Romans 13.7 to render 'honour to whom honour is due'. Among the early leaders were doctors, colonial judges, retired officers from the services, lawyers, peers, baronets, and gentlemen, many of whom were linked by a network of intermarriage, built in part on that of the relatively small Irish Evangelical aristocracy and gentry. These leaders often took a prominent part in affairs, owning the meeting place, assuming responsibility for discipline, inviting and entertaining the preachers.[14] Their role, and their membership of what Beatrice Webb was to call 'the class that gives orders', tended to undercut the Brethren assertion that all believers were equal, and to replace the clergy-laity distinction by others just as rigidly observed, if less formally defined.

The gentility of early English Brethrenism proved a recurring target of criticism. Early assemblies were caricatured as 'asylums for the aristocracy' who could not endure to join the Dissenters.[15] Similarly, Philpot described the movement's aristocratic ethos as 'a

---

[12] Mrs. Groves, *Memoir*, 45 (Journal, 8 August 1829). Groves did not keep to his own rule, however: the following month we find him commenting appreciatively on the natural beauties around him (Mrs. Groves, *Memoir*, 52).

[13] *CWit* 1 (1834), 460-8.

[14] Embley, 'Early Development', 217-18.

[15] Reported in *I* 2 (1839), 512n.

kind of Madeira climate, which suits the tender lungs of gentility'.[16] Philpot, whose favourite divine was William Huntington, the converted coalheaver, condemned the Brethren for their aristocratic, and therefore educated and talented, leadership: 'it cannot be said that God has chosen the poor of this world to commence that spreading movement which originated at Plymouth'.[17] Yet this gentility did make the movement attractive to many who would have been repelled by the vulgarity of much contemporary Evangelical Dissent.[18] It also contributed to the distaste for Dissent as democratic and schismatic, which was usually even stronger than the criticism of Anglicanism; a theological factor in their disapproval of the political campaigning and internal practice of Dissent was the anti-democratic belief that power came from above, not from the people, and that rulers exercised their power by divine appointment.

Lord Congleton, who epitomised the gentility of much early Brethrenism

The movement's ethos is also apparent in the attitudes of leaders towards the poor. Darby displayed a genuine, if somewhat paternalistic, concern for them, and he was evidently much loved by the poor at Calary. Professedly at home among them himself, in 1832 he urged believers at Plymouth to be 'much among the poor' and so imitate Christ.[19] The industrial poor, in particular, had a place in his heart and his evangelistic vision.[20] In a letter of 1848, a year of marked industrial unrest, he noted after visiting Yorkshire how 'people are employed like machines'. However, for him, the solution to 'the real distress which weighs on the working class in the manufacturing districts', and the best comfort for believers among them, was the Second Coming.[21] His concern was with their spiritual needs, and his solution to their problems likewise a spiritual one; there is little evidence of his adopting an approach like that of William and Catherine Booth (the founders of the Salvation Army) in the 1860s and after, which recognised the need to meet the physical needs of the poor before they could be expected to be receptive to the gospel message. Müller's work in educating the poor and caring for orphans, who were much more likely to be drawn from the lower classes, brought him into extended contact with them, although

---

[16] [J.C. Philpot], 'Editors' Review: the Christian Witness', *GS* 8 (1842), 83.

[17] *Ibid.*, 78-9.

[18] Embley, 'Early Development', 216.

[19] Darby, *Letters*, 1.14 [1832].

[20] *Ibid.*, 1.135 (17 June 1848).

[21] Darby to P[ierre].S[chlumberger]., 8 July 1848 (BGT folder 5, f.11).

it is questionable whether he ever shed his somewhat paternalistic attitude. Chapman proved more able to get alongside the poor in Barnstaple, deliberately taking a house in a part of the town where they would not feel out of place when visiting him. Other leaders also developed an effective ministry among the poor in preaching and visiting. Bowes found poorer Scots responsive to his message, perhaps because he combined evangelistic passion with a willingness to speak out on issues of social justice. But the only significant leader to be drawn from the lower ranks of society appears to have been Gribble, who had been a draper, and he does not appear to have been a part of the network of leaders which centred on the conferences of the 1830s, perhaps in part because of his bankruptcy.

5.1.2 Brethren and the Civil Order

Darby's earliest writings were called forth in reaction against the Erastianism of the Irish religious Establishment. In this the Brethren were at one with the early Tractarians, whose emphasis on the church's divine institution and consequent independence of state control was called forth by government proposals in 1833 to reduce the number of Irish bishoprics. But Brethren were to develop a rather different view of the relation of church and state, arising out of their particular understanding of the church as 'heavenly' and the believer as being no longer a citizen of this world. Its central feature was the call for believers to withdraw from participation in worldly affairs.

Separation from the world entailed withdrawal from the exercise of civil and political office.[22] The rationale for this received expression in *The Christian Witness*; an article probably written by Newton posed the question: 'Is the Exercise of Worldly Authority consistent with Discipleship?'[23] The answer given was negative: among other reasons, worldly powers would always be opposed to Christ. Salvation, by contrast, involved 'extrication' from the principles and systems at work in this age. A few years earlier, Borlase had asked '"How far may we mingle with the world?" Even as far and as often as we can witness for Jesus.'[24] Belief that the Christian's only involvement with the world was as a witness to it has persisted in some Brethren circles to the present.

The most famous exposition of such withdrawal, also emanating from Plymouth, was Hall's pamphlet *Discipleship*. Since the world rejects Christ, it argued, the believer who is separated to Christ is thereby separated from the world. Christ's example of separation and his commands both make separation mandatory. Indeed, Christ's kingdom, far from being of the world, is in opposition to it. Nevertheless, the believer is to be subject to the higher powers. Hall offers what became another frequently used argument – that the Scriptures instruct believers concerning their duties as fathers, husbands, and masters, but not as rulers. The fact that God has not provided such guidance is an indication that it is impossible to act as a Christian in such a position. This was because rulers had to govern according to law rather than grace. Hall also stressed the discontinuity between the Testaments against the use of the Old Testament to justify war, which he saw as directly contradicting the teaching of Christ.

---

[22] Interestingly, early Italian Brethren did not share this negative attitude towards political involvement (Cf. Daisy D. Ronco, *Risorgimento and the Free Italian Churches, now Churches of the Brethren* (Bangor, Wales: privately printed, 1996)).

[23] *CWit* 4 (1837), 251-65.

[24] *CWit* 1 (1834), 467.

Hall was not alone in his pacifism: such an opinion was widely held by early members, and there are numerous instances of officers resigning their commission upon associating with Brethren. This was the issue which precipitated Groves' break with the Church of England, after he had been challenged concerning Article 37, which asserted the legitimacy of a Christian bearing arms when called upon by the civil authorities.[25] However, we should distinguish the approach adopted by these Brethren, which regarded the use of force as legitimate for governments but inappropriate for believers, from that adopted by groups such as the Quakers, which regarded all use of force as wrong in principle. A refinement of the Brethren view was provided by Groves, who argued that war was not essentially sinful and that Christians would have to engage in it in a future dispensation, but that it was inappropriate for them to do so in this one.[26]

Ironically, the Brethren combination of withdrawal from involvement in civil affairs and obedience to those in power led one early critic to describe them as 'thorough Jacobites': he noted their belief in non-resistance to authority, passive obedience, the divine right of rulers, and their opposition to democracy, whether in the legislature or in the church.[27] In these aspects, Brethren presented a challenging contrast to most Dissenting denominations, which became increasingly vocal on political matters from the 1830s.

5.2 The Doctrine of the Church[28]

It would be possible to see early Brethren ecclesiology as having two foci, one provided by what they saw as the ideal set out in the New Testament and the other by the realities of the contemporary religious world. It was shaped as much by reaction against the latter as by an attempt to conform to the former.

We have already seen Darby's earliest definition of the church, in his 'Considerations addressed to the Archbishop of Dublin'. Although this dates from his High Church period, his thinking was to develop along the lines there foreshadowed and proved definitive for many Brethren, whether or not they followed him in 1848. In this section we shall summarise the main distinctive features of Brethren ecclesiology: the Spirit's role in constituting the church, the church's heavenly nature and destiny, the tension between

---

[25] For fuller exposition of Brethren attitudes to pacifism, see Peter Brock, 'The Peace Testimony of the early Plymouth Brethren', *CH* 53 (1984), 30-45; Elizabeth Kay Wilson, 'Brethren Attitudes to Authority and Government: with particular reference to pacifism' (Master of Humanities dissertation, University of Tasmania, 1994).

[26] Dann, 'Groves', 163, quoting the *Memoir*.

[27] Cyprian Thomas Rust, *The "Brethren." An examination of the Opinions and Practices of the new sect usually denominated "Plymouth Brethren"* (Colchester: I. Brackett, 1844), 63.

[28] I have treated Brethren ecclesiology at greater length in 'The Church's Ruin and Restoration: The Development of Ecclesiology in the Plymouth Brethren and the Catholic Apostolic Church, c.1825-c.1866' (PhD thesis, King's College, London, 1997). See also Clarence B. Bass, 'The Doctrine of the Church in the Theology of J.N. Darby with special reference to its contribution to the Plymouth Brethren movement' (PhD thesis, University of Edinburgh, 1952), revised as *Backgrounds to Dispensationalism*; Shih-An Deng, 'Ideas of the Church in an Age of Reform: The Ecclesiological Thoughts of John Nelson Darby and John Henry Newman, 1824-1850' (PhD thesis, University of Minnesota, 1994); Rowdon, *Origins*, Appendix 1.

unity and separation, and the theory of the church's irreparable ruin. Throughout these the interplay between ideal and reality will be evident.

5.2.1 The Spirit and the Church

Crucial to Brethren ecclesiology was the doctrine of the Holy Spirit; it was his presence which alone could make their theory workable.[29] As Darby explained in 1847, 'The church of the living God is the body of saints formed on earth in unity with Christ in heaven as the Head, by the Holy Ghost sent down from heaven to form them into unity with Christ at the right hand of God.'[30] Initially, Darby's emphasis was more on the church's heavenly nature, but he began to place an increasing stress on its constitution by the Spirit. Since the Spirit was not sent down until Pentecost, believers before that point did not form part of the church.

The Spirit's role in ministry will be considered below, but here I want to focus on Brethren interest in Irvingite claims to exercise supernatural gifts such as tongues and prophecy, because this is a subject of intense interest to some contemporary Brethren. Brethren and Irvingites breathed the same radical atmosphere, and many early Brethren were well informed about Irving's views. Darby, probably accompanied by Wigram, went in 1830 to investigate what was happening in the West of Scotland, where it was claimed that the gifts had been restored; Irvingites and Brethren mixed at the early Powerscourt conferences; and some who had been influenced by Brethren later joined the Irvingite movement.

However, most Brethren concluded that the manifestations connected with Irving's ministry were not from God. Newton explained why, in an article written in the light of events at Salcombe.[31] His fundamental objection was to Christological error in the Irvingite prophecies (Irving had taught that Christ at his Incarnation assumed *fallen* human nature) which overthrew the doctrine of the atonement. Since apostles should be infallible, the movement's claim to have apostles was nullified by the sanctioning of such error. He also insisted that Christians, as those indwelt by the Spirit, were able and responsible to 'try the spirits' (1 John 4.1), a procedure which Irvingites rejected when undertaken by outsiders. In an appendix, Newton catalogued the failed prophecies which had been uttered, especially by Robert Baxter, whose defection from Irving's church in 1832 had caused a sensation in the Evangelical world. Wigram was probably responsible for an article which appeared during 1835, 'The Verity of the Revival of the Apostolic Church in Newman-street and elsewhere examined'.[32] He did not think the manifestations genuine, but did not rule out the possibility of the gifts being restored before Christ's return; their non-continuance had resulted from the church's unbelief, and he claimed to have experienced some such phenomena himself. In his view, Irvingites erred in focusing on the form of the New Testament church at the expense of its motivating principle (the abiding presence of the Holy Spirit, according to an editorial note[33]). Other writers felt

---

[29] Deng, 'Ideas of the Church', 73.

[30] D[arby]., *MiscW*, 4.157.

[31] 'The Doctrines of the Church in Newman-Street considered', *CWit* 2 (1835), 111-28. Newman Street was where Irving set up a congregation after his deposition from the National Scotch Church in Regent Square.

[32] *CWit* 2 (1835), 154-87.

[33] *Ibid.*, 185n.

bound to explain why their views were not to be confused with Irvingism. Hargrove, for example, had carefully examined Irvingism and devoted a section of his apologia for secession to explaining the differences.[34] He, like Newton, considered that Irving's Christology subverted the doctrine of the atonement, and accused Irvingites of interposing the church and its ordinances between the believer and the Bible, with the church taking the place of Christ. Prophecies contradicted one another and remained unfulfilled, and the whole system was worldly in character.

Darby produced several anti-Irvingite works, including 'Remarks on a Tract circulated by the Irvingites entitled "A Word of Instruction"', and 'A Letter to a Clergyman on the Claims and Doctrines of Newman Street'.[35] A little-known work was entitled 'Are the Newman Street teachers (Catholic Apostolic) sent of God?'[36] The original, *The Claims of the Teachers who have come from Newman-street, London, to be received as sent of God, considered*, was published in Dublin during 1835 in response to Hardman's attempts to proselytise members of the flock at Aungier Street. An unfriendly reviewer criticised it as 'the production of the leader of a little party, who, having been a great disturber of the peace of other churches, is much alarmed that some who have gone a few steps further than himself, are about to disturb the peace of the little heterogeneous body with which he is connected'.[37] Darby's main arguments were that the gifts sanctioned Irving's unorthodox Christology, and that the claim to inspiration was disproved by failed and contradictory prophecies. The same consideration which led Darby to accept the final authority of Scripture, even apart from the church, predisposed him to reject the manifestations as denying the individual Christian's right to understand the Scriptures with the Spirit's aid and so judge the veracity of claims to the gifts. He considered that they represented a Satanic attempt to discredit the testimony to the Second Coming, and to frighten believers from expecting the Spirit to work in and through them.

Whilst Brethren soon came to reject Irvingite claims, and also to reject the very possibility of such gifts being given, they continued to accept the presence of gifts such as wisdom, knowledge, and faith, which were regarded as essential to the teaching ministry. Accordingly they denied that belief in the principle of gifting by the Spirit as the source of ministry entailed belief in the restoration of miraculous gifts.[38] Groves' mature view (during the late 1840s) was fairly typical: the supernatural gifts had been given for the church's infancy, and withdrawn when the New Testament was completed, as a sign of the church's progress towards maturity.[39] All the same, it was the possession of charismata rather than authorisation by virtue of appointment to office which dominated their understanding both of ministry and of the conduct of worship; one writer draws attention to the 'laundered charismaticism' operative in such contexts as the Breaking of Bread, inspiring individuals to contribute to the worship.[40]

---

[34] Hargrove, *Reasons*, xxii-xxxix.

[35] Darby, *CW*, 15.1-15, 16-33.

[36] *BT* n.s. 2 (1898-9), 110-11, 126-7, 142-3, 158-9, 172-4, 188-92; also published separately. Kelly confessed that 'none of us had the scent' of this work (W. Kelly to P., 23 June 1898, Chapter Two archive).

[37] 'Irvingism in Ireland', *CE* n.s. 4 (1835), 521.

[38] Dorman, *Principles of Truth*, 63.

[39] Mrs. Groves, *Memoir*, 444.

[40] Ian S. Rennie, 'Aspects of Christian Brethren Spirituality', in Loren Wilkinson (ed.), *Alive to God: Studies in Christian Spirituality presented to J.I. Packer* (Downers Grove, IL: IVP, 1992), 201-2.

5.2.2 The Church as a Heavenly Entity

We have already noticed the distinction made by Darby between the church as heavenly and Israel as earthly. The relationship in the thinking of many Brethren between their understanding of their position as believers seated in heavenly places in Christ, their understanding of the church as composed of such believers, and their critique of existing religious bodies is expressed by Darby, reflecting on his 'deliverance':

> I had found peace to my own soul by finding my oneness with Christ, ... I was in Christ, accepted in the Beloved, and sitting in heavenly places in Him. This led me directly to the apprehension of what the true church of God was, those that were united to Christ in heaven: I at once felt that all the parish [system] was not that.[41]

Not only was the church heavenly in nature, but it was heavenly in destiny.[42] As such, it exercised no earthly power, but shared the rejection which had been the fate of its Saviour and Head: 'Outside the camp, here below, answers to a heavenly portion above'.[43]

One of the earliest statements of Brethren doctrinal distinctives stressed the church's heavenly character as associated with Christ, from which followed the idea of separation from the world. The writer (possibly Darby) summed them up as '*Separation from the world, union of the saints, and the liberty of, and dependence on the Holy Ghost, according to the word.*' The result of such an understanding was that Christ's blood and righteousness was 'preached much more in connexion with Christ's resurrection and sitting at the right hand of God; so that generally much more habitual and well grounded peace is possessed than amongst others'.[44]

5.2.3 Unity and Separation

A truth which Brethren have always claimed to uphold is that of the unity of all true believers. This was frequently founded upon the insistence that they should receive all whom Christ had received (Romans 15.3-7). As Tregelles explained, the title of believers to heaven is as those who have been washed in the blood of the Lamb; in his view, '*The basis of our union in glory is quite sufficient for our union on earth; and even as we shall then be manifested on that ground, so ought we now to stand manifestly joined together on that alone.*'[45] If the blood of Christ was sufficient to unite believers to God, then it was also sufficient to unite them to one another. Similarly, Dorman asserted: '... I must stand where *all* the saints of God *may* meet me, if they please, *on earth*, and where they *all must* meet me in *heaven*'.[46]

Writers have debated whether the stress on separation from the religious world formed a part of the teaching and practice of the earliest Brethren. Often their approach and

---

[41] Darby, *Letters*, 1.515 (Memorandum, 1868).

[42] Elmore, 'Two Peoples', 201.

[43] J.N. Darby, *Synopsis of the Books of the Bible* (5 vols; Kingston-on-Thames: Stow Hill Bible and Tract Depot, 1943-9), 1.159 (on Leviticus 16), cf. 5.260-1 (on Hebrews 13).

[44] Anon., *Copy of a Letter from ***** to the Rev. *** ([Worcester: E.B. Rouse], n.d.), 2-3. A pencil note on the copy in the Chapter Two archive dates the work to 1834 and attributes it to Darby.

[45] [S.P. Tregelles], *The Blood of the Lamb and the Union of Saints* (London: Central Tract Depôt, n.d.), 12.

[46] Dorman, *Principles of Truth*, 35.

conclusions are dictated by their own views on the matter, as Rennie points out with reference to interpretations of Groves:

> In the present reconstruction of their history, very many open brethren have sought to portray Groves as so charitable in relations with other evangelicals that he was something of an ecumenical evangelical. This interpretation fails to hold in tension his love for all in whom he believed that he discerned the life of Christ, and his eschatological beliefs, with their corresponding ecclesiastical rigor when it came to assessing institutional Christianity.[47]

Ironside denied that separation was part of the pioneers' message,[48] while Lang asserted that the early meetings welcomed believers to communion without requiring separation from existing religious connections, and that Darby himself followed this practice when in Switzerland.[49]

However, Lady Powerscourt evidently saw identification with Brethren as entailing separation from the Establishment.[50] It is also clear that the Plymouth meeting fairly soon adopted a stance of separation from other religious bodies. Newton came to regard catholicity (the belief that the visible church should be comprehensive, including all professing believers) as evidence of apostasy; in this dispensation, Newton taught, true believers were always a small remnant who separated themselves from the professing church.[51] That Darby had changed his views by 1836 is evident from the letter which Groves wrote to him that March; subsequently we find Darby insisting that 'from that corruption they must be separate who are to be in God's unity; for He can have no union with evil. Hence, I repeat, we have this great fundamental principle, that separation from evil is the basis of all true unity.'[52] In similar vein, Wigram suggested that 'it is by realising the power of our union with Christ, that we shall separate from the world, and this will unite us to one another'.[53]

Separation was not only from the unbelieving world, but from the Established Church, which was regarded as hopelessly mixed up with the world; from religious societies; and from Dissent, which was seen to have resorted to worldly methods to maintain itself and to remedy the injustices under which it laboured. Strong gave reasons for his secession which were fairly typical: the connection of the church with the world through its status as established, the unscriptural nature of parts of the Anglican liturgy, the belief that printed prayers hindered the Spirit's operation, and the division of true believers entailed by such devices as subscription to the Thirty-Nine Articles.[54] To justify secession, Brethren had to clear themselves of the charge of schism. This was usually done by effectively asserting that the bodies from which they had separated could no longer be correctly described as churches, if indeed they had ever merited that designation. They also had to answer the accusation of proselytism, again by engaging in some

---

[47] Rennie, 'Brethren Spirituality', 208n.

[48] Ironside, *Historical Sketch*, 17.

[49] Lang, *Groves*, 109-10.

[50] Mrs. Madden, *Daly*, 158.

[51] Cf. Newton, *Catholicity*.

[52] Darby, *CW*, 1.356-7. Hargrove enunciated the same principle (*Reasons*, xi).

[53] In [J.N. Darby et al.], *Collectanea: being some of the subjects considered at Leamington, on the 3d of June and four following days in the year 1839* (Edinburgh: J.S. Robertson, 1882), 76.

[54] Anon., 'Secession of Leonard Strong', 282-7.

redefinition. A clear presentation of early thinking was offered by Brenton, himself a clerical seceder. 'Schism is the sinful dividing of the body into parts. Sectarianism is the sinful and unnatural formation of the parts into distinct bodies.'[55] Seeking visible unity was right, but it was erroneous to seek outward uniformity without inward spiritual unity. Visible unity could not be adequately demonstrated by occasional joint meetings, for it should be presented to the world at the Lord's Table. Rebutting the charge of proselytism, which he defined as getting others to join a party, Brenton insisted that Brethren merely sought to persuade others of the truth.[56] As far as Dissenters were concerned, Borlase was typical in sympathising with their separation from the Establishment, but not with the bodies which they formed, since these were formed on incorrect principles, and thus excluded genuine children of God.[57] As Dorman explained, a dissenting body was united on the basis of those points in which it differed from other Christians.[58]

In the face of a heightened sense of denominational differences, many Evangelicals were concerned to secure some visible expression of cross-denominational unity. In 1842, the Birmingham Congregational minister John Angell James proposed an alliance of Evangelicals against the unholy triumvirate of 'Popery, Puseyism and Plymouth Brethrenism'.[59] The inclusion of the last of these, although soon dropped as a priority by the Evangelical Alliance, shows how much of a threat Dissenters believed Brethren to present. It is not surprising, therefore, that many Brethren regarded the new body as no better than a well-meant human expedient. Of the Alliance's first conference in August 1846, Craik wrote:

My own mind is nearly decided that it *cannot* succeed. I object, first, to the basis; secondly, to the united acting of such a body. Either there is membership on the grounds of profession and conduct, or there is membership open to all. In the former case, the Alliance becomes a Church, in the latter, a mere secular body. Who are to be the agents of such a body? Not angels, but human beings, professedly belonging to some one of the various bodies among which believers are distributed. The thing is, in my judgment, utterly hopeless.[60]

Nevertheless, prayer meetings for union of believers were held at Bethesda soon afterwards, with special reference to the conference in London, and Craik himself was impressed by the prayer meetings for the Alliance which he attended. The following July, he spoke on the hindrances to spiritual growth which resulted from taking a position separate from Christians in general.[61] Hargrove, who was by now moving back towards a more traditional ecclesiological perspective, could say at the Alliance's inaugural conference in 1846 that in his view it gave expression to the fundamental principle (of a fellowship which transcended denominational barriers) for which early Brethren stood.[62]

[55] L.C.L. Brenton, *Sectarianism and the Lord's Table. An appeal to the Christians in Ryde* (Ryde: Hartnall, 1845), 3.

[56] *Ibid.*, 4, 6-8.

[57] *CWit* 1 (1834), 354.

[58] W.H. Dorman, *Truth for the Times: A Letter to the Dissenters* (London: Simpkin, 1842), 13.

[59] Ruth Rouse and Stephen Charles Neill (eds.), *A History of the Ecumenical Movement 1517-1948* (London: SPCK, 1954), 319.

[60] Tayler, *Craik*, 225. Membership was of individuals rather than congregations or denominations.

[61] *Ibid.*, 225, 229.

[62] Stunt, *Awakening*, 292.

For such Brethren, the Evangelical affirmation that all true believers were invisibly united was congenial to their thinking, although they would have gone further than others in seeking to provide opportunity for visible expression of this at the congregational level. By contrast, Darby condemned the Evangelical idea of invisible unity as an evasion of the challenge of Christ's description of the people of God as 'the light of the world' (Matthew 5.16); as he asked, 'Of what use is an invisible light?'[63] All that such a concept did was to confirm that the church was ruined.

5.2.4 The Ruin of the Church

Three articles in *The Christian Witness* for 1834 deserve note as indicating how this concept was being developed at Plymouth and elsewhere. J.L. Harris, in 'Retrospect and present state of prophetic inquiry',[64] doubted that revival of the church from its apostasy was promised to Christians, or that God intended to mend what man had marred. Borlase, in 'Separation from Apostasy not Schism',[65] asserted that an apostate dispensation always remained such, even when revivals occurred in it. Wigram, writing 'On the Cause, Means, Mode, and Characteristics of the Present Apostasy',[66] suggested the inevitability of the immediate fall of each new dispensation. All these notes were to appear in Darby's exposition of this topic, which was the fullest. His understanding of the church's ruin had been fermenting since his 'deliverance', as he gradually became detached from Anglicanism. However, it came to mature development following his dispute with Wesleyan perfectionism in Switzerland in 1839, and represents an application of Calvinist anthropology to the realm of ecclesiology: Israel's history paralleled that of the individual, and the individual's history represented that of the church. Restoration was neither possible nor promised; God's purpose involved replacement. In Bass's words,

> What is known in present times as the church, as expressed in denominational systems, is not the true church of God, for, refusing to meet in the simplicity of His name, it is now in ruins: not merely corrupted, but utterly, hopelessly, quite irreparable. God has discarded the church, as He set Israel aside, and His testimony is borne in the world by the assembly, which has existed from the beginning, for it alone meets "in His name."[67]

The essence of the ruin was the loss of the Holy Spirit as present in power in the church: as the early church let slip the expectation of the Lord's immediate return and settled down to life in the world, it lost sight of its heavenly nature and destiny. The results of this were twofold: firstly, it disavowed dependence on the Spirit and introduced the 'clerical principle', by which ministry was restricted to certain official appointees rather than being the prerogative of those appropriately gifted by the Spirit. Secondly, the church fell into apostasy as it became entangled with, and ultimately

---

[63] Darby, *CW*, 1.140.

[64] *CWit* 1 (1834), 264-82.

[65] *Ibid.*, 332-57.

[66] *Ibid.*, 389-404.

[67] Bass, 'Doctrine of the Church', 181.

indistinguishable from, the world around it, a result which received symbolic expression in the establishment of Christianity under Constantine.[68]

Darby expounded his understanding of the church's ruin in two pamphlets responding to attempts by Swiss Dissenters to form churches, *On the Formation of Churches* (1840) and *Some Further Developments of the Principles set forth in the Pamphlet, entitled, 'On the Formation of Churches'* (1841).[69] His main argument was that believers neither could nor should attempt to form churches on the primitive pattern. Attempts to form churches, like the perfectionism which he had just opposed so successfully, sprang from a failure to recognise the depth of the ruin wrought by sin, in the one case corporate, in the other individual. (He had been burdened by a sense of the church's corporate ruin before he could articulate his understanding of what had happened, and prior to his deliverance he had spent six or seven years weighed down by the knowledge of his ruined state as an individual.) Just as salvation came not through acknowledging God's law as good and attempting to keep it in one's own strength, but through Spirit-given awareness of one's fallen condition, confession of sin, and looking to God for saving grace, so too the path for God's people began with recognition and confession of their ruined state, and looking to him for grace to act accordingly. As with individuals, so for God's people corporately what was right for an unfallen condition was not the right path now; obedience, not imitation, was their duty. What was right for Moses when the law was first given was not right for Nehemiah when God's people were returning to him after their apostasy. God's people must seek direction from him which was appropriate to their circumstances, and Scripture provided this: the call to separate from evil and the promise of Christ's presence with two or three gathered in his name. Whilst it was no longer possible to have formally recognised officers in the church, believers could look to the Holy Spirit to distribute the gifts which would edify God's people: they might preach the gospel and celebrate the Lord's Supper, since neither activity required human ordination.

Elsewhere, Darby explained that although ruined, the church still existed.[70] The Holy Ghost remained, and so, therefore, did the essential principle of the church's unity. He continued to gift individuals within the body, although its local manifestation was ruined. Gifting was universal in its application, and gifts were given directly by God; thus they were still in evidence. By contrast, office, which was local in application, was dependent upon apostolic appointment and thus no longer in evidence.[71]

Not all Brethren, however, shared Darby's belief that the church on earth was irreparably ruined. Darby's focus was on the church's universal aspect, whereas many who eventually sided with Open Brethren stressed the local congregation: they might agree that the church universal on earth was ruined, but they saw no reason why God should not prosper attempts to build local churches according to a scriptural pattern.

5.3 Church Order

The Brethren movement was characterised during its first few years by a degree of fluidity regarding questions of church order, which complicates the attempt to distinguish

---

[68] Darby expounds this in 'On the Apostasy. What is Succession a Succession of?' (1840), *CW*, 1.112-123. Similar views were expressed in [Newton and Borlase], *Answers*.

[69] Darby, *CW*, 1.156-205.

[70] *Ibid.*, 3.272.

[71] *Ibid.*, 1.131.

gatherings which became Brethren assemblies from others which followed many of the same practices. There are several possible explanations for this fluidity. Firstly, many of the earliest Brethren were reluctant to adopt a 'church' position; in part this sprang from belief in the church's ruin, but before that, some appear to have viewed the gatherings as possessing a 'para-church' status. Meetings at Limerick and Plymouth, for example, were initially arranged at times which did not conflict with those of local congregations, dual allegiance was practised, and individuals were allowed to share in fellowship at the Lord's Table without being required to give up their ecclesiastical connections or clerical status.[72] Secondly, Coad suggests that lack of concern to establish new structures and ensure adequate provision of ministry resulted from the widespread belief that the Second Coming was imminent.[73] A third factor would surely have been the developing consciousness of the church's ruin, which often produced a lack of clarity about what positive action to take.

However, by around 1840 there appears to have been a much greater 'family likeness' about Brethren meetings, as the movement developed a clearer sense of its own identity. This often included separatist attitudes towards existing churches, although there was still scope for some variation, as Coad comments:

> the Bristol group adopted an open and brotherly attitude to other Christian groups, while Darby and Newton actively rejected other churches. On the other hand, on matters of church government it was Plymouth and Bristol who insisted on a structured order, with Darby the odd man out. Finally, there was a growing breach between Newton and Darby on prophetic interpretations, while the Bristol group were essentially pragmatic, concentrating on evangelistic and practical philanthropy.[74]

It is common to assert that the Brethren movement represented a return to the New Testament, but such a statement can mislead. Not all Brethren sought to replicate the New Testament pattern for church life: apart from the 'non-restorationist' outlook highlighted by Callahan, Coad has pointed out that others regarded much New Testament practice as merely temporary, and not intended as a pattern for every later generation to follow.[75] Darby would exemplify the former, and Groves (and, later, Craik) the latter. Darby taught that since the professing church was now ruined, it would be inappropriate to attempt to follow the apostolic pattern; rather, believers should follow the directions given in Scripture for such an eventuality. It seems that he linked following New Testament principles and their outworking in one divinely-revealed pattern more closely than Groves, who also denied that any church now was formed exactly on a New Testament pattern, but added that in any case there was no mandatory system laid down in Scripture: 'I do not say that no system can be made out of the New Testament, but I am quite sure that no *imperative* one can, nor one from which difference of circumstance may not make it at once allowable and holy, in some respects to differ.'[76] Groves insisted only that such a system should not be contradictory to the spirit and essence of the gospel. But all streams

---

[72] Darby, *Letters*, 1.18 (received 30 April 1833), 3.301-2 [185-].

[73] Coad, *History*, 56.

[74] Roy Coad, 'The Shaping of the Brethren Movement: Britain, a Historical Synopsis' [Lectures on Brethren history given at Regent College, Vancouver, 2-6 July 1990], 12 (CBA Box 32/49).

[75] Coad, *History*, 255.

[76] A.N. Groves, *Liberty*, 80-1.

of Brethren united on two points: a distinctive approach to corporate worship which centred on the Breaking of Bread and stressed the Spirit's leading, and an understanding of local leadership which dispensed with the need for ordination as a prerequisite for ministry.

5.3.1 The Emergence of Distinctive Patterns of Worship

From the very beginning, the Lord's Supper (or, as it came to be known by Brethren, the 'Breaking of Bread') was as central to Brethren worship as abuses of it had been to the pioneers' critiques of the Establishment. Groves in Dublin came to recognise that 'believers, meeting together as disciples of Christ, were free to break bread together as their Lord had admonished them; and that, in as far as the practice of the apostles could be a guide, every Lord's day should be set aside for thus remembering the Lord's death, and obeying his parting command'.[77] At Dublin, the Breaking of Bread initially followed a prescribed order, though in due time this was replaced by open worship.[78] Hereford, too, began with the leaders arranging beforehand who should break bread, minute books indicating that this continued until the late 1840s at least. But in 1830, Müller at Teignmouth had introduced open ministry in connection with weekly observance of the Lord's Supper, and this gradually became the norm, the vast majority of assemblies moving in the direction of making worship completely unstructured and spontaneous. In its developed form, the Breaking of Bread was conducted in the light of three fundamental principles: belief in the presidency of the Spirit by whose descent the church had been formed (which was interpreted as precluding human presidency or pre-arrangement), the open and unstructured nature of the service (which allowed any male believer to take part as they felt led), and the focus upon Christ's death and the benefits won for believers thereby. Gospel meetings, too, were not infrequently conducted in this way.

The immediate activity of the Spirit was also central to Brethren understanding of ministry, a term which they saw as denoting the content and activity of Christian proclamation within the company of believers (gospel preaching was not generally seen as constituting 'ministry'). In his tract, *On Ministry in the Word,* apparently written in response to the growth of 'any-man ministry' thinking in London, Wigram described the Brethren approach to ministry as stated, by which he meant that 'in every assembly those who are gifted of GOD to speak to edification will be both limited in number and known to the rest', but not exclusive, because the recognition of some as teachers did not preclude the exercise of ministry gifts by others.[79]

It is possible that Quaker influence helped to shape the Brethren approach to worship and ministry; Stunt suggests that Quaker belief in the 'inner light', as modified by a stress on the authority of Scripture, gave rise to an 'impulsive' approach to ministry, in which believers spoke in public without prior preparation, as led by the Spirit.[80] However, the shift from pre-arranged to open ministry sometimes pre-dated the Quaker accessions, as in Dublin from 1831. Furthermore, joining Brethren could be interpreted as a reaction *against* aspects of Quaker ecclesiology in the quest for closer conformity to the New Testament, which included the observance of baptism and the Lord's Supper. The

---

[77] Mrs. Groves, *Memoir*, 39.

[78] Anon., *Interesting Reminiscences*, 7-8, 18.

[79] [G.V. Wigram], *On Ministry in the Word* (London: Tract Depot, [c.1844]), 2.

[80] Stunt, *Brethren and Friends*, 23.

'impulsive' approach never became universal. Groves was unhappy with it, as he was with anything which seemed too rarified to admit of tangible realisation; he regarded it as an attempt to set up something more 'spiritual' than God had instituted. Just as believers laboured to obtain their daily bread, so too spiritual food required the labour of preparation; Timothy, he pointed out, was exhorted to give himself to study of the Scriptures. The only time when believers were promised God's help in speaking without prior preparation was when called before hostile authorities.[81] Newton had been in the habit of preparing his sermons. One of his colleagues, T.P. Haffner, in the course of confessing his errors before the saints at Ebrington Street in 1847, recalled a recent conversation with him on the subject:

> he said, that before coming to the Lord's table, he did not see it at all wrong to be prepared with what he had to say to the saints; that if they were in a right state, he believed *that* was the way that God by His Spirit ... would teach ... oh! with what humiliation do I now appear in the presence of God, for having so long retained in my bosom the knowledge that our poor brother did thus *practically* deny the *present* leadings and guidance of the Spirit of God ...[82]

Open and 'impulsive' ministry became the norm at the Breaking of Bread, but prepared ministry became increasingly widespread at other meetings, with the exception of conversational Bible readings. Over the years, the spontaneous approach to ministry at the Breaking of Bread has proved a difficult one for many to understand, and a measure of uncertainty appears to remain regarding what it means to be led by the Spirit in worship; not infrequently magazines feature articles or replies to questions dealing with this topic.

5.3.2 Leadership and Growth

A useful exposition of early Brethren thinking concerning leadership is offered by Rowdon, who notes their rejection of existing patterns of appointment to office, whether apostolic or congregational, of distinctions between clergy and laity, and of 'one-man ministry'.[83] Evidently, it was easier for the pioneers to critique existing practice than to formulate a practicable approach of their own. Craik and Müller hammered out some workable principles during their retreat early in 1839, which appear to have been similar to the approach adopted by Newton: in post-apostolic times, the assembly was to recognise Spirit-appointed elders by acknowledging their gifts and submitting to them.[84] Darby asserted that attempts to restore the forms found in the New Testament were doomed to failure in the church's ruined condition, and amounted to apostasy. Nevertheless, 'any-man ministry' was not to be countenanced: although no appointments to office could now be made (because of the lack of apostles to make such appointments), gifts remained, which should be acknowledged and received. From the late 1830s, these men were agreed on the question of formal appointment to office (as opposed to recognition); where they differed was on the question of whether authority resided in those recognised as gifted or

---

[81] Mrs. Groves, *Memoir*, 416, 418 (June 1847).

[82] Tregelles, *Three Letters*, 30n. Tregelles argued that Brethren had changed their views on the question of impulsive ministry.

[83] Harold H. Rowdon, 'The Early Brethren and Ministry', *JCBRF* 14 (January 1967), 11-24.

[84] Dickson, *Brethren in Scotland*, 149-50.

in the congregation as a whole, Darby inclining to the latter view and the others to the former.[85]

Darby's hardening anti-clericalism, arising out of his disillusionment with the Church of Ireland's restrictive attitude towards the activities of laymen as part of the Home Mission, is reflected in 'The Notion of a Clergyman Dispensationally the Sin Against the Holy Ghost'.[86] In this, he rejected the very principle of a clerical class in the church on the ground that it ran contrary to the principle of dependence on the Spirit: 'The notion of a clergyman consists in acknowledging that, as the source of authority, which, they admit, is not appointed by God at all.'[87] Furthermore, the appointment of clergy by the state under the parochial system entailed the church's involvement with a world which had rejected God, and the silencing of the gifts of the Spirit given to lay members. These considerations rendered secession imperative. Bowes also expressed his disapproval of a 'hired ministry' as unscriptural, but other Brethren tended to place more stress on the positive aspect of the topic: that no ordination was necessary to minister in the church, and that church life should offer opportunities for all whom God had gifted to employ their gifts to build up the flock.

Although there was widespread opposition to the appointment of settled pastors, the reasons for this varied. The Dublin gathering renounced the concept of a recognised eldership, probably as a result of Darby's influence.[88] Likewise, the newly-formed assembly at Tottenham denied the possibility of ordination to office on the basis that the lapsed state of the church had resulted in the loss of the higher authority necessary for ordination.[89] By 1841 Darby was rejecting such appointments on the basis that there were no longer any apostles.[90] A different reason was given at Bethesda, where we have seen that Craik and Müller refused to appoint pastors because such appointments were liable to stifle the exercise of gifts by others in the church. Groves, however, considered that

> recognized pastors and teachers are *essential* to the good order of all assemblies; and as such required and commanded of God, and though I should not object to unite with those who had them not, if it were the result of the Lord's providence in not *giving* them any, I should feel quite unable to join *personally* those who rejected them as unnecessary or unscriptural.[91]

In spite of the widespread rejection of the practice of formal appointment to office, there was still an informal exercise of leadership, often by a former clergyman. Of ninety such seceders listed in Appendix V, twenty-six joined the Brethren during the 1830s, most of them former Anglicans. Such men would have had experience in ministry which

---

[85] Burnham, *Conflict*, 82, 160.

[86] Darby, *CW*, 1.36-51 (written in 1834 but not published until 1871).

[87] *Ibid.*, 1.41. Cf. R.M. Beverley's assertion that 'In human priesthood will be found the master principle of the apostasy.' (*The Church of England examined by Scripture and tradition: in an answer to lectures by the Rev. John Venn, of Hereford, on the Christian ministry* (London: R. Groombridge, 1843), 41.)

[88] Anon., *Interesting Reminiscences*, 8.

[89] Embley, 'Origins and Early Development', 107, following William Robinson, *The History and Antiquities of the Parish of Tottenham* (London: Nicholls and Son, 1840²), 2.297-304.

[90] Darby, *CW*, 1.166-7; cf. 4.282-3, 323-4, 329-30.

[91] Mrs. Groves, *Memoir*, 414 (Journal, 6 June 1847).

must have left its mark on their pastoring and preaching, not least in the depth of some of the theological thought which was taking place. There was also a pattern of able men settling in an area and giving themselves to pastoring and teaching. Examples from this period include Newton and his colleagues at Plymouth, Chapman at Barnstaple, Craik and Müller at Bristol, and Hall at Hereford; likewise, in 1839 Cronin was described as 'the resident superintendent' of the newly-formed assembly at Stafford.[92]

Some early halls were built with accommodation for those who gave themselves full-time to ministering among them, as at Woolpit, where Henry Heath exercised such a ministry from 1848-69

Some were members of the professional classes. Such folk were among the first to adopt new ideas within Evangelicalism.[93] They were often gifted in public speaking, and able to provide direction to the young assemblies. The wealthy among them were able to bankroll the movement's expansion at home and abroad. Many were able, as gentlemen of independent means, to devote much of their time to the work.

The informality of such a system, however, could lead to two opposite abuses, 'autocratic dictatorship where strong individuals have been present, and democratic disorder elsewhere'.[94] It also meant that the leadership was often unrepresentative of the membership: at Hereford, for example, the leaders were drawn from the small minority who belonged to the professionals and the gentry, rather than the 80% who belonged to the lower classes.

5.4 The Study of Biblical Prophecy

In 1846, Darby suggested that:

---

[92] R.M. Beverley to Robert Howard, 8 July 1839 (LMA Acc.1017/1526). Given Darby's links with, and input to, this gathering, this suggests that his opposition to such functions may not always have been as definite as it later became.

[93] Bebbington, *Evangelicalism*, 104.

[94] Lang, *Groves*, 153.

that which characterized their testimony at the outset was the coming of the Lord as the present hope of the church, and the presence of the Holy Ghost as that which brought into unity, and animated and directed, the children of God; and they avowed their dependence on it. The distinct condition of the saints of the present dispensation, as filled with the Spirit abiding with them and risen with Christ, marked their teaching, while the great truths of the gospel were held in common with other true Christians, only with the clear light which God Himself directly, and these other truths, afforded.[95]

On many occasions since then, Brethren have presented a similar picture; but whilst eschatology soon became an important aspect of Brethren belief, and the movement took shape in an atmosphere of zealous investigation of biblical teaching on the subject, it is questionable whether it formed a primary part of the motivation of most of the earliest pioneers. It could be argued that they were looking backwards, to the New Testament era, as much as forwards, and that eschatological views shaped, rather than stimulated, the response of early Brethren to the ecclesiastical situations in which they found themselves.

Nevertheless, prophetic study undoubtedly formed a significant part of the developing movement's activity, and it is worth elaborating a little on the background. The Enlightenment belief in human progress, which meshed in well with the optimistic postmillennial eschatology of many Puritans and missionary pioneers,[96] appeared to have been discredited by events. In 1798, the economist Thomas Malthus had predicted a gloomy future for humanity, on the basis that population growth would always outstrip the means of production. Revolution, war, disease, and civil unrest strengthened the feeling that the social order was fast collapsing and beyond human efforts to secure its redemption.[97] Thus many Evangelicals came to reject the idea that the world would be converted in preparation for the return of Christ. Instead, they foresaw a decline in vital religion, coupled with a rise of infidelity and wickedness which would culminate in the appearance of the Antichrist; many considered the rise of democratic conceptions of government to be a preparation for this. The millennium would be inaugurated by Christ's return (hence the term 'premillennial' referring to the Second Coming), which would represent a supernatural breaking into the present order of things and which would be personal and visible – something which previous Evangelicals had not usually taught.[98] Thus they decried what they regarded as the attempts of missionary societies to convert the world by human agency, and placed little value upon efforts to introduce measures for social reform. Many expected the destruction of Christendom as a visible entity, and, as might be expected, saw their own days as those immediately preceding Christ's return.

Premillennialism existed in two main varieties, historicist and futurist. Historicists, believing that prophecy foretold events relating to the whole course of human history, sought correspondences between events of their day and prophecies in Scripture, assisted by the hermeneutical principle that a day in prophecy equalled a year in history.

---

[95] Darby, *CW*, 20.13, cf. 3.343, 20.305.

[96] Postmillennialism looked for an unprecedented worldwide ingathering of souls, precipitated by mass conversions among the Jews; this would form the millennium, and be followed by Christ's return. Cf. Iain H. Murray, *The Puritan Hope: A study in Revival and the interpretation of Prophecy* (London: Banner of Truth, 1971).

[97] Stunt, *Awakening*, 251.

[98] Bebbington, *Evangelicalism*, 84.

Ingenious mathematics and inventive hermeneutics combined to lead a number of historicists to the conclusion that the Second Advent was imminent, and date-fixing was widespread (Darby appears at one point in his early ministry to have foretold it for 1842, and Irving for 1868[99]). Unfortunately, historicism was widely discredited by the failure of its representatives to reach agreement on major points. By contrast, the futurists, who emerged during the 1820s, eschewed such activities. For them, prophecy indicated no events to be expected before the Lord's return, which constituted the next event on the prophetic timetable (though plenty was said about what should happen after it, especially by those who believed in a period during which the saints were removed from the earth, the 'Great Tribulation'). Some adopted a 'partial rapture' theory, asserting that only those believers who were prepared and expectant would be raptured (i.e. caught up to heaven with Christ); we shall see later how this interpretation was to prove a recurrent cause of unrest among Open Brethren.[100]

For this generation, as for many in the generation preceding it, prophetic study was looked on as a serious intellectual pursuit, and one which attracted widespread interest in times of uncertainty and apprehension.[101] This was particularly so among the higher classes, who, as well as having most to lose from current trends, were likely to be the first to adopt new interpretations of Scripture and history; unlike many previous millenarian movements, this one understood eschatology as upholding the existing social order; any reversals would be spiritual, as unfaithful church leaders received their due condemnation, rather than economic or social. Societies and journals were founded to further prophetic study; the most significant journals included the Irvingite *Morning Watch* (1829-33), Irish *Christian Herald* (1831-5), *The Investigator* (1831-6), and the Brethren *Christian Witness* (1834-41). The residential conferences already noted brought together leading Evangelicals for the same purpose.

This eschatological speculation was to have significant practical effects. The initial impact of the French Revolution had been to give impetus to missionary concern,[102] thus bolstering the effect of postmillennialism. However, the more pessimistic outlook associated with premillennialism, especially its futurist variety, produced a shift in perception of mission: from being a preparation for the conversion of the world, it became a rescue mission to save a few souls from the coming destruction; different (and perhaps more short-term) objects meant that often different methods and strategies were adopted. At home, too, the impact of the revolution in eschatological thinking was felt in secessions from existing churches; this had begun well before the emergence of premillennialism, and owed much to other factors, but those who believed that the faithful must be called out of Babylon (Revelation 18.4) were often led to set up new church structures to replace the apostate ones which they had left. In this context we should view Brethren and Catholic Apostolics, among others.

---

[99] See Coad, *History*, 119; Smith, 'Darby in Switzerland', 90n; Andrew Landale Drummond, *Edward Irving and his Circle* (London: James Clarke, [1937]), 130.

[100] Amillennialism should be mentioned for the sake of completeness, but it was held by very few Brethren before the 1950s. It understands the millennium as a symbolic description of the period between Christ's ascension and his return, during which the gospel is preached to all nations.

[101] Although there are several important books on the subject, a valuable introduction to this topic remains Stephen C. Orchard, 'English Evangelical Eschatology 1790-1850' (PhD thesis, Cambridge University, 1969).

[102] Stunt, *Awakening*, 20.

5.4.1 The Adoption of Dispensationalism

Almost immediately after his 'deliverance', Darby's study of Isaiah 32 had led him to conclude that there were separate futures for the heavenly church and the earthly Israel, a distinction which was at the heart of what became known throughout the Evangelical world as 'dispensationalism'. It belongs with the concept of the Christian as a citizen of heaven, awaiting the Lord's return from there, and the church as a heavenly entity. For Darby,

> the distinction between the Jewish and Gentile 'dispensations' of God's dealings with men was 'the hinge upon which the subject [prophecy] and the understanding of scripture turns'. This was vitally to influence Darby's view of unfulfilled prophecy and of ecclesiology; indeed, it would hardly be an exaggeration to claim that it was the mainspring of his thought.[103]

However, during the late 1820s his concerns were more with ecclesiology than with eschatology, as a result of his personal situation.[104]

Around 1830 this began to change. As a result of his dispensational thinking, Darby gradually abandoned the historicist approach to prophetic interpretation. He became increasingly convinced of the vital importance of prophetic study; by 1833 we find him advising that the proposed Brethren journal, *The Christian Witness*, should have 'something more of direct testimony to the Lord's coming, and its bearing also upon the state of the church'.[105] He began to advocate a pretribulational rapture, though as yet he was uncertain whether this would be secret or public.[106] During the mid-1830s, his remnant world-view, which owed something to the beleaguered situation of Evangelicals in Ireland as well as to his ecclesiology, coalesced with his eschatology to produce a developed dispensational scheme in which ruin was both inevitable and irreparable, and the believer's responsibility was to separate from a world rushing to judgement and destruction, in the expectation of the Lord's immediate return. Nebeker suggests that Darby's belief in the church's heavenly nature was probably what led him to react not only against the subservience to the state of much Irish Evangelicalism, but also against its eschatological legitimation, a postmillennial optimism which expected the triumph of its cause over the forces of infidelity and Romanism. Darby would have seen such ideas as expressions of worldly principles, and it was the world which had crucified Christ.[107]

According to Darby, 'A dispensation is any arranged dealing of God in which man has been set before his fall, and having been tried, has failed, and therefore God has been obliged to act by other means.' Salvation was always by grace, but the mode of administration of God's dealings with his people on earth differed in each dispensation. Invariably failure was immediate and ruin the result; thus the faithful took on the character of a remnant.[108] Restoration was impossible, but God made a new beginning using the previous dispensation's faithful remnant. God's heavenly dealings centred upon the church, and his earthly dealings upon Israel. Since prophecy had reference to earthly

---

[103] Rowdon, *Origins*, 51, quoting Darby, *CW*, 2.18.

[104] Stunt, 'Influences in Darby's Early Development', 68.

[105] Darby, *Letters*, 1.25-6 (received 19 August 1833).

[106] Burnham, *Conflict*, 122-3.

[107] Gary L. Nebeker, 'John Nelson Darby and Trinity College Dublin: A Study in Eschatological Contrasts', *Fides et Historia* 34 (2002), 87-109.

[108] [Darby et al.], *Collectanea*, 41.

events, the church as a heavenly body was not strictly a subject of prophecy.[109] Indeed, the church age was described by Darby and his followers as a 'parenthesis' in God's dispensational purposes, during which his earthly dealings were in a sense suspended; the church existed upon earth, but its nature and destiny were heavenly.[110]

Groves shared Darby's pessimism, and in 1833 he formulated a dispensational scheme, summarised in the chart below.

Table 5.1: The dispensational scheme of A.N. Groves

Dispensation	Characteristics	Nature
Abrahamic	Faith and hope	Elective (i.e. blessing only for those chosen)
Jewish	Sight and enjoyment	Universal
Gentilic	Faith and hope	Elective
Millennial	Sight and enjoyment	Universal

Source: A.N. Groves, *On the Nature of Christian Influence* (Bombay: American Mission Press, 1833), 6-7, 26.

It was the failure to distinguish between dispensations, Groves asserted, which had resulted in attempts to carry on Christian work on the basis of worldly principles. By 1848, however, he considered practical teaching more important than the elucidation of dispensational theories.[111] Groves's scheme appears to have dropped out of sight, perhaps because his absence from Britain meant that he could not participate in the prophetic conferences; I have not come across it in any other writing.

Newton, like Darby, came to accept a premillennial understanding of prophecy, but differed in placing the rapture at the end of the Great Tribulation. By 1834 he had rejected Darby's division of New Testament passages into 'Jewish' and 'Christian' (the 'Jewish interpretation') and his belief that the church represented a 'parenthesis' in God's earthly dealings. He criticised as 'virtually Marcionites' those (presumably including Darby) who were saying that the instruction given through the twelve apostles was Jewish in character and not intended for the church.[112] Newton preferred to affirm the unity of God's people in all dispensations and the church's place in prophecy. Since certain events were to be expected before Christ's return, Newton examined contemporary political developments closely to see how they might be preparing the way for such events. Darby

---

[109] E.g. Darby, *Letters*, 1.131 (1 May 1848).

[110] E.g. Darby, *CW*, 13.155. For fuller expositions of Darby's dispensational views, see Bass, *Backgrounds*; Elmore, 'Two Peoples'.

[111] Dann, *Father of Faith Missions*, 252.

[112] Cox, *Earnest Expostulation*, 25. Marcion was a second-century heretic who drew a radical disjunction between Old and New Covenants, and whose opposition to anything savouring of Jewish thought led him to pare the New Testament canon down to Luke and ten Pauline epistles. Space does not permit an exposition of Darby's view of the role played by St Paul as a recipient of divine revelation, but Taylor Brethren today see the Pauline epistles as its summit, Paul having been entrusted with revelation concerning the gospel and the church, and their current leader (sometimes allegedly referred to as 'our Paul') as continuing in the Pauline succession.

had only come gradually to such views, and Newton's rejection of them must therefore be regarded as immediate and decisive.

5.4.2 *The 'Secret Rapture'*

The doctrine of the secret rapture of believers to heaven before the Great Tribulation and the battle of Armageddon has become a commonplace of much fundamentalist thinking, especially as popularised by works such as the *Scofield Reference Bible* (first published in 1909), Hal Lindsey's *Late Great Planet Earth* (1970), and the *Left Behind* series of novels by Tim LaHaye and Jerry B. Jenkins (1995 onwards). However, the doctrine as now taught is not quite the same as that taught by early Brethren, and even that took some years to appear in a developed form. It was certainly not part of the earliest Brethren thinking on prophetic matters; for example, a brief summary of Darby's prophetic views dating from 1829 makes no mention of the rapture.[113]

One of the problems is that although Darby was the first to lay out the main aspects of this doctrine, he said little about his sources, although he did throw out a few hints concerning them.[114] Modern writers on the topic are liable to press historical evidence into service to support their particular prophetic views. Those who share Darby's belief in a pretribulation rapture of believers seek to demonstrate that the doctrine appears in the writings of the early church Fathers, or rest content with its being a clearer exposition of biblical teaching on prophecy than any which had preceded it. Darby may then be portrayed as one through whom God restored to the church an understanding which had previously been lost. However, Darby's originality is open to question: according to Newton, around 1832-3 Darby acknowledged his indebtedness to a comment on 2 Thessalonians 2.1-2 from a clergyman from Cork by the name of Tweedy.[115] More importantly, Stunt has recently demonstrated how Darby could well have been influenced by two continental Roman Catholic writers, Lambert and Agier.[116]

Those who insist that the church must go through the Great Tribulation before being caught up to meet her Lord ('post-tribulationists') often seek to cast discredit upon the origins of the 'secret rapture' doctrine.[117] Many rely upon Tregelles' account of this:

> I am not aware that there was any definite teaching that there would be a *secret* rapture of the Church at a secret coming, until this was given forth as an 'utterance' in Mr. Irving's Church, from what was there received as being the voice of the Spirit. But whether any one ever

---

[113] Darby, *CW*, 2.23.

[114] Cf. T.C.F. Stunt, 'Prophetics, Pentecostals and the Church', *H* 54 (1975), 304; *idem*, 'Tribulation', 93. Darby stated that few writings contained so much truth, especially regarding prophecy, as Irving's (*CW*, 15.34), but this could be taken to mean that they reflected his own thinking rather than being a source for it.

[115] 'Fry MS', 238-9.

[116] Stunt, 'Influences in Darby's Early Development', 61-8.

[117] A recent example of this approach is Dave MacPherson, *The Rapture Plot* (Simpsonville, SC: Millennium III Publishers, 1995), on which see Timothy C.F. Stunt, 'The Tribulation of Controversy: A Review Article', *BAHNR* 2.2 (Autumn 2003), 91-8.

asserted such a thing or not, it was from that supposed revelation that the modern doctrine and the modern phraseology respecting it arose.[118]

The argument is that the charismatic manifestations in which such an idea was first promulgated were not divine in origin but demonic, and that Darby and his followers engaged in a conspiracy to conceal its origins. However, Tregelles, although usually careful in his handling of sources, was not offering eye-witness testimony, and there is no other evidence to corroborate his suggestion. Sandeen goes so far as to condemn Tregelles' statement as 'a groundless and pernicious charge'.[119]

A more recent attempt to demonstrate that Irving was indeed the originator of dispensationalism and of the concept of the pretribulation rapture has been made by Mark Patterson. In an article written jointly with the sociologist and writer on restorationist movements, Andrew Walker, Patterson argues that the source was not the charismatic manifestations, but the writings of Irving and others of his circle, notably those contained in the quarterly *The Morning Watch*. Whilst he warns against taking Darby's failure to indicate his sources as an indication that his ideas represent original insights into the teaching of Scripture,[120] the most that Patterson's evidence allows us to claim with any certainty is that both Darby and Irving were drawing on ideas and hermeneutical approaches which were 'in the air' during the late 1820s. Parallels between the thinking of Darby and Irving could be due to the use of a book by 'Ben Ezra' (the pseudonym of a Chilean Jesuit, Manuel Lacunza (1731-1801)), translated by Irving in 1826 and published as *The Coming of Messiah in Glory and Majesty*. Darby's appreciation of Lambert and Agier was probably linked to his awareness of Ben Ezra, whose work was a seminal influence on both of them.

More important for our purposes than the doctrine's origin is its success. What made it so compelling was not its ability to offer more convincing exegesis of certain key passages such as Matthew 24.36-41 or 1 Thessalonians 4.16-17, so much as the neatness of its fit with the rest of the eschatological system propounded by Darby. It is integrally related to his concept of the church as heavenly and to his formulation of the distinction between the church and Israel.

Not all Brethren adopted Darby's system, though. Newton disagreed strongly, not only with Darby's exegesis of particular passages, but also with the implications for other aspects of Christian theology, such as the unity of the people of God in all ages. Newton was also concerned that Darby's 'Jewish interpretation' could have the effect of discouraging the ordinary believer in their reading of Scripture and so lead them to place unwarranted trust in their teachers, who in this way would become intermediaries between God and the believer. In his view, this was neither more nor less than popery and amounted virtually to a giving up of Christianity.[121]

---

[118] S.P. Tregelles, *The Hope of Christ's Second Coming: How is it Taught in Scripture? And Why?* (London: Samuel Bagster and Sons, 1886²), 35n.

[119] Sandeen, *Roots of Fundamentalism*, 64.

[120] Mark Patterson and Andrew Walker, '"Our Unspeakable Comfort": Irving, Albury and the origins of the pre-tribulation rapture', in Stephen Hunt (ed.), *Christian Millenarianism from the Early Church to Waco* (London: Hurst, 2001), 98-115; cf. Mark Rayburn Patterson, 'Designing the Last Days: Edward Irving, The Albury Circle, and the Theology of *The Morning Watch*' (PhD thesis, King's College, London, 2001).

[121] 'Fry MS', 238.

We also find something like a post-tribulational understanding being advocated by Müller at Bristol and Chapman at Barnstaple; I doubt that Müller would have built his orphan houses if he had shared Darby's expectation of the imminent Second Coming. Bowes appears to have held postmillennial views until the end of the 1840s.[122] Coad refers to an unspecified tract of 1839 which affirmed that 'amillennialists' could be, and were, Brethren.[123] Nevertheless, Darby's views were to be the most widely taught among Brethren, and they have exercised immense influence beyond the movement's borders.

5.5 The Centrality of Mission?

5.5.1 The Brethren – A Missionary Movement?

In recent years, it has become commonplace to present Brethren as a missionary movement. This view has been reinforced by works outlining the history and spread of Brethren missions, especially as undertaken in fellowship with the editors of *Echoes of Service*.[124] Noting the high proportion of later Open Brethren who have engaged in overseas mission, one writer suggests that no other group (with the exception of the Moravians in the previous century) had given mission the priority which the early Brethren did.[125] It is true that after 1860 Open Brethren began to make mission a high priority, but the early decades do not, on the whole, present an inspiring example. Apart from Groves' missionary work in Baghdad and then in India, and the works supported by the SKI, such as that carried on in Demerara by Leonard Strong, relatively few Brethren apart from Darby seem to have headed for the overseas mission field during the early period, and this in an era which could be described as the heyday of Evangelical mission.

One explanation for this lack of missionary zeal may lie in the apparent failure of Groves' mission to Baghdad, and the subsequent lack of progress in Madras, with Cronin and Parnell both returning home. These appear to have foundered on unfavourable views about the rightness of missions to the heathen. For example, Clulow, a colonial judge who retired from Madras to Plymouth, 'had come to accept the strange view now gaining wide currency amongst Brethren that it was *not* the responsibility of the Church now to promote missions to the heathen, that being the task assigned to another dispensation!'[126] Having financed the outward passage of Bowden and Beer, who had responded to an appeal for missionaries made by Groves at Barnstaple in 1835, and promised them £50 a year, Clulow withdrew his support.[127] In spite of Chapman's interest

---

[122] Dickson, *Brethren in Scotland*, 260.

[123] Roy Coad, 'An assessment of the Brethren movement: the abiding insight in the context of the world Christian community' (Lectures on Brethren history given at Regent College, Vancouver, 2-6 July 1990), 19 (CBA Box 32.49).

[124] Stunt et al., *Turning the World Upside Down*; Fred[eric]k A. Tatford, *That the World may Know* (10 vols; Bath: Echoes of Service, 1982-6).

[125] Ken Newton, 'Seeing the Bible Through Mission Eyes', in Harold H. Rowdon (ed.), *The Brethren Contribution to the Worldwide Mission of the Church: International Brethren Conference on Missions held at the Anglo-Chinese School, Singapore, 9-15 June 1993* (Carlisle: Paternoster for Partnership, 1994), 13.

[126] E.B. Bromley, *They Were Men Sent from God: A Centenary Record (1836-1936) of Gospel Work in India amongst Telugus in the Godavari Delta and neighbouring parts* (Bangalore: Scripture Literature Press, 1937), 41.

[127] *Ibid.*, 40-1.

in Spain, which he visited in 1834 and 1838, the missionary interest of their home assembly at Barnstaple was not strong, even though it was one of the more outward-looking assemblies.[128] One wonders whether failure reinforced the conviction that this was not an age for mission.

Furthermore, many missionary society recruits at this period were from lower classes than those providing early Brethren leadership. For all their professed unworldliness, it appears that few leaders were as ready as Groves was to give expression to this by giving up their position and prospects in order to go abroad for the sake of the gospel.

5.5.2 *Motives for Mission*

In 1830 Groves expressed the two primary objectives of Brethren mission:

> The two great objects of the Church in the latter days, independent of growing up herself into the stature of the fulness of Christ, seem to me to be the publication of the testimony of Jesus in all lands, and the calling out the sheep of Christ who may be imprisoned in all the Babylonish systems that are in the world.[129]

Motivation to achieve these objectives was provided by the Great Commission (Matthew 28.18-20) and by a sense of the imminence of Christ's return. Indeed, mission served to hasten the Lord's return: 'I consider the *testimony* of Jesus is to be published through every land, before the Bridegroom comes; this makes my heart feel an interest in heathens, that we may hasten the coming of the Lord.'[130] In Darby's opinion, those who believed in Christ's imminent premillennial return had a stronger motivation for mission, as they sought to gather out the elect from the world before the coming judgement.[131] However, such a motivation also predisposed early Brethren against adopting a long-term approach.[132] Thus Newman portrayed Brethren mission as very 'short term' in its vision.[133] The imminence of the Second Coming and the consequent urgency of the commission to preach the gospel precluded the adoption of any kind of long-term strategy for reaching an area. Early Brethren reacted against the postmillennial hope which had motivated eighteenth-century missionary pioneers such as William Carey, believing that their task was simply to rescue a few individuals from the Babylon of apostate religion. However, I am not convinced that all Brethren missionaries took this approach. Even Groves was convinced by what he saw of educational work in India that such institutions, if not able to claim apostolic sanction, nevertheless represented a potentially valuable adjunct to more directly evangelistic work.[134]

Mission also offered Groves the possibility of combining his eschatological hope with the opportunity of realising his convictions about Christian unity. Part of the

---

[128] *Ibid.*, 57-8; Peterson, *Chapman*, 66-7.

[129] Mrs. Groves, *Memoir*, 78 (Journal, 29 September 1830). On Groves' missiology, see Stephen John Chilcraft, 'Anthony Norris Groves' theory and practice of mission' (MA dissertation, Birmingham Christian College, 2003).

[130] Mrs. Groves, *Memoir*, 233 (Journal, 13 December 1833).

[131] Darby, *CW*, 2.25.

[132] Rowdon, *Origins*, 187.

[133] Newman, *Phases of Faith*, 34-5.

[134] Mrs. Groves, *Memoir*, 307 (Journal, 28 July 1835).

attraction of Baghdad for him resulted from his belief that the final drama of history would
be played out in the Near East,[135] but he also believed that, if anywhere, it would be
beyond the traditional confines of Christendom that believers could abandon their
denominational differences (the chief hindrances to the spread of the gospel) and exhibit
true unity.[136]

5.5.3 Thinking Radically about Mission

Groves' most influential role in Brethren mission was perhaps as a source of inspiration
rather than as a thinker or a winner of converts. Veitch comments that his work in
Baghdad bore fruit not in terms of numbers of converts but in inspiring others to offer for
missionary service.[137] His *Christian Devotedness* also influenced a number of leaders to
adopt a simple lifestyle and to see their material possessions as a trust from God to be
stewarded wisely. Dann notes Parnell, Newman, and Müller among them, and much later
the American Brethren writer William Macdonald, whose *True Discipleship* was to be very
influential on the development of Operation Mobilisation during the 1970s.[138]

In *Christian Devotedness*, Groves expressed the conviction that the church should
cease to provide for the future, thus recovering a sense of dependence on God. In line with
this, he disposed of his own fortune. Like Irving, he sought to realise a sense of
dependence on the Spirit, visible expression of the fellowship of believers, and
apostolicity in ministry.[139] In August 1829, he wrote:

> I am persuaded that missions never will prosper till we cease to labour as gentlemen and are
> content to be one with the people; till we cease to trust our power of human reasoning, and until
> our confidence be in the persuasive power of the Holy Ghost, till we cease to confide in human
> learning, and trust entirely to the knowledge of the truth of God.[140]

Groves' approach shaped that of Müller and Craik to 'living by faith', and hence also that
of Hudson Taylor, founder of the China Inland Mission and a formative influence on the
development of 'faith missions' in general.[141]

In an important evaluation of the biblical and historical bases for the concept of
'living by faith', Rowdon defines it as the practice of making one's needs known only to
God and looking to him to meet them instead of relying on any guarantee of a regular
income.[142] Darby objected to 'sending any one into the Lord's field with a salary of so

---

[135] Rowdon, *Origins*, 187.

[136] E.H. Broadbent, *The Pilgrim Church* (Basingstoke: Pickering & Inglis, 1985 [1931]), 354.

[137] Veitch, *Brethren*, 28.

[138] Dann, *Father of Faith Missions*, 51, 81, 86, 513.

[139] Stunt, *Awakening*, 126, 142.

[140] A.N. Groves [ed. A.J. Scott], *Journal of Mr. Anthony N. Groves, missionary, during a journey from London to Bagdad, through Russia, Georgia, and Persia. Also, a journal of some months' residence at Bagdad* (London: James Nisbet, 1831), 60.

[141] Klaus Fiedler, *The Story of Faith Missions* (Oxford: Regnum Lynx, 1994), 55-6; Lang, *Groves*, 13-19.

[142] Harold H. Rowdon, 'The Concept of Living by Faith', in Anthony Billington, Tony Lane, and Max Turner (eds.), *Mission and Meaning: Essays Presented to Peter Cotterell* (Carlisle: Paternoster Press, 1995), 340.

much per annum', considering that engaging individuals to work in this way left no scope
for them to exercise faith in God to provide for their needs.[143] The fullest survey and
analysis of this concept, however, has been provided by Larsen, who demonstrates that
its content changed significantly over time.[144] He notes that its earliest exponents
grounded it in pragmatic as well as biblical considerations, adducing such things as the
likely response of those whom they sought to reach. Also, they tended to be flexible in
its application: Müller, for instance, adopted this approach for himself and his work, but
was quite happy to engage salaried helpers for the orphanages. Initially it was applied to
all believers, not merely Christian workers; it did not preclude their receiving a regular
salary; and an essential precondition was the disposal of all possessions.

Charismatic gifts were another issue raised by the ideal of apostolic dependence on
God rather than upon human resources (in this case, education and language study) which
had been inculcated by Irving and Groves. Fridays in Baghdad were spent in fasting, Bible
study and prayer for manifestations of the Spirit's presence and gifting.[145]

> Groves ... made numerous references in his journal to the subject. He felt that lack of faith was
> the reason why the miraculous gifts were not in evidence, and reasoned that since miracles were
> intended to impress unbelievers they were most likely to appear among missionaries to the
> heathen – if only those missionaries exercised faith in God's promises. Feeling the diversity of
> languages to be a great barrier to missionary work, he raised the question whether the gift of
> tongues would be among the gifts poured down in the latter days.[146]

On one occasion Groves expressed the view that the need for language study, by contrast
with the availability during the New Testament era of the gift of tongues, was evidence of
the church's departure from God.[147] To that extent, he evidently believed that the
apostolic pattern of activity could not be replicated. Unlike Groves, who felt that the
argument that none could go forth as missionaries unless endowed with supernatural gifts
was refuted by his experience of seeing numbers converted, Parnell was convinced of the
necessity of supernatural gifts for mission, and had published a pamphlet on the subject
(now apparently lost). The lack of evident fruit in India, which he saw as due to the
absence of supernatural gifts, was one reason why he returned to England in 1837.[148]

In general, Brethren shared with many radical Evangelicals a principled opposition to
religious societies. Harris was typical in objecting to such bodies because they fell short
of being the church, and thus could not accomplish that which the church was intended to
accomplish. Because they involved appeals to the world for funds, they were necessarily
constituted and organised on worldly lines, and did not recognise the Spirit's gifting and
direction, hindering his leading by the control of their agents. Societies represented a
tendency to resort to activism rather than to repent and seek God's way of meeting this
need. They owed their existence to the church's failure to fulfil its duty, but encouraged

---

[143] Darby, *Letters*, 1.32 (22 November 1839).

[144] Timothy Larsen, '"Living by Faith": A short history of Brethren practice', *BAHNR* 1.2 (Winter 1998), 67-102.

[145] H. Groves, *Congleton*, 42.

[146] Rowdon, *Origins*, 78.

[147] A.N. Groves, *Christian Influence*, 33n.

[148] H. Groves, *Congleton*, 55-6; Rowdon, *Origins*, 79.

insubordination to its authority.[149] However, not all were opposed to the idea of founding societies or other para-church institutions, especially if conducted along 'faith lines'. This is evident from the widespread support given to the SKI. Some Brethren were willing to support other radical Evangelical agencies such as the Continental Society, and in time many became devoted supporters of the British and Foreign Bible Society.

Initially Groves had been content to reinforce the work of denominational societies in India, and his recruitment trip to Europe in 1835-6 had this objective in view, but his activity was a factor in some serious problems which developed in the Church Missionary Society's work during the mid-1830s, and he concluded that it would be better to form a new work on scriptural lines.[150] In 1840, he put forward an alternative to the society-based approach to mission, which he criticised as lacking in church character.[151] A prospective missionary should either have the confidence of the church or churches sending him forth, or, lacking that, the strength of calling and trust in God which would enable him to go out without any human source of support on which to rely. Churches were better placed than societies to know the missionary's strengths and weaknesses and maintain pastoral care, and would be more strongly motivated to support one they knew well.[152] Elsewhere he explained the advantages of such an approach:

> My grand object in England or in India, is to promote the principle of *Congregational Missions;* the design of which is, to make the connexion as close as possible between those who go forth and those who send; so that as far as possible, they may be personally acquainted, and at least acquainted by intimate personal interest; and that the Missionary may stand in the liberty wherewith Christ has made him free, and not be entangled in the bondage of any home system.[153]

Missionaries could earn all or part of their living, thus avoiding the appearance of preaching because they were paid to do so; having no clerical status to maintain, they could live more cheaply. Groves estimated that on this basis, mission could be carried out at one-third of the current cost, and more missionaries be sent out. Nevertheless, he rejoiced that societies were doing the Lord's work, albeit imperfectly: 'The grand point to be arrived at is, that the Church act so as to prove that the work societies endeavour to accomplish with the world's help, can be done better, because more scripturally, by the Church herself.' Hinting at the movement's lack of missionary zeal, he prayed 'that those in England or elsewhere who may excel in many things, may be equally distinguished by their pre-eminence in this also'.[154] In later years, they were; but Groves would not see this in his lifetime.

---

[149] J.L. Harris, 'Religious Societies', *CWit* 4 (1837), 87-100.

[150] Bromley, *Men Sent from God*, 25; Ken J. Newton, 'Anthony Norris Groves: (1795-1853) A Neglected Missiologist', 6 (Typescript, [1993], CBA Box 32/46).

[151] A.N. Groves, 'Letter on Missions to the Heathen', *CWit* 7 (1840), 127-41.

[152] The principle of local commendation would become a keystone of Brethren missionary policy, but some claimed that the principle of local financial responsibility was not given the same degree of attention.

[153] A.N. Groves, *The Present State of the Tinnevelly Mission. With an historical preface, and reply to Mr. Strachan's criticisms; and Mr. Rhenius's letter to the Church Missionary Society* (London: James Nisbet, 1836²), 31.

[154] Groves, 'Letter on Missions', 141.

PART 2

1850-1914:
A Maturing Movement

CHAPTER 6

Evangelism and Expansion

It has been suggested that Open Brethren post-Bethesda were 'like the happy country that has no history' because of their freedom from further such divisions.[1] This is a neglected period of the movement's history, so far as scholarly study is concerned, but to treat it as uneventful would be to misread it. Apart from the tensions which would erupt into division in the 1890s, this was the age when it expanded, developed a distinctive and widely-recognised identity, and fostered an array of agencies to assist assemblies in outreach and to provide them with reading material. In Part I we noted the tendency to interpret the growth as spontaneous and therefore as divine in origin; during the 1840s and 1850s there was some measure of spontaneous formation of new meetings,[2] but certain factors in the movement's growth from 1850 onwards can be isolated. These include the revival of 1859-60 and its consequences, the vigorous outreach undertaken at all levels, and the adoption of a concept of the Christian life in which activism was central. These are discussed in this chapter and the next.

6.1 The Extent of Growth

6.1.1 The Overall Picture

Lay evangelism had been developing throughout the nineteenth century. At its beginning, we find Dissenters of all denominations making increasing use of itinerant lay preachers to open up work in new locations, and the 1830s and 1840s had seen the emergence of an urban lay evangelism which expressed itself through the founding of agencies such as city missions, and which was indifferent to denominational barriers and disaffected with the clergy who represented such systems.[3] The second half of the century was the main period of Open Brethren mission and growth, and the movement's success owed much to its lay character.

Quantifying the growth is difficult. The main nationwide statistical evidence is provided by the 1851 Census of Religious Worship and the lists of assemblies published at intervals, but each source has its shortcomings. The 1851 Census, which measured the number of attendances on Sunday 30 March, gave a total of 132 places of worship in England and Wales which were identified as 'Brethren', although the returns did not differentiate between Open and Exclusive gatherings.[4] It was acknowledged that some assemblies were not included in this figure, either because they gave no denominational designation or because companies met in private homes and so were unknown to local enumerators. (The latter problem also occurred with other denominations, such as the Primitive Methodists.) Checking the returns so far published, which cover about half of

---

[1] 'A Younger Brother' [A. Rendle Short], *The Principles of Christians called "Open Brethren"* (Glasgow: Pickering & Inglis, [1913]), 98.

[2] Coad, *History*, 168.

[3] John Kent, *Holding the Fort: Studies in Victorian Revivalism* (London: Epworth, 1978), 101.

[4] Unfortunately, the census report for Scotland provides no information: Brethren are not listed as a separate category, and the original returns have long been lost.

England (and the whole of Wales, although no assemblies were reported there), leads me to believe that at least a third more assemblies submitted returns which were not identified as Brethren, and to that figure we must add those assemblies which did not submit returns. Later address lists indicate that Exclusive gatherings were more likely than Open ones to meet in homes, so the under-representation of Exclusive Brethren may be greater than that of Open Brethren. Of the returns which I have traced, one-third appear to be Exclusive and two-thirds Open, but it would be unwise to take this as a guide to the relative strengths of the two wings.

The published statistical summaries included one giving the attendance for various denominations in over seventy large towns and London boroughs, of which only twelve listed a Brethren presence.[5] However, the incompleteness of the returns is evident from the fact that no designated Brethren presence was recorded in cities which are known to have had an assembly at the time, such as Liverpool, Manchester, and Plymouth. Among the largest gatherings were Rawstorne Street, London (500 in the morning, 350 in the evening)[6] and Barnstaple (363 in the morning (including children), 104 in the afternoon, and 137 in the evening),[7] as well as those at Plymouth mentioned earlier. Most others were much smaller.

It has been established by researchers that the 1880s saw the first real evidence of decline in urban church attendance;[8] however, Open Brethren were to continue growing long after this. Lists of assemblies are available from 1897 onwards (the earliest known Exclusive list appeared in 1873), and although these are incomplete and disclaim any official character, they still enable approximate estimates of the movement's strength and spread, and totals from them are tabulated in Appendix IV.[9] Based on the respective totals of assemblies listed and of assemblies known to have existed when a list was issued but not listed in it, I would estimate that the 1897 and 1904 lists were at least 90% complete.

The number of Open assemblies grew from a minimum of 838 in 1887 (it is impossible to ascertain how many unlisted assemblies existed at that point) to 1,185 in 1897 and 1,337 by 1904. All areas would have seen growth, but it was especially strong in South-West England, Scotland, and Ulster. The availability of address lists for virtually all types of Brethren in existence during the period from 1892 to 1901 provides a unique opportunity of comparing their relative strengths. The results are tabulated below by country; a breakdown by region and county appears as Appendix III.

---

[5] Horace Mann, *Census of Great Britain, 1851. Religious Worship in England and Wales [abridged]* (revised ed.; London: George Routledge, [1854]), Table F, 113-33.

[6] PRO HO129/15/21, supplied by Gerald West.

[7] Wickes (ed.), *Devon*, no. 1008 (PRO HO129/295).

[8] Sheridan Gilley, 'The Church of England in the Nineteenth Century', in Sheridan Gilley and W.J. Sheils (eds.), *A History of Religion in Britain: Practice and Belief from Pre-Roman Times to the Present* (Oxford: Blackwell, 1994), 300.

[9] Lists were also published by G.A. Sprague of London in 1886 ([A.M. Sparks], 'A List of Assemblies', *EH* 1 (May 1886), 8) and 1887 ([A.M. Sparks], 'List of Assemblies', *EH* 2 (February 1887), 4), and an appendix containing corrections to the latter ([A.M. Sparks], 'List of Assemblies', *EH* 4 (1889), 44); no copies of these appear to have survived, but totals from the 1887 list appeared in the article on it and are included in Appendix IV.

Table 6.1: Relative strength of different types of Brethren by country, 1892-1901

	Open	Churches of God	Total Exclusive	Kelly	Lowe	Raven
England	723	58	928	200	161	567
Wales	32	4	26	8	2	16
Scotland	274	70	145	13	6	126
Ireland	156	2	63	7	9	47
Total	1185	134	1162	228	178	756

Sources: Open: [J.W. Jordan], *List of Some Meetings in the British Isles and Regions Beyond Where Believers professedly gather in the Name of the Lord Jesus for Worship and Breaking of Bread in remembrance of HIM, upon the first day of the week* (London: the author, [1897]). **Churches of God**: index pages of lists are reproduced in Julian N. Clarke, 'The Origins, Development, and Doctrine of the Churches of God: a study in Brethren history and hermeneutics' (BA (Hons) dissertation, Manchester University, 1984), 15 (1898 England and Wales, 1901 Scotland). **Kelly**: [F.E. Race and W.J. Hocking], *List of Meetings of saints gathered to the Lord's Name in Great Britain and Ireland* (London: T. Cheverton, 1892). **Lowe**: Thos. R. Dix, *List of Meetings* ([London: n.p., 1901]). **Raven**: John J. Besley, *List of Meetings* (n.pl.: n.p., [1901]). Although the Kelly list is dated a few years earlier, they are unlikely to have experienced significant change between then and 1901. No lists are available for Stuart Brethren, but Noel (*History*, 734) suggests that typically they numbered about thirty-five meetings worldwide. For an outline of the various Exclusive groups, see section 8.2, and for the Churches of God, see section 7.4.

Overall, Open and Exclusive assembly numbers were about even, with Open Brethren stronger in Scotland and Ireland, and Exclusives stronger in England, although we have no way of knowing how average assembly sizes compared. The high numbers of Exclusive meetings were due in part to the fact that they underwent a succession of splits from 1880 onwards, and therefore many towns would have had meetings from two or three of the main divisions where there had been one previously. In England, Exclusives were much stronger than Open Brethren in the East Midlands (where Open Brethren were very weak), the South-East (apart from Buckinghamshire and Hertfordshire), the North-East, and Cornwall, Dorset, Gloucestershire, and Wiltshire; they were also slightly stronger in the West Midlands. Outside London, Open Brethren had high concentrations of assemblies in Devon and Somerset, Gloucestershire, Hampshire, Surrey, Kent, East Anglia, and Lancashire. Elsewhere in Northern England there were relatively few Open congregations outside the main conurbations. The Churches of God were concentrated in the industrial Midlands and Northern England.

In Scotland, Open Brethren assemblies were heavily concentrated in Ayrshire, Lanarkshire, and Aberdeenshire. They were much stronger than Exclusive Brethren in most areas, though not in most southern counties (excepting Wigtown), East and Midlothian, Perthshire, or Shetland, where Exclusives were considerably stronger. The Churches of God were concentrated in the industrial Lowlands. The remarkable concentration of Open assemblies in Ulster is noteworthy, and is still evident today. As for Wales, it is noticeable that there were very few assemblies of any type in rural areas.

One of the main catalysts for Brethren expansion was the revival which affected Ulster and the North-East of Scotland in 1859-60, and the attempts made to conserve and export the blessing to other parts of Britain. The nature and extent of continuity between pre- and post-1859 Open Brethrenism are still none too clear, but what does seem incontrovertible is that the social composition of the movement began to change fairly significantly, though this was more evident in some areas than others. The gentility of the 1830s gave way to a new, more populist ethos which reflected the predominant social grouping among the accessions to the movement from the late 1850s onwards. In time, this affected the leadership as well, and hence the theological outlook of much of the movement, as less sophisticated approaches to Scripture paved the way for a patternism which stressed exact conformity to every recorded detail of New Testament church practice.

The revival's main impact was in the Protestant counties of Antrim and Down, Dublin, Cornwall, and the Western Lowlands and North-East of Scotland, and it resulted in 10% of the population professing conversion in Ireland, Scotland, and Wales.[10] In Britain as a whole, the churches gained around a million members, and to this should be added the unknown proportion of converts who were already church members.[11] Resulting large-scale accessions from Presbyterian congregations in many localities of Scotland and Ulster would have done much to dilute the Anglican ethos of early Brethrenism.

In subsequent years, revivalism attempted to perpetuate the lay ethos and vigorous outreach of the revival itself, as a means of conserving and spreading the blessing; *The Revival,* an interdenominational magazine, was started in 1859 as a means of informing believers about what was going on, and publicising the activities of notable evangelists. R.C. Morgan, its founder, had associated with Brethren at Bath from 1851-5, although he never joined them in membership and could not accept certain conditions of fellowship 'which he felt tended to cripple him in the freedom with which the Divine Son had made him free'.[12] The magazine provides valuable evidence of the extent of Brethren involvement in the revival and in revivalist activity thereafter. A number of Brethren in various parts of Britain, Exclusive as well as Open, were happy to co-operate in interdenominational work, and we shall see that Brethren evangelists formed an integral part of the revivalist network, but there were others who appear to have been taking opportunities to proselytise among revival converts. In a rare critical note, Morgan expressed disapproval of Darby's instructing young converts following the preaching of the Exclusive evangelist Charles Stanley in Islington. He warned new believers against Darbyism on the basis that it excommunicated Müller and those in fellowship with him, even though Müller's *Narrative* had been a catalyst for revival in Northern Ireland.[13]

Revivalism probably had more impact on Open Brethren than the revival had done, even in counties which had been most directly affected. For example, a Congregational minister in Kingstown (now Dun Laoghaire, just outside Dublin), Joseph Denham Smith (1817-89), saw considerable fruit from his evangelistic preaching during 1859-60, with crowds of up to 2,000 gathering for evangelistic meetings.[14] Merrion Hall was therefore opened in Dublin during 1863, along the lines of the newly opened Metropolitan

---

[10] Janice Holmes, *Religious Revivals in Britain and Ireland 1859-1905* (Dublin: Irish Academic Press, 2000), 3, 19; J. Edwin Orr, *The Second Evangelical Awakening in Britain* (London and Edinburgh: Marshall, Morgan & Scott, 1949), 76-7.

[11] Fiedler, *Faith Missions,* 114; Orr, *Awakening,* 207.

[12] G.E. Morgan, *"A Veteran in Revival". R.C. Morgan: his Life and Times* (London: Morgan & Scott, 1909), 21.

[13] *The Revival,* 19 May 1860, 155; 26 May 1860, 162.

[14] On Denham Smith, see Pickering (ed.), *Chief Men,* 124-6.

Tabernacle of C.H. Spurgeon, to provide both a home for a city-centre assembly and also a venue for large-scale evangelistic efforts.[15] For many years it was the hub of Dublin revivalist activity.

As part of this activity, means of outreach previously regarded as exceptional were widely adopted: open air preaching, the setting up of mission halls for gospel preaching, the emergence of full-time itinerant evangelistic preachers, and the appearance of women preachers. Open Brethren in particular shared in all this, and harvested many of the converts.[16] The result, according to Coad, was that the movement's character became that of a 'gospel mission'.[17] Theologically, there was an increased emphasis on conversion as involving a crisis experience, to the extent that Coad suggests that many Open Brethren confused the two.[18] Yet some later expressed unease at what they saw as the substitution of human revivalism for God-sent revival, and the movement appears to have been divided in its attitude: whilst Dickson observes that Scottish Open Brethren continued the revivalist emphasis on instant salvation and assurance based on acceptance of Biblical propositions, and the use of revivalist techniques and hymns,[19] others expressed themselves rather negatively about such things as substitutes for true revival.[20]

The American evangelist D.L. Moody made his first visit to Britain from 1873-5, accompanied by the songleader Ira D. Sankey. Their missions were as important for the Open Brethren as the 1859 revival, not so much in terms of numbers converted as in terms of their impact on the evangelistic methods employed and the hymns sung. Their stress on experience and Moody's relatively undoctrinal preaching, reinforced by Sankey's experience-orientated hymnody, would have reduced the significance of doctrinal barriers dividing various streams of Evangelicals. All this would have contributed to a homogenising process, and thus have paved the way for increased co-operation between Open Brethren and other Evangelicals (although in Scotland, and perhaps elsewhere also, many Brethren later became less amenable to such involvement[21]). Thus Müller, who preached for Spurgeon at the Metropolitan Tabernacle, also helped follow up the evangelistic campaigns of Moody and Sankey by instructing their converts.[22] This process had begun before their visit, but undoubtedly became much more widespread afterwards, and the two Americans did much to foster the activist ethos of much late-century Evangelicalism; among Open Brethren, this tended to displace the more contemplative approach of many early leaders.[23] Furthermore, the opportunities for service, the openness for ministry from any gifted brother, and the movement's increasingly revivalist theology would have attracted many converts.[24] Brethren would

---

[15] Beattie, *Brethren*, 85; Anon., *Jubilee Year. Brief History of Merrion Hall, Dublin, 1863-1913* ([Dublin]: n.p, [1913]); Anon., *Merrion Hall Dublin: One Hundred Years of Witness 1863-1963* ([Dublin: n.p., 1963]).

[16] Bebbington, *Evangelicalism*, 116-17.

[17] Coad, *History*, 185. The traffic was not all one way, however: Moody spent time studying the Scriptures in company with Brethren such as Darby, Henry Moorhouse, and F.C. Bland, and adopted a form of the Bible reading in his own ministry.

[18] Coad, *History*, 279.

[19] Dickson, *Brethren in Scotland*, 79.

[20] See section 10.1.3.

[21] Dickson, *Brethren in Scotland*, 86-7.

[22] Müller, *Autobiography*, 526, cf. 530.

[23] This remained strong among those Exclusive Brethren who followed Darby and Stoney.

[24] Orr, *Awakening*, 202.

also have benefited from the widespread improvement in working-class living standards and the associated desire to attain social respectability, which would include church attendance: assemblies combined an aura of gentility which had not been completely dissipated by revivalism with a lay orientation which provided opportunities of service and fulfilment. Not all of this growth was due to conversions. The phenomenon of 'transfer growth' was widespread, and often encouraged by some who sought to persuade believers to leave their compromised and worldly churches and throw their lot in with the new movement, which thereby acquired a reputation for sheep-stealing and proselytism.

Open Brethren liked to portray the movement leading to the formation of assemblies as a spontaneous one, the result of divine action rather than revivalism or strategic church-planting. For example, the biography of the Ulster evangelist David Rea (1845-1916) records of his preaching at Darkley (Armagh) during 1875-6 that he sought to teach converts in special early-morning meetings each Sunday, and they became dissatisfied with existing churches as a result of comparing them with the New Testament; the result was that they began to practise believer's baptism and weekly Breaking of Bread without having heard of Brethren.[25] However, it was from the Brethren itinerant William M'Lean of Peterhead that they learned these practices, so in this case things were not as spontaneous as might be thought. It seems clear that, for the most part, growth during the period from 1850 to 1914 was the result of vigorous and planned outreach, in which certain individuals played key leadership roles by virtue of their wider influence. The rest of this chapter explores how that influence was exercised, the outreach strategies which were adopted, and where these proved most successful.

6.1.2 Growth amid Opposition in Scotland and Ireland

Initially, boundaries between Brethren and other movements were rather fluid; the founder of the Churches of Christ, Alexander Campbell, visited Great Britain during 1847, and concluded that Brethren provided the closest parallel to his own movement because of their primitivism. There were contacts between the movements during the 1840s and 1850s, made easier by the lower social status of Brethren in Scotland. There the two were liable to be confused, but from the 1860s Brethren became increasingly predominant.[26]

As many of the Bowesite assemblies died out during the 1850s, the Open Brethren movement in Scotland is largely rooted in the 1859 revival, further more localised awakenings which followed it in the North-East, and the revivalism which attempted to perpetuate such awakenings. Dickson describes the revival movement in Scotland as urban, anti-institutional, and non-denominational, arguing that it prepared the soil for Brethren growth.[27] In Lanarkshire, for example, he discerns a pattern whereby individuals became dissatisfied with their own churches and were attracted to Open Brethrenism by the quality of fellowship and the lay administration of baptism and the Lord's Supper. The county had a number of assemblies dating back to the 1850s, some with roots in the Evangelical Union, a denomination which was itself the product of revivalism.[28]

---

[25] Tom Rea, *The Life and Labours of David Rea* (Kilmarnock: John Ritchie, [1917]), 29-32. On Rea, see also *BM* n.s. 17 (1916), 120.

[26] On contacts between these movements see Louis Billington, 'The Churches of Christ in Britain: A Study in Nineteenth-Century Sectarianism', *Journal of Religious History* 8 (1974), 44.

[27] Dickson, *Brethren in Scotland*, 27.

[28] *Ibid.*, 42, 53.

Many revival converts rejected the restrictions placed upon them in the older churches and founded new ones, wishing to give fuller scope to the Brethren emphases on lay activity and intellectually-stretching Bible study;[29] growth would follow as they engaged in vigorous outreach. However, this process was slower to begin in the North-East because churches there were more sympathetic to the revival, thus lessening the frustration felt by many converts.[30] A few assemblies began spontaneously, others as a result of the activities of English revivalists, many of whom belonged to the Brethren and whose emphasis on Bible study led to the formation of small groups for the purpose.[31] Large-scale transfers from other churches, especially the Free Church of Scotland and the Baptists, were not uncommon, especially when Open Brethren began work in a district. The most notable instance of this occurred on the island of Westray in Orkney, where 150 believers (two-thirds of the Baptist church there) made such a move in 1867-8 as a result of the ministry of Rice Hopkins (1842-1916)[32] and J.A. Boswell (1840-1925), which combined powerful evangelistic preaching with advocacy of Brethren worship practices. Not surprisingly, this resulted in longstanding bitterness and accusations of proselytism and sowing discord.[33]

Open Brethren became particularly strong in Ayrshire (building on an existing tradition of Presbyterian Dissent), Lanarkshire and Glasgow, as well as the fishing communities of the North-East; according to Dickson, growth in the Lowlands was facilitated by the conjunction of Brethren culture with that of Lowland communities.[34] In terms of social class, their main strength was among the skilled working classes and lower middle classes.[35] Aberdeenshire was the main rural area where assemblies achieved any measure of strength in Scotland; this had been true of the earlier Scotch Baptist movement, and was also the case with the Baptists from the 1860s.[36] Other rural counties in which Brethren flourished for a while were Wigtownshire and Shetland. However, by contrast with the Baptists, Brethren failed to penetrate the Gaelic-speaking community, even though some early evangelists were native Gaelic speakers.[37] North of the Caledonian Canal, during this period the only assemblies were at Wick and Thurso, apart from clusters of meetings around Inverness and in Orkney and Shetland; none of these were in Gaelic-speaking areas. Some areas of Northern Scotland were staunchly Roman Catholic, but elsewhere ferocious opposition was experienced from the Presbyterian community, to the extent that one report asserted that 'The Pope is not half so frightful in

---

[29] Coad, *History*, 169; Neil Dickson, 'Scottish Brethren: Division and Wholeness 1838-1916', *CBR* 41 (1990), 21; cf. *idem*, *Brethren in Scotland*, 61.

[30] Dickson, *Brethren in Scotland*, 85.

[31] Neil Dickson, 'Brethren and Baptists in Scotland', *BQ* 33 (1990), 372-3.

[32] On Hopkins, see Ian McDowell, 'Rice Thomas Hopkins 1842-1916: an open brother', *BAHNR* 1.1 (Autumn 1997), 24-30.

[33] Baptists were prone to this because of the similarity between many Brethren practices and those of the Scotch Baptist churches. Among these were plural leadership, open worship and weekly celebration of the Lord's Supper (Dickson, 'Brethren and Baptists', 373-6).

[34] Dickson, *Brethren in Scotland*, 379. Dickson instances such features as an egalitarian spirit (cf. *ibid.*, 308), the desire for self-improvement through education, the architecture of gospel halls, and the social side of assembly life, as reflecting aspects of the host culture.

[35] *Ibid.*, 289-92.

[36] D.W. Bebbington (ed.), *The Baptists in Scotland: A History* (Glasgow: Baptist Union of Scotland, 1988), 35, cf. ch. 14.

[37] Dickson, *Brethren in Scotland*, 99.

these regions as the Brethren'.[38] In the area around Inverurie, Hugh McIntosh, a probationer for the Free Church of Scotland ministry issued a pamphlet entitled *The New Prophets* in 1871 which was widely circulated, churches being supplied with copies for free distribution; thus the evangelist Donald Munro (1839-1908) and his colleague received little support when preaching there.[39] In 1874, an evangelist working in the village of Halkirk in Caithness reported that the Free Kirk minister there had called a special meeting to warn the flock against the dangerous character of Donald Ross. Ross, as we shall see, played a crucial role as an evangelist in the growth of Open Brethren in North-East Scotland.[40] The minister's stratagem backfired because of the ill-will between the various Presbyterian communities, as the Church of Scotland folk aligned themselves with the evangelist and against the Free Kirk.[41] This was not the only time when denominational divisions served to open the door for Brethren to gain a hearing. As one evangelist reported in 1897, 'dissension among the denominations is opening the way for God's easy, artless, unencumbered way of Salvation'.[42]

Donald Ross

Factors which gave rise to Presbyterian opposition included the Open Brethren practice of believer's baptism, and the fact that assemblies were better able to assimilate the revivalist impetus than the Presbyterian churches.[43] Some opposition came from Evangelicals in the denominations who approved of the revival but not of lay preaching: it is noteworthy that revivalism was much more 'churchly' in character in much of Scotland than it was south of the border.[44] Yet reports during the 1870s also refer to widespread ignorance of the gospel in parishes whose ministers were warning against the new heresy. This says something about the nature of the preaching which prevailed in the

---

[38] *NA*, August 1874, 30.

[39] [John Ritchie], *Donald Munro, A Servant of Jesus Christ* (Kilmarnock: John Ritchie, n.d.), 54. On Munro see also *BM* n.s. 9 (1908), 120.

[40] On Ross see section 6.3.1; Pickering (ed.), *Chief Men*, 120-2; C.W.R[oss]. (ed.), *Donald Ross, pioneer evangelist of the North of Scotland and the United States of America* (Kilmarnock: John Ritchie, n.d.).

[41] *NA*, July 1874, 28; August 1874, 30.

[42] 'TLWW', *W* 27 (1897), 88.

[43] Beattie, *Brethren*, 293; Crawford Gribben, 'The Worst Sect that a Man can Meet', 3 (typescript, published as '"The worst sect a Christian man can meet": opposition to the Plymouth Brethren in Ireland and Scotland, 1859-1900', *Scottish Studies Review* 3 (2002) 34-53).

[44] Orr, *Awakening*, 200-1.

Highlands at the time; its high Calvinist ethos and introspective spirituality, which fostered suspicion of claims to assurance of salvation, would undoubtedly have been a significant factor in opposition to revivalism and hence to Brethren outreach.

The Scottish historian Crawford Gribben suggests that as the movement became more populist, it also became more rigorously primitivist and began to reject traditional Calvinist teaching.[45] Among those who joined the Brethren from the background of the revivalist and non-Calvinistic Evangelical Union was the Arminian evangelist Alex Marshall (1847-1928), whose *God's Way of Salvation* (1888) sold over five million copies in English alone by 1928.[46] However, this trend should not be overstated. *The Northern Witness* (later *The Witness*) and *The Believer's Magazine* both continued to uphold most of the 'five points of Calvinism'; even limited atonement, the most controversial, was maintained in the sense that while Christ's death was seen as a propitiation for the sins of the whole world, it was for the elect alone that Christ died in a substitutionary sense. Calvinist influence may also account for a perceptible difference of emphasis in the evangelistic preaching of Scottish and Irish Brethren when compared with Darby's published evangelistic sermons; in line with many of the more strongly Calvinist preachers of their day, the former show a much more marked stress on divine judgement upon sin, whereas Darby's preaching is more characterised by an emphasis on the love of Christ for the sinner.

Opposition undoubtedly fostered the growth of a strongly separatist outlook among Open Brethren in Scotland and in Ulster: 'The persecution and reproach attached to this movement was of such a nature that only those who had known conviction of sin and conversion to God, who were really born again and knew their sins forgiven, could survive such an ordeal.'[47] In rural areas, it might extend to trade boycotts, thus forcing Brethren to move home in order to find work.[48] An anonymous writer commented that when he left the Church of Scotland thirty years earlier (presumably to help form the Free Church of Scotland) there had been no criticism of his joining another denomination, but when he separated from *all* denominations in obedience to 2 Corinthians 6.18, he encountered fierce opposition from religious people, and the minister even preached a sermon against heretics. The moral was that:

> You may leave one denomination and join another, without incurring the world's displeasure. You may say many "strong" things, and preach on almost any subject you like; you may even teach "separation" as a general principle, and get the ears and the blessings of the people all the time, so long as you remain even in a "nominal" fellowship with the world's churches. But the moment you learn that, in the estimation of God, "to obey is better than sacrifice" (I Samuel

---

[45] Gribben, 'Worst Sect', 11.

[46] On Marshall, see Hawthorn, *Marshall*; W 58 (1928), 411-12.

[47] Robert Chapman, *The Story of Hebron Hall Assembly, Larkhall, 1866-1928. A Short History of the Inception, Progress and Personalities of the Assembly* (Kilmarnock: John Ritchie, 1929), 14. Nevertheless, Larkhall was to become the largest assembly in Scotland, with a membership of 400 by 1914, and that in an area well supplied with Evangelical ministries and congregations (Chapman, *Hebron*, 45-6, 64; Alex Strang, *Centenary of Hebron Hall Assembly Larkhall 1866-1966* (n.pl.: n.p., [1966]), 3).

[48] Cf. John A. Anderson, *Autobiography of John A. Anderson, M.D. China Inland Mission* (Braemar: the author, 1950[2]), 19.

xv.22), and seek to act out what you see to be the will of God regarding separation from the unconverted, the opposition of the world breaks out.[49]

In such an environment, there was no room for the half-hearted or those inclined to compromise.

For many assemblies, revivalism had shaped their ecclesiology as well as their evangelism. As Dickson comments,

> Brethren itinerant preachers had found undenominational revivalism congenial because of their lack of a developed institutional sense, their concept of an unsophisticated unity based on a minimalist Evangelical message, and the urgent priority which they gave to evangelism. Assemblies formalised these features, along with several other emphases of contemporary popular piety, into an ecclesiology.[50]

This does not mean that they were necessarily happy to accept the existing church scene and work with other churches: Ross, for example, found that revivalism, and in particular the twin problems of clerical antagonism and of what to do with those converted through his ministry, forced him to consider the need for a gathered church.[51] As one convert recalled, 'We went to church, and sometimes got a word to help us in spiritual life, more frequently a cold blanket thrown over us to damp out "Revivalism," and not infrequently, a tirade against "presumption" in being too sure of our salvation.'[52] During their stay in a locality, evangelists of Ross's stamp concentrated initially on gospel preaching, but would then begin meetings for Bible study and prayer with their converts. This brought them all face to face with such subjects as baptism, the Lord's Supper, and church life, and evangelists and converts appear to have learned together.[53] All felt themselves squeezed out of the churches, a perception which strengthened the negative attitude of these evangelists towards the ministers; the seceders were joined by converts from the 1859 revival who had been reawakened, a fact which gave strength to the accusations of proselytism.[54]

As a result, North-East Scotland, an area which had experienced much revivalist activity, saw the foundation of almost thirty assemblies in the early 1870s, Baptist churches being especially hard hit by losses to the new movement.[55] Although Brethren evangelists had been active in the area during the 1860s, it was as part of the interdenominational revivalist network, and they worked with existing churches rather than forming Brethren assemblies. Those founded during the following decade were therefore initially independent of Brethren elsewhere; indeed, as Ross recalled:

---

[49] Anon., 'What the World Opposes', *BM* n.s. 1 (1900), 8.

[50] Dickson, *Brethren in Scotland*, 89.

[51] *Ibid.*, 93.

[52] Anon., 'Assembly Life Experiences. Letters of an Octogenarian. No.1. – Conversion and Early Life', *BM* n.s. 20 (1919), 9.

[53] F. Cordiner, *Fragments from the Past: An account of people and events in the Assemblies of Northern Scotland* (London: Pickering & Inglis, 1961), 70; [Ritchie], *Munro*, 71.

[54] Dickson, *Brethren in Scotland*, 96-7; [John Ritchie], *James Campbell, A Servant of Jesus Christ* (Kilmarnock: John Ritchie, n.d.), 57.

[55] Dickson, *Brethren in Scotland*, 97-8.

We knew nothing of gathering to the name of the Lord Jesus, but we did certainly know that what claimed to be the Church was doing a gigantic work for the devil in deceiving the people, and we were now experiencing its enmity and hatred to God's work. Those converted at the meetings were disgusted with the churches and unconverted ministers, and we were being much exercised about what was to be done. We had heard of "Brethren," but only as bad, bad people, and we resolved to have nothing to do with them.[56]

The significance of this independence was not lost on later writers such as John Ritchie,[57] himself a product of this wave of activity, who commented that they 'refuse to be made responsible for errors that were taught, and for divisions that were made before they were born'.[58] The American pastor and itinerant Bible teacher H.A. Ironside (1876-1951), whose family roots were also in the North-East assemblies, stated that Exclusive Brethren (who already had a number of assemblies along the North-East coast[59]) had approached them with a view to establishing fellowship, but that when asked to 'judge the Bethesda question', they refused to condemn George Müller. It was a while later that Ross and others attended a conference in Glasgow and received a welcome on the strength of the blessing known to have attended their outreach.[60]

According to Dickson, Open Brethren in the area grew at times of awakening (the 1880s, 1895, and 1921) and contracted as a result of migration, whether to Aberdeen or overseas.[61] Since much of the movement's growth had been among artisans and the lower middle classes,[62] it is not surprising that emigration, which affected these classes primarily, was to be one of the main factors which slowed growth in Scotland, although it was also a factor in the growth of vigorous Brethren movements elsewhere in the English-speaking world, especially in Canada, the United States, Australia and New Zealand. It was not only the rank and file who crossed the seas; a number of leading evangelists also did so from the 1870s, including Marshall, Munro, and Ross (to North America), and Hopkins (to Australia), while others made lengthy ministry tours.

In the light of their own history, North American writers have sometimes portrayed Open Brethren in North-East Scotland as a third grouping, neither Open nor Exclusive. Their eschatology and ecclesiology (in particular their acceptance of the idea of the ruin of the church) are said to be closer to Exclusive than to Open thinking.[63] To some extent

---

[56] C.W.R[oss]. (ed), *Donald Ross*, 48.

[57] On Ritchie, see J. Grant, 'John Ritchie (1853-1930)', *BM* 111 (2001), 148-9; Pickering (ed.), *Chief Men*, 216-20.

[58] John Ritchie, *"The Way which they call Heresy." Remarks on Mr. W. Blair Neatby's book,* "A History of the Plymouth Brethren" (Kilmarnock: John Ritchie, n.d.), 100.

[59] Cf. Neil Dickson, 'Open and Closed: Brethren and Their Origins in the North East', in James Porter (ed.), *After Columba – After Calvin: Community and Identity in the religious traditions of North East Scotland* (Aberdeen: Elphinstone Institute, 1999), 151-70.

[60] Ironside, *Historical Sketch*, 71-3. J.A. Boswell, who had evangelised in this region and who later joined the Churches of God, asserted that Darby had recognised this independence of origin and had insisted that they could not be treated as associated with evil in the way that Open assemblies elsewhere had been ('The Open Position', *NTr* 12 (1900), 74).

[61] Dickson, 'Open and Closed', 159.

[62] *DSCHT*, s.v. 'Brethren'.

[63] Cf. Robert H. Baylis, *My People: The Story of Those Christians Sometimes Called Plymouth Brethren* (Wheaton, IL: Harold Shaw, 1995), 87; Kenneth V. Botton, 'Regent College: an experiment in theological education' (PhD thesis, Trinity International University, 2004), 34-6, following Ross

this may be reading the divisions in North American Brethrenism back across the Atlantic, but there was undoubtedly a difference of outlook which has persisted to the present. However, I would prefer to see things in terms of a spectrum of opinions within Open Brethren, rather than positing two separate movements.

Similar issues surface in a consideration of Open Brethren growth in Ulster, a province with its own long tradition of popular revivalism.[64] The 1859 revival itself mostly affected the Presbyterian community, which had been prepared over the previous three decades by the widespread penetration of conversionist theology and active evangelistic outreach, including open-air preaching.[65] J.G. M'Vicker (1826-1900) was a Presbyterian minister who was converted in the revival and later joined Open Brethren.[66] Speaking in 1898, he recalled what he saw as the progress and stability of the work, putting this down to the solid teaching which the converts had previously received: 'The word was laid ready to burn and the breath of God kindled it.'[67] Open Brethren presence in the province was largely the result of this movement.[68] Dozens of men paired up to engage in full-time itinerant evangelism throughout the province. For example, David Rea and William M'Lean saw assemblies established in County Armagh as the result of evangelistic campaigns at Darkley (1875), Ballinderry (1878), Killeen (1878), Halfpenny Gate near Moira (1879), and Ahorey (1881). Rea was responsible for the emergence of assemblies in a number of other locations, either alone or with another evangelist. W.J. Matthews and James Campbell worked together from 1878 to 1891, planting assemblies (mostly in County Tyrone) at Cookstown (1879), Larrycormick (1880), Kingsmills near Stewartstown (1880), Dunmullan near Omagh (c.1883), and near Newtownstewart (mid-1880s). Each man paired up with others after this and saw considerable fruit from their work; indeed, it was claimed that Campbell had been responsible for the commencement of no less than forty assemblies in Northern Ireland.[69] Brethren also benefited from the visit of Moody and Sankey to Belfast in 1874; conversions at their meetings included a large number of young men afterwards gathered into assemblies.[70]

The unpleasant and occasionally violent nature of some of the opposition, which came from both sides of the sectarian divide,[71] was undoubtedly a factor in the greater rigidity and separatism of Open Brethren in Northern Ireland.[72] More positively, opposition could provoke curiosity in the local populace, as at Rathfriland, County Down, in the 1890s, where a series of uncomplimentary articles appeared in the local newspaper. Folk might then come and see what the fuss was about, hear the gospel, and

---

Howlett McLaren, 'The Triple Tradition: The Origin and Development of the Open Brethren in North America' (MA thesis, Vanderbilt University, 1982).

[64] David Hempton and Myrtle Hill, *Evangelical Protestantism in Ulster Society 1740-1890* (London and New York: Routledge, 1992), 146.

[65] *Ibid.*, 148.

[66] On M'Vicker, see section 6.3.1; Pickering (ed.), *Chief Men*, 113-5; [Max I. Reich] (ed.), *Selected Letters with brief memoir of J.G. M'Vicker* (London: Echoes of Service, [1902]).

[67] [Reich] (ed.), *M'Vicker*, 33.

[68] Beattie, *Brethren*, 283.

[69] William Gilmore, *These Seventy Years* (Kilmarnock: John Ritchie, [1954]), 21.

[70] Beattie, *Brethren*, 289.

[71] E.g. the reports in *BM* 3 (1893), 23 (Catholics and Orangemen hindering the spread of the gospel); 'TLWW', *W* 17 (November 1887), v (three tents burnt down that summer).

[72] Coad, *History*, 172.

be converted.[73] However, some evangelists were more willing to co-operate with existing churches, notably David Rea. Although he had left the interdenominational Irish Evangelization Society in 1877, in order to be free to teach and practice the whole Word of God (points at issue included believer's baptism and the Breaking of Bread), he was happy to have clerical support and participation in his campaigns, even though this earned him the criticism of some younger brethren.[74]

WOODEN PREACHING HALLS AS USED IN IRELAND.

Wooden-sided tents, a few of which are now in use in this country, are a modification of the portable wooden buildings that have been used for gospel preaching for some years in Ireland. There, however, the buildings are of much greater length; they have not an oiled canvas roof, but one of a more solid description, and they are kept in one place for a considerable time. The Irish Evangelization Society use these Wooden Halls, planting them in R.C. districts, and the testimony given in them — of course amid opposition and not without danger — has often been used of God to deliver souls from "the power of darkness."

Portable 'wooden tents' or 'wooden halls' like this one dating from the turn of the century were widely used by evangelists in Ireland; one was constructed as recently as the 1960s. Similar constructions were used in England and Scotland, but with an oiled canvas roof instead of a wooden one

There had been extensive Brethren outreach elsewhere in Ireland, but Irish Evangelicalism appears for the most part to have given up its hopes of making inroads into the Catholic majority for a more realistic approach which focused on the needs of the Protestant community, concentrated in Ulster.[75] However, the 1859 revival did make some impact on the rest of Ireland. In some areas, such as Kerry, the Anglo-Irish landed gentry were among the first to be affected. From these upper-class converts emerged some effective evangelists, including F.C. Bland (1826-94), Richard Mahony, and W.T. Crosbie (1817-99), the 'Three Kerry Landlords'.[76] The movement failed to establish a presence in the Gaelic-speaking areas in the West; whilst the Church of Ireland had made strenuous outreach efforts in these localities, they remained strongly Roman Catholic. Brethren presence in Ireland was mainly in areas with a significant Protestant population from which to draw converts, and so the greatest concentration of meetings in the South was in the area around Dublin. Work among Roman Catholics remained difficult and at times dangerous until well into the twentieth century.[77] Catholics were forbidden to enter Protestant church buildings, so tent and open-air work were used, but that put evangelists in positions of vulnerability. In Cork during the Edwardian period, open-air meetings led

---

[73] 'TLWW', *W* 27 (1897), 4.

[74] Rea, *David Rea*, 60, 105, 142-3, 159, 227.

[75] Hempton and Hill, *Evangelical Protestantism*, 188-9.

[76] On Crosbie and Bland, see Pickering (ed.), *Chief Men*, 62-4, 89-93.

[77] Cf. a report in 1957 of opposition, led by a priest, to outreach in Cork (*PS* 8.5 (March-April 1957), 183-4).

by Commander Salwey were defended by the police, many of whom were converted; however, he was eventually expelled from Ireland on account of his persistence in such activity.[78] More often, such methods were deemed inadvisable because of the opposition which they could arouse. Brethren shared the whole Protestant community's sense of isolation and apprehension, which was strengthened by the gathering political and civil unrest, and many assemblies shrank or disappeared from the late nineteenth century onwards as members emigrated to safer areas.

6.1.3 Success in England and Wales

Although a striking precedent for Brethren assemblies existed in North-West Wales early in the nineteenth century, in the form of a group of churches with Scotch Baptist affinities and premillennial convictions led by J.R. Jones of Ramoth,[79] the first assembly in South Wales for whose existence we have firm evidence was founded in Cardiff in 1852.[80] By the mid-1930s, when Beattie was writing the articles for *The Believer's Magazine* on which his book was based, there were to be about two dozen assemblies in Cardiff, and eighty-five in the whole of South Wales.[81] Although the 1859 revival had its main impact among the Welsh-speaking community, and in subsequent decades Nonconformity functioned as the bearer of Welsh culture, Brethren assemblies founded in the following years were almost entirely English-speaking, and in urban South Wales. It seems, therefore, that the Brethren presence in the principality owed more to English revivalism than to Welsh revival.[82] It is noticeable that the rapid growth of the South Wales coal mining industry from the middle of the century was followed a generation later by Brethren growth.

The impact of the 1904 revival is not easy to assess, and it is indeed possible that the movement largely passed the assemblies by; the periodicals made less mention than one might have expected of its Welsh manifestations. Some assemblies entered the address list for the first time after 1904, and these may owe something to that movement, but of those for which founding dates are available, many more owe their origins to revivalist activity and suburban migration during the 1920s.

---

[78] Ruth Salwey, *The Beloved Commander* (London: Marshall, Morgan & Scott, 1962), 46, 60.

[79] No links are known between these congregations and Brethren, but Brethren saw them as another precedent for their own way of gathering. Some associated with the Disciples of Christ, and others with the Baptist Union of Wales (cf. J. Emlyn Jones, 'Primitive Christianity in Wales', *H* 12 (1935), 39-40, 62, 100-1, 121, 141-2).

[80] This was the assembly later known as Adamsdown Hall (E.C. P[robert], *Sesquicentenary of Gospel Work and Witness. Adamsdown Gospel Hall, Clyde Street, Cardiff. 1852-2002* (n.pl: n.p., 2002), 6).

An assembly may have existed in Wales before 1852. An evangelist whom Tregelles met in 1844 and corresponded with thereafter, the bard Eben Fardd, adopted Brethren views and translated his *The Blood of the Lamb and the Union of Saints* into Welsh. Even before they met, both were in contact with Dr John Pugh (Ioan ap Huw Feddyg) of Aberdyfi, who was already associated with Brethren (Fromow, *Newton and Tregelles,* 32-4; T.C.F. Stunt to the author, 3 March 2004, following E.G. Millward, 'Eben Fardd a Samuel Prideaux Tregelles', *National Library of Wales Journal,* Winter 1952, 344).

[81] Beattie, *Brethren,* 162.

[82] Cf. Orr, *Awakening,* 91-2.

We turn now to look at the movement's growth in England. Snapshots for London are provided by the 1851 Religious Census, another conducted in 1887,[83] and the work of Richard Mudie-Smith, who co-ordinated the conduct of a third during 1902-3.[84] The last of these, which was the most thorough, indicated that generally Nonconformist strength was concentrated in upper working-class and middle-class suburbs;[85] Brethren assemblies, however, were distributed fairly evenly, apart from the wealthy and fashionable areas, but were strongest in lower-middle class districts, with a marked concentration in North and North-East London, where this period saw massive expansion in suburban housing provision. Here John Morley played a strategic role, bringing in some of the revival preachers, and introducing leaders to one another.[86] In 1867 he was responsible for the commencement of an assembly in the Iron Room at Clapton, which by 1879 had grown to 400 and by 1888 to over 700. This was one of several large assemblies which flourished in the wake of the Moody and Sankey campaigns.[87] Among those in fellowship or who preached there regularly were itinerants such as Denham Smith, Shuldham Henry, and C. Russell Hurditch (1839-1918), while from 1880 to 1900 M'Vicker functioned as a pastor, and appears to have been responsible for much of the ministry: in 1887, he was preaching the gospel each Sunday and expounding 1 Corinthians each Friday.[88] Clapton was the first link in a chain of assemblies: along with the Leyton assembly (which began in the early 1880s), it was responsible for the commencement of work at Folkestone Road, Walthamstow, in 1884 (which grew to 350 members within four years), and this assembly initiated another nearby at Higham Hill around 1900. Each of these in turn planted others in its locality. To some extent, this process was facilitated by the outward migration of the working classes to the new suburbs, assisted by the intensive suburban services operated by the Great Eastern Railway. But the evangelistic zeal and vision of these assemblies must also be honoured. South of the Thames, there was only one assembly (an Exclusive gathering at Kennington), until William Lincoln (1825-1888), the Anglican minister of Beresford Chapel in Walworth, seceded in 1862 and was baptised at a nearby Baptist chapel.[89] As well as publishing the address delivered upon his secession, he produced a lengthy apologia, *The Javelin of Phinehas*, which delineated from an eschatological perspective what he saw as the evils of the state-church system. His adoption and implementation of Brethren views was a gradual process, probably hastened by some of his flock who moved faster than he did, objected to his continuing domination of the worship, and seceded in 1864 to form an assembly at Camberwell.[90] Although Beresford Chapel did achieve recognition as a Brethren assembly, Lincoln insisted on controlling the preaching, and

---

[83] Anon., *The Religious Census of London* (London: Hodder and Stoughton, 1888).

[84] Richard Mudie-Smith, *The Religious Life of London* (London: Hodder and Stoughton, 1904).

[85] Hugh McLeod, *Class and Religion in the Late Victorian City* (London: Croom Helm, 1974), 27.

[86] Coad, *History*, 175.

[87] Rowdon, 'Brethren Identity', 168.

[88] Coad, *History*, 167, 175; [Reich] (ed.), *M'Vicker*, 145 (letter of 9 March 1887).

[89] On Lincoln, see Anon., 'Notes of the Life and Ministry of Mr. William Lincoln', *EH* 3 (1888), 84-7; Beattie, *Brethren*, 88-90; Coad, *History*, 177; William Lincoln, *Address ... to the Congregation of Beresford Episcopal Chapel, Walworth, On Sunday Evening, November 23rd, 1862, upon the occasion of his Quitting the Communion of the Established Church* (London: James Paul, [1862]); Pickering (ed.), *Chief Men*, 107-10; Timothy C.F. Stunt, 'William Lincoln', *W* 101 (1971), 166-9.

[90] A. Stunt, C. Morgan, and F. Stunt to W. Lincoln, 14 October 1864 (typed transcript, CBA Box 162(348)); T.C.F. Stunt to F.R. Coad, 13 June 1968 (CBA Box 165).

doing most of it himself, always providing a biblical exposition at the Breaking of Bread.

By 1874, there were eighteen Open assemblies in the London postal area, but there were over thirty Exclusive meetings in London with an estimated 3,000 in fellowship.[91] The main period of Open Brethren expansion was to follow: by 1904, assemblies were scattered throughout much of the new suburban developments which ringed the capital, as well as the older belt which lay immediately outside the area covered by the cities of London and Westminster; in total, there were 80 assemblies in the London postal area and a further fifteen in Middlesex, much of which was by now absorbed into the metropolis.

In Bristol, a group of assemblies grew up, centred on Bethesda, several with men who served as pastors; some were linked by a united oversight which met each week.[92] Between 1850 and 1875, membership of this group of assemblies grew from 600 to 1,000.[93] One offshoot, Unity Chapel (founded during the 1850s and exhibiting some affinities with Baptist churches[94]), grew to over 500 members by the end of the century before contracting under the searching ministry of G.H. Lang (1874-1958).[95] Tent missions conducted by J.A. Vicary resulted in the formation of assemblies at St Paul's (1875), Lawrence Hill (1880), Totterdown (c.1880), Bishopston (1886), and Horfield (c.1905). By contrast, Bethesda's central location would result in decline, with under a hundred in fellowship by 1914.[96]

Initially, the movement continued to expand in its rural strongholds of East Anglia and the South-West; probably the highest concentration of assemblies in the world was in Devon, where as many as ninety Open gatherings may have been in existence by the time of Chapman's death in 1902. But from the 1870s onwards it also established quite a strong presence in London and the industrial areas of the West Midlands, Lancashire, Yorkshire and the North-East. For example, by 1904 there were twenty-five assemblies in the Greater Manchester area (from Stockport in the south to Oldham and Bolton in the north), distributed throughout the city, suburbs, and surrounding towns; in Liverpool and the Wirral, there were eighteen assemblies by the same date. This reflects the fact that Brethrenism was becoming much more of an urban movement. Indeed, Britain as a whole was becoming more of an urban (or perhaps suburban) society: the proportion of the population living in towns and cities rose from 48.3% in 1841 to 70.2% in 1881.[97]

This shift in the centre of gravity was accentuated as the movement in England faced rural decline whose consequences were potentially as serious as those of emigration from Scottish and Irish assemblies. A downturn in the agricultural sector of the economy from the 1870s meant that many village assemblies were struggling as a result of the loss of their most able members, often skilled artisans such as millers, blacksmiths, shoemakers, or tailors, who moved to the towns in search of employment. A survey in 1913 noted the decline of village life during the preceding three or four decades and the resulting poverty of many assemblies. Whilst they had not been as badly hit as many rural chapel communities because they were less dependent on the assistance offered by

---

[91] Darby to Mr P., January 1874 (BGT folder 15, f.19).

[92] See Linton and Linton, '*I Will Build my Church*', ch. 3.

[93] *Ibid.*, 36.

[94] Orr, *Awakening*, 107.

[95] Linton and Linton, '*I Will Build my Church*', 40. On Lang, see *H* 37 (1958), 186-7; *W* 88 (1958), 253-4; G.H. Lang, *An Ordered Life: An autobiography* (London: Paternoster, 1959).

[96] Linton and Linton, '*I Will Build my Church*', 58.

[97] Geoffrey Best, *Mid-Victorian Britain 1851-75* (London: Fontana, 1979), 24.

the larger town congregations, the writer of the survey called for a change of approach, urging itinerant workers to go where there was no guarantee of finance or fellowship, and calling for settled pastors who would preach by action as well as word.[98]

6.2   Evangelistic   Strategies

In the 1851 Religious Census returns, Brethren who gave their building any name usually included the words 'Room' or 'Chapel'. The introduction of 'Gospel Hall' as a title for many assembly premises was a result of 1859 and the revivalism which attempted to perpetuate it.[99] Its great advantage was held to be that the working classes who would not enter a traditional place of worship because of its respectability would feel free to attend a service in a Gospel Hall. This change in nomenclature reflects a change in the movement's ethos. The first generation was made up to a considerable extent of seceders from other churches. After 1859, such secessions continued to occur, especially when the movement first took root in a particular region, and a number of assemblies owed their existence to such movement, but at the same time we see a much greater emphasis on evangelism. From being a movement whose most obvious distinguishing characteristic was perhaps the intense discussion of theological issues, Open Brethren became a movement whose primary *raison d'être* was evangelism.

Spontaneous growth, in which a meeting was formed without contact with the wider movement, did occur from time to time. The stress laid upon this by older historians may arise from a desire to give due weight to the Spirit's work in the movement; however, it risks under-emphasising three factors: the climate in which the movement emerged, which made it likely that such 'spontaneous' growth would take place, the existence of a network of links between evangelists, and the evidence that certain revivalist strategies were widely and successfully deployed.

6.2.1 Planting New Assemblies

Beattie's book demonstrates a recurring pattern, in which evangelistic meetings in a locality led to a regular outreach being established by a neighbouring assembly and eventually the formation of an independent assembly. While widespread, this was by no means the only way in which Brethren assemblies came into existence. Of the assemblies commenced during this period, I have been able to establish the causes for the founding of about 650. New assemblies could result from an evangelistic campaign (190), longer-term outreach (193), migration (41; often in search of employment), planting by another local assembly (79), secession from the denominations (78), accessions from Exclusive Brethren (34), or schism (26).

We have already seen how church planting by local assemblies proved successful in North-East London. This method of expansion was particularly suited to urban areas, where distances involved were not great and a close watch could be kept on the new work. Such initiatives were sometimes undertaken when an assembly had grown to the extent that it was likely that members would become less involved in the work: in such circumstances, it was often deemed more fruitful to dismiss a group to form a new

---

[98] 'A Village Worker', 'Village Work. – A Survey', *Counties Quarterly*, 1913 no. 4, 26-7.

[99] Coad, *History*, 185. Other bodies, such as undenominational missions, also used the title; this illustrates the difficulty of identifying which gatherings counted as Brethren assemblies.

assembly elsewhere, especially if they had been travelling from another community.[100]
Doing this also made space for further accessions to the parent gathering. For example,
groups were dismissed from Elim Hall in Glasgow to start new assemblies in 1903, 1904,
1909, 1911, 1917, and 1932; yet as late as the 1940s there were still 400 in
fellowship.[101] Outreach might be undertaken for several years, and premises acquired,
before 'a table was set up' (i.e. the Breaking of Bread began to be observed) and an
assembly formed.

Such clusters of assemblies could also appear in rural areas on occasion. For example,
in the Aylesbury area, the work of John Elphinstone Taylor (1843-1912), founder of the
Buckinghamshire Mission, resulted in the foundation of eight assemblies between 1875
and 1900.[102] Taylor is otherwise unknown to us, a representative of the many unsung
heroes to whom assemblies owed their inception, and a reminder that the story of
Brethren must not be reduced to biographies of the 'big names'. In Surrey, Dr Sydney
Austin left the Church of England and commenced an assembly at Lingfield in 1875.[103]
Under his guidance, it engaged in outreach to many surrounding villages and hamlets; of
these, assemblies later appeared at Tatsfield (1887), Westerham (by 1888), Crockham
Hill (fl.1897), Oxted (1897), Nutley (1898), Blindley Heath (fl.1904), Crawley (1905),
Crowhurst Lane End, Edenbridge (1907), and Staffords (or Staffhurst) Wood, Limpsfield
(by 1921). Some were founded by others, but it seems likely that they built on Austin's
work.

One of the most frequent causes of the creation of a new assembly was the evangelistic
campaign, sometimes conducted in a public building but often using a tent. Tent
campaigns could prove quite a draw, especially in rural areas, evoking the kind of interest
otherwise associated with such attractions as travelling circuses. In these, as in other
methods of pioneer evangelism, it was seen as best for the evangelists to work in pairs
rather than alone. Apart from the existence of precedent for this in the mission of the
Seventy (Luke 10.1), it provided mutual support. These missions often resulted in the
formation of assemblies composed of new converts, along with a leavening of mature
believers drawn by the life and teaching of the movement, for which evangelistic
campaigns could act as a 'shop window'. Reports of evangelistic meetings in the 1890s
often mentioned not only professions of faith, but believers exercised regarding
separation from their churches. Such work was put on a more organised basis from the late
1890s, as assemblies in particular areas banded together to support such work.

Individuals or couples might begin outreach work on their own initiative when
moving to a new area, as at Stanwick in Northamptonshire during the 1890s, or as a result
of observing assembly practice elsewhere; for instance, the assembly at Cockenzie, near
Edinburgh, began in 1884 after fishermen from the community, away with their boats,
had visited assemblies at Lerwick and Peterhead: some were baptised, and on their return
set about replicating what they had seen.[104]

Secession was another way in which assemblies might come into existence.
Sometimes individual Brethren were responsible for giving clearer light to meetings of

[100] 'AC', *BM* n.s. 11 (1910), 94.

[101] Anon., *Elim Hall, centenary 1882-1982* ([Glasgow]: n.p., 1982).

[102] [C. Russell Hurditch], 'Notes for the Month', *FT* 17 (1899), 216; letter in *H* 57 (1978), 100.
Taylor worked in the county from around 1863 ('Opening of Willesden Hall', *FT* 11 (1893), 68).

[103] Anon., *The Work of the Lord in a Surrey Village: a testimony carried out at Lingfield, with a
short biographical sketch of Sydney Charles Austin* (London: Pickering & Inglis, n.d. [1925]).

[104] Anon., 'How It Began. Cockenzie – Port Seton', *PS* 5.7 (July-August 1953), 195-6.

believers, which resulted in their adopting Brethren views and practices and beginning outreach in their locality. Group secessions, often following times of revival blessing in the parent church, could also lead to the formation of an assembly, as at Gateshead (1870), Carlisle (founded in 1873 after the Presbyterian William Reid's preaching had attracted Christians from other churches, leading to revival and then a secession to form the assembly, which he later joined[105]), Sunderland (c.1875), and Warrington (1883). An unusual case was the assembly at Galston, Ayrshire, formed around 1870: here Primitive Methodists had migrated from Cornwall for employment reasons; their lay ethos, and their isolation from the rest of their denomination, freed them to study the Scriptures for themselves, with the result that they began to adopt Brethren views. The crisis was precipitated when one member advocated Christadelphian ideas, and those who rejected such teaching formed the nucleus of a Brethren assembly.[106] Secessions from interdenominational bodies, such as 'Christian Unions' (of which more later), might also produce an assembly, as at Kilbirnie (1889).

Occasionally, the secession might be from an existing assembly, as at Adam Street, Belfast, in 1892. This could be an acrimonious business, with implications for surrounding assemblies as they considered whether they could receive those from each side of the dispute; thus announcements of the institution of new assemblies often included the words 'commenced in fellowship with' and the name of the parent gathering(s). More often, secessions were the fruit of teaching meetings, often in a neutral venue, aimed at Christians who belonged to the sects or 'systems', as Brethren often called them. These would feature teaching on Brethren distinctives, the objective being to persuade believers to leave their churches and associate with those gathered to the Lord's name alone. Ritchie appears to have seen such meetings as a healthy contrast to the tendency of interdenominational workers to suppress contentious aspects of truth. Reporting a series of lectures on the Tabernacle given in Kilmarnock which attracted believers from all churches, he claimed: 'We find that preaching the whole truth does not *drive* the people away as is generally supposed; it *draws* all who are worth having.'[107] Men such as William Kelly could draw vast crowds to their lectures, which were often published. Smaller reading meetings might be arranged in homes, as at Hinton St George in Somerset, where in 1863 the rector's widow invited the scholar and teacher Thomas Newberry (1811-1901) to give Bible readings; these continued each week for a year, and covered issues such as baptism, the Breaking of Bread, and church truth, resulting in an assembly being formed.[108] Such meetings might attract believers who would not dream of entering another church.[109] Underlying this activity during later decades was the belief expressed by Rendle Short that in a day of increasing apostasy, believers would have to stand together, and the hope that Brethren could therefore receive considerable accessions

---

[105] Beattie, *Brethren*, 192-3.

[106] John S. Borland, *History of the Brethren movement in Galston. On the occasion of the jubilee of the opening of the Evangelistic Hall On November 26, 1898* (Kilmarnock: n.p., 1948); idem, '"How it Started". Error led them to the Truth', *PS* 5.6 (May-June 1953), 161-2.

[107] 'TLWW', *BM* 5 (1895), 60.

[108] F.G. Russell, 'How it Started: Hinton St George', *PS* 4.4 (September-October 1951), 111-12. On Newberry, see Pickering (ed.), *Chief Men*, 80-2; Veitch, *Story*, 72.

[109] For a description of such a meeting, see Andrew Miller, *The Brethren: a brief sketch of their Origin, Progress and Testimony* (London: G. Morrish, [c.1879]), ch. 2.

from other denominations.[110] Sadly, by the time he wrote, the numbers of such accessions were already declining.

6.2.2 Evangelistic Methods

Although the assembly at Hereford did not split in the wake of the Bethesda controversy, it did divide in 1850, ostensibly over whether Sunday evening meetings should be devoted to gospel preaching or to teaching for believers; Percy Hall, whose evangelistic zeal appears to have declined somewhat, took the latter view, and set up another meeting.[111] Whilst many assemblies had Sunday evening gospel meetings before 1859,[112] it is likely that the revival and attempts to perpetuate it led to the practice becoming more widespread. Evangelistic activity rapidly came to centre on this meeting, which was regarded as the assembly's united testimony. Other evangelically-minded denominations also adopted the practice, which was facilitated by the introduction of gas lighting in urban streets. Huge congregations could be attracted: at Walthamstow in the late 1880s up to 1,000 would attend, and that in an assembly which had only existed for a few years.[113] Gospel meetings proved attractive to some of the working classes whom Mann's Census report had noted as indifferent to organised religion and resentful of approaches which reinforced their own sense of social inferiority. At Eastbourne from about 1871, a Miss Brodie (the daughter of a previous rector) and her brother gathered people in a school and talked, rather than preached, the gospel. Such down-to-earth gospel proclamation in everyday language attracted many who found it easier to understand than the sermons of the local Anglican clergy, and in due time an assembly resulted.[114]

There might be more than one address in a gospel meeting; at Bearwood in Birmingham in the late nineteenth century it was not unusual to have two, followed by three more addresses in the open air. However, the question of whether the preacher should prepare beforehand, arising from the spontaneous or 'impulsive' approach to ministry advocated by Darby and others, provoked some debate. One writer warned against making this a cover for a slapdash approach, but considered that no rules could be laid down for or against the practice of speaking without prior preparation. If a speaker was soaked in Scripture and filled with the Spirit, he would speak to profit even if he had not had time to prepare beforehand.[115] Another fruit of this concept, open meetings, at which no arrangements were made as to who should speak, died out fairly rapidly, and their passing was rarely mourned: 'by far the greatest number of those who contend for open meetings for gospel preaching, are persons whose only chance of securing an audience, is to take advantage of the opportunities such meetings afford.'[116] It came to be

---

[110] [Short], *"Open Brethren"*, 99-100.

[111] Beattie, *Brethren*, 38-9.

[112] The 1851 Religious Census recorded attendances at morning, afternoon, and evening services; of the 132 locations identified as Brethren, 103 had an evening service (Mann, *Census*, Table L).

[113] *EH* 3 (1888), 117; T.H. Morris, 'The Work of the Lord at the Queen's Road Hall, Walthamstow', *EH* 3 (1888), 161.

[114] Beattie, *Brethren*, 130; Victor G. Walkley, *A Church set on a Hill: the story of Edgmond Hall, Eastbourne 1872-1972* (Eastbourne: Upperton Press, 1972), 10-12.

[115] 'QA', *NW* 11 (1881), 47.

[116] [John Ritchie], 'Gospel Meetings', *BM* 3 (1893), 44; cf. [A.M. Sparks?], 'Pre-Arrangement in Gospel Meetings', *EH* 6 (1891), 1-2.

widely recognised that the principles which should guide the assembly in its meetings for worship and ministry were not applicable to gospel meetings. However, the Welsh Revival, in which unplanned meetings were the norm, may have given this approach a temporary boost as some assemblies sought to turn what began spontaneously into a regular custom.[117]

A more frequent source of problems was the placing of responsibility for inviting speakers into the hands of one individual, who might fail to take care that no speakers would undercut the assembly's distinctive doctrinal and ecclesiastical position, whose chosen speakers might be of such poor calibre as to drive away potential hearers, or who might introduce devices such as choirs and musical instruments which were not acceptable to the assembly.[118] This practice sprang from the belief that the gospel meeting was not an assembly meeting, strictly speaking, and that as an evangelistic activity it was the concern of individuals so burdened: minute books from the 1880s onwards occasionally record requests from individuals to be allowed the use of the assembly's premises for such meetings. Eventually it became widely accepted that such meetings were the responsibility of the assembly as a whole; all believers were encouraged to play a part, whether publicly or by prayer and personal contact with the unsaved.[119] Some assemblies, particularly in Northern Ireland but also in Scotland, held a series of nightly gospel meetings for a week or two each year, preceded by preparation and led by full-time evangelists.

It was a point of honour in assembly life to 'take nothing from the Gentiles' (cf. 3 John 7), and so no collection would be taken at meetings where unsaved folk were expected.[120] But assemblies were less agreed about the use of music in the services. At one extreme was the opinion that only Christians could sing hymns, either to, or in the presence of, unsaved folk, who should not be asked to sing what was not true in their own experience; thus gospel meetings should be confined to Bible readings, prayers, addresses, and an invitation to remain behind for conversation on spiritual matters.[121] Music might attract crowds but, it was argued, it was unable to convert sinners; great danger lay in its capacity to evoke a merely emotional response which could harden individuals against the gospel.[122] But most assemblies did sing, and from the 1860s publishers produced a succession of hymnbooks designed for such meetings, although many assemblies preferred to adopt *Sacred Songs and Solos*, which had been compiled by Sankey during the 1873-5 campaigns in Britain.[123] He had started the fashion for massed choirs in evangelism, and his book was widely used throughout the Evangelical world. Some assemblies, especially after the turn of the century, went so far as to include musical items in gospel meetings. However, some mission halls, especially in Scotland, which joined the Brethren closed down brass bands and other similar musical groups, believing that these were unscriptural.[124]

In later decades, it was recognised that assemblies would have to work to maintain interest and attendance at gospel meetings, especially as churchgoing was beginning to

---

[117] 'ASQ', *BM* n.s. 6 (1905), 59-60.

[118] Cf. *W* 33 (1903), 98-9.

[119] 'ASQ', *BM* n.s. 11 (1910), 47-8.

[120] *BM* 4 (1894), 10; 'AC', *BM* 8 (1898), 106.

[121] 'QA', *NW* 11 (1881), 143.

[122] 'YBQB'; *BM* 4 (1894), 57.

[123] John S. Andrews, 'Brethren Hymnology' (typescript, [1990]), 5-7; Coad, *History*, 186.

[124] Dickson, *Brethren in Scotland*, 154-5.

decline. The need for halls to be comfortable and well-lit was often stressed, as was the value of open-air work and literature distribution in connection with the meetings. Publishers offered an overprinting service for assemblies, whereby leaflets or evangelistic monthlies could include the times of meetings and an invitation to attend. All the same, the problem of gospel meetings with no unsaved present began to appear. One suggested solution was to visit local people to find out why they did not attend, and rectify anything relating to the room in which the meeting was held, its location, or the quality of the preaching.[125] Another sign that evangelism was not proving as effective as it had done is that from the 1890s, reports of outreach work begin to record, in default of any more encouraging results, that 'saints were helped'.

From about 1890, there are signs of nostalgia for earlier days, brought on in part by a perceived shallowness in contemporary evangelism, which was sometimes compared with the deep conviction of sin manifest in 1859. Leaders began to recognise the problem of unsaved individuals in assembly fellowship. Behind this development was seen the hand of Satan, seeking to fill assemblies with lifeless professors who gained access because standards had been lowered. An unsigned letter to *The Witness* on 'New Methods' lamented the replacement of Bible exposition by anecdotes (a feature of Moody's preaching) and the recounting of pre-conversion experiences 'which were better forgotten as they have been forgiven'. The aim seemed to be to make services bright rather than soul-searching, but '"A happy evening" is about the last thing an unconverted soul needs, and about the last thing he would get were Paul the preacher.' Furthermore, sensationalism acted like a drug, the dose needing continual increase; the result was indifference to spiritual things.[126] It was also alleged that there was now a far higher proportion of spurious responses, the fruit of adopting new and unscriptural methods.[127] Some, notably Ritchie in *The Believer's Magazine*, began to distinguish between revival (which awakened Christians first of all) and revivalism (got up by human effort).[128] What was needed to secure divine blessing was a return to prayer, preaching, separation and vital fellowship.

A variation on the gospel meeting was the 'Gospel Tea Meeting'. The urban underclasses could be reached by such means as free meat teas followed by a gospel address, evidence that Brethren were aware, like William Booth, that it was useless to expect attention to the gospel from a man with an empty stomach. However, while some Brethren outreach to the poor was well-received, some seems to have been either *de haut en bas* or undertaken by the poor themselves (as in many of the working-class assemblies founded in Scotland following the revival); there is relatively little evidence that class barriers were effectively surmounted in fellowship or evangelism. Brethren may have been radical in some ways, but they remained socially quite conservative, and this limited the effectiveness of their evangelism. In addition, nineteenth-century Evangelical religion provided an avenue of upward social mobility, as converts from the lower classes would have sought to better themselves; it is noticeable how many self-taught Bible scholars there were in assemblies.

Once the Religious Worship Act of 1855 allowed religious meetings to be held in places other than churches or buildings specifically licensed for worship, neutral venues,

---

[125] 'AC', *BM* 9 (1899), 35, cf. 9.94.

[126] Anon., 'New Methods', *W* 19 (1889), 92-3.

[127] George Adam, 'Power for Service', *W* 37 (1907), 64; [John Ritchie?], 'The Gospel and Modern Evangelisation', *BM* 9 (1899), 121-3.

[128] John Ritchie, 'Revival. II. – Where and How Revival Begins', *BM* n.s. 3 (1902), 97.

such as theatres, provided another opportunity of reaching those who would never be induced to enter a Gospel Hall.[129] Revivalists of all denominations used such facilities, Brethren among them. One series of meetings, conducted by the Canadian evangelist J.J. Sims in Glasgow during 1893, filled St Andrew's Hall (the largest venue in the city) with over 4,000 people, and was noted as different in character and size from any previous Brethren outreach.[130] Such large-scale ventures would become a prominent feature of Brethren evangelism in the years after the First World War. Meetings might also be held in homes, schools and churches, though critics often warned ministers against being too ready to grant permission for Brethren evangelists to use their premises and thus gain an entry to the congregation.

Many individuals and assemblies engaged in open-air work. In Glasgow, for example, workers from a number of assemblies banded together to travel to a different village each Saturday, suitable trains being intimated in the pages of *The Witness*. More frequently, assemblies would hold open air meetings before the gospel meeting, using them as a means of attracting folk in. Open-air work often attracted hecklers, and in the 1890s meetings at Bearwood, Smethwick, had to be moved to ground owned by the assembly after political agitators caused disruption.[131] A variation on the theme of open-air work was provided by baptismal services: assemblies which lacked their own baptistry could turn the lack into an evangelistic opportunity, as baptisms often took place in rivers or at the sea, thus guaranteeing an audience of curious spectators.

The foundation of all evangelism was seen to be personal witness, and believers were encouraged to buy up every opportunity. In the mid-1850s, it was Emily Gosse's habit, according to her son, to engage in personal evangelism. Although terminally ill with cancer, she 'scarcely ever got into a railway carriage or into an omnibus, without presently offering tracts to the persons sitting within reach of her, or endeavouring to begin a conversation with someone of the sufficiency of the Blood of Jesus to cleanse the human heart from sin'.[132] She was also a noted writer of evangelistic tracts. Tract distribution was, for Brethren as for other Evangelicals, a favourite means of personal evangelism, and Brethren publishers turned out vast quantities in all shapes and sizes. In the late 1880s, Ritchie suggested the formation of 'Tract Distribution Bands', and was pleased to report that five years later, he knew of over 250 such bands in association with assemblies in Britain.[133] From about 1900, around large cities such as London and Glasgow, groups of young believers might engage in outreach work on Saturday afternoons, banding together to undertake tract distribution and open air work. Whilst this kind of work was rarely enough by itself to lead to the formation of an assembly, it may have helped prepare the ground for more intensive work by itinerant evangelists. Longer tours were undertaken from the 1880s by groups of young men led by Ritchie: each summer, a particular county would be selected, and the group would move from place to place, distributing tracts, visiting homes, and holding open-air meetings, for which the minimum of notice would be given so that the clergy had no chance to hinder the work![134]

---

[129] Cf. Bradley, *Call to Seriousness*, 58.

[130] 'TLWW', *W* 24 (1894), 1, 19.

[131] Barton, *Bearwood*, 13.

[132] Edmund Gosse (ed. Peter Abbs), *Father and Son: A study of two temperaments* (Harmondsworth, Middlesex: Penguin, 1983), 70. On Emily Gosse (1806-57), see *ODNB*.

[133] *BM* 3 (1893), 46.

[134] [John Ritchie?], 'Village Work', *EH* 3 (1888), 102.

The tracts used varied from the fairly traditional to what can only be described as tasteless novelties. There were tracts for use on the train; at race meetings and football matches; outside public houses, theatres and dance halls; during elections; for formalists and infidels: in fact, tracts for every conceivable occasion. Among the latter were Gospel coins, brass tokens with texts stamped on them: 'Being metal, they cannot be torn up or used to light the fire with, but must remain about the house as a persistent, silent messenger, with indelible words of warning and of grace.'[135] Another report referred to an individual buying a supply of envelopes and overprinting them, 'This is for you. Please open and read'; these were then filled with tracts and flung from the window of a train as it passed by isolated houses.[136] In similar vein, the evangelist John Knox M'Ewen described his bicycle tours, in the course of which 'I go through the villages blowing my whistle and scattering tracts broadcast'.[137] More often, they were left on park benches, offered to fellow train-travellers, or distributed in connection with open-air work. Text posters, too, were used, and some Brethren were evidently not above fly-posting: one worker carried a supply of posters, paste, and a brush, to place them on walls, fences, or trees.[138]

FIXING "WAYSIDE WORDS ON A TREE.
An incident of frequent occurrence during the Gospel Tours.

Charles Morton (1849-1900) was one evangelist who engaged in flyposting, though it is questionable how many passers-by there would have been to read the posters being put up here

From the 1880s, horse-drawn 'Bible carriages', such as the Beulah Gospel Carriage and the Caledonian Bible Carriage, facilitated longer evangelistic forays. Workers would embark on a tour, lasting through the spring and summer, and as far into the autumn as the weather allowed. Moving from place to place, they would preach in the open air and distribute literature, the carriage serving as their living quarters for the duration. Something of the potential of such work can be gleaned from the report of one tour made by John Brunton in the Midlands and South Wales during 1887: in six months, he sold or

---

[135] Advertisement in *EH* 1 (January 1887), 15.

[136] *BM* 1 (1891), 70.

[137] 'TLWW', *W* 25 (1895), 84.

[138] *BM* 1 (1891), 82; cf. John Ritchie, 'Evangelistic Tour among the Villages', *NW* 10 (1880), 77-8.

distributed almost 15,000 Bibles and New Testaments, 55,000 gospels and other Scripture portions, and 77,000 wall cards, texts and biblical almanacs.[139] To support such workers, believers from nearby assemblies would join them at weekends. Folkestone Road, Walthamstow, even had an Evangelistic Cycling Club, formed to support the work of the assembly's 'gospel car'.[140]

Nobody looking at this carriage could fail to get the message!

In 1851, an estimated two million plus children, including 75% of working-class children aged five to ten, were enrolled in British Sunday Schools. Brethren made use of this means of outreach, but it is unlikely that Sunday schools ever became the focus of religious life in the way that they did in some Anglican and Nonconformist congregations in Northern England. Nevertheless, some assemblies could sustain enormous schools, such as that at the Octagon, Taunton, which at the turn of the century numbered over 1,000 children.[141] During the pre-war years, some evangelists found it increasingly difficult to reach adults, and so began to try contacting them through young people instead.[142] By this time there was also a growing recognition, even among more conservative assemblies, of the particular needs of children. For some in this category, who sought to follow the pattern of Scripture as closely as possible, children's work gave rise to great heart-searching in connection with the use of modern methods of communication. One correspondent in *The Witness* asked whether magic lanterns, acrostics and Bible word searches dishonoured the Word; did the Holy Spirit use the senses, or the Word only? Responses varied: one thought that such methods lacked Scriptural precedent and amounted to a profanation of the Word, while another defended them as aids to understanding and challenged critics to say what methods they used. John Ritchie pointed out that even adults found it helpful to examine models such as those of

---

[139] *EH* 3 (1888), 68.

[140] *FT* 13 (1895), 198.

[141] *LOH* 21 (1933), 78.

[142] E.g. *W* 43 (1913), 28.

the Temple (or, he might have added, the Tabernacle), and asked whether critics of such methods had ever tried to retain the attention of a group of children. However, the inquirer persisted in his objection, characterising such things as lacking Biblical principle, precept, or precedent.[143]

Outreach was also directed to other specific groups within the community. Mission to the rapidly-increasing Jewish population, for example, was carried on at Spitalfields in London,[144] as well as in Liverpool and Glasgow, from the late nineteenth century onwards. Student work also made its appearance in Bristol: in 1913, A. Rendle Short and W.R. Moore arranged a series of Sunday evening meetings for students, with large attendances.[145] By the end of the century, women's meetings also appear to have become quite widespread.

6.3   Evangelistic   Agencies

Although evangelism was often regarded as a matter of individual responsibility, and evangelistic meetings as not being strictly assembly meetings, the assembly became the primary evangelistic agency. However, there were a number of travelling evangelists who assisted the assembly in its outreach, and by the end of the century co-ordination and support agencies were beginning to appear.

6.3.1 Full-time Evangelists

In many ways, full-time evangelists and teachers provided the nearest thing to clerical leadership in the Brethren movement. The wealth of writing on the subject enables us to construct an ideal type of the late nineteenth-century Brethren evangelist: he would have proved his calling and gifting while still in secular employment, being then commended to the work by his home assembly; learning by apprenticeship to a more experienced itinerant, he would be a diligent Bible student (though not otherwise widely educated), a zealous visitor, and a solemn and passionate preacher; a man of individual initiative, but ready to work with another evangelist as often as possible, he would itinerate as led by God, staying or moving in accordance with the response to his message; he would take a position of separation from the religious systems of the world, and while not a 'religious professional' he would devote his whole time to the work, living 'by faith'.

However, it is possible to divide these evangelists into several overlapping sub-groups: those who settled in a particular locality, 'gentlemen evangelists' from a higher social class, those converted or active in the 1859 revival, those whose appeal was more popular, and those who belonged to Exclusive meetings. We shall examine each of these in turn, but in doing so it is important to remember that much evangelistic work was done by ordinary assembly members in their spare time.

A minority of evangelists continued the early pattern of settling in one place and working in and around it; a good example would be Major R.S. Tireman, who built up and pastored Unity Chapel in Bristol from the late 1850s.[146] However, most itinerated, often quite extensively. Itinerancy was a strength of the Brethren movement as much as it had been of the Methodist movement before it, in that these men did much to give assemblies

---

[143] *W* 19 (1889), 30, 46, 62, 77-8, 93.

[144] E.g. *W* 23 (1893), 46.

[145] *W* 43 (1913), 333.

[146] Linton and Linton, *'I Will Build my Church'*, 39-40.

a sense of cohesion arising from a common vision and understanding of Scripture. Nevertheless, the system did have significant weaknesses, especially when the itinerant was the one who decided where and for how long to work, rather than the assembly inviting him to work among them for a specific period: complaints were often voiced that smaller rural assemblies, who would often have valued help in outreach or lacked opportunities to receive solid teaching, tended to be overlooked, while assemblies in towns received repeated visits.[147] Another problem was that if an evangelist was in the habit of taking firm bookings for months ahead, it could happen that he might see the beginnings of blessing in a particular place but be unable to consolidate it because of a prior commitment elsewhere. Thus some preferred not to accept bookings but to move from place to place as they felt led, and to stay as long as God was blessing their labours; assemblies were free to communicate their need to these servants, but that was not treated as an invitation.[148]

Orr's analysis of the hundred individuals included in Pickering's *Chief Men among the Brethren* indicated that a third were converts of, or workers in, the 1859 revival.[149] Some were already members of the Brethren, while others joined soon afterwards, doubtless attracted by the lay ethos, flexibility and pragmatism, freedom to overleap denominational barriers, and scope for those of working class-background, which corresponded with the ethos of the revival; their accession would have helped to strengthen the orientation of assemblies towards mission.[150] However, there were some tensions as interdenominational revivalism came face-to-face with Brethren who had developed a distinctive identity apart from the denominations. The English evangelists in particular were willing to preach anywhere and to work through existing churches, and tended to avoid mentioning Brethren ecclesiological distinctives,[151] a fact which earned them criticism from the 'tighter' assemblies represented by *The Believer's Magazine*. Scottish evangelists were active in North-East England as well, imparting to the assemblies they founded something of the Scottish separatist flavour.

Coad suggests that the revival preachers fell into two types: gentlemen and popular, each with a ministry to a different audience.[152] At the hub of the network of gentleman preachers was one who never actually belonged to the Brethren himself, Reginald Radcliffe (1825-1895).[153] An Anglican from Liverpool, he advocated the adoption of the methods of Moody and Sankey,[154] and encouraged a number of evangelists who would associate with assemblies. Another was Gordon Forlong (1819-1908), who emigrated to New Zealand in 1876, but who had often worked alongside Brownlow North in Scotland during the 1859 revival.[155] He was instrumental in the conversion of a number of Brethren leaders, including Marshall and J.R. Caldwell (of whom more later). A third example was Russell Hurditch, who was responsible for planting a number of assemblies, mostly in London; several were marked in the 1897 assembly list as associated with the

---

[147] Cf. the letter from a small assembly in *W* 20 (1890), 28-9.

[148] 'AC', *BM* 8 (1898), 35, 70; [John Ritchie], 'It was too short', *BM* n.s. 10 (1909), 9.

[149] Orr, *Awakening*, 202.

[150] Cf. Dickson, *Brethren in Scotland*, 72.

[151] Dickson, 'Scottish Brethren', 14.

[152] Coad, *History*, 172-3.

[153] On Radcliffe, see *BDEB*; Mrs. Radcliffe, *Recollections of Reginald Radcliffe* (London: Morgan and Scott, [1895?]).

[154] G.C. Needham, *Recollections of Henry Moorhouse* (Chicago: F.H. Revell, 1881), 16.

[155] On Forlong, see Pickering (ed.), *Chief Men*, 68-9.

Evangelistic Mission, which he had founded in 1865. This body attracted cross-denominational support, even from Exclusive Brethren, and in some ways Hurditch could be regarded as part of the undenominational network rather than that of Brethren; not all his congregations were listed as assemblies.

Among the popular evangelists two stand out. John Hambleton (1820-89) had been a comedian before his conversion in 1851; encouraged by Radcliffe, he began preaching to a small group meeting in his house, who studied the Scriptures and evangelised, in time also breaking bread together.[156] Hambleton typifies the Brethren attitude towards the culture of their day: as a former actor, he was very negative towards the theatre and offered an aggressive witness at Stratford-upon-Avon's Shakespeare tercentenary celebrations in 1864. At his baptism (conducted by Hurditch in private grounds at Tunbridge Wells), 'when in the water, [he] testified against this Babylonish world, and against what appeared to him the evidences of it in the statuary in the grounds, and in the fountain in which he was being baptized'.[157] The other popular evangelist to note is Henry Moorhouse (1840-80): he was converted through the interdenominational evangelist Richard Weaver and introduced to evangelistic work through Hambleton, earning the nickname 'the boy preacher' because of his youthful appearance.[158] It is said that his emphasis on the love of God, especially in a series of sermons on John 3.16 preached in Moody's church in Chicago, had a significant impact on Moody's preaching. More importantly, he began Bible readings in the city which helped to mould the way that Moody and others in his network studied the Bible; Moorhouse also suggested that Sankey should accompany Moody on his first visit to Great Britain. These evangelists often worked interdenominationally, and so helped to link Open Brethren to the wider revivalist network.[159]

In Scotland, the evangelist who did most to shape the Brethren movement was Donald Ross (1824-1903). A member of the Free Church of Scotland, his evangelistic career took him to Aberdeen as the first superintendent of the North-East Coast Mission, founded in 1858 to reach the fishing communities. The antipathy of the clergy to lay preaching resulted in his thought taking on an increasingly anti-clerical cast, something which would be a prominent feature of the magazines he edited from 1870 onwards. Gradually he became convinced that something was radically wrong with the churches, but what was he to do with the converts? His first step was to resign as superintendent of the mission; in his letter of resignation, he intimated his intention of working inland, away from the mission, depending on God to supply his needs and answerable to no human board of directors. Several missionaries joined him, and the result was the formation of the 'Northern Evangelistic Society', which worked in Northern England as well as in Scotland.

The opposition he experienced was a factor in his growing disillusionment with the Free Church, and eventually he left it: its mixed membership of saved and unsaved, and its opposition to the work which he was doing (which was seeing plentiful conversions),

---

[156] On Hambleton, see John Hambleton, *Buds, Blossoms and Fruits of the Revival; a testimony to the great work of God in these last days* (London: Morgan & Chase, n.d.); Pickering (ed.), *Chief Men*, 101-4.

[157] *The Latter Rain* 3.131 (1 June 1870).

[158] On Moorhouse, see John Macpherson, *Henry Moorhouse: The English Evangelist* (London: Morgan and Scott, n.d.); Needham, *Moorhouse*; Pickering (ed.), *Chief Men*, 166-70.

[159] Cf. Holmes, *Religious Revivals*, 143.

meant that he no longer felt able to support it.[160] Ross's thinking was developing fast, and he dissolved the Northern Evangelistic Society, encouraging the evangelists to live by faith: 'The Northern Evangelists are henceforth individually to be dependent on Jesus only in their work.'[161] Exercised about the Breaking of Bread, he concluded that no ordained president was needed, and so began to meet with Brethren, probably about 1870. Some of Ross's evangelists appear to have taken this step before he did, and Open assemblies owing their existence to other workers had also appeared at both Aberdeen and Peterhead in 1868.[162] Almost immediately, Ross began to publish several monthlies, partly in order to make known what he was discovering about the state of Christendom and its opposition to the revival work. Ross was a forceful preacher, applying the message to his hearers and urging them to respond. Influenced by holiness teaching, he stressed the need for holiness as a precondition for revival. Yet he was also a firm Calvinist, described by another evangelist as 'the walking Shorter Catechism'.[163]

Another group of evangelists were converted before and during the 1859 revival in Ulster. James M'Quilkin was a weaver who spoke widely on the revival as its 'first convert'; like a number who joined the Brethren at this time, he found that an orthodox Calvinist upbringing had not given him a saving relationship with Christ, a fact which affected their attitudes towards the existing churches. M'Quilkin's first convert was Jeremiah Meneely, and they, with others, began to pray (inspired by Müller's testimony to answered prayer in his *Narrative*) for the Spirit to be poured out on the area around Ballymena where they lived.[164] Their prayers were answered when, early in 1859, at a meeting which some of them had convened, large numbers were brought under a deep sense of conviction of sin. One who was converted through these men was M'Vicker, who as a local Presbyterian minister was longing for spiritual vitality. He recollected that the Spirit worked for fifteen years to bring him to cease trusting in his own efforts and rely entirely upon God's promises, a period which ended with his conversion. Soon after, he was baptised by Meneely, adopted Brethren views, and was deposed from the ministry. Moving to London in 1879, he associated himself with the Clapton assembly, giving himself to teaching and pastoral work there until his death.

Exclusive Brethren had a number of effective evangelists as well. The former schoolmaster, C.H. Mackintosh (1820-96), of whom we shall say more in the next chapter as an author, was an active evangelistic preacher in Ireland during and after the 1859 revival. Others included George Cutting (1844-1934), author of the widely used booklet *Safety, Certainty and Enjoyment* ([c.1905]) W.T.P. Wolston (1840-1917), an Edinburgh doctor;[165] Andrew Miller (1810-83), who expressed his grief at the decline of evangelistic concern among the assemblies which he visited;[166] A.H. Burton (1853-1937), who chaired the 'Prophecy Investigation Society' and was a co-founder in 1917 of the 'Advent Testimony and Preparation Movement', both of which were

---

[160] Donald Ross, 'A Clear Statement', *W* 69 (1939), 5-6 (written c.1871). McIntosh (*New Prophets*, 19) quoted one of these evangelists as saying that 'The communion table sends more people to hell than all the distilleries in Scotland.'

[161] *NEI* 2 (1872), 64.

[162] Dickson, *Brethren in Scotland*, 98; *W* 60 (1930), 116.

[163] C.W.R[oss]. (ed.), *Donald Ross*, 130.

[164] Müller, *Autobiography*, 448-50.

[165] On Wolston, see Pickering (ed.), *Chief Men*, 141-2.

[166] On Miller, see *ibid.*, 74-6.

interdenominational in nature;[167] C.J. Davis (1842-70) of Aberdeen, who worked among peasants suffering as a result of the Franco-Prussian war, some of whose writings were collected after his death and issued by Open Brethren publishers from 1876 as *Aids to Believers*;[168] and Charles Stanley (1821-88) of Rotherham, author of a whole range of tracts and of a rather breathless account of his evangelistic encounters, *Incidents of Gospel Work: shewing, how the Lord hath led me* (first published in 1889).[169]

6.3.2 Evangelistic Organisations

The 1870s saw the development of Echoes of Service as a service agency for Brethren mission overseas, and it grew rapidly during the last two decades of the century. This acted as a catalyst for the realisation that needs were great in Britain also, especially in rural areas; many villages were perceived as sunk in ritualistic darkness (reflecting the rise in the proportion of High Church clergy in the Church of England). The planting of a new assembly at Hoxne in Suffolk in 1897 was reported as taking place amidst the not unusual combination of 'ritualism on the one hand and hyper-Calvinism on the other'.[170]

Awareness of the need led to calls for the creation of bodies to co-ordinate and resource mission at home. Early in 1899 a plea was made at the Leominster Conference for missionaries and other full-time workers by J.L. Maclean, one of the editors of *Echoes of Service* (in which a letter was subsequently published), who contrasted the zeal of assemblies in sending workers abroad with their comparative indifference to needs at home.[171] A businessman named William Page of Croxley Green, near Watford, discussed the need with Maclean and called a meeting in London for 4 May to discuss the possibility of co-ordinated outreach in London, Middlesex and Hertfordshire. The result was that the agency which later became known as Counties Evangelistic Work held its first campaign that summer. A similar meeting took place that day in Bristol, leading ultimately to the formation in 1904 of the Western Counties and South Wales Evangelization Trust, which also acted as a trustee for assembly property. News of outreach in the West of England and South Wales was shared through *Counties Quarterly*, a forerunner of *The Harvester*. Several other publications kept assemblies provided with information for prayer and practical action: *Counties Evangelization* (1899-1907 or later), *Evangelization of Eastern Counties* (1905-12), and *The South-Eastern Counties Evangelization* (1904-10 or later).[172]

Page stimulated similar efforts elsewhere by attending meetings, providing information and offering assistance. In 1900, the first gospel carriage was purchased for use in Essex; by 1905, there were eleven, and four tents, provided by Page. The 'South-Eastern Counties Evangelization' work began in 1904, covering Kent, Surrey, and Sussex. In the same year a similar venture in Hampshire, Berkshire, and Oxfordshire,

---

[167] On Burton, see F.W. Pitt (ed.), *Windows on the World: A record of the life of Alfred H. Burton B.A., M.D.* (London: Pickering & Inglis, n.d.).

[168] On Davis, see Noel, *History*, 134-5.

[169] On Stanley, see Pickering (ed.), *Chief Men*, 126-8.

[170] *W* 27 (March 1897), 57 (cover).

[171] Ernest H. Grant and A.A. Gibbs, 'South-Eastern Counties of England (Counties' Evangelistic Work)', *PS* 1.7 (November-December 1946), 69. Grant was secretary of this work from 1906-53.

[172] The only known copies of these are in the minute books of Counties, Westbury. For the history of the Counties works, see Brian Mills, *A Story to Tell: Evangelism in the Twentieth Century* (Carlisle: OM, 1999).

'South-Western Counties', began when Sir George Pigot had a gospel car built, William Page offered to provide another, and the fellowship of assemblies was sought.[173] Many assemblies responded readily, but not all: in 1904, Page issued a circular, *Evangelists and Assemblies*, urging the legitimacy of organisation for evangelistic purposes and alleging that objections to it sometimes cloaked a lack of concern for the lost.

Please Distribute in the Assembly. No. VIII., Jan. 1909.

Evangelization of Eastern Counties
(Essex, Suffolk, Norfolk, and Cambs.)

In fellowship with Assemblies of Christians gathered unto the Name of the Lord.

REPORT
OF
Summer Work, 1908.

The oversight of this work is in the hands of the following brethren, who from time to time take counsel together, and with the evangelists engaged in the work :

W. T. BILSON, *Leytonstone*.
A. BOAKE, *Loughton*.
E. J. BOAKE, *Loughton*.
B. BULLIMORE, *North Walsham*.
G. GOODMAN, *Woodford*.
J. HIXON IRVING.
A. M. KYD, *Clapton*.
HINDLEY JONES, *Southend-on-Sea*.
W. MARRIOTT, *Melton Constable*.
W. H. MATTHEWS, *Ilford*.

G. J. NEWTON, *Saffron Walden*.
A. PAGE, *Aylsham*.
W. S. PHILLIPS, *Fakenham*.
E. B. ROCHE (Dr), *Norwich*.
W. SMITH, *Gt Yarmouth*.
W. STAGG, *Ilford*.
W. STUNT (*HON. TREASURER*), *to whom contributions on behalf of the work may be sent, addressed Hillside, Springfield, Chelmsford*.

Publications such as this one included reports from evangelists as well as details of financial contributions. Although it was subtitled 'In fellowship with Assemblies', the overseeing brethren (here listed on the cover) were sometimes misunderstood as acting 'instead of assemblies'

Other similar initiatives were developing elsewhere. The Ayrshire Gospel Tent was first used in 1888, the practice being to arrange two six-week campaigns each year.[174] In England, Essex assemblies began to work together in evangelism about 1890, and those in Kent a few years later. Leading Suffolk brethren used to meet to discuss assembly matters, and their burden to reach the county's needy localities led to the decision in 1895

---

[173] *W* 64 (1934), 167.

[174] <www.ayrshiregospeloutreach.org.uk>, Ayrshire Gospel Outreach, accessed 3 April 2005.

to seek the fellowship of assemblies in providing and working a tent.[175] Six Yorkshire brethren issued a circular letter in 1899 to share with assemblies the conclusions of a meeting at Leeds: this had agreed that the best methods of outreach were visiting, open-air meetings and tent missions, and pointed to the challenges posed by Romanism, Spiritualism, and infidelity; working with only one tent and one carriage until 1927, twelve assemblies were planted in the county during that period.[176] These bodies sought to avoid infringing the autonomy of evangelists and assemblies; they did not direct the evangelists, but circulated reports, gathered information regarding needs and openings, and channelled funds. Christians were encouraged to give their Saturday afternoons and holidays to work alongside the evangelists. Assembly support, however, varied from area to area, being noticeably weaker in the Eastern Counties (perhaps because a Gospel carriage was already at work here). However, deputation meetings were soon found to be an effective means of stimulating interest.

All these initiatives were intended to lead to the formation of assemblies; the first which resulted was that at Uxbridge in 1899, and a number were founded in subsequent years. Evangelists would teach 'assembly truths' as well as proclaiming the Gospel, with this objective in view. In the next chapter, we shall examine how the movement was given a sense of cohesion, what it believed, and what assembly life was like.

---

[175] J.W. Ashby, 'Surveys of Service. Eastern Counties' Gospel Tent', *BM* n.s. 36 (1935), 92-4.

[176] H. Beaumont, *Seventy Five Years of Telling Yorkshire: a history of the Yorkshire Tent and Bible Carriage Work* ([Wyke, Bradford: the author, c.1974]), 2, 4.

CHAPTER 7

The Development of Open Brethren Identity

Brethren in the 1830s were probably not too bothered about finding a name for themselves, partly because they expected the Second Coming very soon, and partly because many of them really did see the gatherings to which they belonged as havens for all consistent believers. When they used the simple designation 'Brethren', they did so as a description rather than a title – 'brethren' with a small 'b'. 'Christian Brethren' appears to have first been used as a description of the movement as early as 1839.[1] Initially it would not have been used as a quasi-denominational title, nor in any sense which excluded other believers.

However, perhaps inevitably, there was a tendency to move from 'brethren' to 'Brethren' or even 'The Brethren'. Analysis of the titles used by Brethren meetings responding to the 1851 Religious Census bears this out. Of ninety-one returns (excluding duplicates), twenty-three used the designation 'Brethren', seventeen used only 'Christians', seventeen used 'Plymouth Brethren' (some adding 'Christians'), fourteen used 'Christian' and 'Brethren', and sixteen accepted no designation. Some of these labels were affixed by the local enumerators rather than the respondent for the assembly, and some respondents only used titles such as 'Plymouth Brethren' under protest. Half the returns I have been able to analyse came from Devon, where seventeen of the twenty-three occurrences of 'Brethren' were found, but apart from this it is not possible to detect any regional preference for one name rather than another.

The Census report highlighted a tension which has yet not been resolved to the satisfaction of all Brethren, and which has been reflected in the debates about nomenclature: for many, their only distinguishing principle was that they rejected any distinguishing principles which would separate them from other believers, but paradoxically they maintained a separation from bodies (and sometimes believers) which did not take the same stance.

> Those to whom this appellation is applied receive it only as descriptive of their individual state as Christians – not as a name by which they might be known collectively as a distinct religious *sect*. It is not from any common doctrinal peculiarity or definite ecclesiastical organization that they have the appearance of a separate community; but rather from the fact that, while all other Christians are identified with some particular *section* of the Church of God, the persons known as "Brethren" utterly refuse to be identified with any. Their existence is, in fact, a protest against all sectarianism; and the primary ground of their secession from the different bodies to which most of them have once belonged, is, that the various tests by which, in all these bodies, the community of true Christians with each other is prevented or impeded, are unsanctioned by the Word of God. They see no valid reason why the Church (consisting of all true believers) which is *really one*, should not be also *visibly* united, having as its only bond of fellowship and barrier of exclusion, the reception or rejection of those vital truths by which the Christian is distinguished from the unbeliever. ... The Brethren, therefore, may be represented as consisting of all such as,

---

[1] Coad, *History*, 160n.

practically holding all the truths essential to salvation, recognize each other as, on that account alone, true members of the only Church.[2]

In spite of the tendency of many such believers to accept the designation 'Brethren', giving any name to assemblies as a group was resisted by some writers as sectarian. Advising believers how to fill in the 1911 Census return, *The Believer's Magazine* told them not to give their religion as 'Brethren', which was sectarian, but as 'Christian'.[3] The name 'Plymouth Brethren' was explained as having first been used of the Brethren at Plymouth.[4] That being so, its use of assemblies elsewhere was seen as faintly ridiculous. Acceptance of the title 'Open Brethren' was seen as accepting a position on a level with the sects, and it was also argued that it had been coined by Exclusive Brethren in the context of charging assemblies with theological indifferentism. Believers were advised to refer to their assembly as 'Christians meeting in ____ Hall'.[5] However, many assemblies did come to exhibit, and often to cultivate, a distinctive and easily-recognisable identity. This chapter explores the means by which this was created and fostered.

7.1 Means to the Development of a 'Brethren' Identity
7.1.1 Publishers[6]

Beginning with the Tract Depot in Plymouth, founded in 1838, Brethren had been served by publishers drawn from their ranks.[7] By 1840, London had a Brethren publisher and bookseller, the Central Tract Depot in Warwick Square, an indication of the movement's growing presence in the capital. This was strengthened in 1853 when William Yapp (1807-74) moved from Hereford to London. He set up a publishing and bookselling business in the West End, in which he was joined by James Hawkins (d.1919); Yapp gave his name to 'yapp edges' on Bibles, overlapping covers which were turned down at the corners.[8]

However, the two major Open Brethren publishers were founded in Scotland. Both owed much to Donald Ross, and their early productions continued his revivalist, populist, and separatist emphases. From 1870 Ross founded a string of monthlies which will be discussed in the following section, as well as maintaining bookshops in Aberdeen,

---

[2] Mann, *Census*, 41. The report was apparently based on a tract by William Kelly (Malcolm Leonard Taylor, '"Born for the Universe": William Kelly and the Brethren Mind in Victorian England (Aspects of the Relationship between Science and Theology)' (MPhil thesis, University of Teesside, 1993), 97.

[3] Anon., 'Filling in the Census Paper', *BM* n.s. 12 (1911), 48.

[4] Anon., '"The Plymouth Brethren." How the Name Originated, and has been Perpetuated', *BM* 9 (1899), 18.

[5] Cf. *BM* n.s. 15 (1914), 48, 71.

[6] On this section, see further John A.H. Dempster, 'Aspects of Brethren Publishing Enterprise in Late Nineteenth-Century Scotland', *Publishing History* 20 (1986), 61-101; Dickson, *Brethren in Scotland*, 274-8. A contemporary survey of Exclusive Brethren writings was [William Reid], *Literature and Mission of the so-called Plymouth Brethren* (London: James Nisbet, 1875; reprinted London: Chapter Two, n.d.).

[7] Rust, *"Brethren"*, 12.

[8] On Yapp, see *GL* 6 (1875), 1-12; Pickering (ed.), *Chief Men*, 138-40.

Edinburgh, and then Glasgow.[9] He emigrated to North America in 1879, but Henry Pickering (1858-1941)[10] came from Newcastle to manage the Glasgow shop in 1886, and appears to have become its owner in 1892. William Inglis became a partner in 1893, and thus emerged a company known to generations of Brethren as a vital source of sound literature: Pickering & Inglis. Inglis died in 1908, and Pickering moved to London in 1922, but the firm retained a strong Scottish connection throughout its existence.

Henry Pickering   John Ritchie

The other main publisher, John Ritchie, exemplified the robust and independent approach of Brethren in North-East Scotland. Born in 1853, he was converted in 1871 through the preaching of Donald Munro in Inverurie. He shared Ross's interest in the use of publishing as a means of spreading the revivalist impulse and message.[11] Ritchie gave up his secular employment to engage in evangelism, and worked the Caledonian Bible Carriage for a few years in the mid-1880s.[12] His burden for souls is evident from the pages of *The Believer's Magazine*, but around 1880 he also established a publishing company at Kilmarnock. In time, this became identified with conservative Open Brethren. The company is still active today, catering for the same constituency.

As well as a steady flow of material expounding Open Brethren distinctives, publishers such as Pickering produced a variety of material on fundamental Christian truths. Some of this was written by non-Brethren writers, but Brethren publishers tended to produce their own responses to issues of the day, such as the growth of ritualism and 'higher criticism', rather than utilising those produced by non-Brethren Evangelicals.[13] Many books appeared as part of series or 'libraries', such as the 'Witness Manuals', a series of restatements of basic doctrines in non-technical and non-controversial terms, issued by Pickering & Inglis from 1912.[14] Evangelistic material was produced in vast quantities, including tracts and posters. It was possible to have some of these overprinted (or 'localised') with details of the local assembly's activities. Other tracts were produced for

---

[9] Dempster, 'Brethren Publishing', 65-9.

[10] On Pickering, see Anon., 'Helpers During these 60 Years', *W* 60 (1930), 15; *BDE*; *H* 17 (1941), 46; *ODNB*; *W* 71 (March 1941), insert.

[11] Dickson, *Brethren in Scotland*, 99.

[12] Dempster, 'Brethren Publishing', 75-6; Dickson, *Brethren in Scotland*, 138.

[13] Dempster, 'Brethren Publishing', 82-3.

[14] *Ibid.*, 74; cf. *W* 42 (1912), 32.

distribution among believers, dealing with contemporary issues such as Biblical inspiration, Christian unity, sectarianism, political involvement, 'higher life' teaching,[15] and eternal punishment.[16] For Sunday schools, it was possible by the 1890s to buy hymnals, reward books, lesson schemes, leaflets, registers, books of recitations, magazines, pictures, bookmarks, text sheets, and tea-meeting tickets.[17] Finally, we must not forget the text posters (for use in meeting rooms), charts, writing paper (emblazoned with suitable Scripture texts), and assembly requisites such as roll books and account stationery.

From a commercial standpoint, the main Open Brethren publishers were outstandingly successful, as is evident from their longevity. One reason, suggested by Dempster, is that they realised that although there was a limited number of potential purchasers, there was a virtually unlimited number of potential recipients. Once the purchasers were persuaded to buy for the benefit of the recipients, sales were assured.[18] Thus believers were exhorted to buy evangelistic items for distribution to the unsaved, Bible story books for children, books on Brethren distinctives for their own edification and that of believers in the sects, and study aids for those aspiring to minister. Another reason for success is that Brethren appear to have been enthusiastic readers; not only were they keen to learn but, for the men, there were a whole range of opportunities of putting to use what they learned, through public preaching and teaching, as well as through participation in conversational Bible readings. A third factor is that both Ritchie and Pickering were successful entrepreneurs and effective communicators; Pickering did much to popularise the use of visual aids in Brethren children's work, his books of children's talks remaining in print until the late twentieth century. There was always something new in the pipeline to maintain interest, and both companies held annual summer sales from the 1880s onwards.

There were other Open Brethren publishers, but they were much smaller than these two. One of the longest-lived was R.L. Allan of Glasgow, who issued Brethren material from 1863 until his death in 1919, when the firm was taken over by Pickering & Inglis.[19] That year they also took over a former Exclusive publisher in London, Alfred Holness.[20] The dominance of the two main publishers, as well as their extensive output, thus played a vital role in helping this radically-decentralised movement to achieve a relatively high degree of cohesion. However, not all approved of the Brethren publishing explosion. M'Vicker expressed apprehension that the movement's original biblicism was being endangered by it: '"Brethren" are beginning to write libraries like those who went before them, as if their Bible was too hard for plain people to understand. I almost wish such

---

[15] 'Higher life' denoted holiness teaching as expounded as Keswick and similar conferences.

[16] Cf. *BM* 1 (September 1891), cover advertisement.

[17] Cf. *BM* 6 (November 1896), cover advertisement.

[18] Dempster, 'Publishing', 91; cf. P.G. Scott, 'Richard Cope Morgan, Religious Periodicals and the Pontifex Factor', *Victorian Periodicals Newsletter*, No. 16 (June 1972), 1.

[19] *BM* n.s. 20 (1919), 24. The name survives, having been bought back by Nicholas Gray (formerly of Pickering & Inglis) from Zondervan (who had become the parent company of Pickering & Inglis) in 1989; most of the output consists of hymnals and Bibles for a small group sometimes known as the Cooneyites (Nicholas Gray to the author, 28 July 2004; see also the website at <www.bibles-direct.com>). The latter have no historical connection with Brethren, and whilst sharing the Brethren lay ethos and rejection of 'sectarian' designations, would not espouse an Evangelical understanding of salvation.

[20] *W* 56 (1926), 453.

books were all burnt, if that would have the effect of keeping those who read them more at their Bibles.'[21]

M'Vicker may have had a point: few movements have been quite so dominated by their writers. This is evident from the effect of the widespread practice of identifying authors (especially Exclusives) by initials only.[22] Sometimes this indicated that they were sufficiently well-known not to need their name to be given. Usually, however, it appears to have been an expression of respect for the teaching authority of those whom God was using to bring fresh light from the Scriptures. Darby was referred to as 'J.N.D.', Mackintosh as 'C.H.M.' and so on; Pickering frequently signed his editorial contributions to *The Witness* 'HyP', and in more recent times it was not unknown for the Biblical scholar F.F. Bruce to be referred to as 'F.F.B.'. Although this practice was justified on the ground that it threw the spotlight on the Lord rather than on his human instruments, Brethren history does seem to indicate that the reverse occurred; this use of initials gave a mystique to the writers which must have aided the reception of their views.

7.1.2 Periodicals

The 1850s saw the beginning of an explosion in the number of daily, weekly, and monthly publications, and most of the monthlies were of a religious character.[23] Almost from the moment that the division between Open and Exclusive Brethren took place, therefore, the latter realised the need for a periodical which was aimed at outsiders, easily affordable, and which expounded Brethren teaching.[24] They issued four which sought to meet the need:[25] the *Bible Treasury* (1856-1920, edited almost from the start by William Kelly[26]), *Things New and Old* (1845-90, edited by Mackintosh[27] and then Miller), *The Present Testimony and Original Christian Witness Revived* (1849-81, edited by Wigram and intended to fill the gap left by the demise of *The Christian Witness*), and *The Girdle of*

---

[21] [Reich], ed., *M'Vicker*, 87 (29 August 1876).

[22] A key to many of these is included in Arnold D. Ehlert, *Brethren Writers: A Checklist with an Introductory Essay and Additional Lists* (Grand Rapids, MI: Baker Book House, 1969).

[23] Best, *Mid-Victorian Britain*, 248-9.

[24] W. Trotter to J.N. Darby, 19 June 1851 (CBA 5540(328)).

[25] Dempster, 'Brethren Publishing', 81, following Scott, 'Morgan', 3.

[26] William Kelly (1820-1906) was the son of an Ulster farmer and was educated at Trinity College, Dublin, where he, like Darby, was attracted by High Church teaching. Moving to the Channel Islands, he left the Established Church in 1841 after an Evangelical conversion. He sided with Darby in the divisions of the 1840s. Kelly acquired a reputation as an exegete and textual critic of no mean ability, maintaining a correspondence with a range of biblical scholars and critics; the division among Brethren was no barrier to his helping Tregelles in the latter's textual work. Bruce considered him the best Greek scholar the Brethren movement had produced ('QA', *H* 52 (1973), 119). Kelly edited Darby's works from 1865-83, although he did not share Darby's paedobaptism and separated from him in 1880. See *BDEB*; E.N. Cross, *The Irish Saint and Scholar: A Biography of William Kelly 1821-1906* (London: Chapter Two, 2004); *ODNB*; Taylor, '"Born for the Universe"'.

[27] Mackintosh gave up his position as a schoolmaster in Westport to concentrate on writing. He proved to be a lucid and popular writer, with a gift for the telling phrase: not an original thinker, he mediated Darbyite theology to the wider church. See Beattie, *Brethren*, 142-3; Edwin N. Cross, 'Charles Henry Mackintosh 1820-1906' (typescript, 2001, Chapter Two archive); Pickering (ed.), *Chief Men*, 110-12.

Truth (1857-66). According to Miller, by 1880 there were eleven Exclusive monthlies published in London alone, some with a circulation of 40-50,000.[28] Open Brethren may well have been influenced by these simply because for many years there were no other periodicals for them to read. Even when Open Brethren periodicals did appear, these often carried advertisements for exegetical and devotional works by gifted Exclusive writers such as Bellett, Darby, Kelly, Stoney, or C.A. Coates (1862-1945): no comparable Open Brethren writers appeared for many years, and so Exclusive thinking gained a firm foothold in many Open assemblies.

In Scotland, Open Brethren often read Bowes' periodical, *The Truth Promoter* (1849-75).[29] In England, ironically, the most influential periodical among Open Brethren, at least until they began issuing their own, may have been a non-Brethren one: *The Revival*, edited by R.C. Morgan.[30] Morgan founded it in 1859 with the intent of providing sympathetic coverage of the revival which was not available through the existing media. Influenced by Finney's idea that it was possible to 'organise' a revival by ensuring that there were no hindrances in the church and by engaging in vigorous evangelism, British evangelists began to do this in response to events in Ireland. Morgan's paper followed and promoted the work of these travelling revivalist preachers. To counteract a drop in circulation as revival fires cooled, it was reinvented as a symbol of interdenominational evangelism in 1869, and the following year renamed *The Christian*. From the 1870s, occasional articles from it appeared in *The Northern Witness* and *The Witness*.

The first periodical produced specifically for Open Brethren was *The Golden Lamp* (1870-90), whose main editors were William Yapp and then Henry Groves (1818-91), but this contained no news items or announcements.[31] Two other Brethren periodicals were edited by Hurditch, *The Latter Rain* (1866-75, when it was incorporated into the interdenominational *Word and Work*) and *Footsteps of Truth* (1883-1905).[32] Neither included much on Brethren distinctives, perhaps because of Hurditch's own very open attitude towards other denominations. A long-lived periodical was *The Believer's Pathway* (1880-1949), commenced by William Shaw of Maybole, Ayrshire; initially devotional in character, it became a magazine for Christian workers. Perhaps the most useful English periodical in terms of news and notices was another London-based monthly, *The Eleventh Hour* (1886-95). English magazines appear to have started, like the Scottish ones, as a result of individual initiative; but unlike them, they tended to cease when the individual in question had to lay down their editorial responsibility. For instance, *The Eleventh Hour* ceased publication when its editor, A.M. Sparks, became seriously ill.[33] Thus, in the absence of a major means of ensuring coherence, English Open Brethren became marked by a greater variety of outlook than their counterparts in Scotland and Ulster. However, this was overcome in some measure by the appearance of magazines intended to circulate information about evangelistic work at home and overseas, the most notable example being *The Missionary Echo* (from 1872), which became *Echoes of Service* in 1885 and is still published.

---

[28] Miller, *Brethren*, 163.

[29] See Dickson, *Brethren in Scotland*, 15, 39.

[30] See Scott, 'Morgan'.

[31] On Groves, see Pickering (ed.), *Chief Men*, 98-100; Stunt et al., *Turning the World Upside Down*, 35-7.

[32] [C. Russell Hurditch], 'Notes for the Month', *FT* 17 (1899), 64.

[33] *EOS* 26 (September Part II, 1898), inside back cover.

It was Ross who first attempted to use magazines in order to provide a measure of doctrinal and practical unity. Unlike those edited by Ritchie, most of those which Ross founded did not survive, although the *Northern Assemblies* (1873-4, intended for those in fellowship) provides invaluable information concerning assembly activities as well as papers on Brethren doctrine.[34] One which did survive would become one of the most important Brethren periodicals: successively known as *The Northern Evangelistic Intelligencer* (1871-2), *The Northern Intelligencer* (1873-4), *The Northern Witness* (1875-86), and (from 1887) *The Witness*, it continued to appear until 1980, when it was incorporated into *The Harvester*.[35] Edited from 1876-1914 by J.R. Caldwell, a silk manufacturer and gifted Bible teacher in the Glasgow area,[36] its circulation grew rapidly, reaching 6,000 around 1886 and almost 20,000 by 1914.[37] During Caldwell's editorship, the magazine's ethos changed dramatically: Ross's forthright separatism gave way to a more urbane, thoughtful, and nuanced exposition of moderate Brethren thinking which won the magazine an increasing number of non-Brethren readers.[38]

J.R. Caldwell

The other main periodical during these decades was *The Believer's Magazine*, commenced by Ritchie in 1891. Ritchie's conversion in North-East Scotland had located him within the movement which gave birth to the forerunners of *The Witness*, and he

---

[34] The only known copies (Nos. 2 and 23 are missing) are bound with the *Northern Evangelistic Intelligencer / Northern Intelligencer / Northern Witness* for 1872-6, in a volume held by the Christian Brethren Archive. My thanks to Dr Neil Dickson for allowing me to consult it before its lodgement there.

[35] For the periodicals issued by Pickering & Inglis and John Ritchie, see Dempster, 'Publishing', 71-2.

[36] On Caldwell see the brief memoir in John R. Caldwell, *Epitome of Christian Experience in Psalm xxxii; with the Development of Christian life ...* (Glasgow: Pickering & Inglis, [1917]); Pickering (ed.), *Chief Men*, 150-4.

[37] The Publishers, 'Concerning "The Witness"', *W* 44 (1914), 109; but see H[enr]y P[ickering], '1870 – About "The Witness" – 1927', *W* 57 (1927), 213, which gives a circulation figure of 16,000 for 1914.

[38] However, Dickson points out (*Brethren in Scotland*, 147) that the variety of opinions initially allowed by Ross gradually disappeared; Caldwell may have taken a fairly open line on many issues, but he was reluctant to allow expression of dissenting opinions.

became a frequent contributor. The sustained opposition which Brethren experienced from the churches provoked a negative response, and so Ritchie was, like Ross, a separatist from the start. It seemed to him that Open Brethren periodicals were moving away from such an outlook, leaving a clear gap in the market which needed to be filled. Several periodicals devoted to ministry had ceased, and others (including *The Witness,* although he did not mention it) had changed their position and character.[39] What he did not say, but which may have influenced his thinking just as much, was that while *The Witness* was more open than Ritchie wished, a narrower periodical, *Needed Truth,* made its appearance in 1888; thus he may have been attempting to capture the Scottish movement's 'middle ground'.[40] Ritchie saw a need for a magazine which would expound fundamental truths, and also those truths which separated believers from the world and gathered them to Christ's name, apart from the sects. His production was to be aimed at young believers and older ones 'who need the bread of life broken small'.[41] From the beginning, *The Believer's Magazine* was marked by a sense that the movement's spiritual tone was not what it had been in his early days, and his populist outlook led him to ascribe this to such causes as over-dependence on human learning and failure to maintain separation, believing

> that Gospel work was never more vigorous, that conversions were never more abundant or real, that the unconverted were never got in larger numbers to hear the Word, than in the days when assemblies stood clean and clear from all the systems of the world's religion, walking in the path of separation and fearlessly testifying to the truth that produces and maintains it, having the vials of the religious world's wrath poured out without mercy or measure on their devoted heads.[42]

The Believer's Magazine was not Ritchie's first magazine, that honour falling to *The Young Watchman* (commenced for children in 1884), but it was to prove the most influential, shaping and reflecting the outlook of many more separatist assemblies.

The different outlooks among Open Brethren came to be aligned increasingly with particular periodicals, although readership and authorship often extended beyond the constituency in question. The fact that both *The Witness* and *The Believer's Magazine* had very stable editorships would have enabled them to build a firm base of subscribers and contributors, as well as establishing a clear 'party line'. Editors were accorded an authoritative position, even if they disclaimed it for themselves, and were able to exercise this not only by selection of articles and contributors, but also (and perhaps more significantly) through regular question-and-answer columns dealing with a range of exegetical, doctrinal, ecclesiastical, and ethical questions.[43] Initially, it was the editors

---

[39] [John Ritchie], 'A Friendly Talk about our Six monthly Magazines', *BM* n.s. 18 (December 1917), inside front cover. We shall see below that Caldwell's views on the issues of separation and reception to fellowship had indeed changed. However, his response to the appearance of *The Believer's Magazine* was to assert his intent to continue on the same lines as *The Witness* had done for twenty years, expounding the whole truth in love, without giving undue prominence to any aspect (*W* 20 (1890), note inside front cover), an implicit rejection of Ritchie's charge.

[40] Dickson, *Brethren in Scotland,* 171.

[41] [John Ritchie], 'To Our Readers', *BM* 1 (1891), 1; [*idem*], 'The Story of "The Believer's Magazine" – 1890-1908', *BM* n.s. 9 (1908), 144.

[42] [John Ritchie], 'Helps and Hindrances to Gospel Work. Part IV. – Decline in Gospel Power, and its Causes', *BM* n.s. 7 (1906), 104.

[43] Dickson, *Brethren in Scotland,* 147-8.

who provided the replies, but both magazines gradually opened these to others; by about 1900 *The Witness* was even prepared to print answers giving two different sides of a question, albeit with a concluding editorial summary.

In the absence of any denominational structure, periodicals fulfilled a vital role as channels of communication.[44] Their functions included the provision of teaching (both on distinctives and on fundamental Christian doctrines), devotional material, aids to Bible study (until the 1930s at least, *The Believer's Magazine* and *The Witness* issued a coloured chart, dealing with some prophetic, typological, or hermeneutical theme, with the January issue of each year), and the communication of news and intimation of meetings. Some periodicals were designed for evangelistic distribution, and others for the specific requirements of Christian workers. Readers were exhorted to circulate them to friends and acquaintances, a note in *The Witness* urging: 'If you derive help from reading this *Witness*, send for a dozen or more *free* to hand to fellow-Christians.'[45]

7.1.3 Hymnody

As with many denominations, hymnody provided Brethren with an opportunity to express their fundamental convictions and distinctive beliefs. Hymnbooks were being produced for assembly use from the 1830s, often as individual ventures; this was common in Nonconformity before the emergence of strong denominational organisations facilitated the production of denominational hymnals. Early compilations included J.L. Harris, *A Collection of Hymns* (1834); R.C. Chapman, *Hymns for the Use of the Church of Christ* (1837); G.V. Wigram, *Hymns for the Poor of the Flock* (1838); Edward Denny, *A Selection of Hymns* (1839); and J.G. Deck, *Psalms and Hymns and Spiritual Songs* (1842).[46] Chapman, Darby, Deck, and Denny were all to become noted hymnwriters whose compositions have remained in use among Brethren and sometimes beyond them also. Their output majored on the themes of adoration of Christ, especially in the context of the Lord's Supper, anticipation of his return for believers, and aspiration after heaven on the part of those who were already seated in heavenly places in Christ; the world was seen as a wilderness through which they longed to complete their passage.

A second wave of books appeared in the wake of the interdenominational revivalist movement, and from this point the practice became widespread of using one book for the Breaking of Bread and another for the gospel meeting. This symbolises the tension between the maintenance of a distinctive identity and the desire for fellowship with other believers: the former type of book would contain many distinctively Brethren hymns expressing their theology of worship and the Lord's Supper, while the latter would be composed of gospel and general hymns, many of which would be well-known in other Evangelical circles. Indeed, for gospel meetings many assemblies would have used an interdenominational book, such as *Sankey's Sacred Songs and Solos*, rather than one of those available from Brethren publishers.

Among books designed for use at the Breaking of Bread, *The Believer's Hymn Book*, published by Pickering and Inglis in 1884, was especially popular in Scotland, Ireland, Northern England, and North America.[47] It has proved remarkably long-lived, remaining

---

[44] Dempster, 'Brethren Publishing', 63.

[45] Note in the margin of *W* 42 (1912), 29.

[46] Baylis, *My People*, 17.

[47] *W* 63 (1933), 40. Caldwell was one of the compilers.

in use until the present. Another book which continues in use is *Hymns of Light and Love*, published by Echoes of Service in 1900; this included gospel hymns as well as hymns for meetings of believers. Balancing the desire for distinctive expressions of Brethren aspirations, a certain catholicity of spirituality is evident in the use made by such collections of translations of hymns by German mystics and Pietists produced by Emma Frances Bevan (1827-1909), many of which appeared in her *Hymns of Ter Steegen, Suso and Others* (1894, 1897).[48] Daughter of an Anglican archdeacon, she associated with Open Brethren following her marriage and became known as a translator, versifier and interpreter of German mystical and Pietist writers.

Among Exclusives, revised editions of *Hymns for the Little Flock* appeared in 1856 and 1881 (as well as various further revisions catering for different Exclusive groupings); some assemblies which moved to Open Brethren nevertheless continued to use it. Such a fact indicates that during this period the two streams shared a common understanding of the Breaking of Bread, a service which lay at the heart of their ecclesiology and spirituality. Exclusives also produced collections designed for gospel meetings, such as W.T.P. Wolston's *Gospel Hymnal* (1871) and its successor, *The Evangelist's Hymnal* (1906), although these do not appear to have been used among Open Brethren.

When these books are compared with other major collections from the period, such as the Baptist *Psalms and Hymns* (1900), the Anglican *Hymns Ancient and Modern* (1861) and *English Hymnal* (1906), or those issued by various branches of Methodism, it becomes clear that Brethren hymnody was developing largely in isolation from other Victorian hymnody. The continued emphasis on the atonement contrasts with an increasing stress elsewhere upon the incarnation, and relatively few well-known hymns by contemporary non-Brethren writers found a place in Brethren collections until many years later. (It was not until 1959 that *The Believer's Hymn Book*, for instance, received a supplement containing a large number of such hymns.) Such developments both reflected and helped to shape a distinctive spirituality among assemblies, which often appeared somewhat esoteric to outsiders. In Exclusive circles this was reinforced by the editorial surgery often practised upon hymns by non-Brethren writers, which was intended to render them suitable vehicles for the expression of Brethren spirituality.

7.1.4 Conferences

In Chapter 2, we noted the important role played by the early conferences for leaders. These virtually ceased after the events of the 1840s, although one on prophetic subjects was held in Freemasons' Hall, London, in 1865.[49] Different types of conference now emerged, some arising out of the needs of young converts and local assembly members for solid teaching, and others designed to allow those occupied in the Lord's work to consult together on matters of practice as well as doctrine.

The earliest known example of the former type of conference was at Tottenham in 1853, advertised in the *Missionary Reporter*.[50] However, it was in the wake of the 1859 revival and other subsequent local awakenings that such gatherings really became widespread. The first large conference appears to have been the twice-yearly Dublin

---

[48] On Bevan, see *BDEB*; *ODNB*.

[49] Anon., *Report of Three Days' Meetings for Prayer and for Addresses on the subject of the Lord's Coming, held in Freemasons' Hall, May 30th, 31st, & June 1st, 1865* (London: William Yapp, 1865).

[50] Anon., 'The Missionary Reporter', *H* 15 (1938), 262.

Believers' Meetings, commenced in 1862 and sponsored by the coffee-house magnate Henry Bewley (1814-76).[51] Revival had led to a desire for those engaged in Christian work to confer together on doctrinal and practical issues relating to the awakening, but the workers were soon swamped by attendances of up to 1,200 people, and so the focus of the public meetings shifted to the provision of teaching for converts.[52]

The development of this type of conference was facilitated by the rapid expansion of the railway network and the spread of the Saturday half-holiday. By the end of the century, few assemblies would have been without their 'annual', often held on a Saturday afternoon and evening. These were the Brethren equivalent of the Nonconformist church or chapel anniversary. Public holidays and fast days (local holidays on which pre-communion preparatory meetings were held by Presbyterian churches) provided further opportunities for such gatherings: in Scotland many would have held conferences on New Year's Day, while in Ulster many took place on 12 July; the most famous, at Ahorey, County Armagh, began in 1881, and was held in a large tent adjoining the assembly's hall.[53]

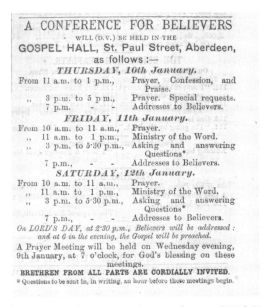

A CONFERENCE FOR BELIEVERS
WILL (D.V.) BE HELD IN THE
GOSPEL HALL, St. Paul Street, Aberdeen,
as follows :—
THURSDAY, 10th January.
From 11 a.m. to 1 p.m.,   Prayer, Confession, and Praise.
,,   3 p.m. to 5 p.m.,   Prayer. Special requests.
7 p.m.   -   -   Addresses to Believers.
FRIDAY, 11th January.
From 10 a.m. to 11 a.m.,   Prayer.
,,   11 a.m. to 1 p.m.,   Ministry of the Word.
,,   3 p.m. to 5·30 p.m.,   Asking and answering Questions*
7 p.m.,   -   -   Addresses to Believers.
SATURDAY, 12th January.
From 10 a.m. to 11 a.m.,   Prayer.
,,   11 a.m. to 1 p.m.,   Ministry of the Word.
,,   3 p.m. to 5·30 p.m.,   Asking and answering Questions*
7 p.m.,   -   -   Addresses to Believers.
On *LORD'S DAY*, at 2·30 p.m., *Believers will be addressed :* and at 6 in the evening, the Gospel will be preached.
A Prayer Meeting will be held on Wednesday evening, 9th January, at 7 o'clock, for God's blessing on these meetings.
BRETHREN FROM ALL PARTS ARE CORDIALLY INVITED.
* Questions to be sent in, in writing, an hour before these meetings begin.

A typical programme for the Aberdeen conference (*NW* 8 (1878), 15)

In Scotland, the twice-yearly Glasgow Believers' Meetings began in 1865.[54] These were modelled on the Dublin meetings,[55] and became one of the largest Brethren conferences, attracting congregations of up to 2,500. Initially majoring on teaching, a

---

[51] Holmes, *Revivals*, 77; Pickering (ed.), *Chief Men*, 146.

[52] A.P. Moore-Anderson, *Sir Robert Anderson, K.C.B., and Lady Anderson* (London: Marshall, Morgan & Scott, 1947), 20.

[53] Rea, *David Rea*, 93.

[54] See [C.J. Pickering], *1865-1965: The Half-Yearly Meetings of Christians, Glasgow* (n.pl.: n.p., n.d.).

[55] *The Revival*, 30 November 1865, 318.

missionary rally was added in 1887, a sale of work for missions in 1894, and a
missionary meeting for sisters in 1900. Ministry included Bible readings on a pre-
arranged passage and teaching for young converts. From the start of Open Brethren
outreach in North-East Scotland, conferences were held, with an emphasis on practical
ministry intended to benefit young converts and others. The most important was that
convened at Aberdeen from 1873.[56]

Such gatherings frequently attracted many who did not belong to assemblies, and thus
provided a kind of shop window for the movement. Great care in ministry was therefore
needed; according to one correspondent in 1904, too much self-criticism might make
other believers feel that they were better off remaining where they were.[57] It was also
likely that a number of unconverted would be present, and so some conferences included
gospel preaching. It was not uncommon for conferences to be followed by applications
for fellowship by individuals converted at them. The presence of so many believers in one
place also made conferences a prime occasion for sharing information about outreach
work at home and abroad, and many would include reports from 'the Lord's servants' (full-
time workers). The occasion might also be taken to run a meeting for Sunday School
workers.

Conferences provided evangelists, missionaries, and teachers with their main
opportunities for cementing cohesiveness: many travelled round the assemblies,
exercising a quasi-apostolic role in teaching and advising as well as evangelising, and
their pronouncements on these occasions would have been treated with great respect, as
well as being reported in the periodicals. Cohesion was also fostered in more informal
ways. Conferences in Scotland fulfilled similar functions to the twice-yearly communion
seasons of the Presbyterian churches, during which the communion would be preceded and
followed by several days of special preaching services. These gatherings were the nearest
the Brethren came to adopting the Victorian habit of sermon-tasting, and they made the
most of their opportunity. All over Britain, believers from other local assemblies would
attend each other's conferences in the same way that Nonconformist congregations
attended one another's chapel, ministerial, or Sunday School anniversary services. This
entailed the provision of refreshments for vast quantities of people, and the opportunities
for conversation during meal-times formed a major part of the social life of many
Brethren. This was all the more valuable for young people in areas where marriage to non-
Brethren was discouraged.[58] Overnight hospitality, too, was provided in some places
where conferences lasted several days.

Many early conferences operated with an open platform, there being no pre-arranged
chairman or speakers: arrangement was regarded as infringing the presidency of the Holy
Ghost.[59] As an advertisement for one to be held at Inverurie in 1872 stated, 'There is no
programme of speakers or subjects, speaking in the Holy Ghost is the thing wanted, and
is the only kind worth listening to. Such speakers are invited to take part.'[60] The
'impulsive' concept of ministry had penetrated deep into areas which professed to be
unaffected by, and unconnected with, English events and controversies. However, it was

[56] See [Matthew S.R. Brown et al.], *Aberdeen Christian Conference Centenary 1874-1973*
(Aberdeen: Alex P. Reid, 1972); Cordiner, *Fragments*, 67-9.

[57] *W* 34 (1904), 163.

[58] Don Franks, *The Saltisford Story* ([Warwick]: n.p., [1999]), 3.

[59] B., letter in *NA*, January 1874, 3-4.

[60] *NEI* 2 (1872), 64.

claimed that the open platform was widely abused by those who liked the sound of their own voice, and so it was gradually replaced by pre-selected speakers.[61] Subjects even began to be announced beforehand, a development which attracted criticism from some who were concerned that this implied a loss of spiritual ardour and an attempt to conform to the practices of the denominations.

Caldwell summarised the issues in an article on '"Believers' Meetings"' in *The Northern Witness*.[62] In his view, open meetings tested a gathering's spirituality. They required firm rule (he suggested that a number of overseeing brethren sit together in full view of the congregation) as well as liberty. Pre-arrangement risked excluding an unknown individual with a message from God, neglecting subjects on which brethren differed. (Allegations were sometimes made that certain topics, such as separation, gathering to the name of Christ alone, and the hope of the immediate (i.e. pretribulational) Second Coming, were being ruled out of order by conference organisers.[63]) Another risk was that those responsible for arrangements would book speakers who said what people wanted to hear. Along similar lines, *The Believer's Magazine* occasionally lamented the decline in searching ministry, alleging that it was becoming more anecdotal and less solidly biblical and expository.[64] Nevertheless, the trend to pre-arrangement and a closed platform continued until almost all conferences adopted them.

Conferences for Christian workers also became a feature of Open Brethren life from the 1870s. Some were Saturday afternoon gatherings of men in oversight of assemblies in a city such as London or Glasgow, at which pressing issues might be discussed and a common approach formulated; these would have been especially helpful to inexperienced leaders from newly-formed assemblies. Conferences for Sunday School workers were also arranged: that at Bridford Mills in Devon was held annually from 1887 until at least the 1950s.[65] The first of the London conferences for them was held in 1907 at Exeter Hall; these would become important twice-yearly events, attracting up to 2,500 people in the inter-war years.

Other conferences were residential, and intended particularly for those in full-time service. One of the first ministry conferences in England was that begun by Henry Dyer at Yeovil around 1871, which became an annual event.[66] Originating out of an 'open home' for Christian workers, it continued as a residential gathering and maintained the open platform into the 1950s, long after it had fallen out of favour in most other places.[67] The most notable workers' conference was that begun at Leominster in 1874, where William Yapp had taken over a hotel as a venue for such gatherings.[68] Yapp showed wisdom in choosing a relatively out-of-the-way location, recognising the impossibility of keeping

---

[61] Neil Dickson has pointed out to me that during the 'Needed Truth' controversy of the late 1880s and early 1890s, speakers often used conferences as opportunities for airing their own views; he suggests that this was another factor leading to the decline of the open platform.

[62] J.R.C[aldwell]., '"Believers' Meetings"', *NW* 15 (1885), 108-9.

[63] Anon., 'Truths which are being lost', *BM* n.s. 10 (1909), 21.

[64] E.g. G.H. Lang, 'ASQ', *BM* n.s. 13 (1912), 23.

[65] *W* 88 (1958), 37.

[66] Beattie, *Brethren*, 75; Pickering (ed.), *Chief Men*, 178.

[67] Pickering (ed.), *Chief Men*, 69; *PS* 9.1 (November-December 1957), 27.

[68] Anon., 'Leominster Conferences', *EH* 1 (June 1886), 2.

a hundred men together for five days in any venue near London.[69] He had been concerned about division among Open Brethren and thought that it might help if leading brethren could be brought together for a few days. These gatherings took place several times a year until 1906, and always began with a time of confession and prayer; they included Bible study on topics related to the church and its work, but also times for mutual counsel, fellowship, and encouragement. Frequently a number of missionaries were present, although in time occasional conferences were convened especially for them by the editors of *Echoes of Service*. Among those who took a leading role were Robert Chapman, Henry Dyer, Henry Groves, Henry Heath, and J.L. Maclean.

7.1.5 Letters and Lists

Whilst the practice of issuing letters of commendation appears to have been initiated in Scotland by Ross during the 1870s as an attempt to exclude those holding fundamental error from assembly fellowship,[70] it can also be seen as a manifestation of the late-Victorian drive for more efficient and systematic ordering of corporate affairs. Doubtless it is also rooted in the traditional Dissenting practice of issuing such letters to individuals moving house and wishing to transfer their membership. Such letters were designed to assure assemblies that the bearers were believers in good standing with their home assembly.

They were meant to have the weight of the assembly behind them, rather than coming from an individual, and were to be handed to the steward at the door on arrival, so that visitors could be welcomed during the Lord's Supper. They were expected to include some information about the bearer's spiritual state and gifting, in order to ensure that they received appropriate pastoral care and found scope for service in their new home. Biblical support for the practice was found in such verses as Romans 16.1 and 2 Corinthians 3.1, although more judicious Brethren conceded that there was little basis in these texts for making such a practice a universal requirement.

Although they never became universal, as is evident from questions concerning the reception of believers who lacked such letters, they were an important means by which admission to fellowship was regulated. Advertisements for assemblies often requested that visitors bring a letter of commendation from their home assembly. Blanks could be bought from Pickering & Inglis, and also from John Ritchie, who advertised packs of fifty, some for those visiting another assembly temporarily and some for those moving to a new area.[71] Some complained these letters risked becoming a mere admission ticket, guaranteeing the unspiritual individual with a letter a seat at the Lord's Table while excluding the spiritual individual without one.[72] More subtly, the practice had potentially sectarian overtones: it implied the existence of a discrete and recognisable network of congregations who corresponded with each other in this way, whose separateness was reinforced by the fact that believers from other denominations would not always have been able to obtain the kind of letter required.

---

[69] *EH* 2 (September 1887), 6.

[70] Dickson, *Brethren in Scotland*, 157.

[71] *BM* n.s 12 (February 1911), ii.

[72] Cf. the criticisms of the ex-Exclusive Harold St John (Patricia St John, *Harold St. John: A Portrait* (London: Pickering & Inglis, 1961), 107).

Lists of assemblies also helped to bind the movement together, although the compilers expressly disclaimed any official status and acknowledged their incompleteness. J.W. Jordan's preface to his 1897 list warned against its being 'taken as a *guarantee* that these Meetings are in a spiritual condition before God, or used as a *clique* of fellowship';[73] nevertheless, he assured readers that he had taken care to exclude meetings known to hold or teach error concerning the person and work of Christ. Such lists were reissued every few years, and could be updated from announcements in *The Believer's Magazine* and *The Witness*.

GOSPEL HALL
68 Townhead Street
Kirkintilloch

....

To believers gathered in the name of the Lord Jesus Christ

in ....

Beloved brethren in Christ, grace and peace from
God the Father and Jesus Christ our Saviour.

We commend to you our ....
....
who........in fellowship with the Lord's people here and
.........on a visit to your locality.

Receive .... worthily of the saints.

On behalf of the assembly, we are affectionately your
brethren in the Lord.

....
....

A typical pro-forma letter of commendation printed for use by a particular assembly; this one is from a later period, but the wording is essentially unchanged

7.2   Doctrinal   Distinctives

The account of the movement which appeared in the report of the 1851 Religious Census described them as 'consisting of all such as, practically holding all the truths essential to salvation, recognize each other as, on that account alone, true members of the only church'.[74] These essential truths received unceasing emphasis during this period, and as time went on and Nonconformist denominations were increasingly affected by liberal theology, the firm adherence of Brethren to fundamental truths won them adherents from other churches. Professor Rendle Short's best-selling *Principles of Christians called "Open Brethren"* (1913) was intended to explain to young people the principles on which assemblies were based.[75] It devoted chapters to the deity of Christ, the inspiration and authority of Scripture, the gospel, and believer's baptism, before proceeding to expound

---

[73] [Jordan], *List of Some Meetings*, 3.

[74] Mann, *Census*, 41.

[75] [Short], *Principles*, 10.

Open Brethren distinctives such as weekly observance of the Lord's Supper (with open ministry), rejection of ordination, and the opening of the Lord's Table to all sound and godly believers. His presentation was influenced by his interest in apologetics and his work among students, but his selection was not untypical.

Although Open Brethren were in principle non-credal,[76] they recognised that in certain circumstances it was necessary to produce written statements of what they regarded as fundamental beliefs. One example was the formation of property trusts. One of the first was The Western Counties and South Wales Evangelization Trust; formed in 1904, it drew on experience gained with the formation in 1898 of what became the Stewards Trust to hold property overseas on behalf of missionaries. The Western Counties deed, which was widely adopted as a model in other areas, and that of the Midlands Evangelization Trust (1916) made reference to widespread departure from the gospel and the ineffectiveness of some local trusts to prevent this affecting assemblies. It was hoped that by setting up a trust in which Evangelical fundamentals and Open Brethren distinctives were spelt out, it would be possible to prevent property from falling into the hands of individuals or groups who denied any of these. The Western Counties deed accordingly listed:[77]

1. The inspiration, authority, and sufficiency of Scripture.

2. The Trinity.

3. The Incarnation, sacrificial death, resurrection, ascension, and return of Christ.

4. The Fall of man.

5. The need of the Spirit to work in regeneration and sanctification.

6. Justification by faith and the new birth, the latter resulting in holiness and good works.

7. The continued conscious existence of the human spirit after death, the resurrection of the dead to eternal punishment or eternal blessedness.

8. The observance of believer's baptism, and of the Breaking of Bread on the first day of each week, so far as circumstances allow.

9. Reception to the Lord's Table of all believers known to be sound in faith and godly in life.

10. 'The conducting of meetings for worship under the guidance of the Holy Spirit, with opportunity for the exercise in the assembly of all true gifts for edification, subject to the Lordship of Christ.'

It is undeniable that, for all that some critics attempted to prove the contrary, the assemblies stood firmly within the Evangelical camp. Space precludes an exposition of Brethren teaching on fundamental themes, but there were certain distinctive emphases which became characteristic, and which were formulated or elaborated during this period; we shall look at these now.

---

[76] By the turn of the century, positive references to early creeds were beginning to appear, especially to their Christological affirmations. Writers found these valuable in countering theological error (e.g. W.H. Bennet, '"An Uncertain Sound." A Congregational Confession of Faith', *W* 38 (1908), 69-70; [John Ritchie], 'The Humanity of the Lord Jesus', *BM* n.s. 7 (1906), 49, which quoted the Chalcedonian Definition of 451, wrongly describing it as the Creed of Nicea). Earlier negative references to creeds were formulated in a different context, that of opposition to the imposition of doctrinal tests which were human productions and which excluded true believers.

[77] Trust Deed of The Western Counties and South Wales Evangelization Trust, 22-5 (Counties archive, Westbury).

7.2.1 The Person and Work of Christ

Not long after Bethesda, Exclusive Brethren were to experience further controversy as a result of differing views concerning the sufferings of Christ, arising from a series of articles by Darby in *The Bible Treasury* in 1858-9[78] and another article in August 1866. Darby spoke for all Brethren when he affirmed his acceptance of standard Christian teaching on the atonement: 'The blessed Lord's offering Himself without spot to God and being obedient to death, being made sin for us, and bearing our sins in His own body on the tree; His glorifying God in the sacrifice of Himself; and His substitution for us; and His drinking the cup of wrath'.[79] However, apart from Christ's suffering at the hands of sinners, and his vicarious suffering at Calvary as the sin-bearer, Darby taught a third class of sufferings, in which Christ entered into the experience of God's governmental wrath against the sin of the Jewish remnant. He felt that this clarified fundamental teaching concerning the atoning work of Christ, and distinguished this from the idea, which he asserted was held by Newton, that Christ was actually in a condition which deserved that wrath.

Reaction was vigorous: even the irenic Chapman refused to receive into fellowship any holding this doctrine of a 'third class of sufferings', whether in its earlier (Newtonian) or later (Darbyite) form.[80] Hall and Dorman were among those who charged Darby with teaching Newton's errors, and when they failed to secure an investigation into the charge, both seceded. They and others pointed out the contrast with Darby's insistence upon investigation of Newton's teaching some years before, but Darby was insistent that his teaching was not the same as Newton's:

> My doctrine is exactly the opposite of Mr. N's. He taught that Christ was born in a state of distance from God, and could only meet God on the cross; but that, by His piety, He escaped many of the consequences of His position by birth. On the contrary, I believe that He was born, and lived up to the cross in the perfect favour of God; and that in grace He entered in spirit, into the sorrows and troubles of His people, and particularly at the end, when His hour was come.[81]

The doctrine itself had no discernible impact on Open Brethren thinking, and it is debatable how much most Exclusive members understood or adopted it, but it did result in the accession of some former Exclusives.

More widespread in both sections of the movement was a tendency to underplay the humanity of Christ. Around 1861, Mackintosh employed some ill-chosen expressions in the first edition of his *Notes on Leviticus*, which appeared to countenance the notion that Christ's humanity was not like ours but was a 'heavenly humanity'; he had to be extricated by Darby and others from the resulting controversy.[82] Open Brethren, among whom Mackintosh's works circulated widely, continued to espouse a mild form of this view, partly by way of reaction against Irving's assertion that in becoming incarnate Christ took to himself *sinful* human nature, and partly because of the apologetic necessity

---

[78] The 1867 revision of these is reprinted in Darby, *CW*, 7.139-237.

[79] Darby, *CW*, 7.147.

[80] Chapman and W. Hake to W.H. Bennet, 10 March 1869, in Hake (ed.), *Letters of Chapman*, 11.

[81] Darby, *Letters*, 1.482 (17 February 1867).

[82] See Darby, *CW* 10, 135-6 (from 'Further Remarks upon Righteousness and Law: with answers to different objections').

of countering denials of Christ's full deity.[83] The latter necessity meant that Christ's deity received far more attention than his humanity from many contemporary Evangelicals, not just Brethren.[84] That Brethren remained within the spectrum of Evangelical belief concerning the person and work of Christ is confirmed by the popularity of their Christological expositions of the Old Testament in non-Brethren circles.

7.2.2 *'Justification in the Risen Christ'*

Justification in the Risen Christ was the title of a tract by the Exclusive evangelist Charles Stanley (1821-88). His concern was that the usual Evangelical teaching placed the believer back under bondage to the law. Foreshadowing modern criticisms of the Refomers' teaching, Stanley rejected the idea that 'God would be righteous in reckoning the breaker of the law righteous because another kept it'.[85] By contrast, he asserted that Scripture taught that justification involved not only pardon but also positive righteousness, and that it was based on the principle of incorporation into Christ rather than imputation of Christ's righteousness to us. (As Newton summarised it, God justifies us on the basis of our perfect righteousness as incorporated into Christ.[86]) In him, the life forfeited by us through sin was given up on the cross, and the due condemnation of the law executed. His resurrection brings us into a state of absolute righteousness, on the basis of which we are justified. The righteousness which is ours in the risen Christ is the rule of our life as believers, rather than the law. Stanley's approach was shared by many Exclusive teachers. According to Neatby,

> The theology of the Brethren is the ordinary theology of Evangelicals of a firmly but moderately Calvinistic type; but there are fairly important variations, of which some of the most significant relate to the doctrine of justification. Darby taught that the Righteousness of God, as spoken of in Romans, is to be understood as God's personal righteousness, and not as His provision and bestowal of righteousness.[87]

Neatby's primary focus was on Darbyism, but there is evidence that such teaching affected Open Brethren too.[88] An influential example was Robert Anderson, whose book *The Gospel and its Ministry* took a similar line. For him, the contrast was 'not between

---

[83] For an overview of Brethren thinking on the humanity of Christ, which also explores the background to Newton's teaching, see F.F. Bruce, 'The Humanity of Jesus Christ', *JCBRF* 24 (1973), 5-15.

[84] Doreen Rosman links this tendency in early nineteenth-century Evangelicals with a faulty anthropology: 'Their failure to appreciate the humanity of Christ was indicative of their inability fully to accept their own humanity.' (*Evangelicals and Culture* (London and Canberra: Croom Helm, 1984), 246.)

[85] C.S[tanley]., *Justification in the Risen Christ; or, "The Faith which was once delivered to the saints"* (London: G. Morrish, n.d.), 11.

[86] Benjamin Wills Newton, *Remarks on a Tract entitled "Justification in the Risen Christ."* (London: Houlston, 1896²), 28.

[87] Neatby, *History*, 230. Darby himself acknowledged that such an interpretation 'sets one on a basis apart from current evangelicalism' (*Letters*, 1.359 (1863)).

[88] E.g. William Lincoln, 'The Righteousness of God', *NW* 14 (1884), 6-8.

personal and vicarious law-keeping, but between righteousness on the principle of law-keeping, and righteousness which is entirely apart from law; between righteousness of man, worked out on earth, and righteousness of God, revealed from heaven'.[89]

Linked with this approach to the doctrine of justification was a strong stress on assurance, which owed much to the radical Evangelicalism of Malan and others, perhaps as mediated by the revivalist preachers. Such a message would have been particularly attractive to many weighed down by the introspective spirituality of some contemporary Calvinism which risked regarding claims to assurance of salvation as tantamount to presumption.[90] However, Lincoln was aware that assemblies themselves were deeply divided over whether assurance necessitated knowledge of the exact moment of one's conversion.[91] The stress on assurance also left the movement open to criticism from such quarters for an alleged superficiality which minimised the agony of conviction of sin. More moderate Evangelicals who espoused the dictum of the commentator Thomas Scott (1747-1821) that growth was the only evidence of life would also have tended on that account to introspection[92] and so would have been suspicious of Brethren teaching.

7.2.3 Sanctification[93]

In the 1830s, the conception of the life of discipleship as one of conformity to the example of Christ exercised considerable influence on Brethren teaching and practice; for example, it was a factor in the decision of many to withdraw from the Army or the Navy. However, it appears to have declined in prominence by the second half of the century (although it would reappear in the debates at the time of the First World War concerning taking up arms). Open Brethren produced few written expositions on the theme of sanctification, and certainly nothing to compare with influential works on the topic such as the Reformed Anglican J.C. Ryle's *Holiness* on the one hand, or those by Keswick speakers on the other. As Rowdon points out, Open Brethren would therefore have been influenced by Darbyite thinking.[94] The relative lack of such exposition and the consequent absence of a solid theological understanding of the nature and dynamic of Christian holiness may be one reason why questions submitted to the periodicals displayed a recurrent tendency to legalism, interpreting the Christian life in terms of conformity to external rules and regulations.

Brethren teaching on sanctification had two foci, 'positional' and 'practical'. Positionally, the believer was already sanctified by virtue of being 'in Christ' and, as such, set apart for God; thus a favourite designation for fellow-believers was 'saints'. Robert Anderson spoke of this set-apartness as being the primary aspect of

---

[89] Robert Anderson, *The Gospel and its Ministry: A Handbook of Evangelical Truths* (London: James Nisbet, 1907[13]), 109.

[90] James G. Hutchinson, *Sowers, Reapers, Builders: A record of over ninety Irish evangelists* (Glasgow: Gospel Tract Publications, 1984), 243.

[91] William Lincoln, 'Is it necessary for a Person, in order to be assured of Salvation, to know the exact day, hour, and moment of his Conversion?', *NW* 14 (1884), 73-6.

[92] Cf. Bradley, *Call to Seriousness*, 21-2.

[93] See also Dickson, *Brethren in Scotland*, 266-74; Harold H. Rowdon, 'The Brethren Concept of Sainthood', *VE* 20 (1990), 91-102.

[94] Rowdon, 'Brethren Concept of Sainthood', 92.

sanctification, and as absolute and complete as justification.[95] This positional emphasis, which overshadowed the practical side of sanctification, was rooted in early nineteenth-century high Calvinism.[96] For example, Walker had taught that sanctification was not a process but an act, bringing individuals into a particular relationship with God at conversion and separating them to him; Walker also denied that grace mended the old nature, a point which would reappear in much Brethren teaching.[97] Similarly, Hawker, who had refused to preach the need for believers to pursue holiness, had asserted that sanctification was imputed to believers.[98] Such an emphasis was regarded as freeing believers from continually looking within to discover evidences of spiritual life.

The stress on positional at the expense of practical sanctification may be related to a fundamental aspect of Brethren teaching, the insistence that sanctification involved the gift of a new nature at conversion rather than the renovation of the old nature.[99] The old nature was irreparably ruined, and although it remained alongside the new nature, believers were called to put it off.[100] It was by virtue of their union with Christ by faith that they had become partakers of all that he was.[101] Writers often acknowledged that this should be manifest practically in a desire to grow more like Christ, but the implications of this were not always worked out in a consistent way. Mackintosh tended to stress the church's heavenly nature and its detachment from the earthly sphere; a negative consequence of this for some (due, no doubt, more to the continuing pull of the old nature than the teaching of 'C.H.M.') was a certain tendency to be so preoccupied with heavenly status that they failed to work out the implications of this for earthly life. Thus Brethren heavenly-mindedness came, ironically, to be known by outsiders as able to co-exist quite happily with earthly well-being.

A more balanced treatment of the topic, reminiscent of Puritan thinking, was provided by Henry Soltau in two articles 'On Sanctification' in *The Northern Witness*.[102] He explained that believers were both perfectly sanctified and called to increase in holiness. Whilst the old nature remained after conversion, the Holy Spirit worked in and with the new nature, enabling believers to mortify the flesh and to walk by the Spirit. We shall see later that there is evidence that Brethren were influenced by holiness thinking during and after this period; this, in addition to the two viewpoints outlined here, indicates that sanctification was not a topic on which the movement spoke with one voice.

---

[95] Anderson, *Gospel and its Ministry*, 121.

[96] Rennie, 'Aspects of Brethren Spirituality', 204-5.

[97] Carter, *Anglican Evangelicals*, 101-2.

[98] *BDEB*; Joseph Cottle, *Strictures on the Plymouth Antinomians* (London: T. Cadell, 1823), 21, 79-80.

[99] C.J. Davis, *"A Few Counsels regarding some Prevalent Errors. By an Elder."* A Lecture, having special reference to the above, delivered in the Ball-Room, Aberdeen (Aberdeen: Tract Depot, [1869]), 51-2. Although Davis was Exclusive, some of his writings were published by Open Brethren and may be taken as similar in outlook.

[100] Cf. [John Ritchie], 'Sanctification', *BM* 3 (1893), 85-7.

[101] [C.H. Mackintosh], *Sanctification: what is it?* (London: George Morrish, [c.1861][2]).

[102] H.W. Soltau, 'On Sanctification', *NW* 8 (1878), 40-3, 51-3.

7.2.4 The Law of God

Brethren thinking on the role of the Law of God in its moral aspect in the believer's life placed them in a small minority among British Evangelicals, who reacted sharply by charging them with antinomianism, seeing Brethrenism as a recrudescence of the antinomian thinking for which high Calvinists such as Robert Hawker and William Huntington had been notorious. Technically, the charge was correct, in that Brethren denied that the Law served as the believer's rule of life.[103] However, it was misleading to imply, as some did, that Brethren did not care about pleasing God, and scurrilous to allege that Brethren teaching allowed believers to adopt an immoral lifestyle. For all the weakness of their teaching on practical sanctification, Brethren were very clear that the believer's great object in life was to glorify and enjoy God. Furthermore, Brethren thinking about the law was also linked with their dispensationalism (though which gave rise to the other is not clear); this was certainly the case for A.N. Groves.[104]

Related to the question of the law was that of the Sabbath, observance of which had become a distinguishing mark of Victorian Evangelicalism, and especially in Presbyterian Scotland, where the Law in its moral aspect was understood as binding upon believers.[105] In Brethren thinking, Sunday was the Lord's Day, not the Christian Sabbath; they claimed that the early Fathers saw the two as distinct.[106] Thus Caldwell interpreted the Sabbath as foreshadowing the believer's rest in Christ; whilst it was the privilege of the believer to observe the first day of the week, it should neither be observed after the manner of the Sabbath nor imposed upon unbelievers.[107] One strain of thought, represented by Craik, saw exercise and fresh air as conducive to spiritual concentration, and a legitimate use of part of the day, especially for those who had no opportunity on other days.[108] Nevertheless, this was not a day for doing what one wished; *The Believer's Magazine* urged believers to lay aside work, recreation, sightseeing, and leisure travel on the Lord's Day, pointing out that after worship, study, teaching, visiting the needy, and evangelistic outreach, there was no time for anything else![109] However, the insistence that such things should be taught more often in ministry and at conferences implies that an increasing number in assemblies did not spend their whole Sundays in the manner advocated. This is corroborated by the appearance of complaints about believers absenting themselves from the evening Gospel meeting.

7.2.5 The Last Things

Whilst we must not overstate the role played by eschatological thinking in Brethren origins, the reported judgement of Lord Congleton that 'Brethrenism would never have taken the course it did without premillennialism'[110] is undoubtedly true; it set them apart from contemporary notions of progress, and shaped the missiology and the attitude to social involvement of many leaders. As with soteriology, Brethren eschatology majored

---

[103] E.g. William Hoste, 'Sanctification by the Law as a rule of Life', *W* 39 (1909), 161-2.

[104] Dann, 'Groves', 106, 118.

[105] Bradley, *Call to Seriousness*, 103-6.

[106] Henry Craik, *New Testament Church Order. Five Lectures* (Bristol: W. Mack, 1862), 76-80.

[107] J.R. Caldwell, 'Shadows of Christ. – IV. The Sabbath', *W* 25 (1895), 55-7.

[108] Craik, *Church Order*, 79.

[109] 'AC', *BM* n.s. 9 (1908), 119; cf. 'AC', *BM* n.s. 1 (1900), 83.

[110] *The Record*, 11 April 1860, quoted in Rennie, 'Aspects of Brethren Spirituality', 208n.

on the motif of replacement (of the old by the new) rather than that of renovation. The majority eschatological view among Brethren, Open as well as Exclusive, was that of dispensational premillennialism. However, there were some who held other views; in 1887 a conference was convened at Leominster to discuss areas of disagreement, such as whether intervening events were to be expected before the Second Coming.[111] Chapman, who was one of the signatories to the letter of invitation, appears to have rejected the concept of a literal Millennium and to have asserted that Christ's coming for believers would follow rather than precede the Great Tribulation. Eventually, he appears to have adopted some form of belief in a partial rapture (see below), although he did not risk division by teaching this in the assembly at Barnstaple.[112] Similarly, for much of his ministry Müller expected the Antichrist to appear before the Second Coming, and would thus also have expected believers to go through the Great Tribulation.[113] As he testified in 1893 to the spiritual help which he and his wife received from reading Newton's writings, this is not surprising. However, it appears that during the last few years of his life he adopted traditional Brethren eschatology.[114]

It is striking that the Brethren went through the most religious period in Britain's history, when Nonconformity experienced unprecedented growth, believing that everything was lost and the outlook was black. The explanation for this lies in their profound sense of disillusionment with the existing order, which found expression in their prophetic views. In spite of the majority belief that no events were to be expected before the Rapture, late nineteenth-century Brethren shared in the widespread Evangelical preoccupation with the 'signs of the times'. Such developments as the increase of theological liberalism and outright infidelity, the prevalence of error, the rise of democracy and lawlessness (which were often bracketed together), the passion for pleasure and amusement, the return of the Jews to Palestine, and the growth of militarism among Western nations were all seen as indicators that the end was approaching.[115] A steady stream of books and booklets on the topic flowed from Brethren presses, and it was not unknown for evangelistic lectures to be given on such subjects.

Towards the end of this period, partial rapture teaching became a topic of controversy. This asserted that only those believers who were living holy and watchful lives would be raptured and share in the millennial reign, the rest having to be purified through enduring the unparalleled torments of the Great Tribulation. Although generally rejected by Brethren, principally from a fear that it made the believer's hope something based on works rather than grace, occasional references to it indicate that it was accepted by a minority.[116] What really brought it to the attention of assemblies was when Lang, a former Exclusive Brother, began to advocate it because he felt that the usual Brethren teaching fostered careless living rather than holiness. After his exposition at a

[111] For a report of the conference, see Anon., 'A Conference on Differences in the Interpretation of Prophecy', *GL* n.s. 11 (1888), 39-47.

[112] Peterson, *Chapman*, 108, 134, 171-2. However, this was denied by Henry Pickering, who visited Barnstaple to ascertain Chapman's views ('WW', *W* 60 (1930), 137-8). Chapman's thinking may have been continuing to develop.

[113] Groves, *Müller*, 8.

[114] J.H. Burridge, *George Müller and the Great Tribulation* (Birmingham: the author, n.d.), 16-17.

[115] E.g T.R[obinson]., 'Signs of the Approaching Day', *W* 22 (1892), 33-5.

[116] For examples, see 'AC', *BM* n.s. 8 (1907), 131; 'QA', *W* 18 (1888), 94-5; 'QA', *W* 24 (1894), 51-2; 'YBQB', *BM* n.s. 14 (1913), 130.

Missionary Study Class houseparty in 1912, doors of ministry began to shut to him.[117] Although one of the deepest and most prolific theological writers among Open Brethren, he became a somewhat marginalised figure, although he claimed that Chapman, Groves, and Lady Powerscourt had all held similar views.[118]

One other aspect of eschatological belief calls for extended comment – annihilationism or 'conditional immortality', as it was labelled at the time. Exclusive Brethren frequently charged Open Brethren with sheltering teachers of this error and alleged that many assemblies were infected by it.[119] Open Brethren just as frequently rebutted both the charge and the teaching.[120] A number of articles and pamphlets appeared in defence of the doctrine of eternal punishment, the fullest being *Facts and theories as to a future state: the Scripture doctrine considered with reference to current denials of eternal punishment*, issued about 1879 by the moderate American Exclusive F.W. Grant (1834-1902) and reprinted by Open Brethren in Britain. Unfortunately, while Open Brethren sought to exclude those who held or taught conditional immortality, it appeared in their circles more often than they acknowledged, although less frequently in Britain than it appears to have done in North America, if Darby's frequent allusions to it are anything to go by. However, the private methods allegedly used to spread this teaching make it difficult to assess the extent of its influence with any accuracy.

The doctrine first appeared in England during the 1840s, and it gained a foothold in the Church of England from the 1850s; during the early 1870s, there was some controversy regarding the requirement that clergy subscribe to the Athanasian Creed, which included clauses affirming belief in eternal punishment.[121] Similar controversy affected Nonconformity, especially among Congregationalists and Baptists; it was a major factor in the 'Downgrade' controversy of the late 1880s which led Spurgeon to withdraw from the Baptist Union in protest at that body's alleged tolerance of unorthodox teachers. Dickson notes that during the early 1870s annihilationism caused controversy in Scottish Brethrenism, and there were many later references to it in *The Believer's Magazine* and *The Witness*.[122] Brethren belief in the sole authority of Scripture would have assisted advocates of conditional immortality to gain a hearing when presenting their case on biblical grounds. H.P.E. de St Dalmas, who had been involved in the investigations into Newton's teaching at Plymouth in 1845, had come to his views as a result of a word study using Wigram's concordances. He thought that conditional immortality teaching was making more headway among Open Brethren than in any other denomination because of their biblicism, and asserted in 1901 that one London assembly had excommunicated more than a dozen members for this belief in a year.[123]

---

[117] Cf. A. Rendle Short to G.H. Lang, 29 July 1913 (CBA Box 74).

[118] G.H. Lang, *Firstborn Sons, their rights and risks* (London: S.E. Roberts, 1936), 214-15; idem, *Groves*, 290.

[119] E.g. W. Kelly, 'The Doctrine of Christ and Bethesdaism' [c.1883], in *Pamphlets* (Sunbury, PA: Believers Bookshelf, 1971), 483.

[120] E.g. 'ASQ', *BM* n.s. 7 (1906), 11-12; W.H.B[ennet]., '"Open Brethren"', *W* 23 (1893), 149; T.C., 'Eternal Punishment', *EH* 6 (1891), 107-8.

[121] Owen Chadwick, *The Victorian Church. Part II: 1860-1901* (London: A. & C. Black, 1972²), 150.

[122] Dickson, *Brethren in Scotland*, 156-7.

[123] H.P.E. de St Dalmas, 'Notes and Comments', *Words of Life*, 5 (1901), 3; idem, '"Without the Camp"', *Words of Life*, 5 (1901), 247.

One assembly which experienced serious difficulties over annihilationism was that at Bethesda, Bristol. In *George Müller and his Successors*, Groves' mentally-unstable but frequently perceptive third son, Edward (1836-1912), portrayed the downside to Müller's long tenure as *de facto* patriarch. Groves' jaundiced perspective may have been occasioned by having been put out of fellowship at Bethesda in 1900 for advocating annihilationist views.[124] He referred to controversy on the subject about 1869 after a popular evangelist preached there, who was subsequently discovered to hold such views and excluded from fellowship.[125] The biographer of Edward White recorded that around 1871 three members were excluded from fellowship for holding such views: J.F.B. Tinling (who had been an effective interdenominational evangelist in India and England, and who may be the evangelist referred to by Edward Groves), Groves' unmarried sister Agnes, and an unmarried daughter of Henry Craik.[126] Four meetings were held during 1872 to deal with the issue.[127] Groves later expressed the view that 'what "separation from Bethesda" was to the Exclusive, so separation from the denial of Eternal Torment is to Bethesda – *its speciality in the way of discipline*'.[128] Chapman referred to the issue in a letter to Müller, which may have been responding to events at Bethesda: he believed that many who held this error were nevertheless regenerate, and distinguished between those in whom such error was rooted (who would spread it) and those merely influenced by it (who could be instructed).[129]

Also during the early 1870s, a number of Open Brethren leaders issued a denial of Exclusive charges, though I have not traced a copy of this.[130] Elsewhere, it seems that an Open assembly in Edinburgh may have split over this issue at the same time.[131] In 1893, the Exclusive writer W.W. Fereday cited three cases of Open meetings which had sheltered false teachers of Newtonianism, annihilationism (in this case, money allegedly secured

---

[124] Groves, *Müller*, 199-200, 211. Groves may have been influenced by de St Dalmas, who was living in Bristol by this time; after being excluded from Bethesda, Groves attended Highbury Chapel, Cotham, where de St Dalmas also worshipped (ibid., 46, 222). The latter may have been the unnamed former Exclusive teacher who influenced a number of young men at Bishopston Gospel Hall towards annihilationist beliefs; when these were condemned, they left for local Nonconformist churches (ibid., 147-8). Another source appears to have been a W. Chesterman, who had been excluded from an assembly in Bath and sent Groves a pamphlet denying the immortality of the soul (ibid., 187). A third source (perhaps the most important) may have been his own experience; separation from his parents and virtual incarceration in a boarding school at Bideford, Devon, run by the mentally-unstable William Hake, as well as several periods of insanity which necessitated his confinement in mental hospitals, appear to have contributed towards the development of a keen sense of human suffering, which may have predisposed him towards conditionalism.

[125] Groves, *'Bethesda'*, 126.

[126] Freer, *White*, 101; Groves, *'Bethesda'*, 124-6; idem, *Müller*, 31.

[127] Arthur T. Pierson, *James Wright of Bristol: a memorial of a fragrant life* (London: James Nisbet, 1906), 162.

[128] Groves, *Müller*, 200.

[129] Chapman to Müller, 8 April 1871, in Hake (ed.), *Letters of Chapman*, 15-16.

[130] Early in 1906, it was said that this happened thirty-three years previously ('ASQ', *BM* n.s. 7 (1906), 11-12).

[131] Cf. the announcement of a new meeting commenced 'in separation from the non-eternity doctrine' (*NEI* 2 (1872), 88).

this leader's position), and universalism respectively.[132] Occasional references to it also appear in assembly records, as at Hereford in 1883 and 1904. Another, slightly later, case was that of the Indian missionary pioneer Bowden's son-in-law, W.H. Stanger of Barnstaple, who left Brethren on adopting these views a number of years before his death in 1926.[133] In 1913 *The Believer's Magazine* and *The Witness* alerted readers to a pamphlet on the topic, *Is Man Immortal?*, being sent to those in oversight from Brighton.[134] That annihilationists continued to seek converts among Brethren is evident, both from their own statements and from warnings issued by Brethren. Similar reactions were evident to the extreme form of dispensationalism propagated by E.W. Bullinger. Apart from a tendency to write off much of the New Testament as not applicable to believers in this age, Bullingerism was notable for its espousal of a form of annihilationism. An assembly in Strathmore Road, Croydon, was split by it in 1906,[135] and articles against such views continued to appear into the 1930s.

7.2.6 Brethren and Scripture

Brethren have always been renowned for their biblical knowledge, and the movement has produced a number of scholarly exegetes. We have already noted Kelly, Tregelles, and Wigram, but Darby too has been described by F.F. Bruce as 'a well-informed and discerning textual critic'.[136] He produced translations of the Scriptures into English and (with the help of others) French and German. Brenton translated the Septuagint; Craik produced a Hebrew grammar; C.E. Stuart (1823-1903), an Exclusive leader, was another noted Hebrew scholar.[137] By the end of this period, the Greek scholar W.E. Vine (1873-1949) was beginning to write,[138] and we shall see later that the tradition has continued.

With such an impressive line-up of textual scholars and commentators, it is significant that Brethren have not produced systematic theologians. This may be due to the way in which Scripture was studied, often by means of Bible readings which worked through a passage or book of Scripture, and also to their aversion to theological systems which excluded true believers from fellowship. Yet the systematising impetus found expression in the development of a distinctive hermeneutic, making considerable use of allegory and typology. Examples of this would include Mackintosh's works on the Pentateuch, and those by Soltau and Jukes on the Tabernacle, the priesthood, and the sacrificial system. Other favourite parts of Scripture, for this purpose, included the Song of Solomon and the Epistle to the Hebrews; the latter provided a divinely-inspired

---

[132] W.W.F[ereday]., *A Letter by W.W. Fereday regarding the so called "Open Brethren"*, London: Chapter Two, 1997 (first published 1893), unpaginated.

[133] *W* 56 (1926), 378.

[134] [John Ritchie], 'Annihilationist Doctrines. A Warning Regarding Recent Pamphlets', *BM* n.s. 14 (1913), 72; cf. *W* 43 (1913), 172.

[135] 'IML', *W* 39 (1909), 180; 'WML', *W* 36 (1906), 87-8.

[136] F.F. Bruce, 'John Nelson Darby', *H* 24 (1947), 6.

[137] On Stuart, see Pickering (ed.), *Chief Men*, 128-31.

[138] On Vine, see *BDE*; Percy O. Ruoff, *W.E. Vine: His Life and Ministry* (London and Edinburgh: Oliphants, 1951). A trained classicist and former schoolmaster, his best-known work was the *Expository Dictionary of New Testament Words* (4 vols, London: Oliphants, 1939-41). This has remained in print as a standard Evangelical reference work.

exposition of typological themes and thus, from one perspective, could serve as a key to the whole of Scripture. One writer explained why Brethren saw this as so valuable:

> ... most, if not all, the spiritual truths in connection with the church of God which are ours in the present day ... were typified in a very remarkable way by the Spirit of God in the different parts of the tabernacle, and the varied vessels connected therewith, as also by the materials used and the exact measurements given for all its parts. ...

> What gives the tabernacle so great an interest for the people of God in the present day is the fact that it was instituted in the wilderness, and was peculiarly suited for wilderness circumstances. Believers are now passing through a wilderness experience on the way to Canaan in a spiritual sense ....[139]

The idea of this life as a sojourn in the wilderness was a very common one in Brethren hymnody and devotional writing, and fitted with their withdrawal from worldly affairs as citizens of another country. Although the writer may have been somewhat over-optimistic, even in his own day when visual aids were less common than they are now, in asserting that 'There are few subjects in the Word of God that prove more interesting to young Christians than that of the tabernacle in the wilderness',[140] meetings at which lectures were given on models or charts of the Tabernacle were a frequent feature in Brethren assemblies.

The typological approach was not unique to Brethren: the Anglican Henry Law (1797-1884) produced best-selling volumes on *The Gospel in the Pentateuch*, and the Presbyterian Patrick Fairbairn (1805-74) wrote a standard work on *The Typology of Scripture*. But typological exposition became a hallmark of Brethren ministry. However, Brethren appear to have developed their approach in ignorance of the typological exegesis of the Fathers of the early centuries, although they would have shared with them a belief in Christ as the key who unlocked the meaning of all Scripture.

Typology and dispensationalism both focused on the search for patterns in Scripture, a search based on belief that in history God acts consistently and according to a pattern. Thus students would search for corresponding events, persons and places in the various dispensations, an approach which lent itself to presentation in chart form. This approach may have enabled Brethren to circumvent the challenges to the notion of predictive prophecy posed by contemporary Old Testament scholarship, by removing the fulfilment of prophecy to the post-Rapture era. However, we should not regard dispensationalism merely as a strategy of retreat formulated in response to these; it also represented a positive attempt to interpret Scripture as a unity.

Two other points concerning Brethren thinking deserve mention here. Firstly, Open Brethren, while agreed concerning the status of Scripture as the verbally-inspired Word of God and its consequent reliability on all matters of which it spoke, varied in their understanding of the mode of inspiration. A number accepted the 'dictation theory', in which the writers were pens in the divine hand,[141] although Caldwell explicitly rejected it in favour of an approach which gave fuller weight to the different writing styles of the

---

[139] Anon., *The Types of the Tabernacle and what they teach* (London: Gospel Tract Depot, n.d.), 5, 6-7.

[140] Ibid., 5.

[141] E.g. Thomas Baird, 'The Plenary Inspiration of Holy Scripture', *W* 38 (1908), 80.

authors.[142] Secondly, apart from the tendency to sit light to traditional formulations of belief, another result of Brethren biblicism was opposition to the division of doctrines into essential and non-essential: Caldwell described this as a man-centred approach which sought to establish the minimum needed for escaping hell, rather than seeking to glorify God in proclaiming his truth.[143] All truth was essential, in that it was divinely-revealed and therefore both authoritative and vital for establishing and nourishing believers. Brethren upheld as an ideal the presentation of every aspect of biblical teaching, each in due proportion.

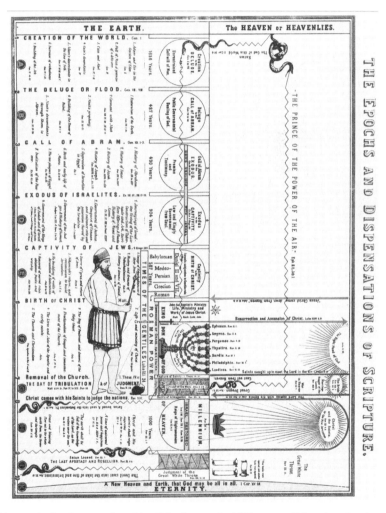

This prophetic chart produced by J.A. Savage in 1893, exemplifies the visual presentation to which dispensationalism lent itself

---

[142] J.R.C[aldwell]., 'Verbal Inspiration, Right and Wrong Views', *W* 39 (1909), 182.

[143] J.R.C[aldwell]., '"Church Government"', *NW* 9 (1879), 182-3.

7.3 The Emergence of Settled Patterns of Assembly Life and Worship

It was during this period that the traditional pattern of assembly life really became fixed. Dickson notes that the move towards greater uniformity in church order was parallel with the dying down of revival excitement; growth now came more through the regular outreach of the assembly.[144] This should not be taken as implying any diminution of evangelistic activity, but rather its institutionalisation as part of a weekly routine, a development which would make adaptation the more difficult many decades later. In the following pages we attempt to paint a picture of what it was like to belong to an assembly during this period.

7.3.1 Joining the Assembly

We are fortunate in possessing a fairly full description by Edward Groves of how applicants for fellowship were dealt with at Bethesda in the 1880s. The process was designed to satisfy the leading brothers, and the assembly as a whole, of the applicant's conversion, personal holiness, and doctrinal soundness. At each step it was possible for objections to be raised. Applicants were asked to meet with two elder brethren at one of the chapels, certain evenings being announced for this purpose. These would then mention the applicants to the 'Friday meeting' which included those engaged in ministry and pastoral visiting, as well as those serving as deacons. Applicants' names were then given out on Sundays in the notices and brought forward at the next monthly Church Meeting, and two brethren deputed to meet each one. The brethren brought their report to a following Church Meeting, and if accepted the applicant was then received into fellowship. Those transferring from other churches could be received on the basis of a letter of commendation from their previous church (unless it or its minister was lax in their personal conduct or unsound in doctrine), although this requirement was dispensed with when the individual was already well-known.[145]

Not all assemblies would have had such a complex procedure, but the majority would have stressed the need for applicants for fellowship to offer a clear testimony to those in oversight. One problem was that this requirement could make it harder for those with limited powers of expression to be admitted, even though they might be genuinely converted. On the other hand, it was not unknown for assemblies to receive individuals who offered a fluent statement of faith but proved to lack spiritual life, a problem which became more evident as the movement's spiritual temperature cooled.

It is important to note that believer's baptism (near-universal among Open Brethren) was not formally connected with this process; rather, it was viewed as the individual's act of obedience to Christ, an understanding which was paralleled among many contemporary Baptists (although Brethren sought to avoid becoming a 'Baptist sect'). Denying that baptism was a prerequisite for communion, Caldwell asserted: 'If a person is to be baptised, it should be *only* to please his Master, not as a means to joining a Christian community.'[146] All that could be proven from the New Testament, according to another writer, was that believers alone were received into fellowship, and that it was God's will for every believer to be baptised.[147] This view may have owed something to Victorian

---

[144] Dickson, *Brethren in Scotland*, 123.

[145] Groves, *'Bethesda'*, 113-17.

[146] *W* 34 (1904), 99.

[147] A.J.H[oliday]., 'Baptism not a Test of Fellowship', *NW* 9 (1879), 60-1.

individualism, but it owed much more to the conviction that outward acts could be undergone by individuals who were spiritually dead and so must never be made the basis for reception to fellowship.[148] Historically speaking, many of those seceding from their churches during the 1870s reached a clear understanding of the need to separate from the 'mixed communion' of believers and unbelievers before they adopted the practice of believer's baptism,[149] and the former issue remained more important for many of them. On the other hand, in practice many Scottish Brethren did treat baptism as the gateway to fellowship. Ritchie saw baptism as normally coming after conversion and before reception to fellowship, although he too insisted that it was not the door of admission or a test of fellowship,[150] and when the Churches of God parted company with Open Brethren in the early 1890s this was laid down by them as a formal pre-requisite for admission to fellowship.

7.3.2 A Typical Sunday

Brethren Sundays (or, to use their preferred term, Lord's Days) were as full of meetings as those of other Nonconformists, but there was a balance between different types of meeting. Pride of place was given to the Breaking of Bread or Lord's Table, which was the assembly gathering *par excellence*. As such, therefore, it was connected with the privileges and responsibilities of assembly fellowship, and so should not be observed by private groups or by believers unknown to each other, as at conferences. Theologically, the dominant motif was that of 'remembrance' (sometimes used as an alternative name for the meeting), and the worship was contemplative in style.

In the great majority of assemblies, this meeting was completely open, for any to speak as led by the Spirit, within the parameters believed to be laid down by Scripture, such as the silence of women. (This could cause problems where an assembly lacked men, either because it had few men in fellowship or because they were engaged in occupations, such as fishing, which took them away from the assembly for a period of time; it was not unknown, therefore, for men from neighbouring assemblies to come over and break bread in order to keep an assembly alive.) Normally it took place in the morning, worship being regarded as the believer's first priority.[151] Thus the term 'Morning Meeting' became synonymous with 'Breaking of Bread'. However, pastoral needs in some assemblies led to the holding of a monthly Breaking of Bread later in the day, often following the Gospel meeting, for 'sisters in service' (housemaids and other domestic staff) who had to work on Sunday mornings.[152]

Brethren broke bread every Lord's Day, claiming that Acts 20.7 provided apostolic precedent for this. The fact that on that occasion it was observed in the evening was not a problem, for Brethren pointed out that Jews reckoned the day from sunset to sunset: thus this verse was interpreted as supporting the principle of devoting the first available time to worship.[153] Incidental references imply that children often did not attend the Breaking

---

[148] H[oliday]., 'Baptism not a Test', 69-70.

[149] Cf. M'Vicker's reported comments on Brethren seceders in Ulster (*NA*, November 1873, 43).

[150] 'ASQ', *BM* n.s. 6 (1905), 95.

[151] 'AC', *BM* n.s. 11 (1910), 107.

[152] E.g. Christopher Bull, *(A short history of) Shrewsbury Chapel, (Redhill: issued to mark the centenary on 3rd December 1988 of the opening of the Chapel)* ([Redhill]: n.p., 1988), 6.

[153] 'YBQB', *BM* 6 (1895), 106.

of Bread, one parent remaining at home to look after them. Although the periodicals sometimes encouraged the practice of bringing children to observe, it was recognised that they might have to sit at the back of the meeting with other non-participants, where, if unsupervised, they could get up to mischief.[154]

Central to Brethren thinking about assembly life was the distinction made between worship and ministry. Worship was directed to God, and seen as the fruit of the Spirit's leading (preparation of particular contributions was seen as inappropriate). Ministry was seen as directed to man, and (though debate continued about this) the fruit of prior preparation. Although in many assemblies the Morning Meeting was devoted exclusively to worship, by the turn of the century it came to be acknowledged that it was also the most convenient opportunity of providing ministry for believers, some of whom might be unable or unwilling to attend at other times. Ministry following the Breaking of Bread had always been given in a minority of assemblies, and this practice began to be adopted by others. However, there was disagreement as to whether this should be pre-arranged or spontaneous.

Three significant weaknesses in Brethren practice emerged. The first is evident from the responses to a question in *The Witness* on the aim of the Morning Meeting. Although a number appealed to the belief that the presidency of the Spirit could alone ensure acceptable contributions in worship or ministry, none spelt out what this meant or entailed in practical terms.[155] The second was the widespread lack of attention to the need for 'rule', which allowed the domination of the meeting by one man or the expression of too many unedifying 'blessed thoughts'. The third was a rigid patternism, which could lead to assemblies dividing over the details of the conduct of the service.[156]

Ministry meetings were sometimes arranged for Sunday afternoons, especially in larger urban assemblies, where high-quality exposition might attract believers from neighbouring assemblies and denominational churches; Sunday Schools and Bible classes usually took place then also. Believers in rural assemblies might eat their packed lunches on the premises to avoid making long trips home and back between meetings.[157] Gospel meetings, held in the evenings in many places, but in the afternoons in some rural areas, provided the prime opportunity for the assembly to look outward. While not strictly assembly meetings, they were seen as occasions for believers to unite in testifying to the gospel. In many places they were preceded by open-air meetings and tract distribution, with the aim of attracting outsiders. However, occasional complaints were voiced that members did not make the Gospel meeting a priority. It may be that some perceived outsiders as belonging to a lower social class and thus chose not to participate; members with a network of outside social contacts would also have been influenced by the wider trend towards once-only attendance at church on Sundays.

---

[154] For more on the Morning Meeting, see Neil Dickson, '"Shut in with Thee": The morning meeting among Scottish Brethren, 1830s-1960s', in R.N. Swanson (ed.), *Studies in Church History 35* (Woodbridge, Suffolk: Boydell & Brewer, 1999), 275-88. This deals with matters which space has not permitted me to, such as the nature of leading by the Spirit.

[155] 'QA', *W* 32 (1902), 179-80, 193-5; 33 (1903), 17-20, 34-6.

[156] *W* 18 (1888), 126. For sample questions about such matters, see 'QA', *NW* 11 (1881), 95-6; 16 (1886), 80.

[157] E.g. David Sayer, [address on early Brethren in Suffolk] (typescript, [1954]), 5.

7.3.3 Other Assembly Activities

During the week, prayer meetings would be held, and also Bible readings. The latter were another type of meeting in which Brethren excelled. Taking a conversational form, the idea was that a certain passage of Scripture would be studied in detail, each man present being free to contribute. Ministry meetings, too, would be held by many assemblies; a brother would expound a portion of Scripture at length, and there would not be the scope for open discussion which there was at the Bible reading. Such gatherings might be arranged by an individual rather than by the assembly, although using its premises, and itinerant Bible teachers would hold series of ministry meetings over a week or two, to which believers from other assemblies and other denominations would be invited. The advantage of such meetings was that taking a longer passage of Scripture, and expounding it in a coherent manner which brought out its leading themes, avoided the tendency of Bible readings to get bogged down in the detailed examination of individual words of Scripture, a tendency which resulted in young believers losing the thread of the argument of the passage.[158] Not surprisingly, complaints were being voiced by the 1890s that such meetings were often better attended than Bible readings, a fact which was sometimes, and perhaps unfairly, attributed to the desire of many to be spoon-fed rather than doing the work themselves.[159]

Church business meetings were relatively infrequent (although overseeing brethren would probably have met monthly to deal with business and pastoral matters); during this period, such records as we have indicate that the tendency was for such meetings to be held twice or four times a year, perhaps accompanied by a fellowship tea. At them, the oversight would review the assembly's work and spiritual state and there might be opportunity for those in fellowship to ask questions. But the democratic procedures which were so prominent a feature of contemporary Nonconformist church government did not figure largely in the way that assemblies ran their affairs. Indeed, voting on spiritual matters was condemned as an unspiritual imitation of worldly methods.

Whereas many Nonconformist congregations shifted the emphasis of their programme during this period from the cultivation of piety to the enjoyment of fellowship and friendship,[160] Brethren steadfastly upheld the earlier ideal (though some of the latter needs were doubtless met by conferences, which may have been one reason for their popularity). Such activities as bazaars and literary or dramatic societies were all but universally rejected, the nearest approach to such things being occasional sales of work in aid of overseas mission. In the same way, outreach tended to be seen in terms of explicitly 'spiritual' activities such as preaching and tract distribution.

7.3.4 Music

The question of music, and in particular of instrumental accompaniment, excited varying opinions. Some assemblies did begin to use organs in services: the Carlisle assembly decided to purchase a harmonium in 1876, while King George Hall, Greenwich, had an

---

[158] Letter from J.G., *W* 42 (1912), 47-8.

[159] M.A.A., 'Are we "Filled"?', *W* 20 (1890), 70-1.

[160] Cf. Charles D. Cashdollar, *A Spiritual Home: Life in British and American Reformed Congregations, 1830-1915* (University Park, PA: Pennsylvania State University Press, 2000).

organ from its opening in 1878 and choirs from 1881.[161] Others, especially in localities influenced by Presbyterian opposition to the use of instruments in worship, sang without accompaniment. The Larkhall assembly, for instance, used no instrumental accompaniment during this period, although it did have a singing class from 1891 and choirs for outreach work and midweek use from 1897.[162] Even where instrumental music was adopted by assemblies, they usually resisted its introduction at the Breaking of Bread, partly for practical reasons: when a hymn was suggested, there was an inevitable hiatus while the accompanist found a suitable tune. All the same, there was a concern to raise the standard of singing at worship and evangelistic meetings; this led to some assemblies introducing midweek singing practices for those able to give a lead in singing.[163]

Such measures were, however, relatively unusual; when a questioner in *The Witness* requested suggestions for improving the singing in worship and gospel meetings, one respondent observed that 'in our dislike of anything like organisation, we have drifted into slovenliness. In our desire to maintain simplicity, we have degenerated into disorder. In our fear of formalism, we have lapsed into irreverence.'[164] He recognised that larger assemblies would have gifted leaders and would not need instrumental accompaniment, but smaller ones might need this, or a gifted precentor. In summing up the responses, Caldwell noted that some had been 'largely a dissertation against the use of musical instruments'.[165] Similar opposition was voiced by Ritchie answering questions in *The Believer's Magazine*; he regarded instrumental music as a feature of the previous dispensations and of millennial worship, rather than of the spiritual worship offered by the assembly; it was a worldly expedient managed far better by the world's churches; it lacked New Testament warrant; and its prominence in evangelism at the expense of preaching was leading to spurious conversions, as well as secessions of disapproving members.[166] Overall, many felt that introducing expedients such as instruments and choirs went against the essential simplicity which should mark spiritual worship.

7.3.5 Leadership and Office

In nineteenth-century British society, there was a tradition of regarding leadership as an opportunity for public service, something which was expected of a gentleman.[167] Some Brethren leadership practice reflected this way of thinking. According to Coad, leadership passed during the later nineteenth century from the ex-clergy and aristocracy to men from the business world; a successful businessman or farmer might plough back a great proportion of his profits into providing a building, supporting itinerant workers, and even encouraging a man to settle in an assembly as its pastor. The drawback was that his control of affairs might be quite close, thus hindering the development of the

---

[161] Anon., *A record of the Lord's work at the Hall, King George Street, Greenwich (1875-1935)* ([London]: n.p., 1935), 9-10.

[162] Chapman, *Larkhall*, 39, 61.

[163] E.g. Barnstaple (Peterson, *Chapman*, 76-7) and Bethesda, Bristol, during the 1860s (Pierson, *Wright*, 48, 167).

[164] R.W.B., 'QA', *W* 38 (1908), 84.

[165] 'QA', *W* 38 (1908), 115.

[166] 'AC', *BM* 6 (1896), 95; 'ASQ', *BM* n.s. 9 (1908), 96.

[167] Harrison, *Early Victorian Britain*, 94-5, 102.

assembly.[168] Edward Groves alleged that in 1874 his brother Henry had refused to settle at Bethesda because it was impossible for gifts of members to be developed in a church which was treated as a department of Müller's SKI.[169] He was cynical but not entirely inaccurate in observing that

> a forlorn Brethren's meeting was exactly suited for the development of gift in a retired military officer or civilian. Requiring no support of a material kind from those who formed the assembly, he was free to expound Scripture as he pleased, especially if he undertook to make up the deficiency that constantly happened in the matter of rent and expenses.[170]

During the 1860s, many military officers and gentry who had been influenced by A.N. Groves in India returned to England, and provided this kind of informal leadership.[171]

J.G. M'Vicker was one of a number of former clergy who continued to exercise a full-time pastoral ministry

As had happened in earlier years, a number of men exercised a full-time local ministry during this period, for example Samuel Alexander at Berkhamsted,[172] Philip Gosse at St Marychurch, Torquay, Henry Heath (1815-1900) at Woolpit,[173] Lincoln at Beresford Chapel, and M'Vicker at Clapton. The obituary of J.T.M. Ware (1823-77), who pastored the flock at Hopton in Suffolk, even described him as a 'dissenting minister'.[174] Even where there was a body of elders, it was the 'pastor' who would do most of the preaching, as with Chapman at Barnstaple from the 1850s until the last decade of his life.[175] Many of

---

[168] F.R. Coad, 'The Influence of Brethrenism on English Business Practice', in Giorgi and Rubboli (eds.), *Guicciardini*, 109-110.

[169] Groves, *Müller*, 24-5.

[170] *Ibid.*, 375.

[171] Coad, *History*, 168; Stunt et al., *Turning the World Upside Down*, 23.

[172] <www.kingsroadchurch.org/content/about/history>, Kings Road Church, Berkhamsted, accessed 27 March 2005.

[173] On Heath, see Pickering (ed.), *Chief Men*, 72-4.

[174] Betty Woollams, *Stones of Thanksgiving: High Street Chapel, Hopton, 1854-2000* (n.pl.: Oxfootstone, [2000]), 14.

[175] Peterson, *Chapman*, 74.

these ministries lasted for several decades, and it was uncommon for men to move from one 'pastorate' to another.

More often, leadership was provided by men with local roots, and often of the same social class as others in fellowship. Many, probably most, assemblies lacked formally-appointed elders, believing (like Darby) that since the death of the apostles there was nobody in the church qualified to make such appointments. As we noted earlier, Darby's view was that while office and the power to appoint to it were no longer present in the church, gifting was; the assembly should recognise those in its midst whom God had gifted to engage in oversight of the flock, and to submit to them. This informal recognition might take various forms. In some cases, the oversight came to include the whole male membership, in others, those who chose to attend the oversight meetings; in yet others, those already so recognised would invite other potential overseers to join them.

Even Bethesda, Bristol, which owed so much to the pastoral work of Craik and Müller, retreated from the principle that such appointments could be formally recognised. During the 1860s, these men used to invite others to share with them in oversight, convening weekly meetings of the twenty or so involved; deacons were chosen by the congregation.[176] When in the late 1870s a group at Bedminster wished to become autonomous, the Bethesda oversight permitted this on condition that they found a full-time pastor.[177] But by 1900 Bethesda had been influenced by some who had joined it from Exclusive backgrounds; its position was that no appointments could be made, and although those so gifted were to be recognised, by 1917 their lack would be lamented.[178]

In spite of the belief that God still gifted men to serve as overseers in the assembly, the lack of shepherds was a need widely felt. Most assemblies rejected the idea of appointing full-time workers, believing that a plurality of brethren allowed fuller scope for the variety of the Holy Spirit's gifts and avoided the risk of rebuilding a clerically-dominated church order. Yet by the end of this period, it was being suggested at some meetings of leading brethren that assemblies should recognise and support pastors in the same way that they did for evangelists, in order to meet the need.[179]

The diversity of opinions on the question of official recognition of leaders is borne out by the variety of designations adopted by those signing census returns for Brethren assemblies in 1851. A number disclaimed any official position. William Hill, signing the return for a gathering at Droitwich which appears to have been Brethren, added this note: 'As the persons assembling in this room meet only in the name of their Lord & Master Christ, they have no other name than that of Christians, & as their dependence is on His Holy Spirit they have no Minister so-called, but one who has occasionally been led to speak to those assembling has signed the census.'[180] Some signed as elder, deacon, or manager, and several as 'minister of the Gospel' or 'minister of the Word', although this is unlikely to have implied that they held office in this capacity. However, Chapman and

---

[176] [Davies and Chrystal], *Bethesda*, 14-15; Groves, *Müller*, 24.

[177] Linton and Linton, *'I will build my Church'*, 42.

[178] Anon., *1900. Bethesda Handbook, for the use of those in Fellowship* ([Bristol], n.p., [1900]), 8; [Davies and Chrystal], *Bethesda*, 15.

[179] For a critical report of this view, see [John Ritchie], 'Paid Pastors', *BM* n.s. 15 (1914), 47-8.

[180] John Aitken (ed.), *Census of Religious Worship, 1851. The Returns for Worcestershire* (Worcestershire Historical Society n.s. 17; Worcester: Worcestershire Historical Society, 2000), no. 420 (PRO HO 129/391/3).

Jukes adopted the simple designation 'minister', which, because it would have been used by other denominations, may indicate that their position was recognised in a more formal sense.[181]

Handling property and finance was the one widespread exception made to the principle of not appointing to office. For the sake of propriety and accountability, it was deemed wise for certain trustworthy individuals to be chosen and appointed by the assembly to administer its finances and accommodation. Such appointments were acceptable on the basis that they concerned the assembly's material affairs rather than its spiritual ones.[182] Unlike many Nonconformist churches, Brethren tended to stop short of designating these men 'deacons', but the secretary or 'corresponding brother' became a familiar feature of assembly life and often exercised considerable influence by virtue of his role in booking speakers.

7.3.6 The Changing Role Played by Women

Several women played a prominent role in the Scottish movement during the 1860s and 1870s, even becoming part of the wider British revivalist network.[183] Before the Larkhall assembly was set up, some women converted during the 1859 revival used to preach on Sunday evenings to packed congregations; apparently this was not uncommon.[184] This departure from social and ecclesiastical norms was justified on several grounds: exceptional times demanded exceptional measures; female preaching was an instance of female prophesying foretold as a feature of the last days in Joel 2 and manifested on the Day of Pentecost; women were evidently gifted by God for this work; and (a typical expression of revivalist pragmatism) meeting halls were packed with curious hearers, with blessing following. On occasion, women even ministered at the conferences which were becoming such a prominent feature of assembly life.

However, as things cooled down, Scottish assemblies detached themselves from interdenominational revivalism to develop a stronger sense of doctrinal correctness and ecclesiastical propriety.[185] The practice of allowing women to minister publicly ceased to be encouraged, was increasingly called into question, and eventually condemned unequivocally. The New Testament came to be interpreted as a blueprint for assembly life, and women's silence enjoined on the basis of 1 Corinthians 14.33-36 and 1 Timothy 2.8. Only one assembly (at Rhynie, in Aberdeenshire) continued to allow women to preach, which occasioned some tensions during the 1880s, as John Anderson recalled:

> the question of Women's Ministry caused a good deal of disturbance in Aberdeenshire. Godly and gifted women had been the means of much blessing in and

---

[181] Wickes (ed.), *Devon*, no. 1009 (PRO HO129/295); John Wolffe (ed.), *Yorkshire Returns of the 1851 census of religious worship. Vol.1, Introduction, City of York and East Riding* (York: Borthwick Institute of Historical Research, 2000), no. 404 (PRO HO129/519/54).

[182] 'ASQ', *BM* n.s. 3 (1902), 24.

[183] This section is indebted to Dickson, *Brethren in Scotland*, 74-7; idem, *Modern Prophetesses: Women Preachers in the nineteenth-century Scottish Brethren* (n.pl.: Partnership Publications, n.d. [first published 1993]).

[184] Chapman, *Larkhall*, 17-18; Strang, *Larkhall*, 2.

[185] Another factor may have been the decline in the influence exerted by John Bowes, who had been an advocate of women's public ministry (Dickson, *Brethren in Scotland*, 86).

around my home. We studied the matter, taking the Word of God as our sole guide. We found that both men and women in the present dispensation are priests, and as such, offer spiritual sacrifices – that both men and women, filled with the Holy Spirit, spoke at Pentecost – that Christ, while on earth, listened to women's petitions, called for their public testimony, and appointed a woman as the first herald of the resurrection, and that in the New Testament Church it was understood that both men and women might pray and prophesy (*i.e.*, speak forth God's message – 1 Cor. xi. 5). Therefore, notwithstanding the urgent request of leading brethren in both Scotland and England, the Rhynie meeting refused to prohibit women from taking part. The consequence was that we were ostracized, although all visitors from other Assemblies freely stated that the power of the Holy Spirit was realized more in Rhynie than in other meetings.[186]

It is ironic that the assembly had come to such a position as a result of the methodology which Brethren writers usually commended, that of searching the Scriptures and seeking to implement the pattern found therein.

Mrs. Martha Anderson preached in the assembly at Rhynie, Aberdeenshire. Her son James produced an outspoken defence of the practice

Even so, some women did fulfil valuable ministries. Frances Bevan was one of several who wrote hymns, another being Hannah K. Burlingham (1842-1909). Mary Yapp (1830-1911) conducted Bible readings for women alongside the Leominster conferences and elsewhere, wrote on typology, and contributed articles to *The Golden Lamp.*[187] Anne Evans (1820-1902), one of the first seven to break bread at Bethesda, Bristol in 1832, moved to Brimscombe and began a fruitful outreach work, opening mission rooms in the Stroud area.[188] Caroline Blackwell (a noted devotional writer) and another woman appear to have preached in the assembly rooms at Tralee in Ireland in 1872.[189] In the Blackdown

---

[186] Anderson, *Autobiography*, 21-2. Rhynie never appeared in the assembly lists; one wonders whether this was a case of editorial censorship.

[187] Ian McDowell, *Chief Women Among the Brethren* (Chadstone, Victoria: Chadstone Computing, 1992²), no. 11.

[188] T.M.W., 'Some Women Workers.- VIII', *CG*, March 1932, 57; *W* 61 (1931), 287.

[189] Caroline S. Blackwell, *A Living Epistle; or, Gathered Fragments from the correspondence of the late Caroline S. Blackwell* (Kilmarnock: John Ritchie, [1898³]), 485 (letter of 4 August 1872).

Hills, near Exeter, a Mary Rawling was teaching an adult Bible class and offering advice to local brothers at the turn of the century.[190] In the interdenominational context, the most famous was Henrietta Soltau (1843-1934), who grew up in Devon assembly circles, where her father William encouraged her to give addresses to mixed audiences; she later became a convention speaker, and supervised the CIM training home for women in London from 1889 to 1916.[191] But these are fairly isolated instances.

Mary Yapp

The subject of women's ministry received frequent attention in the periodicals.[192] The quest for a more public role was seen as a manifestation of the spirit of the age, with its call for women's rights. The fact that the ministry of women was being blessed did not mean that God sanctioned the principle of such ministry; indeed, it was likely to prove injurious to character, health, and family relationships. Male–female role distinctions were seen as operative in the church just as much as in the home or the social circle, and the equality of Galatians 3.28 as beside the point, since it referred to privileges rather than service. In the assembly, women represented the church in its submission to Christ, and as such they were to be subject and silent. Their ministry was to be one of deeds, not doctrine. Women did no miracles and wrote none of the New Testament books. Biblical arguments in favour of women engaging in public speaking ministry were considered and rejected. Acts 2.16-21 was seen as a special case; anyway, the ultimate rejection of the infant church's testimony led to the replacement of such phenomena by the written word. The equation of women's speaking with New Testament prophecy was rejected: there was no prophecy now, and when women in the New Testament era exercised this gift, they did so privately. Prophecy was replaced by teaching, and writers either asserted that women did not receive this gift, or that they should exercise it privately, as Priscilla had done in Acts 18. Even praying out loud in the assembly with a head-covering was rejected, not

---

[190] G.H. Lang, *God at work on his own lines: as seen in various lands in centuries nineteen and twenty* (Wimborne: the author, 1952), 51-2.

[191] *ODNB*.

[192] See, for example, 'AC', *BM* n.s. 9 (1908), 18; J.R. Caldwell, 'The Ministry of Women', *W* 25 (1895), 141-3, 158-60, 165-7, 185-7; J.G.H., 'The Ministry of Women', *GL* n.s. 10 (1887), 42-7, 67-70; A.O.M[olesworth]., 'The Ministry of Women', *NW* 8 (1878), 148-50, 165-8, and responses, concluding with J.R. Caldwell, 'The Ministry of Women', *NW* 9 (1879), 3-5; 'QA', *NW* 14 (1884), 96.

only because it was deemed out of character with the ministry assigned to women, but also because it would grieve some who disapproved. However, Fereday considered that the principle of an evangelist's direct responsibility to God meant that women could not be stopped from preaching the gospel.[193]

Many women undoubtedly found contemporary assembly practice restrictive. Some writers were sensitive to this, conceding that wider recognition of the varied roles played by women in the New Testament, and a recognition of the contemporary need for such ministries, might lessen the temptation to go beyond what was there allowed. However, Brethren tendency to disparage the philanthropic work which formed such a significant part of the life of many contemporary churches, and of many Evangelical women outside the Brethren, would have denied them other outlets for their abilities and zeal.[194] Indeed, most Brethren who did engage in any publicly-visible philanthropic work seem to have been men.

As for overseas mission, to some extent this provided openings for gifted women denied opportunity of exercising their gifts in assemblies at home. This would have been especially true of pioneer situations, in which assemblies had not been established. My analysis of missionaries sent out from 1874-1913 and whose activities were reported in *Echoes of Service* indicates that out of 1,064 names listed, over half (558) were women.[195] Of these, it appears that 266 went out in their own right, and 292 as wives of male missionaries. Furthermore, the proportion of women increased from 37% in 1874-83 to 57% in 1894-1903 before declining slightly to 55% in 1904-13. The ratio of women to men in mission over these four decades as a whole would have been broadly comparable with that in the home membership.[196] Open Brethren mission, like independent 'faith missions', made far greater use of women than denominational bodies such as the Baptist Missionary Society, but women usually fulfilled the role of supporters rather than leaders, as at home; they would not have taken a leading role in any institutions or informal networks set up by missionaries on the field.

7.3.7 Property

In 1829, A.N. Groves had asserted that 'After sufficient space to accommodate the people, there is nothing worth spending a shilling upon in churches.'[197] Many, perhaps most, later Brethren took a similar view. A perusal of assembly address lists is enough to demonstrate that Open Brethren used a variety of premises. Often they hired premises rather than purchasing them, and a number gathered in such venues as Masonic and Co-operative Halls, venues which could not have been congenial given Brethren opposition to both movements; the assembly at Ebbw Vale even met in the Rational Hall. Others met in public libraries, hotels, cafés, or in rooms above workshops or retail premises. Hiring meeting rooms meant that moves were frequent, which could not have helped visitors

---

[193] W.W. Fereday, 'QA', *W* 20 (1890), 143-4.

[194] Cf. Bradley, *Call to Seriousness*, 123-4.

[195] This would include a minority commended from other countries, but I have no reason to believe that there was any significant variation in attitudes on this subject among Brethren worldwide. My source is the list of missionaries in Stunt et al., *Turning the World Upside Down*, 615-38.

[196] Dickson (*Brethren in Scotland*, 296) found that over the period from 1863 to 1937 60.2% of the members of the eight assemblies whose rolls he analysed were women.

[197] Groves, *Journal from London to Bagdad*, 46.

trying to locate the assembly. Some assemblies met in private homes, especially during their early days. But an increasing number began to acquire premises for their exclusive use, either by purchase or on a rental basis. By the turn of the century, a number were taking possession of chapels which had previously belonged to other denominations. Others converted private dwellings for use as meeting rooms; the assembly at Moat's Tye in Suffolk met in a thatched building which had been a cottage. Many built their own premises; Dickson comments that when working-class assemblies did so, they would erect functional buildings because they had not the means to pay for anything more lavish, and because they were utilising techniques learned in the course of their work, which were practical rather than decorative.[198]

Many assemblies, like other congregations, acquired 'Iron Rooms', prefabricated constructions which were cheap and easy to erect. This example stood at Stapley on the Blackdown Hills in Devon

If acquisition or erection of buildings was a sign that a movement was settling down, then Brethren obviously considered that they were here to stay. Only occasionally did expectation of the Lord's immediate return serve as a brake on the property-acquiring process. More of an obstacle was finance: either the means were lacking, or it was felt that there were higher priorities for their use, such as the support of 'the Lord's servants' at home and abroad. Purpose-built premises were sometimes owned by an individual, possibly the builder, and arrangements could sometimes be complex; for example, at Mumbles, near Swansea, the oversight announced in 1901 that they would like someone to build a new hall and rent it to the church. This is what happened, and it was only after the builder's death that the assembly bought the hall in 1917.[199] As an increasing number of assemblies acquired buildings, the need for sound legal arrangements stimulated the emergence of bodies of trustees, who would hold the property and ensure that it continued to be used for the purposes for which it had been built or purchased.

In the matter of architecture, Open Brethren were gradually affected, if unconsciously, by the increased aesthetic sensitivities of the period. These created a desire among many Nonconformists for more aesthetically-pleasing buildings in more prominent or

---

[198] Neil Dickson, 'Brethren and their Buildings', *H*, October 1989, 12-13.
[199] Anon., *Castleton Chapel [Mumbles] 1881-1981* (n.pl.: n.p., [1981]), 5.

salubrious locations. Commenting delicately on the unpretentious, not to say unattractive, nature of Brethren meeting rooms, Beattie later advanced the opinion that sometimes the testimony would have been better served by a move to more attractive premises. In his view, there could be an element of spiritual pride in the apparent humility of those who clung to their old meeting places.[200] More often, believers were simply unconcerned about the poor external appearance of their halls, an attitude which often elicited the criticism that they spent more money on their homes than on their places of worship. On the other hand, Ritchie lamented a tendency to want more attractive buildings; it was a sign of spiritual decay that what was good enough for the previous generation (which he tended to idealise) was so no longer.[201] Nevertheless, even he balanced this with the challenge that if believers were willing to spend money on their own homes, they should do likewise on their halls.[202] Some saw the evangelistic value of attractive premises: Caldwell applauded the fact that 'Brethren in Scotland seem to be awakening to the need of better places for meeting as more likely to induce unsaved to attend.'[203] But many would have contrasted outward appearances with spiritual vitality, as when Pickering reported on a visit to Paisley:

> we noticed a striking contrast in the magnificent Baptist Cathedral, built by one of the Coats' [*sic*] at a cost of £130,000, where some one hundred and forty members, most aged women, worship; and the old mill store, low in the roof and small in articles of adornment, where some two hundred and fifty born-again men and women seek to gather unto the worthy Name alone.[204]

7.4 Reception, Fellowship, and the 'Needed Truth' Division

The late nineteenth century witnessed a change in the Open Brethren sense of identity and a resurgence of exclusive thinking among them. In part, this was a reaction against a perceived slackness regarding separation, especially on the part of those who had grown up in the movement and who, as second-generation members, had not had to pay the price which their parents had paid for acting on their principles: many of them were, it was alleged, more open to contact with the denominations than they should be. But it owed something to the influence of Exclusive criticisms of what they saw among Open Brethren. There also appears to have been a shift in the reasons for secession from the denominations, from a desire to realise the unity of believers to a desire to separate from ecclesiastical evil and to follow the New Testament pattern of church life.

By this stage, there appear to have been three main views concerning reception to fellowship. The first (whose advocates were often known as 'tight' Open Brethren) was that reception was always and only to full assembly fellowship; there could be no occasional reception of visitors from the sects as that would imply the existence of two 'circles of fellowship'; however, a differentiation was made between the universal body of Christ, to which all true believers belonged, and its expression in the local assembly, for

---

[200] Beattie, *Brethren*, 106.
[201] 'ASQ', *BM* n.s. 6 (1905), 83.
[202] 'AC', *BM* n.s. 7 (1906), 83.
[203] 'WML', *W* 32 (1902), 163.
[204] *W* 24 (1894), 147 (cover).

whose maintenance believers were responsible. Breaking bread was seen as a privilege reserved for members of such gatherings. The second, mediating view allowed for occasional reception, so long as due care was taken by leading brothers to ascertain a visitor's spiritual standing, doctrinal soundness, and godly life. The third saw the universal body of Christ as taking priority over its local expressions and argued that reception of visitors was based on their position as members of the universal body (hence it often appealed to former Exclusives); many adherents of this view left the matter of participation at the Breaking of Bread to the individual. Attitudes of surrounding churches to Brethren in their locality could do much to shape an assembly's thinking on such matters: where the experience of Brethren was that of hostility and rejection, they were less likely to be open to contact with other churches than where relationships were more positive and friendly.

Tension between advocates of different views was frequently evident, but the only major schism to affect British Open Brethren as a movement was the 'Needed Truth' schism of the early 1890s, so named after the periodical in which its views were disseminated (its members prefer the designation 'Churches of God').[205] At its heart were differences in ecclesiological belief and practice, and underlying these were differences in hermeneutical approach. While both sides agreed that Scripture was divinely inspired and therefore authoritative in all matters of faith and practice, they differed over whether the New Testament was to be read as a record of apostolic church life, whose underlying principles could be worked out in different ways at different times, or as a pattern to be followed in detail by churches in every generation. The former answer was that of Craik, Rendle Short, and many other Open Brethren, especially in Southern England; the latter was that of most Open Brethren in Scotland and of a number in Northern England, even if they did not go all the way with what became the 'Needed Truth' grouping.

From the mid-1870s, questions concerning reception to the Lord's Table and order in the house of God were being raised among the new assemblies in North-East Scotland, as is evident from conference advertisements in *The Northern Intelligencer*. Soon after, increasing concern was expressed about the looseness of fellowship among Open Brethren, many of whom followed the practice of 'receiving all whom Christ had received', and the ease with which some moved in and out among the sects. It was argued that such looseness entailed associating with those who moved in circles where human organisation took the place of the divinely-revealed pattern, and where false doctrine was tolerated or even propagated. There was thus a risk of contamination entering assemblies. By contrast, it was asserted, assembly fellowship necessitated prior breaking off of all links with the sects. In the light of such concerns, it was vital to establish means of clarifying who was entitled to share in the Breaking of Bread, and of distinguishing

---

[205] This section is indebted to Dickson, *Brethren in Scotland*, 158-69; Gordon Willis and B.R. Wilson, 'The Churches of God: Pattern and Practice', ch. 8 of Wilson (ed.), *Patterns of Sectarianism*. Other works on the Churches of God include Clarke, 'Churches of God'; Norman Macdonald, 'One Hundred Years of Needed Truth Brethren: A Historical Analysis' (typescript, 1993, Chapter Two archive); [J.J. Park], *The Churches of God: their Origin and Development in the 20th Century* (Leicester: Hayes Press, [1987]); [J.D. Terrell and J.M. Gault], *The Search for the Truth of God: The New Testament answer in Churches of God* (Leicester: Hayes Press, 1992²).

between the church and the world (which was often taken to include Christian believers not in assembly fellowship).[206]

Crucial to this position was an exegetically-based distinction between 'the Church which is Christ's body', to which all the saved belonged, and 'the Church of God' (also known as 'the Fellowship'), which included only those formally 'received' by, or 'added' to, a company of believers gathered to the name of the Lord. In two articles in *The Northern Witness* entitled 'Thoughts Concerning Fellowship',[207] Caldwell distinguished three circles of fellowship: the fellowship of life shared by all believers, assembly fellowship, and fellowship in Christian service. The present was a time of apostasy, in which divine doctrines and commands were being replaced by human ones, something which was true to some extent of all denominations. This had two consequences: firstly, separation from denominations was imperative on those who wished to be obedient to God; secondly, it was no longer possible to regard all believers as part of the circle of assembly fellowship. Those added to the Lord must also be added to the assembly, which involved formal reception.

Rice Hopkins

Another problem exercising many leaders at this time was that of local divisions. Many Brethren were reluctant to countenance the existence of more than one assembly in a locality, especially when this was the result of division. *The Believer's Magazine* would later carry questions about the proper approach to adopt in such circumstances, and the advice generally given was that leading brethren in other assemblies nearby should seek to work with the assembly affected in order to resolve differences and bring about reconciliation. From time to time magazines carried announcements that differences between particular assemblies had been resolved and they were now 'in happy fellowship'. However, if such arbitration failed, it was seen as improper to allow individuals from both sides to enjoy uninterrupted fellowship with other assemblies, a fact which necessitated assemblies' taking sides in disputes. Unfortunately, among Open Brethren there was no formal means of securing a consistent treatment of certain issues

---

[206] For an early expression of such concerns, see [J.A. Boswell], 'Questions connected with Fellowship', *NW*, April 1876, 63; [*idem*], 'Answers to Questions connected with Fellowship', *NW*, May 1876, 78-9.

[207] *NW* 10 (1880), 97-9, 115-8. To Caldwell's distress, these continued to be commended and even reprinted long after he had rejected the views expressed in them.

throughout the country, or a consistent policy regarding whom to receive from any assembly affected by division. Those concerned about this included Caldwell, Chapman (who had sought some measure of unity in doctrine and practice among Devon assemblies[208]), Rice Hopkins (who emigrated to Australia in 1882), Ritchie, and F.A. Banks (1862-88), whose manifesto *The Church and the Churches* was published by Pickering & Inglis in 1883.[209]

At some point during the 1880s, Caldwell retracted his narrower views, expressing regret throughout the rest of his life that he had ever held them. He adopted a more open approach to reception (having always allowed visiting believers from the sects to share in communion) and now also to preaching in other churches, and this would become one of the main differences evident between *The Believer's Magazine* and *The Witness*. A new periodical, *Needed Truth*, therefore began to appear, quarterly from 1888-91 and monthly thereafter.[210] Although its appearance was attributed to the alleged refusal of *The Witness* to publish articles on the subject of 'positional truth', both magazines were initially published from the same Glasgow address.[211] Initially it adopted a moderate position in an attempt to persuade the whole Open Brethren movement to adopt its views; it had no desire to be seen as a rival periodical to *The Witness*. To assist C.M. Luxmoore of London in editing the magazine, there were A.J. Holiday of Bradford, J.A. Boswell of Falkirk, John Brown (1846-1938) of Greenock, and W.H. Hunter (1849-1917) of Manchester.[212] However, increasing opposition appears to have provoked them to adopt a more aggressively confrontational stance.[213]

By now, these issues were being raised in various areas at meetings for overseeing brethren, at which those who would become the chief advocates of the *Needed Truth* position often spoke.[214] A conference for leading brethren throughout the country took place at Windermere in July 1891, but it failed to resolve the disagreement. A division within the assembly at Greenock triggered a wider separation from 1892-4 in which 100-150 new gatherings were formed.[215] Many originated as secessions from Open assemblies, and a number of entire assemblies withdrew from Open circles.[216] About seventy were in Scotland; in England, the movement was concentrated in the industrial

---

[208] [Park], *Churches of God*, 17.

[209] Terrell and Gault, *Search*, 33.

[210] Macdonald, 'One Hundred Years', 8.

[211] [Park], *Churches of God*, 20. Pickering appears to have associated with *Needed Truth* circles for a brief period (*ODNB*).

[212] On Hunter, see Brady and Evans, *Brethren*, 178.

[213] Macdonald, 'One Hundred Years', 7.

[214] E.g. *EH* 3 (1886), 72, 5 (1890), 27; 'TLWW', *W* 21 (1891), 111.

[215] Anon., 'Greenock leads the way' (typescript, n.d.; CBA Box 140(10)).

[216] Among the seceding assemblies were Dykehead (Lanarkshire), Inverness, and Orton (Aberdeenshire) in Scotland; Armagh (Newry Road) and Belfast (Shiloh Hall) in Ireland; Douglas, Isle of Man; Birkenhead (Atherton Hall and Seacombe), Blackburn (Oxford Hall), Derby, Halifax, Hebburn, Howdon (near Newcastle), Jarrow, Leeds (Queen's Square), Leicester (Oak Street), Liverpool (Albert Hall and Churnet Street), Long Eaton, Newhall (Derbyshire), Nottingham (Clumber Hall), Portsmouth (Landport), Preston (Water Street), St Helens, Tutbury (near Derby), and Wigan in England. It is noticeable that most of them were clustered in the East Midlands, Lancashire, and Tyneside; in some cases, assemblies appear to have acted as a group, jointly issuing letters explaining their decision.

areas of the North and the Midlands. Many seceding assemblies issued circular letters to explain the stand they had taken.[217] From March 1894 *Needed Truth* began to carry intimations of new assemblies, indicating that the movement was developing a separate existence. To that end, distribution of literature among Open Brethren was encouraged.

Not all who shared the new movement's concerns actually seceded; some preferred to seek reform by other means. The division split the editors and contributors to *Needed Truth*:[218] Hunter, for example, followed Chapman in deciding not to secede, although he continued to assert the necessity of some kind of central oversight.[219] Some who did secede would in time rejoin Open Brethren, such as Ludovic W.G. Alexander in Edinburgh and Hopkins in Australia.[220] Among sympathisers, Ritchie, who had been expected to become a leader in the new movement, stayed with Open Brethren.[221] One factor was the influence of Marshall, Caldwell, and others, who had been influenced by the new views but eventually rejected them as sectarian; as a result, the secession allegedly received less support than its leaders had expected.[222]

According to two writers from the Churches of God, Terrell and Gault, the new movement's distinctive emphases were:

> 1. That the Church of God in any one town was one Church regardless of how many companies might compose it.
>
> 2. That only believers baptised and added to a Church of God should be received into its fellowship and share in the Breaking of the Bread. Addition to one Church of God means addition to all.
>
> 3. That overseers should be recognised in each Church and, in addition, should act together in matters affecting all the Churches to maintain a unity of practice and doctrine.
>
> 4. That the Churches were inter-dependent on one another and not independent.
>
> 5. That the House of God was composed of all the Churches of God seen together, united in service.[223]

The root problem was seen as the 'independency' of Open Brethrenism. Although the solutions advocated were somewhat different, and based on different passages of Scripture, from those advocated by Exclusive Brethren,[224] the idea that meetings constituted a visible unity and the theory of 'guilt by association' were accepted by writers in *Needed Truth*. In a series of articles published in 1900,[225] J.A. Boswell insisted that Open Brethren meetings constituted a fellowship in which individuals were received from one

---

[217] For transcriptions of a number of these, see [M.S.E.], 'Some Papers and Letters in Connection with the Separation of the 1880's and 1890's' (typescript, n.d.; CBA 15029).

[218] Macdonald, 'One Hundred Years', 21.

[219] [Park], *Churches of God*, 89. Oversight brethren in the Manchester area, where Hunter was active, continued to meet until the 1960s, if not later.

[220] L.W.G. Alexander, *Discerning the Body: An Examination and a Refutation of Needed Truth Doctrines* (Glasgow: Pickering & Inglis, n.d.).

[221] Dickson, *Brethren in Scotland*, 171; *W* 60 (1930), 92.

[222] Hawthorn, *Marshall*, 68; McDowell, 'Hopkins', 28.

[223] [Terrell and Gault], *Search*, 33.

[224] John R. Caldwell, *A Revision of Certain Teachings Regarding The Gathering and Receiving of the Children of God* (London: Pickering & Inglis, n.d.), 5.

[225] J.A. Boswell, 'The Open Position', *NTr* 12 (1900), 25-30, 49-54, 73-8.

another; if care was exercised over the reception of individuals, it should also be exercised over which assemblies to receive as part of that fellowship, since many had started from causes such as schism or failure to exercise godly discipline.

> For a time these meetings are not recognised as *in* the fellowship, but they grow in numbers, and by degrees the fresh element finds its isolated position from the assemblies close at hand irksome. An arrangement is come to with some brethren that the past should be forgotten; the assembly is then published as in the fellowship, very probably only a few, or even one, taking action in the matter.[226]

By contrast, the Churches of God discerned a pattern in the Acts of the Apostles in which people received the word of the gospel, believed, were baptised, and were added to the circle of those walking in obedience to the Lord. Addition was not to the body of Christ but to 'the Fellowship', and thus entailed more than simply being brought to faith in Christ. All members of Christ's body should indeed be added to such a gathering, since it represented the only Scriptural pattern of association; all others represented disobedience, as did all use of ecclesiastical terminology not found in Scripture, hence the need for separation.[227] Only those so added should break bread together. The distinctive feature of the polity of the Churches of God, which has remained unchanged, is that assemblies are linked formally through the unity of the elderhood.[228] The movement's writers distinguish their union of assemblies under a united oversight from Exclusivism, in which they see one assembly functioning as a control centre.[229] The distinction mirrors the circumstances of the origins of each movement, Exclusive Brethrenism having roots in the hierarchical system of Anglicanism, and the Churches of God in the context of Scottish Presbyterianism, in which leadership was provided by a corporate body (the General Assembly) drawn from all sectors of the denomination and including elders as well as ministers.

Just as all who were baptised and added to the circle of those gathered to the Lord's name in a place belonged to the Church of God there, and came under one oversight (even if they met in separate companies), so too all such gatherings in a district (for which the New Testament precedent was the Roman administrative province) were united under one district oversight. District oversights were in turn united as a representative conference of overseers (from which a few men were selected to act as a circle of leaders), thus ensuring that all Churches of God were linked and could act together. At each level, members of the oversight elected others to join their number; there was no wider franchise.

The use of such a district oversight to help resolve division in a local oversight or to overrule local decisions was given formal expression after a disciplinary case led to division in a Church of God at Ayr in 1901, each group claiming recognition from the wider movement. A number of gatherings, including thirty-three of the Scottish ones, led

---

[226] *Ibid.*, 26-7.

[227] Macdonald points out that whilst this was the view of the developed movement, the seceders of 1892-4 did not claim that they were forming 'churches of God' where none had existed previously; he takes this to imply that they acknowledged the ecclesial status of the assemblies they were leaving ('One Hundred Years', 20). The weakness of such a position may have stimulated *Needed Truth* apologists to adopt the later, more negative, approach.

[228] [Terrell and Gault], *Search*, 38.

[229] [Park], *Churches of God*, 13.

by the evangelist Frank Vernal, did not accept that the district oversight could have such a role and left the movement around 1904, many rejoining Open Brethren and thus helping to ensure that the separatist note continued to be sounded there.[230]

The Churches of God soon ceased to grow. Some assemblies which had joined returned to Open Brethren after a few years; English examples include Tutbury and Nottingham's Clumber Hall. The return of groups of members to their former assemblies, sometimes with suitable expressions of contrition, was reported in the magazines.[231] Numbers of assemblies declined to 135 in 1901, eighty-seven in 1910 (due to the Vernal division), and eighty in 1913.[232] Thereafter there were few further reversions to Open Brethren for many decades and the situation stabilised.

Open Brethren were deeply troubled by the emergence of this movement. Indeed, the evidence indicates that they found it more difficult to cope with the existence of the Churches of God than with that of Exclusive Brethren: obituaries sometimes omitted or minimised reference to an individual's connections with the Churches of God,[233] and none who led the newer movement were featured in Pickering's compilation of *Chief Men among the Brethren* (first published in 1918), whereas a number of Exclusive Brethren received generous treatment. A large number of articles appeared in *The Believer's Magazine* and *The Witness*, all expressing opposition, and a variety of arguments were used. Many felt instinctively that the new movement contradicted something which was fundamental to the ethos of Open Brethrenism. In Caldwell's words, 'If we are called upon as the result of a process of reasoning to reject and treat as heathens and publicans, with whom there can be no fellowship in the things of God, the godliest men we know, it is time to review in the presence of God, every step by which such a conclusion has been arrived at.'[234] It was portrayed as a departure from the principle of receiving all whom Christ had received. The old openness, which had provided an opportunity for believers to be led on in the truth step by step as a result of their contact with Brethren, had been replaced by a narrowness which repelled potential accessions: 'Believers who were gradually being led on in the truth stayed away when they learned that their presence was not wanted.'[235] The structures set up were seen as examples of human 'combination' (a term more often used of trades unions at that time) which contrasted with the Church's heavenly character and Spirit-wrought unity,[236] and it was alleged that men were more zealous in maintaining them than in reaching the lost. Regarding district oversight meetings, Ritchie asserted that participants would 'go miles to such gatherings, who

---

[230] Macdonald, 'One Hundred Years', 40, 45; [Park], *Churches of God*, 27-8; [Terrell and Gault], *Search*, 39.

[231] E.g. to Ayr ('TLWW', *BM* n.s. 11 (February 1910), i); Cardiff (*BM* n.s. 1 (August 1900), ii); Bethesda, Linthouse, Glasgow ('TLWW', *BM* n.s. 8 (May 1907), i); Hebburn ('WML', *W* 38 (1908), 36).

[232] Macdonald, 'One Hundred Years', 23, following [Park], *Churches of God*, 150.

[233] E.g. *W* 52 (1922), 204 (Luxmoore); *W* 55 (1925), 119 (Boswell).

[234] J.R. Caldwell, 'The Basis of Reception and Fellowship', *W* 21 (1891), 146.

[235] Alexander Marshall, *"Holding Fast the Faithful Word." Or, Whither are we Drifting?* (Glasgow: Pickering & Inglis, [1910]), 11.

[236] W.H.B[ennet]., 'The Mutual Relation of Assemblies', *W* 20 (1890), 177-81; cf. George Adam, '"The Church of God" and "District Oversight"', *W* 21 (1891), 140-2. Bennet made the point that many in Scotland had separated from Presbyterianism and were therefore not keen to go back to such a church order.

never cross the street to win a sinner to Christ, or help a fellow-saint'.[237] Many challenged what they saw as the 'High Church' claims of the new movement, alleging that the appropriation of the title 'Churches of God' both ignored the fact that the Church of God no longer existed on earth as a visible entity, and unchurched all other assemblies in the same place.[238] Particular exception was taken to Henry Elson's description of it in 1904 as an expression of the kingdom of God 'in advance of anything known for centuries'.[239] Others warned against confusing an assembly's form of church government with its ecclesial status.[240] Some arguments paralleled those advanced when the Brethren movement first emerged. For instance, G.A. Sprague denied that the New Testament offered any example of the faithful being called to separate from an assembly on account of its imperfect standards or bad condition,[241] and Caldwell asked why the seceders thought they could do better in attempting to reconstruct the church than all their predecessors throughout history, who had failed.[242] Propagandists were accused of making misleading statements regarding Open Brethren.[243]

The Churches of God were but the tip of a far larger iceberg which threatened to shipwreck the unity of Open Brethren throughout much of Britain. Ritchie sympathised with their separatism if not with their Presbyterianism and belief in a district oversight, and he sounded a warning note in *The Believer's Magazine* about the danger of over-reacting against their distinctive emphases. He feared that the outcry against separation had resulted in a silence regarding Scriptural teaching about separation from the world and principles of gathering, and that numbers who had been added to assemblies knew nothing of these things and so would feel free to start another meeting when they could not get their own way.[244] Representing the type of Open Brethrenism found in Scotland which distanced itself from the earlier movement, and which was probably dominant outside Glasgow and Edinburgh, *The Believer's Magazine* rejected the widespread openness in reception found among English assemblies. Reception to the Lord's Supper was seen as a privilege rather than a right, part of the privileges and responsibilities incumbent upon those in fellowship with the local assembly. Thus there was only one circle of assembly fellowship, rather than a circle including visitors and a smaller one restricted to permanent members. Rather than welcoming all professing believers, Ritchie insisted that an assembly must know a person before it could receive him.[245] Separation preceded fellowship; to a correspondent exercised regarding even nominal association with the error tolerated in the Church of England, Ritchie quoted the text 'Cease to do evil, learn to do good' (Isaiah 1.16-17) as expressing God's will, assuring his readers that God would give further light to those who take the first step, that of separation.[246]

---

[237] 'AC', *BM* 8 (1898), 71.

[238] 'AC', *BM* 6 (1896), 47; *GL* n.s. 9 (1886), 71.

[239] Quoted in Clarke, 'Churches of God', 31.

[240] Macdonald, 'One Hundred Years', 15.

[241] G.A.S[prague]., 'The Present Ultra-Exclusive Movement', *EH* 9 (1894), 118-19; cf. 'AC', *BM* 7 (1897), 83.

[242] J.R.C[aldwell]., 'The Receiving of Children of God', *W* 41 (1911), 110.

[243] *EH* 8 (1893), 37.

[244] 'ASQ', *BM* n.s. 5 (1904), 132.

[245] [John Ritchie], 'Present Day Perplexities', *BM* 3 (1893), 83.

[246] 'AC', *BM* n.s. 1 (1900), 23-4.

Other Open Brethren adopted a much more open attitude, welcoming all believers, whatever their ecclesiastical allegiance, without requiring them to separate from such connections first. A distinction was made between receiving a believer because of what they were, and receiving them because of where they had come from; it was the former which was seen as the right course of action. Along these lines, M'Vicker argued that the Lord's Table demonstrated the unity of Christ's body, not that of the local assembly or of those with particular views regarding separation and worship; thus all believers were to be welcomed. Separation was from sects, not from believers in the sects.[247] Marshall, who had seen the impact of exclusive thinking during his time in Canada from 1880-90, took issue with Ritchie in *"Holding Fast the Faithful Word." Or, Whither are we Drifting?*, published around 1910. Sketching the origin and growth of *Needed Truth* thinking, and rebutting many of Ritchie's charges, Marshall called for all believers to be received to the Lord's Table because they already belonged to the only 'fellowship' recognised by Scripture.

An issue over which 'tight' and 'moderate' factions diverged was that of 'gathering to Christ's name'. Caldwell regarded this as equivalent to corporately owning Christ as Lord, and rejected the idea that it was only true of some companies of believers whose gatherings had the Lord's presence in a distinctive way. There was no tie which united Brethren apart from that which united all believers in Christ. His fear was that it was a small step from such a restricted outlook to outright denial that Christians in the sects gathered to the name of Christ.[248] *The Believer's Magazine* offered such a denial, pointing to the noticeboards of the sects as proof that they gathered to individuals or distinctive doctrines. Gathering to the name implied that Christ was the centre and the gathering power, and his Lordship in the assembly was recognised.[249] The issue was put into sharp perspective, however, by a missionary in Spain, G.J. Chesterman, who pointed out that while Brethren were arguing about such matters as whether they gathered 'in' or 'into' the name, millions had never heard it.[250] The tension between those who saw evangelism as the primary issue and those whose concerns were more with ecclesiology has continued to cause problems for internal relations among Open Brethren, as we shall see. The next chapter will demonstrate that Exclusive Brethren faced the same problem.

---

[247] [Reich] (ed.), *M'Vicker*, 153 (letter of 8 March 1899).

[248] J.R. Caldwell, 'Gathered into the Name of the Lord', *W* 39 (1909), 157-8; 'Gathering to the Name', *W* 41 (1911), 141-3; also 'QA', *NW* 10 (1880), 63; 'QA', *NW* 14 (1884), 95-6.

[249] 'AQ', *BM* n.s. 9 (1908), 35.

[250] G.J. Chesterman, letter in *W* 20 (1890), 109-10.

CHAPTER 8

Open and Exclusive

William Collingwood is not untypical of Open Brethren writers who wish to put as much distance as possible between themselves and Exclusive Brethren. His comment in 1899 was that 'they retain nothing in common with those they have left, except that they still have the same custom of "breaking bread" on the Lord's-day, and an open ministry'.[1] Collingwood's small work was an apologia for what he saw as original Brethren principles, which he contrasted with the resurgence of narrower views in his own day. However, from a historical standpoint, things are not as simple as that. Although Open and Exclusive Brethren should not be treated as one movement, their shared historical roots and continuing interaction make it impossible to discuss Open Brethren history without some reference to what was happening within Exclusivism. Furthermore, each side was in part shaped by reaction against the views of the other. This chapter therefore surveys the contacts between the two groupings during the period to 1914.

8.1 Looking Across the Fence

In this section, we take a look at the critiques issued by each side of the other. A full treatment is not possible here, neither should this chapter be taken as a balanced and comprehensive account of Open or Exclusive belief as a whole, but the main lines of argument should be evident.

8.1.1 Exclusive Critics of Open Brethrenism

Exclusive charges against Open Brethrenism continued to be dominated by accusations of neutrality towards doctrinal error. The spectre of Bethesda haunted Exclusive writers, and they considered that the subsequent course of Open Brethrenism gave them reason for their concern. It was frequently alleged that Open meetings sheltered teachers of annihilationism. Although Open writers challenged Exclusives to produce any evidence for such claims, and denied them categorically, there does appear to have been a measure of truth in the allegations, as we have seen. One writer, W.W. Fereday, did produce the evidence requested, but ironically he was already contributing to Open Brethren periodicals and would rejoin Open Brethren a few years later.

One thing which stung Open Brethren was the refusal of Exclusives to receive them to the Lord's Table. Andrew Miller explained that Open Brethren

> professedly assembled on the principle of the church of God as before the division, and owned the presence of the Holy Ghost in their midst. ... as this was and is the ground taken, the gatherings must be dealt with as one body. By acknowledging the presence of the Holy Ghost in this way they profess to be one body though many members: therefore, in receiving a single member from a body that professes to be a unity, the whole body, sound or unsound, is, in principle, received. (See 1 Cor. xii.) But in the church of England and in the various forms of

---

[1] Collingwood, *'Brethren'*, 22.

dissent, no such position is assumed. They meet on the ground of a particular system; ... and the members of the different systems remain as so many individuals, and ought to be dealt with as such.[2]

Similarly, the Darbyite leader Stoney wrote: 'When an assembly has professed to be on the ground of the church of God, and has departed from it, we do not receive from it or commend to it.'[3] Kelly regarded Open Brethren as worse than other sects because the others had begun in an attempt to safeguard something good, whereas Open Brethren were determined to shelter guilty Christians from the judgment of Scripture.[4]

The problem was not that Open Brethren as a body taught error, but that they were willing to receive individuals who were in fellowship with false teachers. This was what had occasioned the division at Bethesda, Bristol, in 1848. The Darbyite brother J.S. Oliphant, who withdrew from Bethesda in 1864 because he believed that continuing in fellowship would involve associating with unjudged evil,[5] issued several critical works over a period of half a century. In the 1871 edition of his *Bethesda Fellowship*, he stated the point at issue as being how unjudged doctrinal or moral evil affected an assembly. Open Brethren, he asserted, claimed that it only affected those who accepted it, whereas Oliphant insisted that it affected the whole assembly, citing 1 Corinthians 5 in support of his claim: leaven affected the whole lump. For reconciliation to be possible, those at fault must go back to the first false step they took, and correct their course. This was to be a common Exclusive argument, on the basis of which they insisted that Open Brethren must revisit the events of the 1840s and confess and put away the evil which they had committed at that time.[6]

Open Brethren, it was said, had never really grasped the implications of the truth of the 'one body' as requiring visible expression in terms of a circle of meetings known to one another as sound in faith and order. A.N. Groves, for instance, was described as 'a devoted man, of a practical turn of mind, confused and incapable of analysis';[7] he had failed to see that the principle of unity is not life or light but the 'one Spirit'[8] and 'never had the least real light on the nature of the church'.[9] In Exclusive eyes, Groves stood for the whole of Open Brethrenism. The consequence was that each assembly acted for itself, rather than in concert with others. Thus the accusation of association with evil was complemented by that of independency of spirit: Exclusives charged that Open Brethren often commenced new gatherings without reference to others, sometimes because of local disagreements. The result of independency was practical disunity, as an individual put out of one assembly for false teaching might be readily received in another. They had a point; in 1906 John Ritchie commented that he knew of five such divisions within twenty miles of

[2] Miller, *Brethren*, 61.

[3] J.B. Stoney, *Letters from J.B. Stoney. Second Series* (Kingston-on-Thames: Stow Hill Bible and Tract Depot, n.d.), 3.95.

[4] Kelly, 'Doctrine of Christ and Bethesdaism', 484.

[5] J.S.O[liphant]., *Bethesda Fellowship, ... 1907* (Southampton: n.p., [1907]), 4.

[6] J.S.O[liphant]., *A Letter on Bethesda Fellowship; with an appendix on the true basis of communion* (London: G. Morrish, [1871][2]), 21-2, 28, 75.

[7] Anon., 'A few Remarks from a Private Letter in Reply to a Friend who Enclosed the Paper', *BT* 13 (1880-1), 362.

[8] Ibid., 362.

[9] Anon., 'Teulon's Plymouth Brethren', *BT* 14 (1882-3), 269.

him, none caused by fundamental error, and that it was being openly taught that division was preferable if agreement on cases of discipline or administrative matters proved impossible.[10]

8.1.2 Open Critics of Exclusivism[11]

A prominent Open critic of Exclusivism was Henry Groves, whose *Darbyism* appeared in 1866. According to his brother Edward, he was fired with the desire to reunite Brethren but under-estimated the difficulties involved.[12] Edward offered his own criticisms on Exclusivism in *Conversations on 'Bethesda' Family Matters*. This section relies mainly on these brothers' published opinions concerning Exclusivism, but my reading of the literature leads me to believe that Henry Groves in particular was not untypical of Open Brethren thinking.

Undoubtedly one of the most significant areas of disagreement concerned what were described as the 'high church claims' of Exclusivism. According to Henry Groves,

> Those who discern the signs of the times, will not be slow to perceive that Darbyism is but another form of the high-church ritualistic movement of the day, rising among those called "brethren," which, though less gross and less outward than much which bears that name elsewhere, is not the less real. It has its high-church ecclesiasticism, its exclusive claim to ministry, and its superstitious regard for the ordinance of the Lord's supper ...[13]

Objection was raised to the assumption of the title 'the one assembly of God' and the claim to be standing on 'divine ground', especially in view of the early repudiation of all ecclesiastical pretensions.[14] It was felt that Exclusives wrongly identified the body, into which God receives, with churches, into which we receive.

Open writers pointed to the divisions among Exclusives as proof of the fallacy of their claim to meet 'on the ground of the one body'. Exclusives felt this keenly, and the London party would later formulate an apologetic of advance though division, in which conflict was seen as the means of purging out evil and bringing new truth to light. The alleged Exclusive insistence on uniformity of judgement was felt to be dangerous and productive of division; presciently, in view of later developments, one critic wrote: 'I almost feel history repeating itself, and a pope in embryo waiting the opportunity to arise'.[15] It was even suggested that the trend to centralisation involved the suppression of the gifts of many because the principle of individual responsibility in service was incompatible with the concept of one central authority. That authority was deemed by many to be in Darby's hands: 'Mr Darby left the surplice and the prayer-book behind him, but he always adhered to Infant Baptism; nor could he altogether divest himself of his

---

[10] 'ASQ', *BM* n.s. 7 (1906), 96.

[11] Apart from the pamphlets, two valuable articles are T.C., 'Exclusivism', *NW* 5 (1875), 113-16, and J.R. C[aldwell], 'Exclusivism', *NW* 12 (1882), 154-6, written in the light of the division between Darby and Kelly.

[12] Edward Kennaway Groves, *Müller*, 131.

[13] H. Groves, *Darbyism*, ii.

[14] E.K. Groves, *'Bethesda'*, 168.

[15] T.C., 'Exclusivism', 115.

clerical prestige.'[16] Indeed, with reference to Darby's actions in issuing the 'Bethesda Circular' in 1848, Henry Groves claimed that 'The moment any act of importance has to be performed, the very semblance of a corporate church responsibility is set aside, and the entire guidance of the Spirit is made to centre *in his own individual person.* ... as if Spirit and Apostle, church and council, all centred in one man'.[17]

Not surprisingly, there was opposition to the idea of central control, and especially the alleged dependence upon a central meeting or assembly, such as the London Saturday meeting, an outgrowth of Darby's belief that all believers within the geographical boundaries of a town or city formed one ecclesiastical unit, even if they broke bread in different locations. It was intended initially as a means of communicating decisions taken by local meetings, but in time began to take such decisions itself. Edward Groves observed tartly, 'It is one of the inconveniences of this form of Church government that the printer has to be called in, in order to provide a sufficient number of copies of its decrees.'[18] His brother insisted upon the independence of local assemblies, each responsible directly to Christ: 'God's purpose appears to have been, to keep every assembly as much dependent on Himself alone as every individual is.'[19]

Linked with this was the claim that Exclusives were in error for dealing with believers as bodies, rather than as individuals. Ironically, Exclusives sometimes alleged that a root cause of the evil at Bethesda was that the 'Baptist' congregation there had been received into fellowship with assemblies as a body. In reply, Open writers pointed to the inconsistency of judging Bethesda as never having been a proper Brethren meeting, yet condemning it as if it were. Local autonomy meant that no assembly was bound by the evil tolerated in another. Open Brethren could recognise independently-originating works, but Exclusives could not (the same charge was laid against the Churches of God).[20]

Responding to Exclusive comments about the infectious nature of evil, Open Brethren pointed out that leaven took time to work, and that all individuals in an infected assembly were not necessarily infected straight away. On such a basis, their policy of examining each individual made sense, whereas Exclusives were forced to condemn believers whom they respected personally, because of their ecclesiastical connections. In any case, Exclusives (like Open Brethren) happily received godly individuals from the Church of England or the Church of Scotland, in which error was taught and tolerated, but which had not been imbibed by those being received. A person became a partaker in the evil of the false teacher (2 John 11) only by praying God's blessing on their teaching. Furthermore, it was alleged that error was present in Exclusivism, notably the practice of infant or household baptism (Darby's distinction was not always grasped) and the idea of a post-conversion sealing with the Spirit.

Open Brethren were generally reluctant to revisit the events of the 1840s, although they did so to show where they felt Exclusive writers had given an inaccurate or misleading picture of what had taken place. However, on occasion they claimed that there had been no accusation of heresy until well into the dispute, the problems at Plymouth

[16] E.K. Groves, *'Bethesda'*, 141. Darby distinguished clearly between infant baptism and household baptism, however (see his address, 'Baptism: Romans 5:12', *Basketfuls of Fragments*, December 1999, 16-23).

[17] H. Groves, *Darbyism*, 48.

[18] E.K. Groves, *'Bethesda'*, 136.

[19] H. Groves, *Darbyism*, 7.

[20] Caldwell, 'Exclusivism', 154.

initially being blamed on Newton's clericalism and authoritarianism. In addition, they argued that if these events were to be revisited, then Darby's conduct was quite as reprehensible as Newton's doctrine. More generally, the alleged severity of Exclusive discipline came in for criticism. Quoting Mackintosh, Edward Groves asserted that devotion beyond divinely-appointed bounds was always to be suspected: David was severest in discipline when out of touch with God.[21]

Later on, Open Brethren began to criticise Christological developments among Darbyite Exclusive Brethren. In a series of articles in *The Witness* which drew upon patristic theology, David Anderson-Berry (1862-1926) suggested that if the writers of tracts which he had received had possessed some knowledge of church history they might have avoided errors condemned long ago. He regarded Darbyite Christology as an over-reaction against Newton's teaching, with its implied belief in the sinfulness of Christ's human nature; he saw F.E. Raven's teaching (in which Christ was presented as being God in person and man in condition) as clear evidence of a Docetic tendency in Darbyism.[22]

In spite of the gravity of these charges, Open Brethren could be very positive about Exclusive evangelistic outreach, this being a vision which both sides shared.[23] They were also happy to use Exclusive evangelistic literature such as the tracts written by Mackintosh and George Cutting's best-selling *Safety, Certainty and Enjoyment*.[24] Expository works by Exclusive authors such as Bellett, Darby, Kelly, and Mackintosh were manifestly superior to anything by Open authors, and featured frequently in the advertising pages of *The Believer's Magazine* and *The Witness*, and were often quoted from in articles. It was the system and the alleged pretensions which they opposed, not the expository gifts of the leaders.

8.2 Developments within Exclusivism

There are three main threads to be followed through the history of Exclusive Brethren, and in particular the stream to which Darby and his successors Raven, Stoney, and Taylor belonged: increasing introversion and separatism arising from the development of their assembly-orientated mysticism, increasing veneration of leaders (as seen in the emergence of an overall leader), and more elaborate outworking of belief in the visible unity of assemblies.[25] It is noteworthy that each of the groups which separated from the

---

[21] E.K. Groves, *'Bethesda'*, 137.

[22] D. Anderson-Berry, 'The Person of Christ Historically Considered', *W* 38-9 (1908-9), *passim*.

[23] E.g. Marshall's review of Stanley's *Incidents of Gospel Work* (*W* 22 (1892), 54-6).

[24] Cutting remained with the 'London party' after the Glanton division of 1908, and was responsible for planting a number of meetings in the East Midlands. Open Brethren appreciation of his work is indicated by the appearance of an obituary in *W* 64 (1934), 167, 192.

[25] For Exclusive history during this period, see further W.R. Dronsfield, *The 'Brethren' since 1870* (revised ed.; Ramsgate: Aijeleth Shahar, 1993); A.J. Gardiner, *The Recovery and Maintenance of the Truth* (Kingston-on-Thames: Stow Hill Bible and Tract Depot, [1951, 1963]; references below are to the later edition); Neatby, *History*, chs. 14-15; Noel, *History*; Roger N. Shuff, 'From Open to Closed: A Study of the Development of Exclusivism within the Brethren movement in Britain 1828-1953', BD dissertation, Spurgeon's College, 1996 (part of which was published as 'Open to Closed: The Growth of Exclusivism among Brethren in Britain 1848-1953', *BAHNR* 1.1 (Autumn 1997), 10-23). For a perceptive interpretation, see B.R. Wilson, 'The Exclusive Brethren: A Case Study in the Evolution of a

Stoney-Raven-Taylor gatherings in the divisions surveyed below was connexionally
rather than centrally governed.

Each case has been interpreted as a conflict between evangelistic and ecclesiological
emphases, as has the *Needed Truth* division. Although it is true that the group which
followed Darby became increasingly introverted, mystical, and centralised, it would be an
exaggeration to say that they had no concern for outreach. More seriously, Darby's
concept of the church's irreparable ruin tended to be overshadowed in the teaching of his
successors by a perception that they were involved in setting up a fuller expression of
assembly life than had ever been known hitherto (again, the same point applies to the
Churches of God). Darby himself had strong words for those guilty of such ecclesiastical
pretension, and to the end of his life he remained a passionate and winsome evangelistic
preacher who dreamed of pioneering with the gospel; yet these facets of his ministry
existed in tension with his quest for ecclesiological purity.

8.2.1 Further Controversy over Christ's Sufferings[26]

In his *Bible Treasury* articles on Christ's sufferings, Darby contended that 'Christ did
enter into the sufferings of others without being in the state they were in, and He had deep
sufferings of His own which were not atonement and were not mere sympathy.'[27] As we
saw in the previous chapter, this was taken by others to indicate a third class of
sufferings, the first two being his suffering at the hands of sinful men and his bearing as
an atoning sacrifice the wrath of God against sin. He also asserted that Christ made
atonement during the three hours he was forsaken on the cross, i.e. before his death,
rather than by his death, as Evangelicals had usually taught.

Darby's views were grounded, like Newton's, in typological interpretation of the
Psalms as much as in direct exegesis of the New Testament.[28] Many among his followers
considered them all but indistinguishable from those which had caused such a furore when
advanced by Newton, although Darby considered that his doctrine could be clearly
distinguished from Newton's: Newton taught that Christ was born under the sorrow of the
Jewish remnant, in a state of distance from God, and sought to escape it by prayer and
obedience; Darby that Christ was not born into this state but voluntarily entered into it so
that he could sympathise with others and thus help them.[29]

Some leading brothers, feeling that Darby's ideas were similar to Newton's, sought an
investigation, but this was persistently refused by those closest to Darby. Dorman
therefore seceded in 1866; during 1868-9, he issued a six-part work countering
Mackintosh's *The Assembly of God* (a popular exposition of Exclusive ecclesiology)
entitled *The High-Church Claims of the Exclusive Brethren*. Significantly, he did not use
an Open Brethren publisher, but the interdenominational firm of Morgan and Chase.
Dorman considered it remarkable that a movement which began by repudiating all
ecclesiastical claims should now arrogate to itself the exclusive use of the title 'church of

---

Sectarian Ideology', in Wilson (ed.), *Patterns of Sectarianism*, ch. 9. The following sections draw on
these sources as well as those footnoted.

[26] For a fuller exposition, see Neatby, *History*, ch. 12.

[27] Darby, *CW*, 7.146.

[28] Cf. Darby, *Synopsis*, 2.42 (on Psalms).

[29] Darby, *CW*, 7.222; *idem*, *Letters*, 1.433-4 (9 June 1866), 439-40 (10 June 1866), 442 (18 June
1866), 482 (17 February 1867).

God', and challenged it to produce tangible evidence to back up its claim, such as was available during New Testament times. He regarded the sudden stress on ecclesiology (which dated from a controversy over discipline in 1864) as a diversionary tactic designed to divert attention from the debate about Darby's teaching concerning Christ's sufferings.[30]

In *Grief upon Grief: A Dialogue* (1866), Percy Hall, who would secede in 1870, explained his objection to three aspects of Darby's teaching. Firstly, he understood Darby as asserting that Christ suffered God's wrath after Gethsemane and before Calvary, arising from his identification with the Jewish remnant, yet this suffering did not form part of the atonement. Secondly, on this showing, Hall concluded that God must have shown wrath towards one who was neither personally guilty nor an atoning victim on behalf of others. Thirdly, he understood Darby to be saying that Christ had the exercises of soul proper to a sinful Israelite, and that he was thus placed in a position in which communion with God was non-existent, and his relationship with God lost. Hall felt that Darby was treating the cross itself as part of Christ's non-atoning sufferings, and although he had repeatedly remonstrated with him, he could secure no rejection of the concept of non-atoning suffering.[31]

Darby was minded to desist from breaking bread for the sake of those who had been unsettled by the debate, which may indicate that he recognised the weakness of his position, but Stoney and others urged him not to do so.[32] He considered Dorman's withdrawal as an excuse for looseness, alleging that Dorman broke with those teaching Newtonian doctrine only to associate with others linked by association with the same doctrines.

8.2.2 'The Ramsgate Sorrow': Darby and Kelly Part Company

Near the end of Darby's life, Exclusivism began to divide between those whose scholarship and evangelistic concern kept them in touch with the wider world and those of a more mystical frame of mind, whose spirituality tended to focus on the assembly. There were to be significant divisions in 1879-81, 1883, 1885, 1890, and 1908. Open Brethren claimed that in each case a crucial role was played by the gathering at Park Street in London (to which Darby and Stoney belonged).[33] Regular brothers' meetings there for the London gatherings took administrative decisions relating to the movement as a whole, and so it came to exercise considerable influence. However, A.H. Burton stood on its head the charge that Exclusive Brethren were ruled by the meeting at Park Street, asserting (*contra* Marshall) that it was Newton, not Wigram, who had introduced the idea of submission to a central meeting.[34] Furthermore, Darby had often been abroad when

---

[30] W.H. Dorman, *The High-Church Claims of the Exclusive Brethren. A Series of Letters to Mr. J.L. Harris* (6 parts; London: Morgan and Chase, [1868-9]), 8.

[31] P.F.H[all]., *Grief upon Grief: A Dialogue* (London: Houlston & Wright, 1866²), 6-7, 13, 42-3, 48-9.

[32] Darby, *Letters*, 1.432 (9 June 1866); Stoney, *Letters. Second Series*, 1.137.

[33] For an example of this interpretation, see Veitch, *Story*, ch. 5; this work was an apologetic for the autonomy of each local congregation.

[34] *What is Exclusivism? A review of Mr Alex. Marshall's "Holding Fast the Faithful Word"* (London: James Carter, 1908), 6.

controversial matters were being discussed, and appears to have distanced himself from the manner in which some of the decisions had been taken or circulated.[35]

Darby had increasingly dreaded the prospect of further division and the ever-more exclusive attitude and assumptions of ecclesiastical position made by some within Exclusivism. Wigram, too, was apprehensive: before his death in 1879, he expressed the conviction that Brethren had been 'playing at church' and that God could not go on blessing them in their present state.[36] However, it appears that Darby, nearing the end of his earthly course, was influenced by men like Stoney.[37] Their introspective piety resulted in an unbalanced emphasis on the purity of the assembly.[38] It could have acted as a healthy counterweight to the objective nature of much Brethren teaching, but instead two rival groups emerged.[39] Exclusive evangelists had shared to the full in the activity which marked much British Evangelicalism during the 1860s and 1870s, and had reaped a rich harvest as a result. However, the 'New Lumpists' (cf. 1 Corinthians 5.6-7; so called from their emphasis on securing the purity of the assembly), considered that new converts from the evangelists' work were insufficiently instructed in the movement's distinctive doctrines, and wished to restrict the circle of fellowship to those deemed 'spiritual'. (They may have been reacting against the kind of activism associated with Moody, who believed in setting new converts to work straight away without waiting to teach them first.) Darby long opposed such a restriction, although he appears to have changed his mind by this time,[40] and Wigram was also troubled by it.

There was an Exclusive meeting at Ryde on the Isle of Wight which was universally recognised as being in an unhealthy condition, and a breakaway meeting which included a number of converts from Anglicanism. In 1879 Edward Cronin, who was in fellowship with the Exclusive meeting at Kennington in London, went on a visit to Ryde. He broke bread with the second group, apparently from a desire to get Brethren to recognise it in place of the original meeting (Kelly had already argued that the original meeting was in such a state that it should no longer be recognised, though he considered Cronin's action irregular and unwise[41]). His actions earned him the criticism of more 'churchly' Exclusives, because they saw it as attempting to force the issue, but his own meeting delayed putting him out of fellowship. Park Street therefore declared him out of fellowship, and thus all who broke bread with him. They posted their decision to a number of meetings outside London. However, the same day, and without knowing what Park Street were doing, Kennington finally declared Cronin to have put himself out of fellowship; the London brothers' meeting therefore accepted that Park Street's decision was annulled and Kennington remained in fellowship. Unfortunately, the meeting at

---

[35] E.g. Darby, *Letters*, 3.10 (26 August 1879).

[36] Ironside, *Historical Sketch*, 79, 83.

[37] *Ibid.*, 98.

[38] Near the end of his life, Stoney recalled how at Manchester in 1873 he had shown how Satan had constantly opposed the truth, most recently by means of a form of gospel proclamation which limited it to salvation and excluded church truth; he was out of sympathy with what he described as the 'wave of gospel excitement' (J.B. Stoney, *A Message to the Quemerford Meeting* (n.pl.:, n.p., [1896]), 3).

[39] Ironside, *Historical Sketch*, 122.

[40] Darby to Mr F., 26 February 1863 (BGT folder 11, f.19); Darby to Mr C., 6 July 1870 (BGT folder 14, f.5); cp. Darby to P[ierre].S[chlumberger]., March 1881 (BGT folder 17, f.21).

[41] Marginal note in Kelly's copy of Neatby, *History*, 286 (Chapter Two archive).

Ramsgate received Park Street's first intimation but not that from the London meeting, and itself divided over whether to declare itself out of fellowship with Kennington. When news of the London meeting's decision came through, reunion proved impossible; it was two years before Park Street finally decided which section at Ramsgate to recognise, and when it did, it sided with the New Lumpists. Kelly could see nothing wrong with Cronin's action at Ryde, and accused Park Street of acting independently, though it would be more accurate to say that they were insisting upon other meetings coming into line with them.[42] Several other leading Exclusives rejected Park Street's decision, including Thomas Neatby and Andrew Miller, and the movement divided.[43] Kelly had established himself as a lucid interpreter of Darby's theological views, and it was a disaster when these two giants found themselves on opposing sides. Darby claimed that 'the judgment of Park Street has been accepted almost everywhere in London, and in the whole country',[44] but 25-30% of English meetings appear to have gone with Kelly.

William Kelly, c.1890

Neatby notes that 'though there were exceptions on both sides, the Baptists went nearly solid for Mr. Kelly, and the paedobaptists for Mr. Darby. Considering that the question of baptism had no connexion of any kind with the subjects then in dispute, this is certainly a very interesting circumstance.'[45] However, Darby implied that there was a connection, arguing that the division amounted to an attempt to form a Baptist sect.[46] The New Lumpists, who followed Darby, may be roughly equated with the paedobaptist strand of Exclusivism; their emphasis on church truth would fit well with a belief in infant baptism as introducing to a sphere of privilege (the assembly). Their spirituality also appears to have been quite introverted and even mystical, as was more fully brought out by developments among this grouping during succeeding decades. On the other hand, the more outward-looking and evangelistically-inclined, many of whom followed Kelly,

---

[42] For this charge, cf. J.A. von P[oseck]., *The Word of God, or Private Revelations: Which?* ([Lewisham: the author, 1881]).

[43] Veitch, *Story*, 78.

[44] Darby to P[ierre].S[chlumberger]., September 1881 (BGT folder 17, f.26).

[45] Neatby, *History*, 237.

[46] Darby to P[ierre].S[chlumberger]., 15 December 1881 (BGT folder 17, f.29). Although he elsewhere claimed that there was no connection, he asserted that the issue of baptism underlay Cronin's desire for something new (Darby to Andrew Miller, May 1881 (CBA5540(179)).

tended to regard personal response to Christ as a prerequisite to baptism: such a spirituality would give greater place to the individual as opposed to the family or the body.

There were those who felt that such a division should never have occurred (after all, no fundamental doctrine was at issue).[47] In spite of the differences between the two sides, the leaders retained a high regard for each other: on his deathbed, Darby stressed that he did not wish his followers to make any attack upon Kelly, and Kelly (who could be quite caustic about those he thought were departing from the truth) likewise continued to speak of Darby with warmth and affection, even while recognising his foibles. He regarded Darby as 'a really good & great man' who had been misled by partisan followers.[48] If personality was a factor in the division at Plymouth, it certainly was not so on this occasion.

8.2.3 Controversies over Christian Experience: Grant, Stuart, and Raven

A former Anglican clergyman, F.W. Grant (1834-1902),[49] of Plainfield, New Jersey, had criticised Darby's understanding of the geographical city as the basic ecclesial unit, and the role played in London by the meeting of brothers at Park Street. He also diverged from the teaching being accepted in Britain that reception of eternal life occurred subsequent to the new birth, at the same time as sealing with the Spirit, and asserted that Old Testament believers also enjoyed eternal life. Wilson has noted that the effect of Grant's views was to diminish the distance between those in the assembly and believers outside it, whereas the teaching of his opponents and their successors linked spiritual blessing to assembly life rather than to faith and conversion.[50] In 1884 divison ensued, most North American Exclusives following Grant; the Grant Brethren became known for their outward-looking approach; in time, most of them would reunite with Open Brethren.[51] In Toronto, the Exclusive meeting adopted a fateful strategy in its condemnation of Grant's views, stating that acceptance of the Park Street decision was based not on knowledge of the facts but on the principle of 'one body and one Spirit'.[52] In other words, what mattered was acting in unity with other gatherings and accepting their presentation of the facts of the matter. This principle would cause further divisions within Exclusivism, not always involving Park Street.

The Reading division (1885) concerned the teaching of C.E. Stuart (1828-1903).[53] Stuart was a Hebrew scholar, and on the basis of certain Old Testament types he taught that Christ made propitiation by presenting his blood in heaven after his death. Park Street took the matter up after Stuart's own assembly had exonerated him, thus precipitating another division. A few British meetings (more in Scotland than in England) followed Stuart, as did a number in New Zealand.

---

[47] W.M. Rule, 'All Ye Are Brethren' (typescript, [1931]), 6 (CBA Box 12/18).

[48] Marginal notes to his copy of Neatby, *History*, 309, 287-9, respectively.

[49] See Pickering (ed.), *Chief Men*, 100-01; John Reid, *F.W. Grant: His Life, Ministry and Legacy* (Plainfield, NJ: John Reid Book Fund, 1995).

[50] Wilson, 'Exclusive Brethren', 303-4.

[51] Other works on the Grant Brethren include Baylis, *My People*; McLaren, 'Triple Tradition'.

[52] Veitch, *Story*, 78-9.

[53] See Pickering (ed.), *Chief Men*, 128-31.

The Bexhill division (1890) took place over the teaching of F.E. Raven (1837-1903) of Greenwich, whose Christology was deemed erroneous. Raven did not express himself too clearly, but he appears to have taught that in person Christ was God, but in condition he was man, a view which has been criticised as Apollinarian.[54] He also appears to have denied that Christ derived his human flesh from Mary. Furthermore, he insisted that eternal life should be viewed not as the present experience of all believers, but as something possessed in actuality by Christ, and as an inheritance to be entered into by those who are in Christ.[55] The meeting at Bexhill refused to accept a visitor from Raven's meeting, excommunicated it, and thus forced other meetings to decide which they would support. Raven's supporters sought to show that he did not teach the errors imputed to him; Park Street cleared Raven and cut off from fellowship those who disagreed with him. Although only a minority of English meetings parted company with Raven (some returning to fellowship with the Kelly Brethren), becoming known as Lowe Brethren after their leader, W.J. Lowe (1838-1927), a majority of Exclusive assemblies on the Continent did so.[56] After the division, Raven's teaching appears to have become increasingly obscure and mystical in tone; it was claimed that only the truly spiritual would understand it. Such an assertion would have inhibited questioning or criticism, as nobody would have wished to incur the accusation that they were unspiritual.

In Britain, the Lowe Brethren themselves split in 1909 over a disciplinary case in which the Tunbridge Wells meeting insisted that a local assembly's decisions must be regarded as binding on all others and not open to investigation. Most British Tunbridge Wells meetings reunited with the Kelly-Lowe Brethren in 1940, but those in North America remained apart.

8.2.4 Glanton: Local and Central Responsibility

The Glanton division of 1908 among the Raven meetings had its roots in a division which had affected the Alnwick meeting from 1904, the result of which was that neither party at Alnwick continued breaking bread, but some who confessed their errors were received to fellowship with the nearby Glanton meeting. Early in 1908, they recommenced breaking bread at Alnwick, in full fellowship with Glanton. Some elsewhere thought that Glanton had infringed the principle of local responsibility by its assumption that the Alnwick meeting no longer existed and its consequent actions. Park Street rejected the conclusions of local meetings which had approved Glanton's impartial handling of the matter, and insisted that the remnants of a meeting still existed in Alnwick, and that Glanton should therefore be refused fellowship for receiving believers from Alnwick.

Over two hundred meetings in various countries left at this point, including almost all the outward-looking element; some commentators have seen the division as having presented an opportunity for dissidents, uneasy at the mystical and Christological views

[54] Apollinarius was a fourth-century bishop who taught that in the incarnate Christ the divine Logos took the place of a human mind or soul.

[55] See F.E. Raven, *Letters of F.E. Raven and Fragments from his Ministry* (Kingston-on-Thames: Stow Hill Bible and Tract Depot, [1963]), 26-7 (18 September 1890), 40-7 (paper on 'Eternal Life'), 56-8 (to J. Edmondson, 15 June 1891); also the quotations in Bruce, 'Humanity of Christ', 8-9.

[56] On Lowe, see Anon., *A Brief Account of the life and Labours of the late W.J. Lowe* (London: C.A. Hammond, [1927]).

now being advanced by James Taylor and others, to be removed.[57] Most of the Raven party's evangelists went with Glanton (including H.P. Barker, who later associated with Open Brethren, A.J. Pollock, and W.T.P. Wolston), and this grouping became the most evangelistically active of the Exclusive streams.[58] Most British Stuart meetings united with it in 1909. The remaining Raven-Taylor Exclusives, however, developed a strongly-centralised leadership and a hierarchical structure of meetings which served as a means for disseminating the new teachings propagated by successive leaders.

8.3 The Growth of Concern for Reunion

Exclusive thinking about reunion has often focused on returning to the point of divergence (seen by some as departure) and seeking reconciliation through repentance for sins committed at that point. However, it began to be suggested that what mattered was not the past but the present. As the years went by, some suggested that the 'Bethesda question' should no longer be kept going, and even claimed that Darby had supported such an approach. On both sides of the divide, a growth of concern for reunion was evident, especially among those who had separated from the Raven group or its predecessors.

8.3.1 The Plainfield Conference of 1892[59]

A conference took place at Plainfield, New Jersey, in 1892, between representatives from Open Brethren (including some from Britain) and leaders of the Grant Brethren, on the initiative of the latter, who were questioning whether there was continued reason for excluding Open Brethren from the Lord's Table. Over 1,000 gathered for ten days of prayer and discussion. In a circular issued afterwards, the Grant representatives acknowledged that Open Brethren were not now guilty of association with evil doctrine, but took care in receiving individuals received from gatherings where a false teacher was active and did not allow them to continue in communion with him. However, they were dubious about Bethesda's assertion that the *Letter of the Ten* should be interpreted as expressing this approach. In other words, they were not convinced by Bethesda's explanation of earlier events, but they did approve of its current practice. Scottish evangelists active in North America, such as Marshall, Munro, and Ross, had played a crucial role in altering Grant perceptions of what Open Brethren were like.

Nevertheless, some Exclusives feared that excessive concessions had been made, and further pamphlets appearing from Open Brethren confirmed them in their suspicions that false doctrine was still at work and that those at Plainfield had been misled. There was some justification for Exclusive concerns: the Scottish evangelists who had influenced the Grants were, of course, somewhat different in outlook from English Open Brethren, since they had grown up largely independent of the English movement.[60] In fact, two of them, Ross and Munro, had refused to attend the conference.

The result was that Grant meetings divided over the question of whether to receive Open Brethren who came among them. A number, who upheld the Plainfield circular,

---

[57] Rule, 'All Ye are Brethren', 9-10.

[58] Coad, *History*, 212; Reid, *Grant*, 87.

[59] This section is indebted to Ironside, *Historical Sketch*, chs. 12-13; Noel, *History*, ch. 7; Reid, *Grant*, 102-12.

[60] McLaren, 'Triple Tradition', 52.

adopted the designation 'Independent' rather than 'Open' or 'Exclusive', and extended fellowship to both Open and Exclusive Brethren. Others, who had never accepted the conclusions of the circular, nevertheless welcomed believers from both sides if properly commended. Most Grant meetings had opened their doors to Open Brethren by 1932, rejecting the concept of a 'circle of fellowship' of accredited meetings. A similar phenomenon occurred in Britain as a result of the Devonshire House conferences, to which we now turn. In both cases, such gatherings received to fellowship on the same grounds as did Open Brethren (reception of all believers known to be sound in faith and godly in life), but they refused to be classed with them on account of the differing historical courses which they had followed.[61]

8.3.2 The Reunion Meetings of 1906-7

In 1902, a meeting was proposed for united prayer and the promotion of fellowship through enjoying ministry from both sides; as a result, a conference was held in the Clarence Rooms, London. This was repeated the following year, and in 1904 and 1905 larger conferences were convened at the Caxton Hall.[62]

Early in 1906, calls were issued for a united meeting for humiliation in response to the divisions and the spiritual condition which had produced them. In September, a conference took place at Stourbridge. A statement read at it explained that

> Various sorrows and difficulties having arisen, resulting in the cutting off of a considerable number of the Lord's people both in America and England from a certain fellowship of Saints, have led to great searchings of heart, not only as to the immediate troubles themselves, but also with reference to past divisions and alienation on the part of those who professedly gather in the name of the Lord Jesus.[63]

The objective was not an amalgamation of Open and Exclusive groupings, but a return to the original principle of fellowship, 'the recognition and reception of all Saints as being of Christ's body – owning no circle or company short of the whole assembly of God, refusing only those who by moral conduct, evil doctrine, and deliberate association with either, exclude themselves from its privileges'.[64]

Another gathering was arranged for 28 November – 1 December at Devonshire House in London, a venue chosen as free from association with any one party (it belonged to the Society of Friends). Again, humiliation rather than amalgamation was the declared purpose.[65] This was convened by G.W. Heath[66] and H.D. Woolley, and preceded by a

---

[61] According to Neatby, the Stuart Brethren had pioneered such an approach (*History*, 312-13).

[62] The addresses from these were published as D. Anderson-Berry et al., *Heart-preparation for the Lord's return: a series of addresses delivered at a conference in Caxton Hall, Westminster, by Dr. Anderson-Berry [and others] ... Revised and corrected by the speakers* (London: A. Holness, [1904]), and idem, *"Rivers of living water": a series of addresses [on the Holy Spirit] delivered at a conference in Caxton Hall, Westminster, by Dr. Anderson-Berry [and others] ... Revised and corrected by the speakers* (London: A. Holness, [1905]).

[63] Anon., 'Read at the Conference at Stourbridge, Monday, September 10th, 1906' (CBA2345).

[64] *Ibid.*

[65] Alex Marshall, letter in *W* 37 (1907), 28; cf. 'Devonshire House' [open letter from the convenors, 28 November 1906] (CBA 2292).

meeting of several Exclusive leaders with their counterparts at Bethesda, Bristol.[67] The Devonshire House conferences represented an attempt to break out of the pattern in which agreement on the rights and wrongs of past divisions was regarded as a prerequisite to reconciliation. The focus was to be on the Scriptural principles which should govern reception, rather than their alleged historical outworking. An initial problem was that Open Brethren perceived a lack of even-handedness in the treatment of each side. They called for matters to be handled in a righteous manner, and for Exclusives to recognise that Open Brethren had not injured them, but the reverse.[68] Some voiced the criticism that papers calling the conference had not included any Exclusive expression of regret for the divisions which had occurred, and there was strong feeling that confession was required from both sides, not from Open Brethren alone.[69] There was a measure of suspicion of those who had, until this point, united in accusing Open Brethren of complicity with error.[70] It seems to have been thought by several that Exclusive regrets regarding division did not reach any further back than 1880. Clearly there were some among Open as well as Exclusive Brethren who opposed any attempt to sidestep consideration of past events.

Prayer, conference, and exhortation formed the agenda, and admission to the daytime gatherings was by ticket only, requests for seven hundred tickets being received: 'plenty of combustible material', as one participant from Bethesda put it.[71] Discussion of the events of the 1840s took up rather more time than the convenors had wished, but all united in affirming the rightness of Newton's exclusion.[72] Once again, an obstacle was presented by the Exclusive belief that the *Letter of the Ten* indicated that Open Brethren knowingly received those holding to fundamental error or choosing to associate with such, though this was again denied. Pending further statements from Bethesda discussion of its current position was deferred, but a number of misunderstandings had been cleared up. Amalgamation of meetings was not seen as the way ahead; rather, it was for each individual and each meeting to right themselves before God, preferably in the context of meeting with brothers from other parties locally. A postscript added to the convenors' report after reception of the awaited statement from Bethesda welcomed the indication that it did not in fact practice what Exclusives had alleged were 'Bethesda principles'. In this statement, Bethesda explained that the *Letter of the Ten* could not be withdrawn as the signatories were now all dead; it did not carry the church's authority, and the church was not to be held responsible for the widespread misunderstandings of it. Although produced for a particular occasion, and so no longer relevant, there was nothing in it which present leaders would wish to withdraw. The assembly received all sound and godly believers, and did not practice intercommunion with assemblies where fundamental error was tolerated.[73]

---

[66] Heath was in fellowship with the Open assembly at Sidcup, and was treasurer of the Prophecy Investigation Society and a director of Morgan and Scott (*CG*, November 1938, 257).

[67] Anon., *A short report of the Devonshire House Conference Meetings* (Sidcup: W.T., [1906]).

[68] W.J. Matthews to G.F. Bergin, 26 November 1906 (CBA 2290). Bergin was director of the orphanages at Bristol.

[69] W.H. Bennet to G.W. Heath, 31 October 1906 (CBA 2353). Bennet was an Editor at Echoes of Service.

[70] Lithographed letter from W.H. Bennet, 26 November 1906 (CBA 2291).

[71] D.D. Chrystal to G.F. Bergin, 28 November 1906 (CBA 2294).

[72] G.W. Heath to the editor of *Field and Work*, 25 March 1907 (CBA 2316).

[73] Anon., *A Statement of the position of Bethesda, 1906* ([Bristol: John Wright, 1906]).

Circulation of the proceedings and of the Bethesda statement resulted in many inquiries, in response to which the convenors issued a statement. They repeated that the objective was not amalgamation of meetings or circles of fellowship, but a return to the original principle governing reception. If individual assemblies did this, the question of fellowship would automatically resolve itself. Naïvely, they claimed that there was no Scriptural justification for the divisions which had occurred among Exclusives, nor any doctrinal hindrance to fellowship. All that mattered in reception was an individual's spiritual condition, not which type of meeting they were in fellowship with. Brethren were agreed that Newton's doctrine was unacceptable, and the division was put down by many to Müller's ungracious reception of Darby in 1849.[74] It was claimed that, as Darby had affirmed, there was no justification for charges against Bethesda after they had acted against Newton. Bethesda's recent statement had dispelled the misinterpretation of the *Letter of the Ten* previously current.

> Brethren generally have interpreted the "Letter of the Ten" to mean refusal of a blasphemer, but reception of his upholders and intercommunion with the Meeting sheltering him. The letter really means refusal of a blasphemer and *rescue* of any not holding the evil doctrine from his Meeting, and refusal of all intercommunion, and this has been the practice of "Bethesda" for fifty years ...[75]

Further consideration of the variety of approaches to reception among Open Brethren was needed: some were too lax, and others too strict. Their hope was that the next conference would consider the divisions among Exclusive Brethren.

A further gathering was called for 8-11 May 1907, again at Devonshire House. Not so many attended as previously, only two or three hundred being present. Once again, the feeling was that the conference should concentrate on current principles rather than revisiting historical questions. Those present concluded that the only workable policy involved the direct dependence of each gathering on the Holy Spirit (which was precisely what Open Brethren already taught). Further conferences, it was felt, should be arranged on a local rather than national basis.[76]

An issue which came to prominence through these initiatives concerned the existence or otherwise of any 'circle of fellowship' apart from the body of Christ. This was troubling Open as well as Exclusive gatherings. Writing around the time of the Plainfield conference of 1892 but apparently in response to the 'Needed Truth' division, J.H. Burridge had outlined what became a widely-adopted approach. He explained that as each meeting gathered to Christ and took responsibility for its own spiritual health, receiving all believers without requiring separation, because they already belonged to the church, it would find that it was *ipso facto* in fellowship with others. The primary relationship was with Christ, not with other groups of believers.[77] Some former Exclusive Brethren feared the establishment of any new denomination or circle of fellowship claiming first place in

---

[74] Circular issued by the conveners, February 1907 (CBA 2299); cf. a letter from the Brooklyn meeting, 25 May 1907 (CBA 2324).

[75] Circular issued by the conveners, February 1907.

[76] H.C. Crawley, *A Plea for Unity Among the People Called Brethren: with a resumé of the Devonshire House Conference* (Glasgow: Pickering & Inglis, [1907]).

[77] J.H. Burridge, *Christian Unity: A Treatise on "Brethren," the Church of God, and Ministry* (London: Alfred Holness, [c.1892]), 38-9.

the attention of believers, and rejected the claim to an exclusive title to be gathered in the Lord's name.[78] This perspective was reflected in a number of statements put out by local assemblies. For example, Brethren in Worcester issued a statement in February 1907, rejoicing that as a result of meetings for confession, prayer, and discussion over the previous year they had discovered a real unity and so rejected all 'circles of fellowship'. They were not amalgamating, but were receiving individuals from each other's meetings.[79] Meetings in other areas were taking similar action, with the result that soon over seventy meetings were following the principle of receiving all sound and godly believers who separated themselves from false teachers.[80]

The movement appears to have lost its impetus fairly quickly, perhaps because it was overshadowed by the Glanton division, although meetings of a similar nature may have been held as late as 1921.[81] This may explain why these meetings have been neglected by historians of Brethren. The impetus towards reunion may also have been hampered by the principle that God never restored what had been marred by human failure.[82] Not many Exclusives were convinced by the conclusions of these conferences; Oliphant considered that the fundamental question, that of the effect of association with a false teacher, had still not been dealt with.[83] Some on both sides may have been deterred from following a path to reconciliation because it crossed a minefield of potentially explosive perceptions and issues. Heath's hopes that those meetings leaving the Raven party in the wake of the Glanton division might adopt scriptural ground rather than forming a party of their own were not fulfilled to any great extent, although some individuals and meetings did join Open Brethren over the next three decades and others, while not regarding themselves as Open Brethren, received all who were sound in faith and godly in life.

8.4 Exclusive Accessions to Open Brethren

During this period, a number of Exclusive meetings began to associate with Open Brethren.[84] However, it was the leading teachers making the same move, frequently in

---

[78] Mrs. Neatby, *The Life and Ministry of Thomas Neatby* (Glasgow and London: Pickering & Inglis and Alfred Holness, n.d.), 19.

[79] Printed letter from Brethren in Worcester, February 1907 (Chapter Two Archive).

[80] Anon., *Notes of Conference held at Devonshire House, London, May 9-11th, 1907* (London: S.W. Partridge, [1907]).

[81] Cf. a marginal note by G.W. Robson on a copy of his article 'Somewhat in Conference', *H* 54 (1975), 92 (CBA Box 61).

[82] Letter of G.W. Heath, 12 June 1907 (CBA 2402).

[83] O[liphant]., *Bethesda Fellowship, … 1907*, 3.

[84] As far as I have been able to establish, they appear to have included the following:
Princes Street, Ipswich (by 1882).
Kelly: Prospect Place, Woolwich (1887); Bridgwater (1888); Brentwood (1890s); Rotherham and Chudleigh (1891); Yorke Street, Southsea (1895); Carfax Hall, Clapham; Chadwell Heath; and Whitstable (all c.1900); Union Street, Newport; and Kenilworth (both by 1902); Hale Street, Coventry; and Warwick (both by 1903); and Burton-upon-Trent (by 1910).
Lowe: Ramsey, Isle of Man (1896); Goltho, Lincolnshire (1900s); Berrymead Room, Acton (c.1909); and Falmouth (by 1912).
Stoney-Raven: Bray, County Wicklow (by 1886); Wollaston, near Stourbridge (by 1888); Kenmare, County Kerry (1890s); Uttoxeter (by 1891); Carlton Hall, Westbourne Park, London (1894);

response to divisions within Exclusivism, who had the greater impact. Among them were several well-known Bible teachers. Like Dorman, Thomas Newberry (1811-1901), compiler of the study Bible which bears his name, left Exclusivism in 1866. Thomas Neatby (1835-1911) was a doctor from West Yorkshire, a friend of Hudson Taylor and a noted teacher. He left Darby for Kelly after the Park Street division, and then joined Open Brethren in 1887.[85] It was his son, William Blair Neatby, who produced what for decades was the standard history of Brethren.

W.W. Fereday (1861-1959) was a prolific author who, having left Open Brethren before 1893, associated with them again from around 1900, after being put out of the large and influential Kelly meeting at Blackheath, London; several meetings in London and the Midlands appear to have made the move with him.[86] Soon after, he issued a pamphlet entitled *Fellowship in Closing Days*, in which he noted that there had been six divisions within Exclusivism in the previous twenty years; at that rate, in another twenty years fellowship would become virtually impossible. He rejected the idea of a 'circle of fellowship' which lay at the heart of connexional thinking: any attempt to build a visible body of approved meetings would be divinely judged. Controversially, he alleged that association with evil took place among Exclusives in that the failings of leaders were often hushed up lest discipline should precipitate a division. Anticipating the reunion conferences (in which he was involved), he argued that 'Open' and 'Exclusive' labels should be dropped, and all assemblies recognised which were pure in doctrine and practice, and which guarded against importing evil.

An influential writer on prophetic subjects who appears to have influenced the thinking of C.I. Scofield (compiler of the famous Reference Bible) was Walter Scott (1838-1933). Converted among Baptists in Scotland, he joined with Open Brethren, then moved to the Stuart Brethren, before returning on being excluded for breaking bread with an Open assembly in 1906.[87]

A.T. Schofield (1846-1929) was a Harley Street physician, a pioneering psychiatrist, and lecturer on health topics. He sided with Kelly in 1881 and opposed the inward-looking mysticism of Stoney, moving to Open Brethren about 1909. He was active in the missions of Moody and Sankey and Torrey and Alexander, one of the founders of the Mission to Deep Sea Fishermen, and a member of the Prophecy Investigation Society and the Victoria Institute, a body which aimed to integrate Evangelical faith and commitment to scientific research.[88]

Harold St John (1876-1957) joined Open Brethren from the Lowe Brethren around 1910.[89] St John was one of several former Exclusives who, surprisingly, did much to *broaden* Open Brethren thinking, not least by his catholicity of spirit which drew upon

---

Renshaw Street, Manchester; and Limerick (both by 1904); and Sturton by Stow, Lincolnshire (by 1910).

Stuart: Olive Hall, Hamilton (by 1904).

[85] On Neatby, see Mrs. Neatby, *Thomas Neatby*; Pickering (ed.), *Chief Men*, 43-4. Neatby had published *Two Letters on important subjects relating to Fellowship* (London: the author, [c.1882]).

[86] W.W. Fereday, *Fellowship in Closing Days* (Littlehampton: W. Hignett, [c.1900]³), 4-5, 7-8; cf. *idem*, *A Letter*. On Fereday, see *W* 89 (1959), 182-3.

[87] See D.J. Macleod, 'Walter Scott, A Link in dispensationalism between Darby and Scofield?', *Bibliotheca Sacra* 153 (1996), 155-78; *W* 36 (1906), 150; 63 (1933), 282.

[88] See *CG*, June 1929, 103-7, 110-11; Pickering (ed.), *Chief Men*, 200-2; *W* 59 (1929), 136.

[89] On St John, see Patricia St John, *Harold St. John*; *W* 87 (1957), 117, 141-7.

the resources of centuries of Christian spirituality. To the end of his life he remained a seminal thinker, doing much to ensure the success of the annual conferences of brethren at High Leigh and Swanwick from the mid-1950s.

However, some accessions from Darbyite Exclusivism precipitated sharp controversy through their advocacy of household baptism. Darby taught that baptism introduced the infant to a place of privilege, the circle in which God's grace was at work. The conversion of the head of a household automatically altered the position before God of the rest of the household. Baptism was not the believer's act of obedience and did not involve a personal response to God, for it was a divine act. It might be performed by an evangelist, or by the head of a household. We should note that a number of early Brethren had retained their paedobaptist convictions, although they criticised the Prayer Book teaching of baptismal regeneration, although, after the division between Open and Exclusive Brethren, believer's baptism had become the norm among Open assemblies.[90] Advocacy of a different practice by former Exclusives caused considerable upset, therefore.

The most vigorous protagonist of such views was the ex-Raven brother Russell Elliott (1861-1950), who joined Open Brethren after the Devonshire House Conference of 1906, in which he played a prominent role. His views on baptism resulted in his gradually being frozen out,[91] a development to which he responded with numerous controversial pamphlets during succeeding years. Another was the ex-Raven evangelist Alfred Mace (1854-1944).[92] Attempts were made by others to portray baptism (by whatever mode) as a non-essential matter, on a level with 'meats and drinks' (Romans 14).[93] The heat generated by the controversy was such that some warned assemblies against receiving holders of this view into fellowship, alleging that its advocates had caused secessions from assemblies.[94] A conference of brethren at Newton Abbot in 1910 advised that advocates of household baptism should not be permitted to minister in assemblies or at conferences.[95] From their perspective, Exclusive Brethren saw Open Brethren as insisting on believer's baptism, rather than allowing for diversity of practice as they did. Undoubtedly the debate served to harden the stance of many Open Brethren, especially those represented by *The Believer's Magazine*, which took a clear line on the necessity of baptism preceding reception into fellowship. Issues relating to reception would continue to cause tensions within the movement, but during this period Open Brethren also faced considerable external criticism, which we shall examine in the next chapter.

---

[90] For an overview of early Brethren teaching on baptism, see Harold H. Rowdon, 'The Early Brethren and Baptism', *VE* 11 (1979), 55-64.

[91] Noel, *History*, 568; 'Touchstone' [G.C.D. Howley], 'Russell Elliott', *W* 105 (1975), 66-8.

[92] 'Touchstone', 'Alfred Mace', *W* 96 (1966), 183-6.

[93] For an Open Brethren evaluation of household baptism, see D. Anderson-Berry, 'What is Household Baptism? Conversations on Baptism. – IV.', *W* 40 (1910), 73-6.

[94] E.g 'AC', *BM* 9 (1899), 46; 'ASQ', *BM* n.s. 6 (1905), 95.

[95] 'TLWW', *BM* n.s. 11 (June 1910), iii.

CHAPTER 9

Brethren and their Critics

Not only did Open and Exclusive Brethren have serious criticisms to offer of one another, they also faced criticism from outsiders and former members. This chapter surveys a fairly representative sample of critics from the beginning of the movement through to 1914, and discusses the main charges which they made.

9.1 The Critics

It was not long before Brethren began to attract public criticism. Early Irish responses, some called forth by events at Westport in 1835-6, tended (like English critiques) to defend the principle of religious establishment, since this and related issues, such as ministry, discipline, and the sacraments, figured prominently in Brethren critiques of the Establishment and apologies for secession; a target of the critics was Darby's sense of quasi-apostolic authority.[1]

One of the earliest books on the movement, by Cyprian Rust (who at this stage appears to have been either Independent or Baptist), appeared in 1844 (*The "Brethren." An examination of the Opinions and Practices of the new sect usually denominated "Plymouth Brethren"*). A vigorous critic of what he termed Brethren hobby-horses, he also asserted that Brethren failed to acknowledge that in many respects their church order was similar to that of Dissenting congregations. His shorter work, *'"The Old Paths." A few brotherly hints to "The Brethren:"* more particularly addressed to Mr. W.H. Dorman, Late of Islington* (1842), argued that Brethren were not different enough from other churches to justify their withdrawal from them. The sectarianism of early Brethren was a common target of Dissenting opponents; the Baptist minister Cornelius Elven of Bury St Edmunds commented that while objecting to sects, Brethren were in effect creating a new one. Elven also criticised their objections to a stated ministry, the lack of a congregational voice in church affairs, their failure to take part in religious societies, and their attempt to improve on Christ's order for the church by admitting unbaptised believers to the Lord's Table.[2]

Other seceders also attacked the new movement. From a somewhat introspective Calvinist standpoint, J.C. Philpot (in whose conversion Darby had played a part during 1826-7) produced a review of the *Christian Witness* in 1842.[3] His main target was what he saw as Brethren attempts to put Scripture into practice independently of any deep experience of the Spirit's work in the soul. He attributed this to their faulty view of saving faith, which he characterised as mental assent to the truths of the gospel. Philpot would return to the fray in reviews of Brethren works during the mid-1850s.

---

[1] E.g. Sirr, *Reasons for Abiding*, 29-30.

[2] Cornelius Elven, letter of 18 July 1839.

[3] [J.C. Philpot], 'Editors' Review: the Christian Witness', *GS* 8 (1842), 77-84.

A more moderate Calvinist critique came from C.H. Spurgeon and his associate George Rogers.[4] Spurgeon was one of a number of pastors, mostly non-denominational, who agreed with Brethren in rejecting ordination but asserted the necessity of a recognised pastoral ministry; they therefore rejected the Brethren attempt to ground ministry exclusively in the impulsive exercise of a charismatic gift. It has to be said that Brethren apologists have not always distinguished the issues of ordination and office. Another was H. Grattan Guinness (1835-1910), who associated with Brethren at Merrion Hall, Dublin, from 1864-8; in 1863 he wrote *A Letter to the "Plymouth Brethren" on the Recognition of Pastors*.[5] Most of these men (except Spurgeon) were attracted by aspects of Brethren thinking and practice, and perhaps felt the need as a result to make clear why they did not join the movement, and why their members should not do so. Some of them had themselves seceded from the Establishment. From Norwich, Robert Govett offered an *Address to the Christians called Plymouth Brethren, on Liberty of Ministry and Gift* (1847). A.A. Rees of Bethesda Chapel in Sunderland wrote *Four Letters to the Christians called "Brethren," on the subject of Ministry and Worship* (probably written during the 1860s).

The most vehemently critical works came from Presbyterians.[6] To some extent they may have interpreted the Brethren in the light of previous encounters with Glasites, Haldanites, Scotch Baptists, and Walkerites, but more significant were their apprehension at the threat to church order posed by revivalist practices such as lay-preaching and their concern to stem the losses to Brethren of newly-converted church members. Their tone is often confrontational, sometimes vitriolic, and was to be matched by a similarly robust Brethren reaction. The legacy of mutual suspicion has ensured that many Open Brethren in Scotland and Northern Ireland remain noticeably more separatist in their outlook than their English co-religionists.

The son of the Ulster Baptist controversialist Alexander Carson himself entered into vigorous controversy with the Brethren. James Carson's rambling and sarcastic work *The Heresies of the Plymouth Brethren* (1877) was directed mainly at the writings of Mackintosh. For Carson, Brethren were not to be treated as honourable opponents, and he defended as Christ-like what some had criticised as a lack of charity towards the movement. Whereas the movement had in its early days drawn to it many good men, it was now to be regarded as extremist, as Jesuitical in its concealment of doctrinal novelties, and, he implied, as teaching what could result in immorality.[7] The reliability of Carson's work may, however, be gauged from its description of Darby's translation of the Bible as 'a deliberate attempt to overturn the Deity of Christ'.[8]

One of the most indefatigable opponents of Brethrenism was the Londonderry Presbyterian Thomas Croskery; his perspective is evident from his list of heretical precedents for Brethren views, which included just about every major heretical group in

---

[4] E.g. G. Rogers, 'On Plymouth Brethrenism', *Sword and Trowel*, July 1865, 282-7; [C.H. Spurgeon], 'Plymouth Brethren', *Sword and Trowel*, January 1867, 32; idem, 'The Two Draughts of Fishes', *Metropolitan Tabernacle Pulpit* 8 (1862), 195-6, 202-3;

[5] *BDE*.

[6] For more on these, see Gribben, 'Worst Sect'.

[7] James C.L. Carson, *The Heresies of the Plymouth Brethren* (London: Houlston, 1877), iv-v, [vi].

[8] *Ibid.*, 39.

church history.[9] Another confessionally-minded Ulster Presbyterian, Thomas Houston, opposed Brethrenism as a species of baptistic and lay-led revivalism. He acknowledged his debt to the works by Carson and Croskery.[10] W.T. Latimer[11] of Belfast gave special consideration to the Open Brethren practice of believer's baptism, condemning their rebaptism of converts baptised in infancy and rejecting Brethren baptism as invalid because not performed by a minister.

THE HERESIES
or
THE PLYMOUTH BRETHREN.

BY
JAMES C. L. CARSON, M.D.

Fourteenth Thousand.

LONDON:
HOULSTON & SONS, PATERNOSTER ROW.
1877.

The sales figures achieved by books such as this one testified to the threat which Brethren were believed to present to existing churches

For Peter Mearns, a United Presbyterian minister from Coldstream in the Scottish Borders, it was time the Brethren were 'detected, exposed, and expelled'.[12] He treated their practices before discussing their doctrines, partly because Brethren tended to conceal their doctrines at first and partly because discussion of their practices would assist the church member encountering them.[13] Another Presbyterian cleric to write against the Brethren was William Reid of Edinburgh,[14] not to be confused with another Presbyterian minister of the same name who joined the Open Brethren in Carlisle. The value of this book was lessened by the author's dependence on the Exclusive movement's second-rank spokesmen: Neatby criticised it for relying on Mackintosh, Stanley, and Davis much more than on Darby or Kelly.[15] Reid somewhat implausibly credited Brethren with an

---

[9] Thomas Croskery, *Plymouth-Brethrenism: A Refutation of its Principles and Doctrines* (London and Belfast: William Mullen, 1879), vii. This was not his only anti-Brethren work.

[10] Thomas Houston, *Plymouthism & Revivalism: or, the Duty of contending for the Faith in opposition to prevailing errors and corruptions* (Belfast: C. Aitchison, [1874]²), 35n.

[11] W.T. Latimer, *A Lecture on the Doctrines of Plymouth Brethren* (Belfast: James Cleeland, [1890]³).

[12] Peter Mearns, *Christian Truth viewed in relation to Plymouthism* (Edinburgh: William Oliphant, 1875²), 29.

[13] *Ibid.*, 26.

[14] William Reid, *Plymouth Brethrenism unveiled and refuted* (Edinburgh: William Oliphant, 1876²).

[15] Neatby, *History*, 229.

extensive acquaintance with the work of a whole catalogue of earlier heretical teachers. At a more popular level, the Presbyterian minister James Moir Porteous had a hit in 1874 with his novel *Brethren in the Keelhowes*, which ran into six editions (including one with the Scots dialect translated into English) within a very short space of time. A feature of this work is the robust critique of alleged tendencies of Brethren and other 'Evangelists' towards Arminianism, by which he appears to have meant their belief that human beings co-operate with God in receiving salvation and that Christ died in order to make salvation possible for all, rather than certain for some.[16]

As we can see, many later critics focused on Exclusive Brethrenism. Duncan Mackintosh[17] was not unusual in condemning it as 'one of the most pernicious, exclusive, and tyrannical systems that has appeared in the Christian Church'.[18] Drawing on the year he had spent in fellowship with Exclusive Brethren, Alexander Murdoch[19] used a format which combined elements of the novel and the set-piece dialogue in order to present a simple and moderately-expressed critique.

High Church critics seem to have been better able to offer a balanced evaluation of the movement, perhaps because they were less likely to lose members to the Brethren. One of the most even-handed critiques came from the Principal of Chichester Theological College, J.S. Teulon,[20] whom Neatby singled out as an honourable exception to the run of critics. Noteworthy for his readiness to recognise what the church could learn from Brethrenism and his balance of negative criticism with positive appreciation, he adopted the view that such movements arose because the church had forgotten some part of the truth which needed reviving in order to meet the challenges of the age. In his opinion, Brethren were seeking to testify to truths which the whole church accepted, while rejecting the visible body founded to give such testimony.[21] An unusual critique was offered from another High Church standpoint by the Glasgow Catholic Apostolic, W.R. Brownlie.[22] He emphasised the divinely-revealed order which should obtain in the church; spiritual gifts were to be exercised within the bounds of such order, and in particular in submission to the ministries appointed. By themselves, gifts were no qualification for ministry. Order was also to be seen in the pattern of worship to be followed.

Perhaps the most upset was caused by a work which was not intended as a critique so much as a corrective of various misrepresentations of the movement, Neatby's *A History of the Plymouth Brethren* (1901).[23] Although Neatby appeared to distance himself from Brethren, he was associating with Open Brethren at Kendal when he wrote his book,

---

[16] J. Moir Porteous, *Brethren in the Keelhowes; or, Brethrenism tested by the Word of God* (London: Simpkin, Marshall, 1876[6]), 160.

[17] Duncan Macintosh, *Brethrenism; or the Special Teachings, ecclesiastical and doctrinal, of the Exclusive Brethren, or Plymouth Brethren; compiled from their own writings. With Strictures. Also, a reply to the ex-editor of the British Evangelist* (London: Houlston, [1875][4]).

[18] *Ibid.*, 3.

[19] [Alexander Murdoch], *Life among the Close Brethren* (London: Hodder and Stoughton, 1890).

[20] J.S. Teulon, *The History and Teaching of the Plymouth Brethren* (London: SPCK, 1883).

[21] *Ibid.*, 6, 45.

[22] W.R. Brownlie, *The Gifts of the Spirit and the Ministries of the Lord: Letters to a Member of "the Brethren"* (Glasgow: D. Hobbs, 1877[2]).

[23] For a fuller account of Brethren responses to Neatby, see Tim Grass, 'The quest for identity in British Brethren historiography: some reflections from an outsider', in a forthcoming volume edited by Neil T.R. Dickson and Tim Grass to be published by Paternoster.

which must have made his criticisms all the more painful.[24] One correspondent in *The Witness* even compared his action to that of Ham uncovering his father's nakedness (Genesis 9).[25] What stung Brethren were his charge that they 'took shape under the influence of a delusion', this being the expectation that Christ's return would take place within a few years,[26] his alleged failure to acknowledge any divine hand in the events of the movement's history,[27] and his focus on the divisions which beset Brethren rather than their evangelistic activity (inevitable, given his belief that Darbyism represented normative Brethrenism).[28] Another former insider to offer an influential critique was Tregelles, in *Five Letters to the Editor of "The Record," on recent Denials of our Lord's vicarious Life*, first published in 1864.

9.2 The Issues Raised

External critiques gave more space to doctrinal issues than did Open critiques of Exclusivism. The latter majored on ecclesiological issues and tended to ignore the doctrinal issues raised by outsiders unless these had precipitated secessions, as was the case with the doctrine of the 'third class of sufferings' of Christ. Many outsiders focused on Exclusivism, which was at that time far more zealous than the Open wing of the movement in literary labours, and more in the public eye, not least because of its frequent and acrimonious divisions. However, Open Brethren were deeply influenced by certain aspects of Exclusive teaching, and so it is germane to consider these criticisms in some detail, but the teachings which critics so often condemned were not always as widely-held within the movement as they asserted. We also do well to bear in mind Neatby's caution concerning critical evaluations of Brethrenism as 'generally extremely untrustworthy', often based on unrepresentative sources, and frequently misrepresenting even these.[29]

9.2.1 Theological Issues

In the minds of some, Brethren went astray on a whole range of fundamental doctrines: 'They hold peculiar views upon Faith, Repentance, Justification, Sanctification, the Sabbath, the Church, the ministry, the Moral Law, Prayer, and the Holy Spirit. They are also Anabaptists and Millenarians.'[30]

Some criticised Brethren for departing from the truths rediscovered at the time of the Reformation. Brethren did not intend to do so, and they gave thanks for the rediscovery of such doctrines as justification by faith, but they did not always perceive the differences between their doctrinal formulations and those of the Reformers. This is evident in the way that different writers treated the topic of imputed righteousness, the belief that the

---

[24] Ritchie, *"The Way which they call Heresy"*, 104n.

[25] S.F.B., *W* 32 (1902), 82-3.

[26] W.H. Bennet, *A Return to God and His Word: Remarks on Mr. W. BLAIR NEATBY'S 'History of the Plymouth Brethren'* (Glasgow: Pickering & Inglis, [1914]), 30; Neatby, *History*, 339.

[27] Bennet, *Return*, 27-8

[28] S.F.B., *W* 32 (1902), 82-3.

[29] Neatby, *History*, 229.

[30] Thomas Croskery, *A Catechism on the Doctrines of the Plymouth Brethren* (London: James Nisbet, 1868[6]), 3.

righteousness which is accounted ours by God is the righteousness of Christ, who in his incarnate life was perfectly obedient to the Law and who suffered for us.

Alleged rejection of the imputation of Christ's righteousness as the grounds of our justification was a frequent theme of Reformed criticisms, as was the idea that our justification is grounded upon Christ's resurrection.[31] For Newton, such teaching amounted to justification on the basis of our merits rather than those of Christ. Furthermore, Brethren teaching on sanctification confused the believer's personal condition with their representative condition in Christ.[32] Similarly, whilst applauding the manner in which Brethren linked justification with Christ's resurrection (and paralleling this with similar thinking in Tractarianism and the Catholic Apostolic Church), Teulon criticised them for not giving due weight to Christ's active obedience to the Law during his life which qualified him for his work on the cross, and their confusion of atonement, forgiveness, and justification.[33] It was also alleged that some Brethren taught that atonement was made during his three hours' suffering on the cross, before and apart from his death, and so without the shedding of blood; thus by implication they denied the substitutionary nature of Christ's death.[34] According to Croskery, they 'assign atonement to the sufferings, and deny it to the death'.[35] Others, however, criticised Brethren for confining Christ's substitutionary suffering to the cross and excluding his earthly life.[36] The tendency of some Exclusive writers to underplay the reality of Christ's human nature in the interests of safeguarding his 'heavenly humanity' was also noted.[37] Mackintosh came in for frequent and sustained criticism in this respect.[38]

Brethren eschatology came under fire, especially from those who did not believe in a literal earthly millennium. Houston alleged that 'Millenarian views, however they may foster morbid fancy and enthusiasm, tend to carnalize the minds of Christians, damp the scriptural hope of heaven, and prevent vigorous and sustained exertions for the world's conversion'.[39]

Dispensationalist hermeneutics were criticised since they appeared to lead to the setting aside of those parts of Scripture deemed no longer applicable: Brethren, it was claimed, used the Bible when it suited them and explained it away when it did not. In addition, Brethren were accused of taking liberties with the text in their spiritualising.[40] Early on, Sirr was perceptive enough to recognise that Brethren rejection of a religious

---

[31] E.g. Carson, *Heresies*, 45-52; Croskery, *Catechism*, 16; [A. Haldane], *Errors of the Darby and Plymouth Sect* (London: James Nisbet, 1862²), 11; Houston, *Plymouthism*, 19-20; Tregelles, *Five Letters*, 43. Newton, who opposed such teaching as reminiscent of early Irvingite mysticism, knew of no more destructive tract than Stanley's on *Justification in the Risen Christ* ('Small Notebook 7', 22b).

[32] Newton, *Remarks*, 6-8, 28.

[33] Teulon, *Brethren*, ch. 5; cf. Tregelles, *Five Letters*, ch. 2.

[34] Croskery, *Plymouth-Brethrenism*, 87; Porteous, *Brethren*, 131-2.

[35] Croskery, *Plymouth-Brethrenism*, 103, cf. 87.

[36] John Cox, *Test before you Trust; or, the new doctrine and the old divinity compared* (London: Nisbet, [1862]), 3.

[37] Anon., 'Darbyism', *QJP* 11 (1859), 372; Porteous, *Brethren*, 114-15; Tregelles, *Five Letters*, 21-2.

[38] Carson, *Heresies*, 1-2; Edward Dennett, *The Plymouth Brethren: their rise, divisions, practice, and doctrines* (London: Elliot Stock, 1870²), 44-5; Mearns, *Plymouthism*, 104-5.

[39] Houston, *Plymouthism*, 26.

[40] Anon., 'The Plymouth Brethren', *CO* 62 (1866), 897-9, 901-2.

establishment was grounded in a hermeneutic which downplayed the continuing significance of the Old Testament.[41]

9.2.2 The Church, its Ministry and Order

The hermeneutical basis of Brethren ecclesiology was often challenged. Reformed critics, whose theology emphasized the unity of God's dealings under Old and New Covenants, attacked the Brethren idea that there was no church before Pentecost.[42] Critics also accused the Brethren of treating the New Testament pattern of church order as temporary without any textual warrant for so doing. Teulon commented that Brethren assumed that which was transitory to be permanent and vice versa.[43]

High Church critics challenged the rejection of a doctrine of ministry founded on apostolic succession.[44] The widespread Brethren belief that in the absence of apostles there could be no formal appointments to office was also rejected.[45] Nevertheless, Brethren were regarded as having their own *de facto* leaders, notably Darby, whose role was singled out for comment.[46] Indeed, William Reid of Edinburgh was 'acquainted with no Church, in which the one-man ministry, [sic] obtains greater prominence than in the assemblies of the Brethren'. Educated and able, such men were proof that the Brethren chose their ministers just like the sects which they condemned.[47] On the other hand, some condemned what they saw as 'any-man ministry', which was interpreted as an over-reaction against one-man ministry.[48] Critics also expressed fear for the future of ministry among the Brethren once the present generation of well-educated former clergymen died out: it was likely, they thought, that ministry would become dominated by the ignorant.[49] Spurgeon asserted that if pastors were a gift from God, then attempting to manage without them would result in spiritual poverty; opposition to one-man ministry sprang from conceit regarding their own abilities, and a refusal to submit to divinely-appointed authorities in the church.[50]

The lack of order and planned provision for the needs of the flock was another target of criticism. Sir Robert Anderson told Henry Pickering that he left the Brethren because of 'their unwillingness to provide intelligent ministry at meetings other than the Lord's

---

[41] Sirr, *Reasons for Abiding*, 15-16.

[42] Croskery, *Plymouth-Brethrenism*, 1.

[43] Teulon, *Brethren*, 59-60.

[44] Ibid., ch. 3.

[45] Croskery, *Plymouth-Brethrenism*, 78-9; E.J. Whately, *Plymouth Brethrenism* (London: Hatchards, 1877[2]), 57-8.

[46] E.g. Sirr, *Reasons for Abiding*, 29 ('who, I have heard you say, knows more of the mind of God than anyone else'); William Townsend, *Church & Dissent: being reflections and reasonings that have induced the author, after eighteen years' communion among the Plymouth Brethren, to leave them, and enter the communion of the Church of England* (Lewes: Sussex Express, [1872]), 60 ('the apostle of modern times').

[47] Reid, *Plymouth Brethrenism*, 66, 69.

[48] A.A. Rees, *Four Letters to the Christians called "Brethren," on the subject of Ministry and Worship* (London: Passmore and Alabaster, n.d.[2]), 8.

[49] Mearns, *Plymouthism*, 160.

[50] Spurgeon, 'Two Draughts', 195-6.

Table, and their haphazard way of doing things'.[51] According to Whately, if the presidency of the Holy Spirit was a reality then Paul's directions in 1 Corinthians 14 were superfluous.[52] Mearns commented wryly that if this were true, one would expect better order in the meetings than was actually the case.[53] The impulsive understanding of ministry was also questioned:[54] it was a curious fact that when a leading brother was present, 'it is seldom that any other brother is *moved* to address the meeting'.[55] In fact, it was alleged, what counted in practice was recognised ability and a desire to minister – and that, for Rees, was as it should be.[56]

Some criticised as presumption the Brethren attempt to set up a pure church.[57] By contrast, others criticised the Brethren belief in the impossibility of this on account of the church's ruin, a concept which was also rejected, along with the related concept of unity as something intended to be external and visible.[58] Rust allowed the possibility that national religious establishments might apostatise, but rejected the claim that the apostasy of the entire visible church was foretold in the New Testament.[59] And some later critics suggested that the early belief in the church's ruin was contradicted by later Exclusive claims that the 'assembly of God' as set up by them was the sole representation of the church on earth.[60]

Sirr had early noted that, for all the light which they claimed to have received, Darby's followers could not agree on the question of baptism: 'Can "the apostle of dissent" be unable to settle a question on which so much depends, if the things that are wanting are to be set in order?'[61] For others, it was the developed Darbyite belief in the infallibility of the assembly which was belied by this disagreement.[62]

9.2.3 Proselytism

Perhaps the charge most often pressed against the Brethren, and doubtless one of the main reasons why critics went into print, was that of proselytism. Whately made the acute observation that revival converts were prone to react against the church's normal forms of worship, and that this reaction gave Brethrenism its strength. Opposition increased it still further, but the end result was likely to be a coldness of heart, seen in the cessation of

---

[51] [Henry Pickering], 'Home-Call of Sir Robert Anderson, K.C.B., LL.D.', *W* 48 (1918), 100. On Anderson, see section 11.4.

[52] Whately, *Plymouth Brethrenism*, 52.

[53] Mearns, *Plymouthism*, 150.

[54] Guinness, *Letter to Brethren*, 19.

[55] Mearns, *Plymouthism*, 158.

[56] Rees, *Four Letters*, 6, 33.

[57] Anon., 'Plymouth Brethrenism: its spirit, principles, and practical consequences', *CO* 62 (1866), 605.

[58] Croskery, *Plymouth-Brethrenism*, 28-31.

[59] Rust, *"Brethren"*, 14.

[60] E.g. Dennett, *Brethren*, 23. Dennett was drawing primarily on Mackintosh's pamphlet *The Assembly of God: or, the All-Sufficiency of the Name of Jesus*, which seems to have provoked quite a reaction by its uncompromising stance.

[61] Sirr, *Reasons for Abiding*, 53; cf. *ER* 5 (May 1839), 577-8n.

[62] 'An Inclusive Brother', 'On the Teaching of the Exclusive Brethren', *NW* 5 (1875), 43; cf. Dennett, *Plymouth Brethren*, 52.

Christian activity and the loss of a missionary spirit.[63] Critics spoke of the underhand means used by Brethren to gain converts from Protestant churches, which often involved saying nothing about their distinctives when beginning work in a particular locality, and even joining churches or infiltrating evangelistic enquiry rooms in order to influence the impressionable.[64] Brethren, said Mearns, were 'found in the wake of religious awakenings as constantly as sharks follow ships'.[65] Even Hargrove attacked what he saw as the dishonesty of gaining admission to groups and using influence there to proselytise and sow dissension.[66] A more positive spin was put on the evidence by Teulon, who described the main acknowledged purpose of Brethrenism as not the awakening of sinners but the upbuilding of the saints, an aspect of God's purpose which Evangelicalism had forgotten.[67]

Undoubtedly, the charge was given weight by such writers as Mackintosh, who asserted 'It is not with the systems we have to do. ... Our business is with the saints in those systems, to seek, by every spiritual and scriptural agency, to get them out into their true position in the assembly of God.'[68] Similarly, William Reid of Carlisle averred that the movement was not ruined as critics alleged, since it was growing through accessions of the best members of all churches, which should ask themselves why they were losing so many people in this way.[69] One means by which they were being attracted was illustrated by a report in *The Witness* which referred to the distribution of a tract entitled *A Voice to Christendom* outside the doors of the churches in Hamilton at service time, 'which caused many to awaken from their religious slumbers'.[70] Ironically, on one occasion a complaint appeared in *The Northern Evangelistic Intelligencer* about proselytism of Brethren converts in North-East Scotland by the sects.[71]

9.2.4 Schism

Linked with the charge of proselytism was that of schism, which was seen as an odd way to set about securing the unity of true believers.[72] 'If all Plymouthists were like Mr.

---

[63] Whately, *Brethren*, 119-22.

[64] Anon., *Plymouth Brethrenism: its Ecclesiastical and Doctrinal Teachings; with a Sketch of its History* (London: Hodder & Stoughton, [1874]²), 5; Latimer, *Brethren*, 3; Murdoch, *Close Brethren*, 66-7; Porteous, *Brethren*, 28; Reid, *Plymouth Brethrenism*, 12-13. However, a Brethren defence would be that they kept strictly to the gospel when dealing with the unconverted (William Kelly to A.M.P., in *BT* 9 (1872-3), 96).

[65] Mearns, *Plymouthism*, 42.

[66] Charles Hargrove, 'Thoughts on Fellowship', in Joseph Hargrove (ed.), *Notes on the Book of Genesis, with some Essays and Addresses by the late Rev. Charles Hargrove, Volume III. Essays and Addresses* (London: John F. Shaw, 1870), 52.

[67] Teulon, *Brethren*, 10-11. One reviewer put this down to acquaintance with Brethren who were more interested in testifying to church truth than in preaching the gospel ('Teulon's Plymouth Brethren', *BT* 14 (1882-3), 268).

[68] C.H.M[ackintosh]., *The Assembly of God: or, the All-Sufficiency of the Name of Jesus* (Addison, IL: Bible Truth Publishers, 1982 [1865]), 27.

[69] [Reid], *Literature and Mission*, 19, 21.

[70] 'TLWW', *W* 23 (April 1893), iv; cf. [Spurgeon], 'Plymouth Brethren', 32.

[71] *NEI* 2 (1872), 32.

[72] Anon., 'Plymouth Brethrenism', 599; Croskery, *Plymouth-Brethrenism*, 39-42.

Groves and his brother-in-law, Mr. Müller of Bristol, the other denominations would have nothing to complain of.'[73] But they were not: Brethren were schismatic.[74] High Church writers viewed this seriously, alleging that Brethren 'seek in separation from her [the church] that which might have been sought and found in union with her'.[75] And this divisiveness affected internal as well as external relations. An anonymous writer commented that 'The system which a generation ago began upon a basis of universal fellowship has ended with universal excommunication'.[76] The Brethren made the biggest claims, yet were the most divided of sects.[77] Their sectarianism was proved both by the use of the name 'Brethren' (a charge to which later Brethren were sensitive) and by the frequent internal schisms.[78] Indeed, they had become every bit as proud and sectarian as the systems which they had left.[79] Houston saw this as typical of revivalists, and rooted Brethren separatism in that of John Walker.[80] Teulon noted the odd circumstance that 'the duty of withdrawing from an assembly of the Brethren which has tolerated evil, is regarded as even more imperative than that of separating from the ordinary ecclesiastical institutions of Christendom, since light rejected is worse than original darkness'.[81]

As Croskery wryly mused, 'Is it not significant that the Brethren – the most sectarian and divisive and quarrelsome sect in Christendom – should found their ideas of ministry upon the practice of a Church like that of Corinth, which was remarkable for precisely these qualities?' Such division demonstrated the hollowness of their claim to have a Spirit-appointed ministry: 'If the Holy Ghost appoints the ministry among the Brethren, how is it that they have false teachers, for they are separated from each other by doctrines?'[82] In his view, the sects were more catholic than the Brethren because they recognised each other's standing as genuine churches.[83]

In all this, an element of spiritual pride was detected: 'we alone are separate from the world, we alone are obedient to the Gospel, we alone love the brethren, we alone forsake not the assembling of ourselves together, we are THE SAINTS'.[84] Rust thought they would better be called 'accusers of the Brethren' on account of their claims to superior spirituality and their slandering of the rest of the church.[85] They were 'spiritual Ishmaelites', always at variance with other Christians.[86] They were disturbers of churches, hostile to ministers, and sought to draw converts into their own meetings,[87] manifesting a judgmental spirit, denouncing Evangelical ministers as unconverted, and encouraging church members to sit in judgement on their ministers, and 'they speak of

---

[73] Mearns, *Plymouthism*, 24; cf. the praise offered by Reid, *Plymouth Brethrenism*, 3.
[74] Anon., 'The Plymouth Brethren', *CO* 62 (1866), 906-7.
[75] Teulon, *Brethren*, 45.
[76] Anon., *Plymouth Brethrenism*, 3-4; cf. Rees, *Four Letters*, 7.
[77] 'Anon., 'Darbyism', 371; cf. Spurgeon, 'Two Draughts', 202-3.
[78] Anon., 'Plymouth Brethrenism', 600-1.
[79] Anon., *Plymouth Brethrenism: its Ecclesiastical and Doctrinal Teachings*, 3-4.
[80] Houston, *Plymouthism*, 11.
[81] Teulon, *Brethrenism*, 52.
[82] Croskery, *Catechism*, 8, 9.
[83] Croskery, *Plymouth-Brethrenism*, 32.
[84] Sirr, *Reasons for Abiding*, 87; cf. McIntosh, *New Prophets*, 13, 31.
[85] Rust, *"Brethren"*, 69.
[86] Anon., 'Plymouth Brethren', 905; cf. Macintosh, *Brethrenism*, 7.
[87] Houston, *Plymouthism*, 28.

those who are not awakened after their manner, and who do not embrace their doctrinal views, as unconverted'.[88] There may have been some truth in this charge, especially in Scotland and Ulster; on the other hand, the testimony of at least one such minister, M'Vicker, was that he had been unconverted.

Brethren strongly rebutted the allegation of sectarianism. During its early years, the meeting at Peterhead often made a statement along these lines:

> we are but a fragment of the great Church on earth. We seek to carry out primitive order while acknowledging all who are the Lord's, who do not meet with us; and welcome all whose walk and doctrine would not exclude them. So we cannot be a sect unless we claim what does not belong to us: a position which disowns all others.[89]

But in practice if not in theory, many did disown all others, and found it hard to welcome believers from the sects.

9.2.5 Lack of Outreach

As noticed above in passing, lack of outreach formed another significant area of criticism. A Methodist critic alleged that the movement had arisen as a matter of intellectual conviction and discussion rather than as a result of the need to provide for new converts.[90] Rust put the lack of outreach down to the belief that the gospel was not to convert the world.[91] Whately saw the energies of those who joined the movement from other churches as being diverted from evangelism to proselytism.[92] Dennett noted that evangelistic preaching was left to individuals, and that 'As a Community, they make no provision for evangelisation, and, as far as I can gather, never dreamt of sending a missionary to the heathen.'[93] Whilst such charges were amply refuted in later decades by Brethren missionary concern and evangelistic activism, they do seem to have possessed a certain force during the 1840s and early 1850s. This is confirmed by the lack of interest apparently shown in overseas work, the vigour with which Brethren laid into existing churches, and the amount of time and attention given to matters of internal controversy. Important as these undoubtedly were, both in terms of their theological significance and their impact on the movement's cohesiveness, they do appear to have deflected attention from mission.

This accusation may be linked to the Brethren failure to do themselves justice in terms of the publicity given to their outreach: much Brethren missionary work was conducted by individuals who eschewed connections with established missionary agencies, and the movement as a whole was at this stage distinctly ambivalent about the idea of giving prominence to individuals in reporting missionary activity. Furthermore, it is true that many Brethren, Open as well as Exclusive, regarded preaching the gospel as a matter of

---

[88] *Ibid.*, 27; cf. McIntosh, *New Prophets*, 14-15, 20.

[89] Beattie, *Brethren*, 276.

[90] J. Robinson Gregory, *The Gospel of Separation: A Brief Examination of the History and Teachings of Plymouth Brethrenism* (London: Charles H. Kelly, 1894), 4-5, 17.

[91] Rust, *"Brethren"*, 6.

[92] Whately, *Brethrenism*, 11.

[93] Dennett, *Brethren*, 36; cf. Croskery, *Plymouth-Brethrenism*, 158; [G.T. Stokes], review of a number of Brethren writings in *London Quarterly Review* 27 (1866), 20.

the individual's responsibility before the Lord; although they did not intend to diminish its importance by this, there are hints in the periodicals that some in assemblies tended to treat the support of evangelistic activity, expressed in prayerful attendance at the gospel service, as an 'optional extra'.

Withdrawal from the world was another charge advanced by critics. Some saw it as incongruous that Brethren should appear to reject philanthropy as being in opposition to God's purpose for the world because it made people better without Christ, while yet practising medicine.[94]

9.2.6 Christian Experience

It was often alleged that Brethren understood saving faith in terms of a volitional act, which amounted to intellectual assent to the gospel – faith in propositions drawn from the teaching of Scripture rather than in Christ.[95] McIntosh described the Brethren view of faith as believing that you are saved, an understanding which was unacceptable to Calvinists.[96] Similarly, repentance was allegedly regarded as 'a mere intellectual review of ourselves and our conduct'.[97] Philpot described Brethrenism as 'nothing but the letter of Scripture, tacitly if not openly ignoring, setting aside, or denying the main branches of gracious experience'.[98] It was not a religion for the tried and tempted (which he saw as the characteristic state of the elect), nor could it speak to those who were conscious of their unbelief.

Brethren proclamation of the possibility of instant conversion and assurance came in for plenty of criticism from those in the Puritan tradition, who tended to emphasise the drawn-out nature of the process of conversion as the awakened soul experienced a period of conviction of sin under the condemnation of the Law and a sense of lostness and helplessness before being enabled to look to Christ for salvation. It may have given rise to the allegation that Brethren did not preach repentance, because repentance was associated in many Calvinist minds with belief in the necessity of a pre-conversion period of preparation of the heart. Brethren assertions that assurance was the normative state of Christian experience contrasted with a widespread belief in Presbyterianism that claims to assurance of salvation amounted to presumption, and their preaching on this topic made a great impact.[99] Many Calvinist critics felt that Brethren made assurance of the essence of faith in such a way as to discourage converts from due self-examination and to class weak believers as unsaved.[100] Related to this was the allegation that Brethren did not, in their understanding of Christian experience, give sufficient place to the experiences of trial and difficulty of which the Old Testament was full; this was put down

---

[94] Teulon, *Brethren*, 161-3; cf. Croskery, *Plymouth-Brethrenism*, 151, 156.

[95] Anon., 'Plymouth Brethren', 908; Croskery, *Plymouth-Brethrenism*,108; Houston, *Plymouthism*, 21; Latimer, *Lecture*, 4; [Philpot], 'Editor's Review', 81; Porteous, *Brethren*, 176.

[96] McIntosh, *New Prophets*, 11.

[97] Croskery, *Plymouth-Brethrenism*, 113n; cf. idem, *Catechism*, 15; McIntosh, *New Prophets*, 29.

[98] Review of C.H. Coles, *A Treatise on some Important Subjects, viz., On the Church of God, &c*, and C.H. Marston, *The Spirit of God grieved, and the Church of God sleeping* (1855), 163.

[99] Hutchinson, *Sowers, Reapers, Builders*, 243.

[100] Croskery, *Plymouth-Brethrenism*, 108, 113; Houston, *Plymouthism*, 22; McIntosh, *New Prophets*, 24; C.H. Marston, *Grieving the Spirit; a sermon, preached in Clifton Chapel, Beds, September 14, 1856* (London: Houlston and Stoneman, [1856]), 43-4; [Philpot], 'Editors' Review', 81.

in part to insistence that the Psalms were to be read as typological descriptions of Christ's experience on earth, rather than as reflecting the experience of godly believers in Old Testament times.[101]

Regeneration and sanctification were another area in which Brethren teaching was seen as erroneous: it was charged that for Brethren, regeneration represented the introduction of a new power into the soul, rather than the regeneration of the soul itself, so that the regenerated person became in effect two individuals.[102] Other writers put this in terms of the old and new natures, sanctification having nothing to do with the (irredeemable) old nature: the fear was that such an approach could and did allow some Brethren to excuse sin by saying that it was a manifestation of the old nature, which was no longer the real 'them' and for which they were no longer responsible. Furthermore, the assertion that the new man was sinless left no room for progress in sanctification.[103] Croskery noted the connection of Brethren teaching about the two natures with their belief that Christ left his old human nature behind him in death.[104]

Brethren were repeatedly accused of antinomianism, the denial that the Law of God in its moral aspect has any bearing upon the life of the believer.[105] Lurid hints were thrown out concerning the evils to which such error had given rise, although the Victorian obsession with propriety (coupled, perhaps, with a desire to avoid prosecution for libel) ensured that no specific instances of immorality or other evil conduct were cited.[106] Practically speaking, this was deemed their most serious error, since it amounted to 'religion made easy': they were spared the struggle of mortifying the flesh, since perfect holiness was vicariously imputed to them.[107] There was, in Reid's words, 'a confounding of what we are in Christ representatively, with what we are personally'.[108] Although we may reject Houston's scurrilous allegation that Brethren, not being under the Law, did not therefore believe that they could commit sin,[109] there was some basis for the theological aspect of the charge of antinomianism: firstly, Brethren sometimes spoke of the Law as given for unbelieving Gentiles; secondly, they emphasised far more than many Evangelicals the role of the Spirit in the life and walk of the believer; thirdly, they stressed the completed aspect of sanctification, sometimes at the expense of the believer's responsibility to be progressively sanctified.[110] Neatby noted the tendency to prefer exposition of the believer's privileges in Christ over practical words of exhortation,[111] a tendency noted by Brethren themselves and also found among earlier high Calvinists. However, A.N. Groves had earlier pointed out that Christian believers

---

[101] Marston, *Grieving the Spirit*, 42; [Philpot], 'Editors' Review', 82.

[102] Porteous, *Brethren*, 188, 190; Reid, *Plymouth Brethrenism*, 180.

[103] Croskery, *Plymouth-Brethrenism*, 118, 122; Houston, *Plymouthism*, 25; Latimer, *Lecture*, 9-10.

[104] Croskery, *Plymouth-Brethrenism*, 89.

[105] Croskery, *Catechism*, 3; *ER* 5 (May 1839), 576; Gregory, *Gospel of Separation*, 32, 38.

[106] Carson, *Heresies*, 166-7; Cox, *Test before you Trust*, 30; Croskery, *Plymouth-Brethrenism*, 136-7; Houston, *Plymouthism*, 15-18; Latimer, *Lecture*, 7; Mearns, *Plymouthism*, 71-5; Rust, *"Brethren"*, 34-5.

[107] Anon., 'Plymouth Brethren', 909; Reid, *Plymouth Brethrenism*, 41, 142.

[108] Reid, *Plymouth Brethrenism*, 185.

[109] Houston, *Plymouthism*, 17-18.

[110] Teulon, *Brethren*, 106-14.

[111] Neatby, *History*, 235.

had an even stricter, more extensive, and more heart-searching rule of life, the New Testament.[112]

A potentially serious consequence of Brethren attitudes towards the Law was highlighted by the Strict Baptist C.H. Marston, who spent some months with the Brethren during 1855; in his view, Brethren denial that Gentiles were under the moral Law resulted in a false peace being proclaimed, since it was this Law which the Spirit used to convict of sin: thus he feared that many who had been 'converted' in Brethren meetings had never been truly born again.[113]

One aspect of the Law on which great stress was laid during this period was the observance of the fourth commandment. Whilst Brethren valued the Lord's Day, they did not see the Old Testament Sabbath obligations as transferred to it, a view which, as we have seen, did not go down well in Presbyterian areas.

Many critics condemned the Brethren's alleged refusal as believers to pray for the forgiveness of sins. According to Croskery, Brethren taught that believers were not supposed to pray for forgiveness since all their sins were forgiven at conversion, and unbelievers were not to do so either because they could not pray acceptably; thus pardon was not to be prayed for at any point.[114] However, Brethren made a fine distinction between such prayer and the confession of sins with a view to forgiveness, which was encouraged, although in practice seriously neglected.[115] E.K. Groves asserted that Brethren were happy to confess sin in general terms, but lacked any real sense of sinfulness; bad conduct (of which he gave examples) could therefore co-exist with professions of reliance on the work of Christ. He recorded a number of instances of financial or moral failure among Brethren, observing the lack of a sense of sin which resulted from the way the atonement was applied and the pervasive spiritual unreality.[116] The petition in the Lord's Prayer 'forgive us our sins' would not have troubled them, since majority opinion denied that this prayer was intended for the Christian dispensation; few indeed were those who would have advocated its congregational repetition.

9.3 The Impact of Criticism

In 1883, a clergyman at Killymun, near Dungannon in Ulster, circulated leaflets warning against attendance at meetings held by the Brethren evangelist David Rea, alleging that Brethren did not believe in the necessity of repentance or prayer. Rea's response was to speak plainly on the necessity of both.[117] Brethren clearly did feel it necessary on occasion to respond directly to criticism. A number of writers, especially Exclusives (since they were the main targets of the critics), produced defences of their theology and practice. Darby in particular produced a number of responses to critical works, which may be found in his *Collected Writings*. Some were *ad hominem* responses to particular critiques (and on occasion he could overwhelm opponents by the length of his response), while others presented a more general overview and defence of the movement's

---

[112] A.N. Groves, *Remarks on a Pamphlet, entitled "The Perpetuity of the Moral Law"* (Madras: J.B. Pharoah, 1840), ii, 81-95.

[113] Marston, *Grieving the Spirit*, 41-3. Cf. [Philpot], 'Editors' Review', 80-1.

[114] Croskery, *Catechism*, 14; idem, *Plymouth-Brethrenism*, 104-7; McIntosh, *New Prophets*, 9, 11.

[115] Neatby, *History*, 233.

[116] Groves, *Müller*, 179-85, 213-15.

[117] Rea, *David Rea*, 100.

distinctives. Other writers, for example Kelly and (among Open Brethren) Ritchie, produced similar works. Some first appeared in the pages of Brethren periodicals, but were not always advertised there when published separately.

To some extent, the first generation of histories of the movement, produced from the 1870s onwards, may also be seen as responses to accounts by critics of the movement's rise and development. Critical accounts would have been slanted in the direction of warning readers against contact with the movement, so it is hardly surprising that Brethren responses affirmed and sought to demonstrate the movement's divine origin. Alongside the history, such works included explanation and defence of the movement's distinctive beliefs and practices.[118]

On occasion, critics were urged to acquaint themselves with the movement. The Presbyterian convert to Brethrenism, William Reid of Carlisle, urged inquirers to attend meetings and read the literature for themselves, and offered an extensive survey of Exclusive writings. They would find Darby 'incomparably more profound, as well as more learned' than even the Puritan divine John Owen.[119] In Reid's view, the critics lacked spiritual discernment as well as acquaintance with Brethren works. He also pointed out that many ministers owed a great deal to Brethren, having been converted through reading their tracts or drawing on Brethren expositions in their ministry.[120]

But how accurate were the charges laid against the movement? Even more categorically than Neatby, Coad expressed the conviction that 'there is not one of these books which contains anything of moment that is really relevant to [Open] Brethrenism'.[121] However, I am not convinced that critics were always as wide of the mark as has been alleged. Even Teulon's outrageous charge that permitted occupations were restricted to medicine and some handicrafts appears less so in the light of the agonised discussions in Open Brethren periodicals about Christian involvement in a range of occupations, business practices, and relationships.[122] Furthermore, whilst it is true that the majority of critics had Exclusivism in their sights, a number of these charges would have been applicable by extension to Open Brethren, as critics often pointed out. To my mind, although some focus on doctrinal vagaries which were not followed by the majority of Brethren (especially in the Open stream), most of the accusations contain at least a grain of historical truth, and this is confirmed by the fact that Brethren writers made similar criticisms themselves. In particular, the allegations of schismatic conduct and proselytism should be taken more seriously than has often been done.[123] The problem was

---

[118] For more detail on these works, see Grass, 'Quest for identity'. A prime example of such a work was Andrew Miller, *The Brethren: a brief sketch of their Origin, Progress and Testimony* (London: G. Morrish, [c.1879]); it included several chapters outlining Brethren teaching on issues raised by critics.

[119] [Reid], *Literature*, 8.

[120] *Ibid.*, 17, 42.

[121] Coad, *History*, 228.

[122] Teulon, *Brethren*, 142; cf. Croskery, *Plymouth-Brethrenism*, 151. Even the latest (1997) edition of the *Oxford Dictionary of the Christian Church* perpetuates this howler.

[123] The significance of these may have been underestimated by historians who have presented the movement from a Southern English perspective, whereas the movement was markedly more separatist in Scotland and Northern Ireland. On the other hand, Dickson (*Brethren in Scotland*, 175) comments on the debate regarding the willingness of some to preach in other denominations that 'The defence of

that even when particular criticisms only applied to a minority in the movement, the whole was tarred with the same brush, which served to isolate Brethren still further and so rendered them more prone to doctrinal deviation. The sheer persistence of some of these charges means that they must be taken seriously; some could be accounted for in terms of critics all depending on the same source, but this is not always the case. Many of them may, however, be put down to the inevitable disparity between theory and practice which marks every church. Others may represent expressions of frustration at, or suspicion of, the crude or careless literary style of many Brethren writers: 'they all write in such a *foggy* style, that it is almost impossible to attach to their sentences any definite meaning; they can be crisp and clear enough, indeed, where they want to do so, but elsewhere they are misty and vague'.[124] William Reid of Edinburgh pointed out that Brethren had failed to produce any theological work considered worth stocking by a non-Brethren bookseller, or recognised as a standard outside their circles, even though they had some biblical scholars of note.[125] However, on one point the critics were definitely wrong: some predicted that Brethren would not last long because the movement's growth was due to proselytism rather than evangelism.[126] To the extent that Brethren were motivated by an outgoing evangelistic spirit, they have survived, and at times grown, and will continue to do so. Even at this point, though, critics were right in their contention that Brethren operated with a somewhat different understanding of conversion from that of older Puritan or Methodist proclamation, which included a period of preparation before and outworking after.[127]

The barrage of criticism which late nineteenth-century Brethren faced undoubtedly left its mark on the movement. Coad notes that criticism was strongest in the areas where the Churches of God were to emerge, and concludes that criticism and opposition made Brethren more separatist. This would be corroborated by what we have seen of the relations between Open Brethren and the denominations in Ulster and North-East Scotland. He also observes that the broadcasting of what he calls 'the scandals of the exclusive spirit' confirmed outsiders in their contempt for the movement, noting that many biographies of individuals who had spent some time among Brethren tended to cover up this fact.[128] Overall, criticism helped to strengthen the sense of rejection by the world which was seen as an integral part of following the rejected Christ, and thus to maintain the movement as a separately-existing entity. In the next chapter, we shall look more closely at the attitude of Open Brethren towards the religious world of their day.

liberty for preachers was not an expression of a simple pan-Evangelical ecumenism but could become an argument for a means of proselytising.'

[124] Anon., 'Plymouth Brethren', 905.

[125] Reid, *Plymouth Brethrenism*, 16-17.

[126] Croskery, *Plymouth-Brethrenism* 164-5.

[127] On this topic, which deserves fuller investigation in the light of Brethren teaching in different countries, and its implications for attitudes towards social transformation, see Phyllis D. Airhart, '"What Must I Do To Be Saved?" Two Paths to Evangelical Conversion in Late Victorian Canada', *CH* 59 (1990), 372-85.

[128] Coad, *History*, 230-1.

CHAPTER 10

Brethren and the Wider Religious World

At the turn of the century, one writer summarised the Open Brethren outlook on the world around them. Ritualism and rationalism were both advancing at the expense of Protestantism. Churches, he claimed, equalled the world in the provision of amusement: 'Dramatic entertainments, concerts, raffles, numerous mountebank tricks and performances, kissing (!) and other questionable practices in church, school rooms, and chapel, presided over by the clergyman, and the proceedings opened with prayer, is the run of the day, and all for money!'[1] Few remained who defended the inspiration of Scripture; the Lord's Day was being secularised by church and state; vital religion was dying out. Yet many faithful remained; how they regarded the world around them is the subject of the next two chapters. In this chapter we survey their views of the religious world, and in the next their views of, and engagement with, political, social, cultural and intellectual life.

10.1 Responses to Evangelicalism

10.1.1 Maintaining Separation

Controversy over questions of fellowship had ramifications for participation in interdenominational activity. Throughout much of this period, Open Brethren seem to have been beset by internal controversy over the question of fellowship with other believers. For example, the relationship between Brethren and the Evangelical Alliance was initially marked by suspicion on both sides. This soon began to break down; we find J.E. Howard attending an Evangelical Alliance conference in Berlin during 1857,[2] and others active in the Alliance, such as the Earl of Cavan (1815-87),[3] who was active in a range of interdenominational and evangelistic ventures, and the itinerant missionary F.W. Baedeker (1823-1906).[4] However, other Brethren advocated keeping clear of such bodies on the ground that the only God-ordained association was the church. People joined them, it was claimed, because they wanted union but were not prepared to surrender their cherished traditions and creeds. Caldwell, answering a question in *The Northern Witness*, even claimed (during a period in which he espoused narrower principles of fellowship) that those who supported such movements were in effect 'saying that God's principles of association are a failure, and man has found out a better way'.[5]

Open (and some Exclusive) Brethren had been extensively involved when Moody and Sankey visited Britain, and in England many continued to share in interdenominational

---

[1] W.S., 'The Character of the Times', *BM* n.s. 1 (1900), 21.

[2] [Maria Howard], *Memorials*, 30.

[3] See *BDEB*; C.A.C[oates]., *Frederick John William, eighth Earl of Cavan: a life-sketch* (n.pl.: n.p., [c.1890]); Pickering (ed.), *Chief Men*, 60-2.

[4] On Baedeker, see Robert Sloan Latimer, *Dr. Baedeker: and his apostolic work in Russia* (London: Morgan & Scott, 1908²); Pickering (ed.), *Chief Men*, 142-6.

[5] 'QA', *NW* 10 (1880), 47.

work such as that of the YMCA. However, many in Scotland began to withdraw from such activity, which is understandable in view of the opposition which they were enduring. *The Believer's Magazine* steadfastly refused to allow that such co-operation was either Biblically legitimate or practically fruitful. The fear was that Brethren testimony would become blunted, and that failure to maintain a godly separation from worldly religion would lead to young believers from Brethren families and new converts going back into the systems from which the founding fathers had extricated themselves at considerable personal cost. Preachers were urged not to preach among the sects or in interdenominational gatherings, because of the stipulation that certain topics must not be preached about; they were also warned of the risk of losing the light they had received on such matters as the evil of these gatherings.[6] *The Believer's Magazine* condemned interdenominational efforts as pan-sectarian rather than non-sectarian: churches of all denominations (including those practising such errors as one-man ministry, infant baptism, and mixed membership) were represented on their committees, and the nature of the church and the ordinances were subjects on which silence was enjoined.[7] Ritchie also discerned a tightening hold being exercised by the clergy upon them, which made them no place for Brethren. Commenting on the increasing use of the term 'inter-denominational' instead of 'undenominational', he saw the former as indicative of the desire of ministers to keep a tight rein on what took place in such missions. Since evangelists would now be expected to direct converts to the churches in return for official support, how could Brethren any longer justify preaching in such circles?[8]

Included in this condemnation was a movement which, superficially appeared similar to Open Brethrenism, and represented another form of the reaction against the profusion of denominations: the 'Christian Unions' which sprang up all over Glasgow and Lowland Scotland. These were formed by lay-people, who established mission halls in which the gospel could be preached, and in some cases the Lord's Supper celebrated.[9] These would not be easy to distinguish from Brethren, and indeed a number would develop into Brethren assemblies.[10] Marshall wrote that he knew of a dozen assemblies which had developed from such missions.[11] Ritchie saw these associations as a response to the threat of large-scale secessions of Moody's converts in obedience to what they had learned from Scripture; he regarded them as pan-sectarian, because they linked all the sects together, rather than unsectarian.[12]

A more moderate line was advocated by Caldwell in *The Witness*; noting the recent increase in lay evangelistic initiatives, he welcomed the fact that many of these were conducted apart from the denominations and their leaders were thus free to follow the teaching of Scripture. In other cases, a gifted individual might secede together with his

---

[6] E.g. Anon., 'Undenominational Ground', *W* 19 (1889), 71-2; 'ASQ', *BM* n.s. 6 (1905), 11-12.

[7] E.g. [John Ritchie], 'Undenominational Unions', *BM* 1 (1891), 38-40.

[8] [John Ritchie], '"Inter-Denominational"', *BM* n.s.1 (1900), 43-5.

[9] Dickson, *Brethren in Scotland*, 100-1; John Ritchie, in *BM* n.s. 3 (1902), 48.

[10] For example, Johnstone Evangelistic Association (which became an assembly in 1925), Coatbridge Christian Union (1938), Anniesland Christian Association, Glasgow (1942), and Mauchline Mission Hall, of the Ayrshire Christian Union (c.1955). A number of other mission halls in England and Scotland developed into assemblies, some as late as the 1960s. For details of Scottish ones, see Dickson, *Brethren in Scotland*, 128-9, 194-5, 202.

[11] Marshall, *"Holding Fast"*, 30.

[12] [John Ritchie], 'Undenominational Unions', *BM* 1 (1891), 38-40.

former flock, and begin declaring the truth he had so far learned from Scripture. Perception of the truth often came gradually, and if those concerned were moving in the right direction, the Spirit's blessing upon their work should be acknowledged. Different views might exist concerning the legitimacy of preaching in the sects, but the flocks gathered by such means needed to be fed.[13]

While some, especially those who were part of the revivalist network, were happy to preach in the sects, others condemned the practice. Banks considered that in preaching there was no justification for separating proclamation of the gospel from instruction about the duties which new converts should undertake. Since Brethren separated from the sects because of their desire to obey God fully, why preach among them when it was not possible to declare the whole counsel of God, and when converts would join the sects? 'Why allow your gift as an evangelist, to be utilised for the inconsistent purpose of putting fresh blood into the veins of that which, as a system, you have avowedly left?'[14] As was explained elsewhere, preaching in such places amounted to implicit approval of what went on in them and made it impossible to lead others out.[15]

The Believer's Magazine carried a number of questions on the legitimacy of fellowship with the sects. In Ritchie's view, separation must not be given up; he was utterly convinced

> that Gospel work was never more vigorous, that conversions were never more abundant and real, that the unconverted were never got in larger numbers to hear the Word, than in the days when assemblies stood clean and clear from all the systems of the world's religion, walking in the path of separation and fearlessly testifying to the truth that produces and maintains it, having the vials of the religious world's wrath poured without mercy or measure on their devoted heads.[16]

If true Christians remained in systems from which they should separate, any lack of fellowship was their fault, not that of Brethren.[17] If Brethren went soft on separation, the risk was that

> over most of privileged Scotland ..., if God does not come in, in grace, and reviving power, the inheritance that God has given us, will be lost to our children. The old believers of 25 and 30 years ago, who bought the truth and had to pay something for it, are passing off the scene, and others are letting it slip through between their fingers.[18]

This viewpoint both followed from, and reinforced, a reading of Brethren history which stressed separation as a motivating factor for the earliest leaders.[19]

By contrast, Craik in 1862 had advised Brethren visiting a locality where no assembly existed to seek out the congregation whose order was most Scriptural and whose

---

[13] J.R. Caldwell, 'Our "Identification" with Evangelistic Efforts', *W* 26 (1896), 165-6.

[14] F.A. B[anks], 'John's Third Epistle', *NW* 16 (1886), 27.

[15] 'YBQB', *BM* 6 (1896), 140; 'YBQB', *BM* 7 (1897), 10.

[16] [John Ritchie], 'Helps and Hindrances to Gospel Work. Part IV. – Decline in Gospel Power, and its Causes', *BM* n.s. 7 (1906), 104.

[17] 'YBQB', *BM* n.s. 11 (1910), 35.

[18] Donald Munro, 'How shall we order the child? Part II', *BM* n.s. 2 (1901), 127.

[19] Anon., '"The Plymouth Brethren"', *BM* 9 (1899), 17-18.

gatherings were most likely to edify.[20] Such an approach was criticised in *The Believer's Magazine*: 'The Word of God, that forbids a believer to be connected with a sect, must be as true, in the distant village, as in the town, with its Assembly of Saints gathered unto the Lord's name.'[21] If it was right to be separate in the one case, it must also be right in the other; the advice given was to worship alone, a course which, it was asserted, had been used to gather an assembly. Similarly, frequent condemnations were issued of going to hear preachers from the sects.[22] (Caldwell, whilst calling on those who attended such preaching and those who stayed away not to judge each other, disarmingly admitted that hearing more cultivated preachers might make some discontented with the plainer fare on offer at the Gospel Hall and thus lead to their departure.[23]) The assembly must be in a desperate state to resort to such expedients. Even sending children to a Nonconformist Sunday School was ruled out by such an approach (it appears that unsaved children did not always attend the Breaking of Bread, and that parents would alternate in attendance; the lack of provision for children in some assemblies would have made Sunday Schools attractive).[24] Marrying believers from the sects was also condemned;[25] Ritchie went so far as to say that 'in the Lord' in 1 Corinthians 7.39 referred to a union which was under the authority of Christ, which could only be the case when both partners were obeying him in the matter of fellowship.[26] This is, I suspect, the nearest Open Brethren ever came to explicitly affirming endogamy, the belief that one should only marry within the group, although the Churches of God and the Taylor Brethren would both adopt such a policy.[27]

Speaking at the Glasgow Conference in 1886, A.J. Holiday insisted that separation must be maintained even when those in the sects might display greater zeal than the local assembly. Brethren could not go back on what God had shown them; it was Satan's strategy to get believers to abandon the truth about the position they should take. Such a temptation was especially likely to beset those of the second generation, who had never known any other environment than the assembly, and who would be more likely to leave as a result of meeting earnest Christians in the sects.[28] As W.J. M'Clure, an Irish evangelist who emigrated to North America, explained, the first generation of Brethren had sacrificed much to obey the truth and separate from the denominations. Once assemblies were established, however, it was easier to identify with them: children of the first generation were received into fellowship but as they had not had to make the same sacrifices as their parents in order to join, the truth had less of a grip on them. It was easy for them to lose hold of the truth concerning separation; some even ministered among the sects, or became 'ministers' themselves.[29] By contrast, at a later (and more open) stage in

---

[20] Craik, *Church Order*, 66-7.

[21] 'YBQB', *BM* 3 (1893), 58; cf. 'QA', *NW* 16 (1886), 110.

[22] E.g 'YBQB', *BM* 7 (1897), 10; 'AC', *BM* n.s. 9 (1908), 10.

[23] 'QA', *W* 19 (1889), 140-2.

[24] 'QA', *W* 17 (1887), 15; cf. 'QA', *W* 20 (1890), 142-3.

[25] 'AC', *BM* n.s. 1 (1900), 12.

[26] 'AC', *BM* n.s. 9 (1908), 71.

[27] For the Churches of God, see Anon., 'A summary of the origin, distinctive doctrine and practices of the Needed Truth Assemblies', *W* 92 (1962), 103-4; Clarke, 'Churches of God', 32. Such an idea has persisted among some Open Brethren too; cf. W. Fraser Naismith, 'BQB', *BM* 82 (1972), 27; David West, 'QB', *BM* 113 (2003), 268.

[28] A.J. Holiday, 'Position and Condition', *W* 17 (1887), 1-4; also in *EH* 1 (December 1886), 13-14.

[29] W.J. M'Clure, 'The Place which the Lord chose', *BM* n.s. 10 (1909), 100-2.

his development, Caldwell insisted that to have no more fellowship with believers in the sects than one would have with the world merely served to harden such believers in their sectarianism.[30] (He may well have thought that showing friendship to them would make it possible to proselytise them.) Separatists were aware that something positive was needed to ensure that the assembly remained the most attractive environment for young believers. Spiritual food and opportunities for service were needed.[31] Yet the emphasis on separation tended to overshadow this fact, and this has undoubtedly continued to be one of the chief reasons for the leakage from more conservative assemblies.

In practice, assemblies tended to be more separatist in Scotland and Northern Ireland, whereas many in England (especially in the South) were happy to engage in interdenominational activity. Yet even in those assemblies whose leaders took a separatist line, members would not infrequently have attended meetings outside the assembly, and participated in interdenominational outreach, prayer and Bible study. This is evident, not only from personal recollections of those who grew up during these decades, but also from the frequency with which it was felt necessary in some quarters to warn against the practice.

Both 'tight' and 'loose' factions recognised that the movement had lost much of its early drawing power. Ritchie and others put this down to a failure to maintain a clear position of separation from the sects, but Caldwell spoke for many of more open views when he ascribed it to a Pharisaic attitude towards others which had grieved the Holy Spirit:

> Long ago we made no bones about it when I preached in Baptist Churches, and when Hopkins and Boswell went into all the Churches in Orkney and Shetland, and gathered out many Assemblies. But these were the days of power, and our refusal to receive saints as such, and to co-operate with Church Christians in Gospel work, or in teaching believers, are the two positions that have so separated us, that the talk of receiving believers is a sham; none ever come. They all know they are not wanted. Had we gone where we were invited, and received all who loved the Lord, the Spirit would not have been grieved as He has, and the meetings would have grown to hundreds instead of tens.[32]

Similarly, M'Vicker expressed the conviction that

> Sectarian position and teaching I fear have grieved the Holy Spirit, and robbed "Brethren" of much of their old unction and power. If we cease to own the one *true* Body in all its brokenness, the only justification of our meetings is gone, and the one scriptural and tenable ground – the ground taken by "Brethren" in their most spiritual days – is taken from us. We should thus become simply another among the many existing denominations, distinguished by a little clearer light about the order of worship, a good deal less on some hardly less important subjects, and a great deal of boasting and hard speaking about our brethren.[33]

---

[30] J.R. Caldwell, 'Unity and Separation', *W* 21 (1891), 162.

[31] 'AC', *BM* n.s. 10 (1909), 60.

[32] Quoted in Hawthorn, *Marshall*, 37-8. Caldwell's willingness to preach among the denominations for proselytising purposes must be distinguished from the 'pan-denominational' ecumenism of such men as Russell Hurditch.

[33] [Reich] (ed.), *M'Vicker*, 153 (letter of 21 October 1887).

Elsewhere, he offered a sobering reason for this decline: 'I greatly fear that numbers of false professors have been gathered in, by means of after-meetings, in many places, to whom points and forms are everything, and the possession of God's life in the soul nothing.'[34] The difference of opinion, like the perceived lack of spiritual power, continues today.

10.1.2 Brethren and 'Holiness' Teaching

Bebbington notes that holiness teaching, like premillennialism, stressed divine action, breaking into human life and history; he argues that Brethren contributed to the holiness movement the concept of the church's heavenly calling, and the idea of spirituality as essentially withdrawal from the world.[35] All the same, the relationship between Brethren and the holiness movement was often a cool one during this period. To some extent this can be accounted for in terms of an inverse correlation between separatism and social class: the holiness movement initially affected the middle and upper classes (partly because others could not take time away from work to attend its conferences and conventions). Brethren from these ranks of society were more likely to be sympathetic to it, and also more likely to be already engaged in interdenominational activities. Those less ecumenically minded welcomed evidence of God's activity in human lives, as with other instances where God was blessing outside Brethren circles, but tended to assume that the consequence would be that those so blessed would see the truth of the Brethren position and identify with assemblies. As one writer put it, 'These dear believers have been led to see their standing in the *risen Christ*, and that all fullness is theirs in Him. ... Now, may it not be that their next step will be to see their *identity* with the *rejected Christ*, and our gathering together unto Him outside the camp?'[36] The same Bible was a sufficient guide in both spheres, individual and corporate. The writer challenged the movement's tacit silence regarding church truth, insisting that true holiness was linked with true obedience. Similarly, Ritchie's opinion of 'consecration meetings' was that 'Ministry that "separates" from worldliness, personal, social, political, ecclesiastical, and "fills" with Christ, is true "consecration" ministry.'[37]

M'Vicker, who was a shrewd observer of events within and beyond Brethrenism, provides us with a detailed description and balanced evaluation of a holiness meeting, written soon after Moody and Sankey visited Oxford and Cambridge in 1873:

> ... I attended what is called a Holiness meeting, feeling some curiosity to see what was taught and done there. Much of it was good, but much of it, on the other hand, was little likely to produce true holiness. One could not but be distressed at the attempt, sedulously made, to create physical excitement, by standing up and stamping, and clapping the hands, and singing favourite verses over and over again to rapid tunes, and waving handkerchiefs, and uttering volleys of prearranged "Amens" and "Hallelujahs." *Nervous disease* was much more likely to be produced by such means than *Gospel holiness*: and many would be in danger of mistaking the one for the other. Not less painful were some of the testimonies that young Christians were encouraged to

---

[34] Ibid., 180 (letter of 8 February 1892).

[35] Bebbington, *Evangelicalism*, 152, 157-9; *idem*, *Holiness in Nineteenth-Century England: The 1998 Didsbury Lectures* (Carlisle: Paternoster, 2000).

[36] Anon., 'The Higher Life', *BP* 3 (1882), 97-101; quotation from page 98.

[37] 'YBQB', *BM* 6 (1896), 22.

give to *their own spotlessness* ... Still, it must be said, that there was *life* and *interest* all through; and much less in the teaching to object to than I expected. Some who spoke had evidently got true *soul-deliverance*, and *the courage of cleanness*; and, frankly, I feel less distress over even the mistakes and exaggerations of those who are longing for true holiness to God, ... than over the far more serious mistakes of those who cry out against "perfectionism," and are living in daily sin and conscious defeat, arguing that this is all that Christians are to expect on earth, and trying to satisfy themselves with a kind of visionary and imputed holiness which they have outside themselves in Christ.[38]

Other writers also felt that the movement provided a necessary corrective to the Brethren tendency to stress objective truth at the expense of experience – what one writer described as 'glorying in position with little regard as to condition'.[39] But Henry Groves, who lived at Kendal from 1868 and so had opportunity to observe the development of Keswick at first hand, used his biography of Lord Congleton to demonstrate that 'higher life' teaching was unnecessary for those who realised the life which was theirs in the risen Christ – a characteristic Brethren emphasis, often expressed in terms of the believer's call to work out their 'positional sanctification'.

It was the interpretation rather than the experience which presented problems for some; one writer suggested that in some cases people were being converted, while in others they were coming into assurance of faith or apprehending new truth; there might even be some who were being deceived. Christians should not be divided into classes: all were perfect as to their standing, and imperfect as to their state. Perfectionist teaching was criticised primarily for lowering the standard of holiness by restricting 'sin' to known and voluntary acts.[40]

Scotland proved more promising soil for holiness thinking than might have been expected, given the prevailing Calvinist ethos. Bowes had a Wesleyan background, and during the 1860s some Lanarkshire assemblies appear to have adopted perfectionist views.[41] Moody and Sankey, whose visits to Britain helped to shape much Open Brethren evangelistic practice, had themselves been influenced by holiness thinking, which in turn has been seen as indebted to early Brethren for its conviction that a higher level of practical holiness was possible for each believer as an outworking of their standing as already completely sanctified through Christ.[42] Munro and Ross had been influenced by holiness teaching and during the late 1860s and early 1870s they (like Finney) stressed the need for holiness as a precondition for revival; Ritchie was converted and nurtured under such influences. Whilst *The Believer's Magazine* and *The (Northern) Witness* tended to be critical of the theology (if not the experience) of the holiness movements, it appears likely that such movements nevertheless contributed to maintaining the spiritual heat of Scottish assemblies and that Ritchie and others had more in common with them than was acknowledged.[43] The main issue on which Brethren would have differed from Keswick was in seeing entire consecration as accomplished at conversion, rather than through a post-conversion act of surrender.

---

[38] [Reich] (ed.), *M'Vicker*, 121 (to a missionary, undated; cf. 199 for dating).

[39] W.H.B[ennet]., 'The Late Mr. Joseph Stancomb', *W* 23 (1893), 75.

[40] E.g. G.F.G., 'The Higher Life', *NW* 8 (1878), 155-9.

[41] Dickson, *Brethren in Scotland*, 74.

[42] Bebbington, *Evangelicalism*, 157-9; Fiedler, *Faith Missions*, 116.

[43] Dickson, *Brethren in Scotland*, 94-5, 116-17, 266-71.

From the 1880s, Keswick theology was much more moderate in its views. This made it easier for Brethren to attend Keswick and other such conferences, read the literature, and espouse aspects of the teaching. In one area, the Blackdown Hills, Brethren displayed a marked affinity for holiness teaching. The Brealey family, three generations of whom led the Blackdown work, were sympathetic to it, as was Lang, who settled for some years at Clayhidon. Before him, a convert of George Brealey's named Ephraim Venn (1858-1931) trained as an evangelist at the Guinnesses' institute in East London and at Cliff College, which had strong links with the holiness movement in its Methodist expression, returning to plant assemblies in Somerset.[44]

10.1.3 Brethren, Revival, and Revivalism

A considerable proportion of Open Brethren leaders were either converted during the 1859 revival or cut their teeth as part of the developing network of revivalist evangelists which grew out of it. However, in some areas relations between Brethren and interdenominational revivalism were strained, and especially so in North-East Scotland. Here a number of missionaries sought to reach the coastal communities with the gospel during the 1860s, working as far as possible alongside the existing churches. These wished to conserve the fruits of this activity, and when some of the missionaries and their converts began to question accepted ways of doing things, and to set up their own gatherings, they reacted negatively. This, as we have seen, set off an equally negative response from what were rapidly developing into Brethren-style assemblies, and the result was a polarisation which contributed much to the clear separatist position taken by many Brethren in the region.

That being so, we should not be surprised at the ambivalence of many Brethren, especially in Scotland, towards Moody and Sankey when they visited Britain from 1873-5. For example, one writer in Ross's short-lived *Northern Assemblies* rejoiced in the blessing granted, even if some were shaken by the fact that it occurred where it did, but denied that this justified returning to the sects or joining in united prayer meetings and other such activities.[45] In response, S. Trevor Francis (1834-1925) urged participation in such ventures and warned against a narrow approach, asserting that 'God often makes a little truth go a long way.'[46] He was, at the time, assisting the American evangelists in London, and belonged to the meeting at Kennington, which was Exclusive. Other Southern leaders such as Hurditch were more than happy to join in interdenominational outreach; his magazines had a decidedly interdenominational flavour in terms of the events reported.

Some were sceptical of portrayals of Moody which stressed his co-operation with the churches. According to *The Believer's Magazine*, Moody's Bible readings during his first visit to Scotland had caused many to search the Scriptures and so to gather to Christ's name alone, an assertion which, even if overstated, helps to explain the increase in assemblies in Scotland during the 1870s.[47] But as for subsequent ventures of a similar

---

[44] *W* 61 (1931), 67.

[45] J.S., 'Vessels unto Honour', *NA*, April 1874, 13-14.

[46] *NA*, May 1874, 19-20. On Francis, who wrote such hymns as 'O, the deep, deep love of Jesus', 'Saviour, we remember Thee' and 'Let me sing, for the glory of heaven', see *BM* n.s. 31 (1930), 239-40; Pickering (ed.), *Chief Men*, 160-1; *W* 55 (1925), 279.

[47] [John Ritchie], 'Notes on Current Events', *BM* n.s. 1 (1900), 24.

nature, separatists adopted the view that it was not possible to join a united campaign if one had come out from the churches involved.

From acknowledging the possibility that God might be blessing work undertaken outside the movement, Open Brethren moved to ask why he did not appear to be blessing work undertaken within it. Responses to the Welsh Revival of 1904-5 provided a clear instance of Open Brethren heart-searching that God should apparently be pouring out his blessing on other denominations while passing them by, a circumstance which was seen as saying something about the assemblies' spiritual condition. Already, several meetings in London during 1902-3 had considered the lack of spiritual power in assemblies.[48] William Shaw asked 'How is it that a great Revival ... does not take place among us ...?' Brethren saw little result from their outreach, while others with a limited grasp of truth were seeing much more. He warned against thinking that imitation of the methods used in the revival meetings would bring success: 'let us not attempt any imitation of methods lest we find we have *imitated everything except the power!* Let us be delivered from attempting to *work up* that which can only *come down.*' The real problem, he felt, was the worldliness of Brethren.[49]

The periodicals reported fairly extensively on the revival as it affected Brethren, the majority of reports being from Scotland. In Findochty on the North-East coast, Brethren co-operated with the Methodists and the Salvation Army, and saw hundreds of conversions.[50] At Hermon Hall, Glasgow, a whole football team was converted.[51] In Lockerbie, James Anderson reported:

> On Sunday night we had a remarkable time. The Lesser Town Hall was overcrowded; we felt that God was with us. Had not spoken for more than ten minutes when I felt strange – trembling all over. The sorrows of hell seemed to encompass me, and as I spoke the people quailed. The dying love of Christ melted our hearts and the people sobbed. For a few moments we were speechless. The Lord was at hand and I felt He must carry on the meeting, so I quietly left. The people were riveted to their seats; the Spirit moved. Prayer, hymns and testimony went on for an hour and a half, then I returned and closed the meeting in an orderly way. It was a never-to-be-forgotten night, and we are reaping the fruit of it now.[52]

The same page reported at least 200 professions at Broxburn, and 250 at Carlisle. Those who had visited South Wales reported on what they had witnessed, stirring up desire for revival blessing to be poured out elsewhere.[53] Leaders met to consider what they could learn.[54]

Ritchie noted that South Wales assemblies kept apart from the revival as it manifested itself in the chapels, working independently: 'There is a wonderful spirit of hearing, and

---

[48] 'WML', *W* 32 (1902), 84, 164; 'WML', *W* 33 (1903), 84; cf. Anon., 'The Lack of Spiritual Power in Assemblies: Its Cause and Remedy', *EOS* 32 (1903), 243-4.

[49] William Shaw, 'The Revival in Wales: has it a voice for us?', *W* 35 (1905), 27-8; cf. [John Ritchie?], 'Revival and its Counterfeits', *BM* n.s. 6 (1905), 37-8, claiming that some had attempted to replicate what they had seen.

[50] 'WML', *W* 33 (1903), 73.

[51] 'WML', *W* 35 (1905), 35.

[52] 'WML', *W* 35 (1905), 67.

[53] E.g. 'TLWW', *BM* n.s. 6 (April 1905), i-ii; 'WML', *W* 35 (1905), 19, 36.

[54] E.g. at Cardiff ('TLWW', *BM* n.s. 6 (May 1905), iii).

men and women are led to Christ in their homes, in trains, trams, at business, on the streets, everywhere. ... throughout the whole of Wales at present anxious souls are found everywhere, waiting for some one to lead them to Jesus (Acts viii.31).'[55] The revival represented a great opportunity for suitable teachers:

> It is a great opportunity for all who know and love the Gospel in its simplicity and fulness to spread it abroad among those who are awakened to eternal realities, and to establish on the firm foundations of the faith those who are being saved. The life of God in a soul cannot live on excitement, it needs the milk of the Word of God. Everywhere, new born souls are crying out for spiritual food which unconverted Ritualistic and Rationalistic preachers cannot give.[56]

In responding to events, Brethren were trying to tread a tightrope, avoiding rejecting a work of God but also remaining faithful to their understanding of God's principles of church life.

> If the present revival is to be the best ever known, it will only be so by being the most scriptural ever known. There is a double danger at the present time, on the one hand, lest our eyes should be blinded by prejudice to what God is doing; or, on the other hand, lest our grasp of divine principles and methods be loosened, in our anxiety to share at any cost in the manifestations of blessing.[57]

Many therefore welcomed the evidence that God was working, but expressed concern at aspects of the proceedings. *The Believer's Magazine* noted the lack of ministry; feelings, testimonies and singing could not feed the new life or provide guidance concerning conduct.[58] As for the dreams and visions reported from Wales, none stood up to testing, and God did not now communicate with believers by such means.[59] The pragmatic idea that certain methods should be adopted because they worked in Wales was rejected. The fact that God used certain means there, sovereignly setting aside the normal patterns of church life, did not mean that he approved of them; indeed, if the work were more Scriptural in character, he might bless even more.[60] Rather than visiting Wales to see what was happening, it was simpler to be exposed to the teaching of Scripture.[61]

Writers in *The Believer's Magazine* made a clear distinction between God-sent revival and humanly-engineered revivalist excitement. True revivals, according to Ritchie, did not evaporate, neither was there a backwash by way of reaction against all the excitement.[62] Sadly, such excitement could leave an area more difficult to reach than ever.[63] Throughout the twentieth century, Brethren would be perplexed by such matters as revivalism and claims to supernatural manifestations, and divided in their responses, unable to resolve the tension between the supernaturalism and the cerebralism of their

[55] 'TLWW', *BM* n.s. 6 (April 1905), iii.
[56] 'TLWW', *BM* n.s. 6 (January 1905), iii.
[57] W.H[oste]., 'The Revival of 536 B.C.', *W* 35 (1905), 69.
[58] 'AC', *BM* n.s. 6 (1905), 10.
[59] 'AC', *BM* n.s. 6 (1905), 47; cf. R.W.B[roadbent?]., 'Welsh Visions', *EOS* 34 (1905), 119.
[60] [John Ritchie?], 'Revival Times', *BM* n.s. 6 (1905), 25.
[61] Anon., 'The Revival in South Wales', *EOS* 34 (1905), 23-4.
[62] 'TLWW', *BM* n.s. 6 (November 1905), i.
[63] 'TLWW', *BM* n.s. 6 (August 1905), i.

spirituality. Meanwhile, on the back of the revival came another challenge; it was reported from Norway that

> A testing time has been allowed to come upon many of the Lord's people and among assemblies gathered in the simplicity of the Word, by means of a remarkable work which, under the name of "Revival,!" has manifested itself in various places. It is impossible at the present stage to estimate its character or results, but we may mention that "prophesying," speaking with "tongues," and many such gifts are claimed, in association with the corruption and denial of most of the fundamental doctrines of the Word.[64]

10.1.4 The Appearance of Pentecostalism

From the beginning of the Pentecostal movement in Britain, Brethren were in contact with it. Around 1909, a group of young Bible students associated with Brethren in the Preston area, under the leadership of Thomas Myerscough (1858-1932), had entered into the Pentecostal experience. Myerscough became one of the early leaders of the Assemblies of God in Britain, and a gifted Bible teacher; it has been suggested that he was the medium by which Brethren thinking regarding the Lord's Supper influenced the development of the Elim Pentecostal churches.[65] Among those students was W.F.P. Burton (1886-1971), who pioneered Pentecostal mission in Congo. While in Africa, Burton developed a friendship with the Brethren missionary Dan Crawford, and it is claimed that Crawford himself received a baptism of the Holy Spirit, accompanied by spiritual gifts, in 1924.[66] However, such contact rapidly came to be disapproved of: when a question was submitted to *The Believer's Magazine* about a leading brother who both attended and commended Pentecostal meetings, Ritchie responded that such a person should not be recognised as a teacher.[67] As with Irvingism, many Brethren appear initially to have been willing to investigate the possibility of the movement's being a genuine work of God, but ultimately to have concluded that it was not.

Nevertheless, at least one assembly 'went Pentecostal'. A note in *The Witness* in 1911 stated that 'Believers should be warned against a circular, emanating from Stanley Hall, Manchester, advocating "The Tongues" as the evidence of the baptism of the Holy Spirit.'[68] Stanley Hall had appeared in the 1904 address list, and from it was to spring one of the largest Pentecostal churches in Britain. The businessman John Nelson Parr (1886-1976), who was to become a leading light in the Assemblies of God, received his Pentecostal experience there. Having been associated with a holiness meeting, he moved to Stanley Hall after hearing that some of the members were seeking the Pentecostal blessing. At Christmas 1910, one of them received it at the end of the Breaking of Bread,

---

[64] 'TLWW', *BM* n.s. 8 (June 1907), vi.

[65] Richard Bicknell, 'In memory of Christ's Sacrifice: Roots and Shoots of Elim's Eucharistic Expression', *Journal of the European Pentecostal Theological Association* 17 (1997), 65, 85n.

[66] See William K. Kay, *Inside Story: A History of British Assemblies of God* (Mattersey: Mattersey Hall Publishing, 1990), 30, 67; Colin Whittaker, *Seven Pentecostal Pioneers* (Basingstoke: Marshall Pickering, 1983), 165-6.

[67] 'ASQ', *BM* n.s. 9 (1908), 106-7.

[68] 'WML', *W* 41 (1911), 100; cf. *EOS* 41 (1912), 222; 'TLWW', *BM* n.s. 13 (July 1912), iii; 'WML', *W* 42 (1912), 168; *W* 43 (1913), 278.

as did Parr himself a little later. The result was a new sense of evangelistic effectiveness, coupled with healings, miracles, and charismatic manifestations, but also fierce opposition from other churches. From 1917, Parr became pastor of what was developing into a Pentecostal church, after expelling a leader whose Brethren views on such matters as women keeping silence in the assembly and the rejection of instrumental music at the Breaking of Bread made him a barrier to progress. (The man in question also appears to have espoused annihilationist views, and Parr's consistent opposition to such teaching may indicate that these were more of a problem than the man's Brethrenism.[69]) The fellowship later built Bethshan Tabernacle in Longsight.[70]

The main Brethren arguments against Pentecostalism were typical of those used by other Evangelicals. In the biblical record, it was said, miraculous gifts were given at times of new revelation or dire apostasy, in order to gain attention. Scripture represented 'that which is perfect' in 1 Corinthians 13.10; 'To claim to speak with tongues today is tantamount to saying that Holy Scripture is neither complete nor sufficient.'[71] On occasion a more distinctively dispensational argument was used which claimed that the sign-gifts were intended for Jewish believers during an overlap between dispensations, and that after the fall of Jerusalem they passed away.[72] Some Brethren drew on earlier responses to Irvingism: Anderson-Berry included an article on Christ's sinlessness in his series on Christology for *The Witness*, in which he provided an account of Irving's teaching and practice as paralleling more recent phenomena.[73]

The most detailed responses were produced by Robert Anderson (of whom more in the next chapter) and Lang. Anderson's *Spirit Manifestations and "the Gift of Tongues"* proved very popular, running to a fourth edition by 1909. He regarded Pentecostalism as 'marked by doctrinal error, and energised in part by spiritual influences of a sinister kind'.[74] Every dispensation was ushered in by miracles; the supernatural gifts which inaugurated the Christian era were intended primarily for the covenant people (he discerned a pattern in Acts whereby God addressed himself 'to the Jew first'), but when the Jews were set aside, the miracles ceased and there was no reason to expect their revival. Anderson examined the Irvingite manifestations, quoting at length from the prophet Robert Baxter (1802-89), whom he had known for many years.[75] Pentecostalism was dangerous because it drew attention away from Christ and from Scripture; objective truth was de-emphasised in favour of subjective experience. The phenomena themselves

---

[69] Cf. Brady and Evans, *Brethren*, 136.

[70] Ibid.; John Nelson Parr, *"Incredible"* (Fleetwood: the author, [1972]).

[71] T.B[aird?]., 'QA', *W* 43 (1913), 22.

[72] E.g. W.E. Vine, *Spiritual Gifts: With special reference to "Tongues" and "Healings"* (Bath: Echoes of Service, n.d.).

[73] D. Anderson-Berry, 'The Sinlessness of Jesus', *W* 38 (1908), 159-61.

[74] Robert Anderson, *Spirit Manifestations and "the Gift of Tongues"* (Glasgow: Pickering & Inglis, n.d.[5]), 2.

[75] Baxter was a parliamentary solicitor and an Anglican Evangelical. He influenced the development of the Irvingite movement by his prophecies during 1831-2, before causing a sensation by recanting belief in the gifts and going into print on the subject in *A Narrative of Facts, Characterizing the Supernatural Manifestations, in Mr. Irving's Congregation, and Other Individuals, in England and Scotland and Formerly in the Writer Himself* (London: James Nisbet, 1833) and *Irvingism, in its Rise, Progress, and Present State* (London: James Nisbet, 1836). Newton, Darby, and other Brethren all made considerable use of Baxter's writings.

displayed characteristics of hysteria, and did not conform to the guidelines in 1 Corinthians 14, which laid down that gifts were under the control of the individuals concerned, tongues were not intended for all and they were inferior to other gifts. Around 1911, Lang issued *The modern Gift of Tongues: Whence is it?* He too thought the movement as a whole was Satanically-inspired, and added the belief that it was intended to paralyse God's work in preparation for the rise of Antichrist. Like Anderson, he believed that some features were to be understood in psychological rather than spiritual terms, and the loss of control in the movement was a major aspect of his critique. Comparing it with Irvingism, Lang noted the occurrence of Christological error. He was not a cessationist in principle, but did not accept that Pentecostal phenomena were the same as those recorded in the Acts of the Apostles.

10.2 Responses to other Theological Developments

From the 1860s, the Victorian religious consensus began to break down, as the impact of higher criticism and developments in philosophy and scientific thought combined to render traditional beliefs increasingly untenable for many. In 1863, Craik had airily dismissed the controversy raging over Bishop Colenso's views on the authorship and composition of the Pentateuch, expecting few to be convinced by such opinions.[76] But it was not long before Brethren changed their tune, as what had been minority views rapidly became the accepted orthodoxy. The 'Downgrade Controversy' over the nature of biblical inspiration and the normative status of biblical doctrine, which surrounded C.H. Spurgeon and the Baptist Union from 1887, served to reinforce Brethren convictions about the future of Christendom. Protest was a hopeless task; God had not promised to bring about a better state of things in the sects, and separation was imperative lest believers become like them. 'The fundamental principles [sic], the entire constitution is wrong, and it is impossible for you to remedy that.'[77] In any case, the future of the professing church had been prophetically foretold.

In 1907, R.J. Campbell, minister of the Congregationalist City Temple in London, achieved notoriety with his book *The New Theology*. This outlined a fairly extreme liberalism which blurred the distinction between God and humanity and portrayed the church's mission in terms of this-worldly betterment. It was, perhaps, a concentrated version of Nonconformist political triumphalism, riding on the back of their successes in the 1906 General Election.[78] In line with the tremendous popular attention excited by Campbell's thought, Brethren devoted several booklets and articles to refuting it. *The Believer's Magazine* ran a series of articles in 1907-8 on fundamental truths, while *The Witness* carried one entitled 'Fundamental Facts' during 1908, perhaps by way of presenting a positive alternative to Campbell's eviscerated version of the faith. Like many Brethren since, Ritchie wondered why it was that many Evangelicals remained in denominations affected by error rather than speaking out against it.[79] In such a climate, it was relatively easy for Open Brethren to find a reason for their existence as a distinct entity: as Alexander pointed out, most other Christian groups in Britain had been affected by higher criticism to some extent, and so it was for Brethren to move out with the

---

[76] Craik, *Church Order*, 15-16.

[77] [John Ritchie?], 'A Hopeless Task', *BM* 6 (1896), 30.

[78] Bebbington, *Evangelicalism*, 198-9.

[79] [John Ritchie?], '"The New Theology" and the Foundation of the Faith', *BM* n.s. 8 (1907), 25.

gospel.[80] In the decades which followed, they would do just that, with conspicuous success.

Romanism and ritualism, the other main enemies in the theological world, had been the subject of critical works for rather longer. As early as 1845, J.E. Howard had delivered *Eight Lectures on the Scriptural Truths most opposed to Puseyism*. Contrasting Judaism and Christianity he evaluated the movement in the light of biblical teaching on worship, priesthood, baptismal regeneration, unity, the church's failure, and its heavenly hope. In the summer of 1851, Craik delivered a course of lectures at Bethesda on the subject of Romanism.[81] Developments within Anglicanism along such lines elicited frequent critical comment; a missionary in Italy, J.S. Anderson, offered a series of articles on 'The Rome-Grade' in *The Witness* during 1899. Brethren recognised the popularity of ritualism's appeal to the senses, something which was not likely to be true of their worship: indeed, they gloried in the contrast. One major aspect of Evangelical polemic against Ritualism was absent, though: the futurist cast of Brethren eschatology meant that they opposed attempts to seek correspondences between particular prophecies and current events or trends, on the basis of the principle first enunciated by Darby that while prophecy concerned earthly matters, the church, which was heavenly in its essential nature, would have been removed from the scene by the rapture when the time came for these prophecies to be fulfilled. As far as many Brethren were concerned, all worldly religious systems, and not just that of Rome, would form part of the mystical Babylon spoken of in Revelation, and believers in them were urged to 'come out' (cf. Revelation 18.4).

Some of the new sects also received their share of attention, although Mormonism does not appear to have continued to cause the kind of problems evident in the early history of the Hereford assembly.[82] 'Millennial Dawnism' (Jehovah's Witnesses) merited a series of articles in *The Witness* during 1911. There was even a reference in *The Believer's Magazine* to their infiltrating Brethren after-meetings and speaking to folk as they left the hall.[83] But the most sustained condemnation was reserved for Spiritualism. A series of articles by Ritchie appeared in *The Believer's Magazine* during 1909, expounding biblical teaching, stressing the movement's demonic character, and warning believers against attending spiritualist meetings and séances. Hypnotism, palmistry and thought reading were included in the condemnation, along with more obviously spiritualistic activities.[84] After the First World War, there would be many lectures and pamphlets on the topic of spiritualism, responding to the upsurge of interest in it. It seems possible that the popularity of Spiritualism accounted for some of the strength of Brethren opposition to Pentecostal phenomena.

It would be misleading to conclude from this chapter that Brethren spent their time scanning the newspapers for evidence of 'change and decay' without lifting a finger to help those affected. In the following chapters we shall see that in spite of an inbuilt bias

---

[80] L.W.G. Alexander, 'Lift up your Eyes and Look', *W* 44 (1914), 11-13.

[81] Tayler, *Craik*, 257.

[82] For encounters with Mormons, see 'IML', *W* 40 (1910), 37 (trying to poach converts at the end of a tent mission in Deepcar, Sheffield); 'TLWW', *BM* n.s. 7 (August 1906), iii (opposing outreach at Wyke, Bradford, after some had been converted).

[83] *BM* n.s. 12 (1911), 84.

[84] *BM* n.s. 10 (1909), 32-3, 43-5, 55-7, 68-9.

in their theology towards other-worldliness, some were active in practical philanthropic work, and we shall explore Open Brethrenism as a mission-orientated movement.

CHAPTER 11

Brethren and Society

We abstain from the pleasures and amusements of the world. If we have evening parties, it is for the purpose of studying the word and of edifying ourselves together. We do not mix in politics; we are not of the world: we do not vote. We submit to the established authorities, whatever they may be, in so far as they command nothing expressly contrary to the will of Christ.[1]

So wrote Darby in 1878, and his description would have been true of the great majority of Brethren, Open as well as Exclusive. However, they still had to interact with the world, and in this chapter we shall explore various aspects of that interaction. Among other things, we shall discover that it included some significant expressions of practical Christianity, and that, although Brethren often seemed to undervalue the created order, the movement did not lack a vein of artistic sensitivity.

11.1 Social Concern

An earlier historian of the 1859 revival, Edwin Orr, has suggested that it had three phases: prayer, outreach, and the application of an awakened conscience to the social issues of the day.[2] It has to be admitted that Brethren did not enter fully into the third of these. Whilst Darby and others wrote extensively on social trends, their motivation was not so much engagement with the issues themselves as a desire to demonstrate the imminence of the Second Advent. Such an outlook continued to be manifest in *The Witness*, which included articles on significant contemporary events drawing the moral that the Lord's return was approaching rapidly.

At first sight, too, Brethren attitudes to philanthropic activity appeared rather dismissive. Caldwell expressed the opinion that it represented a Satanic distraction of believers from their task of spreading the gospel; the enemy sought 'to substitute for the simple testimony of Christ a system of world-improving machinery, the object and aim of which is the well-being of man in the world and in the flesh, and from which the object and aim of the heart of God is excluded'.[3] Indeed, it was misery which often awakened sinners to their need of God. Philanthropy aimed at improving the condition of the poor, but the world's real problem was its rejection of Christ; all that reform could achieve was to make men more comfortable on the road to hell. As another writer put it in explaining why believers should be cautious about joining worldly philanthropic societies, '[Paul's] object was not to save the wreck, but to save out of it'.[4]

All the same, it was acknowledged that practical assistance could often open doors for the gospel, although believers should not compromise their principles or enter into

---

[1] Darby, *Letters*, 2.439 (to an editor of the *Français*, 1878).
[2] Orr, *Awakening*, 146.
[3] J.R. Caldwell, 'Christ; or, World-Reformation. Which?', *NW* 16 (1886), 81.
[4] *GL* n.s. 2 (1879), 120.

'unequal yokes' (cf. 2 Corinthians 6.14-18).[5] Brethren did not espouse the Nonconformist 'Social Gospel', but at their best they did believe in the necessity for practical expression of Christian compassion. This was especially evident in missionary practice: Groves had sought to relieve the suffering of victims of floods and plague in Baghdad during 1831-2, and workers frequently found medical work a valuable adjunct to more direct evangelism.

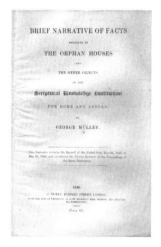

Müller issued an annual report detailing donations and sharing news of God's blessing on the work (notably in terms of conversions among the orphans), but remained committed to the principle of not making direct appeals for funds

Care of orphaned and needy children was an area in which Brethren made an enormous contribution. By the 1870s, Müller's work at Bristol had grown to the point where his orphanages on Ashley Down were catering for over 2,000 children at a time. Another pioneer in this field, Thomas Barnardo (1845-1905), associated with Brethren following his conversion in Dublin during 1862.[6] Initially intending to become a medical missionary with the CIM (itself a Brethren-influenced 'faith mission'), his focus was diverted to the needs of the poorest children and young people of London's East End. Although he became an Anglican late in the 1880s, and would describe Brethren as 'an excellent street through which to pass, but a bad street in which to abide',[7] his outlook was affected by his time among them: his mission included a Brethren-type fellowship in which baptism and the Lord's Supper were observed without clergy to conduct the services. A third example of Brethren involvement in orphanage provision was J.W.C. Fegan (1852-1925).[8] He was an evangelist and teacher as well as founder of the famous children's homes, and his work in the Kent village of Downe, where his parents lived, won the respect of its most famous residents, Charles Darwin and his family.

---

[5] E.g 'QA', *W* 31 (1901), 35-6.

[6] On Barnardo, see *BDE*; *ODNB*; Gillian Wagner, *Barnardo* (London: Eyre & Spottiswoode, 1980).

[7] J. Wesley Bready, *Doctor Barnardo: Physician, Pioneer, Prophet* (London: George Allen & Unwin, 1930), 55.

[8] On Fegan, see Pickering (ed.), *Chief Men*, 187-92.

Others, less famous, were equally involved in work which combined medical assistance with evangelism. Dr J.A. Owles, for instance, ran a medical mission in Liverpool from 1866;[9] other such ventures were commenced in centres such as Glasgow and (in the twentieth century) South-East London, while in Shoreditch there was for some years around the turn of the century a mission seeking to reach Jews through such means.

For all their contact (in lodging-house evangelism and city outreach work) with the evils of drink, Brethren were ambivalent towards the Temperance cause. They condemned drunkenness and often advocated teetotalism, but disapproved of temperance societies. The mission of believers was not to reform the world but to witness to it. Joining such groups involved the believer in an unequal yoke, and temperance advocates often rejected the gospel. In their message, morality and effort replaced regeneration.[10] Ritchie wryly noted that the world could reform people better than believers could, but the latter had the higher task of spreading the gospel; furthermore, reform was not a necessary prerequisite to conversion.[11] Those Brethren who did not drink alcohol (and they were fewer than some, including Ritchie, would have wished[12]) usually made an exception for the Breaking of Bread. Although some assemblies were agitated by individuals pressing for non-alcoholic grape juice to be used, they were discouraged from making this a test of fellowship. Ritchie did not mind what wine was used (often it was port or claret) so long as it was the fruit of the vine. This was deemed typologically significant, Genesis 49.11 being quoted as evidence; hence currant juice (blackcurrant juice?) should not be used. In spite of occasional claims to the contrary, 'We never heard of a genuine believer, however weak, being led to love strong drink by sipping the wine at the Lord's Supper.'[13] However, there were some who advocated the Temperance cause, such as the former Baptist pastor W.J. Grant (1849-1930) of Kilmarnock,[14] and John Wardrop (1809-92), a leading figure in the Wishaw assembly and former member of the Evangelical Union.[15]

Social concern was also evident in the practice of Brethren landlords, some Irish examples being particularly noteworthy. The Earl of Cavan sought to improve the living conditions of the Achill Islanders on the West Coast of Ireland (who had earlier been something of a *cause célèbre* in Evangelical mission to Roman Catholics), providing a pier and securing a regular steamer service.[16] Edward Denny, who owned almost the whole town of Tralee, was known for his personal frugality and generosity as a landlord.[17] Yet their personal concern never led them to engage in sustained theoretical reflection on the causes of deprivation or the action which government should take. There was no visionary writing comparable to the Salvationist William Booth's 1890 work *In Darkest England and the Way Out*. In this respect, Brethren failed to explore adequately the implications of their radical approach to Christian faith and fellowship. My suspicion is

---

[9] See J. Allden Owles, *Recollections of Medical Missionary Work* (Glasgow: Pickering & Inglis, [1909]).

[10] Anon., 'Teetotalism and the Gospel', *BP* 3 (1882), 124-7; W.H. Broom, 'Objections to a Christian joining Temperance Societies', *NI* 3 (1873), 122-6.

[11] 'YBQB', *BM* n.s. 3 (1902), 94.

[12] 'AC', *BM* n.s. 3 (1902), 35.

[13] 'AC', *BM* 9 (1899), 118; cf. *BM* n.s. 8 (1907), 132.

[14] [Henry Pickering], 'More Helpers during our 60 Years of Issue', *W* 61 (1931), 13.

[15] Beattie, *Brethren*, 201-4; Dickson, *Brethren in Scotland*, 326.

[16] Pickering (ed.), *Chief Men*, 62.

[17] On Denny, see *BDEB*.

that there were two major inhibiting factors: the Victorian social and religious ethos, which they unconsciously imbibed, with its somewhat passive acceptance of social distinctions and economic inequalities, and their heaven-focused eschatology, which left little place for development of a distinctive attitude to the created order.

One Brethren missionary provides a striking exception to the rule of non-involvement in political affairs. In 1908, C.A. Swan, who had served in the Portuguese colony of Angola, was asked by the Quaker philanthropist William Cadbury to return under conditions of strict secrecy to collect information concerning the continuing slave trade. The results were published as a book, *The Slavery of To-Day or, The Present Position of the Open Sore of Africa*, complete with case studies and shocking photographs. Swan laid his information before the British Government in the hope that it would urge the Portuguese to apply the anti-slavery legislation which already existed.[18]

11.2 Education

During the late nineteenth century, Brethren were extensively involved in the field of education in England and Wales. Apart from the day schools supported by the SKI, on which that body's annual reports are a rich source of information, a number of Open and Exclusive assemblies started up similar ventures independently.

Some schools were for Brethren families, especially in rural areas where clergy played a dominant role in village schools. For example, the local clergyman exercised a controlling influence upon the day school at Burrington in North Devon, and since the founders of the assembly there did not wish their children to be taught error, Müller helped establish a school in 1846 on the assembly's premises.[19] That at Hopton in Suffolk was a response to the establishment in the village in 1855 of a National School (these were run in accordance with Anglican principles and required children to attend the Church of England); initially independent, it was supported by the SKI from 1874, closure coming at some point after 1903, possibly because continuance would have entailed upgrading the premises.[20] The venture evidently proved worthwhile, the SKI report for 1877-8 noting that many from the school had been received into assembly fellowship.[21] On occasion, things could work the other way round: the establishment of one school, at Warsash near Southampton, resulted in the founding of an assembly there.[22]

The Blackdown Hills Mission provides a somewhat different example of Brethren involvement in education. This rural area north-east of Exeter was portrayed by Brethren writers as backward, poor, anarchic, and ignorant of Christianity. George Brealey (1823-88) first visited it in 1863, as a salaried evangelist, and saw conversions through his ministry there. When his converts wished to be baptised and to observe the Lord's Supper on Sundays, conclusions which they had reached for themselves, he gave up his position and devoted himself to planting assemblies in the villages. The educational work for which the mission became noted began when illiterate converts expressed concern for their children (although some of the pupils were adults), and Brealey combined

---

[18] David J. Jeremy, *Capitalists and Christians: Business Leaders and the Churches in Britain, 1900-1960* (Oxford: Clarendon, 1990), 148-9.

[19] Sidney Ford, 'How it Began: Burrington, North Devon', *PS* 1.6 (September-October 1946), 60.

[20] Woollams, *Stones of Thanksgiving, passim.*

[21] *Brief Narrative*, 39th Report (1877-8), 40.

[22] 'WML', *W* 33 (1903), 117.

superintendency of this aspect of the work with vigorous itinerant evangelism. Several schools were maintained, that at Bishopswood surviving until 1947 when the inadequacy of the facilities in the face of improved standards necessitated closure.[23]

Schools in urban areas seem to have been intended more for the (unchurched) poor, perhaps following the pattern set from 1844 by Lord Shaftesbury's 'Ragged Schools'. The second objective of the SKI was to fund day schools for the poor in which instruction would be combined with Christian teaching. Initially, these were all in the Bristol area, but in time Müller supported wholly or in part schools throughout South-West and Southern England and South Wales, and in mission fields such as Italy and Spain. The first SKI-supported school at Cardiff opened in 1873 as the result of repeated requests for a school to counter Roman Catholic influence; in eleven months, it had 491 scholars on its books, and several other schools were opened in the city.[24]

The staff and pupils of the SKI's schools at Purton, Gloucestershire, in 1898. Here the SKI trained many of its teachers

From 1870 a succession of legislative enactments made primary education compulsory; this was reflected in a sharp increase in the number of day schools in Britain wholly or partly supported by the SKI, peaking at around fifty from 1874-1882, with a marked trend towards complete rather than partial support.[25] The increase reflected the movement's increasing size, and the large numbers of converts joining assemblies could have been responsible for a 'Brethren baby boom'. However, this was followed by a sharp decline in 1883 (to sixteen). Some assemblies took on the responsibility of supporting

---

[23] On Brealey and the Blackdown Hills Mission, see *BDEB*; W.J.H. Brealey, *'Always Abounding;' or, Recollections of the Life and Labours of the late George Brealey, the Evangelist of the Blackdown Hills* (London: W.G. Wheeler, [1897[3]]); R.H. White, *Strength of the Hills: The Story of the Blackdown Hills Mission* (Exeter: Paternoster, 1964).

[24] *Brief Narrative*, 36th Report (1875), 30.

[25] In 1877-8, for example, the SKI supported day schools in Britain in Cornwall (Callington), Devon (four at Barnstaple, Bishopswood and three others on the Blackdown Hills, Chittlehamholt, East Brent, three at Exeter, High Bickington, two at Plympton, Plympton Underwood), Dorset (Shaftesbury), Gloucestershire (four in Bristol, King's Stanley, two at Purton, Saul, Stroud), Hampshire (Portsmouth), Herefordshire (Howle Hill, two at Ludlow), Somerset (Yeovil), Suffolk (Hopton), Warwickshire (Kenilworth), London (Bow, Brentford, Cubitt Town, three at Kilburn, North End, two at Walham Green) and five in Cardiff.

such work themselves, as was the case with the Bethesda Sunday Schools in 1884. More important factors were the need for financial retrenchment (between 1877 and 1882 more was spent on schools than on mission support), as well as the problem of finding teachers who were suitably qualified both spiritually and educationally: faced with a lack of resources, in the early 1890s Müller decided to close almost all the schools supported by the SKI.[26]

Middle-class Brethren preferred to send their sons (and sometimes their daughters) to suitable boarding schools, and some Brethren schools of this nature were established. For example, W.E. Vine's father founded a boarding school at Blandford in Dorset, which moved to Exeter in 1875. Vine himself taught there until moving to Bath in 1911.[27] Middle-class urban Brethren would not have sent their children to a school attached to a local assembly, even if they lived in an area where such a school existed, as they could afford more socially-appropriate education. Rural assemblies, by contrast, would usually have been more uniformly working-class in composition; their members had to reckon both with the dominance of the clergy in local schools and with the fact that they could not afford to send their children away to school.

A typical middle-class Brethren family, that of W.E. Vine

11.3 Involvement in Society

11.3.1 Separation

In exploring the ways in which Brethren were involved in the world, we must begin by noting their relatively consistent stress on withdrawal from it in its political aspect:

... whilst God has legislated for the behaviour of husbands and wives, parents and children, masters and servants, and thus touches upon every department of social life, He is absolutely silent, as far as instructions to the Christian are concerned, with regard to the sphere of politics.

---

[26] Bergin, *Ten Years After*, 2; cf. SKI reports, and William Blake, 'An Outline of the Family History of the Assembly of Christians now meeting in the Gospel Hall, Henry St. Ross' (manuscript, [1929]), fos. 98-101 (CBA 5626(1)).

[27] Ruoff, *Vine*, 15.

... Is it not a reasonable, indeed an unavoidable inference, that God does not contemplate His children occupying such positions in this evil age?[28]

There were occasional exceptions: Lord Congleton, who had initially refused to take his seat in the House of Lords after his father's death in 1842 because of the oaths required, came to the view that judicial oaths were not forbidden by Scripture; feeling bound to obey the royal summons, he changed his stance.[29] At a local level, we find a few more. The Earl of Cavan was Deputy Lieutenant for the county of Somerset, a Justice of the Peace and Lieutenant-Colonel of the 2nd Somerset Militia.[30] But their rarity during this period indicates the movement's fundamentally other-worldly character. In spite of the considerable number of Evangelical Members of Parliament early in the nineteenth century, some of whom had exercised great influence on policy and had earned respect for their readiness to take an independent stance on matters of principle,[31] Brethren during this period did not seek election to the Commons.

Such withdrawal was grounded in their understanding of Scripture as providing a blueprint for every area of the believer's life in the world just as it did for church life, which included the example of separation from worldly affairs set by Christ on earth. According to Scripture, believers were citizens of heaven, resident aliens in this God-rejecting world who should not become entangled with its affairs. Most Brethren reasoned that just as the church lost its heavenly character when it became mixed up with a Christ-rejecting world, so too individual believers would find such involvement injurious to spiritual life. One exception, however, was the Irish landlord G.F. Trench, whose *God in Government; or, The Christian's Relation to the State* (published around 1870) argued that whilst Christians should not seek political involvement, they should get involved when necessary; in any case, he claimed, believers would make the best government ministers.

Non-involvement did not betoken a lack of awareness of current affairs. The periodicals often commented on major events, seeking to discern what God might be saying through them to believers and to the nation. The Boer War was seen as a divine chastisement upon the British Empire and a call to awake from indifference. In interceding for the authorities, readers were urged to confess their sins and those of the people, which Caldwell listed as ritualism, rationalism, godlessness, pride, covetousness, drunkenness, and immorality.[32] Pickering saw the death of Edward VII in 1910 as a reminder of the brevity of life and a challenge concerning the neglect of assemblies to pray for rulers and those in authority (a recurring theme), especially for their salvation.[33] However, Brethren looked beyond these events to the Lord's return, and their interest in them was often motivated by an attempt to discern signs of its imminence.

---

[28] J.R. Caldwell, 'The Coming Political Struggle', *W* 40 (1910), 5; cf. *idem*, 'The Christian's Relation to the World's Government', *NW* 9 (1879), 88-9; [John Ritchie], 'Politics; or Should a Christian Vote?', *BM* 2 (1892), 63-5.

[29] Groves, *Congleton*, 90.

[30] *BDEB*.

[31] Bradley, *Call to Seriousness*, 164-6.

[32] J.R. Caldwell, 'The War: viewed from a divine standpoint', *W* 30 (1900), 5-6; cf. J.R[itchie]., 'The War in South Africa: Thoughts and Reflections for God's People', *BM* n.s. 1 (1900), 13-14.

[33] H[enr]y P[ickering]., 'The Death of King Edward VII', *W* 40 (1910), 85-6.

Speakers and writers from the late nineteenth century onwards summed up the Brethren attitude to the civil powers as Pray, Pay, and Obey: as commanded in the New Testament, believers should pray for those in authority, pay the taxes demanded of them, and obey the 'powers that be' as holding office by divine appointment.

Prayer for those in authority was consistently enjoined, and its neglect almost as consistently lamented. The element of retreat from the world in Brethren spirituality was exemplified by the Glasgow solicitor Alexander Stewart's hymn 'Lord Jesus Christ, we seek Thy face', with its depiction of believers as

> Shut in with Thee, far, far above
> The restless warring world below ...

Such an outlook, coupled with a tendency to see life in this world as an opportunity for outreach to others, would have resulted in a preoccupation with more directly 'spiritual' concerns in prayer meetings, at the expense of intercessory concern for world affairs.

The insistence that a believer should pay whatever taxes were demanded of him meant that Brethren did not participate in the campaign against paying for Anglican education through the rates which saw hundreds of Nonconformists convicted from 1902 onwards for withholding payment, and some imprisoned. The issue was raised in a letter to *The Witness*, but the response was that the believer had no right to pick and choose the uses to which the authorities might apply his payment; it was legitimate for a believer to seek repeal of the legislation concerned (this in itself was something of a concession compared to earlier views), and understandable that he would not wish to have his children taught error, but withholding payment savoured of insubordination to the 'powers that be'.[34] Indeed, Brethren aloofness from political involvement was probably reinforced by observing the conflict over education between true believers in the Establishment and Nonconformity.[35]

The strong belief that rulers held office because God had put them there meant that Brethren opposed voting, not merely as entanglement with worldly affairs, but also because voting people out of office represented an attempt to bring down men whom God had placed there. Rulers might be evil men, for whom Christians would not vote, but nevertheless unwittingly fulfil God's purposes by their actions in office. Power was from above, not from beneath, as in democracy, in which the will of the people was decisive.[36] Democracy was seen as a preparation for the coming of Antichrist, who would overthrow all divine institutions. Brethren thus had no time for socialism, whether in its political or 'New Theology' forms. According to Ritchie, it was godless and lawless, having nothing in common with Christianity.[37]

Linked with the belief that rulers held office by divine authority was the movement's social conservatism. The periodicals were often fulsome in their praise of reigning or recently-deceased monarchs (always coupling this with the hope that royalty might come to a knowledge of saving grace or the recounting of evidence that they had done so), and tended to support the retention of capital punishment (on the basis of what they regarded

---

[34] *W* 33 (1903), 130, 146-7.

[35] Cf. [Short], *Principles*, 124.

[36] G.A., letter in *W* 29 (1899), 64-5.

[37] 'AC', *BM* n.s. 11 (1910), 11.

as biblical principles[38]). The stratified society of the Victorian era was one into which Brethren fitted easily, and the potentially radical nature of their ecclesiology was not developed in ways which challenged this. Indeed, failure to observe proper social etiquette, even in the context of the assembly where all were theoretically on the same level as believers, was deprecated. Most Brethren leaders would have observed the appropriate conventions for relating to particular social groups, although Darby provides a striking example of winsome non-compliance in this respect. He had been loved by the poor of his Wicklow parish, and ever after retained an ability to get alongside them, often preferring to stay with them when itinerating rather than with the 'leading brethren' of the meetings. A sidelight is thrown on the matter of social delicacy by an 1881 advertisement for a 'House of Rest' at the resort of Rothesay on the island of Bute, intended for those who considered hydropathic establishments too expensive and too worldly for believers, but who were nevertheless not of the class who would feel at ease in a city mission-type seaside home.[39] One area which turned out to be an exception to this conventionality was that of pacifism, though I suspect that pacifism may have been more acceptable among some social classes than others. Another was evangelism; Ritchie, reporting on an evangelistic tour, asked 'Is Gospel work to die of respectability, or are men to be allowed to go down to hell unwarned, because we havn't [sic] been "introduced to them?"'[40]

All the same, differences of social class and related differences such as those in education, ambition and social outlook may have made for tensions between different streams of the movement: there appears to be a polarity between the openness of the more refined Open Brethren and the separatism of the more working-class gatherings in Scotland, Ulster, and Northern England. Men from different streams would have found it difficult to relate to one another at a human level, and that could not have helped in discussion of controversial issues.

11.3.2 Brethren in Business

As with other Nonconformists, business provided one way in which Brethren could interact with society with little restraint or objection.[41] Indeed, the frequency of warnings in the periodicals against debt and condemnations of bankruptcy resulting from injudicious speculation indicate that some Brethren were less restrained and less ethically-sensitive than they should have been.

Businessmen undoubtedly provided the movement with a considerable proportion of the finance needed for expansion and outreach.[42] Examples would include Huntingdon Stone of Peek Freans;[43] the baker Charles Aitchison (d.1906) of Glasgow, who left

---

[38] Thus Caldwell argued for it on the basis that the world was not governed according to grace as the church was ('Subjects & Rulers', *W* 22 (1892), 167-8).

[39] *NW* 11 (1881), 144.

[40] John Ritchie, 'Evangelistic Tour Among the Villages', *NW* 10 (1880), 78.

[41] For a fuller discussion of this theme, see F. Roy Coad, 'Brethren Businessmen and Social Responsibility', in Anon. (ed.), *Christians in the Business World* (Leicester: UCCF Associates for the Historians' Study Group, 1982), 19-25.

[42] Coad, *History*, 178.

[43] See section 12.2.

£150,000 in his will to be distributed through the Aitchison Trust;[44] and, best known, the Carlisle building contractor John Laing (1879-1978).[45]

Many others combined active business involvement with extensive preaching, teaching and writing, as well as shouldering the burden of oversight in their home assemblies. Among them we may list another biscuit manufacturer, Jonathan Carr (1806-84), who moved from the Quakers to the Brethren in Carlisle during the 1870s;[46] the engineer W.H. Dorman (son of the early Brethren leader) of Stafford; and Caldwell, who combined his writing and teaching activity with being a silk manufacturer. He wrote more about business principles than any other contemporary member of the Brethren, offering a fairly typical exposition of Brethren thinking.

The unequal yoke principle was applied by Caldwell and others in a number of areas: worship and service, business, share ownership, membership of groups such as the Freemasons, marriage, friendships, and leisure activities all came under scrutiny.[47] According to Caldwell, 'The principle of the "yoke" is that one is committed to the action of the other.'[48] This presented a problem for the believer: for instance, 'If the evil ways of an ungodly partner result in profit, how can the Christian share that profit, and yet be clear in his protest against the evil?'[49] Unions were also seen as entailing such commitment, and believers were often warned not to join them, even if it meant losing their jobs. On occasion, it did: the obituary of the evangelist James Campbell recorded how, probably during the 1870s, 'Not seeing his way clear to join the Trades Union, his fellow-workers struck. On asking the cause the foreman replied, "You are the cause of the strike." He graciously replied that he was unwilling to cause any difficulty, lifted his tools and left, since which time he had laboured unceasingly and won hundreds of souls for the Master.'[50] Caldwell saw compulsory union membership and the principle of combination (workers banding together to take action to secure pay increases and improvements in working conditions) as preparing the way for the introduction of the mark of the beast.[51] The same was true of the developing Co-operative Movement, which was seen as 'one of the drag-nets of the last days whereby Satan is preparing the way for the final edict that men shall neither buy nor sell who have not the mark of the beast'.[52]

---

[44] Pickering (ed.), *Chief Men*, v.

[45] On Laing, see Roy Coad, *Laing: The Biography of Sir John W. Laing, C.B.E. (1879-1978)* (London: Hodder and Stoughton, 1979); *DBB*; *ODNB*.

[46] On Carr, see *DBB*; *ODNB*.

[47] E.g. John R. Caldwell, *Separation from the World, Jehoshaphat, and other papers* (Glasgow: Pickering & Inglis, n.d.), 48-50; J. Ritchie, 'The Unequal Yoke: An address to young believers', *NW* 13 (1883), 115-19; cf. [*idem*?], 'Unequally Yoked in Business', *BM* 6 (1896), 99; 'QA', *NW* 10 (1880), 62, 95.

[48] 'QA', *NW* 17 (1887), 96.

[49] Caldwell, *Separation*, 48.

[50] 'WML', *W* 34 (1904), 55.

[51] Caldwell, *Separation*, 50; 'QA', *NW* 10 (1880), 158-9; 'QA', *W* 22 (1892), 96. A rare example of a pro-union brother was Henry Bostock (c.1833-1923) of Stafford, founder of the Lotus shoe company (*DBB*).

[52] 'QA', *W* 33 (1903), 164.

11.3.3 Pacifism and War

From the 1880s onwards, there is evidence of an unresolved tension concerning pacifism which would break out into open hostility during the First World War. On the one hand, several high-ranking military officers were associated with the Brethren; on the other, the periodicals at this stage advocated pacifism and withdrawal from the armed services. Although a number of the earliest Brethren had resigned their commissions on conversion, this did not continue to the same extent; we have noted already the influence exercised on the movement by a leavening of retired military men on their return from India. Others were to continue this tradition. Among the ranks of Brethren soldiers were General John Halliday (1822-1917), who became the senior General in the Army in India, and his son-in-law Major-General Sir Charles Scott (1848-1919), who served for thirty years in India until 1910 and was involved in the Soldiers' Christian Association.[53] Another military family included Captain Charles Orde-Browne of Woolwich (whose daughter married William Dobbie), his son-in-law Colonel George Wingate (1852-1936), and his son Major-General Orde Wingate (1903-44).[54] In 1892, the Farnborough assembly reported that a room of its new building was lent to soldiers for prayer, a number of them being in fellowship.[55]

Against the background of increasing militarism, the periodicals followed a clear pacifist line, in common with much Nonconformist thought. Caldwell, answering a questioner in *The Northern Witness*, asserted that a Christian should not be engaged in war. Pointing to the absurdity of conflict between Christian nations, he explained that believers served the Prince of Peace, and while God's people were a national entity in Old Testament times, they were not so now.[56] Some years later, he advised those converted while serving in the army to seek an honourable way out; the fact that the testimony of others in the army was being blessed did not make their position a right one.[57] Ritchie also took a pacifist line: he advised believers against becoming volunteers, as they were ambassadors of peace; furthermore, the companionship and occupations would prove injurious to spiritual life. He had never heard of an active Christian doing such a thing.[58] A few months before war broke out in 1914, he asserted that a believer should never take up arms, even in self-defence; such an action indicated a lack of faith in a sovereign God, and all too often defensive action became offensive.[59]

11.4   Science

Probably the most significant scientific event of the nineteenth century was the formulation and widespread acceptance of the theory of evolution. This harmonised with the dominant belief in human progress, which left its mark on much Nonconformist thought. Such a belief was the antithesis of Brethren expectations for the world, which were couched in terms of degeneration into the last great apostasy. Thus Brethren

[53] *BM* n.s. 20 (November 1919), iv; Pickering (ed.), *Chief Men*, 198-9, 208; *W* 49 (1919), 180.

[54] On Dobbie, see section 16.2.1; Sybil Dobbie, *Faith and Fortitude: The Life and Work of General Sir William Dobbie* (Gillingham, Kent: P.E. Johnston, 1979); *ODNB*.

[55] 'TLWW', *W* 22 (August 1892), iv.

[56] 'QA', *NW* 15 (1885), 95-6.

[57] 'QA', *W* 28 (1898), 202-4.

[58] 'YBQB', *BM* 6 (1896), 106.

[59] 'AC', *BM* n.s. 15 (1914), 11.

condemned the Great Exhibition of 1851, which exemplified the Victorian spirit of progress, as not fitting for Christians to attend. Quoting Darby, one writer suggested that two signs of the approaching end were the increase of evil and the gradual withdrawal of Christians from the world. In what were the closing days of this dispensation, days to be marked by widespread apostasy, it was imperative for believers to walk wisely.[60]

That being so, we might expect Brethren responses to evolutionary theory to partake of the nature of a 'last ditch stand', but the evidence is that the scientifically-minded among them engaged with evolutionary theory in a thoughtful and surprisingly open manner. Whilst they usually rejected evolution as an explanation of the origins of life, they sometimes put forward a version of the 'gap theory', in which they clamed that between Genesis 1.1 and 1.2 there was an unspecified interval during which the created order then existing was judged in some unspecified manner, after which a re-creation occurred.[61] This allowed them to accept the evidence adduced in connection with scientific theories concerning the earth's age, and to integrate the dinosaur phenomenon (of great interest during the nineteenth century because so many palaeontological discoveries were being made) into their theology and world-view.

Philip Gosse (1810-88) was perhaps the most accomplished Brethren scientist of the period, although his reputation suffered an unjustified eclipse as the result of his son Edmund's misleading portrayal of him as a crabbed bigot in *Father and Son*.[62] He was made a Fellow of the Royal Society in 1856, and was a recognised authority on the ecology of the seashore. Derided for putting forward the theory (in *Omphalos*) that the world was created with the appearance of having existed for much longer than was in fact the case, his work nevertheless represented a serious attempt to come to terms with contemporary scientific discoveries. However, he does seem to have viewed certain conclusions widely drawn from them as inimical to Christian faith, which may explain why, after Darwin's ideas were published in *The Origin of Species*, Gosse allowed their previous friendship to cool.[63]

Brethren sensitivity to the issues raised by evolutionary theory receives further corroboration from occasional autobiographical references. Laing testified to wrestling as a young man with the intellectual challenges of the theory of evolution, reaching the controversial conclusions that the six days of Genesis 1 represented geological periods and the chapter itself was a poetic account.[64] His struggles may have been a factor in his later support for attempts to raise the standards of Evangelical scholarship. As a student, Arthur Rendle Short thought through the relationship between Christianity and science, with the aid of Henry Drummond's *Natural Law in the Spiritual World*, a work which combined acceptance of evolutionary theory (for which it was condemned by Brethren) with warm Christian faith. He saw no conflict between science and revelation since the

---

[60] Anon., *A Word to all True Believers in the Lord Jesus Christ, with reference to the great Industrial Exhibition For 1851* (London: J.K. Campbell, 1851), 4, 6-8. Cf. J.G. Bellett, 'The Great Exhibition', *BM* n.s. 25 (1924), 69-71.

[61] 'YBQB', *BM* 5 (1895), 46; 'YBQB', *BM* n.s. 11 (1910), 22.

[62] Ann Thwaite's recent biography, *Glimpses of the Wonderful: The Life of Philip Henry Gosse 1810-1888* (London: Faber and Faber, 2002), is a lucid attempt to redress the balance. See also *BDEB*; L.R. Croft, *Gosse: The Life of Philip Henry Gosse* (Walton-le-Dale, Preston: Elmwood Books, 2000); *ODNB*.

[63] Croft, *Gosse*, 8.

[64] Coad, *Laing*, 36.

same God was the author of both Scripture and the laws of nature. As a result of his experience, and his conviction that most apologists were distinctly unconvincing to young people with a scientific education, Short manifested a lifelong interest in apologetics and a concern for work among students, and his apologetic motivation led him to regard matters of church order as comparatively insignificant.[65]

Exclusive writers such as Darby and Kelly produced a stream of apologetic works responding to developments in the fields of science and biblical criticism. However, few Open writers during the nineteenth century treated such topics directly, illustrating the assertion that in the second half of the nineteenth century it was the Exclusives who possessed the best writers and thinkers.[66] One was J.E. Howard, who delivered *Seven Lectures on Scripture and Science* (1865). Howard was made a Fellow of the Royal Society in 1874 for his work on quinine; he was also active in the Victoria Institute.[67]

The most prolific Open Brethren apologist during this period was Robert Anderson (1841-1918), who became head of the C.I.D. at Scotland Yard and was eventually knighted.[68] His approach is in some ways reminiscent of that of C.S. Lewis, being marked by an appeal to common sense rather than specialist expertise. Anderson plainly considered that the best form of defence was attack: a reviewer in *The Witness* described him as 'always an advocate, never a judge, an Apollos for accuracy, not a Barnabas for consolation, trenchant rather than conciliatory, with a chronic inability to see another side to any question',[69] while Hurditch's daughter Grace remembered him as one 'who knocked down his biblical opponents like ninepins'.[70] His apologetic writings included *Daniel in the critics' den* (1895), *The Bible and modern Criticism* (1902), *Christianised rationalism and the higher criticism* (1903), and *The critics criticised; or, the Higher Criticism and its counterfeit* (1904). The most popular, however, was *The silence of God* (1897), which was often reprinted over the next thirty years.

Medicine proved to be the most congenial branch of science for Brethren, probably because many trained as doctors with the intent of becoming missionaries. (It would be an interesting exercise to work out whether the proportion of doctors among Open Brethren members is as unusually high as the proportion of missionaries.) This was certainly true of Arthur Rendle Short (1880-1953). Being precluded from missionary service on health grounds, he achieved distinction as a practitioner and Professor of Surgery in Bristol.[71] His brother Latimer also entered the medical profession. Other notable medical men included the consulting physician David Anderson-Berry (1862-1926),[72] A.T. Schofield, whom we encountered earlier, Frank Bergin (d.1949), consultant radiologist at Bristol

---

[65] W.M. Capper and D. Johnson (eds.), *The Faith of a Surgeon: Belief and Experience in the Life of Arthur Rendle Short* (Exeter: Paternoster, 1976), 34-7; [Short], *"Open Brethren"*, 57, 60. Interestingly, he appears to have accepted creationism in the last year of his life (Letter from John Rendle-Short, *H*, November 1988, 23).

[66] Writing was not the only Open Brethren mode of apologetics, however; we have seen that Müller intended his orphan houses to be a living demonstration of the reality of God.

[67] [Maria Howard], *Memorials*, 47, 49.

[68] On Anderson, see Moore-Anderson, *Robert Anderson*; *ODNB*.

[69] *W* 42 (1912), 59.

[70] Coad, *History*, 182.

[71] On Short, see Capper and Johnson, *Faith of a Surgeon*.

[72] See Pickering (ed.), *Chief Men*, 209-11.

General Hospital from 1919, and J.J. Morison (1856-1933), a police surgeon who became an expert on poisons.[73]

Sir Robert Anderson   Professor A. Rendle Short

An interesting feature of Brethren attitudes to medicine is their love of homeopathy. A leading homeopath in 1850s London, Dr John Epps (1805-69), was connected with Brethren.[74] Müller had his orphans treated homeopathically, and Craik used homeopathic remedies.[75] Lang practised as an amateur homeopath, and wrote an (unpublished) apologia for homeopathy, 'The Patient to the Doctor', in which he testified that one recipient of his attentions had been the family cat.[76] In Glasgow, Hunter Beattie used homeopathy, in which he had a longstanding interest, from about 1910 as part of his evangelistic work in the city.[77] Others included Dr James Wardrop, also in Glasgow,[78] and Dr Robert McKilliam (1837-1915), John Ritchie's Sunday School teacher in the Free Church of Scotland and later a noted speaker among Brethren as well as editor of a prophetic magazine, *The Morning Star*.[79] Although most of these were doctors, the possibility of practising homeopathy as a lay person would have been attractive to those who rejected the concept of a recognised caste of experts, whether clergy or doctors. Another reason for its popularity was probably Müller's influence.[80] As recently as 1989, the assertion by the Assistant General Secretary of the Christian Medical Fellowship in a book review that homeopathy was 'occult' drew several indignant rebuttals from Brethren practitioners.[81]

---

[73] Rowdon files, now deposited with the CBA.

[74] Croft, *Gosse*, 109; on Epps, see *ODNB*.

[75] Groves, *Müller*, 235; Tayler, *Craik*, 281.

[76] G.H. Lang, 'The Patient to the Doctor' (typescript, n.d.; CBA Box 72).

[77] Henry Beattie, 'My Father: Hunter Beattie (1875-1951)', *BM* 87 (1977), 196-7; *BM* 61 (1951), 220.

[78] 'Dr. James Wardrop of Glasgow', *CW* 30 (1915), 131.

[79] Cross, *Irish Saint and Scholar*, 45-6; Dickson, *Brethren in Scotland*, 73, 128, 261; Pickering (ed.), *Chief Men*, 175-7, 216.

[80] Timothy C.F. Stunt, 'Homeopathy and Brethren', *W* 103 (1973), 127-8.

[81] Review, *H*, January 1989, 26; letters, *H*, March 1989, 19; Q. Muriel Adams, R.A.F. Jack, and Andrew Fergusson, 'Homeopathy for and against', *H*, November 1989, 12-14; 'Homeopathy – a Correction', *H*, January 1990, 23.

11.5 Culture and Leisure

Early nineteenth-century Evangelicals tended to see most sports and leisure activities as occasions for sin; while many changed their thinking, the Brethren continued to manifest quite a negative attitude towards such pursuits. Favourite targets were novel-reading and sport. Intensity seems to have characterised Brethren family life to an even greater extent than that of other Evangelicals of a similar social class. Thus one questioner in 1893 felt it necessary to ask Ritchie whether a believer should go to see 'a menagerie of wild beasts': Ritchie's response was that enjoyment of the created order was permissible, but frequently such places involved the believer in associating with the ungodly; furthermore, the believer could not condone brutality (such as lion-hunting).[82]

Two illustrations may be given of the intensity of a middle-class Brethren upbringing. Charles Hargrove's son, also Charles (1838-1918), forsook his Brethren roots, becoming a High Anglican, then a Dominican monk, and finally a Unitarian. His parents regarded his conversion to Catholicism as God giving him over to a delusion because of his unwarranted intellectual speculation, and his memoir indicates that they saw the smallest sins as evidence of an unregenerate state.[83] The second illustration is provided by Edmund Gosse's *Father and Son*, which indicates a similar concern on the part of parents for the spiritual wellbeing of their child, leading them to restrict severely the range of activities and companionships deemed permissible. Although much about Gosse's account is open to question (to put it mildly), it was intended not as an objective biographical portrait, but a record of 'a struggle between two temperaments, two consciences and almost two epochs'.[84] It records his perception of his father and the impact of their relationship on his quest for a sense of his own identity. As such it remains salutary reading, in spite of its serious inaccuracies.[85] On the other hand, there were some cultured families among whom a more world-affirming approach to life was evident. Rendle Short, for example, was a keen teenage cricketer and not only graduated in geology but found it a source of relaxation. In the mid-1850s, the Jeckell family were recorded as spending their holiday in reading, boating, drawing, singing, and even (in the evenings) dancing.[86]

Novels form an interesting example of changing cultural attitudes among Brethren, especially if we extend our view beyond the First World War. It has been suggested that Evangelicals generally accepted novels once their members became better educated or more professionalised.[87] Initially Brethren had condemned novel-reading, and it has been claimed that prophetic study served as a surrogate activity,[88] but the practice was probably more widespread than was openly acknowledged. (Sir Walter Scott seems to have been a particular favourite of Brethren readers.) Even fictional works for children were condemned. The main objections appear to have been that novels often depicted and

---

[82] 'YBQB', *BM* 3 (1893), 130.

[83] L.P. Jacks, *From Authority to Freedom: the Spiritual Pilgrimage of Charles Hargrove* (London: Williams & Norgate, 1920), 74, 148-50.

[84] Gosse, *Father and Son*, 35.

[85] Other negative pictures by leavers during this period include William Bowyer [Honey], *Brought out in Evidence: an autobiographical summing-up* (London: Faber and Faber, 1941), 79-80; Howard Spring, *And another Thing* ... (New York and London: Harper and Brothers, 1946), 114-17.

[86] Soros and Arbuthnott, *Thomas Jeckyll*, 30.

[87] Dempster, 'Brethren Publishing', 89, following Cunningham, *Everywhere Spoken Against*, 52.

[88] Cunningham, *Everywhere Spoken Against*, 54.

glorified sinful lifestyles and that a God of truth could not be glorified by stories which, because they were not true, must be classed as lies. Religious novels were singled out as particularly deserving of condemnation in the latter respect. Novels were also seen as generating an unwholesome excitement by their over-dramatised representations of life. Those who read them would find themselves becoming like the characters they admired and adopting the writers' underlying (worldly) values, with a consequent loss of spiritual power.[89] Such descriptions fit the popular sensational novels better than serious works of literature, and this may indicate the largely working-class nature, and likely reading material, of the magazines' audience.

By the late 1920s, however, novels would be appearing from Pickering & Inglis, who also published the 'Lily Stories', described as 'pure literature' and intended for use in home and hospital visiting. They were intended to counteract the 'penny dreadfuls' and were later ingenuously described as 'not novels, but true to life stories'.[90] Ritchie's contempt was withering: in an advertisement detailing his own publishing plans, he dismissed them as '"Novelettes" which are now advertised as **Pure Gospel Books**, to be hawked from door to door, consisting of **Fictitious Love Tales**, with a **tincture** of their "Gospel," thrown in at the close to **colour** them and make them palatable to those accustomed to read what may be found in any **Worldly Romance**',[91] and condemned them as depraving believers and destroying their appetite for the Scriptures. In time, however, novels would also appear on Ritchie's list, albeit in the form of Sunday School prizes.

Sport was also discussed frequently in the question pages of *The Believer's Magazine*, which seems to have been read by a more working-class clientele than *The Witness* (which did not have so much to say on the topic) by the 1890s: this may be another instance of the way in which working-class Brethren took a more world-rejecting line than their middle-class co-religionists or Nonconformists in general. In one answer, Ritchie warned against using sporting and leisure activities as adjuncts to outreach: in the YMCA, such things tended to swamp the spiritual side of its activities.[92] He recognised the value of bodily exercise; the problem lay more in the association with unbelievers which was a part of many sporting activities. He suggested that the contemporary passion for 'bicycling' be harnessed in the service of village evangelism, thus combining exercise with spiritual activity.[93] Sports clubs failed the 'unequal yoke' test; indeed, if a Christian proved congenial company to his fellow club-members, it indicated that he was not in a healthy spiritual condition.[94] It was beyond Ritchie's understanding how a believer could be happy to play games with the unsaved, 'assisting them to trifle away

---

[89] 'QA', *NW* 15 (1885), 64-5; [John Ritchie], 'Novel Reading: A Snare to Young Believers', *BM* 2 (1892), 116-17; 'YBQB', *BM* 3 (1893), 34. For Brethren attitudes to literature, as well as portrayals of them in literature, see Neil Dickson, '"All one hears of are its miseries": the Brethren and literature', *BAHNR* (forthcoming), a revised version of a series of articles which first appeared in *Aware* during 1991.

[90] *W* 66 (January 1936), ii.

[91] *BM* n.s. 26 (November 1925), vi.

[92] 'AC', *BM* n.s. 8 (1907), 142.

[93] *BM* 9 (1899), 32-3.

[94] 'YBQB', *BM* n.s. 7 (1906), 23.

their day of grace in frivolity'.[95] Neither, he asserted, should a believer be guilty of 'trifling away his ransomed days'.[96]

It was Caldwell, however, who posed the question, 'What Amusements are Innocent?' The answer appeared to be 'very few, if any'. For him, 'the essence of idolatry [was] feasting and playing, away from the realised presence of God'.[97] Believers should only go to worldly parties, therefore, in order to speak for God. Games, too, were off-limits if they resulted in companionship with the ungodly; games of chance amounted to an implicit disbelief in divine providence, while competitive games ('games of emulation') were clearly opposed to the Spirit of Christ (Galatians 5.20). 'What games there are which would not involve the believer in one or other of these three evils I know not.'[98] Indeed, if believers were walking with God and looking out for opportunities of serving him and ministering to those in need, there would be no time left for 'the empty amusements wherewith the world is seeking to kill the time that is hurrying it to destruction, and to shut out the thought of God and of eternity'.[99] Social events were also warned against: wedding receptions (the believer would feel it appropriate to leave before the entertainment), works outings (one's testimony might be put at risk), and even picnics (these provided opportunities for levity and inappropriate physical intimacy). Thus some assemblies arranged alternative activities for their young people. At Selly Oak in Birmingham, for instance, Bible studies ensured that they would not fall prey to the attractions offered by an urban Saturday night.[100] On the other hand, a conference celebrating the opening of the Woldingham Iron Room in Surrey was preceded by an impromptu cricket match.[101]

Just as it would be unfair to characterise all Brethren as excessively intense in their attitude to leisure pursuits, so too we should avoid treating them all as culturally unaccomplished. Some missionary writers gave evidence of real ability; doubtless their descriptive skills made their spoken presentations on deputation all the more compelling. Other Brethren poured out their poetic soul in hymn-writing and devotional poetry. A full survey of Brethren hymnodists is not possible here,[102] and much of their work did not last, but attention should be drawn to Emma Frances Bevan, whom we noted earlier.

Curiously, several Brethren achieved distinction as artists. Gosse's drawings of marine life reached a wider public through his books. William Collingwood was a member of the Royal Academy and a noted watercolourist. John Linnell (1792-1882), who associated with Brethren at Orchard Street, London, from 1843 to 1848, was a painter and engraver.[103] Swaine Bourne (d.1923), who founded the assembly at Bearwood, near Smethwick, and his son, Kendrick Swaine Bourne (1872-1960), designed and produced

---

[95] [John Ritchie], 'Words of Help and Cheer to Young Believers', *BM* 2 (1892), 141.

[96] 'YBQB', *BM* 6 (1896), 94.

[97] Caldwell, *Separation*, 56.

[98] *Ibid.*, 60.

[99] *Ibid.*

[100] 'TLWW', *W* 24 (1894), 20.

[101] *EH* 2 (July 1887), 4.

[102] See John S. Andrews, 'Brethren Hymnology', *EQ* 28 (1956), 208-29 (updated version, typescript, [1990]; CBA Box 30 (19)), and the literature there cited.

[103] On Linnell, see David Linnell, *Blake, Palmer, Linnell and Co.: The Life of John Linnell* (Lewes: The Book Guild, 1994); *ODNB*.

stained glass, and their firm's work graces churches in various parts of England, including Anglican buildings in Halesowen and Gosforth, a Baptist chapel in Aberystwyth, and a Unitarian chapel in Glossop (what their fellow Brethren would have thought of that can only be imagined).[104] One could wish that these men had set down in writing how they integrated their artistic pursuits with their theological views. The same is true of the architect Thomas Jeckyll (1827-81), who achieved fame as a restorer of Norfolk Anglican churches from 1847. His willingness to undertake such commissions betokens an ability to dissociate religious convictions from professional life which was unusual among Brethren.[105]

---

[104] On the Bourne's, see Jean Johnson, 'Brethren in Bearwood: the earliest days', paper delivered at the BAHN Conference, Gloucester, 11 July 2003; *W* 91 (1961), 76.

[105] On Jeckyll, see Soros and Arbuthnott, *Thomas Jeckyll*. Although he spelt his name differently, his father was George Jeckell of Wymondham. Thomas, whose association with Brethren is inferred from his spending part of 1848 living with Wigram in London, appears to have left Brethren by 1853.

CHAPTER 12

The Brethren Movement as a Missionary Agency

Beyond any other British denomination, Open Brethren have become noted for their missionary outlook. It is not possible here to survey the places where missionaries served, and in any case that has been done already. Neither is it possible to survey the many areas where a viable indigenous work has developed. This chapter will focus on the building of a strong home base, exploring the various means by which missionary vision was fostered and missionaries supported, and discussing further the distinctive pattern of 'living by faith' adopted by so many Brethren workers.[1]

12.1 Maintaining Interest and Channelling Support

12.1.1 The Emergence of Facilitating Bodies

Indirectly, the Bethesda controversy led to the appearance of periodicals and bodies concerned with prayer and financial support of missionaries. During the years when it was at its height, no new missionaries were sent out by assemblies and Brethren at home were too preoccupied to support those already serving abroad. The preoccupation with issues of fellowship undoubtedly resulted in a loss of interest in mission, but it may also have been a consequence of insufficient missionary zeal: reviewing the *Memoir* of A.N. Groves, *The Missionary Reporter* (see below) claimed that if Brethren 'had early spread themselves over the surface of the vast regions of the heathen world, they might have learned to love one another in very contrast to the darkness around'.[2] Another factor hindering the development of a missionary vision was the view of some early Brethren that it was not the church's task in this dispensation to promote mission among the heathen.

The only leader to keep up a practical interest during the late 1840s and early 1850s appears to have been Müller, who had an extensive network of contacts through the SKI, which channelled support to workers overseas.[3] A.N. Groves saw the impact of the controversy on missionary support (some missionaries in India had to be assisted by local Anglicans), and determined to awaken assemblies to their responsibilities and establish means by which missionaries could be supported. Returning to his home assembly at Tottenham in 1852, he pleaded for more support for mission work.[4] In response, the solicitor James Van Sommer (1822-1901), who had moved from the assembly at Hackney to that at Tottenham, commenced *The Missionary Reporter* the

---

[1] For a survey and assessment of Open Brethren mission, see H.H. Rowdon, 'The Brethren Contribution to World Mission', in Rowdon (ed.), *Brethren Contribution*, 37-46.

[2] *MR* 2.16 (1 April 1856), 142; for a later expression of this opinion, see T.M. Sparks, 'Editorial', *LOH* 1 (1911-12), 49.

[3] Bromley, *Men Sent from God*, 94; Coad, *History*, 167; Stunt et al., *Turning the World Upside Down*, 27-9. In the year 1850-1, the SKI assisted twenty-four workers in Britain and Ireland and twenty-one overseas; the figures for 1860-1 were seventy and thirty-seven respectively, and those for 1870-1 ninety-five and ninety-one.

[4] Stunt et al., *Turning the World Upside Down*, 27.

following year.[5] Its objects were the provision of information regarding independent missionaries at home and abroad (these included non-Brethren such as the German J.G. Oncken, who pioneered Baptist work in Central and Eastern Europe) and the dissemination of the view that if the church is itself a missionary society, local churches ought to concern themselves with mission. Regrettably, lack of support resulted in it ceasing publication by 1862.[6]

Mission was ever-present in the spirituality of many Open Brethren. As the wording on this prayer card explains, 'These cards are intended to remind us of the servants of Christ whose faces we have seen, and whose fellowship we have enjoyed but who are now absent, serving the Lord.'

---

[5] On Van Sommer and *The Missionary Reporter*, see Anon., 'The Missionary Reporter', *H* 15 (1938), 262; T.C.F. Stunt, 'James Van Sommer, an undenominational Christian and man of prayer', *JCBRF* 16 (August 1967), 2-8; W.T. Stunt, 'James Van Sommer: Missionary Enthusiast', *EQR* 9.4 (October-December 1957), 18-23.

[6] *ME* 1.1 (January 1872), endpapers. No issues after January 1858 are known to have survived. The last issue may have appeared in December 1861 (J.W. Forrest, 'The *Missionary Reporter*', *JCBRF* 21 (May 1971), 28).

1860 saw the appearance of *Letters of Interest,* edited by Yapp, who was later joined by his brother-in-law, Maclean. It appeared until 1863, and annually from 1866-83 as *The Gospel in Italy,*[7] providing information regarding the development of work in Italy, a country whose political struggles had attracted considerable British attention. This country also excited keen interest among contemporary Evangelicals, partly because of some celebrated cases of persecution of Protestants and partly because British Brethren were linked with the Italian movement through two of its leading figures, Count Guicciardini (1808-86) and his convert T.P. Rossetti (1825-83). Guicciardini had come to England after his conversion; Rossetti was a political refugee who was converted through Guicciardini while in this country. Both returned to their native land and engaged in church-planting.[8]

After Yapp died, Maclean continued to issue *Letters of Interest,* in association with Henry Groves and Henry Dyer, thus laying a foundation of editorial co-operation for a new publication, *The Missionary Echo* (1872), edited initially by Groves and Maclean. This became known as *Echoes of Service* from 1885, and is still published each month.[9] From about 1890, a daily prayer guide was produced, which came under the auspices of Echoes of Service in 1913; this too is still issued.[10] It says a great deal about Open Brethren that their most successful English-language periodical has been one devoted to overseas mission.

From the start the magazine acted as a channel of funds for missionaries. Some were apprehensive about this, fearing that missionaries might come to depend on the channel rather than on the Lord; the belief that missionaries were 'supported by Bath' (where the offices of Echoes of Service were located from 1873), and therefore not in need of funds, was a recurrent misunderstanding which had to be corrected in the periodicals. It was also difficult to establish any New Testament precedent for an organisation such as Echoes of Service. Those with such concerns tended to prefer a direct link between the assembly and the worker, as it enabled a more meaningful relationship to be built up.[11] By 1909, the Editors were corresponding with approximately 600 workers, a six-fold increase since 1886.[12] Inevitably, therefore, the Bath office became a bigger operation, with additional editors and office staff joining it. Such developments would contribute to apprehensions raised during the 1920s.[13]

E.K. Groves also preferred direct links between workers and assemblies, but for rather different reasons. He alleged that *The Missionary Echo* was commenced because his brother Henry recognised the effects on assemblies of leaving missionary support in the hands of Müller and the SKI. (Müller, too, had found it necessary to stress in his annual report for 1862-3 that the workers supported by his organisation were not to be regarded

---

[7] Stunt et al., *Turning the World Upside Down,* 28, 38. Copies are preserved in a bound volume, 'The Lord's Work in Italy' (CBA 7341).

[8] On Guicciardini and Rossetti, see *BDEB.* On the Italian movement, see Ronco, *Risorgimento and the Free Italian Churches;* Stunt et al., *Turning the World Upside Down,* 341-7.

[9] Throughout this book, where *Echoes of Service* appears in italics, the reference is to the magazine; where not, to the agency.

[10] Anon., 'The "Echoes" Prayer List', *LOH* 20 (1931), 179.

[11] [John Ritchie?], 'Godly Giving', *BM* 3 (1893), 89; cf. 'AC', *BM* 8 (1898), 47.

[12] Ruoff, *Vine,* 18. In terms of the number of overseas workers supported, Echoes had overtaken the SKI by 1880.

[13] See section 17.4.

as its missionaries.) However, Edward thought the new institution was open to the same objection as the old one: in both cases there was a risk that a worker who expressed unacceptable opinions would have his support cut off. He therefore felt it better for each assembly to support its own missionaries.[14] Nonetheless, Echoes grew rapidly, even more rapidly than the constituency which it served; it became common for newly-founded assemblies to appear in the list of donors printed in each issue of the magazine, an indication of how deeply-rooted missionary concern had now become.

The association with Bath began when Maclean moved there in 1873. The offices in Widcombe Crescent became something of a nerve-centre for Open Brethren mission, and by virtue of their wide-ranging acquaintance with assemblies at home and missionary work overseas, the Editors came to exercise considerable (if undefined) influence.[15] Not only were they consulted regarding missionary matters, but some shared in discussion of problems in British assemblies. A number also proved to be expository preachers of a high calibre. All served without remuneration, and many gave their whole time to the work. Gradually Echoes of Service came to be entrusted with responsibility for overseas property as well as money. Because missionaries in some countries were not legally permitted to hold property or funds in their own names, the Continental Lands Company was formed in 1895 and the Stewards Company in 1898, to ensure that mission properties would continue to be used for their intended purpose.[16]

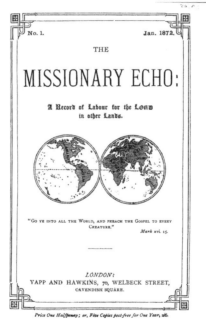

No. 1.   Jan. 1872.

THE

MISSIONARY ECHO:

A Record of Labour for the Lord
in other Lands.

"Go ye into all the World, and preach the Gospel to every Creature."
Mark xvi. 15.

LONDON:
YAPP AND HAWKINS, 70, WELBECK STREET,
CAVENDISH SQUARE.

Price One Halfpenny; or, Five Copies post-free for One Year, 2/6.

The cover of a facsimile of the first issue of the *Missionary Echo*

---

[14] Groves, *Müller*, 146.

[15] For this paragraph, and details of the Editors to 1972, see Stunt et al., *Turning the World Upside Down*, ch. 3.

[16] *LOH* 14 (1925), 160; McLaren, 'Triple Tradition', 88.

A similar body to Echoes emerged in Scotland. The first missionaries from Scottish assemblies appear to have been commended in 1876, and in the early 1880s a fund was commenced, the Home and Foreign Mission Fund, which in time also offered advice to prospective candidates and their assemblies, as well as considering policy issues relating to sending and support. Among those involved was Caldwell of *The Witness*, but Ritchie also began to receive funds for mission work through *The Believer's Magazine*, and so the Lord's Work Trust was established to channel such gifts and circulate missionary information. Both magazines also carried regular reports of missionary work at home and overseas.

12.1.2 Missionary Conferences and House-parties

Almost from the start of this move, leaders at home felt the need to confer about mission-related issues, and to include missionaries in their deliberations. The precursors of later residential missionary conferences took place in Leominster, where in 1873 a former hotel was turned into a conference centre for the Lord's servants by Yapp, who had settled there in 1863. Concerned at the divisions among Open Brethren, Yapp 'thought if only he could get leading brethren together, not to platform meetings, but to sit at the same table, have a few days' social fellowship together with private prayerful consideration over Scripture and various urgent questions, it might do good'. Onlookers expected his venture to fail, but in the event the Leominster conferences proved to meet a felt need, being held several times a year until 1906, and often including a number of missionaries.[17] From 1893, too, occasional small conferences of leading brethren and missionaries met to discuss in confidence policy issues relating to mission, and from 1902 such a gathering preceded the London Missionary Meetings each year.[18]

More high-profile were the missionary meetings intended for ordinary assembly members. The most famous were those held each year over several days in London from 1895, which grew out of a monthly missionary prayer meeting.[19] Held initially at Devonshire House, growth in attendance led to moves to Kingsway Hall in 1913 and to Westminster Central Hall from the early 1920s.[20] A factor attracting large attendances (up to 3,000) was the presence of many missionaries, all on furlough being invited by the convenors.

From the 1890s, local and regional missionary conferences also became popular. Existing gatherings, such as the Glasgow Half-Yearly Believers' Meetings, also added missionary meetings to their programme. Few assemblies of any size would have omitted to hold regular missionary meetings, though smaller and out-of-the-way assemblies sometimes complained about the difficulty of securing missionary speakers. Such gatherings, especially the larger ones, were where many first became conscious that God was calling them to serve overseas.

---

[17] B[rewer]., *Early Days*, 91-3; quotation from page 91.

[18] Stunt et al., *Turning the World Upside Down*, 47-8.

[19] This was first held in 1894 ('TLWW', *W* 24 (1894), 84).

[20] Beattie, *Brethren*, 119.

12.1.3 The Missionary Study Classes

An agency which did much to develop and sustain missionary interest in the assemblies was the Missionary Study Class (MSC) movement. With this was linked the name of Rendle Short: although he was not the pioneer of this movement, he did much to ensure that it caught the attention of Open Brethren throughout much of the British Isles. A formative influence on his thinking was the Student Volunteer Movement, founded in the United States in 1886 to foster missionary commitment among students.[21] The concept of small groups for study of mission-related issues had also been anticipated in the Church of England, with the Church Missionary Society producing text books for class study.[22]

Assemblies in Lancashire were to the fore in this development: since 1895 they had held an annual missionary conference, and they began to form groups for study and prayer concerning missionary matters. The idea of producing a magazine was also mooted. A missionary on furlough, Mrs Walter Fisher, was responsible for the earliest known such group, however, at Grosvenor Hall, Dublin (1899). In 1903 she started a class in Bristol for women, to which men were later admitted. Short first became involved in 1905 as a missionary candidate. He decided that such classes were worth replicating, and inserted a request in *Echoes of Service* during 1910 for secretaries of similar groups to contact him. As a result, he linked up with the Lancashire work and the planned local magazine became a national one, with the purpose of linking the study groups (renamed Missionary Study Classes) as well as providing information.[23] *Links of Help* carried features on various fields of missionary activity and items on what classes could do practically by way of mission support, as well as continually reinforcing the missionary challenge. It ran from 1911 until the end of 1935, when it was absorbed into *The Harvester*. Although the new magazine faced opposition from those who feared that it was intended as a competitor to *Echoes of Service*,[24] Vine and the other Editors of Echoes of Service showed support for the new venture by proof-reading each issue and eliminating indiscretions. In connection with it, H.G. Hall opened a depot in Bolton, from which maps, diagrams, pictures, and essays could be borrowed by class leaders.

By 1912, about sixty MSCs had come into being. Their first residential conference, on the lines of those of the Student Volunteer Movement, took place that summer for consideration of fundamental doctrines and presentation of the missionary challenge.[25] Short was the convenor, and considered that time away from normal life made young people more open to considering whether God might be calling them to missionary service (in this he was proved right by the number of candidates who dated their call to such gatherings). Such conferences also provided a spiritually profitable way of using holidays, and gave speakers a chance to open up neglected lines of teaching.[26] Lang

---

[21] Capper and Johnson, *Faith of a Surgeon*, 140, 153; cf. Rouse and Neill (eds.), *History*, 328-9.

[22] Stunt et al., *Turning the World Upside Down*, 558.

[23] H.G. Hall, 'The Story of "Links"', *LOH* 12 (1923), 12-14; Linton and Linton, '*I Will Build my Church*', 242; A. Rendle Short, 'The Early Days of the M.S.C.', *LOH* 18 (1929), 50; cf. *LOH* 9 (1920), 108; 11 (1922), 2. Interestingly, Preston in Lancashire was an early centre of missionary interest among Assemblies of God; Myerscough appears to have played a significant role, and Burton was one of the best-known missionary recruits. Thus Brethren missionary vision helped to shape the missionary activity of another movement.

[24] Hall, 'Story of "Links"', 12.

[25] Capper and Johnson, *Faith of a Surgeon*, 125-7; A. Rendle Short, letter in *LOH* 1 (1911-12), 144.

[26] A. Rendle Short, 'The Beginning of the Holiday Conferences', *LOH* 18 (1929), 66-7.

certainly did that at the first conference with his exposition of the partial rapture theory, which closed the door to his further involvement; this rejection may have helped to shape his negative perception of the movement.

Criticism was not slow in coming. As Short summarised it:

> 'Was this the thin end of the wedge? Would it grow to a widespread revolt of the young against the older and divide meetings? Where was the Scriptural warrant for M.S.C.'s? Was missionary study going to take the place of Bible study? It was rumoured that the sisters took a very prominent part in the M.S.C.'s; were apostolic injunctions going to be defied? Was an unscriptural amalgamation, or federation of M.S.C.'s under one central committee, in existence?'[27]

The appearance of such a movement clearly gave rise not only to ecclesiological concerns about the legitimacy of such a body, but also to tensions within assemblies. Apart from the tension between old and young (which may have been made worse by the development of work for particular age-groups during this period and the failure of many older leaders to train and bring forward their potential successors), there were fears that missionary study would squeeze out Bible study.

Looking back, Short claimed that overseas interest had been in decline from about 1895 to 1905. He asserted that after the interest generated by F.S. Arnot[28] and others had dissipated, contributions through Echoes of Service had dropped and then remained static. At home, he claimed that there had been a lack of aggressive gospel work, and a failure to provide for the needs of young believers resulted in a serious leakage of that generation (this was indeed a major factor behind the welcome given to the MSC movement by older leaders). He saw an upturn from 1905, as revival of interest in overseas work resulted in increased financial contributions and new missionary recruits.[29] It is true that finance had apparently failed to keep pace with the increasing number of missionaries. In 1910, 239 English assemblies (about 27% of the total) had sent gifts through Bath, and the MSC movement and *Links of Help* represented attempts to respond to the shortfall.[30] However, Short's analysis was flawed: in fact, the number of new missionaries peaked in 1899 at fifty-four and remained generally higher thereafter than it had been before 1895. In addition, it was during the same decade that the evangelistic work which became known as Counties Evangelization got going in various parts of England with widespread support. There is no noticeable diminution in the rate at which new assemblies were coming into existence during the period concerned, which implies that home mission was being carried on as vigorously as ever. Home and overseas work do appear to have risen and

---

[27] A. Rendle Short, 'The Early Days of the M.S.C.', *LOH* 18 (1929), 51.

[28] Arnot (1858-1914) was, along with Dan Crawford (1869-1926), one of the pioneers of assembly mission in Central and Southern Africa. He presented the needs of Central Africa with great forcefulness during a return to Britain from 1888-9, with the result that a group of thirteen went back to Africa with him. Few survived long, and the death of so many new recruits was undoubtedly a factor inspiring some of the large number of missionaries who went abroad during the 1890s. On Arnot, see *BDCM*; *DSCHT*; *ODNB*; Pickering (ed.), *Chief Men*, 183-7. On Crawford, see *BDCM*; Pickering (ed.), *Chief Men*, 220-3.

[29] See A. Rendle Short, 'The Early Days of the M.S.C.', 50-1; *idem*, letter in *H* 14 (1937), 234; *idem*, 'What is the Use of these Missionary Study Classes?', *LOH* 12 (1923), 3-4.

[30] T. Baird, 'Startling Statistics', *LOH* 1 (1911-12), 34.

fallen together, but not necessarily at the points claimed by Short; furthermore, the level of financial support may not have been an entirely accurate indicator of the level of missionary interest, which was due partly to assemblies' lack of experience in supporting full-time workers of any type and the impact of the concept of 'living by faith' (see below). All the same, the relationship between the two spheres was not without its problems; an article in 1888 claimed that interest in foreign work had led to a neglect of support for home work which contrasted with the situation two decades earlier, with the result that some discouraged workers had joined the sects. The author also suggested that such neglect could have contributed to present problems, which was probably an oblique reference to the debates raging over reception and fellowship.[31]

The faces of these 10 Ambassadors for Christ remind us of their "work of faith, and labour of love, and patience of hope, in our Lord Jesus Christ," as they witnessed that "God so loved the World, that He gave His only begotten Son, that WHOSOEVER BELIEVETH in Him should not perish, but have everlasting life."—*John iii, 16, Rom. x. 14, 15 ; 2 Cor. iv. 7 ; Rom. xii. 1 ; Phil. ii. 10 ; Rev. v. 13.*

A wide range of visual aids such as this early 1920s map were available as posters and as postcards

---

[31] Anon., 'Furtherance of the Gospel', *EH* 3 (1888), 133; cf. *EOS* 22 (1893), 264.

All these ventures depended on the tireless and strategic activity of advocates of the missionary cause. One example would be Thomas M'Laren (1832-1908) of Glasgow. He was involved in the inception of *Echoes of Service*, and contributed frequent articles to *The Witness* on mission themes, presenting statistics concerning the needs and offering suggestions for individual and assembly action.[32] Others included Charles Brewer of Leominster (1826-1915), who produced the forerunner of the Echoes of Service prayer list from 1890, and H.G. Hall, who was behind the vision of the Lancashire assemblies. Several, such as Rendle Short, had wanted to serve overseas themselves but been prevented by health or family reasons, and such work offered them a means of sharing in the missionary task. Others, such as Arnot, were forced to spend periods at home because of ill-health and used the opportunity to spread the challenge among the assemblies.[33]

12.2 The Impact of Brethren Missiological Thinking

The Brethren concept of 'living by faith' was to influence many of the interdenominational missions founded during this period. One of the best known was the CIM. Its forerunner was the Chinese Evangelisation Society (CES), founded at Tottenham in 1849 and dissolved in 1860, and whose most famous recruit was Hudson Taylor. Taylor had worshipped with Brethren in Hull from 1851-2 and also had strong links with the assemblies at Hackney and Tottenham, and was associated with the CES from 1854-7. In 1865, he founded the CIM, adopting Müller's faith principles; most of its early financial support came from Brethren assemblies or the SKI. By 1895, it had no less than 641 missionaries, some of them Brethren, and a number of other Brethren served in China independently.[34] Its first secretary was Richard Hill, Jr, whose father had been an early leader in the Plymouth area.[35] Other examples of faith missions inspired by Brethren practice included the North Africa Mission (1884), whose secretary was E.H. Glenny of Barking.[36]

Many faith missions were in some way connected with Fanny and Grattan Guinness. He was a gifted evangelist who joined Open Brethren when he married Fanny, who although a Quaker had Brethren leanings. Although he became an elder at Dublin's new Merrion Hall during the mid-1860s, this was a relatively open assembly, refounded as a result of the revival preaching of Denham Smith and others, and welcoming non-Brethren such as the Free Church of Scotland minister Horatius Bonar to preach, and Guinness was always ill at ease with what he felt was a narrowness and lack of evangelistic vision among the Brethren movement at large.[37] The Guinnesses opened a missionary training institution in East London, but appear to have passed out of the Brethren orbit.

---

[32] *W* 38 (1908), 116.

[33] Stunt et al., *Turning the World Upside Down*, 557.

[34] Edwards, *Christian England*, 3.349; Fiedler, *Faith Missions*, 24, 35, 37. The origins and development of the CIM and other faith missions are charted in Fiedler, *Faith Missions*, to which this chapter is indebted.

[35] David J. Beattie, 'The Brethren Movement: Its Rise and Progress. XXX', *BM* n.s. 37 (1936), 154.

[36] Stunt et al., *Turning the World Upside* Down, 477, 486; W 56 (1926), 279.

[37] Fiedler, *Faith Missions*, 34, 38, 173; Moore-Anderson, *Robert Anderson*, 21. On Guinness, see also *ODNB*.

In spite of the impact of Brethren ideas on these agencies, many Brethren disapproved of missionary societies as lacking New Testament precedent and interfering with the worker's direct responsibility to the Lord. However, a significant exception to this disapproval was the British and Foreign Bible Society. Many Open Brethren missionaries worked with this body in Scripture translation from the late nineteenth century onwards, and many more made extensive use of the materials which it produced. References to it in the periodicals were always couched in positive terms, and its work was commended as worthy of support. It is likely that this was because it had a clearly restricted remit and did not see itself as called to found churches (of whose structures Brethren might have disapproved).

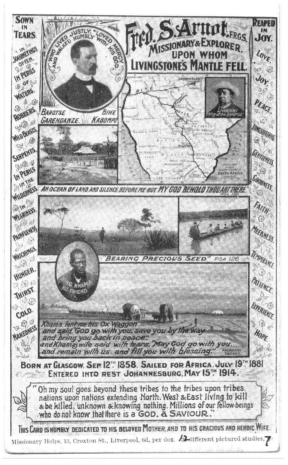

This card, produced to mark the death of F.S. Arnot, illustrates the hero status accorded to those who gave their lives to spreading the gospel of Christ

Larsen has pointed out that 'living by faith' became an identity-marker among Open Brethren.[38] Although they rejected the concept of an ordained ministry, they do seem to have placed those who 'lived by faith' on a pedestal, perhaps giving insufficient consideration to their needs as human beings. One regrettable consequence appears to have been a slowness on the part of many individuals and assemblies to adopt a disciplined approach to the support of full-time workers. E.K. Groves claimed that refusal to issue appeals for funds led to a failure to see the need for serious and systematic giving.[39] Coad believes that the emphasis on 'living by faith' was responsible for a reluctance to support full-time workers at home or abroad on a systematic (salaried) basis,[40] although this may have owed as much to a fear that such workers would form something suspiciously like a clerical caste. It is unfortunate, therefore, that Brethren during this period do not seem to have been aware that putting those who 'lived by faith' on a pedestal could have similarly injurious effects, possibly leading to disparagement of those who received a regular income or salary or who were not full-time in Christian work. It would be worth investigating the extent to which 'living by faith' was a reflection of the contemporary cult of respectability and independence. This upheld the ideal of not being dependent on the resources of others, and of suiting expenditure to income.[41] Insistence that workers were accountable only to God may be seen as paralleling the disapproval of dependence on charitable handouts.

The supernaturalism of 'living by faith' was also evident in attitudes towards training. While Brethren recognised the value of training in specialist fields such as medicine and dentistry, they insisted that the essential qualifications for service were spiritual ones, which emerged in the course of service at home.[42] Missionary training institutions were thus almost as suspect as theological colleges, and seen by some as lacking biblical warrant. However, Huntingdon Stone (1857-1916) opened a missionary training home at Greenwich where candidates were able to live while receiving instruction in missionary principles and medical training (for which he paid the costs), and engaging in practical outreach in the locality. It was estimated that he had helped 500 young people prepare for missionary service, and he left his fortune of £250,000 to Echoes of Service, to be disbursed within ten years.[43]

For many Brethren, their supernaturalism meant that their expectations regarding missionary work were located within the context of their anticipation of the rapture (although a significant exception was Dan Crawford, whose anticipation of the evangelisation of the whole world before the Second Coming was a factor in his adoption of postmillennialism[44]). The hope of hastening the Second Coming by reaching (though not converting) the whole world was a major reason for the faith missions' focus on previously unreached areas, and their willingness to use anyone, whether or not ordained. Brethren missionaries pioneered many such areas, especially in Africa. Denial of the

---

[38] Larsen, "'Living by Faith'", 68-9.

[39] Groves, *Müller*, 179.

[40] Coad, *History*, 56.

[41] Best, *Mid-Victorian Britain*, 254, 280, 290.

[42] E.g. 'AC', *BM* n.s. 11 (1910), 107-8.

[43] Anon., *Greenwich (1875-1935)*, 8; *W* 45 (December 1915), 158. See also *EOS* 45 (1916), 391-2. Stone was connected with the biscuit manufacturer Peek Frean, one of whose founders was John Carr, brother of Jonathan (Coad, *Laing*, 29).

[44] Dan Crawford, *"Touching the Coming of the Lord"* (Aylesbury: Hunt, Barnard & Co., n.d.).

necessity for ordination or formal appointment to office, ability to tolerate differing viewpoints on such potentially divisive issues as baptism (perhaps more in evidence abroad than at home), and recognition of unity as already existing, which enabled them to transcend denominational divisions, and the practice of direct dependence on God apart from human organisations, were all aspects of Brethren thinking which became important in the development of the faith mission ethos.[45] In the next section, we shall see that from the 1920s some of these came into question at home as well as overseas, with ramifications for the movement's sense of identity.

---

[45] Fiedler, *Faith Missions*, 171-2, 277-8.

PART 3

1914–1945:
Holding the Torch for Evangelicalism

CHAPTER 13

Growth and Decline

13.1 The Impact of Post-war Social Change

Brethren after the Great War found themselves in an unfamiliar landscape. The society of 1918 was significantly different from that of the Edwardian era. The social profile of women was now higher, as a result of the extension of the franchise and the growing acceptance of women working outside the home; the increase in employment opportunities for women was a factor in the improved living standards among the poor. Another feature was the weakened sense of deference towards one's social superiors, coupled with a vacuum left by disproportionately high losses among the officer classes during the war.[1] Society no longer had quite the same feeling of stability, and the industrial unrest which had begun shortly before the war was to become a recurring feature of life during this period. Trade Unionism grew in influence, and the Labour Party enjoyed its first (brief) taste of government in 1924.

In the religious sphere, the decline of the practice of Christianity among the middle classes was marked, a development hastened by the existence of a growing range of leisure pursuits and the fashionable status of agnosticism during the 1920s; after the strains of the war, many threw themselves into the pursuit of pleasure.[2] The predominant mood was one of optimism and of a desire for reconstruction, epitomised in the formation of the League of Nations. Churches joined the campaign for reconstruction, a high watermark of their involvement being the 1924 Conference on Politics, Economics, and Citizenship (COPEC), masterminded by William Temple, who was to be Archbishop of Canterbury from 1942 until his death two years later. Brethren stood apart from all such discussions, and their social outlook was in part shaped by reaction against such things.[3]

The growth of the welfare state meant that many Nonconformist churches found themselves occupying a more marginal position in society than they had been used to, as the state took over the provision of many services which the churches had helped to provide and which had given them a means of integrating into the local community.[4] However, since Brethren had never provided much in the way of leisure activities, and their welfare provision in depressed areas continued to be needed, they were little shaken by this.

For many, these years formed a relaxed interlude between the war and the 1930s, which would be marked by economic insecurity in parts of the United Kingdom and an ever-deepening sense of foreboding regarding German and Russian intentions. Religiously,

---

[1] Gilley and Shiels (eds.), *Religion in Britain*, 466; Adrian Hastings, *A History of English Christianity 1920-1990* (London and Philadelphia: SCM and Trinity Press International, 1991), 19.

[2] Kenneth Hylson-Smith, *The Churches in England from Elizabeth I to Elizabeth II. Volume III: 1833-1998* (London: SCM, 1998), 147, 155.

[3] Cf. 'WW', *W* 55 (1925), 34. This paragraph focused on the conference's theological unorthodoxy, as seen in its denial of the Fall and of the need for atonement and regeneration, and its inclusion of modernists and Unitarians.

[4] Hylson-Smith, *Churches in England III*, 154-5.

the 1930s would see a revival in the fortunes of Christianity among the upper classes and the *intelligentsia*,[5] but it is noticeable that whereas in the nineteenth century Brethren had been well represented among the upper classes, they had little share in this revival and indeed appear to have remained either ignorant or critical of it; since its most popular manifestations were High Anglicanism and Roman Catholicism, this is not altogether surprising.[6] If we fault Brethren for their lack of engagement with contemporary thought, it must be acknowledged that they were no worse than most other Evangelicals. It has been suggested that Evangelicalism had become intellectually withdrawn and defensive by the 1930s because the best nineteenth-century Evangelical brains had gone abroad,[7] a thesis which bears investigation with reference to Open Brethren. However, a major factor accounting for this withdrawal was the influence of the Fundamentalist movement, which was significant during the 1920s and 1930s.[8] With this came a rise in the popularity of premillennialism among Evangelicals at large, blunting the edge of their social concern.[9]

13.2   Effective Evangelism

The previous Open Brethren assembly in the village of Hurlford, near Kilmarnock, had become extinct. Outreach continued by such means as tent meetings, gospel meetings in a hall, and tract distribution, but the village proved a hard place. However, a tent campaign in 1933 was given a flying start by an opening conference and an open-air march of witness. Halfway through the campaign, conversions began to occur. As a result, more than fifty were baptized, and before it ended the Breaking of Bread was taking place in the tent. A nucleus of the converts, with a few believers from other assemblies, procured a hall in which to meet, thus attracting some Christians from other denominations who had been helped by the tent meetings.[10]

Such a story highlights several recurrent elements in contemporary Open Brethren church-planting. Opening conferences could often draw a crowd of supporters from local assemblies, giving the mission a high profile locally. Baptisms during the campaign of converts and believers from other churches, sometimes in a temporary baptistery dug in the tent, and the commencement of a regular Breaking of Bread before it ended were also common. Along with Bible readings conducted towards the end of the mission on matters of Christian living and assembly practice, these ensured that sufficient momentum was generated for a new assembly to 'hit the ground running' (when a hall was opened in a new locality, a campaign usually marked the occasion for the same reason). At Driffield, for example, a mission in 1924 using the Yorkshire Tent resulted in the formation of an assembly which within weeks was attracting forty-six to the Breaking of Bread, 160 to

---

[5] Hastings, *English Christianity*, 253-4.

[6] *Ibid.*, 194; Hylson-Smith, *Churches in England III*, 181.

[7] Oliver Barclay, *Evangelicalism in Britain 1935-1995: a personal sketch* (Leicester: IVP, 1997), 15.

[8] For discussion of Fundamentalism and its impact on Brethren, see Bebbington, *Evangelicalism*, ch. 6; Ian M. Randall, *Evangelical Experiences: A Study in the Spirituality of English Evangelicalism 1918-1939* (Carlisle: Paternoster, 1999); *idem*, '"Outside the Camp": Brethren Spirituality and Wider Evangelicalism in the 1920s', *BAHNR* 2.1 (Winter 2000), 17-33; Shuff, 'Open to Closed'.

[9] Randall and Hilborn, *One Body in Christ*, 100-01.

[10] For the full report, see G.G., 'A Village Campaign and the Results', *BM* n.s. 35 (1934), 53-4.

the Sunday School, and 310 to the Gospel meeting.[11] There was also less reluctance to give numbers of converts in reports during this period, and it was not unusual to read of twenty, thirty, or forty being baptised and added to an assembly as the result of a campaign.

The attraction of believers from other denominations was another typical feature; such missions strengthened the impression that Brethren were 'going places', and the clear presentation of the gospel, especially when it included a stress on assurance of salvation, would have drawn many who were frustrated by the deadness and liberalism of their own churches.

This report also exemplifies the extensive coverage given by the periodicals to outreach efforts. *The Witness* increased the size of each issue from twenty to twenty-four pages in 1929, in order to include more reports of evangelistic work; *The Believer's Magazine* also carried (briefer) reports, and *The Harvester* began with the intent of carrying full reports from the workers themselves. Such coverage would have stimulated assemblies to extend fellowship to new works, and also to go and do likewise.

There is another typical feature in this report – or rather, not in it – which presents a problem for researchers. It made no mention of the existence of a Church of God in the village. Such reporting illustrates the tendency to denominationalism evident among Open Brethren during this period; even the existence of earlier Open meetings in the same town was sometimes omitted in reports and announcements of new gatherings. Intimations concerning the founding of new assemblies must therefore be treated with care; apart from the tendency (surprising among Brethren, who began by sitting light to material resources such as buildings) to notify the opening of a new hall in terms which implied the founding of a new assembly, the presence of Exclusive or 'Needed Truth' gatherings in a town was usually ignored, reports giving the impression that an assembly had been planted where no similar gathering had previously existed.

The inter-war period was the heyday of large-scale missions, such as those organised by the assemblies in Liverpool. Late in the First World War, assemblies had held united prayer meetings; in the winter of 1917 they began weekly meetings for believers. A desire for united outreach led to tent meetings being held during the following summer, and a big tent in a central location was used for the summer of 1919. This mission proved outstandingly successful, with over 500 professions; there were two baptismal services in the tent, at which sixty-one and thirty-one were baptised respectively, as well as other baptisms in local halls. United activity proved a catalyst, not only for the outreach of the assemblies themselves, but also for that of the Anglican Cathedral, which began its own 'People's Service'. The Boaler Street assembly, for example, saw its membership rise from 110 in 1919 to 300 in 1923. From 1928, the big tent was occasionally pitched in an unreached district of the city, with the objective of seeing an assembly formed as a result. Cinema services, follow-up meetings for converts, and meetings for believers kept the momentum going through the winter. Attendance began to fluctuate in the 1930s as the range of alternative attractions increased, but missions were held as late as 1939.[12]

Cardiff assemblies purchased their own tent in 1924, a 'Canvas Cathedral' capable of seating 2,300. Meetings included a song service at the beginning, designed to create a congenial atmosphere for the preaching. Saturday evenings and Sunday afternoons saw

---

[11] *H* 1 (1923-4), 316.

[12] [Henry Pickering], 'Magnetism and Evangelism', *W* 53 (1923), 81; F.C. Grant, 'Liverpool Tent Campaign', *W* 49 (1919), 164; *H* 5 (1928), 61; 8 (1931), 14; 16 (1939), 210.

meetings for believers, many of whom had few opportunities for receiving good teaching.[13] Many other places began holding such missions, including Bristol, Bolton, Birmingham (all by 1918), Aberdeen (1919), Plymouth (1926), St Albans (1927), Norwich (1929), Nottingham, and Newport.

The Cardiff Big Tent, typical of those used in many cities
during the inter-war years

A planned approach was adopted by assemblies in highly-urbanised Lancashire. In 1919, a united meeting at Bolton drew about 500 brethren from local assemblies to consider ways and means of reaching out, and a follow-up meeting decided to organise large-scale campaigns. Brethren were conscious that over half the sixty towns with a population greater than 10,000 had no Open assembly, and tent work began the following year, not only in large cities such as Manchester, Liverpool and Birkenhead, but in towns such as Oldham and Todmorden; hundreds of conversions resulted from the first season. The villages were not neglected, bands of workers visiting them to share the gospel.[14] Some evangelists who worked in Lancashire proved themselves masters of the big mission, such as Phil Mills and Fred Elliott, and went on to evangelise all over the British Isles.

It is noteworthy that the Open Brethren and Pentecostal communities both grew in numbers during the 1920s, and that both made extensive use of large-scale evangelistic missions. The effectiveness of such campaigns may have been due in part to the movements' non-clerical ethos, but there may have been a class factor at work here: their evangelists were, perhaps, people to whom the 'man in the street' could relate, and whose preaching he could understand, better than that of the clergy. Pentecostal congregations did not share Brethren objections to recognised ministerial leadership, but many of their ministers would, like Brethren evangelists, have shared the social and cultural background of their flocks and their prospective converts.

The rise of 'cinema services' did not betoken any softening of Brethren opposition to cinema-going (or to the use of films by churches), but it did prove a highly successful means of mounting high-profile evangelistic meetings in the days when going to the cinema was a frequent leisure activity for most people. They began during the First World

---

[13] John McAlpine, *Forty Years Evangelising in Britain* (London: Pickering & Inglis, 1947), 58.
[14] *LOH* 8 (1919), 81; 9 (1920), 20, 135.

War, one of the earliest locations being Stranraer (1915).[15] Soon large cities and smaller towns across the United Kingdom caught the vision: in Liverpool, Brethren began with a one-off service on a Sunday night in 1918, which became twenty-seven consecutive Sundays.[16] In Glasgow, Alex Marshall began holding cinema services in 1919, and it was noted that most of the congregation would be gathered off the streets; the cinema would be full well before the service was due to start.[17] South Grove Hall, Walthamstow, moved their regular Gospel meeting to a cinema in the late 1920s, and were rewarded with a jump in attendance to over 500, three-quarters of whom were believed to be unsaved.[18] Nevertheless, assemblies could find themselves faced with unforeseen problems; in 1929 Woodcroft Hall in Burnt Oak, Middlesex, found that two-thirds of their congregation of 600 were careless, laughing 18-25 year olds; finding themselves unable to cope with the disruption the first week, they took the precaution of stationing workers to keep order, with a corresponding improvement in behaviour.[19]

By the 1930s, the cost of hiring cinemas, especially once they were allowed to show films on a Sunday, was becoming too much for most assemblies and cinema services were decreasing in popularity, but during the Second World War one bombed-out assembly in Bristol rented a cinema for a few months and saw attendances of up to 500, mostly outsiders. Arresting subjects were announced, and the service began with hymns projected onto the screen.[20] Although reports indicate that there was some fruit from these services, the impact was probably in terms of novelty value as much as anything, as had been the case with the previous century's theatre services. Ritchie warned that such efforts would yield little permanent fruit unless followed up by effective preaching,[21] and by and large he appears to have been right.

By contrast, Counties Evangelization had started from a concern for rural areas, and such bodies continued to be concerned about the well-being of small rural assemblies. Evangelists had been encouraged to offer their services to such during the winter season, conducting missions in assembly premises and engaging in follow-up work when it was impossible to pioneer with a tent and carriage. Sometimes such missions could be very fruitful and do a great deal to rejuvenate a struggling assembly. By the mid-1930s, it was claimed that about fifteen new assemblies or gospel works had been commenced in West Somerset since the war.[22] On Saturday afternoons from about 1910 until the 1960s, up to fifty workers would go out to villages around Bristol; open-air work would be followed after tea by an evangelistic meeting.[23] In London, similar outreach was undertaken, the area around the metropolis being divided into six sections, each with its band of willing workers.[24] At the end of each summer, report meetings would update local believers and serve as stimuli to prayer, giving and involvement. Tract bands also continued to be active, *The Believer's Magazine* reporting their activities in Scotland through the 1920s.

---

[15] 'WML', *W* 45 (1915), 164.

[16] *W* 49 (1919), 82.

[17] [Henry Pickering], 'Cinema Services', *W* 50 (1920), 211.

[18] *H* 6 (1929), 3.

[19] *H* 7 (1930), 10.

[20] A Rendle Short, 'When They Come Home', *W* 75 (1945), 54.

[21] [John Ritchie], 'A Look Round Among Evangelistic Efforts', *BM* n.s. 22 (1921), 45.

[22] *H* 11 (1934), 175-6.

[23] Linton and Linton, *'I Will Build my Church'*, 255.

[24] *H* 10 (1933), 62-3.

The Pilgrim Preachers, passing through Barnet Fair in 1919

The inter-war years saw a number of new types of evangelism. One group which received plenty of publicity was the 'Pilgrim Preachers', a newspaper's nickname for a group whose treks through Britain attracted considerable media attention.[25] The brainchild of Ernest Luff of the Open Air Mission and the Brethren businessman P.W. Petter, their objective was to testify to the imminence of the Second Coming and proclaim the gospel, by means of tract distribution, personal conversation, and meetings in the open air and (where possible) in churches. Their first tour was from Bath to London in April 1919; two months later sixteen of them with banners made their way from Norwich to London, holding meetings which drew up to 3,000 people; the following year they worked from Land's End to John O'Groats. Bicycles became their preferred mode of transport. Their tours were always extensively reported by Open Brethren periodicals (although not all participants were Brethren), and continued until 1938. A number of clergy proved sympathetic and made their churches available, probably because they shared the belief in the imminence of the Lord's return, but on one occasion the Preachers were refused permission to engage in open-air witness outside St Paul's Cathedral, which did nothing for Brethren perceptions of Anglicanism as spiritually dead.

The increasing popularity of missions and special meetings for children and young people was possibly a response to adult unresponsiveness, but it may also have been a manifestation of a growing child-centredness in society at large. Large Sunday Schools were not unknown; Ely, in Cardiff, had 1,200 on their books in 1936,[26] Warrington claimed an average attendance of 1,000 in 1933,[27] and many others ran into several hundreds. An increasing proportion of additions to the assembly were the result of

[25] See John W. Newton, *The Story of the Pilgrim Preachers and their 24 Tours throughout Great Britain: With many Stirring Scenes, Genuine Conversions, Peculiar Positions, and Soul-stirring Experiences* (London: Pickering & Inglis, [1938]); P.W. Petter, *The Story of The Pilgrim Preachers and their Message* (London and Edinburgh: Marshall, [1921]).

[26] *W* 67 (1937), 20.

[27] *H* 11 (1934), 9.

children's and youth work; for instance, Bearwood, in Smethwick, reaped such a harvest which tripled their membership between 1924 and 1939.[28] However, the proportion of scholars converted was often disturbingly low. An excellent illustration of this is provided by the statistics for the Sunday School of the assembly at Church Lane, Stafford, for the years 1919-40, during which the meeting doubled in size. Two thousand children passed through the Sunday School; approximately 400 professed conversion during children's missions; all children of members came into fellowship, though a number later left; by contrast, under 2% of children from non-Christian homes came into fellowship, and all who did had had social contact with Christians during adolescence in homes, Covenanter camps and other such settings.[29] So how were assemblies to retain their young people? Those in the Birmingham area, noting that only a tenth of scholars were converted and joined assemblies, and that many dropped out after the age of fourteen, began a youth rally in 1920.[30] With the appearance in some assemblies of such agencies as Crusaders and Covenanters,[31] and the proliferation of youth camps and house parties, there were a variety of ways in which teenagers could be retained. Henry Pickering had thought in 1921 that very few were now converted after sixteen in assemblies,[32] but F.A. Tatford was optimistic that assemblies, unlike denominations, were seeing increasing numbers of young people.[33] Student work was undertaken in a few places, although this was soon left to the developing Inter-Varsity Fellowship, one of whose chief advocates was Rendle Short.

At the other end of the age range, meetings for elderly men were started by an assembly in St Leonards during the mid-1920s, with many conversions resulting – all because some sitting outside the hall had refused invitations to the regular gospel meeting.[34] The most widely-used approach, however, was that of the Women's or Mothers' meeting, which came to be regarded as one of the most effective assembly agencies for conversions.[35] Although such meetings began late in the nineteenth century, they appear to have experienced growth during this period. That at Adamsdown Hall, Cardiff, grew to around 400 by 1923, and the Ely (Cardiff) meeting to the same size by 1936.[36] By 1934, it was noted that there were ywenty-three such meetings in the Cardiff district, which were having a knock-on effect on attendance at Sunday School and gospel meetings; most

---

[28] Barton, *Bearwood*, 22.

[29] Venables, *Meeting Room, Stafford*, 9.

[30] Anon., 'Young People's Rally', *W* 50 (1920), 212.

[31] Both were interdenominational youth organisations. Crusaders catered for the 'grammar school' stream and were more independent of the local church, Brethren involvement being on an individual basis; Covenanters (which was Brethren in origin) was perhaps more working-class in its ethos and its classes were under the oversight of the church to which they were attached, partly in reaction to the 'unattached Christians' produced by Crusaders (T.C.F. Stunt to the author, 3 March 2004). Laing was extensively involved in both, founding the first Covenanter class in 1928 at Woodcroft Hall, Burnt Oak, Middlesex (Coad, *Laing*, 121, 123).

[32] *W* 51 (1921), 95.

[33] F.A. Tatford, 'How Can We Keep our Young People?', *W* 68 (1938), 29-31.

[34] K.H.E., 'An Aged Man's Meeting', *CG*, March 1932, 51-2.

[35] J.H.H. Biffen, 'A Missionary's View of Home Work', *W* 66 (1936), 181; 'WW', *W* 59 (1929), 163.

[36] P[robert], *Adamsdown*, 12; *W* 67 (1937), 20.

assemblies had some who had come into fellowship as a result.[37] It would be interesting to explore whether such meetings were more likely to grow in areas where there was greater resistance to married women working outside the home.

Revival was in the air. From 1919, Ritchie ran a series of articles on preparation for revival in *The Believer's Magazine*. Observers noted exceptional response to missions, although admitting that it was not as much as had been hoped for.[38] The healthy proportion of young people in assemblies was also apparent.[39] North-East Scotland and East Anglia saw small-scale revival, especially among fishing communities, in 1921.[40] Open Brethren participated in some of the meetings, and assemblies along the coast of Aberdeenshire and Morayshire saw many conversions; indeed, some new assemblies were founded in the wake of the revival, as at Wick in 1923. In a letter describing what was happening, Marshall urged believers to seek what God was longing to give.[41] Yet there was also an element of caution in Brethren reaction, as there had been in 1904-5; Ritchie, noting the blessing in North-East Scotland, expressed the hope that a ministry of truth might follow the evangelistic fervour.[42] The concurrent upsurge of revivalist activity was something of a mixed blessing, and there was a degree of tension between younger activists and older separatists; the latter had often paid a high price for their convictions, and expressed apprehension at the lack of depth and openness to interdenominational co-operation evident in much Brethren outreach.[43] Concern was also expressed regarding the increased proportion of spurious or temporary professions of faith. Pickering investigated this problem, examining the fruits of a number of Brethren and non-Brethren missions. He concluded that high numbers of professions might be due in part to the preacher's personal magnetism, coupled with the deployment of methods which operated primarily upon the will (a legacy of Finney, via Moody and Sankey): such means as decision cards, inquiry rooms, and appeals for hands to be raised all attracted his criticism. In a follow-up article, he explained that he was not against special efforts *per se*, since he thought every assembly should have them regularly, but what concerned him was adoption of the world's methods and undue reliance upon the preacher.[44] *The Believer's Magazine* was also wary of big missions, preferring regular assembly outreach; thus it gave less space to reporting such events, and Ritchie gave way to expressions of nostalgia for old-style evangelists. On occasion, an evangelist might find that few traces of a previous campaign remained when he returned to the area: in 1924, one evangelist conducted a mission in Wigtownshire which saw twenty-five professions of faith, but on returning to the area five weeks later he found very few traces of the work.[45] Part of the reason for this in rural areas would have been the relative lack of workers to shepherd

---

[37] *H* 11 (1934), 171.

[38] E.g. Anon., 'Home Echoes', *CG*, February 1922, 217-21; Anon., 'The Revival Movement', *CG*, March 1922, 239.

[39] Dickson, *Brethren in Scotland*, 198.

[40] See *ibid*., 189-91; Stanley C. Griffin, *A Forgotten Revival: East Anglia and NE Scotland – 1921* (Bromley: Day One, [1992]); 'TLWW', *BM* n.s.23 (January 1922), ii.

[41] *W* 52 (1922), 16-17.

[42] *BM* n.s. 23 (1922), 10.

[43] Randall, *Evangelical Experiences*, 146.

[44] [Pickering], 'Magnetism and Evangelism', 81; *idem*, 'Mesmerism in Modern Evangelistic Work', *W* 53 (1923), 50. For similar views expressed by Ritchie, see 'YBQB', *BM* n.s. 24 (1923), 42-3.

[45] *H* 1 (1923-4), 345.

converts and inquirers: in 1935, J.W. Ashby looked back over thirty-four years conducting tent missions in East Anglia and judged that whenever an assembly had been planted as a result of his work (which had happened in nine instances), it was because there had been a suitable local brother able to follow up the mission with winter meetings and to lead on inquirers and converts.[46]

13.3 'Two by two': Brethren Evangelists

Some evangelists combined secular employment with spare-time outreach work, but most who engaged in any itinerant activity devoted their whole time to it. In 1937 it was estimated by Fred Broadhurst of Liverpool that there were over 250 full-time workers in Britain and Ireland, most of whom would have been evangelists.[47] They got everywhere, including the parts that other evangelists did not, could not or would not reach. For example, in 1933 there were reports of Scottish evangelists working on the islands of Eigg and Fair Isle.[48] Their activity was most intense in Ulster, where in 1932 about twenty tents were being worked by evangelists who usually paired up for the purpose.[49] As well as having biblical precedent (Luke 10.1), this provided an ideal 'apprenticeship' opening for a younger evangelist, mutual support, and practical assistance in the task of erecting and dismantling the tents. Evangelists in the North of England also worked often in pairs, but workers with Counties Evangelization tended to work singly, except where a young worker was gaining experience.

Evangelists were expected to be totally committed to their work during the summer season. Those working with Counties Evangelistic Work (as Counties Evangelization was known from 1928) were advised in 1929 that, for reasons of security and accessibility to inquirers, they should not leave the work to preach elsewhere.[50] Sometimes the minutes record the wish of the oversight (a body of men with an interest in the work who met regularly to review its progress) that evangelists would focus on areas with little or no real gospel proclamation, a perennial problem being the tendency of some evangelists to gravitate to the vicinity of supportive assemblies.[51]

The advent of motor transport enabled itinerant evangelists to cover more ground, if in less depth. Motor vans were used in many parts of Britain, some featuring ingenious arrangements to facilitate the holding of meetings. *Links of Help* ran articles in 1921, complete with plans and photographs, explaining how to build a portable hall and a motorised carriage.[52] However, a number of Counties evangelists continued to be reliant on horse power until the late 1930s, when it was decided that future caravans should be designed for motor haulage because of the difficulties of securing horses to move them from place to place.[53]

---

[46] J.W. Ashby, 'Surveys of Service: Eastern Counties' Gospel Tent', *BM* n.s. 36 (1935), 93.

[47] *H* 14 (1937), 276.

[48] 'TLWW', *BM* n.s. 34 (July 1933), endpapers; *W* 63 (1933), 93.

[49] *BM* n.s. 33 (September 1932), iii.

[50] South-Eastern Counties minutes, 18 March 1929; Counties Evangelistic Work minutes, 19 March 1929.

[51] E.g. Counties Evangelization minutes, 5 March 1928.

[52] 'Co-Worker' [H. Grosvenor Cooper], 'Motor Caravans for Gospel Work', *LOH* 10 (1921), 180-1, 191; *idem*, 'Portable Halls for Gospel Work', *LOH* 10 (1921), 116-18.

[53] Counties Evangelistic Work minutes, 12 February 1937.

Counties Evangelization continued to extend its area of operation. In 1917, a similar work which had begun in South-West Essex in 1903 came under the Counties banner.[54] By 1944, the accounts indicate that work was being undertaken in Lincolnshire, Leicestershire, and Warwickshire. However, as a body it was subject to recurrent misunderstanding and criticism; this often focused on the oversight, which functioned as a self-selecting body. Individuals known to have an active interest in the work were invited to associate themselves with the oversight, as was the practice in many assemblies. A pamphlet was issued in 1929 which dealt with misunderstandings about the work and how it was directed, and the point had repeatedly to be made that Counties provided equipment and acted as a link with assemblies but did not control evangelists' movements: having been invited to serve in a county for a season, they were relatively free to choose where to go.[55] The oversight might exercise direction regarding how the work was to be done (by such means as issuing pamphlets with practical guidance) but left the evangelist free to decide where to do it (though in pre-motorised days, they were sometimes expected to progress along a predetermined route, partly for practical reasons, moving from place to place when their work was done). It also sought to vet prospective evangelists, to stimulate prayer support and assembly interest through deputation meetings and cards indicating the whereabouts of workers, and to channel finance. Generally speaking, relationships between the oversight and the evangelists seem to have been satisfactory, though it is interesting that the evangelists were not invited to oversight meetings. That this did not often lead to problems is undoubtedly due to the fact that the work was overseen by men with a heart for evangelism, and who thus would have possessed an instinctive sympathy with the evangelists.

Opposition continued to be a problem for most workers, the three main sources being what were sometimes called Ritualism, Rationalism, and Russellism (the doctrine of the Jehovah's Witnesses). During the 1920s, communist opposition was recorded in some areas, and one evangelist (R. Lauriston) described the Durham mining villages as 'permeated with socialism and spiritism'.[56] Other problems included Highland Calvinism, as at Embo and Brora in Sutherland (combined with a superstition which alleged that there had been no fish off the pier at Embo since the evangelist had 'dipped' converts there!).[57] Elsewhere there were the challenges of liberalism, Roman Catholicism, and (in West Wales) the emotionalistic legacy of the Welsh Revival.[58] On rare occasions, opposition came from other Evangelicals, such as the Salvation Army at West Rainton, Durham, in 1923.[59] Even experienced workers might find things far from idyllic. Teresa Anderson, the wife of a Counties evangelist, had worked at the Mildmay Mission Hospital in East London, but the behaviour of the children in the village of Sandridge, near St Albans, in 1943 came as a shock to her: 'It did not seem possible that such wickedness could be, for the children did not stop at anything, it seemed, and yet I had seen and worked amongst

[54] Counties Evangelization minutes, 25 June 1917.
[55] Counties Evangelistic Work minutes, 27 May 1929; cf. an editorial note in *W* 59 (1929), 285.
[56] *H* 3 (1926), 87.
[57] *H* 3 (1926), 91; cf. 'TLWW', *BM* n.s. 25 (1924), i; *W* 54 (1924), 225.
[58] E. Lewis and A.E. Ward, *H* 5 (1928), 123.
[59] *H* 1 (1923-4), 12.

those little "East Enders," and they were supposed to be the worst of all. I would rather
have ten "East Enders" to one of the village children'.[60]

13.4 Where did the Movement Grow?

The number of Open Brethren assemblies in the British Isles grew steadily from 1,337 in
1904 to 1,775 in 1933. If the average size of an assembly was thirty members (and this
may be on the low side), then Open Brethren would have had over 53,000 members at
their peak, a figure which fits well with a late 1920s estimate that Brethren of all types
numbered 80,000 members, five-eighths being Open Brethren.[61]

Table 13.1: Total numbers of new and disappearing assemblies by decade,
1915-44[62]

	England	Scotland	Wales	Northern Ireland	Republic of Ireland[63]	Total
1915-24	180 (97)	73 (35)	23 (10)	27 (13)	10 (7)	313 (162)
1925-34	242 (174)	56 (68)	43 (10)	16 (7)	7 (13)	364 (272)
1935-44	126 (104)	26 (29)	10 (9)	12 (1)	1 (4)	175 (147)
Total	548 (375)	155 (132)	76 (29)	55 (21)	18 (24)	852 (581)

Some measure of strategic thinking was evident in the publicity given to the needs of
unreached areas (although in some cases this failed to acknowledge the existence of
Exclusive meetings). For example, in its first volume, *The Harvester* highlighted the
needs of the Scottish Highlands, North Wales, and Lincolnshire.[64] Evangelists seeking to
plant churches in such areas could count on plenty of sympathetic reporting of their work
and its needs; thus Ieuan Elias reported regularly on the work at Rhosllanerchrugog, and
John Nicholson likewise kept readers abreast of the work he was doing in Stornoway.

---

[60] Teresa L. Anderson, *A Sister's Letter to Sisters* (Surbiton: Counties Evangelistic Work, [c.1943]),
unpaginated.

[61] *Whitaker's Almanack* for 1935, in Noel, *History*, 735; apparently Whitaker used no figures later
than 1929.

[62] New assemblies include those whose commencement date is known, and those appearing in
address lists or magazine announcements for the first time; disappearing assemblies (figures in
brackets) include those known to have closed, or those appearing in address lists or announcements for
the last time. I have not included assemblies moving from or to Exclusive Brethren or other
denominations. It should be noted that these figures are inevitably skewed by the irregular intervals at
which new assembly address lists appeared; 1933 being the last for eighteen years, a higher number of
assemblies than might be expected made their final appearance in it, producing an inflated figure for
disappearing assemblies during the decade 1925-34.

[63] Strictly speaking, Ireland only became independent in 1922, and was initially known as the Irish
Free State.

[64] Anon., 'Wales and its Need', *H* 1 (1923-4), 161-2; 240, 300.

Further evidence of strategic thinking is provided by the convening of a conference in 1928 on the topic of evangelising Wales, held at Llanfairfechan, itself the location for a newly-planted and predominantly Welsh-language assembly which resulted from the commencement of 'Plas Menai'.[65]

13.4.1 Growth

Overall, analysis of assemblies founded in England and Wales during this period indicates that of the 49% for which the reasons for their commencement are known, about 40% were the result of outreach over a period of time, often several years, by individuals or assemblies. Special missions accounted for 23%, planting of an assembly with a nucleus who were members of the parent (or 'hiving off' as it was called) for 9%, as did migration of believers to new areas. Schisms, accessions from other denominations, and transfers from Exclusive Brethren each accounted for about 6%. In Northern Ireland, about a third of all new assemblies appear to have been the result of longer periods of outreach – far more than owed their origin to special missions; although these continued to be very frequent, their function appears to have been altering, from that of stimulating the commencement of new assemblies to that of adding converts to existing ones. This may reflect the fact that Brethren were now represented in most Protestant parts of the province.

The environment which saw most new assemblies was the suburbs. For many, the 1920s were a decade of material prosperity and improved living standards, and new housing estates sprang up like mushrooms outside most major cities. House-building figures increased from about 150,000 a year during the 1920s to 300,000 in 1934-8, most of these going up in the South-East.[66] Assemblies sprang up in the wake of such activity, particularly in Southern England and the Home Counties, but pockets of growth also occurred in the West Midlands, the Wirral, Lancashire, Yorkshire, Durham, Lanarkshire and the Scottish Lowlands, and Belfast. For the most part, new urban and suburban assemblies owed their inception more to the efforts of existing gatherings in the locality rather than to agencies such as Counties Evangelistic Work. When approached by the Chadwell Heath assembly in 1935 concerning the needs of the new London County Council estate at Becontree, Counties indicated that they saw their work as being primarily in the villages.[67] This, coupled with the decentralised nature of Open Brethren, meant that until the 1970s, and the explicit widening of Counties' remit to include urban work, there was no co-ordinated regional attempt – apart from Lancashire, Yorkshire, and Lowland Scotland, where assemblies co-operated in strategically-directed outreach – to present the needs of, and respond to, new housing developments and churchless city districts in the way that there had been regarding the villages.

Examples of new suburban assemblies include Aspley Hall in Nottingham, opened in 1931, which was the first place of worship to be built on a new housing estate that was intended to accommodate 10,000 people. It was the result of local assembly outreach, including a tent mission.[68] In Stoke on Trent, Swan Lane Gospel Hall originated in the mid-1930s when the assembly at Bowstead Street realised that its Sunday School was

---

[65] *W* 58 (1928), 475.

[66] Hastings, *English Christianity*, 244.

[67] Counties Evangelization oversight minutes, 22 February 1935.

[68] *H* 9 (1932), 55.

shrinking as families moved out to a new estate.[69] Likewise, in 1937 members of Fenton Hall, Leeds, commenced an outreach work in the Scott Hall area of the city to respond to the outward migration of members as well as the general population; this became an autonomous assembly in 1952.[70] Spectacular results attended the establishment of Woodcroft Hall, Burnt Oak, Middlesex (1927). This work began with five couples meeting to consider the possibilities for work on a new estate, and an assembly began with twenty believers. A Sunday School soon had 1,500 children on its books, there being few other facilities for them on an estate with a population of almost 20,000, and the estate was divided up among members for purposes of evangelistic visiting, and a couple were also set aside to spend half their time as visitors on behalf of the assembly. Outreach included such innovations as a men's club, featuring meals followed by discussion. The assembly grew rapidly, some transferring from other churches, some moving into the area, and some being converted through its outreach. One migrant, William Smith from Irvine, Ayrshire, was appointed as pastoral visitor and eventually became a full-time worker. Groups of members were sent out to plant assemblies at Kingsbury (1935) and Stanmore (1936).[71]

To aid new assemblies, Laing had some standard designs produced for halls, and provided the finance for a number of these to be erected by his company. For example, that at West Road, Bury St Edmunds, was built in 1939 when the company was constructing a new runway for the airfield at Mildenhall.[72] Gradually assemblies throughout the British Isles awakened to the need of adequate and attractive premises; an article by Laing in *The Harvester*, 'Hovels or Halls', pleaded for this and criticised the use of the term 'Gospel Hall' as a hindrance to outsiders.[73] The author advocated building a chain of halls about two miles apart in a large town (anticipating the adoption of such a policy from the 1970s by the Ichthus Fellowship in South-East London), regarding the best size for an assembly as between 100 and 200. He also expressed a preference for owning (the property being vested in a trust) rather than renting, on the grounds that this enabled a more suitable building to be acquired, and that when it was paid for, more funds would be available for evangelistic work. The long-term perspective evident here contrasts strikingly with early belief in the imminence of the Second Advent; Brethren had clearly decided that they were here to stay – for a while, at least.

Remarkable growth occurred in South Wales during this period, a phenomenon also evident in the Pentecostal denominations. From forty-one assemblies in 1904, Brethren in the principality grew to ninety-nine in 1933, almost all in the southern counties of Carmarthen, Glamorgan, and Monmouth. Intensive missions and long-term gospel work both played vital parts, and some assemblies proved particularly effective in such work. For example, Mackintosh Hall in Cardiff gave birth to assemblies at Heath (1920), Tavistock St (1922), Roath (1924), Taffs Well (1928; itself the parent of an assembly at Nantgarw as early as 1932), and Rhiwbina (1930), as well as supporting other outreach

---

[69] *Trent Vale Times* 10 (October 1986), 5 (CBA Box 36).

[70] <www.scotthall.org.uk/Newpages/personal/aboutpersonal/infopersonal/pastpersonal.htm>, accessed 3 April 2005.

[71] Coad, *Laing*, 117-20; *H* 10 (1933), 44; 26 (1949), 9.

[72] Stuart and Megan Walker, *The Origins and History of West Road Church, Bury St. Edmunds, from 1847 to the present day* ([Bury St Edmunds: the authors, 2003]), unpaginated.

[73] *H* 14 (1937), 56-7.

works, its own membership peaking at about 350 in 1923.[74] Yet even within this area, wide variations were evident between individual assemblies, as one observer noticed in 1929:

> Amongst the Assemblies in South Wales progress varies considerably. Some with a keen interest in the spread of the Gospel, and who are not afraid of spending money on special campaigns yearly, continue to grow, but amongst others there is a tendency to mark time, to magnify the present distress, to complain of the difficulty of getting people in to the meetings, and with some, perhaps, to be more ready to strive for shibboleths than for souls.[75]

Surveying the wider scene, some full-time workers in the 1920s perceived a lack of real interest in gospel work:

> in general, the assemblies are not alive to their responsibility in this direction, as shown by the small number of new workers entering the home field, and the lack of assembly contributions towards the support of labourers at home ... The great spiritual revival which many thought would certainly follow the war, appears as far off as ever.[76]

In the view of some such writers, the seeds of decline were already present in the movement; some might say that its subsequent history has proved their pessimism correct.

13.4.2 Decline

As early as 1916, *The Witness* had run a series of articles on 'Decaying Gatherings'. These generated a considerable volume of correspondence, which offered a wide range of diagnoses of the reasons for decline.[77] Nothing conclusive resulted from airing the issues, but it is clear that Brethren were increasingly concerned about the possibility that the decline which they had thought would be the experience of the 'sects' might also be their experience before too long.

Following the end of the union of Britain and Ireland in 1922, Brethren in the Irish Free State were set for decline. Nationalist unrest had relatively little direct effect on the assemblies, although during the Easter Rising of 1916, Grosvenor Hall, Dublin, reported that it had suspended all meetings except a daily prayer meeting,[78] and other assemblies in troubled areas may also have been similarly affected. Merrion Hall, which in 1920 had Dublin's largest Protestant congregation, was briefly occupied by the military in 1922.[79] More significant was the indirect effect, as Protestant businessmen from England and Scotland returned home.[80] For example, the assembly at Ballina, in the North-West, had

---

[74] Anon., *Mackintosh Evangelical Church. 100 Years of Worship and Witness* (n.pl.: n.p., [1997]); Don Roberts, 'A History of the Cardiff Assemblies' (typescript, 1992, private collection).

[75] Edwin Willie, *H* 6 (1929), 21.

[76] H.W.E[vans]., 'Editorial', *H* 4 (1927), 34-5; cf. W[illia]m Rouse, 'Home Workers' Bible School and Conference at Llanfairfechan', *H* 3 (1926), 104-5.

[77] For the correspondence, see *W* 46 (1916), 94-5, 106-7, 117-20.

[78] Anon., 'Notes on the Rebellion in Ireland', *BM* n.s. 17 (1916), 72.

[79] *GG*, March 1921, 50; *W* 52 (1922), 230.

[80] Henry Pickering, letter in *W* 59 (1929), 58; Stunt et al., *Turning the World Upside Down*, 339.

been attended by many landed gentry, most of whom left for England by the early 1920s.[81] Some assemblies had been founded and led by, and were largely composed of, such folk, and these leaderless and often isolated gatherings would have been the first to fade from the scene. There had been a decline in the number of assemblies from forty-four in 1904 to twenty-seven in 1951. The Roman Catholic Church rapidly asserted its position as the religion of the vast majority of people, and in some areas priests and their congregations could make life extremely difficult for Protestants of all shades, and public evangelism potentially dangerous.

Even in Scotland, growth levelled off in the 1930s, a peak of 379 assemblies being attained in 1933. More significant than the rate at which assemblies were closing was a marked decline in the rate at which new ones were appearing, from seventy-two in the decade 1915-24 to twenty-five from 1935-44 (1945-54 saw this decline further, indicating that the war was not the major factor). Furthermore, of those which did appear during the period, some were mission halls and other undenominational bodies which became recognised as assemblies, rather than new plants. Emigration caused some concern, especially in the industrial and mining areas of Ayrshire and Lanarkshire. Dickson estimates that at least 10% of the membership of Scottish assemblies may have emigrated during the period from 1860-1967.[82] The large assembly at Larkhall (Lanarkshire), which had hitherto experienced consistent growth, saw its membership decline as families moved elsewhere in Britain or emigrated in search of work.[83] A similar pattern was evident at Roman Road, Motherwell.[84] To help such folk, the Christian Emigration Service was 'begun at the suggestion of missionaries, and with the approval of elder brethren meeting at Westminster, to encourage young men and women to seek *situations* in distant lands and assist in mission work'.[85]

Throughout the British Isles, rural assemblies were beginning to find the going hard. I suspect that fewer assemblies were being founded in rural areas, in spite of the concern of Counties Evangelization and its sister bodies to reach the villages. Those assemblies which existed already were growing older, younger members not infrequently found themselves having to move in search of employment, and the needs of the countryside were often overlooked in the euphoria which greeted the movement's success in establishing itself in suburbia. Such trends, which had appeared in most other denominations during the late nineteenth century, were telescoped in Brethren circles as rural decline and suburban growth coincided to a greater extent. Occasionally, an assembly would close because of the death of the last remaining brother, who might well have soldiered on alone for years (an assembly could not continue to break bread if all its members were sisters, because of the prohibition on women's public ministry).

Inner-city assemblies, too, would have been affected by the beginning of slum clearance programmes, which resulted in large-scale migration to new housing estates. Assemblies may have been weakened to the point where the need to vacate premises would result not in a move but in closure. In London, for example, during this period meetings closed at Recreation Hall, Manor Park (1932); South Grove Hall, Peckham (1933); Carton

---

[81] Cecil Wilson, 'My Father: John A. Wilson (1888-1969)', *BM* 88 (1978), 258-9.

[82] Dickson, *Brethren in Scotland*, 307.

[83] Chapman, *Larkhall*, 77.

[84] Anon., *Roman Road Hall, Motherwell: Centenary 1875-1975* ([Lanark]: n.p., n.d.), 14.

[85] Anon., 'Christian Emigration Service', *LOH* 16 (1927-8), 273; *W* 57 (February 1927), endpapers.

Hall, Baker Street; Sussex Hall, Brixton; and Fleet Street (all 1936); East Ham (1937); The Cut, Lambeth (1938); Archel Road, Kensington; and King's Highway, Plumstead (1939; a pity, given the evocative location!); and Carfax Hall, Clapham (1940). Furthermore, a *laissez-faire* approach meant that work might decay in inner cities for want of concerted effort to maintain it.

Clearly, the upbeat air of the 1920s was giving way to a more sober, and on occasion apprehensive, estimate of the assemblies' spiritual health and future prospects. In this, Brethren doubtless shared in the wider change of outlook, which was affected by the gathering political storm-clouds. This change was to interact with the continuing concern to define themselves over against other similar movements, which we shall examine in the following chapter. In addition, a key factor, although one whose extent is difficult to quantify, may have been the loss of expectancy among workers; Pickering claimed in 1934 that whereas four decades previously a Sunday without signs of spiritual interest in response to gospel work would cause disappointment in many assemblies, it was now being seen as the norm.[86] Many, it seems, were concluding that they had entered 'the day of small things'.

---

[86] H[enr]y P[ickering]., 'Do We Look for Conversions?', *W* 64 (1934), 134.

CHAPTER 14

'Whither are we Drifting?':
Changes in the Brethren Ethos

Two threads run through the story of Brethren identity during this period, of confidence and (paradoxically) loss of confidence. On the one hand, Brethren evangelism appeared to be highly successful in many areas, and the movement looked set to attract many from denominations affected by liberal theology; on the other hand, there was an underlying sense of unease, sometimes expressed in terms of opposition to new developments. As with much non-Brethren Evangelicalism, there was an eschatologically-inspired sense of apprehension at what the future might hold, both for the movement itself and for Christianity (and the world) in general. The much talked-of 'Open Brethren identity crisis', which hit the movement from the 1960s onwards, has many of its roots in the inter-war period: Open Brethren found themselves trying to clarify their relationship with Exclusive Brethren on the one hand, and non-Brethren Evangelicals on the other.

14.1 Open and Exclusive

According to Henry Pickering, 'In faith and practice they differ so little that it is no uncommon thing for believers to transfer from one to the other with little demur'; at least a dozen well-taught former Exclusive teachers, he claimed, now ministered among Open Brethren.[1] This was a somewhat disingenuous remark, given that Pickering & Inglis were one of the publishers engaged in a pamphlet war during the 1920s and early 1930s, with Open and Exclusive writers pointing out the defects in each other's position and arguments. It is a curious fact that, as far as I have been able to ascertain, almost none of them discuss the attempts at *rapprochement* which took place in 1906-7.

The main charges made by Exclusive writers continued to be those of independency and of neutrality regarding false doctrine. A number of Exclusive writers were responding to Rendle Short's *Principles of Open Brethren*, and were concerned that fellow-Exclusives were adopting Open principles, and in particular a belief in the independence of each local assembly. Some were; and some meetings went over to the Open side.[2] The crux decisions were to invite Open Brethren as preachers, and to open the Lord's Table to all sound and

---

[1] 'WW', *W* 55 (1925), 54.

[2] Examples during this period include:

Glanton: Water Street, Stafford (by 1917); Shottery, Warwickshire (early 1920s); Etloe Hall (1927) and Milton Park Hall, Bristol (1932); Etnam Street, Leominster (c.1930); Pitlochry (mid-1930s); Sligo (c.1938).

Kelly: Fitzwilliam Street, Sheffield (by 1918).

Lowe: Cemetery Road, Sheffield (early 1920s); Horsham (c.1923); Warnham, Sussex (c.1925).

Stuart: Fort William (1919-22); Gospel Hall, Carluke (by 1927).

A number of other assemblies appearing during this period used the same premises as earlier Exclusive meetings had used, but I have not been able to confirm continuity.

godly believers.[3] The assembly at Church Lane, Stafford (which had begun associating with Open Brethren somewhat earlier), reacted against its Exclusive origins with a vengeance; two members were licensed by the diocesan bishop to conduct Anglican services, and several were on the local Methodist plan.[4] Doubtless similar activity went on elsewhere, especially in rural areas.

Concern to define themselves over against Exclusive Brethren is also evident in some of the Open Brethren histories which appeared during the 1930s. That by the Scottish solicitor T.S. Veitch, *The Story of the Brethren Movement* (1933), argued that the divisions which had shattered Exclusivism had all resulted from insistence upon uniformity of doctrine and practice, the benchmark being Darby's meeting at Park Street in London. In the preface, George Goodman commended the work as seeking 'to tell the truth, that those who desire information and help in the confusion of Exclusivism may find it and act before the Lord'.[5] As in David Beattie's *Brethren: the story of a great recovery*, an underlying concept was that of the autonomy of assemblies, each directly responsible to God and led by his Spirit. Beattie's work first appeared as a lengthy series of articles in *The Believer's Magazine* from 1934-8, which the editor, William Hoste, hoped would recall Brethren to first principles.[6] Beattie contacted assemblies throughout the British Isles for information, and his work demonstrated what he regarded as the spontaneous and divinely-instigated emergence of like-minded gatherings all over the country, again, perhaps, intended as a contrast with the centralisation and division which Open writers considered the hallmarks of Exclusive history. Interestingly, little notice was taken by either writer of the reunion of Kelly and Lowe gatherings in 1926, which they ought on their principles to have welcomed. By contrast, Napoleon Noel's two-volume *History of the Brethren* (1936) portrayed Open Brethren as the ones who were hopelessly divided as a result of their attachment to the principle of independency.

Open Brethren also went into print in response to developments among Taylor Brethren from 1929, when James Taylor denied the eternal Sonship of Christ in meetings at Barnet.[7] His teaching drew on that of his predecessor, and had been maturing in his mind for twenty-five years. Put at its simplest, Taylor affirmed the eternal deity of Christ, but asserted that he did not become the Son of God until the Incarnation. Open Brethren had already expressed their belief that Christ was eternally the Son as well as eternally God,[8] and a number of articles appeared condemning Taylor's teaching, the most detailed probably being a series by Hoste in *The Believer's Magazine* during 1932, also published separately as *Divine Relations before the Incarnation* (c.1932). Works by moderate Exclusives critical of Taylor's teaching were also reviewed positively by Open Brethren,

---

[3] Cf. Linton and Linton, '*I Will Build my Church*', 69 (with reference to Etloe Hall).

[4] Venables, *Meeting Room, Stafford*, 15.

[5] Veitch, *Story*, iv.

[6] *BM* n.s. 34 (1933), 283. The appearance of these two works in the same decade is intriguing; was it merely a case of competition between the two leading publishers, or was Beattie intended as a more conservative portrayal of Brethren history than Veitch?

[7] E.g. correspondence in *BM* n.s. 33 (1932), 118, 185, 207; H[enr]y P[ickering]., 'The Denial of the Eternal Sonship of Christ', *W* 62 (1932), 253 (which associated Taylor's view with those of Unitarians and Modernists); W.E. Vine, 'The Eternal Sonship of Christ: In view of Present Denials', *W* 62 (1932), 217-18.

[8] E.g. W. Hoste, 'The Eternal Sonship', *H* 1 (1923-4), 3.

such as W.J. Hocking's *The Son of His Love* (1934).[9] Open Brethren continued to be appreciative of the writings of many other Exclusives; thus the Taylor brother George Cutting, whose evangelistic booklet *Safety, Certainty and Enjoyment* had run to eight million copies by 1932, was described in *The Witness* as 'beloved by all for his works' sake'.[10]

The literary ferment reflects the fact that a number of accessions from Exclusive ranks took place during this period, of individuals as well as assemblies. For example, Harold Barker (1869-1952) had been provoked by the Glanton division to review what had happened at Bethesda. If that had been of the flesh, might the same also be true of previous divisions? In the light of intra-Exclusive controversies, he began to wonder whether there was really any ground for their charges against Open Brethren. Around 1916 he joined Open Brethren, although it appears that he later returned to the Glanton meetings, possibly because of the lack of true 'worship' in Open circles.[11]

However, such accessions were not without their problems; Russell Elliott continued, as did some others, to advocate the practice of household baptism, and articles against it appeared in *The Believer's Magazine* and *The Witness*.[12] Generally it was deemed unacceptable to advocate the practice in ministry, but belief in it did not constitute a bar to fellowship. Former Exclusives undoubtedly influenced Open Brethren in a variety of ways; some reacted against aspects of Exclusivism, such as the perceived tendency to centralisation, while others sought to spread aspects of Exclusive teaching among Open assemblies. As a result, some Open Brethren were decidedly cautious in the welcome they gave to these defectors.

14.2 The Influence of Trends in Evangelicalism

Evangelicals were at their weakest during the 1920s. Feeling threatened by Anglo-Catholicism (then the dominant Anglican school), the social gospel, liberal Evangelicalism (which sought to retain what it saw as the basic Evangelical emphases while accepting many of the results of modern critical study of the Bible), and the opposition of denominational hierarchies, many Evangelicals adopted a somewhat introverted posture.[13] It became easier for them to join together in conventions and para-church agencies, while lamenting the state of the religious world outside. This was usually interpreted in eschatological terms, as prefiguring, and probably paving the way for, the final apostasy. Adventism, the belief that the return of Christ was imminent, gained considerable ground in Evangelical circles. The return of the Jews to Palestine in 1917 gave a tremendous and unlooked-for fillip to the newly-formed Advent Testimony and

---

[9] *BM* n.s. 36 (1935), 215-16.

[10] *W* 62 (1932), 188.

[11] See Eric H. Barker, 'My Father: Harold P. Barker (1869-1952)', *BM* n.s. 88 (1978), 2-3; Harold P. Barker, *Why I Abandoned Exclusivism* (London: Pickering & Inglis, n.d.); 'Touchstone', 'Harold Primrose Barker', *W* 98 (1968), 186-8.

[12] E.g. W. Hoste, 'Household Baptism', *W* 51 (1921), 117-19; [Henry Pickering], 'Household Baptism', *W* 52 (1922), 178-9.

[13] See Hastings, *English Christianity*, 200-01; Martin Wellings, *Evangelicals Embattled: Responses of Evangelicals in the Church of England to Ritualism, Darwinism and Theological Liberalism, 1890-1930* (Carlisle: Paternoster, 2003).

Preparation Movement, in which Open and moderate Exclusive Brethren (such as John Weston and A.H. Burton) were active.

Another feature of Evangelicalism was the rise of the Fundamentalist movement, whose influence in Britain was at its greatest during the 1920s. It might have been expected to attract considerable support from Brethren, given its robust proclamation of such doctrines as the deity of Christ, the substitutionary nature of the atonement, the necessity of the new birth, and the premillennial Second Coming. However, reactions were mixed. Some welcomed the movement's stand for truth, but others insisted that all truth was vital, not just certain truths denominated 'fundamental'; Ritchie suggested that fundamental truths tended to be those most closely associated with the message of salvation.[14] Another response was to portray Brethren as the true Fundamentalists.[15]

Although Brethren did not often associate with any Fundamentalist para-church movements, they shared many Fundamentalist concerns, as well as the Fundamentalist mentality, which was marked by increasing separatism in the face of perceived threats from theological liberalism. Magazines noted many of the more notorious utterances of modernist churchmen.[16] *The Witness* also carried several series of weighty articles on fundamental truths, such as Christology (1922), 'The Gospel We Preach' (1935), and a pair of compilations by Pickering in 1925 of quotations from liberal theologians and Scripture references for fundamental doctrines.[17] The growth of modernism and ritualism appears to have led him to a more positive attitude towards other Evangelicals, who were seen as fellow-swimmers against the tide of apostasy. In *The Witness*, he often praised such men (although he also wondered how they could remain in their theologically-mixed denominations), and he began to publish more of their writings. By 1928, he was advertising books and booklets on the fundamentals, and in the 1930s there was a noticeable broadening in the range of authors published by him. Writers appearing on the lists of Pickering & Inglis included American Fundamentalists such as W.B. Riley and A.C. Gaebelein, W. Graham Scroggie and G. Campbell Morgan (he had a Brethren background), as well as H.C.G. Moule and H.P. Liddon (who was not even an Evangelical, but whose Bampton Lectures on *The Divinity of our Lord and Saviour Jesus Christ,* reissued in 1924 as edited by George Goodman, provided a timely defence of traditional Christological teaching in the face of challenges to it within and beyond Open Brethren). Conversely, some of them on occasion wrote to, or even for, *The Witness*, such as the Canadian Anglican W.H. Griffith Thomas. Pickering also included articles made up of extracts from the writings of faithful men, often nineteenth-century churchmen such as Lightfoot, Moule, Ryle, and Westcott, as well as Nonconformists such as Maclaren and Spurgeon. In a series of 'Ministry by Mighty Men of God', which ran from 1932-5, no less than half the writers were non-Brethren.

[14] [John Ritchie], 'What are "The Fundamentals"?', *BM* n.s. 26 (1925), 39.

[15] [Henry Pickering?], 'Who Are "The Fundamentalists?"', *W* 53 (1923), 129; [*idem*?], 'Who are the True Fundamentalists [sic]', *W* 54 (1924), 404.

[16] E.g. H[enr]y P[ickering]., 'How Should we Act Towards Evolutionists and Modernists', *W* 58 (1928), 331-2; A.W. Philips, 'Doctrine in the Church of England: a disquieting Document', *BM* n.s. 39 (1938), 69-71.

[17] H[enr]y P[ickering]., 'Modernism or The Old Faith. What is Meant? Which Shall We Choose?', *W* 55 (1925), 181-3; [*idem*], 'What is Meant by The Old Faith. Modernism and the Old Faith. Part II', *W* 55 (1925), 201-4.

An increasing number of apologetic works were also published. Two examples in particular stand out: Rendle Short's writings and Pickering's *The Believer's Blue Book* (c.1929). Short issued several apologetic works arising from his concern for students: *The Historic Faith in the Light of Today* (1922; with Bertram Colgrave), part of which was incorporated in *The Bible and Modern Research* (1931), *Why Believe?* (1939), and *Modern Discovery and the Bible* (1942); most were published by the Inter-Varsity Fellowship (IVF). Just as the Blue Book was intended as a reliable record of parliamentary proceedings, Pickering's work, which first appeared as a series of articles in *The Witness* from 1922-6, was intended to provide a reliable statement of Open Brethren beliefs; it discussed the inspiration of Scripture, the deity of Christ, the Resurrection, whether a Christian can fall away and be lost, which is the true church, baptism and the Breaking of Bread, and the Second Coming.

Modernism and changes in the liturgy (a revised Prayer Book was controversially rejected by the House of Commons in 1928) made Brethren feel that it was worth reaching out to believers in the sects, who, it was thought, were hungry for sound teaching.[18] A former Anglican clergyman, E.P. Luce, held a number of meetings during the late 1920s, explaining why he had seceded (in 1922).[19] Assemblies in cities such as Bristol, Exeter, London, Rochester, and Norwich took large public halls for series of meetings dealing with basic truths, aimed at non-Brethren believers; even the village of Woolpit, Suffolk, saw largely-attended meetings at the Brethren Room on such topics.[20] Underlying such activity was the belief, shared with Fundamentalists, that the outlook for denominational Christianity was dire, and that in the face of imminent judgement believers in mixed denominations should withdraw from them. Hoste and Vine edited a symposium, *Light for Dark Days* (1928), expounding New Testament church principles and calling on believers to leave mixed denominations. Assemblies, it was hoped, would prove a haven for many such. A report of a mission at Seven Kings, near Ilford, in 1914 had recorded 'A number converted, 25 baptised, and some led out of Babylon'.[21] Sadly, hopes that others would follow the same path were to remain largely unfulfilled, a fact which helped to provoke a loss of confidence after World War II.

Another feature of contemporary Evangelicalism was the proliferation of interdenominational conventions for the deepening of spiritual life. Initially, Brethren criticised the unity displayed at Keswick on the ground that attenders were united for a week but remained in their separate sects for the rest of the year;[22] compromise in the realm of church order would have been seen as reflecting compromise in matters of spiritual experience. During the early 1920s some concern was also voiced that some speakers were drifting from the Fundamentals; there was controversy over some utterances

---

[18] F. Glover, 'The Menace of Modernism', *H* 2 (1925), 186; A. Rendle Short, 'Back to the Faith', *LOH* 10 (1921), 51.

[19] E.P. Luce, 'Why I Left the Church' (typescript, [1927], personal collection); cf. a report of his meetings at Chatham in *H* 4 (1927), 54. Luce contrasted one-man ministry (often by unconverted men) with the freedom of the Spirit to gift whomever he chose; he rejected denominationalism, fundraising for support of clergy and missionaries, and the way that baptism and the Lord's Supper were observed.

[20] H[enr]y P[ickering]., 'Standing for the Fundamentals', *W* 58 (1928), 311-12; Short, 'Back to the Faith', 51.

[21] 'WML', *W* 44 (November 1914), 49.

[22] 'WW', *W* 56 (1926), 394.

at the convention, and the basis of the convention was narrowed as a result.[23] However, as early as 1920 *The Gospel Graphic* (an illustrated monthly taken over by Pickering the previous year) was carrying positive articles on Keswick.[24] Pickering & Inglis soon took a bookstall there, and in 1929 they took over publication of the annual report containing the messages given.[25] In 1936, Pickering reported that the former solicitor and itinerant preacher George Goodman 'has been favoured with an invitation to give the Special Bible Addresses to the 5000 intelligent Christians who will (D.V.) assemble at Keswick'.[26] The change of tone is significant as an indicator of changed attitudes in many quarters towards non-Brethren Evangelicalism and to co-operation with it. That year, the local assembly's Breaking of Bread service during Keswick week attracted over 600 visitors (one wonders how they coped), and even if many of them belonged to denominational churches, it does indicate that Brethren were a significant presence at such conventions.[27]

Some continued to critique the Keswick movement's theological distinctives, however; Andrew Borland (1895-1979), whose theological acumen was equalled by few if any Brethren during this period, devoted an editorial in *The Believer's Magazine* to this topic in 1939.[28] Keswick was commended for its exposure of sin and its promise of victory, but Borland considered that its teaching concerning reckoning oneself dead to sin and alive in Christ was already taught in assemblies, minus the unhelpful emotionalism and undue emphasis on experience. Similarly, Hoste asserted that God blessed the convention because generally God's Word was preached faithfully and Christ was set forth as the believer's all-sufficient resource, but questioned the practice of silence regarding disputed issues and the concept of a post-conversion reception of the Spirit by faith through an act of absolute surrender.[29] In spite of the advocacy from the 1920s of some form of Keswick teaching concerning sanctification by George Goodman[30] and the itinerant preacher Reginald Wallis (1891-1940),[31] there was a growing sympathy for a more traditional Reformed approach. *The Witness* ran a warm review of *Christ our Freedom*, a new IVF publication, singling out for praise Martyn Lloyd-Jones's address on 'Christ our Sanctification'.[32] Doubtless it was the Scots who were most in sympathy with

---

[23] E.g. Bebbington, *Evangelicalism*, 219-20; 'WW', *W* 50 (October 1920), 326.

[24] J.S[tephen]., 'All One in Christ Jesus', *GG*, July 1920, 138.

[25] *W* 59 (1929), 162.

[26] *W* 76 (1936), 139. Other Brethren speakers during this period included Northcote Deck, Reginald Wallis, and Montague Goodman (cf. the back-cover advertisement featuring their writings in *W* 66 (July 1936)). Dan Crawford spoke as early as 1912 (Charles Price and Ian Randall, *Transforming Keswick* (Carlisle: OM, 2000), 118).

[27] *CG*, September 1936, 205.

[28] 'Editorial', *BM* n.s. 40 (1939), 203. On Borland, see James Anderson, *They Finished their Course* (Kilmarnock: John Ritchie, 1980), 31-5; The Editors [James Anderson et al.], 'An Appreciation: the late Andrew Borland 1895-1979', *BM* 89 (1979), 211-12.

[29] 'BQB', *BM* n.s. 33 (1932), 143-4.

[30] See, for example, his articles '"Full Surrender"', *W* 53 (1923), 117-19, 139-40, 159-60, which sought to analyse the Keswick experience and explain its somewhat misleading terminology for the benefit of young believers; he considered that for some it was the moment of their conversion.

[31] As in his book *The New Man* (London: Pickering & Inglis, [c.1932]).

[32] *W* 70 (1940), 148. However, when Lloyd-Jones's sermon was reissued as a separate booklet, a reviewer criticised it for failing to recognise that in the New Testament the term refers to the believer's

Reformed views, but even Goodman was fond of quoting the seventeenth-century Puritan theologian John Owen, who wrote extensively on sanctification.[33] Several leading Brethren greeted with enthusiasm the works of the Swiss theologian Karl Barth (1886-1968). Books by him were advertised on the back cover of *The Harvester* in February 1935, and Rendle Short commended Barth's *Credo*, noting that the author had been exiled from Nazi Germany for his views: 'It is years since a book of theology has interested me so much.'[34] A factor in this interest was doubtless Barth's support for the 'Confessing Church', which resisted Hitler's attempt to force the churches into propagating his ideas of Aryan supremacy; Pickering urged prayer for its pastors in their stand for Christian faith,[35] and the periodicals generally displayed keen interest in developments in German church life.

Some feared that encouraging young believers to recognise the true unity of all believers would result in their defecting to the denominations, a tacit admission that there was little to keep them attached to the assemblies. E.H. Trenchard (1902-72), a missionary in Spain, demolished such an argument:

> Are our principles so weak and the teaching of them in the churches so deficient that we cannot trust our young people to listen to ministry outside the "Gospel Hall" without the fear that they will be enticed into system? Something must be wrong here! I am convinced that our principles of an out-gathering in simplicity to the Person of the Lord are clear, logical and scriptural, and when clearly taught to our young people will be enthusiastically held by all with spiritual discernment. The trembling among elders arises from the fact that there is very little consistent teaching in the simple local churches, and a grasp of the "principles" is especially lacking among those who have grown up "in the circle."

> I am convinced if the great truths of the One Body, the dangers of organised Christianity, the Remembrance of the Lord, the liberty of the Spirit, Believer's Baptism, etc., were clearly and systematically taught by capable teachers in the Assemblies, especially to the young generation, we could safely practice the truth of the One Body; (not only talk about it) with the assurance that the number of believers gathering in simplicity would grow and multiply.[36]

All the same, the separatists may have had a point. Reporting the settlement of a former member of the Brethren in a Baptist pastorate, Pickering recorded: 'Assemblies have been used as the training ground, for quite a few who have afterwards assayed to clerical positions in different denominations.'[37]

A movement which was initially linked closely with Keswick, but which gradually diverged from it, was the 'Oxford Group Movement' (initially known as the 'First-Century Christian Fellowship' and in 1939 renamed 'Moral Re-Armament'). This was led by an

---

position as one who is in relationship with God, and is never described as a process (*BM* n.s. 49 (1948), 113).

[33] George Goodman, 'When and How Christ was "Made Sin"', *W* 62 (1932), 9-10; cf. *W* 66 (1936), 6.

[34] *H* 14 (1937), 61-2; for the wider Evangelical interest in Barth's theology during the 1930s and 1940s, cf. Randall and Hilborn, *One Body in Christ*, 212-16.

[35] 'WW', *W* 65 (1935), 113.

[36] E.H. Trenchard, 'Separation – True and False', *H* 9 (1932), 202. On Trenchard, see *BDCM*.

[37] 'Personalia', *W* 58 (1928), 258.

American Lutheran minister, Frank Buchman, and stressed what it called the 'four absolutes': absolute honesty, purity, unselfishness, and love.[38] A few Brethren students at Liverpool University during the mid-1930s were attracted by it as more exciting than assembly life.[39] In response to numerous inquiries, a judicious two-part article on the movement by Rendle Short appeared in *Links of Help* during 1933.[40] He acknowledged that in some ways 'its methods and principles are much more familiar to us than to the churches at large'.[41] Many praiseworthy features were evident: zeal, confidence in God, insistence on repentance of all known sin and on restitution, and the use of informal groups meeting in neutral venues. However, frequently little was said regarding the saving work of Christ, and the message of moral reform was insufficient to save; furthermore, he disapproved of the movement's practices of detailed public confession of sins and of waiting for inward 'guidance', the latter bypassing the study of the Scriptures. In response to a question submitted to *The Believer's Magazine*, Hoste argued that the crucial test of any movement was the place which it gave to the person and work of Christ; the Oxford Group's failed the test, for their teaching majored on the Sermon on the Mount rather than the message of the cross; in addition, they had no doctrinal tests for prospective members, and their explanation of how the Holy Spirit guided believers had more in common with the notion of a 'familiar spirit' than with the Christian belief that the Spirit spoke through Scripture.[42] The cerebral cast of Brethren spirituality was thus reinforced by their reaction against Buchman's teaching, setting the scene for their treatment of the Charismatic Movement.

The faith-healing movement, whose Anglican leader J.M. Hickson came to prominence from 1925, was viewed unsympathetically, partly because of Hickson's erroneous beliefs concerning universalism, prayer for the dead, communion with them and the mortality and sinfulness of Christ's human nature.[43] H.P. Barker wrote a series of critical articles on 'Divine Healing Scripturally Examined' for *The Witness* in 1923; he insisted that Christ healed all (not some) who came to him, and alleged that the movement worked by some kind of auto-suggestion; claims made for healing campaigns were mostly lies. Brethren were also critical of Pentecostal healing missions, such as those conducted by the Jeffreys brothers: criticism focused on the disorder and loss of control inherent in Pentecostal phenomena, and the fact that many went away unhealed, a contrast with what happened during Christ's earthly ministry and pastorally devastating to those concerned.[44] Repeated calls were made for verification of claimed healings. However, as Pentecostalism matured, Brethren criticism moderated; alongside continued criticism of claims that miraculous healings were occurring, it came to be recognised that here was another movement standing firmly for fundamental truths, and there was appreciation of an increased emphasis on seeing lives changed by the gospel.[45]

---

[38] See Barclay, *Evangelicalism in Britain*, 35-6; Bebbington, *Evangelicalism*, 235-40.

[39] Leith Samuel, *A Man Under Authority: The Autobiography of Leith Samuel* (Fearn, Ross-shire: Christian Focus, 1993), 29.

[40] A. Rendle Short, 'The Oxford Group Movement', *LOH* 21 (1933), 2-4, 19-21.

[41] Short, 'Oxford Group Movement', 4.

[42] 'BQB', *BM* n.s. 35 (1934), 163.

[43] 'WW', *W* 54 (1924), 424.

[44] See, for example, G. Goodman, 'I write unto you young men', *H* 5 (1928), 146; William Rouse, 'Healing Campaigns compared with Scripture', *H* 5 (1928), 159-60.

[45] E.g. 'WW', *W* 62 (1932), 112.

14.3 Involvement in Interdenominational Agencies

A number of interdenominational agencies benefited from Brethren involvement, even if those involved were the targets of occasional criticism from their assembly colleagues. The Scripture Union (SU) and the Children's Special Service Mission (CSSM) owed a lot to two Brethren solicitors from Clapton Hall, London, George Goodman (1866-1942)[46] and his brother Montague (1875-1958).[47] George gave up his profession to become a full-time worker in 1919. He had served as a CSSM evangelist, had helped to found the Caravan Mission to Village Children in 1893, and later wrote Bible reading notes for SU for twelve years. Although happy to engage in such interdenominational work, he also issued an important exposition of Open Brethren practice, *God's Principles of Gathering* (1922), because of his concern at the lack of teaching on 'church truth' in assemblies. Although he would later speak at Keswick, during the early 1920s he was evidently wary of Brethren returning to minister in the sects, believing that Brethren truth would do little good mixed with sectarian error.[48] Montague was a council member of CSSM (and also of the Scripture Gift Mission), and authored a number of books for boys (the *Wantoknow* series).

George Goodman   Montague Goodman

Another member of the Brethren to play an important part in the movement was John Laird (1905-88), who hailed from the assembly at Kilmacolm, near Glasgow. Laird would become the General Secretary in 1956 after long service with SU in Britain and in New Zealand, and did much to reorganise it. He combined a lifelong attachment to Brethren with a certain distance from some of its narrower attitudes; as a teenager, visiting York Minster with his architect father, his verdict was, 'Aren't you glad, Dad, that it wasn't Gospel Halls all down through the ages?'[49]

The IVF emerged after World War I, and owed much to Brethren who were, or had been, associated with Bristol assemblies. Rendle Short was heavily involved, providing

---

[46] On George, see Percy O. Ruoff, *The Spiritual Legacy of George Goodman* (London: Pickering & Inglis, 1949); *W* 72 (1942), 91.

[47] On Montague, see *H* (1958), 186; *W* 88 (1958), 245.

[48] G. Goodman, 'Seven Lamps for the Preacher. IV. – The Lamp of Purity', *H* 1 (1923-4), 340.

[49] John M. Laird, *No Mere Chance* (London: Hodder & Stoughton and Scripture Union, 1981), 17.

financial support and helping to establish the idea of a network of Christian Unions.[50] Interestingly, the Bible readings at the IVF's first inter-university conference in 1919 were given by Lang.[51] W. Melville Capper (1908-71), a Bristol obstetrician and gynaecologist, was an enthusiastic supporter of the work of IVF, and helped to found the Christian Medical Fellowship in 1947.[52] Most of the early Scottish leaders were from a Brethren background,[53] and the first women's travelling secretary was Jean Strain, from an assembly in Wimbledon (she went on to marry another IVF worker by the name of Donald Coggan, and eventually to move a long way from her Brethren roots as her husband became Bishop of Bradford and then Archbishop of Canterbury).[54] By the late 1930s, the Christian Union at Cambridge was made up largely of Anglicans and Brethren – an interesting sidelight on the social composition of assemblies during this period.[55]

From Brethren circles, F.F. Bruce (1910-90) and W.J. Martin (1904-1980) were extensively involved in the setting up in 1943 of the Tyndale Fellowship for Biblical and Theological Research, a body intended to promote academic research in the universities by Evangelical theologians (which they saw as an alternative to the idea of an interdenominational college). Their Brethren background may have been a factor in their arguing that the new body should major on biblical, rather than theological, research.[56] Martin, a lecturer in Hebrew and Semitic Languages at Liverpool, also had the vision for the establishment of a residential library, which became Tyndale House in Cambridge (dedicated in 1945).[57] Once again, it was Laing's financial support which enabled the new group to get off the ground.[58]

In spite of the lack of support from Bruce and Martin for the idea of an Evangelical and interdenominational college, London Bible College (LBC) opened its doors in 1943.[59] Montague Goodman and John Laing had been part of an exploratory group investigating the feasibility of such a venture since 1939; Goodman became its first president and chairman of governors, and Laing offered the college a site in Marylebone Road. However, the opinion was voiced in *The Witness* that Evangelical colleges were unlikely to teach assembly distinctives and that it was up to assemblies to take action,[60] a viewpoint which played a part in the post-war creation of an Open Brethren college at Matlock in Derbyshire.

Another agency which did a valuable work, although it was less well-known, was the Christian Colportage Association (CCA). From 1911-31 its Secretary was A.S. Maggs, a

[50] Capper and Johnson, *Faith of a Surgeon*, 11; Douglas Johnson, *Contending for the Faith: A History of the Evangelical Movement in the Universities and Colleges* (Leicester: IVP, 1979), 105, 154-5.

[51] Johnson, *Contending*, 117, 134.

[52] *Ibid.*, 288.

[53] Geraint Fielder, *Lord of the Years* (Leicester: IVP, 1988), 29.

[54] See Anne Arnott, *Wife to the Archbishop* (London and Oxford: Mowbrays, 1976).

[55] Oliver R. Barclay, *Whatever happened to the Jesus Lane lot?* (Leicester: IVP, 1977), 106-7.

[56] Barclay, *Evangelicalism in Britain*, 55.

[57] *W* 110 (1980), 183.

[58] Fielder, *Lord of the Years*, 84.

[59] See Ian Randall, *Educating Evangelicalism: The origins, development and impact of London Bible College* (Carlisle: Paternoster, 2000).

[60] *W* 73 (1943), 196.

member of the Brethren.[61] There were a host of smaller organisations, evangelistic and missionary, which numbered Brethren among their workers, officers or committee members. The lay character of these movements, and of much Evangelical leadership during this period, meant that Brethren were able to fit into such bodies easily, and they made an extensive contribution.

14.4 Cohesion, Separation, and the Beginnings of an Identity Crisis

The 1930s in particular saw increasing heart-searching among leading Brethren as some assemblies began to decline. Fears were expressed that many were compromising with the world, or with its religious manifestations. Coupled with this was a renewed concern for 'assembly truth'. Features seen as indicators of decline included lack of missionary interest, shallowness of ministry, readiness to get involved in interdenominational activities, and worldliness. However, complaints about the last of these tended to lack any clear idea of specific remedial action which could be taken, and some may simply have reflected an inability to adapt to the changing cultural context. But the impact on assemblies of these things appeared fairly clear: J.B. Watson listed 'Seven Things that are Ready to Die': corporate prayer, personal evangelism, family devotions, private meditation, spiritual conversation, hospitality, and the hope of the Lord's return.[62] Elsewhere he considered that an assembly was doing well to get 20% of its membership to the prayer meeting,[63] while W.G.A., in *The Believer's Magazine*, thought that generally about a quarter or a third of the assembly attended its midweek meetings, and only a tenth its Bible readings; the absence from the latter of leaders (who could reasonably be expected to be 'apt to teach') and young people was especially obvious.[64]

14.4.1 Challenges to the Tradition

It does seem that there was a move towards clearer separation in the 1920s, which became more marked as one moved further away from London. There appears to have been a resurgence of 'Needed Truth' type teaching, partly because divisions within that movement and within Exclusivism led to some joining Open Brethren and bringing with them aspects of the thinking of these groups on matters such as separation and centralisation (e.g. John Brown, who had been one of the chief protagonists of the division of 1892[65]). *The Believer's Magazine* carried a number of questions from young believers perplexed at what they saw as the lax conduct of their leaders, especially in the area of co-operation with the sects in evangelism. The widespread use of demarcated seating in some assemblies (believers being asked to sit in front of a board placed part way down the aisle at the Breaking of Bread) may be regarded as further evidence. Finally, it has been suggested to me that Scottish influence (facilitating the spread of 'Needed Truth' teachings) was a factor in Ulster Brethren becoming more separatist during this decade, although the opposition from other Protestants faced by Brethren in the conservative province was probably more important: as late as 1940, a Baptist who

---

[61] *CG*, February 1932, 33.

[62] *W* 61 (1931), 121-3.

[63] 'Problems of the Prayer Meeting', *H* 13 (1936), 219.

[64] W.G.A., 'Assembling Ourselves', *BM* n.s. 45 (1944), 187.

[65] Bruce, *In Retrospect*, 24-6; Dickson, *Brethren in Scotland, passim*; Park, *Churches of God*, 85.

converted to Brethrenism was told to leave home.[66] Of course, a reaction against tighter views was also evident in the literature.[67] This may have contributed to the trend towards increasing interdenominational involvement; the polarisation now evident in British assembly life evidently has deep roots, and was doubtless a factor in the formation between 1918 and 1939 of no less than twenty-three assemblies as a result of schism in Scotland alone.[68]

With clearer separation came strengthening of the received tradition of Brethren teaching; those who deviated from it were liable to censure and speakers who did so might find doors being shut against them. When the missionary J.A. Anderson returned from China in 1921, he joined an assembly in Aberdeen, but was asked to cease attending because objection was taken to his teaching that the Second Coming would not occur until after the Great Tribulation (which believers would therefore have to undergo).[69] At some point he also adopted partial rapture views;[70] along with Pentecostalism and annihilationism, these were effective ways of getting oneself frozen out of assemblies. Lang certainly found the doors shut against him, and even had to explain his views to a meeting of Devon brethren in 1918.[71] This may have been a factor in his insistence that excommunication of true believers should not take place on doctrinal grounds.[72] By contrast, Bruce was known by 1941 to hold a post-tribulational view of the Second Coming,[73] but does not appear to have suffered unduly as a result, possibly because of his growing reputation as a biblical scholar and his adroit handling of controversial issues; perhaps the tendency of Lang and other protagonists of minority viewpoints to press their views on others in season and out of season was more of a problem than the nature of the views themselves. Another instance of what might be termed 'eschatological defensiveness', however, was provided by the articles responding to Alexander Reese's lengthy critique of Darbyite views, *The Approaching Advent of Christ* (1937), which linked Reese's views with 'modernism'.[74]

---

[66] Robert Plant, *They Finished their Course in the 90s* (Kilmarnock: John Ritchie, 2000), 191.

[67] E.g. J.R. Caldwell, 'Three Gatherings of Saints', reprinted in *W* 59 (1929), 177-8; William Shaw, '"Not on our List"', *W* 59 (1929), 201-2; cf. the reprinting in 1929 of Alexander's *Discerning the Body* and Caldwell's *Revision of Certain Teachings*.

[68] Dickson, *Brethren in Scotland*, 198.

[69] Anderson, *Autobiography*, 190-1, 250-1.

[70] *Ibid.*, 257.

[71] See his papers in CBA Box 74.

[72] Lang considered that the real reason his views were opposed was his stress on the need for holiness if believers were to attain to the Rapture; most critics (and there were a fair number during the 1920s and 1930s) considered that this imperilled the essence of the gospel and represented a form of salvation by effort. As he considered that Darby's eschatology fostered careless living, so too the Bible college lecturer H.L. Ellison adopted similar views because he considered that the standard Brethren teaching produced no moral effect on him or others (Ellison to Lang, 17 November 1941, (CBA Box 66)).

[73] 'I am sorry to hear he has become a tribulation saint. He is a promising lad, I hope he may be kept on the right path to the end.' (C.F. Hogg to J.B. Watson, 12 July 1941 ('Letters from Friends', Watson Papers, CBA Box 231).)

[74] W.R. Lewis, 'The Approaching Advent of Christ', *BM* n.s. 39 (1938), 45-8; A.W. Philips, 'Mission Field Modernism and "Tribulation" Theories', *BM* n.s. 39 (1938), 7-9; *idem*, '"The Tribulation" & Modernism: A Review', *BM* n.s. 38 (1937), 324-5.

THOSE ONLY IN COMMUNION WILL PASS THIS BENCH.

A 'behind the board' notice; this one was used at Woolpit, Suffolk

Another example of the way in which a 'Brethren tradition' became established concerns the role of women. For many, woman's place was in the home; this argument was advanced against their voting when the franchise was extended to them in 1918.[75] Women among the Brethren undoubtedly exercised a time-consuming and sacrificial ministry in hospitality, visiting, personal evangelism, teaching young believers and pastoral counselling. The semi-private nature of such ministry meant that few were well known, although *The Christian Graphic* did run a series on 'Some Women Workers' during the early 1930s. Public participation was rarely deemed acceptable. Even leading in prayer was deemed to contravene the injunction to silence; Pickering knew of very few assemblies where women prayed audibly.[76] A thorny issue was the matter of female missionaries giving reports of their work when home on furlough; even this seems to have been rare.[77] Occasionally voices were raised in support of allowing women to speak; Petter's *Assembly Service* allowed that in certain circumstances women might pray or speak in public, but *The Witness* considered this unscriptural.[78]

The quest for ecclesial purity, which was rooted in unease at social change and emphasis on what marked Brethren out from the world around them, led to a number of schisms in Scottish assemblies between the wars, and also to the need for leaders to take counsel together to ensure uniformity of action.[79] As part of this quest, some sought to recreate in detail what they considered to be the correct manner of breaking bread, even at the risk of splitting congregations, and Pickering and his contributors more than once expressed their dismay at the number of questions submitted to *The Witness* on the minutiae of this service.[80]

It is therefore not surprising that some saw an over-emphasis on 'assembly truth' as leading to decline: Alexander claimed that the rot had set in when the original aim of

---

[75] [John Ritchie?], 'The Christian and Politics', *BM* n.s. 19 (1918), 135.

[76] H[enr]y P[ickering]., 'New Testament Companies of Christians', *W* 61 (1931), 181.

[77] 'QA', *W* 65 (1935), 62; 66 (1936), 279.

[78] *W* 60 (1930), 136.

[79] Dickson, *Brethren in Scotland*, 231-3.

[80] 'QA', *W* 58 (1928), 273; cf. *W* 53 (1923), 37. In *BM*, similar concerns were expressed by John Brown, 'A Review of "The Weekly Feast of Olden Time, A Foreshadow of The Weekly Feast of Present Time"', *BM* n.s. 33 (1932), 18-19; cf. *BM* n.s. 35 (1934), 78, 105.

finding common ground on which all believers could meet had been lost, and Brethren became preoccupied with church truths rather than with Christ.[81] On the other hand, an editorial in *The Believer's Magazine* expressed concern that speakers at conferences were neglecting 'church truth', and warned of the risk that the distinctive testimony of assemblies was being lost in the desire to align with nondenominationalism.[82] C.S. Kent, who later became General Manager of *The Times,* issued a pamphlet entitled *Whither are we Drifting?* in 1933. He claimed that co-operation in interdenominational work was leading to a labour shortage in assembly work; all service could and should be performed within assembly fellowship, as the assembly was the only corporate unity recognised in the New Testament. 'If the present trend continues, the very existence of many assemblies may be imperilled.'[83] *The Believer's Magazine* announced that it was celebrating its golden jubilee year with a series on assembly truths. 'The old moorings seem to have been left. Distinctive guidance in many quarters is lacking. Leaders whose ministry we value and whose example we can follow are passing on, and few are rising to fill the vacant places. In some quarters old paths are no longer cherished.'[84] In 1942, Borland wrote of many having a superficial grasp of the assembly position, but lacking any deep appreciation of why assemblies existed or concern for their distinctive testimony. He suggested that growth had been due to a clear grasp of such truths, and decline partly to departure from them.[85] A few years earlier, he had issued *Old Paths & Good Ways in personal, family, and church life* (1938). In it, he expressed the opinion that in spite of continuing numerical growth, assemblies had entered the third stage of the life of a religious movement, a long decline, following inception and growth. The decline was evident in growing indifference to assembly principles, and manifest in personal piety (a superficial grasp of Scripture, and a stress on justification at the expense of sanctification), family religion (parents were often more concerned about the temporal welfare of their offspring than their spiritual state), and church life (ministry lacked depth, and the spirit of worship had been lost). However, it was personal spirituality which he regarded as the root issue.

Of course, those who adopted a distinctive position had perforce to be known by a distinctive name; yet many Brethren were highly reluctant to accept any label which set them apart from fellow-believers, although they clearly felt it necessary to meet apart from them. It was feared that appropriation of the term 'Brethren' (especially when capitalised) betokened a sectarian spirit, and the preferred mode of self-designation was 'those known as Brethren'.[86] However, Dickson has shown that in Scotland the need to safeguard assembly interests by such means as the creation of property trusts and the wish to accommodate legal requirements in such matters as marriage ceremonies led to acceptance in certain contexts of the name 'Christian Brethren' and even of the title

---

[81] L.W.G. Alexander, 'Decadence or Revival', *W* 46 (1916), 135-6.

[82] *BM* n.s. 40 (1939), 35.

[83] C.S. Kent, *Whither are we Drifting?* ([Sutton: the author, 1933²]), 11.

[84] *BM* n.s. 40 (1939), 228.

[85] [Andrew Borland], 'Facing Facts', *BM* n.s. 43 (1942), 1.

[86] Cf. George Goodman, *W* 62 (1932), 269 (we are only brethren in the sense that all believers are); C.F. Hogg, 'Are the People commonly called "Brethren" a Sect?', *W* 62 (1932), 197-8, later issued separately (there is no such body as Open Brethren; each assembly is independent); H.G. Lloyd, letter in *BM* n.s. 15 (1914), 48 ('Open Brethren' is a title on a level with those of the sects); W.E. Vine, *W* 62 (1932), 245-6 (opposing the titular use of 'Brethren').

'pastor' for those men conducting weddings on assembly premises.[87] Doubtless similar factors were at work elsewhere.

Two areas in which the concern for a clearer self-definition was evident were those of theological training and assembly leadership. Continuing suspicion of theological colleges is not surprising, given that few maintained an Evangelical stance during this period. Ritchie considered that the useless knowledge acquired from tutors who were 'practically unbelievers' only served to spoil promising young preachers and made them of no further use. Demand for an educated ministry merely meant that congregations wanted men who would fill the church and carry out their plans. What was needed was an understanding of sinners and experience of vital spiritual work.[88] However, Harold St John and W.E. Taylor did run two ten-week courses at Netherhall, Largs, in 1929 to teach young workers how to handle Scripture correctly and to assist them in improving their public ministry.[89] The need for training gradually came to be acknowledged more widely, as was the possibility that assemblies might lose those capable of exercising a scholarly ministry because of opposition to higher education.[90]

As for local leadership, some potential leaders were killed during World War I, but probably rather more went abroad as missionaries. Another factor limiting the flow of new leaders was that some assemblies continued to be influenced by the Exclusive refusal to recognise any formal appointments to office, among them Bethesda, Bristol, and Southcroft Hall, Streatham. The former was content to assert in 1917 that the way was open for gifted individuals to come and minister among them as led.[91] The oversight at the latter discussed the issue during the 1920s with a view to inviting others to join them, but could not agree whether the oversight included all those who cared for the saints, or merely those who were invited to join the existing overseers.[92] Even where new leaders were emerging, some older leaders were apparently reluctant to allow younger men to have their head during the 1930s. Local oversights tended to function as self-perpetuating bodies, existing elders inviting suitable men to join them; in practice, it was the oversight's recognition, rather than that of the assembly, which ensured that a man was regarded as an elder. The combination of these factors ensured that the movement was heading for a leadership crisis. In some assemblies, lack of competent leadership could result from population migration, and thus be a factor in an assembly's decline.

14.4.2 Centralising Tendencies

The inter-war period is notable for the evidence of centralising tendencies at work in such matters as the creation of property trusts, the co-ordination of outreach, and the consulting together of overseeing brethren. Some were the result of Exclusive influences, but most were due to a denominationalising tendency which was most evident among the most open gatherings. We have already noted the formation of trusts to handle overseas property during the 1890s, as well as the Western Counties and South Wales

---

[87] Dickson, *Brethren in Scotland*, 315.

[88] 'YBQB', *BM* n.s. 24 (1923), 97-8; 'Training for the Ministry', *BM* n.s. 24 (1923), 109.

[89] *W* 59 (1929), 94.

[90] E.g. 'WW', *W* 73 (1943), 180.

[91] Davies and Chrystal, *Bethesda*, 19.

[92] Southcroft Hall, Streatham, Business Meeting minutes, 4 December 1923, 6 January 1924 (CBA Box 100).

Evangelization Trust (1904) and the Midland Evangelization Trust (1916). After World War I, there were calls for greater co-ordination of home work in a manner paralleling that for overseas work, the aim being to release resources for pioneering activity.[93] The Counties organisation was sometimes viewed as seeking to centralise and control such work, although the original vision had been to resource assemblies to do the work themselves.[94]

Another centralising tendency operated through the meetings of elder brethren which were occasionally convened at Devonshire House. In 1915, they discussed the movement's weakness in the areas of caring for and feeding local assemblies.[95] In 1923, another meeting discussed the controversy arising out of the views of the ex-Raven brother Theodore Roberts, whose Christology was deemed suspect after he referred in a letter to an Evangelical periodical, *The Christian*, to Christ's ignorance of the date of his Second Advent. The following year, a group of thirteen leading brethren signed a statement criticising Roberts' teaching and his view of biblical inerrancy, and asserting that he had been put out of fellowship by his local assembly.[96] Lang defended him as orthodox in intent if unguarded in expression, and complained that the interference of brethren from outside ran counter to belief in the autonomy of each local assembly and was evidence of a growth in Exclusive thinking among Open Brethren, as evidenced by what Lang saw as centralisation of discipline and a decree of universal excommunication.[97] In turn, Lang was criticised by Hoste, Roberts' former fellow-elder at Willesden Green, for depreciating the importance of doctrine as a test of fellowship.[98]

Regional meetings of elder brethren had been common from the late 1880s and provided opportunity for the protagonists in the 'Needed Truth' division to state their

---

[93] L.W.G. Alexander, 'Present-Day Evangelism', *W* 50 (1920), 288-9.

[94] E.g. by Ritchie, 'The Christian's Observatory and Outlook', *BM* n.s. 27 (1926), 53-4; 'YBQB', *BM* n.s. 24 (1923), 110-11.

[95] *EOS* 44 (1915), 22; 'WML', *W* 45 (June 1915), 84. This weakness was a recognised factor in leakage from assemblies ([John Ritchie?], 'Practical Points in Assembly Order', *BM* n.s. 21 (1920), 40).

[96] Lang Papers (CBA Boxes 68, 71); Noel, *History*, 255-6. Roberts appealed to Mark 13.32 in support of his views, and it is an indicator of the upset caused by this controversy that decades later this was one of the texts which reviewers of commentaries would check for soundness.

[97] See G.H. Lang, *Departure: a warning and an appeal addressed by one of themselves mainly to Christians known as Open Brethren Including discussions upon the Constitution, Government, Discipline and Ministry of the Church of God and of the Principles and Practice of Service in the Gospel* (Miami Springs, FL: Conley & Schoettle, 1986³), Appendix B. The controversy over Roberts' views reflected one within mainstream theology over the 'kenosis' theory, concerning the extent of Christ's self-emptying during his incarnation, which had been rumbling on since the late nineteenth century; this was an attempt to explain how Christ could have made what were deemed to be incorrect statements concerning such matters as the authorship of certain Old Testament writings (Wellings, *Evangelicals Embattled*, 172-3). Roberts' teaching was regarded as incipient modernism, and some of the concern to reiterate the fundamentals of the faith evident during the 1920s could be attributed to a desire to respond to it and to similar statements by churchmen. Cf. A. Borland, 'Kenosis', *BM* n.s. 29 (1928), 107-9, 127-9 (from a series of expositions of Philippians); J.W. Jordan, 'Omniscience. Omnipotence. Omnipresence', *W* 54 (1924), 231-4.

[98] William Hoste, '"Fellowship and Error"', *W* 52 (1922), 202; *idem*, '"Reception and Fellowship"', *W* 52 (1922), 226; *idem*, 'Discipline and Evil Doctrine', *W* 52 (1922), 237-9.

views. Some were convened as required, while others were monthly or quarterly fixtures in the calendar. Such meetings sought to co-ordinate outreach and consult concerning assembly matters. A regular meeting for overseeing brethren in the London area ceased in 1890, at the time of this controversy,[99] but from 1910, a quarterly meeting in London dealt specifically with matters of mission support. This began as a result of meetings of elder brethren at Devonshire House which expressed a desire for closer fellowship in this sphere.[100] A few took on some oversight functions, as in Manchester,[101] and the United Oversight at Bristol survived until 1937.[102] On one occasion, Brethren in Lancashire appear to have come close to adopting a Methodist-style circuit organisation: around 1920, a large conference in Bolton appears to have approved the idea of a committee to supply and examine assembly lay preachers, but the meeting broke up after one brother condemned it as a departure from revealed truth.[103]

There was apprehension at such developments, especially in view of the direction in which centralising tendencies were taking some groups of Exclusive Brethren, and a fear that some former Exclusives were seeking to spread their views among Open assemblies. In 1927, one Glasgow writer claimed that the original division in the Brethren movement had arisen as a result of the introduction of the idea of an organisation of recognised assemblies under a central authority, something which had been repeated in the 'Needed Truth' division.[104]

14.4.3 Conferences and Holidays

Even during World War I, newly-commenced missionary conferences in regional centres proved a big attraction, and the London Missionary Meetings remained popular. The reduction in working hours and the increased ease of travel meant that conferences flourished after the war ended. New ones began, such as the Bath Believers' Meetings (1919)[105] and the twice-yearly series of Saturday meetings in London (1921),[106] which soon came to be held in Bloomsbury Baptist Church. Established gatherings also prospered; the twice-yearly London Sunday School Teachers' Conference, commenced in 1907, was attracting over 3,000 by the mid-1920s to hear practical and motivational messages from recognised experts in the field.[107]

All over Britain, conferences were attracting record attendances, as at Belfast during Easter 1934, when up to 2,800 attended, a record which was broken the following year when 3,200 flocked to the Monday's meetings;[108] this conference was notable for maintaining an open platform rather than advertising pre-announced speakers. The

---

[99] *EH* 5 (1890), 1.

[100] G.J. Hyde to W.E. Vine, 10 November 1920 (Echoes of Service archive).

[101] Coad, *History*, 218; cf. references in minute books of local assemblies, e.g. Bright Hall, Eccles (CBA Box 3).

[102] Linton and Linton, *'I Will Build my Church'*, 79.

[103] Brady and Evans, *Brethren*, 78.

[104] Robert Barnett, '"Brethren" History and its Lessons for us To-day', *W* 57 (1927), 127-8.

[105] Stunt et al., *Turning the World Upside Down*, 57.

[106] Robert Rendall, *J.B. Watson: A Memoir and Selected Writings* (London: Pickering & Inglis, 1957), 57.

[107] *LOH* 13 (1924), 321, 372.

[108] 'TLWW', *BM* n.s. 36 (1935), 166; *W* 64 (1934), 118.

proximity of several conferences did not seem to cause a problem: on 1 January 1938, within a limited area, one at Motherwell attracted 1,200-1,300, with well over a thousand attending another at Kilmarnock, and the largest ever attendance recorded at Ayr. Two days later, there were over 700 at Prestwick, 700 at Larkhall, 600 at Newmilns, and other meetings in Glasgow, Auchinleck, and Kilbirnie.[109]

The congregation at a conference in Cholmeley Hall, Highgate, North London, c.1933

Some lamented the decline of the open conference, especially in *The Believer's Magazine*.[110] A major contributory factor was the high incidence of unedifying ministry, often from men who loved the sound of their own voices. All agreed that this was a problem in practice, but there was disagreement over whether the principle of open conferences should be jettisoned. Nevertheless, its intimation columns reflected the trend towards pre-arrangement; thus 80% of Scottish conferences announced in the January 1925 issue featured pre-arranged speakers whose names were included.

After 1918, Saturday night youth rallies became popular in the larger conurbations, where they could attract considerable numbers, but also in the rural county of Herefordshire, where young Christians from small assemblies must have found great encouragement in being with a larger group, the Herefordshire Christian Young People's Movement.[111] Day conferences for young people became popular and could attract crowds of over 1,000; the best-known were held at Brockenhurst, Ware (later Hertford), Childerditch, near Brentwood, and Bromsgrove, near Birmingham. These were usually held in the open air, and thus offered participants, who enjoyed the relative novelty of travelling to the conference by charabanc, the chance of a ramble as well as teaching.

Longer residential conferences also became popular. The widespread introduction of paid holidays from the 1930s was matched by a corresponding wealth of provision, as the burgeoning advertisement columns of *The Witness* indicate. South Grove Hall, Walthamstow, began a holiday conference for its new converts in 1929, which later

---

[109] 'TLWW', *BM* n.s. 39 (1938), 53.

[110] E.g. Anon., 'The Ministry of the Word at Conferences', *BM* n.s. 32 (1931), 52-6; A. Toll, 'The Ministry of the Word at Conferences', *BM* n.s. 32 (1931), 134-8.

[111] *W* 86 (1956), 121.

opened up to believers from other assemblies.[112] From 1932, Frederick Tatford arranged annual fortnight-long conferences in hotels for young people (though one wonders how many could afford these). 1939 saw the first of the holiday conferences at Glossop for young people, which lasted until 1968. Up to seven MSC houseparties in various locations took place each year during the 1920s. For those who did not wish to attend a conference, it was possible to book a holiday at a Christian boarding house. In 1920, Plas Menai at Llanfairfechan became the first of a new genre of Christian guest houses, a development which spread far beyond Brethren. It was commenced as the MSC holiday home, where conferences could bring together young people interested in mission with missionaries on furlough.[113] In Scotland, Netherhall at Largs, formerly the home of the scientist Lord Kelvin, opened its doors from 1927, as a more permanent replacement for the conferences held annually at St Andrews from around 1920.[114] At Plas Menai, conferences were hosted regularly for home workers and missionaries, combining relaxation with spiritual refreshment. A similar conference for home workers began in Bristol in 1920, building on the increased local interest in their work; this combined private meetings for the workers to consult together with public report sessions, as well as giving them opportunity to preach the gospel in local assemblies.[115] Annual three-day conferences at Lurgan in Ulster welcomed workers at home and overseas, as well as responsible brethren from assemblies; public meetings were held in the evenings.[116]

14.4.4 Magazines

Periodicals helped to maintain the cohesion of Open Brethren, but also allowed it to be challenged (gradually and within limits) by articles reflecting minority perspectives. Editors were usually also frequent conference speakers; this kept them in touch with their readers, but also gave them further opportunity of exercising influence, both from the platform and also as their advice was sought by local leaders.

The Believer's Magazine never gave circulation figures, although Ritchie's assistant from 1927 and then successor as editor, J. Charleton Steen, did admit that during 1928 the circulation had increased by 'many thousands'.[117] It may well have dropped in Ritchie's latter years, when failing health and inability to adapt to the changing conditions obtaining after World War I meant that he tended to repeat articles, indulge in nostalgia, and engage in vituperation against those in the movement who pursued a less clearly separatist line. This increase appears to have continued for a year or two after, but it is unlikely that *The Believer's Magazine* ever reached the figures achieved by its competitor, *The Witness,* during this period. Relationships between the two were somewhat strained, and were not helped by occasional veiled insinuations during the

---

[112] *CG*, August 1929, 149.

[113] Anon., 'A Missionary Study Holiday Home', *LOH* 9 (1920), 48-9.

[114] Anon., 'W.E. Taylor', *CW* 57 (1939-40), 150-1; Dickson, *Brethren in Scotland*, 208-9; G.H. Milln, 'The Largs Holiday Home', *LOH* 16 (1927-8), 29.

[115] Linton and Linton, *'I Will Build my Church'*, 238; various dates are given for the commencement of these, but *W* 51 (1921), 13, reports the first one.

[116] 'TLWW', *BM* n.s. 38 (1937), 306.

[117] *BM*, n.s. 29 (December 1928), iv. The lack of coverage of Echoes of Service in *The Believer's Magazine* during Ritchie's editorship is noteworthy.

1930s that *The Witness* (not mentioned by name) was making concessions to modernism.[118]

William Hoste (1860-1938)[119] became editor following Steen's death in 1931. His brother D.E. Hoste was from 1903 the director of the CIM, but William had adopted Brethren views while studying for the Anglican ministry at Ridley Hall, Cambridge. Among his works were *Bishops, Priests and Deacons* (1921), an examination of New Testament teaching on church leadership. An able writer on theological topics, he was nevertheless somewhat dogmatic in presenting his views, and played a leading role in the Roberts controversy. The next editor was Borland, who filled the role with distinction from 1938. A graduate in English from Glasgow University, he was probably one of the first university students from an Ayrshire assembly.

J.B. Watson

The Witness saw its circulation rise from 20,000 in 1919 to a peak of 31,800 in 1936.[120] It prospered under the editorship of Henry Pickering from 1914-41 and J.B. Watson from 1941-55.[121] Watson was a Cumbrian who had been a fellow-elder with Pickering at Grove Green Hall, Leytonstone; throughout his extensive ministry he continued full-time employment as a customs official. Whereas Pickering was essentially populist in his approach, Watson was more reflective and helped *The Witness* to maintain its influential position in the rapidly-changing world after 1945.

In response to a question during 1919 regarding the relationship between home and overseas outreach and the danger of neglecting home workers, Hoste had suggested compiling a list of the latter and the publication of reports from them in 'some kind of home *Echoes*'.[122] From 1919 on, discussions took place regarding the possibility of issuing such a publication, with W.J. Wiseman (1890-1970), a former yacht designer who had been able to retire in order to devote himself to Christian work, being invited to start it by a conference of home workers. Several evangelistic agencies were issuing their own,

---

[118] Cf. *W* 70 (February 1940), ii; Pickering put such insinuations down to jealousy at the success of *The Witness* (*W* 64 (1934), 282).

[119] On Hoste, see *BM* n.s. 39 (1938), 86-90, 112; *BM* 101 (1991), 68-9.

[120] H[enr]y P[ickering]., 'Our Plans and Prospects for 1919', *W* 49 (1919), 20; *W* 66 (February 1936), iii.

[121] On Watson, see *W* 85 (1955), 173, 193-201; Rendall, *Watson*.

[122] 'QA', *W* 49 (1919), 47-8. This was how the first editors saw it (*H* 1 (1923-4), 356).

more or less regular, reports, including *Counties Quarterly*, the organ of the Western Counties and South Wales Evangelization Trust, which had first appeared in 1900. From 1922 this became known as *The Harvester*. When Wiseman accepted a position as the British and Foreign Bible Society's agent in Constantinople, it was decided to amalgamate *The Harvester* with another publication reporting home work, *Home Witnessing*, itself an amalgamation of *Wayside Witnessing* (1919) and the *Home Missionary* (1921).[123] The original intent of the relaunched *Harvester* was to report gospel work in Britain and provide helpful articles for workers, and it may be seen as another manifestation of the post-war surge of evangelistic activity among Brethren.[124]

The Harvester was initially published from the Echoes of Service office, and although the Editors of *Echoes of Service* denied that they were trying to concentrate affairs at Bath, Lang alleged that some feared that its promoters wanted it to be the one magazine covering work in Britain, which they thought could lead to a list of accredited home workers.[125] The Counties agencies were also ambivalent about merging their own publications into this one, perhaps feeling that more regionally-orientated publications would secure more support for the work.[126]

After a few years, the magazine's composition changed, with a decline in the amount of space devoted to reports on outreach (few workers were submitting reports and these were alleged to be of limited interest to readers).[127] Circulation fluctuated: almost 5,000 in 1929, over 3,500 in 1933, 6,000 in 1934 and over 8,000 in 1936, but it must have been helped by continuing to absorb other magazines, including *Rays of Light* (commenced in 1922 by Liverpool assemblies), *Marching Orders* (1934, one of whose editors was Harold St. John), and *Links of Help* (1936).[128] The last of these was still printing over 5,000 copies per issue in the mid-1930s, but was experiencing financial difficulties and also seems to have lost its cutting edge as a stimulus to mission support.[129] Pickering, who was by now responsible for it,[130] may have wished to cut his losses in a difficult economic climate.

The third major Open Brethren publisher, apart from John Ritchie and Pickering & Inglis, was Paternoster Press. This was founded by Howard Mudditt, the son of missionaries to China, on a 'faith' basis during the mid-1930s.[131] Unlike the first two, its origins were English, being based initially at Walthamstow and then in central London. It

---

[123] Counties Evangelization minutes, 24 October 1919; W.J. Wiseman, 'Our Beginnings', *H* 38 (1959), 24; cf. *H* 13 (1936), 1; *LOH* 12 (1923), 97. Regrettably, no copies of any of these can be traced except for one issue of *Counties Quarterly* in the CBA.

[124] W.R. Lewis, 'Editorial', *H* 1 (1923-4), 1; cf. 7 (1930), 65.

[125] *EOS* 52 (1923), 280; *H* 1 (1923-4), 48; Lang, *Departure*, 74; *idem*, undated memorandum (CBA Box 68). The Editors had in fact expressed a wish to see the amalgamation of the regional magazines (*EOS* 51 (1922), 23).

[126] Counties Evangelization minutes, 6 February 1923; Evangelization of South-Eastern Counties minutes, 5 March 1923.

[127] *H* 13 (1936), 243; 15 (1938), 1.

[128] *H* 6 (1929), 96; 11 (1934), 181, 222; 12 (1935), 227; 13 (1936), 31, 73; *LOH* 23 (1935), 185.

[129] *LOH* 21 (1933), 25.

[130] *W* 62 (December 1932), ii.

[131] For the company's history, see Anon., '"When God really calls, he provides"', *A*, March 1993, 2; B. Howard Mudditt, 'The Paternoster Story', *H*, May 1985, 6-7; June 1985, 6-7; July 1985, 12-14; September 1985, 5-7.

took over publication of *The Harvester* in 1937. F.A. Tatford (1901-86) became an editor in 1933, and sole editor in November 1939.[132] Until 1939 he also acted as London area correspondent for *The Believer's Magazine*. He combined firm allegiance to traditional Open Brethren teaching, especially on prophecy, with a readiness to think radically concerning matters of outreach and church practice, and a measure of impatience with others who were more cautious. Not a man to suffer fools gladly, he had on occasion to apologise for critical comments made in his editorials. Tatford altered the character of the magazine and made it a powerful force in Open Brethren circles. The changes he introduced were not to everybody's liking, however, and a number of full-time workers decided in 1945 to commence a new magazine, *Precious Seed*.[133] Such action is evidence of growing tension between those who wished to remain faithful to traditional patterns of activity and who upheld a consistent separatism, and those who wished to adapt to what they saw as changing times and who were becoming more aware of the extent of common ground which they shared with Evangelicals in the denominations. This tension was also apparent in the area of attitudes to the world, as the next chapter will show.

---

[132] On Tatford, see James Anderson, *They Finished their Course in the 80's* (Kilmarnock: John Ritchie, 1990), 187-90; John Macnicol, *Twentieth Century Prophet* (Eastbourne: Prophetic Witness, 1971).

[133] For more on *Precious Seed*, see section 20.1.1.

CHAPTER 15

Brethren and the World

During the years from 1914 to 1945, it became increasingly evident that some Open Brethren were changing their attitude to the world and to the question of their involvement in its affairs. Lang claimed that many now voted and some accepted positions of power; no longer did Brethren always resign from the forces; they were unequally yoked in trade federations, unions, scientific and other learned bodies, co-operative societies, and business partnerships; smoking was on the increase; worldliness in dress and reading was evident; some accepted contracts to build theatres, cinemas, or public houses (a veiled attack on Laing, whose firm had done so since the First World War) and two had even built a Spiritualist church.[1] Revealingly, one of his complaints about the rules governing the selection and approval of missionary candidates was that they restricted the Christian worker's personal freedom, 'and they partake of the modern spirit of government, which, by discouraging individualism, is reducing initiative and enterprise'.[2] His portrayal may have been somewhat exaggerated, and certainly unrepresentative of the great majority of Brethren who would have maintained the traditional detachment from the world, but he offers a revealing sidelight on the cracks appearing in the wall of separation from secular affairs which Brethren had built.

15.1 Social and Economic Thinking among Brethren

The spirit of capitalist enterprise remained an important factor in British economic and political life during the inter-war years, and the individualistic nature of Open Brethren spirituality, which frequently stressed that Christian service was a matter of individual responsibility to God, fitted well with this. After World War I, *The Witness* began to carry considerable numbers of trade advertisements from individuals, encouraging readers to patronise them, thus offering implicit approval to the way of life of the Brethren small business proprietor.

Linked with their individualism was a profound disapproval of socialism, which they saw as contrary to the principle that power is from above, not from the people, and a consequent reluctance (for many, outright refusal) to become involved in the democratic process. In 1931, *The Witness* even reprinted Darby's tract 'Progress of Democratic Power, and its Effect on the Moral State of England',[3] which attacked the democratic tendencies of reforming legislation from 1832 onwards and the concomitant rise in infidelity, popery and centralisation of government, all of which were seen as preparing the way for the final rebellion against God. The revolutions in Russia during 1917 did much to confirm Brethren in their outlook, and developments in the Communist world continued to receive plenty of coverage in *The Witness*, in part because of the belief that

---

[1] Lang, *Departure*, 106.

[2] G.H. Lang, *Past, Present, and Future: Guidance and Warning for Followers of the Lamb* (Walsham-le-Willows, Suffolk: the author, [1943]), 11.

[3] *W* 61 (1931), 135-6; for the original, see Darby, *CW*, 32.333-6.

Russia would play a major role in end-time events.[4] The former socialist H. Musgrave
Reade, in his *Christ or Socialism* (reprinted by Pickering & Inglis in 1923), argued that
socialism was essentially materialistic in outlook and tended toward anarchy and the
rejection of moral restraints. There was, he concluded, no such thing as 'Christian
Socialism'. An unsigned article on '"Christian socialism"' in *The Believer's Magazine*
during 1917 condemned it as a delusion, involving an unequal yoke and manifesting a
spirit of revolt against authority.[5] Such attitudes contrasted with the influence of
Christian Socialism among some High Anglicans, and with the Church of England's
thinking about social policy.

Likewise, most Brethren remained suspicious of trades unions as foreshadowing 'the
mark of the beast' (Revelation 13.16-17),[6] and it was rare for them to mention, let alone
give serious consideration to, the economic injustices which had been catalysts for the
development of the trades union movement. Few had the stomach for involvement in such
bodies, but one who did achieved high office: James Barbour, from Cowie in
Stirlingshire, was elected President of the National Union of Scottish Mineworkers.[7]

However, it is noteworthy that some Brethren appear to have joined the Freemasons,
or at least not to have left them on conversion. Among them, it seems, were some
exercising oversight responsibilities in assemblies.[8] Probably the most famous known
Freemason among Open Brethren was Sir Robert Anderson. Whilst it was not unknown
for Nonconformist members and ministers to belong to Masonic lodges, the Brethren
stress on separation from the world, and the application of the 'unequal yoke' principle to
such things as business partnerships, makes such an accommodation with it remarkable.
It is one more instance of the fact that in practice Brethren were not always as 'separated'
as they were in theory.

The innate conservatism of most Brethren meant that righting social injustices was
seen as a matter for God alone, something which would occur during the Millennium and
which believers should not try to bring about by their own efforts. As one writer put it: 'If
I could introduce a great improvement in the world, even the Millennial blessedness, by
political action equivalent only to lifting my little finger, I would refuse to do it because I
want my Saviour to have the glory in the day of His power.'[9] As a result, Brethren
expressed apprehension concerning the development of state provision for
unemployment, sickness and old age; Pickering even saw this as an indication of the last
days, and as contradicting the creation ordinance of work.[10] The 1927 Health Insurance
Act was seen by some as forcing Christians to disobey the injunction to separation in 2
Corinthians 6.14-17.[11] A few years later, Pickering had to assure a questioner that
receiving the Old Age Pension did not amount to an 'unequal yoke'.[12]

---

[4] E.g. W.J. M'Clure, 'What Prophecy Reveals about Russia', *W* 62 (1932), 181-2; 'WW', *W* 55 (1925), 154 (where Bolshevism was identified as the Antichrist).

[5] *BM* n.s. 18 (1917), 65-6.

[6] Dugald Cameron, 'The Christian and Trade Unionism', *H* 14 (1937), 202; Henry Hitchman, *Some Scriptural Principles of the Christian Assembly* (Kilmarnock: John Ritchie, [c.1930]²), 165-7.

[7] On Barbour, see *BM* 95 (1985), 157; Dickson, *Brethren in Scotland*, 250, 322-3.

[8] 'BQB', *BM* n.s. 28 (1927), 180-1; n.s. 34 (1933), 47; 'QA', *W* 53 (1923), 36-7.

[9] T. Fred Hemsley, 'QA', *W* 50 (1920), 325.

[10] 'WW', *W* 50 (1920), 259.

[11] 'WW', *W* 57 (1927), 34.

[12] 'WW', *W* 61 (1931), 66.

Often there was little sense of vocation in secular employment: full-time work was seen as the ideal to which to aspire, a curious twist of thought in a denomination which at this point categorically rejected the idea of formally-recognised and stipended pastoral ministry.[13] Work tended to be what you did in order to provide you with the financial resources to live, and to engage in, or support, 'spiritual' activities such as evangelism and overseas mission. It was also regarded as a sphere for personal witness, but not often as an activity possessing its own inherent value as a mode of fulfilling the divine mandate to be stewards of creation. In a sense, for Brethren (as for many of their colleagues, albeit for rather different reasons) real life began at clocking-off time. Here, too, they were not unique among contemporary Evangelicals, few of whom had, or saw the need for, a developed theology of work.

Tatford provided a contrast to the tendency to idealise 'full-time workers' (though Tatford's own remarkable capacity for work ensured that his output surpassed that of many of the latter). He had wanted to be a missionary but saw the value of witness in a business context; for many years, he combined responsibility in a number of government departments (culminating in a high position with the UK Atomic Energy Authority) with editing, writing, and speaking up to 400 times a year. Yet even he had a somewhat restricted outlook; his article 'Christian Practice in Business' expounded New Testament teaching on master-servant relationships and opposed Christian involvement in trades unions (but not professional associations), but said nothing about larger economic issues.[14] This narrow vision was a feature of Brethren writing on the business world during this period. For example, George Goodman's article 'Can a Christian Succeed in Business?'[15] majored on the personal and ethical qualities of the believer, but did not discuss the Christian's approach to the big issues. Rendle Short's talk on 'The Christian and Modern Business', given at a MSC conference in 1934, appears to have been something of a first in its attempt to apply Christian thinking to such matters – and he was not even a businessman.[16]

Gradually, however, Brethren began to write about economic and other 'secular' issues; a 1937 series of articles in *The Harvester* on 'The Challenge of Today' (doubtless inspired by Tatford) dealt with social responsibility, class distinctions, militarism, politics, trades unions, and recreation. There was little that was revolutionary in the views expressed, but it was significant enough that such a series of articles should have been published at all. By the Second World War, *The Harvester* (which under Tatford's editorship was developing into the most open-minded of Brethren periodicals) was including articles expressing the conviction that Christ's Lordship extended to all areas of society, and that therefore it was legitimate for believers to be involved in them. One such article, in 1937, provides a striking early indication of changing Brethren thinking about social action: 'If the gospel is to be effectively preached, it must be accompanied in some measure by the alleviation of distress. This is not the advocating of a social gospel,

---

[13] From a sociological perspective, we might compare this with the practice of another non-clerical body, the Jehovah's Witnesses: they have combined rejection of ordination and the insistence that every member is a minister with veneration of those who have given their whole time to the work as 'pioneers'.

[14] *H* 14 (1937), 243.

[15] *H* 16 (1939), 56-7.

[16] *LOH* 22 (1934), 132-3.

but rather the practical application of the gospel of Christ.'[17] The writer pointed out that such needs were recognised overseas, so they should be here too. All too often, however, the challenge of the world was seen in terms of external matters: a series of articles during 1938 looked at personal issues such as smoking, dancing, flirting, fashion, sport, gambling, insurance, fighting, and Freemasonry. Brethren were a long way from developing any fully worked-out approach to involvement in the social order.

15.2 Some Brethren Businessmen

Brethren businessmen played a major role in the movement's development during these decades, comparable to that played by former clergyman during the years before 1859, and by aristocrats and gentry during the late nineteenth century. An analysis of the speakers at the twice-yearly Bloomsbury meetings for believers from 1925-35 indicated that of a total of forty-seven speakers, 68% were businessmen and only 32% full-time workers.[18] Many of the former brought to assemblies an increased openness to co-operation with Evangelicals in the denominations and a degree of pragmatism regarding the adoption of innovative evangelistic methods, as well as tightening up the administrative and organisational side of Brethren life.

It is curious to note a parallel to the collection of numerous directorships by some businessmen in the emergence of what might be termed the 'Brethren bureaucracy'. Some individuals served on numerous committees and trusts associated with the movement. Such a phenomenon was not absent from the wider Evangelical scene, but it was more significant among assemblies because their lay ethos meant that such men did not have to direct such a large proportion of their energies to para-church organisations. Laymen, and usually businessmen, could play major roles in shaping and directing the movement, in a way which was less often possible among other Nonconformist denominations because of the tendency of clergy to take most of the leading roles.

The best-known Brethren figure in the business world must surely be Sir John Laing. The government contracts which he undertook during the First World War contributed considerably to the company's growth. Laing was consulted by successive governments on a range of industry-related issues, especially during the Second World War. He also became known as a vigorous supporter (in terms of practical involvement as well as finance and direction) of all kinds of outreach activity, inter-denominational as well as assembly-based. Another builder was A.H. Boulton (1884-1985) of Bebington, who, like Laing, became known for the quality of the houses he built in the Wirral, 'Boulton's little palaces'.[19] He would be commended for his services to the housing industry by Sir Winston Churchill and Harold Macmillan. In several cases he was responsible for financing the erection of halls for Brethren assemblies, sometimes building them as part of his new housing estates. He also took an active interest in mission at home and abroad, being consulted by the Editors of Echoes of Service and taking a leading role in the MSC movement, as well as serving as President of Liverpool City Mission from 1938-64.

---

[17] Richard S. Long, 'The Christian and Social Responsibilities', *H* 14 (1937), 9.

[18] *LOH* 23 (1935), 25.

[19] On Boulton, see Anderson, *They Finished their Course in the 80's*, 11-12; F.P. Gopsill, *Centenary of Archie Henry Boulton 1884-1984* (n.pl.: n.p., [1984]); Gordon Read and David Jebson, *A Voice in the City* (Liverpool: Liverpool City Mission, [1979]), 128.

An intriguing figure is William Marriott (1857-1943), Traffic Manager and Locomotive Superintendent of the Midland and Great Northern Joint Railway (M&GN).[20] He commenced an assembly in his house (as did other businessmen elsewhere) at Melton Constable in Norfolk, where the M&GN had its headquarters, having held meetings there from about 1885. Marriott retired at seventy and undertook gospel work in France; the assembly survived his death, but not the closure of almost all the M&GN system in 1959. Another famous Brethren railwayman was Cecil J. Allen (1886-1973).[21] Allen worked for the Great Eastern Railway and its successor, the London and North Eastern Railway, from 1903-46 as an inspector of materials, but became widely known as an author on railway topics. He was a hymnologist and composer, and served as organist at the London Missionary Meetings for many years, as well as being Vice-President of the Crusader movement.

The petrol engine manufacturer Percival W. Petter (1873-1955) founded, with his brother Ernest, what later became Westland Aircraft in 1914 and, unusually for Brethren, served as Mayor of Yeovil from 1925-7.[22] Petter's confirmation in the Church of England did not stop him from remaining active among Brethren, some of whom were sympathetic to his attempts in the 1930s and 1940s to stop what he saw as the nation's drift away from its Protestant constitutional basis. A founder of the Pilgrim Preachers in 1919, he produced a useful if not entirely traditional work on *Assembly Service* ([1930]).

15.3 Practical Action

Although Brethren philanthropic work was not conducted on any large scale (with the exception of the Orphan Homes in Bristol), some unusual ventures were undertaken, such as the home for believers fleeing the Spanish Civil War (1936-9) which was opened by Petter at Merriott in Somerset,[23] or the medical missions opened during the 1930s at Mottingham and Downham, near Bromley, both on large new housing estates.[24] One area in which Brethren began to get involved was that of care for the elderly. Eventide homes really proliferated from the 1950s, but some pioneered such provision between the wars. For example, Boulton built a number of bungalows next to Bethesda Hall, Bebington, for retired missionaries or full-time workers.[25] Laing had a dozen flats built on an estate in Edgware for retired missionaries and full-time workers.[26] Unity Chapel, Bristol, opened a home for the elderly in 1925,[27] and the Ilford builder W.H. Knox built one at Hornchurch a decade later.[28] Ernest Luff of the Pilgrim Preachers opened several at Frinton on the Essex coast.[29]

---

[20] *W* 74 (January 1944), iii.

[21] See his autobiography, *Two Million miles of Train Travel* (Shepperton: Ian Allan, 1965).

[22] See *DBB*; *ODNB*.

[23] *H* 14 (1937), 206.

[24] See Andrew Fergusson, *He Sent them Out* (Bromley: Bermondsey and Brook Lane Medical Mission, 1988).

[25] Gopsill, *Boulton*, unpaginated.

[26] Coad, *Laing*, 133.

[27] Linton and Linton, *'I Will Build my Church'*, 69.

[28] *H* 13 (1935), 205.

[29] See Donald Bridge, *God has resources: from the Pilgrim Preachers to the Ernest Luff homes* (Exeter, Paternoster Press, [1982]).

It would probably be fair to say, however, that much philanthropic activity undertaken by Brethren represented a response to a particular emergency rather than arising from any thought-out world-view. This is evident in their response to economic depression. When crisis hit the coal industry in 1921, several churchmen sought to intervene. However, they were not agreed on the solutions to the problems facing the industry, and such disagreement confirmed to Pickering that it was unwise to interfere in temporal affairs, which were the domain of unbelievers. 'The spiritual aspect of the conflict is the only side that comes within the province of a spiritual magazine.'[30] Rarely did the periodicals offer any practical suggestions as to what action should be taken. However, their innate conservatism is indicated by their readiness to criticise action taken by strikers.

The depression of the later 1920s and 1930s did not affect all areas of Britain equally. This is reflected in the fortunes of assemblies, some of which were unaffected, while others in coal-mining areas such as South Wales and Durham were hard-hit as most of their wage-earners were laid off. Some South London assemblies met in 1928 to plan how to help fellow-believers in assemblies in the worst affected areas;[31] a moving picture of the destitution which overtook some mining communities was provided by reports in *The Harvester* during 1925 of the church-planting work of Ieuan Elias at Rhosllanerchrugog.[32] He described vividly the poverty which surrounded him, and readers responded with donations of money and clothing. Gifts for needy Scottish miners were also faithfully recorded each month in the donation columns of *The Witness*.

The depression may have accelerated some of the centralising trends at work within the movement. We have seen that there were a number of amalgamations of periodicals, but the only Open Brethren publisher to go under appears to have been the Hulbert Publishing Company, which suddenly collapsed in 1930[33] – and that may have been due in part to rumours (strongly denied) about its proprietor's alleged Pentecostal sympathies.[34] Other publishers weathered the storm, as did the service agencies, though the latter found their income significantly affected. Of course, the fact that their workers 'lived by faith' meant that such bodies had minimal liabilities, since they had no need to go into debt to pay salaries.

15.4 Political Involvement

Even the political realm saw Open Brethren beginning to participate, although this was decidedly unusual and magazines tended to repeat traditional condemnations of such activity. What few seem to have realised, however, was that non-involvement and support of the *status quo* could be interpreted as just as much a political statement as voting or party activism. By 1945, the veteran writer L.W.G. Alexander expressed the view in response to a questioner that political involvement was a matter for the individual to

---

[30] 'WW', *W* 51 (1921), 48.

[31] Southcroft Hall, Streatham, Business Meeting minutes, 4 December 1928 (CBA Box 100); cf. Anon., *Seventy-Five Years of Christian Witness 1902-1977* ([London]: Victoria Hall Evangelical Church, [1977]), 4.

[32] E.g. *H* 3 (1926), 102.

[33] 'WML', *W* 60 (July 1930), 168.

[34] Cf. a reference to Hulberts as a depot for 'Foursquare Publications' (*W* 58 (1928), 473), and the denial that the Elim Foursquare Alliance had purchased Hulberts (*H* 5 (November 1928), back cover).

decide, and made no mention of the traditional Brethren proscription of such activity.[35] It was during this period that the first of several Brethren Members of Parliament was elected. The former Exclusive Sir John Sandeman Allen (1865-1935) was an insurance magnate, Conservative MP for West Derby, Liverpool, and vice-president of Liverpool City Mission.[36] The Conservative Party has often proved a congenial environment for politically-involved Brethren because of the stress of both ideologies on the individual, and the Brethren belief in the powers that be as holding office by divine appointment and corresponding rejection of Socialism as godless and as preparing the way for the Beast because of its assertion that power is from the people.

Some Brethren ruled out not only political involvement, but also any kind of position in which the Christian served as an executive of government policy, such as the police. Thus Hoste laid down the believer's calling to be a witness rather than an agent of the government, though he admitted that there were many openings for consistent service in municipal and government offices.[37] Yet several Brethren served as Chief Constables in local police forces, such as John Williamson, Chief Constable of Northampton from 1924-56.[38] Several also achieved high office in local government, such as Sir James Bird (1863-1925), Clerk to the London County Council.[39] It is also noteworthy that arguments against the appropriateness of involvement in politics and government were not often extended to the legal profession, in which Open Brethren were always well represented.

15.5 Cultural Engagement

During the 1920s, it became quite fashionable to declare oneself an atheist or an agnostic. Brethren did try to respond to some of the intellectual challenges of the contemporary world, as is evident from their apologetic writings. But only a minority engaged with contemporary culture to any extent, and rare indeed must have been the home where T.S. Eliot's writing lay next to *The Witness*. However, a few were more culturally aware, such as Bertram Colgrave (1889-1968), who lectured in Anglo-Saxon and Middle English at Durham from 1920-55,[40] and Kenneth Luckhurst (1904-62), who was secretary of the Royal Society of Arts for twenty-five years.

At a more down-to-earth level, there are signs of an increasing degree of accommodation with the world during this period. An example of this is the issue of leisure activities. Games and rambles began to appear on houseparty programmes, the report of one MSC conference asserting, somewhat defensively, 'it was clearly demonstrated that these pursuits, rightly conducted, proved no hindrance to the more important part of the programme, but rather helped it'.[41] The value of sport as a means of

---

[35] 'QA', *W* 75 (1945), 55. Similarly, E.W. Rogers, whilst disapproving of political involvement, regarded it as a matter for the individual conscience, to which the principles of Romans 14 applied ('BQB', *BM* n.s. 46 (1945), 142).

[36] See Read and Jebson, *Voice in the City*, 129; *W* 65 (1935), 167.

[37] 'BQB', *BM* n.s. 30 (1929), 143.

[38] *W* 104 (1974), 275.

[39] *W* 55 (1925), 59.

[40] *W* 98 (1968), 236.

[41] *LOH* 8 (1919), 27.

healthy exercise was recognised by many,[42] although such a development was not without its critics.[43] Writers such as the psychiatrist A.T. Schofield affirmed the value of some kind of relaxing hobby, in an age when books with such titles as *Profitable Hobbies and Handicrafts,* and the pursuits to which they introduced their readers, were all the rage; hobbies were seen as employing God-given talents, as helping believers achieve a balanced outlook on life, and as providing a point of contact with the unsaved.[44] In 1933, *The Believer's Magazine* carried an article on the topic of leisure which regarded the fruits of human civilisation as neutral in themselves, rather than inherently evil.[45] The writer, a businessman and local councillor in Ayrshire, encouraged believers to relax in order to be able to serve God better, and to avoid the opposite errors of worldliness and asceticism.

Unworldliness did not mean unconcern with health issues. Apart from the longstanding interest in homeopathy, the 1920s saw the publication of books and articles on various aspects of the subject, and the columns of *The Witness* and its stablemate *The Christian Graphic* contained advertisements for such products as 'Surridges' Stamina' ('Many well-known Brethren are deriving benefit from its use') and 'Bowden's Indian Balm', the latter recommended by Caldwell and Chapman (according to Fereday, 'a special blessing seems to rest upon the preparation' – probably the best possible advertising slogan for attracting Brethren purchasers).[46] In this, Brethren probably reflected an increased health-consciousness evident in society at large.

The education which middle-class Brethren sought for their children provides another example of how they accommodated to prevailing cultural patterns. Several boarding schools advertised in *The Witness* and drew many of their pupils from Brethren homes. During the previous century, Brethren schools had often represented a withdrawal from the world, being patronised by parents who wished to insulate their children from such dangers as the local clergyman's religious instruction. However, during this period it is more likely that such institutions were simply a Brethren version of a phenomenon which attracted many middle-class children, the private school. Furthermore, it should be noted that other Brethren served with distinction in the state system, such as Andrew Borland and the Fife headmaster John Rollo (1905-81), who was largely responsible for a series of English textbooks for secondary schools.[47]

For all this increased openness to the world around them, it took a while for Brethren to accept the wireless. At first, they condemned it as bringing the world into the Christian home, and as likely to draw people away from attendance at meetings in order to tune in to

---

[42] E.g. Cedric Harvey, 'The Christian and Sport', *H* 15 (1938), 127. A member of Balham Grove Hall purchased ground for two tennis courts in 1919; they saw weekly use until 1933, partly as a means of retaining the interest of young people ([Eric Priestley], *1876-1976* ([London: Endlesham Hall, 1976]), unpaginated). For all his disapproval of games in connection with assembly work, it is recorded that on one occasion Lang (with Broadbent) was a spectator!

[43] E.g. W.H. Bishop, 'Foundation Truths for Young Believers. IV. – Concerning Recreation', *H* 4 (1927), 51; W. Harrison, 'Sport and Recreation', *CW* 55 (1937-8), 223-4 (sport was invented by those who do not fear God as a diversion from doing so); 'YBQB', *BM* n.s. 20 (1919), 46.

[44] A.T. Schofield, *Christian Sanity* (new ed., London: Marshall Brothers, 1926); cf. Dr H. Chave Cox, 'The Christian and Himself', *H* 14 (1937), 223-4; Kenneth W. Luckhurst, 'The Christian and Recreation', *H* 14 (1937), 250.

[45] Edwin Adams, 'How to Use the World without Abusing it', *BM* n.s. 34 (1933), 132-3.

[46] *CG*, February 1930, 39.

[47] On Rollo, see Anderson, *They Finished their Course in the 80's,* 169-71.

famous preachers (whose doctrine would often have been suspect, in any case).[48] However, in time W.H. Clare began to make representations to the BBC for broadcasting facilities comparable to those offered to other denominations.[49] The advent of war sealed the acceptance of the wireless by Brethren, Rogers pointing out to a questioner its necessity for receiving government instructions as well as news.[50] For Brethren, as for everyone else, the return of war was to bring massive and unexpected changes in every aspect of life. These, as we shall see in Part IV, helped to speed the breakdown in the consensus regarding separation from the political and social world whose beginnings we have examined in this chapter.

---

[48] E.g. 'WW', *W* 53 (1923), 104.

[49] Anderson, *They Finished their Course in the 80's*, 31. Here we see another instance of how all kinds of factors contributed to the 'denominationalising' of Open Brethren.

[50] 'BQB', *BM* n.s. 40 (1939), 287.

CHAPTER 16

Brethren in Two World Wars

It is widely acknowledged that two World Wars had an immense effect on the social fabric as well as the economic health of the United Kingdom. Religious historians also discuss their impact on the churches. However, the impact of these events upon Brethren has rarely been considered in detail.[1] This chapter explores how the onset of war revealed deep divergences of opinion among Open Brethren, as well as stimulating heart-searching concerning the reasons for their existence as a movement.

16.1 Brethren in World War I

We noted earlier that the Brethren attitude to the state could be summed up as 'Pray, Pay, and Obey'. There had been few Brethren writings since the early decades of their history which examined the relationship between the state, the believer, and the church. The wars in which Britain had been involved, such as the Crimean War (1854-5) and the wars in South Africa (1880-1 and 1899-1902), had not, apart from the last of these, assumed sufficient significance to provoke much thought on these issues.[2] Consequently, when war broke out in 1914, it not only caught them out as it did many others, but it found them lacking a living tradition of discussion of the issues on which they could draw in formulating their response. Arguments formulated in the 1830s were rehabilitated to serve in very different conditions, and it is not surprising that some found them less than convincing. It was all very well to quote Romans 13 and to insist on the believer's duty to obey the powers that be, but leaders disagreed over how far that obedience should extend.

16.1.1 Periodical Coverage

As soon as war was declared, both main periodicals devoted the great majority of their columns to war-related issues. In *The Believer's Magazine*, Ritchie offered an initial reaction to 'The War in Europe'.[3] He saw Satan as its ultimate instigator, and called for believers to confess their sins and those of the people. The war might prove to be a mercy if it resulted in access for the gospel to many of the nations involved where it was little known; it would end when people learned that God is sovereign. Ritchie called for special

---

[1] An exception is Dickson, *Brethren in Scotland*, 220-7, 238-9, 316-17.

[2] The second war in South Africa was seen as divine chastisement on Britain for national sins such as the growth of ritualism and rationalism, godlessness, and a boastful spirit (J.R. Caldwell, 'The War: viewed from a divine standpoint', *W* 30 (1900), 5-6). It was also a call for saved and unsaved to awaken from their indifferences (W.S[haw]., 'A Few Reflections on the War in South Africa', *W* 30 (1900), 7-8). God was speaking to the nation through its military reverses, and believers should respond by confessing their sins and those of the people, as Daniel did (J.R[itchie]., 'The War in South Africa: Thoughts and Reflections for God's People', *BM* n.s. 1 (1900), 13-14).

[3] *BM* n.s. 15 (1914), 97-9.

prayer for Christian soldiers, who may have 'to deal death to their fellow-saints in opposing ranks'.[4]

Many church leaders proclaimed the fight against Germany to be a holy war, and the initial call to national self-examination soon gave way to condemnation of German atrocities.[5] For their part, Brethren managed to combine the conviction that believers should not meddle in political affairs as citizens of heaven with a sense of the British Empire's unique status. To those who shrank from praying for the Empire, W.H. Hunter explained that in it there was liberty for gospel preaching and safety for the Jews, and the British word was widely regarded as trustworthy; furthermore, the King and the Government had done nothing to stir up strife but had tried to pursue peace.[6] There was thus an underlying sense that the war was being undertaken for a just cause. On the other hand, privilege (and the Empire was seen as highly privileged in terms of the gospel) brought responsibility, and failure to fulfil that responsibility brought divine chastening: 'it has been through lack of spirituality and real dealing with God among His own in all lands, that this war has been allowed to come upon us'.[7] 'Let there be no mistake about it: we as a nation are being dealt with by God, and the sooner we search our ways before Him, the earlier His hour of deliverance will come.'[8]

Whilst stopping short of explicit endorsement of believers engaging in military service, *The Witness* reported work among soldiers extensively and fulsomely, asserting that 'If only one quarter of the professions are genuine, a wonderful work has been done.'[9] By contrast, it published virtually nothing by or about conscientious objectors. As well as articles on the war and its impact on Christian work, there were discussions of the spiritual forces at work behind the war, and examinations of biblical prophecy, such as two series during 1915, by George Hucklesby on 'The Approaching end of the Age' and by Vine on 'The Roman Empire in Prophecy'. A growing sense of apprehension was evident, which even the armistice and the founding of the League of Nations did not dispel; indeed, the latter was seen as foreshadowing the revived Roman Empire of prophecy.[10] Believers were urged to use every opportunity to engage in evangelism and care for the needy, and to be constant in prayer.[11]

Many saw the war as an indicator of the approaching End, and Pickering even spoke at Carfax Hall, Clapham, in London, on 'How Daniel's Prophecy is being Fulfilled Before our Eyes Today'.[12] However, most Brethren were careful to qualify this perspective with the denial that current events could be matched up with specific biblical prophecies, and to assert that Armageddon would involve a different line-up of nations from the present war, whilst admitting that current events could be preparing the way for fulfilment of

---

[4] *Ibid.*, 99.

[5] Hylson-Smith, *Churches in England III*, 152-4, 170.

[6] W.H. Hunter, 'The Great War', *BM* n.s. 15 (1914), 110-3.

[7] 'A Colonial', 'Christians and the War', *BM* n.s. 15 (1914), 127.

[8] John Ritchie, 'The Chastisement of Nations', *BM* n.s. 15 (1914), 135.

[9] 'WML', *W* 45 (February 1915), 19.

[10] 'WW', *W* 49 (1919), 52, 100.

[11] [John Ritchie], 'Need in the Homeland', *BM* n.s. 15 (1914), 132; [*idem*], 'Privileges and Responsibilities of Saints in the Present time of crisis and of need', *BM* n.s. 15 (1914), 120.

[12] 'WML', *W* 46 (October 1916), 133.

prophecy.[13] In any case, the futurist premillennialism dominant among Brethren expected the Second Coming without any intervening prophetic events. Robert Anderson warned against what he called 'the politics of prophetic interpretation', reminding believers that such puzzle-solving was not fitting when many around them were mourning the loss of loved ones, and asserting that 'The habit of studying prophecy in the light of history and the newspapers, while legitimate within certain narrow limits, always tends to draw away the mind and heart of the Christian from the hope of the Lord's return.'[14] More bluntly, Thomas Baird told those who proclaimed that current events were signs of the imminent Second Coming that 'All such scare announcements dishonour God, discredit prophecy, demean the ministry, and deceive the people.' He condemned 'deceit and scaremongering' of an impressionable and jumpy public, reminding Brethren that no signs were to be looked for before the Rapture.[15]

Several writers sought to discern the spiritual causes behind the war. Broadbent, in an address delivered to a missionary conference in Birmingham, pinned most of the blame on recent developments in German theology: rejection of God as creator and acceptance of evolution had paved the way for rejection of biblical teaching concerning the Fall and redemption; the application to the war of the philosophy of Nietzsche resulted in the conclusion that there was no need to take the needs of humanity or the fear of God into account, with the practical outworking being a policy of terrorising the enemy in order to achieve a speedier result.[16] Lest any should think his presentation one-sided, he also warned that evolutionary theory, the root of the evil, was widespread in Britain also. Ritchie asserted that German rationalism (as seen in higher criticism and atheistic philosophy) and militarism (evident in the pre-war armaments race) were to blame for the war.[17] Pickering apportioned blame among all the major players: Russia had been guilty of cruelty to the Jews, Germany of higher criticism, France of atheism, and Britain of love of pleasure and neglect of God.[18]

Occasional articles dealt with pastoral issues thrown up by events. There is evidence that some took the promises of protection in Psalm 91 to be directly applicable to their loved ones on the battlefield, and were shaken when some were killed.[19] George Goodman, in a reflection on Hebrews 11.24-30, 'Faith on the Battlefields', explained that believers were not immune from suffering, but that God was in control. Some escaped the sword, and some died from it; but all were commended for their faith.[20] By contrast,

---

[13] E.g. 'ASQ', *BM* n.s. 15 (1914), 119; *BM* n.s. 18 (1917), 71; W.W. Fereday, 'The Present Crisis: its relation to the prophetic Scriptures', *W* 44 (1914), 154; W. Scott, 'Prophecy and the Crisis', *W* 44 (1914), 135-6.

[14] Robert Anderson, 'Christians and the Crisis', *W* 44 (1914), 134-5.

[15] T. Baird, 'The Misuse of Prophecy', *W* 47 (1917), 48-9.

[16] E.H. Broadbent, 'Some Spiritual Causes Behind this War', *LOH* 4 (1914-15), 172-3. Nietzsche's glorification of ruthless power was also singled out for comment by A.T. Schofield, 'The World-Rulers of Darkness' (*W* 46 (1916), 85-6).

[17] [John Ritchie?], 'A Divine Deliverance', *BM* n.s. 19 (1918), 133; *idem*, 'The War in Europe', *BM* n.s. 15 (1914), 98.

[18] H[enr]y P[ickering]., 'The European Upheaval', *W* 44 (1914), 133-4.

[19] 'Trustees, Stafford', f.8.

[20] *W* 46 (1916), 37-8.

opposition was expressed to the popular belief that those who died in battle went to heaven.[21]

Some writers dealt with the implications of the war for mission. T. Mortimore Sparks, the first editor of *Links of Help*, acknowledged that it seemed like a disaster: so-called Christian nations were being humiliated before the heathen, and three-quarters of the world's 'Christian' population was at war. Britain's failure to help other nations in need was being visited upon it. Yet all was not lost: opportunities were there for reaching Muslim soldiers; missionaries were at the front ministering to casualties; God was bringing the nations together that they might hear the gospel; converted soldiers would bear witness and themselves be refined through trial; sorrow could lead to close examination of the quality of national life and the reconsecration of believers; and Turkey's actions would result in its loss of influence, thus removing the last obstacle to the return of the Jews to Palestine.[22]

16.1.2 Debates over Pacifism

In answer to the question, 'Should Christians Enlist?', Colonel A.O. Molesworth stated that it was for each individual believer to be persuaded in his own mind.[23] This, however, was precisely the problem: Open Brethren were not united in their response to issues raised by the war, and the divisions which resulted would leave scars which were slow to heal. Questions concerning the believer's responsibility received varying answers in *The Witness*,[24] and although *The Believer's Magazine* was consistent in its conviction that non-combatant service was the best choice, it appears that with the introduction of conscription in 1916 Ritchie began to recognise this as an issue on which believers might genuinely differ.[25] Both, however, began to include special sections in their obituary columns reporting those killed in action.

A range of views appeared among Open Brethren: from the number who enlisted, it is clear that some saw service in the armed forces as justified; some allowed believers to serve as non-combatants and thus to support the war but without taking life;[26] some ruled out any kind of involvement in the war effort.[27] Those who refused to take up arms usually acknowledged that war was a necessary, if perhaps inhuman, part of the exercise of human government, but that it was an inappropriate activity for Christians to engage in;[28] very few, if any, held that all war was inherently evil.[29] In support of their position, they

---

[21] Anon., 'O.H.M.S.', *LOH* 7 (1917-18), 75; John Gray, 'The Latest of Satan's Lies', *W* 46 (1916), 138.

[22] T. Mortimore Sparks, 'The European War (from a Missionary Point of View)', *LOH* 4 (1914-15), 88-90.

[23] *W* 44 (1914), 155.

[24] See the range of answers given in 'QA', *W* 45 (1915), 31-4.

[25] Dickson, *Brethren in Scotland*, 223.

[26] 'YBQB', *BM* n.s. 15 (1914), 118; cf. n.s. 17 (1916), 47.

[27] Hunter Beattie, *The Christian and War* (Glasgow: the author, n.d.), 62-64.

[28] Such a view has been called 'vocational pacifism' (Neil Summerton, 'The just war: a sympathetic critique', in Oliver Barclay (ed.), *Pacifism and War* (Leicester: IVP, 1984), 196-9).

[29] Such a view was expressed in W. Blair Neatby, *The Christian and War* (London: Friends' Tract Association for Friends' Home Mission and Extension Committee, 1915), but by this time he appears to have been associating with the Society of Friends rather than Brethren.

argued that it was inappropriate for those who were ambassadors of the gospel of peace; that believers were citizens of heaven rather than of an earthly state; and that fighting was precluded by the commitment to following Christ's example.[30] If a true believer enlisted, 'he has incurred the guilt of disloyalty to Christ; he has resumed his allegiance to the citizenship of his birth, and he has repudiated the heavenly citizenship to which the grace of God called him'.[31] In killing an opponent, the Christian soldier would either be sending a soul to hell or killing a fellow-believer.[32]

The conscription legislation of 1916 left three choices open to Brethren who were called up: they could serve in the armed forces, or if seeking exemption they could join the non-combatant units such as the Royal Army Medical Corps, or if opposed to any kind of participation in the war they could seek absolute exemption. A number were granted exemption from military service, but few succeeded in obtaining complete exemption from any kind of national service.[33] If not granted such exemption, and unwilling to serve in a non-combatant unit, they would be imprisoned (the fate of 30% of all objectors during the war). Although there were hundreds of Brethren objectors (only the Christadelphians and the Quakers had more), they found it more difficult at the tribunals which heard objections, because they lacked any kind of central body to negotiate on their behalf, and because there was no unity of approach among objectors.[34] The variety of courses which individuals might take may help to explain the lack of unity among Brethren during these years.

G.H. Lang's independent mind, grasp of the legal system, and determined adherence to principle equipped him to assist conscientious objectors in applying for exemption

The resulting liability of Brethren full-time workers to be called up raised issues which went to the heart of Brethren identity. It was difficult for any Brethren agency to help without incurring misunderstanding and criticism; the Editors at Echoes of Service had to explain that a circular they issued regarding applications for exemption was purely for information and was not intended as an authoritative document, nor were they trying to

---

[30] 'QA', *CWo* 30 (1915), 93; 'YBQB', *BM* n.s. 15 (1914), 130.

[31] W.H. Hunter, 'Ought a Christian to Join the Forces of the Crown', *BM* n.s. 15 (1914), 124-5.

[32] John Rae, *Conscience and Politics: The British Government and Conscientious Objection to Military Service 1916-1919* (London: Oxford University Press, 1970), 74.

[33] *Ibid.*, 130.

[34] Wilson, 'Brethren Attitudes', 51-2, 59.

put ministering brethren on a level with clergy.[35] Concern was also expressed when, at George Goodman's suggestion, some leading brethren decided to act as a committee to issue certificates with a view to obtaining exemption for full-time workers, paralleling moves among other denominations to have their workers recognised as ministers.[36] Lang recalled that

> Under the Military Service Acts of 1916 and 1917, evangelists and others ministering in the assemblies were being called to the forces. In several cases, in different districts, it was argued before the magistrates that evangelists were entitled to exemption as being "regular ministers of a denomination." The barrister who took these cases said to me: "We have to show three things: that we are a denomination; that we have regular ministers; that this man is one of them."[37]

Lang, who was active in pleading the cases of conscientious objectors and appeared at tribunals on their behalf, was not the only one who considered it inappropriate to claim exemption as recognised ministers: Brethren were not a denomination, and did not support the idea of a one-man ministry or a clerical caste.[38]

Bitter controversy over pacifism beset Open Brethren in Glasgow, where the evangelist Hunter Beattie became an ardent pacifist campaigner, issuing an occasional publication, *The Word of the Cross*, from October 1915, after local leaders had failed to give clear guidance to believers concerning the right course of action in time of war. After handing out copies of the first number at a conference, he claimed that he was threatened with arrest by leading men.[39] In his opinion, dissidents were being silenced:

> The handful of self-appointed leaders who apparently seek to dominate the servants of Christ, as well as the assemblies of God, have closed doors and barred platforms to any man with a message, unless his message is to encourage the saints to fight and slay their fellow-men. He who teaches the Truth of Scripture which brethren have held and taught UNTIL NOW is not wanted, save among a few here and there where the words and example of Christ have still some authority.[40]

Those in question may have been apprehensive lest anything said at meetings should be deemed to have contravened the 1914 Defence of the Realm Act; Beattie himself claimed that he had often preached at Tylefield Hall with plain-clothes detectives listening for any actionable statement.[41] To him, neutrality on this issue was impossible, and he condemned *The Witness* for attempting to maintain such a position; in a letter, he described Pickering as 'sitting on the fence agreeing with both sides, saying nothing that will bring upon him the offence of the Cross'.[42] Such a stance had, in Beattie's opinion,

---

[35] *EOS* 45 (1916), 356.

[36] Timothy C.F. Stunt, 'Some Centralizing Tendencies among open Brethren before the Second World War' (typescript, 1999), unpaginated.

[37] Lang, *Past, Present, and Future*, 9.

[38] Lang, *Ordered Life*, 174-5; cf. his papers (CBA Box 64); 'Notes for April', *BM* n.s. 19 (April 1918), ii.

[39] Hunter Beattie, *The Christian and War*, 7.

[40] *Ibid.*, 67.

[41] *Ibid.*, 122.

[42] Beattie to Lang, 28 May 1915 (CBA Box 71); cf. Hunter Beattie, *The Christian and War*, 132-3.

pulled the rug from under the feet of those claiming exemption from military service, and was being used against them.[43] In a Glasgow newspaper, *The Sunday Post*, Pickering and another businessman, C.P. Watson (who was treasurer of the Home and Foreign Missions Fund and a Justice of the Peace), repudiated Beattie's views as unrepresentative of Brethren, and listed 297 from Glasgow assemblies who were 'doing their bit'.[44]

16.1.3 The Impact on Assemblies

Meetings went on much as normal in most assemblies, although a few had premises requisitioned.[45] Open-air meetings were prohibited, and streets darkened.[46] However, the intense excitement of the early months proved a hindrance to gaining a hearing in evangelism. Later on, it became evident that many assemblies were themselves affected by prevailing attitudes; Marshall could not recall a time when there was so little evangelistic fervour among them.[47] Nevertheless, a number of assemblies did engage in special outreach, as at Cholmeley Hall, Highgate, which began work among French and Belgian refugees within weeks of war breaking out.[48] In Oxford, German prisoners of war were allowed to attend the Breaking of Bread, and were given a supply of German Bibles by the assembly.[49] In some assemblies, a monthly Gospel service was held which featured the reading of the names of those associated with the assembly who were serving at the front. Relatives would be invited to come and hear their loved ones mentioned and prayed for. New Park Hall, Barking, found their list growing to 185 names, and saw this as a worthwhile means of outreach.[50]

Many assemblies responded to the King's calls for prayer and humiliation, perhaps partly because of their reverence for royalty. They observed the calls to prayer addressed to the nation, but not with other denominations and not in a way which implied belief in a national relationship with God.[51] Neither did they participate in the 'National Mission of Repentance and Hope', called by the Anglican Archbishops in 1916. So, for example, in September 1914 the Bearwood assembly held a meeting to intercede for victory, in January 1915 it observed the King's proclamation of a day of intercession, in 1917 a royal proclamation regarding the food shortage was read during the Sunday meetings, and in July 1919 a thanksgiving service was held, again in obedience to royal command.[52] Other assemblies and groups of assemblies met at intervals for united prayer.

---

[43] Hunter Beattie, *The Christian and War*, 135.

[44] Cutting preserved in CBA Box 74.

[45] E.g. Lattimore Hall, St Albans (1915); Portman Rooms, Baker Street, London (1916); Dalmellington, Ayrshire (1917).

[46] [John Ritchie], 'Records of Work, and Notes for Workers', *CWo* 31 (1916), 62.

[47] Alex Marshall, 'Success in Evangelism', *LOH* 7 (1917-18), 84.

[48] 'WML', *W* 45 (February 1915), 20.

[49] K. Savage, *Steadfast in the Faith* (Oxford: Rewley Press, n.d.), 8.

[50] E.B. Glenny, *New Park Hall, E.H. Glenny memorial, Axe Street, Barking: centenary year 1846-1946: a century of Christian witness* (n.pl: n.p., 1946), 30; for other examples, see Anon., 'O.H.M.S.', *LOH* 5 (1915-16), 175; 7 (1917-18), 122.

[51] *EOS* 43 (1914), 446; 'A National Call to Prayer', *BM* n.s. 19 (1918), 12; 'Testimony for the Lord in Many Lands', *BM* n.s. 19 (February 1918), I; 'WML', *W* 45 (February 1915), 19.

[52] Barton, *Bearwood*, 19-20.

Training camps proved a fruitful venue for evangelism, and there were many reports of conversions, doubtless because those who were there knew what awaited them once they arrived on the Continent. By 1915, South-Eastern Counties Evangelization was receiving more requests than it could cope with from assemblies who wanted evangelists to come and work in local camps.[53] The Cumberland tent was pitched at a training camp in Yorkshire in the summer of 1915; it was open during the day as a reading and writing room, with magazines and newspapers available, and services were held each evening.[54] A number of assemblies opened reading rooms on their premises.[55]

Alex Marshall in the uniform of the Soldiers' Christian Association, with whom he served during World War I

Several evangelists and missionaries became Army Scripture Readers or worked among the troops. Marshall worked among British internees in Holland, and later among the forces in France.[56] The former missionary James Anderson (not the same person as the Rhynie Anderson) was awarded the MBE for his work as assistant secretary of the Soldiers' Christian Association in France from 1915-19.[57] When a training camp designed to house over 100,000 soldiers was opened at Ripon, the evangelist G.W. Ainsworth, who lived nearby, became an unofficial chaplain to it, preaching nightly there to large crowds. Clare gave up his business in Birkenhead to work full-time among troops in the Shropshire army camps. As a result of Bible readings in his home, an assembly was formed which, unlike others dependent on military personnel, outlasted the war.[58]

Assemblies were formed during the war in training camps for soldiers (Abergele, Nigg, Perham Down, and Rugeley), the munitions complex at Gretna, a non-combatant corps camp at Newhaven, and the internment camp for conscientious objectors at Princetown, demonstrating the versatility of the Open Brethren way of 'doing church'. All except the

---

[53] Evangelization of South-Eastern Counties minutes, 5 January 1915.

[54] George Winter, *With Tent and Caravan: the story of thirty-seven years' evangelizing in North-West England* (Penrith: Reeds, 1950), 34.

[55] E.g. Waterloo Hall, Weston-super-Mare (Stephen Somerset Short, *Waterloo Hall, Weston-super-Mare: centenary booklet* ([Weston-super-Mare]: n.p., 1977), 13).

[56] Hawthorn, *Marshall*, 142-5.

[57] *W* 59 (1929), 66.

[58] Anderson, *They Finished Their Course in the 80's*, 30.

last were noted in *The Witness*. Princetown, located in what had been Dartmoor Prison, was not, possibly because the constituency which supported *The Witness* was not over-sympathetic to those who refused to serve their country even as non-combatants.[59] The camp was opened in March 1917, and by the autumn 1,200 detainees were living there. Brethren among them soon began to break bread and engage in a full round of assembly activities. However, they appear to have felt let down by elder brethren. Jesse Webb, replying on behalf of the assembly to Watson and Pickering, whose repudiation of conscientious objection had made public news, stated that

> ever since the outbreak of war, the majority of elder brethren – those to whom we have looked
> for guidance & instruction in the things of God, & who have for years taught us the truths of
> Separation, & of our heavenly calling & citizenship – have maintained an almost unbroken
> silence in regard to the Christians' [sic] attitude to military service. Others have left it to the
> individual conscience, affirming "Let every man be persuaded in his own mind". This has been
> more like the work of an hireling (John 10 v 12-13) than that of overseers (Acts 20.v 28-29.)
> ...[60]

Watson, who had lost a son in the war, was unmoved: 'He who would stand by (if there be such an one) and not protect by force of arms his womenfolk, the weak and the helpless, from such cruelty is no Christian but a dastard.'[61] The objectors' sense of isolation was relieved by Lang, who paid regular visits to minister, although he encountered some difficulty in arranging for baptisms to take place: the assembly at Paignton was unwilling to host them, and that at Tavistock withdrew permission because of local hostility to conscientious objectors.[62] All Princetown detainees were discharged in April 1919, and the assembly presumably ceased to exist.

16.2 Brethren in World War II

In 1937, a letter in *The Harvester* pleaded for teachers to break their silence and offer help to young believers facing difficult decisions, lest assemblies be caught unawares and divided as they had been in 1914.[63] Clearly the divisions which had affected Brethren during the war were still fresh in the minds of many leaders during the 1930s, and they were determined to avoid a repeat. Open Brethren therefore held a number of consultations, lobbied government departments, issued pamphlets, and in a variety of ways sought to prepare young men for a considered response to the increasing likelihood that they would be called up for military service. Yet in spite of this preparation, this war affected the movement more deeply than the previous one had done; as well as the greater physical damage to assembly property, it produced deeper self-examination and hastened the onset of the 'Brethren identity crisis'.

---

[59] See Lang Papers (CBA Box 66) and, for information regarding the camp itself, Rae, *Conscience and Politics*, 185-90.

[60] Letter of 21 or 22 January 1918 (CBA Box 74).

[61] Watson to Jesse Webb, 11 February 1918 (CBA Box 74); cf. Watson's obituary in *BM* n.s. 19 (May 1918), iv.

[62] Lang, *Ordered Life*, 173-4; W. Alford to Lang, 26 March 1918; N. Tapley to Mrs. Smith, 27 May 1918 (both CBA Box 66). For another example of such hostility, see Franks, *Saltisford*, 19.

[63] A.D. Western, letter in *H* 14 (1937), 130.

16.2.1 Preparation for War

From 1937, there was a stream of articles in *The Believer's Magazine* dealing with principles, proposals, and questions related to the likelihood of war; once again, it pursued a consistent line, arguing that war was sometimes necessary for governments but not lawful for believers. By contrast, *The Harvester* carried articles on both sides of the debate.

The oversight in some assemblies gave considerable thought to the position of their young men who wished to be exempted from military service. For example, that at Hebron Hall, Carlisle, consulted locally and nationally and distributed to those concerned a pamphlet by the Bible teacher E.W. Rogers (1893-1977), *The Christian Believer and Military Service*. This originated as a paper read to a meeting of brethren in November 1937, and argued along traditional lines that it was inappropriate for believers, as citizens of heaven, to fight. God now deals with nations in grace, taking a people out of them. 'As to the world of sinners the Christian should now share the love of God towards them; as to the world system the Christian is enjoined not to love it: such love to sinners and non-love to the system will readily determine a non-combatant attitude.'[64] This love was to be extended to enemies, in accordance with the Sermon on the Mount. Rogers advocated joining the non-combatant corps; he had done so in the last war 'because it involved no oath, and incurred no active co-operation in the conduct of the war'.[65]

A similar approach was adopted by Lang in *The Christian Relation to the State and to War*, first published in 1936. Lang stressed the separation between the realm of the state and that inhabited by the believer; as aliens, believers cannot take oaths of allegiance to the state. This separation meant that no negotiation was possible with the authorities (which Brethren were beginning to do), as it implied that the state had rights in the realm of religion. However, even the dogmatic Lang acknowledged that the lack of explicit New Testament teaching on the subject meant that one who joined up from conviction that this was the right thing to do should not be reproved.

On the opposite side, articulate defences of military service were offered. W.G.S. Dobbie (1879-1964), who was to become famous in 1940 as the 'defender of Malta', where he had gone as Governor, argued for the compatibility of *Christianity and Military Service* in 1936. Dobbie used the argument from silence in the opposite way from many Brethren, concluding that there was no hint in Scripture that the soldier's calling was unlawful. Furthermore, in the New Testament the soldier was used as a picture of what was involved in living the Christian life, which would not have been the case if it was wrong for believers to be soldiers. The Christian may not use carnal weapons for spiritual ends, but may do so as a citizen and a servant of the state.

> If, then, the use of force, even to the extent of taking human life, is in certain circumstances approved of God, the calling is in itself lawful, and it must be lawful for a Christian. It is unthinkable that a Christian should feel unable to undertake a lawful and necessary (though unpleasant) duty, while he is content to leave it to non-Christians to carry it out for him.[66]

---

[64] [E.W. Rogers], *The Christian Believer and Military Service* (Kilmarnock: John Ritchie, [1937]), 7-8.

[65] *Ibid.*, 16.

[66] W.G.S. Dobbie, *Christianity and Military Service* (London: Pickering & Inglis (for the Officers' Christian Union), [1936]), 12.

Dobbie also assured British citizens that arms would never be used in a selfish war of aggression, only for defence and the maintenance of peace. To be a member of these forces was, in his view, an honourable calling.

Another argument for military service appeared when *The Harvester* ran a pair of articles in response to the question 'Should a Christian Fight?'. Captain Reginald Wallis, in answering 'Yes',[67] made the point that believers were citizens of heaven, but also of earth, where the sword was a necessary means of dealing with evil.

Scottish Brethren in particular considered the issues carefully. A meeting of elder brethren in Glasgow during October 1938 drew about 500, and resolved to petition the Government to request exemption for young believers, expressing their willingness to engage in works of mercy in an emergency.[68] Early in 1939, another meeting drew brethren from all over Britain; it laid down that believers should refuse to take life, but that they should be willing to help in other ways, and left it to the individual to decide whether or not to offer their services to medical agencies such as the Red Cross. ARP duties were deemed legitimate so long as they did not interfere with attendance at the Breaking of Bread or involvement in Christian service.[69] A petition was drawn up in May 1939 requesting provision for Brethren to serve as non-combatants in an ambulance corps, but this proposal was later deemed unworkable.[70] Regional meetings of elder brethren took place in some areas. For example, a group of West Sussex assemblies met to discuss the part Christians should play in a national crisis; they urged younger members to train immediately in forms of potential service which would not involve taking life.[71]

16.2.2 After War Broke Out

There was not the degree of concentration by the magazines on war-related issues that there had been in 1914-15; articles continued to appear on a wide range of 'normal' subjects. However, *The Witness* was marked by a stronger sense of the imminent End than was *The Believer's Magazine*, which included few articles on the political climate or on the relation of current events to biblical prophecy. Although Tatford ran a series in *The Harvester* during 1939 which contended that the stage was being set for the fulfilment of prophecy, there were markedly fewer such articles, and fewer public meetings on prophetic subjects, than there had been during World War I: this was also true of Evangelicalism as a whole, and was probably a reflection of the more restrained attitude of the churches generally.[72] Borland, in 'Prophecy and the War', warned against unfounded dogmatism on such issues (as in the assumption that these were definitely the last days) and false optimism, suggesting that the church might yet have to undergo almost universal persecution.[73]

---

[67] *H* 15 (1938), 152-4.
[68] W.F.N[aismith?]., 'The Christian and the State', *BM* n.s. 39 (1938), 329.
[69] *H* 16 (1939), 121.
[70] *H* 17 (1940), 37.
[71] *H* 16 (1939), 37; cf. *BM* n.s. 40 (1939), 39.
[72] Hylson-Smith, *Churches in England III*, 176.
[73] *H* 17 (1940), 75.

It seems that, whereas most in Scotland refused military service,[74] most in England were willing to serve. Overall, a higher proportion of Brethren than previously appear to have enlisted or accepted non-combatant service. A few Brethren achieved high rank, among them Dobbie, Orde Wingate, and Air-Commodore P.J. Wiseman (1888-1948).[75] The model for 'Q' in the James Bond books and films was a member of the Brethren – Charles Fraser-Smith (1904-72), a former missionary in Morocco, who invented a range of gadgets for use by secret service agents during the war.[76]

Many full-time workers were exempted as 'ministers', tribunals being noticeably more impartial this time round.[77] Lang claimed that in both wars there were strong protests from many in assemblies against claiming exemption on grounds which implied that the Brethren were a denomination with a recognised body of ministers.[78] However, Tatford evidently sought to avoid this: he was extensively involved in making representations on their behalf, securing the assurance from the Ministry of Labour that full-time evangelists counted as regular ministers, even though Brethren were not a denomination.[79]

16.2.3 The Impact on Assemblies

In 1941, Pickering summed up the impact of war conditions on assembly life.

> Particularly in those cities of our island where the effects of enemy air action are being most felt, local Assemblies are experiencing hard conditions in their endeavours to maintain their activities. The curtailment of opportunities for meetings, the shrinkage in effective personnel through removals, the absence of young men with the Forces, the evacuation of Sunday School scholars, the "black out" and its consequent travel problems, and, in some cases, the handicap of temporary and unsuitable premises necessarily occupied because their Halls are no longer usable, make the carrying on of this spiritual work a struggle.[80]

When war broke out, many local authorities ordered tents erected for evangelistic missions to be taken down immediately.[81] A later directive from the Ministry of Home Security allowed the resumption of tent work, as long as tents were not pitched in the neighbourhood of military or air establishments and they observed the lighting

---

[74] Dickson, *Brethren in Scotland,* 239. Note the more united stance of Scottish Brethren, compared with the division evident during the 1914-18 war. Clearly the memory of the impact of that division on the movement had resulted in attempts to reach a consensus of opinion. However, one exception was Robert Walker of Chryston, whose *The Christian and War: An Examination of the Pacifist Position* (Chryston: the author, 1942) argued in favour of believers undertaking military service.

[75] *W* 78 (1948), 130.

[76] See David Porter, *The Man who was 'Q': the true story of Charles Fraser-Smith, the 'Q' wizard of World War II* (Exeter: Paternoster, 1986).

[77] Wilson, 'Brethren Attitudes', 59.

[78] Lang, *Past, Present and Future*, 10.

[79] *H* 16 (1939), 217; 17 (1940), 1.

[80] 'WW', *W* 71 (1941), 185. The article appeared just after Pickering's death.

[81] Counties Evangelistic Work minutes, 23 February 1940; South-Eastern Counties Evangelistic Work minutes, 16 February 1940.

restrictions,[82] but there were fewer tent missions; apart from the difficulty of holding evening meetings during the blackout, in 1939 the Army had requisitioned most of the marquees belonging to Counties Evangelistic Work, paying them a very good price in compensation.[83] A number of evangelists therefore turned to reaching the armed forces.[84]

New assemblies continued to be formed. Some probably owed their origins to service personnel, as at Amesbury (1940), Tisbury (1941), Andreas, Isle of Man (1943), and Catterick Camp (1944). Others were formed by evacuees, as at Wantage (1940-6) and Wokingham (1940). There were also closures. Some were temporary (because of shortage of workers or requisitioning of premises), but a number were permanent. Evacuations led to a few permanent closures,[85] destruction of premises by bombing led to very few others.[86] Most noteworthy among the latter was Bethesda, Bristol (closed 1940), although before this it had shrunk to a mere twelve members.[87] Most assemblies which lost their premises continued to function.[88] Some assemblies struggled on for several years, finally closing because of their inability to find a suitable alternative venue.[89]

A number of assemblies began to hold regular meetings for servicemen, and considerable fruit resulted, although the work was not given quite such a high profile as it had been previously, partly because the national mood was less jingoistic, and partly for security reasons.[90] Hebron Hall, Carlisle, held a soldiers' meeting after the regular gospel meeting; servicemen chose the hymns, rendered musical items, and gave short talks; serving refreshments provided opportunities for personal conversation. Some conversions resulted, although attendance dropped when the cinema opened.[91] The minutes record the intriguing request that 'Sisters of discreet years be asked to undertake the work of catering at these meetings'.[92] Elsewhere, meetings for servicemen were held in neutral venues, as in Glasgow, where the Astoria Ballroom was used.[93] Campaigns aimed at servicemen took place, as did church parades. In Bristol, George Harpur ran Sunday services for ARP workers which attracted up to 1,000 attenders.[94]

As in World War I, advertisements appeared in the periodicals, welcoming soldiers seeking fellowship and listing the nearest assemblies to a number of training camps. Many opened their premises as rest rooms where service personnel could read, write, relax, and obtain light refreshments, with an epilogue at some point during the evening.

---

[82] *W* 70 (1940), 72.

[83] Mills, *Story*, 31-2.

[84] Beaumont, *Telling Yorkshire*, 7.

[85] E.g. Archel Road, Kensington; Mortlake; Kings Hall, Willesden (all 1939).

[86] Assembly Hall, East Ham (1940); Romeo Street, Liverpool (1941).

[87] Linton and Linton, *'I Will Build My Church'*, 75.

[88] These included Stokes Croft, Bristol; Victoria Hall, Clydebank; Cherry Street, Coventry; Cranmer Hall, Croydon; Fore Street and Heavitree, Exeter; Crete Hall, Liverpool; Paragon Hall, Hackney; and Maberly Hall, Dalston.

[89] E.g. Canterbury (1945), Deal (1946), and East Kilbride (1947).

[90] *The Witness* reproduced a Ministry of Information warning about the danger of giving away information regarding the location of forces units; in the last war, even parish magazines had been used by the enemy as sources of such information and lives lost as a result (*W* 70 (August 1940), ii).

[91] Winter, *Tent and Caravan*, 29-30.

[92] Hebron Hall, Carlisle, Minutes, 12 March 1940 (CBA Box 144).

[93] 'WML', *W* 72 (October 1942), iii.

[94] Anderson, *They Finished Their Course in the 80's*, 60.

Refreshments for such work were often supplied by local believers from their own rations.[95] The evangelist Willie Scott ran a remarkable rest room at Leswalt, near Stranraer, from 1942, opening, funding, running, and even baking for it himself.[96]

The soldiers were not the only ones to benefit from the links made; for instance, the Lancaster assembly played host to a Non-Combatant Corps company stationed at Lancaster Castle from June 1943. There were more of them than civilian members, but they integrated fully into its life, sharing in evangelism, making improvements to the hall (which they used as a rest room), and one becoming an elder.[97] It was common for soldiers visiting assemblies to be invited home to lunch after the Breaking of Bread, and advertisements indicated homes where they could be sure of welcoming fellowship.

Some Brethren became Army Scripture Readers, and Montague Goodman and Robert Laidlaw became Field Directors of the Army Scripture Readers and Soldiers' and Airmen's Christian Association (later known as the Soldiers' and Airmen's Scripture Readers Association).[98] They travelled the British Isles presenting the needs (for readers and rest-rooms) and the opportunities, seeking to secure the support necessary for a massive extension of the organisation's work. Although it was not a Brethren body, its lay ethos made it attractive to Brethren, and its meetings had been advertised in *The Witness* from 1931; long after the war it still featured prominently in their evangelistic concerns.

The needs of foreigners were not overlooked. The assembly at Tillicoultry, Clackmannanshire, held meetings for Polish soldiers stationed locally.[99] Refugees from overseas, especially Eastern Europe, were contacted through meetings in their own languages, former missionaries taking a leading role in these.[100] Prisoners of war were also reached, some attending local assemblies: at Nutley, Sussex, Ransome Cooper (1881-1979), who had combined employment as an analytical chemist with self-financed itinerant work in Germany and Eastern Europe, held services for German prisoners in the local assembly, which resulted in many conversions.[101] Cooper himself would go on to found The Gospel to Britain's Guests, which sought to reach European 'voluntary workers' in Britain.[102] In several cases, links were formed which resulted in assemblies in Britain sending food and other items to destitute believers in Germany after the war. However, such outreach could provoke local opposition, as Elmfield Hall, Harrow, found when they attempted to minister to Italian prisoners of war from a local camp:

> These men, far from home and totally demoralised, were allowed to walk around the area on Sundays. Some Elmfield members, seeing this as an opportunity to show Christian grace, invited them to Elmfield and/or their homes for refreshments, help in learning English and simple

---

[95] Linton and Linton, *'I Will Build my Church'*, 82.

[96] For a description of his work, see James Anderson, *Willie Scott: 55+ Years of Service* (Glasgow: Gospel Tract Publications, 1986).

[97] Penelope Andrews, *The Moorlands Testimony 1897-1980* (Lancaster: n.p., 1980).

[98] Ian Dobbie, *Sovereign Service: The Story of SASRA 1838-1988* (Aldershot: SASRA, 1988), 82-3; *H* 16 (1939), 237.

[99] Stephen Johns, *The Gospel Hall, Tillicoultry: a short history* (Tillicoultry: Gospel Hall, 1990), 15.

[100] E.g. Alec McGregor and Stuart Hine (Anderson, *They Finished Their Course in the 80's*, 71-3).

[101] On Cooper, see Anderson, *They finished their Course*, 51-7; *W* 110 (1980), 127.

[102] On the Gospel to Britain's Guests, see Ransome W. Cooper, *The Gospel to Britain's Guests* (Stirling: Stirling Tract Enterprise, n.d.); *idem*, *The Gospel to Britain's Guests: The story of the first year* (Stirling: Stirling Tract Enterprise, n.d.).

services. (Hymns in Italian were hastily written and set to tunes from Italian operas.) Some became believers partly because of the loving attitude of Elmfield. This loving attitude wasn't always shown by the local residents though – they took a very dim view of this 'fraternising with the enemy' and some windows in homes were broken, homes daubed and fences and gates smashed – an opportunity for Christian grace to the locals![103]

Initially the number of conferences and other meetings advertised in the periodicals was cut back severely; a number were reinstated during the early months, a period which became known as 'the phoney war', only to be cancelled again later in 1941 after bombing had commenced in earnest. Transport difficulties forced some assemblies to hold their Breaking of Bread in the afternoon, as many cities ceased to run bus services on Sunday mornings.[104] Elsewhere, it was the gospel meeting which was moved to the afternoons, though this was not generally considered as good a time for attracting outsiders.[105] The difficulties attending travel meant that some areas made increased use of local preaching gifts.[106] Many assemblies held special prayer meetings regularly, and observed special days of prayer.[107] However, these were distinguished from national days of prayer called by King George VI, which some felt assumed the rightness of the British cause and were founded on the unbiblical concept of national, as opposed to individual, repentance.[108]

Rendle Short urged assemblies not to curtail all their activities; if places of entertainment could continue to function during the blackout, it should be possible for assemblies to maintain evening meetings.[109] However, some found almost their entire Sunday School evacuated, such as Southcroft Hall, Streatham, most of whose scholars were sent to the Chichester area in the autumn of 1939, although the Sunday School reopened in April 1941.[110] By contrast, other assembly Sunday Schools gained large numbers of evacuees; that at Edgmond Hall, Eastbourne, doubled, although here too the evacuees moved on.[111] In fact, youth and children's work was probably the area of assembly life which saw most changes during the war years. In 1942, the government indicated that it wished everyone between the ages of fourteen and eighteen to join some kind of approved youth organisation which would make cultural, moral and recreational provision; membership was initially to be voluntary although it was anticipated that this would become compulsory.[112] In response, a number of urban assemblies set up youth organisations which could be recognised by local education authorities (e.g. Cardiff,

---

[103] Anon., 'Elmfield – A Church Serving North Harrow for Christ', <www.elmfield.org>, accessed 3 April 2005. The use of operatic airs is an indicator of changing attitudes to culture.

[104] E.g. Hebron Hall, Carlisle (Assembly Business Meeting minutes, 3 November 1943 (CBA Box 144)); Clumber Hall, Nottingham (*H* 19 (1942), 152).

[105] E.g. Southcroft Hall, Streatham (Business Meeting minutes, 24 September 1939, 14 August 1942 (CBA Box 100)); cf. 'WW', *W* 71 (1941), 185.

[106] Cf. *H* 17 (1940), 155.

[107] A number of leading brethren called for assemblies to hold prayer meetings on 3 September 1942 ('Special Call for Prayer', *BM* 52 (1942), 135; cf. *H* 19 (1942), 115; *W* 72 (1942), 76).

[108] E.g. the strongly-pacifist A. Fingland Jack, 'National Prayer', *H* 17 (1940), 164.

[109] A. Rendle Short, 'The Churches in War-Time', *H* 16 (1939), 238.

[110] Southcroft Hall, Business Meeting minutes.

[111] Walkley, *Edgmond Hall*, 34.

[112] *BM* 52 (1942), 80; letter in *W* 72 (1942); 'WW', *W* 72 (1942), 52.

Glasgow, Liverpool, and Redhill).[113] Practical activities were included in the programme, so that it would conform to government requirements. The war thus hastened the rise of youth clubs which combined practical and physical activities with spiritual input in the form of an epilogue.

Some were apprehensive at these developments, perhaps with Communist and Nazi youth organisations in mind; they feared that such bodies would strengthen the state's hold upon the young and that the need to seek official recognition would necessitate compromise in the way the work was carried out. However, George Venables, a county youth worker in Stafford from 1942, saw these clubs as a means of overcoming the tendency to lose children once they reached teenage years. He admitted that the introduction of a 'social' side brought dangers with it, but considered that there was much greater danger in doing nothing.[114] Even *The Believer's Magazine* commended such ventures and urged assemblies to give more place to youth in their life, noting the failure of traditional Bible classes to keep hold of their members.[115]

The evangelistic impetus continued to find means of expression in the most challenging circumstances. In the Channel Islands, which were occupied by Germany from 1940, a weekly service was held for French slave workers who had been brought to Guernsey to build fortifications; even though contact was formally forbidden, there was no interference, and several conversions were known to have occurred.[116]

As the war lengthened, assemblies, like everyone else in the nation, found themselves being worn down by the unremitting tension and pressure. With this was coupled a new and devastating threat:

> Many Assemblies in Great Britain are carrying on their work in circumstances of great difficulty, labouring indeed under handicaps of a most formidable sort. The withdrawal by national demands of practically all the younger brethren, the calls made on older brethren by civil defence work or the longer hours and increased arduousness of business and labour in war time, the dislocation due to movement from one part of the country to another of workers in various trades, the destruction of a number of Halls through enemy action, and (in the London area) the new form of enemy air attack – all these have had and are having serious weakening effects on Assembly activities.[117]

It was claimed that at least twenty London assemblies had their premises damaged by flying bombs, some being totally destroyed.[118] Yet even this had its heartening side. Those who had lost everything in air raids found practical fellowship shown them by fellow-Brethren. Air raid relief funds run by *The Believer's Magazine* and *The Witness* were well supported financially, and a local fund was opened to assist those affected by air raids on Belfast in 1940, and this is unlikely to have been the only one. Brethren in some

---

[113] Anon., *Mackintosh*, 15-16; *H* 19 (1942), 102; 21 (1944), 119; 'TLWW', *BM* 52 (1942), 80, 128.

[114] George Venables, 'Post-War Plans in the Sunday School', *H* 20 (1943), 67; cf. Anon., *A New Testament Church in 1955: High Leigh Conference of Brethren* (Stanmore: T.I. Wilson, [1955]), 42.

[115] James Hislop, 'Disappearing Bible Classes', *BM* n.s. 44 (1943), 182-3.

[116] *PS* 4.5 (November-December 1951), 156.

[117] 'WW', *W* 74 (1944), 64.

[118] 'WW', *W* 74 (1944), 80. They included Cranmer Hall, Croydon; Latimer Hall, East Ham; and Denmark Hall, South Norwood.

quieter areas also made known their willingness to offer hospitality to those who needed a short break.

16.2.4 Planning and Questioning

Well before the end of the war, government departments began to plan ahead for the country's peacetime needs in such areas as housing and education. Tatford, in an article on 'Post-War Planning', observed that it was all the rage, except in assemblies, and called for a more co-ordinated approach to such matters as funding improvements to buildings, large-scale evangelistic campaigns, and radio broadcasts.[119] Further articles followed, dealing with open-air work, overseas mission, and Sunday School and women's work. The series represented something of a health-check for assemblies, and generated a lot of correspondence. Some feared that to engage in planning risked grieving the Spirit, as well as resting on questionable hopes of a coming period of peace. However, many seemed open to fairly radical changes in such matters as the pattern of assembly meetings in order to improve the provision of biblical teaching: several correspondents even suggested that the Breaking of Bread could take place earlier in order to make time for a ministry meeting afterwards.[120]

A series of meetings of overseeing brothers from all types of Open assembly took place in London during 1944-5 to consider current problem areas. They began with the Gospel meeting (training for preachers was advocated as a way of improving the poor quality of the preaching), the Breaking of Bread, youth work, literature, and evangelism.[121] As part of the series, the Editors at Echoes of Service convened a two-day meeting to discuss the challenges of post-war outreach at home as well as in 'liberated lands'.[122] Similar regional meetings took place, as in Devon in February 1943 and Suffolk (twice) during 1945; the first focused on relationships with believers in the denominations, the expectation being that many would wish to join assemblies, while the second Suffolk meeting stressed the need for prayer for revival, interpreting the concern about the spiritual condition of assemblies as evidence that the Holy Spirit was at work.[123]

Most of these issues were not directly war-related, but the war engendered a climate in which those burdened for the future of assemblies could speak more frankly on issues which had long been matters of concern. Everything was deemed open to question, and everyone seemed to want to participate in the debates. On some issues, diagnosis may have been easier than treatment, and the meetings were not directly responsible for many great changes. But change was in the air.

The gospel meeting was a particular target of fire from various quarters. In 1932, J.B. Watson had commented on the basis of wide experience that

---

[119] *H* 20 (1943), 50-1.

[120] *Ibid.*, 82.

[121] *H* 21 (1944), 94, 105, 125, 142; 22 (1945), 33, 46; 'TLWW', *BM* 54 (1944), 127.

[122] 'Looking Ahead', *H* 21 (1944), 142. At the 1943 London Missionary Meetings, Vine had predicted an increase in the number of open doors for the gospel ('The Opened Door', *W* 73 (1943), 170).

[123] Anon., 'Where do we Stand?', *BM* 53 (1943), 168; Anon., 'Forward Movement', *BM* 55 (1945), 186-7; Anon., 'Post War Problems', *BM* 55 (1945), 105-7.

The weekly Gospel Meeting at many of the Halls associated with Assemblies is, to state it mildly, ineffective. No one with any experience of these meetings can deny that in very many instances they are negligible as a means of reaching the unconverted outsider. They simply provide the preacher with the disheartening task of fishing in an empty pool.[124]

Such challenges were occasionally heard during the 1930s,[125] but became much more frequent during the war. It was often asserted that the majority of assemblies which still held one saw no conversions through it, and some suggested replacing it with a more informal style of meeting in which more members contributed. The small assembly at Kenton, Middlesex, tried this from December 1939 and found that in time the hall was filled and conversions from non-Christian families resulted.[126] However, a more serious issue was raised by H.L. Ellison, himself a relatively new recruit to Brethren, when he pointed out that it was no longer possible to assume that hearers possessed a knowledge of basic Christian beliefs; a stronger element of teaching was called for, which would entail using a different set of preachers.[127] More generally, immediate preparation was deemed essential if assemblies were to be able to engage in vigorous outreach once the war ended. As Watson noted, this included such things as reserving sites on the estates of pre-fabricated houses now being built. Failure to take similar action after the last war had, he said, resulted in lost opportunities.[128]

Oliver Barclay, in his recollections of the Evangelical world from 1935, has expressed the opinion that by 1945 conservative Evangelicals were more confident, less defensive, more aware of the thinking of others, more forward looking, and more doctrinally minded.[129] Whilst this might have been true in part for some Brethren, there was widespread concern at the condition of the movement as a whole and apprehension for its future. Many considered that the root problem was the spiritual condition of assemblies: '*it is not new methods we need but new men*'.[130] They therefore began to pray for revival, and this move would gather momentum in the immediate post-war years. Tatford posed the provocative question, 'Are the "Brethren" a back number?' He warned against a blinkered approach which failed to acknowledge that God was blessing outside assemblies. 'There is a very real danger that, in the coming days, the assemblies will miss their opportunity unless there is a real awakening and a determination to do the Lord's will and to reject all else.'[131] The extent to which his words were heeded will become apparent in the final section of this book.

[124] J.B. Watson, 'How to Improve the Gospel Meeting. Equally applicable to most other meetings', *W* 62 (1932), 121.

[125] E.g. M. Goodman, 'Why are There so Few Conversions Today? What is the Remedy', *W* 67 (1937), 29-30.

[126] R.L. Hathaway, 'The Gospel Meeting', *H* 21 (1944), 52-4.

[127] H.L. Ellison, 'What about our Gospel Meetings?', *H* 21 (1944), 99-100.

[128] 'WW', *W* 74 (1944), 96.

[129] Barclay, *Evangelicalism*, 59.

[130] E.W. Humphreys, 'Are Our Gospel Meetings Failures', *BM* 54 (1944), 123.

[131] F.A. Tatford, 'Are the "Brethren" a back number?', *H* 21 (1944), 54.

CHAPTER 17

Overseas Mission and Home Identity

It is interesting to note how many of the problems facing those responsible for missionary support reflect problems faced by the movement at home, in its principles, practices, and relationships with other denominations. Growth, too, mirrored growth in the movement at home.

17.1 The Growth of the Work

Examination of the lists of workers in *Turning the World Upside Down* indicates that the numbers of workers commencing their service dropped during 1917-18, but after the war there was a surge of new recruits: 93 began their work in 1920 and 72 in 1921; thereafter forty to fifty went out most years. During the Second World War numbers again declined, only nine candidates going out in 1942. Over the period as a whole, there was a slight increase in the proportion of new workers who were men, from 39% in 1914-23 to 43% in 1934-43. In some fields, the shortage of men was severe: in 1926 Hoste drew attention to the needs of India, for which the Daily Prayer Guide issued by Echoes listed about fifty couples, forty-nine single women, and only seven single men.[1]

Table 17.1: Number of workers listed and annual income: Echoes of Service, 1914-45

	1914	1918	1924	1929	1934	1939	1945
Number of workers	680	c.700	c.900	?	937	1020	984
Total new workers	21	10	32	25	42	32	13
New workers from Britain and Ireland	14	0	17	9	24	20	1
Income (£ 000s)	28	47	68	57	33	36	74

Sources: Echoes of Service, 1885-2003 annual reports, photocopied in 'ECHOES Receipts and allocations 1885-1986' (Echoes of Service); [Short], *Modern Experiment*, 90; *PS* 1.2 (February 1946), 10.

It was increasingly recognised that missionary candidates would benefit from relevant training, practical as well as theological. When Huntington Stone died in 1916, his training home at Greenwich ceased to exist, but in 1920 H.E. Marsom and his wife were asked to establish a training home for young women in Widcombe Crescent, Bath. The curriculum included biblical and medical lectures, and practical training at Twerton Gospel

---

[1] W. Hoste, 'Candidates. IV', *H* 3 (1926), 86.

Hall. A similar venture for men operated at Bristol, where about ten were trained under the superintendence of Rendle Short.[2] It is not known when these ventures ceased, but during World War II an evening class for candidates was run in central London by Watson and Rogers.[3]

For those who were not necessarily committing themselves to full-time service, correspondence study proved popular. In 1901, C.F. Hogg (1859-1943)[4] returned from missionary service in China to specialise in Bible teaching, and jointly with W.E. Vine ran a Bible correspondence school for some years from 1908.[5] Although a noteworthy biblical scholar, Vine's influence among Brethren was exercised chiefly though his role as an Editor at Echoes of Service from 1910, through the time which he gave to answering correspondents' theological queries, and through books setting out a mainstream perspective on *The Divine Plan of Missions* (c.1927) and *The Church and the Churches* (c.1931), both of which originated as series of articles in *Echoes of Service*.[6]

17.2 Maintaining Interest

In spite of the growth in the number of workers listed by *Echoes of Service*, and in attendance at the London Missionary Meetings (which reached 4,000 in 1935[7]), there were suggestions that interest at home was not all it might be. Vine, who as an Editor had an unequalled grasp of the state of British assemblies, wrote in 1937 that only two-thirds had any real missionary concern, and referred to recent meetings of brethren for consultation and prayer regarding the decline in interest.[8] (The mission-orientated ethos of Brethren is evident in that what Vine regarded as a decline was, I suspect, still a rather higher figure than that for other denominations.) A letter from Rendle Short acknowledged that during the previous seven years a diminution of interest had been apparent, suggesting as a reason the preoccupation with building an unprecedented number of new halls, especially in suburban areas; missionary interest had slumped before and revived, and it was time for that to happen now.[9] A few years later, Alec Pulleng (1897-1986), who would become an Editor in 1950, cited as evidence of a pre-war decline of interest the decline in circulation of both *Echoes of Service* and *Links of Help* (which had merged with *The Harvester* in 1936); there had also been a lessening of interest in MSCs (many had ceased to exist), and gifts via Bath had fallen from £67,000 in 1924 to £30,000 in 1937. Whilst the period 1918-33 had seen a net increase of 284 in the number of missionaries on the *Echoes* list, that for 1933-43 was just twelve. Missionaries on furlough had noticed the difference in assemblies at home.[10] The many letters in response were generally in agreement with his contention. The real problem, it was often asserted,

---

[2] H.E. Marsom, 'Missionary Training Home, Bath', *LOH* 11 (9122), 110; Ruoff, *Vine*, 21; Latimer J. Short, 'Arthur Rendle Short: His Missionary Interests', *EQR* 6.1 (January-March 1954), 29-30; Stunt et al., *Turning the World Upside Down*, 56.

[3] Anderson, *They Finished Their Course in the 80's*, 79.

[4] See Hutchinson, *Sowers, Reapers, Builders*, 161-4; *W* 74 (1944), 6.

[5] A.M., 'Correspondence School of Bible Study', *W* 39 (1909), 195.

[6] Ruoff, *Vine*, 19, 86.

[7] *CG*, January 1936, 11.

[8] W.E. Vine, 'Missionary Interest: An Urgent Problem and How to Meet it', *H* 14 (1937), 194.

[9] *H* 14 (1937), 234.

[10] A. Pulleng, 'Foreign Missions', *H* 21 (1944), 66.

was the spiritual condition of assemblies and believers at home, and so recognition of the inadequacy of support for mission fed into the growing sense that all was not well with assemblies.

Nevertheless, believers were active in practical expressions of support for missionaries. Homes for those on furlough were opened in a number of places, the earliest I know of being at Bracknell (c.1895).[11] These were usually overseen by committees drawn from local assemblies. Laing set aside houses for missionary use on the estates he built.[12] Arrangements were also made for the education of children of missionaries. From 1871 the Park School at Yeovil had educated daughters of missionaries and others under the direction of W.H. Bennet's wife.[13] In 1913, a home for missionaries' children was opened at Bury St Edmunds: children attended local schools but a home environment was provided for them, which enabled their parents to remain abroad.[14] On a smaller scale, sewing classes proved a popular activity for women in many assemblies, although there were occasional complaints in *Links of Help* that items were sometimes sent out which were not appropriate to the needs of the family which received them!

Promoters continued to play a vital role in maintaining interest. Apart from Rendle Short, another was James Stephen (1883-1940), who trained at Greenwich but returned to Scotland as an evangelist, becoming editor of *Links of Help* from 1933. The Lancashire evangelist Fred Elliott (1877-1961) had been unable to become a missionary to the Congo, but his obituary claimed that over thirty had received a call to missionary service through his preaching.[15]

There was also discussion of the relationship between interest in home work and interest in overseas work; did one detract from the other, or was there a symbiotic relationship between them?[16] Recurrent affirmations were made of the essential unity of work at home and abroad, but these counted for relatively little in the face of the existence of separate agencies responsible for each, with separate report meetings, although this distinction was inevitable given the distinctive issues faced by those settling in a new country, adjusting to an unfamiliar culture, and learning a foreign language.

17.3 Missionary Study Classes

We have already outlined the origins of the MSC movement and discussed its impact in reinforcing a sense of distinctive identity through study of Open Brethren principles. The movement continued to grow rapidly, with over 200 classes by 1920.[17] Nevertheless, not all approved, and a number of criticisms would be voiced, especially in the 1920s: the concept lacked Scriptural sanction; classes were not led by elders and were encouraged to act independently of the oversight; women were allowed to speak; Bible study was displaced; it amounted to a sectional activity within the assembly and within the community of assemblies (remember that after the 'Needed Truth' controversy, many were

---

[11] 'IML', *W* 39 (March 1909), 53.

[12] Coad, *Laing*, 133.

[13] Stunt et al., *Turning the World Upside Down*, 45.

[14] *LOH* 3 (1913-14), 17. For the home's history, see Walker and Walker, *West Road*.

[15] *W* 91 (1961), 196.

[16] E.g. 'QA', *W* 49 (1919), 47-8; W. Rouse, 'Home Missions as related to Work in Other Lands', *H* 3 (1926), 98-100.

[17] Herbert G. Hall and J. Curtis Brewer, 'A Reminder', *LOH* 9 (1920), 101-2.

allergic to any suggestion of a 'circle within the circle', whether in the local assembly or in the whole body of Christ); classes were federated in what appeared to exist as a corporate entity, with its own name, headquarters, and legislative council (a central council for the movement had been formed in 1918[18]), and distinct from local assemblies; and games formed part of the programme at holiday conferences.[19]

Vigorous defences were mounted. Vine, who had become editor of *Links of Help* in 1920, claimed that

> Before the *Missionary Study Class* work began there was a manifest tendency on the part of young believers to drift away from assemblies into denominations, or into the world. The effect of this work, however, has been to stem the tide, and today there is a large number of young Christians who are found adhering, in devotion to Christ, to Scriptural principles relating to the Church.[20]

Rendle Short asserted that young people were now actively interested in the assembly's work; they knew 'why they are where they are'; they were more interested in mission, participating by prayer, giving, and (in some cases) going; and a number had been changed at the holiday conferences.[21] However, most defences appeared in *Links of Help*, where the writers were preaching to the converted. It was some while before *The Harvester* began to run articles on the movement. *The Witness*, whilst intimating its conferences and generally supportive of it, ran few articles on it or by its leaders. *The Believer's Magazine* referred to it only indirectly and critically.

17.4 The Fear of Centralisation

During the 1920s, concern was expressed regarding perceived tendencies towards centralisation of various aspects of Brethren activity. Counties Evangelization came in for criticism from *The Believer's Magazine*, it being alleged that dependence on the agency replaced dependence on God, and that it virtually controlled the movements of evangelists.[22] Such a role was seen as interfering with the direct responsibility to God of his servants. Parallel to this was a controversy regarding similar tendencies seen as affecting the realm of missionary support. The most eloquent expression of concern came from Lang, who caused a storm with his book *Departure* (1925), the substance of which was incorporated into *The Churches of God* (1928). His fundamental argument was that the New Testament, which was to be regarded as the divine pattern for all matters of individual and corporate life and service, knew of no visible corporate entity in connection with God's work save that of the local assembly, a point which he claimed none of his critics

---

[18] *LOH* 8 (1919), 49.

[19] Anon., 'The Enthusiast meets the Critics', *LOH* 9 (1920), 62-3; H.G. Hall, 'The M.S.C. and its critics', *LOH* 4 (1914-15), 175, 192; [W.E. Vine], 'Recent Criticisms', *LOH* 15 (1926), 194-5, 211-13. The introduction of sport into conference and camp programmes was criticised in *BM* n.s. 20 (1919), 46 (as the thin end of the wedge) and *W* 50 (1920), 303-4.

[20] *LOH* 11 (1922), 65.

[21] A. Rendle Short, 'What is the Use of these Missionary Study Classes?', *LOH* 12-13 (1923-4), 3-4.

[22] 'The Christian's Observatory and Outlook', *BM* n.s. 27 (1926), 53-4; 'YBQB', *BM* n.s. 24 (1923), 110-11.

had grasped.[23] An individualist himself, he insisted that Christian service was always a matter of individual responsibility before the Lord; human organisation tended to replace dependence on God with dependence on, and control by, other people.[24]

Lang's argument was that, just as the Old Testament contained a detailed blueprint for the Tabernacle and its worship, so the New Testament contained a comprehensive pattern for church life. Since the essential conditions in which mission was undertaken (notably the condition of the human heart) did not change, neither should the institutions or methods employed. Recourse to humanly-devised methods was only necessary if the church changed its mission – which, of course, it had no right to do. The trend towards federation of churches resulted from the Satanic purpose to thwart the spread of the gospel, the human lust for power, the misconception of the church's mission as Christianising the nations, and the desire to avoid suffering and to frustrate persecution.[25]

Lang's opposition to centralisation, which he saw as evidence that Open Brethren were becoming a denomination, was avowedly motivated by his eschatological views, in which visible corporate unity prepared the way for the false religion to be set up under the Antichrist;[26] but his Exclusive background would also have made him wary of tendencies to centralisation such as had manifested themselves among those who had followed Darby, Stoney, and Raven. Rejecting the distinction made by Echoes of Service between principles (which were laid down in Scripture) and methods (which were not), he claimed that development beyond the New Testament pattern was evidenced in such matters as pre-arrangement and control of ministry (which served to exclude ministry deemed unwelcome or controversial – such as his own), regional co-ordination and control of outreach, formation of property trusts (compromising the local assembly's independence by reducing it to a tenant of its premises), and centralised oversight of missionary work.[27] Brethren might try to explain that Echoes of Service and other similar bodies were not missionary societies but, as Lang later pointed out, 'A monthly magazine, lists of accredited workers, a monthly statement of moneys received, with regular remittances to workers, make this systematic service almost indistinguishable in the eyes of outsiders from any *pro forma* Mission.'[28] Such centralising developments, borne of expediency, paralleled the apostolic church's first steps to decline, and must therefore be resisted at all costs.

The controversy struck at the heart of Brethren supernaturalism and the belief in 'living by faith'. It is difficult to discern how much impact it had, but it stung the Editors sufficiently for Vine to write to a few senior missionaries late in 1925, enclosing a copy of *Departure* and seeking their opinion.[29] Brethren at Bath were fighting on two fronts: as well as having to respond to Lang's criticisms, they faced the call of a number of businessmen for the introduction of a committee of management.[30] Whereas Lang

---

[23] G.H. Lang to E.H. Broadbent, 30 March 1926 (CBA 5629).

[24] Lang, *Departure*, ch. 8.

[25] G.H. Lang, *Church Federation: A Study in Church Life and Order, with special reference to Denominational Federating* (Walsham-le-Willows, Suffolk: the author, 1942³), 3-5, 27.

[26] Lang, *Departure*, 61.

[27] *Ibid.*, chs. 8-9.

[28] Lang, *Past, Present, and Future*, 10.

[29] Handley Bird to G.H. Lang, 8 June 1926 (CBA Box 66); letter of W.E. Vine and W.R. Lewis, 26 November 1925 (Echoes of Service archive).

[30] Herbert G. Hall to W.E. Vine, 12 December 1925 (Echoes of Service archive).

considered the introduction of business methods to be part of the problem, they saw it as crucial to the solution. Lang was not the only former Exclusive to get into hot water for his views (another was Russell Elliott), but his criticisms touched the heart of Open Brethren identity in a way that Elliott's advocacy of household baptism and pamphleteering criticism of opposition did not. It seems likely that Vine's book on missionary principles, *The Divine Plan of Missions*, was in part a riposte to Lang; in the Preface, Vine's fellow-Editor W.R. Lewis asserted that

> not all new methods are necessarily "departures." Ezra's "List" of those who left their friends and homes to build the house of God, and Nehemiah's "Treasurers" were something new in their day. Doubtless a Daniel would make good use of the former in the way of intercession, and many of the Levites who otherwise had been overlooked were able through the distribution from the treasury to continue their service for the Lord without their eyes being taken from the One Who was their inheritance.[31]

Lang continued to press his arguments at every opportunity, causing further upset in 1939 with the publication of his biography of A.N. Groves, which the Editors at Bath regarded as a stalking-horse for an attack on their approach to mission.[32] Even today, some assemblies will not deal with agencies such as Counties or Echoes of Service.

The controversy also resulted in the departure from Echoes of Service of the missionary traveller E.H. Broadbent (1861-1945). He had become an Associate Editor in 1919, visiting assemblies and conferences to speak about the work and assisting study classes, but not involved with financial matters. However, he was asked to resign in 1928. The official explanation of the severance was that since he was not based at Bath, the inevitable differences of opinion which arose between him and the other Editors were not resolved as they should have been.[33] In his diary, Broadbent recorded that

> I received a letter from Vine and Lewis requiring me to be dissociated from them in the Editorship of "Echoes" on account of my resistance to what appears to me to be the gradual development of this service into a systematized Missionary Society, threatening the independence of the churches in this country and leading to the formation in other lands of Mission Stations instead of churches; in all of which they are not in agreement with me. I replied accepting their action in severing our connection. Although this is the end of a long period of fellowship in service it has in no way tarnished our brotherly affection and esteem for each other.[34]

Pickering reported this diplomatically in *The Witness*:

---

[31] W.E. Vine, *The Divine Plan of Missions* (Waynesboro, GA: Christian Missions Press, n.d. [c.1927]), 5.

[32] W.R. Lewis to J.J. Rose, 27 September [1946?] (CBA Box 69).

[33] See *EOS* 57 (1928), 279, for the official announcement; Stunt et al., *Turning the World Upside Down*, 64.

[34] Diary, 3 October 1928, fos. 229-30 (CBA 3067). According to Lang, Broadbent had expounded these views publicly (G.H. Lang, *Edmund Hamer Broadbent: Saint and Pioneer* (London: Paternoster, 1946), 81-5).

As noted in *Echoes*, the connection of Mr. E.H. Broadbent as Associate Editor has been terminated. He has expressed himself at several Conferences as afraid of the centralisation of mission work, the official list of missionaries, and of the danger of mission stations becoming "pastorates," instead of the pioneering spirit ever entering "regions beyond" as pictured in the Acts. We have long thought that the burden of handling £50,000 of missionary trust money yearly, and conducting correspondence, advising, and guiding 1000 missionaries was not sufficiently realized, and *special prayer* should be made for guidance as to arrangements in future.[35]

The phrasing of this announcement, and the fact that Pickering was willing to publish articles by Broadbent on missionary methods around this time, indicate a measure of sympathy with his concerns.[36] In these articles, Broadbent challenged the tendency to centralisation and the consequent weakening in local assemblies of a sense of responsibility for the work. Features which he considered lacked biblical warrant included lists of accredited workers (a clerical caste in the making); the publication of amounts distributed; the formation of 'Christian Missions in Many Lands' as an umbrella body to deal with civil authorities in certain countries, which amounted to a missionary society; and the founding of a property trust.

Shortly after this the most influential historical work by a member of the Brethren, Broadbent's *The Pilgrim Church* (1931), appeared, again thanks to Pickering. This presented the history not of institutional Christianity but of attempts to carry out New Testament teaching.[37] Broadbent saw church history in terms of a continual creation of independent Bible–based congregations, which were oppressed by institutional Christendom. The moral which he drew from the story was that departure from New Testament practice led invariably to disaster; he called for a return to New Testament church order so that the unity of believers might be manifest to the world and divine blessing be poured out on the church's evangelism. Lang claimed that the book had been written to counter a doctrine of expediency emerging among Brethren, which claimed that it was necessary in changed cultural circumstances to establish service agencies of a type unknown to the New Testament (such as Echoes itself).[38] However, since it had its genesis much earlier, this is probably reading too much into it.

Unlike Lang, Broadbent remained an acceptable and frequent speaker at Brethren conferences, and his movements continued to be reported. This was probably for two reasons. Firstly, although he considered that his public teaching differed significantly

---

[35] [Henry Pickering], 'Personalia', *W* 59 (1929), 22.

[36] E.H. Broadbent, 'Methods of Mission Work, Ancient and Modern', *W* 58 (1928), 267-9; *idem*, 'Christians and Missionary Work', *W* 59 (1929), 33-5. In 1931, Pickering asked whether Echoes was departing from 'faith lines', instancing such practices as the issuing of a circular by an assembly detailing financial support required for its newly-commended missionaries; the Editors informing the sending assembly of a missionary's need for furlough and the assembly's asking for help from others; and the publication of circulars detailing funds required for a return to the field ('WW', *W* 61 (1931), 137).

[37] It began as an address to an MSC conference at Malvern, before 1920 (*LOH* 20 (1931-2), 188).

[38] Lang, *Broadbent*, 90. Lang and Broadbent were near neighbours after Lang moved to Suffolk in 1929: when not travelling in Eastern Europe, Broadbent farmed at Gislingham and oversaw the small assembly there. He had been made an Honorary Life Governor of the British and Foreign Bible Society in 1920 (*W* 75 (1945), 64).

from that of most in the movement,[39] it was not singled out for criticism, whereas Lang's had been the subject of public scrutiny since before the war because of his advocacy of the partial rapture (a doctrine which Broadbent did not accept). Secondly, there were differences of personal style: Lang had a habit of putting his finger on sore spots in Brethren practice and challenging their legitimacy, as well as pressing his views on people in a dogmatic manner, and his tendency to view disagreements on policy matters as foreshadowings of eschatological apostasy made it difficult for him to avoid writing off those with whom he disagreed. Whilst Broadbent's views on many issues were similar, he adopted a more low-key approach.

17.5 Involvement with Other Missions

The special relationship between Brethren and the British and Foreign Bible Society continued, even forming the subject of a *Witness* article in 1938, in which W.J. Wiseman, by now the society's Secretary for Equatorial Africa, pointed out that some of its translations were the work of Brethren missionaries, and that in turn it helped them by subsidising production and distribution costs.[40] Other Brethren associated with it included Broadbent, George Goodman (who served on its general committee from the mid-1930s),[41] Laing,[42] and J.W. Wiles, a lecturer in English at Belgrade University from 1913 and the society's agent there from 1920-41.[43]

1 Widcombe Crescent, Bath, where the Echoes of Service offices were located until 2004

---

[39] Broadbent, Diary, f.233.

[40] W.J. Wiseman, 'The Bible Society and The Brethren', *W* 68 (1938), 133. For translations in which Brethren missionaries were involved up to 1972, see Appendix III to Stunt et al, *Turning the World Upside Down.*

[41] *W* 72 (1942), 91.

[42] Coad, *Laing*, 192-3. Laing became a Vice-President in 1954 (*W* 108 (1978), 82).

[43] *W* 80 (1950), 68.

Generally speaking, however, majority opinion favoured a clear separation from other agencies and denominations on the field, parallel to that maintained in much of the United Kingdom (where support for agencies which circulated the Scriptures also formed an exception to the rule).[44] There was occasional debate on this matter during the 1930s, and one suspects that missionaries did not always tell Bath everything that they did and everyone with whom they worked, since such information might not have been acceptable to their supporters at home.

Developments in Brethren support and practice of mission during this period reflect the way in which their sense of identity was developing at home. It is clear that there was a tendency to centralisation and denominationalisation, in which businessmen played a prominent role. This development could be viewed as an attempt on their part to apply to spiritual work sound business principles concerning rationalisation. The result was internal tension, between those who upheld traditional autonomy and strict separation from other religious bodies and agencies, and those who wished to modernise and co-operate with other Evangelicals. In the next section, we shall see that such tensions were to grow, to the point that it is almost more accurate to speak of a plurality of Open Brethren movements.

---

[44] A debate on this ran in *The Believer's Magazine* during 1936.

PART 4

1945 Onwards:
Change – and Decay?

CHAPTER 18

Responding to Social Change

18.1 The Fast-changing Social Context

The post-war decades in Britain were characterised by rapid and far-reaching social change to which Brethren often found it difficult to adapt. It is impossible to survey that change here, but I want to pick out a few manifestations which are especially important for an understanding of Open Brethren development. I will comment on changes in the Irish Republic at a later point.

In the field of education, the 1944 Act (1945 in Scotland) had raised the school leaving age to fifteen (raised again to sixteen in 1972) and ensured the provision of secondary schooling for everyone. However, an equally significant development was the dramatic increase in the accessibility of university education, symbolised by the creation of a number of new universities during the 1960s. This meant that many more Brethren young people would attend university, and in so doing come face to face with non-Brethren Evangelicals.

1946 saw the establishment of the 'welfare state' with the passing of the National Insurance and National Health Acts. Small wonder that, with this and the steady rise in housing and living standards for most of the population, the late 1950s and early 1960s were characterised by a spirit of well-being, epitomised by Prime Minister Harold Macmillan's famous phrase 'you've never had it so good'. He was right; the great majority of people had not, and many threw themselves into the enjoyment of the new material opportunities open to them, a trend which would make it more difficult for churches to secure a hearing. This was doubtless a factor in the apparent rapid advance of secularisation in the 1960s. This was symbolised in the ethical sphere by the liberalisation of legislation in three areas: abortion, divorce, and homosexual practice. What Brethren, in common with most other Evangelicals (and indeed many Christians of other persuasions), saw as a moral landslide continued during subsequent decades, but the 1980s saw something new, in the post-war period at any rate: a widening of the gap between the 'haves' and the 'have nots'. There is relatively little evidence that Brethren commented on the justice of this or its implications for their practice of outreach or fellowship. The ethical principles of most Brethren remained firmly conservative and were more fully developed in the area of personal ethics than economic ethics, predisposing many who were politically-inclined to favour Conservatism, with its greater stress on individual initiative and responsibility.

18.2 The Growth of Social Concern and Involvement among Open Brethren

For much of this period, most Brethren, Open as well as Exclusive, were slow to think about the implications of Christian faith for the issues of everyday life. Rowdon suggests that the decline of Evangelical social action earlier in the twentieth century had been due to increasing influence of dispensationalism, reaction against the rise of the 'Social Gospel' during the late nineteenth and early twentieth centuries, the growth of the

missionary movement (which removed many workers from the home scene), and growing
state involvement in welfare. Other factors, related to the Brethren ethos, included the
lack of explicit biblical warrant for engaging in such activity, Christocentricity (which
led them to treat Christ's example as a pattern for how believers should live and what
activities they should engage in), and an other-worldly outlook on life.[1] If, as
Bebbington has claimed, preoccupation with the imminent Second Advent was the
greatest theological obstacle to the development of social concern,[2] then the breakdown
among a proportion of post-war Open Brethren of the pretribulational, premillennial
consensus cleared the way for some to begin engaging in sustained reflection about social
issues. This breakdown reflected a desire to come to some kind of accommodation with the
world, especially in its Christian manifestations, and was reinforced by the increasing
popularity of Reformed theology from the 1950s, which helped to fill the gap left in
some quarters by the rejection of traditional Brethren eschatology.[3] Especially in the
version expounded by the Dutch politician Abraham Kuyper (1834-1920), Reformed
theology had developed a doctrine of 'common grace'. This asserted that God gave his
good gifts to all, not just to the elect, and that the capacity for creativity and invention
was a gift of God, present in every human being. Furthermore, God was at work in the
world to restrain evil and promote well-being, using human civil and political
institutions to that end. Such a theology was potentially revolutionary in its
implications for Brethren attitudes to the world, because it affirmed that unbelievers were
capable of doing works which, whilst not of any value in terms of salvation, were
nevertheless to be regarded as good and praiseworthy – quite a contrast with the earlier
tendency to dismiss such works as 'filthy rags' contributing only to a sense of human
self-righteousness. Where such a view gained acceptance among some Open Brethren (and
the writings of Francis Schaeffer may well have contributed to this, as they did for other
British Evangelicals), it facilitated a less aggressive attitude towards unbelievers, and
also a willingness to co-operate with secular bodies (notably statutory agencies in fields
such as health care and social work) in expressing social concern.[4]

In 1960, a letter to *The Witness* from Alan B. Wood of Caterham asked:

---

[1] Harold Rowdon, 'Historical Reflections on Community Involvement', *PP* 5 (October 1997), 7-9.

[2] Bebbington, *Evangelicalism*, 264.

[3] For an example of this new approach, see Peter Cousins, 'The Church and the World', in David J.
Ellis and W. Ward Gasque (eds.), *In God's Community: Essays on the Church and Its Ministry*
(Wheaton, IL: Harold Shaw, 1979), ch. 12. The inclusion of such a chapter in this symposium is highly
significant.

An intriguing case-study is provided by Brethren attitudes towards Britain's entrance into the
European Economic Community (EEC) in 1973. Suspicion of the EEC was probably a legacy of
nineteenth-century British imperial isolationism, which treated most political and theological
developments on the continent of Europe with suspicion; many Brethren came to regard the EEC as
paving the way for the revived Roman Empire of premillennial prophetic schemes. However, *The
Harvester* marked January 1973 with a special issue which focused on the Brethren in Europe and
explored the new openings which Britain's entry might make possible (cf. the similar perspective of
T.P.H. Wickham, a Brethren missionary in Spain, in 'The Challenge of the Common Market', *W* 102
(1972), 43-5, arguing that matters of prophetic interpretation were beside the point in the face of
Christian duty). This was all the more significant for occurring in the first issue edited by Roy Coad;
Tatford had been a staunch advocate of the traditional view in his many books on prophecy.

[4] For the implications of this for Brethren evangelism, see section 21.5.

It has been a principle held very firmly by the Brethren for a long time that there is little, if any, virtue in taking much interest in the affairs of the world apart from the resurgence of Israel and the decadence of society. It is a rare thing to read in *Echoes of Service* the effect of political happenings on the work and witness of missionaries. Is it possible that we are in error in taking such little interest? ...

On matters where there is a lack of Christian ethics and love for humanity are we right in keeping silent?[5]

In subsequent years, a growing minority would take a similar view. The greater emphasis on a more fully-developed approach to life in this world is evident in a 1973 *Harvester* article by Brian Griffiths of the London School of Economics, who later became an adviser to Margaret Thatcher when she was Prime Minister. He claimed that there was no distinctive Christian attitude to political and economic issues, because most were not matters of principle but about what was politically possible in a given situation. However, his conclusion is worth noting: 'As Christians we must have some sort of idea of the sort of society and world we wish to create and live in and it is up to us, at the very least, to confront our nation with this choice; better still and with God's help to be instrumental in making the hopes a reality.'[6] No longer was such involvement universally condemned as trying to pre-empt the millennium. In the same way, Brethren contributed to wider debate in an Evangelical symposium on *Pacifism and War* which appeared in 1984; this included a defence of pacifism by R.E.D. Clark (a retired Chemistry lecturer), as well as definition and critique of the concept of the 'just war' by Neil Summerton, a senior civil servant with academic expertise in this field. Environmental issues, too, began to figure in the pages of *The Harvester* from the mid-1970s,[7] aided by the fact that two Brethren with a professional interest in this area had impeccable credentials: Charles Fraser-Smith, who had become a pioneering agriculturalist in England after returning from missionary service in Morocco, and Harold Darling, who was Principal of an agricultural college, Wye College (Ashford), and belonged to a large and influential Ulster Brethren family.

In the 1960s, the Christian Brethren Research Fellowship (CBRF) pioneered Open Brethren responses to developments in fields such as education; Randle Manwaring had urged Christians to get involved in all areas of society as salt and light.[8] By 1988, *The Harvester* was running a series on ethical issues, 'Doing Right', discussing such topics as war, politics, and trades unions in a way which demonstrated a much greater willingness to be involved in the world than would have been acceptable under Tatford's editorship. More remarkably, in 1990 a member of the Brethren, Peter Cousins, became editor of *Third Way*, an Evangelical magazine which devoted considerable space to coverage of the arts and social and political issues.

All the same, those who did try to apply Christian thinking to social, moral, and ethical issues sometimes felt like voices crying in the wilderness. The best-known moral activist among Brethren, Charles Oxley (1922-87), is a case in point. A former member

---

[5] *W* 90 (1960), 432.

[6] Brian Griffiths, 'The challenge of power: an economist's view', *H* 52 (1973), 2-3.

[7] E.g. C.F. Fraser-Smith, 'The Peril of Pollution', *H* 56 (1977), 168-9.

[8] Randle Manwaring, 'The Christian and Culture', *JCBRF* 3 (October 1963), 4-10. For the history and significance of the CBRF (later Partnership), see section 20.2.3.

of the Churches of God, he moved away from their policy of non-involvement in social issues in some spectacular ways. Firm convictions about the shortcomings of contemporary secular education led him to set up Christian schools at Tower College (1948) and Scarisbrick Hall (1964) in Lancashire, and Hamilton College (1983) in Scotland. He campaigned in the areas of broadcasting and personal morality (becoming Vice-Chairman of The National Viewers' and Listeners' Association, founded by Mary Whitehouse). Later he succeeded in infiltrating the Paedophile Information Exchange, although he never felt that the Home Office responded adequately to the information he obtained.[9] Oxley was concerned that many Evangelicals, Brethren in particular, were reluctant to face up to contemporary issues. He sought to remedy this as a member of the Swanwick Conference committee, but met resistance from some who could not accept the idea of inviting non-Brethren speakers (one wonders whether the real reason was that they were uncomfortable about the idea of Christians engaging in moral campaigning in the public arena). Yet Oxley, for all his readiness to break new ground (for Brethren if not for other Evangelicals), exemplified the tendency, shared with many other Evangelicals, to focus on personal ethical issues.

The 1961 Swanwick conference had advocated Christian involvement in society,[10] and at that of 1962 Stephen Short exhorted Christians to work for the realisation of God's will, not only through evangelism but also through working for righteousness in every area of life.[11] However, the only one before the 1980s to take an ethical theme was that of 1965, which examined the 'New Morality', often also known as 'situation ethics', a way of thinking which claimed that traditional ethical principles, including those which Evangelicals regarded as clearly taught in Scripture, needed to be re-thought in the light of the principle of love for others. And even in the sphere of personal ethics, only *The Harvester* carried any response to the onset of the AIDS crisis in the 1980s.[12]

18.3 The Burning Issues

18.3.1 Politics and Trades Unions

The London Missionary Meetings in October 1951 saw their largest-ever attendance, even though they clashed with a General Election, an indication that most Brethren still did not vote.[13] Many continued to reject political involvement out of hand.

> The suggestion that the Spirit of God may lead a man walking in truth and godliness to seek the
> world's suffrage in order to get a seat on its councils, or in parliament, is, in our judgment, so

---

[9] See Anderson, *They Finished their Course in the 80's*, 137; David Raynor, *The Standard Bearer: A biography of Charles Oxley* (Weston Rhyn, Oswestry: Quinta Press, 2001).

[10] Anon., *Personal Life and Behaviour in a Pagan Society: Addresses given at a Conference of Brethren at Swanwick* ([n.pl.: n.p., 1961]).

[11] Anon., *The Rule of God in The Life of Man. Addresses given at a Conference of Brethren at Swanwick. September, 1962* ([London: G.W. Robson], n.d.), 52-3.

[12] John Allan, 'AIDS: The Challenge to Christian Action', *H*, May 1987, 15-20. More recently, Dr N.J. Gourlay has combined a sensitive pastoral approach with firm convictions in 'HIV/AIDS', *BM* 112 (2002), 133-4, 165-6.

[13] A. Naismith, 'London Missionary Meetings. October 1951', *EQR* 4.1 (January-March 1952), 17.

completely at variance with the Scriptures as to be unworthy of serious consideration. It is not a question as to whether Christian men have occupied such positions, but were they led of God?[14]

According to P.F.W. Parsons of Wimbledon, politics represented a distraction from the Lord's work. Voting amounted to 'an attempt to decide who is to rule, instead of leaving that question to God', and involved assuming the position of rulers rather than subjects. Democracy was 'the very abandonment of government, a human substitute for the government of God'. The New Testament was not interested in reform movements, but in inner change.[15]

But views were no longer so uniform. When a contributor to *The Believer's Magazine* during 1962 denied that Christians should vote at local or national elections,[16] he drew a response defending Christians who voted, based on the fact that the believer remained a citizen of an earthly country;[17] further letters evidenced mixed reactions. Borland, in summing up the issues as editor, warned against dogmatism, but in view of the Christian's priorities and the risks involved in political activity, he thought it preferable to keep apart from politics.[18]

Before the 1964 election, *The Harvester* printed a pair of articles on the theme 'Should a Christian vote in the General Election?' Edwin Lewis argued: 'Of course he should!' Constitutional government was a safeguard against misuse of power, the believer had a duty towards others, and those who accepted state benefits should fulfil their responsibilities as citizens. Parsons took an opposing line: 'Most definitely not!' Once again he asserted that it was for God to set rulers in office, not for us. 'Voting is ... an attempt to decide who is to rule, which is evidently God's prerogative. In exercising the vote we indirectly assume the role of rulers and depart from the role of subjects.' Believers were not of this world, and the New Testament was not concerned with such matters.[19] In 1986, a writer in *Precious Seed* reiterated the traditional view that the believer's responsibility was to pray, pay, and obey.[20] For some, even campaigning on particular moral issues was suspect. A writer in *Assembly Testimony* smelt eschatological apostasy in the Keep Sunday Special Campaign's activities, because it brought together members of a wide variety of churches in a kind of ecumenical relationship; he urged readers to keep apart from the movement.[21]

On the other hand, in 1986 Jonathan Ingleby outlined 'A Christian Approach to Political Involvement' in a series of *Harvester* articles. An indication of how far some had moved from a traditional Brethren position was provided by *Aware* in April 1992. In the run-up to a General Election, John Allan in his first issue as editor included several articles on political themes, taking it for granted that 'Christians will have a role in the decision-making process'.[22] Furthermore, he challenged the narrowness of the range of

---

[14] James Scott, 'The Christian and the World', *H* 24 (1947), 86.

[15] P.F.W. Parsons, 'The Christian and the Powers that Be', *BM* 65 (1955), 105-9, 111.

[16] 'BQB', *BM* 72 (1962), 186.

[17] *BM* 72 (1962), 284.

[18] *BM* 72 (1962), 299, 310-11, 328, 346-8.

[19] *H* 43 (1964), 56-8; the quotation is from page 57.

[20] Malcolm Horlock, 'My Responsibility to Civil authorities', *PS* 37 (1986), 69-72.

[21] John B.D. Page, 'Is Sunday Special?', *AT* 202 (March-April 1986), 51.

[22] John Allan, 'Change in the Air', *A*, April 1992, 1.

issues with which Christians had been prepared to engage.[23] An unsigned article argued that politics was needed to cope with, and limit the effects of, structural evil.[24] This would have been an unfamiliar concept to most Brethren of the time, although they had always manifested a gut feeling that the structures of the world did indeed represent manifestations of evil, in the sense of a refusal to bow to the Lordship of Christ, and would one day provide the means for the rise of Antichrist: as early as the 1830s, Wigram had claimed that 'the higher I get in the world, the nearer I get to Satan'.[25]

In spite of widespread disapproval of political involvement, several Brethren were politically active at local or national level. Three became Members of Parliament (all Conservative, all knighted, and all in time left the Brethren): John Henderson, Brian Mawhinney, and Peter Mills. Henderson, a former businessman, was MP for Glasgow Cathcart from 1946-64.[26] Mawhinney, a medical lecturer who had been brought up in Apsley Street Hall, Belfast, was MP for Peterborough from 1979-97, and then Cambridgeshire North-West, serving as chairman of the Conservative Party from 1995-7.[27] He had been encouraged to enter politics by Cecil Howley, although his home assembly expressed disapproval; the hostile reception which he received on his first visit there after appointment as a Minister of State at the Northern Ireland Office indicates that Ulster Brethren, for all their traditional outlook, were capable of entertaining strong political opinions.[28] Mills was MP for various Devon constituencies from 1964-87, a Parliamentary Secretary at the Ministry for Agriculture, Fisheries and Food, and involved in formulating European agricultural policy.[29] At a regional level, Ian Clark oversaw the relatively successful transition of Shetland into an oil-dominated economy in the early 1970s.[30] In a more restricted setting, Laing was president of his local Conservative Association from 1945-68,[31] and doubtless others were involved in politics at this level; indeed, the greater scope for Independent candidates in local government may have made it easier for Brethren to be involved, since they would thus be spared the need to commit themselves to upholding all aspects of a party manifesto. The movement's innate conservatism, however, meant that most Brethren were slow to criticise government policy too stridently. Although church leaders from the Archbishop of Canterbury downwards came into high-profile disagreement with the Prime Minister, Margaret Thatcher, over the morality of the Falklands War of 1982, *The Harvester* was the only British Brethren periodical to discuss the war; whilst expressing the view that it 'should never have happened', Coad's editorial majored on expressing sorrow on account of the extensive British input to Brethren expansion in Argentina.[32]

Traditional attitudes, especially those of individual responsibility and separation from the world, can be seen at work in Brethren thinking about trades unions. In 1947, there

[23] John Allan, 'How should a Christian vote?', A, April 1992, 3.
[24] Anon., 'Should Christians be involved in politics?', A, April 1992, 4.
[25] [Darby et al.], Collectanea, 85.
[26] See Anon., Who Was Who 1971-1980 (London: A. & C. Black, 1989²); Dickson, Brethren in Scotland, 323-4; Jeremy, Capitalists and Christians, 392-410; W 105 (1975), 276.
[27] Anon., Who's Who 2003: An annual biographical dictionary (London: A. & C. Black, 2003).
[28] Brian Mawhinney, In the Firing Line (London: HarperCollins, 1999), 24, 31-2, 89-90.
[29] Anon., Who Was Who 1991-1995 (London: A. & C. Black, 1996).
[30] L. Wilson, 'Witnessing in Shetland', H, February 1981, 2-5.
[31] Coad, Laing, 172.
[32] H, June 1982, 1.

had been a debate about union membership and the 'closed shop' in the correspondence pages of *The Harvester*. Some years later, Bruce misjudged his readership when he claimed not to have realised that disapproval of union membership survived in any assemblies, and called for mutual acceptance of different views on the subject.[33] More in line with the majority view was a series of articles in *The Believer's Magazine* during 1976, in which John Heading (an Aberystwyth academic) looked at the issues in the light of recent legislation concerning the 'closed shop' and the opportunities provided for exemption from union membership. He applied the unequal yoke of 2 Corinthians 6 to union membership, as committing members to leadership decisions, and expressed the belief that membership could lead individual believers into situations where they would not be serving their employer in the manner enjoined by the New Testament; strikes, he considered, were wrong, and believers should be content with what they had. In addition, compulsory union membership entailed political affiliation, and foreshadowed the imposition of the mark of the Beast.[34] One Scottish writer took a more moderate line, being in favour of Christians in unions, but not of striking.[35] The letters generated by his article expressed a range of opinions, from seeing unions as unequal yokes to defending striking.[36] It should also be noted that even when the consensus of opinion was opposed to union involvement, there were a few exceptions in practice, although Dickson notes that those involved in politics and union affairs in Scotland usually left the Brethren.[37]

18.3.2 Care of the Needy

During the 1950s and 1960s, a number of areas took steps to open homes for elderly believers. Although the provision made by the 'welfare state' was expanding rapidly, many would not have found it congenial to reside in a home populated mostly by unbelievers. Some homes were initially run on 'faith lines', most notably those founded at Frinton in Essex by Ernest Luff, but the increasing complexity and rigidity of government legislation, as well as the changing attitudes among Brethren to accepted business principles, meant that these eventually adopted a more conventional approach to financing, although some still rejected local authority support in order to ensure freedom to run in the way that they wished.

Another result of continuing change in this field has been the changing roles of agencies such as the George Müller Foundation.[38] It continues to support Christian workers by donations through the SKI, but the residential homes for which it was famed were replaced by non-residential family centres. In 1983, it began working among elderly people, with a care home and sheltered accommodation. The family centres have in turn closed, but its website and Annual Reports now include details of a wide range of projects undertaken in partnership with local churches throughout the Bristol area, by no means all of them Brethren; such a development reflects increasing government recognition of the role of 'faith communities' in social action. Nonetheless, the distinctive refusal to make financial needs known except by prayer continues.

---

[33] 'AQ', *H* 44 (1965), 171.

[34] John Heading, 'The Case Against Union Membership', *BM* 86 (1976), 234-7, 281-3, 299-300.

[35] John Dempster, 'Union membership and the closed shop', *W* 108 (1978), 108-10.

[36] *W* 108 (1978), 213-15.

[37] Dickson, *Brethren in Scotland*, 322.

[38] Julian Marsh, 'The George Müller Foundation', *PP* 25 (January 2004), 25-6.

Even the traditionally-orientated *Believer's Magazine* called its readers in 1985 to be more compassionate towards the poor, challenging them to preach to and assist the needy, criticising elaborate church buildings and ostentatious dress ('we demand a middle class dress while all the Scriptures ask is that the males have uncovered heads, the females covered heads and gaudy apparel be eschewed by all'), and urging them to live at the level of those they were seeking to reach; however, there was nothing in all this which could not have been said by John Ritchie.[39] But in 2000 it carried a notification of the commendation by Hillbank Evangelical Church in Dundee of a couple for work among local homeless and underprivileged.[40]

In all this, we must recognise that assemblies lagged well behind individuals in expressing social concern, except when it was a matter of providing for their own members. When *Harvester* readers were asked in 1973 what practical social service their churches performed in the community, there were no replies.[41] Similarly, a 1974 *Believer's Magazine* article on the assembly's impact through social service focused on outreach; there was little consideration of other aspects of service to the community.[42] Corporate social activity was adopted initially because of its perceived value in securing a hearing and creating openings for the gospel – as had been the case in the late Victorian period, when a number of urban assemblies had engaged in such activities as visiting lodging-houses and running free breakfasts for the very poor. Brethren were slow to adopt the newer Evangelical view, expressed in the influential *Lausanne Covenant* (1974), that evangelism and social action were equal partners in Christian outreach to the world.[43] Indeed, I would think that even now relatively few hold this view in any thought-out way. Whilst they have shared in the upsurge of concern for famine and disaster relief which was evident in British society from the 1960s,[44] this concern has not often provoked radical thinking about lifestyle and material consumption. I suspect that such concern is more a continuation of the older tradition of concern for the needy which found expression in the post-war Liberated Lands Fund and the 'Inasmuch' Relief Fund, both Brethren agencies, which sought to provide material assistance to believers in Germany, Austria and other desperately needy European countries.

However, involvement in community issues, coupled with a more relational approach to evangelism, has been a key to growth for some progressive congregations. For example, in 1992 the assembly at Greenford in Middlesex won considerable local respect by heading up a campaign against the attempt of the pharmaceutical company Glaxo,

---

[39] T[om]. W[ilson]., 'Editorial Searchlight', *BM* 95 (1985), 129.

[40] *BM* 110 (2000), 383.

[41] 'Readers' Forum', *H* 52 (1973), 205.

[42] James Anderson, 'Our Assembly. No. 11', *BM* 84 (1974), 358-9. However, the same author had previously advocated helping senior citizens, providing hospital transport, and caring for alcoholics and ex-offenders ('The Welfare State', *BM* 77 (1967), 250-2).

[43] For the text of the *Lausanne Covenant*, see <www.gospelcom.net/lcwe/statements/covenant.html>. Largely drafted by John Stott, it affirmed the dual mandate of the church to evangelise and to engage in social action. For a summary of how this approach has developed, see David Bosch, *Transforming Mission: Paradigm Shifts in Theology of Mission* (Maryknoll, NY: Orbis, 1991), 403-8.

Coad ran a series of articles expounding Lausanne's thinking in *The Harvester* during 1976-7, but some would merely have perceived this as evidence that the magazine editors were no longer in touch with their constituency.

[44] Hastings, *English Christianity*, 516.

whose world headquarters were located there, to secure closure of a road running past the church.[45] Such an approach to evangelism, which relies on discovering the felt needs of a local community and then seeking to meet them, could be seen as a response to the increasing marginalisation of the churches in society, and to the failure of traditional evangelistic methods to make real contact with the unchurched. It is probably too early to say how successful such an approach has been; there are signs that in some cases it has helped assemblies to end the pattern of decline which forms the theme of the next chapter, but some conservatives fear that the cost involved is too great, alleging that in it the gospel is compromised.

18.3.3 Fiction and Football

The two cases of fiction and football illustrate a continuing shift in Open Brethren attitudes to cultural and leisure pursuits. Brethren opposition to fiction gradually declined, partly because as the social composition of the movement came to include a greater proportion of middle-class members, many of whom did not share the earlier disapproval of novels. By the 1950s Pickering and Inglis, who had been publishing the *Lily Stories* for some decades, were advertising novels as part of their list.

Patricia St John

A few years earlier, Patricia St John (1916-93), daughter of Harold St John and a Brethren missionary, had begun her career as a children's novelist, producing classics such as *Treasures of the Snow* and *The Tanglewoods' Secret* which were acclaimed by Evangelicals of all types.[46] From the mid-1970s, *The Harvester* carried occasional articles on various aspects of the arts, and in 1991 (as *Aware*) it featured a series by Neil Dickson on Brethren and literature, exploring how Brethren were portrayed, as well as discussing Brethren writers and attitudes. For him, such a study posed an unsettling question:

---

[45] Harold Rowdon (ed.), *Ten Changing Churches* (Carlisle: Paternoster for Partnership, 1999), 24.

[46] On Patricia St John, see *A*, January 1994, 20-22; Patricia St John, *Patricia St John Tells Her Own Story* (Carlisle: OM, 1995).

While the Brethren give texture to the social background, the writers also use them as a commentary on a type of Christianity. In general they proclaim that the Brethren are narrow, ferocious, often hypocritical and, when not being merely bizarre or comical, irrelevant. ... Is this another way in which fiction tells wicked lies, or do these writers speak the truth?[47]

The only literary figure of any significance to have remained among Brethren was Robert Rendall (1898-1967) of Kirkwall, Orkney, who was by turns draper, archaeologist, crofter, poet, biblical expositor, and conchologist.[48] It is interesting, though, that even Rendall found that the poetic muse deserted him when he tried to write about 'Christian' themes.[49] Others who had been brought up among Brethren but rejected their heritage (and often any kind of Christian faith) include the poet Patricia Beer, who wrote of her upbringing in *Mrs Beer's House* (1968), and the Ulster philosophy lecturer Max Wright, whose *Told in Gath* (1990) is a revealing yet profoundly depressing account of loss of faith which draws considerably on Edmund Gosse's *Father and Son*.

Sport is not now so widely condemned as it was a century earlier, and a Scottish international footballer, Brian Irvine, was a member of Deeside Christian Fellowship, Aberdeen, during the 1990s.[50] Some assemblies have formed their own football teams, including those at Newcraigs (Kirkcaldy), Northwood Hills, Hellesdon (Norwich), and Wandsworth.[51] The last-named, for example, formed 'Westside FC' in 1996, which grew to include seven teams playing in local leagues, and was open to non-Christian players. Glenwood Church, near Cardiff, which was founded in 1977, chose to build a sports hall rather than a more traditional religious building, because this was seen as more 'user-friendly'.[52] In more traditional circles, however, football (or any other sport) is unlikely to figure in assembly activities apart from youth camp programmes. An Uxbridge writer included entertainment and sport among the 'careers that cater for the soulish side of man' and which were therefore deemed off-limits for believers.[53] Even the enjoyment of sport as a leisure activity is still rejected by some; when one Harrogate teenager was converted in 1981, he sensed instinctively, without being taught about separation, that sport and the lifestyle which went with it were 'not in keeping with the life of a Christian' and gave up playing cricket and watching rugby.[54] Nevertheless, churches which have included

---

[47] Neil Dickson, 'The Brethren and Literature. 1. Fiction's wicked lies', *A*, June 1991, 22.

[48] For Rendall, see Neil Dickson (ed.), *An Island Shore: Selected Writings of Robert Rendall* (Kirkwall: The Orkney Press, 1990), 17-49; *H* 46 (1967), 125; *W* 97 (1967), 286-8.

[49] John Allan, 'John Allan on Robert Rendall', *A*, May 1991, 20-1.

[50] Dickson, *Brethren in Scotland*, 342.

[51] See, respectively, 'Newcraigs Evangelical Church', <www.newcraigs.co.uk>, accessed 3 April 2005; Rowdon (ed.), *Ten Changing Churches*, 78; 'Meadow Way Chapel', <www.meadow-way.org.uk>, accessed 3 April 2005; [John Baigent], *The West Side Story: One Hundred Years of Christian Witness 1902-2002* (London: West Side Church, [2002]), 9.

[52] Alfred Harker, 'The Glenwood Story', *H*, July 1981, 5-8. Harborough Evangelical Church did the same thing (*H*, July 1988, 18).

[53] D.C. Hinton, 'Young Believers. Milestones (5) Leaving School', *BM* 94 (1984), 132. The term 'soulish' was popularised by the writings of the holiness teacher Jessie Penn-Lewis and the Chinese church-planter Watchman Nee, who was influenced by Keswick and by Brethren. It refers to attitudes and actions which have their origin in human nature rather than the work of the Holy Spirit.

[54] Robert Plant, 'My Conversion and Call (81)', *AT* 304 (March-April 2003), 45.

sporting activities in their programme have found them a valuable means of making contact with men in a non-threatening context.

CHAPTER 19

Open Brethren and the Religious World

In his study of Open and Exclusive Brethren in England from 1935-70, Shuff has argued that whilst Brethren claims to provide a distinctive expression of the New Testament pattern for church life were both plausible and attractive in the pre-war context of Evangelical isolation and defensiveness against apostasy, they were less so once Evangelicalism began to experience a measure of revival and renewed confidence from the 1950s, not least because this was an eventuality which had not been foreseen in Brethren eschatology, which anticipated the unrelieved decline of Christendom.[1] Brethren involvement in wider Evangelical activity was thus something of a mixed blessing: whilst it enabled them to share their distinctives with others, it also undercut their distinctiveness and therefore their *raison d'être*.[2] This chapter examines Brethren involvement in interdenominational Evangelicalism and the impact on the movement of significant Evangelical trends; the implications of this for Brethren identity will be explored in Chapter 20.

19.1 Open Brethren Involvement in Interdenominational Evangelicalism

19.1.1 The Impact of Billy Graham

The first real interdenominational challenge after the war was presented by the arrival from America of Youth for Christ. In anticipation, one writer gave a glowing description of its American activities, attributing its success to its interdenominational character; the enemies of the gospel were advancing, and in the concentration camps we will discover the true union of all believers, so (he argued) why not do so now?[3] It was British Youth for Christ who first invited Billy Graham to England in 1946, and one of their sponsors was a former Tunbridge Wells brother, Louis Ford.[4] Full coverage of Graham's early visits was provided by *The Witness* and *The Harvester*. Watson was pleased to inform readers that Graham's mother was in fellowship with Brethren, and that Graham himself used to be, and had been as a student at Wheaton.[5]

Graham's visits to Britain were to be epochal in their impact on Open Brethren. Whereas their eschatology had conditioned them to expect Christendom's steady slide into apostasy, here was evidence that God had not finished with the sects but was reviving

---

[1] Roger Shuff, *Searching for the True Church: Brethren and Evangelicals in Mid-Twentieth-Century England* (Carlisle: Paternoster, 2005), 42.

[2] Shuff, *Searching*, 258.

[3] Gavin Hamilton, 'Youth for Christ', *H* 23 (1946), 6.

[4] Leslie James, 'Louis G. Ford – the man God taught to profit', *H* 58 (1979), 356-7. Ford joined the Open Brethren, founded Marine Hall in Eastbourne, and built up a chain of ironmongers' shops.

[5] 'WW', *W* 81 (1951), 12.

them.[6] Many realised as they had never done before that the gospel was being preached – and blessed – outside their circles, and in a measure beyond anything they had ever seen.[7] This led to considerable questioning, and was undoubtedly a factor in the popularity of the various annual residential conferences which served as think-tanks for Brethren seeking fresh vision and direction for their churches.

However, Open Brethren evaluation of Harringay was mixed. On the positive side, Watson drew lessons from it concerning the power of prayer (he noted that it led to sustained effort), the sufficiency of Scripture (Brethren had the right message all the time but preached to the converted), and the challenge of after-care (what sort of a church were Brethren providing for new converts?). He asserted that those who did not join in should not criticise those who did; Graham's visit had come about because many Evangelicals had been praying for an outpouring of the Holy Spirit, and finally some felt it was time to do something. A good number of inquirers had been put in touch with assemblies.[8] A robust defence of involvement also appeared in *The Witness*; according to the author, David Fairhead of Winchester, 'Many have asked themselves whether there is any conflict in assuming an ecclesiastical position which must ever remain a protest against the principles of the denominations and, at the same time, having fellowship with other believers in the denominations in the preaching of the Gospel.' He denied that fellowship in crusades amounted to endorsement of denominational positions:

> Our good brethren who identify the doctrine of separation with a visible detachment from all believers not in Assembly fellowship should not conclude that others are careless as to the mind of the Lord. It is easy to protest against denominationalism and embrace an unscriptural exclusivism. Both are wrong. If brethren of wider sympathies are regarded as inconsistent, what of other brethren who remain in fellowship with them? On their own principles, must they not separate not only from the denominations but from their own brethren?

He pointed out that withholding support for such campaigns placed Brethren alongside nominal Christians and unbelievers, who stood apart from the proclamation of Christ. If the exclusive-minded were to reply that their separation did not imply acceptance of the views of unbelievers, then it also followed that involvement did not imply acceptance of the denominational views of other believers involved.[9]

A pair of articles from opposite perspectives appeared in *The Harvester*. Putting the case against involvement, P.F.W. Parsons argued that Harringay had been supported by mixed denominations, and so converts would be confused about which church to link up with. Furthermore, the message omitted the topic of baptism. Parsons claimed that the response rate, at 2.5%, was not much higher than that to regular outreach. Yet he drew similar lessons to Tatford, whose editorial introducing the articles had highlighted the prominence of prayer, the value of publicity, the careful approach to such things as

---

[6] Harold Rowdon, 'Brethren in Britain, 1945-2000: A Personal Sketch', paper delivered at the BAHN Conference, Gloucester, 11 July 2003.

[7] Cf. Gerald Coates' recollections of the impact of the 1966 Earls Court crusade (*An Intelligent Fire* (Eastbourne: Kingsway, 1991), 53): 'Although the people in the Gospel Hall had little to do with other Christians, they did go to the Billy Graham meetings. We had never seen anything like it. It was obvious that one could be a Christian and not be part of the Brethren or attend a Gospel Hall.'

[8] 'WW', *W* 84 (1954), 119, 159.

[9] David C. Fairhead, 'Fellowship in the Gospel', *W* 85 (1955), 141-2.

personal work, stewarding and music, and the nature of the preacher and his message. Parsons acknowledged that a work of God had gone on, but this in itself was not sufficient ground for Brethren to be associated with it, as there was a divine pattern for service to which they must be faithful; faithfulness was more important than success. He pointed out that Brethren felt compelled to meet apart on Sunday mornings; if they were free to join in such crusades, why could they not also join mixed churches locally? By contrast, Montague Goodman, whose interdenominational credentials were impeccable, thought Harringay 'the most remarkable movement of God in our land since the days of Wesley'. He agreed with Parsons that Graham should have differentiated between churches, but questioned whether assemblies would have been ready to receive and welcome the converts. He saw many signs of imminent revival, and argued that it would be a shame if assemblies lost out on the blessing because they were unwilling to rise to the opportunities or to co-operate with others 'through a spirit of self-complacent isolation'.[10]

Other conservative Brethren took a similar line to Parsons: they readily acknowledged that God had moved at Harringay, and that there were lessons to be learned from it, but argued that this did not justify believers in departing from the divine pattern; the assembly was the appointed sphere for service and the ideal nurturing ground for converts.[11]

Practically, some were quick to take advantage of the opportunities presented by Graham's visits. An Edinburgh brother offered a free bus trip for over-twelves not in the assembly to hear Graham in Glasgow, if they attended the Gospel meeting twelve times. He noticed a good two dozen strangers waiting to have their cards marked one Sunday, so his device had evidently solved the problem of declining attendance at Gospel meetings![12] Furthermore, it was estimated that for the 1954 Harringay crusade, Open Brethren supplied 28% of the counsellors, and 30% for that at Glasgow's Kelvin Hall the following year.[13] Being used to dealing with spiritually needy individuals themselves rather than leaving the minister to do so, they were well prepared for such ministry. Perhaps the clearest expression of approval was the imitation by some assemblies of Graham's methods. A crusade held by Victoria Hall, Wandsworth, saw forty-five professions of faith, dealt with by counsellors. It had been preceded by eight months' advance preparation, including visiting 3,000 homes with literature, floodlighting the hall during the crusade, 'fishing' (going onto the streets and inviting people to meetings), and daily prayer meetings.[14]

The 1966 Earl's Court crusade occasioned some discussion of mass evangelism, now influenced by Reformed thinking as well as the wider Evangelical readiness to question

---

[10] F.A. Tatford, 'FEC'; P.F.W. Parsons, 'Greater London Crusade Reflections'; Montague Goodman, 'More Reflections on the Crusade', *H* 33 (1954), 73-5, 85. Goodman had submitted his article as a response to a circular from Parsons, whom Tatford felt should be given the right of reply.

[11] Anon., 'The Greater London Crusade', *PS* 6 (1954-5), 184-6; S. Clark, 'Some Reasons why I pray for Billy Graham', *BM* 65 (1955), 81; A.M. Salway Gooding, 'An Open Letter', *CWo*, May 1955, 71 (I owe this, and several other references in the chapters dealing with the post-1945 period, to the card-index file of notes on twentieth-century Brethren compiled by Dr Harold Rowdon and now deposited with the CBA).

[12] 'Willie' to J.B. Watson, 12 December 1954, J.B. Watson Papers (CBA Box 231).

[13] *W* 88 (1958), 130.

[14] 'WW', *W* 85 (1955), 52.

such methods. *The Harvester* carried an extended review of John Pollock's biography of Graham, Graham's own book *World Aflame*, and Erroll Hulse's assessment from a Reformed Baptist viewpoint, *Billy Graham – the Pastor's Dilemma*. The reviewer, Jeremy Mudditt, did not agree with everything in the last of these, but expressed appreciation of Hulse's work.[15] Elsewhere, Bruce expressed reservations about some of Hulse's arguments but was enthusiastic about his comments on the importance of local church evangelism.[16] Charles G. Martin, in the *Journal of the Christian Brethren Research Fellowship* was positive, if not in total agreement,[17] but a reviewer in *The Witness* was more critical, rejecting Hulse's Calvinism, asserting that the results were more widespread than many realised, and expressing sorrow that he should seek to undermine a ministry which God was evidently blessing.[18]

19.1.2 Para-church Agencies

As has often been stated, the Open Brethren contribution to interdenominational Evangelicalism was of disproportionate significance, whether viewed in terms of finance, manpower, or ideas and strategies. However, this must be balanced by an awareness of the continuing refusal of many to involve themselves in para-church bodies. H.F.R. Catherwood, who had left assemblies for Westminster Chapel in the 1950s (marrying the daughter of the minister, Martyn Lloyd-Jones), drew attention to the fact that

> ... without the support of members of the Brethren interdenominational movements would find difficulty in surviving, and yet there is probably more opposition to these movements by individual Brethren than by those in the denominations. So deep is this cleavage of opinion that I do not think I have ever seen or heard the subject discussed in open forum.[19]

His explanation of this was that many had taken up work in such movements because they were concerned for evangelism and frustrated with their assemblies, often because these were resisting necessary change.[20]

An example of this ambivalence was provided by Brethren attitudes to the EA. Most Brethren continued to stand apart from formal association with it. A 1964 review of Leith Samuel's *Evangelicals and the Ecumenical Movement* in *Echoes of Service* (which would have reflected mainstream Brethren thinking) rejected the implied suggestion that all churches should join the Alliance: 'In our view any union of churches is contrary to the plain teaching of Scripture.'[21] At the first National Assembly of Evangelicals in 1965, only twenty-six assemblies were represented, even though the Brethren itinerant Bible teacher Stephen Short was one of the main speakers on the subject of unity.[22] When the EA introduced corporate membership, traditional reluctance to affiliate with any body in

---

[15] Jeremy Mudditt, 'Mass Evangelism: Controversy or Challenge?', *H* 45 (1966), 103-4.

[16] 'AQ', *H* 45 (1966), 91.

[17] *JCBRF* 12 (May 1966), 25-7.

[18] *W* 96 (1966), 271.

[19] H.F.R. Catherwood, 'Interdenominational movements', *W* 91 (1961), 384.

[20] *Ibid.*, 385.

[21] *EOS* 93 (1964), 38.

[22] *W* 95 (1965), 464.

any formal sense meant that assemblies were slow to join. By 1998, only 123 assemblies had done so.[23]

Another example was provided by non-denominational evangelistic agencies. The General Secretary of the Christian Colportage Association (now Home Evangelism) from 1948-64, R.A. Bailey, belonged to an assembly,[24] and a number have worked with it as evangelists. But one evangelist, Sid Mountstevens, withdrew from such a body in 1978 after ten years' service, convicted that this involved him in associating with error.[25]

Interestingly, I have not come across any criticism of the Scripture Gift Mission, whose publications were used extensively by Open Brethren of all shades of opinion. This may be because the mission restricted itself to circulating literature, and its publications were largely, if not completely, composed of passages of Scripture. Similarly, most Brethren made an exception for the British and Foreign Bible Society (and its national components), although they voiced their apprehension at the prospect of ecumenical translation projects involving Roman Catholics and sponsored by the United Bible Societies. Advertisements soliciting support for it appeared regularly in Brethren periodicals. The Gideons, however, whilst also devoting themselves to circulating the Scriptures, did on one occasion come in for some criticism. In 1963, Parsons wrote to *The Harvester* to express his disapproval of the movement. In his view, it had an exclusive membership, it was named after a man (who, to compound matters, came to a sad end), and commitment to its activities detracted from assembly work. A number of responses were printed, mostly defending the Gideons.[26] The organisation's lay ethos would have appealed to Brethren, as would the opportunities for service afforded to the business and professional men who made up its membership; but the highly organised structure and the distinctly middle-class ethos of its dinners and meetings would have been difficult for some to accept.

Although Brethren have played key roles in the IVF (now the Universities and Colleges Christian Fellowship (UCCF)) and affiliated bodies such as the Tyndale Fellowship, assembly support has not been universal. Harold St John once told Oliver Barclay, who would become General Secretary of the UCCF, that the IVF was now being given, in considerable measure, the same task as that for which Brethren had been raised up: that of keeping the gospel alive in an age when it was rarely heard in mixed denominations.[27] Not all leading Brethren were so positive, however, nor so convinced of the IVF's doctrinal orthodoxy. Frequently Brethren attacked the IVF with arguments similar to those used earlier against interdenominational and undenominational missions. John Heading, as a student at Cambridge after the war, refused to join the Christian Union as it was 'really a Christian dis-union' whose members all went their separate ways each Sunday, although students in his college met for prayer and Bible study in his rooms.[28]

More stridently, a Cardiff student, Keith R. Jenkins, protested at the annual letter in *The Believer's Magazine* commending Christian Unions to new students, which by 1960 was being written by W.M. Capper and F.F. Bruce. He urged students to stand apart from such bodies (but not the Christians in them), and to get involved with a local assembly.

[23] Joel Edwards to Neil Summerton, 7 January 1998 (CBA Box 132).

[24] *W* 95 (1965), 76.

[25] Sid Mountstevens, 'My Conversion and Call (83)', *AT* 306 (July-August 2003), 94.

[26] *H* 42 (1963), 122, 131, 155.

[27] Barclay, *Evangelicalism*, 68.

[28] John Heading, 'My Conversion and Call (12)', *AT* 233 (May-June 1991), 90.

The IVF was a sectarian inter-denominational society, and joining it contravened the scriptural principle of separation. Many wrong things were allowed in Christian Union meetings, such as women taking a prominent role. Students in Christian Unions would be taught much error, and would be unable to enjoy much real fellowship with members, as their 'lax, modernistic interpretation of the Scriptures' would often differ from what was taught in assemblies. Some truths would not be discussed, such as baptism and breaking bread. Superficial methods of Bible study and praise would be recommended.[29] A reply from two Manchester students recognised that not all was as it should be, but defended involvement on the basis that it was then possible to show others a better way. Jenkins' response was to reject their belief in the need for united witness on the ground of separation; it was not necessary to join the Christian Union to help other students. He also questioned the authority of Scripture within the IVF.[30] He reiterated his views in an *Assembly Testimony* article, in which he also criticised the IVF for aiming at something impossible (the unity of all believers), having an unscriptural constitution (the corporate body contemplated in Scripture is a local church), and placing young believers in positions of authority.[31]

A letter from 'Graduate' in *The Believer's Magazine* raised the vexed question of the relationship of students with the local assembly. Although commended to it, usually they were only seen at the Breaking of Bread. His assembly would have liked to use their gifts, but students were too busy. The Christian Union could expose them to unhelpful teaching, with the result that 'just at that age when they should be absorbing what we believe to be essential teaching, we find them assimilating doubtful and debatable ideologies which to immature minds is [sic] introducing error in the formative stages of Christian character.' So, which had the prior claim: the Christian Union or the assembly?[32] In reply, a recent Brethren graduate recalled his own involvement in both as a student, in an assembly which took an active interest in the Christian Union. He considered that 'Graduate' had been prompted by an underlying sectarianism and argued that if students were at risk of imbibing denominational views, they should be better taught in the assembly so that they could test all things by Scripture for themselves.[33]

Disparagement of Christian Unions has continued in some circles. In 1988 a lecturer at Glasgow University, writing in *The Believer's Magazine*, criticised them as not representing God's norm, and as offering a restricted and artificial fellowship. Many students were so dependent on this that they never entered into the reality patterned in Acts 2.41-2. 'The result is that they are often ruined as far as normal church fellowship is concerned, and, alas, frequently backslide or fall into gross apostasy once they enter ordinary life.'[34] Another article pointed out that Christian Unions were affected by charismatic teaching, and urged students to stand for the whole truth; the proximity of a good assembly should be the primary factor dictating choice of university.[35]

[29] *BM* 70 (1960), 344-5.
[30] *BM* 71 (1961), 24, 29, 90.
[31] Keith R. Jenkins, 'The Inter-Varsity Fellowship', *AT* 52 (March-April 1961), 28-30.
[32] *BM* 77 (1967), 184-5.
[33] *BM* 77 (1967), 376-8.
[34] David Newell, 'Questions young people ask – series two – 4. How should I approach university?', *BM* 98 (1988), 106.
[35] D.E. West, 'Higher Education – Its Prospects and its Evils', *AT* 240 (July-August 1992), 122.

Immediately after the war, Brethren exercised considerable influence in the Christian Unions at both Oxford and Cambridge but, as grants became more widely available and the proportion of students from other denominational backgrounds began to increase, that influence was gradually diluted.[36] The massive expansion of higher education meant that many more Brethren than before were coming into contact with believers from the denominations through Christian Union activities. This, and the lack of suitable assemblies for them to attend in places such as central London, meant that many were prepared to consider worshipping at non-Brethren churches. A sizeable number made the change a permanent one, leading to laments about the loss of students from assembly circles.[37] W.M. Capper and J.M. Houston responded to a letter urging Christian students to commit themselves to assemblies rather than Christian Unions, in order to counter this drift. They claimed (perhaps overstating things) that those most committed to assemblies were also the most active Christian Union members, and conversely that those who drifted from assemblies were half-hearted in their Christian Union commitment.[38] Concern at the continuing haemorrhage led to two Brethren chaplains being appointed by the early 1980s, one at Queen's University, Belfast, where there was a strong Brethren presence among the student body.[39] From 1976, too, *The Harvester* carried an annual list of assemblies located near to higher educational institutions, although this ceased in the early 1990s because there were so many other churches acceptable to many Brethren students, a reflection of the movement's lessening isolation and of its inability to hold on to its youth.

For some, suspicion of Christian Unions was one manifestation of a more general suspicion of higher education. There appears to have been an underlying fear that students would encounter believers from the denominations, become involved in interdenominational activities such as Christian Unions, and thus be lost to assemblies. In addition, some considered that the choice of suitable subjects to study was limited: one writer warned against the study of English (many works of literature were unedifying), modern languages (finding assembly fellowship abroad could prove problematic), Religious Education (because it included the study of comparative religion), geology (because it contradicted the biblical teaching that the earth was just 6,000 years old), philosophy, and politics. When choosing where to study, more important than academic considerations was that of the nearness of a good assembly.[40]

19.1.3 Biblical Scholarship

Another area in which Open Brethren exercised an influence out of proportion to their numerical strength was that of biblical scholarship. The movement's contribution in this field took two forms: there were the colleges which Brethren helped to create and shape, and the scholars whom they nurtured.

---

[36] Barclay, *Evangelicalism*, 66.

[37] See, for example, correspondence in *The Harvester* during 1957; 'WW', *W* 89 (1959), 107.

[38] *H* 36 (1957), 141.

[39] William Walker, who had been a missionary in India, became 'Dean of Residences' for Brethren students as early as 1971 (*EOS* 100 (1971), 206).

[40] D.C. Hinton, 'Higher Education – Its Prospects and Its Evils', *AT* 239 (May-June 1992), 80.

Since LBC[41] was founded in 1943, it has had a steady stream of Brethren as students and as tutors.[42] Some of the better-known among the former were the Bible teachers Stephen Short and John Williams, and Clive Calver, who did not remain among Brethren but later became Secretary of the EA. Among the latter were H.L. Ellison (1949-55), Harold Rowdon (1954-91), and Leslie Allen (1960-83), while Michael Griffiths attended the assembly at Northwood Hills while serving as Principal (1980-9). Brethren Presidents of LBC have included Montague Goodman (1949-58) and Sir John Laing (1959-78), with Derek Warren serving as Vice-President from 1968-99. Chairmen of the board have included Goodman (1946-8), Warren (1977-83), and Professor Sir Robert Boyd (1983-90).[43] There was steady leakage from assemblies among those who had studied at LBC, which in measure vindicated separatist concerns about the college's impact. In a 1974 article, Rowdon expressed disappointment that a greater contribution had not been made by former students to the life of assemblies, especially as Open Brethren had made a comparatively large contribution to the work of the college; a number of Brethren students arrived already frustrated with their church situation, and had gone on to minister in the denominations.[44] Others, however, have become full-time workers or missionaries.

In response to wartime concern at the lack of distinctively assembly-orientated training, Matlock Bible College was founded in Derbyshire in 1948, primarily to train evangelists. David Clifford, its founder, had been inspired by the North American Bible schools he had seen and wanted to create a British equivalent; his vision matched the concern of leading brethren in England and Scotland for a training school staffed by men from assemblies. The college soon established itself in more open circles, and student numbers grew. It moved to Dawlish in Devon in 1955, becoming Moorlands Bible College, and was re-founded at Verwood in Hampshire in 1968 before finally moving to its present location at Sopley, near Christchurch, in 1970. A parallel institution, Moorlands Ladies' College, functioned at Babbacombe (Torquay) from 1964-8. The former Glanton brother Derek Copley, Principal from 1970-97, became well-known in wider Evangelical circles. Moorlands has continued to offer a distinctive balance of evangelistic, academic, and spiritual training, although the Brethren ethos is now much diluted: by 1985, only five out of thirteen full-time faculty and a sixth of the students were from assemblies.[45]

Among academics, the best-known was undoubtedly F.F. Bruce (1910-90), a biblical scholar who became Rylands Professor of Biblical Criticism and Exegesis at Manchester.[46] Bruce exercised considerable influence through editing the *Evangelical Quarterly* from 1949-80, and answering questions in *The Harvester* from 1952-75, as well

---

[41] Now known as London School of Theology.

[42] For this section, see Randall, *Educating Evangelicalism*.

[43] Boyd, a professor at University College, London, was founder and director of the Mullard Space Science Laboratory near Dorking.

[44] H.H. Rowdon, 'With Heart and Mind', *H* 53 (1974), 232-3. In the period to 1968, eighty-four Brethren had studied at LBC, compared to 340 Baptists, out of a total of approximately a thousand students (H.H. Rowdon, *London Bible College: the first 25 years* (Worthing: Henry E. Walter, 1968), 109).

[45] See D.L. Clifford, 'Missionary Training', *H* 27 (1950), 54, 49; C.H. Darch, 'How it all Began', *W* 86 (1956), 95; *H*, November 1985, 28; Alison Notman, *Faith & Vision: The Moorlands Story* (Sopley, Dorset: Moorlands College, [1997]).

[46] On Bruce, see *BDE*; Bruce, *In Retrospect*; *ODNB*.

as though his advocacy of the work of the IVF (in this, he can be regarded as Rendle Short's successor). He was also a prime motivating force behind the setting up of the Christian Brethren Archive around 1980.

A former Anglican clergyman and missionary to Jews in Eastern Europe, H.L. Ellison (1903-83)[47] joined Open Brethren in 1939 on his return to Britain, and soon began to make an impact. With 'an impish delight in setting off theological fireworks',[48] and a readiness to provoke controversy, Ellison got into hot water as an Old Testament lecturer at LBC because of an article he published in the *Evangelical Quarterly* during 1954, 'Some Thoughts on Inspiration',[49] which was accused of Barthianism. In it, he argued that, in itself, Scripture was not life-giving in its character as a record of revelation, but that the Holy Spirit made it the Word of God to us. The expression 'Word of God' should not, therefore, be used of the Bible without careful qualification. As we read it, we do not so much learn *about* God as hear him speak.

H.L. Ellison

The article's appearance, shortly after the faculty had issued a statement clarifying their understanding of the college's doctrinal basis and excluding such an interpretation, could not have been more ill-timed.[50] Ellison's article was imprecisely expressed, and presented only part of the doctrinal picture, but such assertions were bound to raise hackles. He was, therefore, asked to resign. However, from 1963 he lectured for some years at Moorlands, and was to be extensively involved in the *Bible Commentary for Today* (on which see below), evidence that in some quarters a broader outlook obtained. Clearly Bruce should have anticipated the furore over Ellison's article; that he did not has been tentatively attributed by Shuff to his being less acute theologically than exegetically.[51] I think that what Bruce misjudged was not so much the issues (he was well acquainted with Barth's thought) as the response of the constituency; whilst able to tolerate diversity of Evangelical opinion himself, and a lover of intellectual freedom, he seems to have underestimated the threat which Ellison's article was felt by readers to

---

[47] See *H*, October 1983, 2-3; Anderson, *They Finished their Course in the 80's*, 39-41.

[48] Rowdon, 'Brethren in Britain'.

[49] *EQ* 26 (1954), 210-17.

[50] Randall, *Educating Evangelicalism*, 85.

[51] Shuff, *Searching*, 93. Similar criticisms have on occasion been made of some of Bruce's writings.

present. At any rate, he described the episode as the most unpleasant of his entire literary career.[52]

Another member of the college's staff to provoke controversy was Leslie Allen, who published a commentary on Jonah which treated it as parable rather than history.[53] Coupled with Bruce's support for another faculty member, the Baptist Ralph P. Martin (who in 1964 was accused of being too broad in his sympathies after encouraging Evangelicals to read the German theologian Dietrich Bonhoeffer), these episodes suggest that among Brethren biblical scholars there were those who held a less tightly-defined doctrine of Scripture, or were less strict in their understanding of the implications of biblical authority. This would have been true of scholars in many denominations, but not, at that time, of any other wholly Evangelical denomination.

Another example of a freer attitude to Scripture than had been general among Evangelicals appeared in the *Christian Brethren Review* in 1982. J. Keir Howard, a former missionary in Zambia who has since become an Anglican, asserted that what mattered was not inspiration but profitability. There was no hint of verbal inspiration in the original documents, as is evident from the flexibility with which they were quoted and treated in the early church. Howard saw Scripture as 'dynamic, even fluid, in its essence'; through the Spirit's work, what was the Word of God then becomes a Word of God now. 'The Bible thus stands within an ongoing process by which God's Word is brought to his world through his Spirit, who is none other than the continuing presence of that Word which was the fullness of God's self-revelation.' Its function was that of 'bringing men into the sphere of God's continuing activity, not merely recording his past acts'. As such, it was 'a human book with human imperfections': these were not removed when men recorded their apprehension of the Word of God then, any more than they are when it is preached now.[54]

Two other Brethren scholars deserve to be noted, though they too have now left the movement. Hugh Williamson, who became Regius Professor of Hebrew at Oxford, was a veteran of beach missions on the Wirral run by the Hoylake assembly; for fifteen months after graduating, he had also worked alongside the Brethren evangelist Stan Ford.[55] Such a combination of academic expertise with evangelistic activity was unusual, but not quite unique: John Drane, who has achieved distinction as a writer on everything from Pauline theology to the New Age movement, was in fellowship with Glenbrook Chapel, Manchester, as a postgraduate, and worked with the Scottish Counties Evangelistic Movement in the summer.[56]

'Time would fail me to tell' of all the Open Brethren who have made significant contributions to British biblical scholarship. However, it is probably true to say that most of them are archaeologists, linguists or exegetes rather than specialists in the discipline of biblical theology. During the early years of the Tyndale Fellowship and Tyndale House, Brethren argued for primacy to be given to biblical rather than

---

[52] Bruce, *In Retrospect*, 187.

[53] Leslie C. Allen, *The Books of Joel, Obadiah, Jonah and Micah* (Grand Rapids: William B. Eerdmans, 1976), 176-9.

[54] J. Keir Howard, 'Biblical Inerrancy: An Alternative View', *CBR* 31/32 (February 1982), 29-33; he had expressed similar views in a letter printed in *JCBRF* 16 (August 1967), 44.

[55] [R.A.S.], *Hoylake Chapel: the first 90 years* (Hoylake: n.p., [1989]), 41.

[56] *W* 102 (February 1972), insert.

theological studies.[57] Such an outlook is to be expected from a movement which does not place the stress on systematic theology that other denominations have done. Thus Tatford could comment that Brethren usually had a good knowledge of the text and stories of Scripture (though not of biblical history), but a very limited grasp of doctrine, something which he had attempted to remedy in the doctrinal symposium *The Faith*, which appeared in 1952.[58] A regrettable result of the comparative neglect of disciplines such as theology and philosophy has been the paucity of serious responses to contemporary theological trends, such as those represented by *Honest to God* or *The Myth of God Incarnate*, liberation theology, and recent debate about the 'openness' of God.

Some wanted to see more practical benefit in assembly life from all this study. The missionary Ernest Trenchard, himself a careful scholar and author of several Spanish commentaries, traced the history of Brethren biblical scholarship in a 1971 *Harvester* article. In the post-war period, younger men from assemblies engaged in serious study, so now the movement possessed a number of biblical scholars – but they appeared reluctant to minister. He reminded them that they were servants of the Word, called to pass it on to others, and urged them to provide simple but accurate ministry in the assembly.[59] However, when Brethren scholars engaged in the production of a commentary designed for wider use, the results were to prove controversial.

The appearance of a number of Open Brethren biblical scholars, coupled with the fact that many local leaders would have been influenced by IVF publications as students, meant that assembly hermeneutics was no longer isolated from the wider Evangelical interpretative tradition. This, coupled with the rise in popularity of Reformed theology and the publication of commentaries reflecting this perspective by such writers as William Hendriksen and John Murray, hastened the decline of typological interpretation, a phenomenon which was also evident in Evangelicalism at large, and one which some probably saw as the rot setting in. In the 1950s, a reviewer in *The Witness* could lament the lack of typological treatment in the IVF *New Bible Commentary*;[60] by the end of the 1960s, other periodicals could lament its lack in an Open Brethren production, the *New Testament Commentary* (1969). Such a work was first suggested by Watson as early as 1946, although he had lamented the shortage of potential writers.[61] The most enthusiastic welcome came from the North American Brethren Old Testament scholar Carl Armerding in the *Journal of the Christian Brethren Research Fellowship*,[62] although he recognised that certain aspects of the treatment, such as its treatment of the humanity of Christ in Hebrews 4, were likely to prove controversial; 'That such a work could have been done so well' was, he wrote, 'testimony to the continuing vitality of the movement'.[63] A review in *The Harvester* welcomed it, but criticised its treatment of some eschatological passages and expressed surprise at some of the omissions from the list of contributors.[64] Borland, in *The Believer's Magazine*, regretted the editors' failure to draw on the different approach of teachers among Scottish and Ulster assemblies, claiming that the tone of the work

---

[57] Barclay, *Evangelicalism*, 50.

[58] 'FEC', *H* 34 (1955), 1; cf. 35 (1956), 24.

[59] Ernest H. Trenchard, 'Exposition and Scholarship', *H* 50 (1971), 146, 154.

[60] *W* 84 (1954), 138.

[61] 'WW', *W* 76 (1946), 24.

[62] *JCBRF* 21 (May 1971), 57-66.

[63] Barclay, *Evangelicalism*, 66.

[64] *H* 49 (1970), 22.

would not have been familiar to those used to the writings of such men as Hogg, Hoste, and Vine. In his opinion, it contained many interpretations which Brethren would strenuously contest. The Scottish Bible teacher W. Fraser Naismith, continuing the review, criticised the comments on women taking part in meetings, and the denial of Christ's omniscience (in the comments on Mark 13.32), which he regarded as the work's worst error, and one which would have revived memories of the unpleasant controversy over this issue in 1924.[65] *Assembly Testimony* also carried an extended review by its editor, A.M. Salway Gooding, from a similar perspective.[66] It listed a number of teachers who should have been invited to contribute, such as Tatford, David Gooding (a Professor at Queen's University, Belfast, an authority on the Septuagint text, and an influential Bible teacher among assemblies), Borland, Rollo, and Heading. All possessed proven ability to edify (unlike some who did contribute) and were safer guides to the meaning of Scripture. Gooding condemned the eschatological comments (as tending towards post-tribulationism or amillennialism) and the failure to give a clear lead on such matters as women's silence and paid ministers. He, too, thought the comments on Mark 13.32 the work's worst feature, and reprinted an article by Hoste on 'Modern Misrepresentations of Our Lord' which had first appeared during the Roberts controversy.[67]

When the *Bible Commentary for Today* was published in 1979, the Old Testament section included material by non-Brethren contributors. Brethren had often used expository writings by men such as Campbell Morgan, Handley Moule, and W. Graham Scroggie, but in a work which was meant to 'fly the flag' for Brethren biblical scholarship, this might have been expected to be controversial. Surprisingly, little notice was taken of the work; even *Assembly Testimony*, which might have been expected to sound a warning, had its pages occupied by an extended critique of the proceedings of the 1978 Swanwick Conference, as we shall see. The lack of attention by conservatives indicates that the two sides of the movement had grown further apart during the decade since the publication of the *New Testament Commentary*. It was not surprising, therefore, that in 1983 John Ritchie began the publication for the conservative Brethren market of a multi-volume New Testament commentary series entitled *What the Bible Teaches*,[68] now being joined by volumes on the Old Testament.

A significant aspect of changing approaches to biblical interpretation was the suspicion of anything savouring of dispensationalism. Dispensationalism had kept Brethren from liberalism; it had reinforced Brethren separatism, and thus, along with the stress on Scripture as its own interpreter, lessened the scope for liberal critical scholarship to affect Brethren thinking.[69] On the other hand, another Brethren biblical scholar alleged that it had also kept Brethren from understanding the Scriptures:

---

[65] *BM* 80 (1970), 89-90, 141-2, 147-8.

[66] [A.M.S. Gooding], 'A New Testament Commentary', *AT* 105 (January-February 1970), 19-20; 106 (March-April 1970), 41-4; 107 (May-June 1970), 64-7; 108 (July-August 1970), 90-2; 109 (September-October 1970), 112-16; 112 (March-April 1971), 37-41. 'Kenosis' had continued to be a concern for Brethren; Tatford included an appendix on it by George Goodman in *The Faith: a symposium* (London: Pickering & Inglis, 1952), at a time when similar views expressed by Constantine Metallinos were being condemned by Brethren in Britain and North America (see papers in CBA Box 9).

[67] *AT* 114 (July-August 1971), 84-9; 115 (September-October 1971), 105-10.

[68] Dickson, *Brethren in Scotland*, 343.

[69] Shuff, *Searching*, 71.

'Dispensationalism has been the most powerful instrument in alienating Christians of the Brethren movement from two-thirds of their Bible, and has thus proved the single most deleterious factor in Brethren hermeneutics.'[70] For some, its rejection must have come none too soon, in the light of this example of literalistic reading of Scripture and H.P. Barker's possibly tongue-in-cheek response:

Motor Cars in the Millennium

I was interested in your answer in last August's issue about travel in the millennium. Does not Zech. 8:5 prove that there will be no motor cars? How could there be, when Jerusalem will be full of boys and girls playing in its streets?

This fact is not conclusive. If there are motor-cars there will, no doubt, be by-pass roads, and motor traffic may be prohibited in the crowded streets of the city. ...[71]

19.2 The Impact of Wider Evangelicalism on Open Brethren

In earlier chapters, we have examined Open Brethren doctrinal distinctives. These found renewed expression in two books which appeared after the war. A symposium on *The Church* appeared in 1949, edited by Watson and upholding fairly traditional views. Contributors included the Scots Borland, Rendall, and Rollo, but nobody from Ireland. Another symposium was that edited by Tatford, *The Faith*.[72] It offered a moderate statement which upheld most traditional Brethren distinctives without unduly emphasising them. By the 1960s, however, there were clear signs that the doctrinal homogeneity of Open Brethren was lessening significantly, in the face of charismatic and Reformed theologies.

19.2.1 The Reformed Resurgence of the 1950s and 1960s

Many Open Brethren seem to have remained moderately Calvinistic, and the formation of the Banner of Truth Trust in 1957 was welcomed by *The Witness*.[73] *The Believer's Magazine*, *The Witness*, and *The Harvester* all reviewed its books positively in the late 1950s and 1960s. Students in particular seem to have embraced the resurgent Calvinism, and often contributed to the recurrent outbreaks of correspondence on the issues which it generated.[74] A series of articles by W.E.F. Naismith in *The Believer's Magazine* during 1955 defended and expounded the doctrines of election to salvation and limited

---

[70] David J.A. Clines, 'Biblical Hermeneutics in Theory and Practice', *CBR* 31/32 (February 1982), 68.

[71] 'AQ', *H* 31 (1951), 32.

[72] This, and *The Church*, were reprinted by John Ritchie a few years ago. *The Faith* was authored by those who would have been regarded as 'progressives', and its bibliographies were surprisingly broad, that on the atonement including earlier non-Evangelical writers such as Hastings Rashdall and John McLeod Campbell. However, no works by Darby were listed.

[73] Anon., 'A guide to Reading', *W* 88 (1958), 148.

[74] For examples of lengthy correspondence on Calvinism, see *H* during 1980 and *W* during 1960 and 1964-5.

atonement, drawing on writers such as James Haldane and A.W. Pink, although most Brethren writers would not have embraced such a thorough-going statement of the Reformed faith. Reformed theology in its newer, Barthian, manifestation was also greeted with interest by some. For example, Paternoster published the Dutch theologian G.C. Berkouwer's book *The Triumph of Grace in the Theology of Karl Barth* in 1956 to a warm welcome by Bruce, who had himself been influenced by Barth's writings as a student.[75] In *The Believer's Magazine*, Borland gave it a more cautious welcome, though it was clear that he was engaging seriously with Barth's ideas.[76] Ultimately, though, it was the Banner rather than Barth which was to have more influence on Open Brethren, Bruce notwithstanding.

On the other hand, apprehension was expressed concerning 'hyper-Calvinism', by which writers appear to have meant any form of Calvinism more robust than that current among assemblies, or which looked like exercising a divisive influence on the content of evangelistic proclamation. In some quarters, this may have represented a riposte to Calvinist (usually Presbyterian) critiques of Brethrenism. For example, as late as 1950, the Presbyterian Church in Ireland published a hostile pamphlet on the Brethren in a series which included others against Jehovah's Witnesses, Communists, and Elim Pentecostals.[77] Its author condemned the elaborate system of bribery and inducements allegedly operative in Brethren Sunday Schools, asserting that 'In their zeal for the success of a Gospel mission, Brethren have been known to offer sixpence to the first member of the Sunday School who professed conversion.'[78] Its adherents were marked by 'an overweening conceit of their own spirituality and purity' and (the ultimate Ulster Protestant insult) a 'spirit of ecclesiastical "Sinn Fein-ism"', and were 'notorious proselytisers'.[79] Furthermore, he detected a 'spirit of intolerance and ecclesiastical tyranny which leads to quarrels and disunity both in the family and in the fellowship of the Church'.[80] In the face of such antagonism, Watson in a paragraph headed 'Cold War' described this booklet as 'about the most envenomed piece of religious criticism we can recollect having seen of recent years'.[81] It is small wonder that Open Brethren in Ulster have generally maintained a more rigid separation from other Evangelicals than has been the case elsewhere. Continuing opposition to Presbyterianism may also be due to its teaching about the status within the covenant of grace of children of Christian families, contrasted with Brethren stress on the need for personal conversion: many converts from a Presbyterian background seem to have felt that they had been misled into thinking they were all right.

Others in England, including some leaders, were less than enthusiastic about Calvinism. The Bible teacher George Harpur (1910-87) liked to 'have a go' at Reformed theology. In discussion during the 1960 Swanwick Conference, Douglas Brealey, superintendent of the Blackdown Hills work, expressed concern at the resurgence of

---

[75] *W* 87 (1957), 56.

[76] *BM* 67 (1957), 3.

[77] Investigator, *Who are They? The Brethren* ([Belfast]: Committee on the State of Religion in conjunction with the Publication Board of the Presbyterian Church in Ireland, [c.1950]).

[78] *Ibid.*, 27.

[79] *Ibid.*, 24, 25, 26.

[80] *Ibid.*, 27.

[81] 'WW', *W* 80 (1950), 64.

Puritan theology.[82] Howley, writing in *The Witness*, was unconvinced of the value of reprinting Puritan works, or of Calvinist teaching.[83] In the ensuing debate, he was supported by Howard Mudditt, whose sympathies lay more with Methodism. Mudditt claimed that he had ceased to read Reformed books because of the effect they were having on him (which he failed to specify); their authors' idea of reform, he alleged, stopped three centuries ago (whereas the church should be always reforming), and did not appear to extend to the adoption of believer's baptism and the gathered church.[84] Surprisingly, he took no account of the growing and high-profile Reformed Baptist movement, in which several former Brethren were involved and which owed something to Brethren ecclesiology as well as to Presbyterianism in its enthusiasm for plural eldership.

One area in which the impact of Reformed theology was felt particularly strongly was eschatology. Lang wrote to Bruce of a drift to amillennialism among teachers in assemblies, under the influence of O.T. Allis (a professor at Westminster Seminary, Philadelphia, whose influential book *Prophecy and the Church* appeared in 1945), and hoping that Bruce would be able to arrest this.[85] Bruce's own views inclined towards postmillennialism; accepting the interpretation of church history offered by Kenneth Scott Latourette, which treated it as a series of awakenings, each reaching further than its predecessor, Bruce asserted in 1949 that 'a survey of Church history gives us ground for confidence in the future of the Gospel'.[86] In 1961, Question 1,000 in *The Harvester* 'Answers to Questions' feature asked '*Are we right in expecting a millennium?*' Bruce's opinion was that 'Scripture encourages us to believe that on this earth, the place of His rejection, Jesus will ultimately receive universal and joyful recognition as Lord and King'.[87] When asked in 1964: '*Is there any scriptural support for the idea of a secret rapture of the church?*', his laconic reply was: 'There may be, but I have yet to find it.'[88] One wonders what his editor, the strongly pretribulationist Tatford, made of this. Watson appears to have been somewhat stricter with Bruce, who had an article which he submitted to *The Witness* rejected because its eschatological implications were not in line with the views upheld by the magazine.[89] In a 1976 review, Bruce also welcomed Iain Murray's postmillennial survey *The Puritan Hope*, asserting that postmillennialism was more biblical than the expectation of eschatological apostasy.[90] Yet we should not assume that he adhered to a fully worked out postmillennialism; in a private letter of 1968, he wrote:

> My own eschatological views are fluid enough, and I am content for them to remain so. I marvel
> at the precision with which some brethren have the whole order of end-time events taped, and

---

[82] Anon., *The Apostolic Faith in a Pagan Society: Addresses given at a Conference of Brethren at Swanwick* ([n.pl.: n.p., 1960]), 67-8; cf. G.J. Polkinghorne, 'Swanwick Conference of Brethren, 1960', *W* 90 (1960), 429.

[83] 'Touchstone', 'The peril of extremism', *W* 102 (1972), 383-5.

[84] *W* 103 (1973), 29-30.

[85] G.H. Lang to F.F. Bruce, 13 May 1957 (CBA Box 69).

[86] J.B. Watson (ed.), *The Church: a symposium* (London: Pickering & Inglis, 1949), 194; cf. 'AQ', *H* 51 (1972), 42. Elsewhere Bruce balanced the idea of mass ingathering with that of eschatological apostasy ('AQ', *H* 51 (1972), 10).

[87] 'AQ' *H* 40 (1961), 187.

[88] 'AQ', *H* 43 (1964), 55.

[89] F.F. Bruce, 'His Writings', *W* 85 (1955), 199.

[90] *W* 106 (1976), 432.

still more at the dogmatism with which they condemn any deviation from their chosen line. Amillennialism is on the increase among younger brethren – but they are too discreet to trumpet the fact abroad![91]

For some, the rise of amillennialism was the harbinger of a non-literal (and thus liberal or modernist) approach to other parts of Scripture. In 1968 *The Harvester* ran an article by Professor A.E. Wilder-Smith of Chicago, linking the rise of amillennialism in assemblies with an acceptance of the theory of evolution, and paralleling the loss of a literal interpretation of the beginning and the end of history.[92] He was supported by Tatford, who insisted that it was time to stand against undermining of biblical creationism, and 'time that the assemblies realised, not only the origin (or, at any rate, one of the origins), but the ultimate end, of the present amillennial trend which is destroying the hope of so many'.[93] However, Ellison was closer to the truth in his assessment that 'the growth of amillennialism in the British assemblies' was 'due to the growth of Calvinism in evangelical circles generally'.[94]

Some years later, Malcolm Davis of Leeds advanced a similar argument:

> ... amillennialism in relation to prophecy is the thin end of a wedge which leads to rank modernism and liberal theology. For, to consider the matter logically, if one set of Scriptures may rightly be treated in a non-literal manner, as the amillennialists claim is the case with prophecy, why may not every other part of Scripture, including those concerning the doctrines of Christ and salvation, be treated in a similar non-literal manner? ... either Scripture is all literally true in its primary meanings, or it is not worthy of our trust at all.[95]

Asking the question 'Premillennial or Amillennial – Does it Matter?', Davis was convinced that it did. He restated classic Brethren eschatology, and drew some important practical conclusions. Amillennialists, he argued, tended to think in terms of world reform, whereas premillennialists focused on the salvation of individuals in a dying world; amillennialists retained Judaic features of worship, premillennialists kept to the New Testament.[96] The last was perhaps overstated, but he was right to detect a hermeneutical difference underlying the two.

Another defender of traditional views was the Bible teacher G.B. Fyfe of Ealing who, in a clear statement of classic Darbyite eschatology and hermeneutics, wrote:

> ... our "blessed hope" lies entirely outside the ambit of the prophetic scheme which forms such a large portion of Holy Writ. The Church of God is something "out of this world" altogether – its calling, character and destiny are *heavenly*. A key-point to grasp is, that the Church is the

---

[91] F.F. Bruce to Mr [J.R.?] Casswell, 5 February 1968 (CBA Box 9(13)).

[92] A.E. Wilder-Smith, 'Darwinism and Amillennialism', *H* 47 (1968), 148.

[93] *H* 47 (1968), 141.

[94] *H* 47 (1968), 157.

[95] Malcolm Davis, 'Is Scripture Literal?', *PS* 34 (1983), 21.

[96] Malcolm Davis, 'Premillennial or Amillennial – Does it Matter?', *PS* 34 (1983), 63-8. Two other examples of polemic against amillennialism first appeared as series of articles in *AT*, by William Bunting (1961-5) and David McAllister (1995-7). McAllister condemned it as 'an attack on many things that we hold dear', saw it as fundamentally opposed to the nature of assembly testimony, and as logically leading to liberalism ('Amillennialism Examined', *AT* 268 (March-April 1997), 29-31).

subject of revelation and not the burden of prophecy. Prophecy, precisely speaking, has to do with the earth and with the nation of Israel as the centre of God's earthly ways. If this distinction is carefully observed, it will provide a correct premise on which to base our interpretations.[97]

Such opinions still influence conservative assemblies in their relationships with other churches, their attitude to social issues and social involvement. Apart from the fact that the decline of the eschatological consensus, with its inbuilt separatist dynamic, reinforced the tendency of post-war Open Brethren to fragment, the apocalyptic mood of the 1980s and the pre-Millennium anxiety of the 1990s (which would have counterbalanced the challenge to Brethren prophetic interpretation presented by the collapse of Communism) should have proved fertile soil for Brethren eschatology. In the event, though, there were no Brethren speakers able to command the attention of a wider public in the way that men such as A.H. Burton and Frederick Tatford (who died in 1986) had done. Where a modified form of Brethren eschatology was adopted, it owed much more to writers such as Hal Lindsey (author of *The Late Great Planet Earth*) and Tim LaHaye and Jerry B. Jenkins (co-authors of the *Left Behind* series of novels, which have achieved huge sales in Britain as well as North America) – another example of the North American propensity for adopting Darby's eschatology without his ecclesiology.[98]

Continuing opposition to Lang during the early 1950s, which included a number of periodical articles and pamphlets, indicates that certain ideas, such as a particular view of the rapture, were part of what many Brethren regarded as fundamental truth. But many also felt that Lang's views imperilled the gospel by his insistence on the necessity of holiness and the introduction of a reward motive for believers who wished to avoid being left behind at the rapture. However, after Lang's short-lived periodical *The Disciple* ceased in 1958 and he died the same year, partial rapture views were rarely aired, there being no real successor to Lang as their advocate.

F.A. Tatford, the best-known defender of traditional Brethren eschatology during the twentieth century

The way may have been prepared for an acceptance of other eschatological views by a tendency to neglect teaching on such subjects in assemblies and conferences. It is

---

[97] G.B. Fyfe, 'Prophetic Profile – The Last Week. 12. Prophecy and Promise', *PS* 34 (1983), 10.

[98] A British version of this is evident in Tatford's writings, including his periodical, *Prophetic Witness*, which were read far beyond Brethren circles.

interesting to compare the rather muted reactions to the declaration of war in 1939 and the establishment of the state of Israel in 1948 with the breathless excitement greeting the events of 1917, an indication that perhaps some of the steam had gone out of Brethren commitment to their eschatological views. Yet interest in eschatology appears to have revived, partly because of the universal awareness of the threat to human existence posed by nuclear weapons, a frequent topic of comment in *The Harvester* and *The Witness* throughout the 1950s. When, in response to confusion concerning prophetic teaching, Liverpool Brethren arranged a conference on it in 1958, interest was far beyond the conveners' expectations; brethren attended from all parts of country, with up to 1,200 being present.[99] Tatford was concerned about the confusion, and stepped up the quantity of articles on prophetic subjects in *The Harvester* during 1960 by way of response; a similar trend was evident in *Assembly Testimony* and *Precious Seed*. A few years later, Tatford commented: 'In assembly circles, where leading teachers are to be found contradicting one another, the time is probably ripe to call a conference of Bible teachers for the purpose of considering in detail what the Scriptures teach on this important subject and to reach agreement if possible, on what should be taught in assemblies.'[100] But he was too late; it would have been impossible to reach such a consensus without splitting the movement.

19.2.2 *Longing for Revival*

One major stimulus to the commencement of a different type of residential conference was the burden for revival felt by many Evangelicals in the post-war decades, in which Brethren shared. This represented an expression of the spirit of idealism and post-war reconstruction which had already led to meetings of leaders in the early 1940s to discuss the way ahead for assembly outreach, as well as a response to the threats which were seen as hanging over the future of assemblies in particular and of humanity in general. Expectations were doubtless heightened by the fact that after World War I, longing for revival had been followed by a measure of blessing. Such conferences fulfilled a function analogous to that of groups such as the Baptist Revival Fellowship or the Methodist Revival Fellowship, whose own conferences drew together those who shared both a particular churchmanship and a longing for revival. If it did not come in the form expected, Brethren were by no means the only Evangelicals to be disappointed.

The burden for revival began to be apparent in some of the meetings convened during the war to discuss post-war reconstruction, but its first prominent post-war manifestation was a series of meetings at Westminster Chapel during September 1946, under the title of 'Revival in our Time'. This represented an attempt to continue the work of the United Nations Witness Team, a group of young servicemen which had been disbanded in 1945; it was mostly staffed by Open Brethren, and was avowedly connected with assemblies. Over 2,000 attended the closing rally, and many conversions were seen, but the impetus was not sustained and the movement petered out after two or three years.[101]

---

[99] Anon., 'Conference on the Second Coming of the Lord Jesus', *BM* 68 (1958), 136; *H* 37 (1958), 1, 89.

[100] *H* 43 (1964), 145. Cf. *H* 50 (1971), 1.

[101] Frederick A. Tatford (ed.), *Revival in our Time* (London: Paternoster, 1947), 5-6, and memorandum by Metcalfe Collier in front of the copy in the CBA.

A vocal advocate of change as a prerequisite to revival was Montague Goodman. In an article for *The Witness* during 1946, he challenged Brethren to consider whether they had become hardened into a religion, like other renewal movements before them.

> That which began as a glorious emancipation from religious sectarianism is growing to shape itself into but one more sect, and that the strictest of them all. All the marks of a recognizable religious body begin to be seen and have in many places been fully developed, replete with established traditions, shibboleths and inhibitions held as rigidly as by the Pharisees of old, with a fierce intolerance of all who fail to see eye to eye with them. The inevitable consequence being that those who once stood gloriously for the essential unity of the Church are in danger of becoming but one more divisive factor in it.

He warned that just as ritual ordained by God became hateful to him, so too might the Lord's Table. If assemblies wished to avoid the prospect of decline and extinction, they must be ready to revise their judgements and renounce their traditions: 'it may be that we have sought to follow a *pattern* when we should have adhered to *principles*, forgetting that it is principles that are set before us in the New Testament to guide our worship rather than a pattern of procedure for us to copy'. They must also revise their attitude to non-Brethren believers, and cultivate fellowship with them. This was a time of opportunity, with returning servicemen looking for spiritual homes, and a united which church could usher in an unprecedented measure of revival.[102]

Longing for revival was widespread among leaders, and in *The Harvester* Tatford reproduced an open letter from some of them:

> One of the most tragic aspects of Church history is the record of the devitalised and pathetic survivals which have issued from great movements of the Spirit of God ... Nor do the assemblies seem any exception. The great movement, which stirred the Christian world to its depths just over a hundred years ago, now hardly causes a ripple, and is a shadow of its former self, both as regards church life and order, and also in its gospel witness.

> An analysis of the present position shows that some of the basic principles formerly held dear are no longer in evidence. In those early days, godly men of scholarship were attracted from the ranks of denominations and became pillars in the assemblies. Godly clergy had fellowship with their brethren in the assemblies, while still retaining their pastorates. ... The divisive barriers of sectarianism were thus thrown down, and the power of the Holy Spirit was plainly demonstrated in the spiritual unity thus attained. What was then considered fundamental, however, has been completely reversed in many assemblies today. A puny sect of "Plymouth Brethren" has arisen, narrower than most, and spiritual unity has been replaced by a rigid sectarianism which is quite intolerant of all who follow another course.

> ...

> The immediate urgency of the position lies in the fact that thousands of young men and women have returned, and are still returning into civilian life from the Forces, with no formed association in any Christian community. Many of these found Christ during the period of their war service, and had their first experience of Christian fellowship with fellow-believers in the

---

[102] Montague Goodman, 'The Church in the Post-War World', *W* 76 (1946), 42.

services. They are eagerly seeking a spiritual home, and are more than ready to respond to any approach which offers them a continuance of such fellowship: but they are not, generally speaking, attracted to denominationalism in any of its many forms. We are convinced that if this Scriptural way of fellowship and worship were lovingly presented to such young people in all its simplicity, untrammelled by any hint of sectarian exclusiveness, many would eagerly embrace it. The great opportunity which now presents itself will soon pass, and we feel that the time for action has come.[103]

About the same time, 'An Appeal to Christians' appeared in *The Believer's Magazine* and *The Witness*. Noting the character of the times and the inadequacy of the church to meet the need, it observed that 'Unparalleled opportunities present themselves, but there seems a moral and spiritual inadequacy to respond to their challenge.' Stressing that revival began with the individual, this appeal urged believers to put away sin, selfishness, and ambitions and desires which hindered spiritual progress. It called on them to unite in daily prayer for a solution to the problems of the day, but also for revival.[104]

In November 1947, London assemblies convened a special meeting at Westminster Central Hall on the topic of revival, notes of which were also published. Laing chaired the meeting, and opened by expressing the deep sense of urgency of the situation facing the church, and particularly assemblies. He pointed to the external threats presented by apostasy, moral decline, modernism, Romanism, and Communism, and the internal decay which had resulted in some assemblies losing their evangelistic impetus or becoming sectarian. The church must be revived before it could reach out effectively to the world. Interestingly, Watson suggested focusing on work with children and youth, which was still productive, as a means of replenishing assembly strength.[105]

There was a readiness to acknowledge that the lack of blessing being experienced represented an abnormal state for the church. In 1948, Borland penned several articles on this theme for *The Harvester*. Continuing lack of fruit was not the normal experience of God's servants over the last three centuries, and many Christians were praying for revival. But revivals, according to Borland, were 'due to circumstances brought about by Christians themselves' and God used human instruments.[106] An essential prerequisite, therefore, was confession, and investigation of every aspect of one's life.[107] Revival was always needed, especially when (as now) there was a lack of response to the gospel and Christians were worldly, when Christian love was at a low ebb, when interest in outreach

---

[103] *H* 24 (1947), 97. The signatories included Melville Capper, Montague Goodman, John Laing, Stephen Olford, and Tatford himself. Olford (b.1918) was the son of Brethren parents in South Wales who served as semi-official pastor of Nant Coch assembly in Newport (Rowdon (ed.), *Ten Changing Churches*, 55) before becoming a noted Evangelical preacher and pastor.

[104] *W* 77 (1947), 118; the appeal also appeared in *BM* 57 (1947), 291-2. It was signed by H.P. Barker, Borland, Rendle Short, Tatford, Vine, and Watson.

[105] H.F.R. Catherwood, W.W. Vellacott and J.B. Watson, *Revival in our time: A Call to Christians (Notes of a special meeting held by Representatives of the Assemblies of London in the Lecture Hall at the Westminster Central Hall on November 21ˢᵗ 1947)* (London: Conveners of Revival in our Time, [1947]).

[106] Andrew Borland, 'Revival', *H* 25 (1948), 29. Cf. his earlier article on this topic ('Revival', *BM* 51 (1941), 105).

[107] Andrew Borland, 'Factors that Precede Revival', *H* 25 (1948), 63.

was replaced by criticism, when Christians were living loose and superficial lives, when prayer meetings were declining, when children of Christian parents remained unsaved, when worldly ambition replaced spiritual appetite, and when wickedness outside was increasing (fuelled, he thought, by the growth of the leisure industry).[108]

Montague Goodman issued *An Urgent Call to Christian Unity* in 1948, prefaced by a letter from thirty-five brethren commending the call and the proposed response. Signatories included H.P. Barker, Douglas Brealey, Bruce, Tatford, General Dobbie, the evangelist Fred Elliott, Thomas Elwood (a civil servant from Belfast), Eric Hutchings, Laing, Howard Mudditt, Olford, and Rendle Short. Goodman asked why Brethren had become repulsive instead of attractive, and offered several reasons. The fellowship of saints had been replaced by the narrower fellowship of the assembly; New Testament principles of worship had given way to observance of a rigid pattern; and teaching concerning separation had been misapplied.

> Our loyalty to our Lord and to the light we have received upon His Word may indeed lead us into a separate path in matters of worship, but the separation is surely consequential rather than fundamental and while inevitable in view of our differing courses, should be viewed as an aspect of our church life to be rather regretted than rejoiced in.[109]

Goodman argued that objections to associating with other churches had been overstressed. He acknowledged that such objections might sometimes be justified, but he longed to see an assembly in each town which would exemplify the principle of openness to all believers. Undoubtedly this passionately-written document confirmed conservative perceptions of Goodman as dangerously open-minded and worsened the growing polarisation between progressives and conservatives. Borland criticised it as sectarian, unscriptural in its use of terminology, and uncharitable in its language.[110]

Oddly, little notice was taken of the revival which occurred in the Hebrides in 1949-50, and one wonders whether the burden was diminishing, although occasional revival-focused meetings were still held during the 1950s. For example, a special meeting for prayer and humiliation was convened in connection with the 1953 London Missionary Meetings, for missionaries and other brethren. This was arranged at short notice by editorial brethren at Bath, in the light of unspecified 'Disturbing events in the mission field indicating the power of the Devil'. Events in the field were seen as closely related to the spiritual condition of home assemblies, so the fundamental need was seen as that of revival at home.[111] However, concern for revival appears to have been channelled into annual residential conferences drawing men from much of Britain to High Leigh and later Swanwick, as well as the emergent Charismatic and Restoration movements. By 1959, it appears to have largely disappeared, and few magazine articles appeared to commemorate the centenary of the 1859 Revival and explain the Brethren debt to it. For Borland, the 400th anniversary of the Scottish Reformation seems to have been more significant, a lengthy series commemorating it in *The Believer's Magazine* during 1960-1.

---

[108] Andrew Borland, 'When is a Revival Needed?', *H* 25 (1948), 89.

[109] Montague Goodman, *An Urgent Call to Christian Unity* (London: Paternoster, 1948), 14.

[110] [Andrew Borland], 'The Editor's Observations on "An Urgent Call to Christian Unity"', *BM* 59 (1949), 97-9.

[111] A. Pulleng, 'A Day of Prayer', *W* 84 (1954), 10; *idem*, 'The Need of the Hour', *EQR* 6.1 (January-March 1954), 12-13.

19.2.3 The Charismatic and Restoration Movements

In this section, we shall look firstly at Brethren input to the Restorationist movement, and then more generally at Open Brethren and the Charismatic movement. Once again, it was the decline of dispensationalism which was to pave the way for increasing openness to charismatic gifts.[112] These two factors were both prominent in the developing thought of Arthur Wallis (1922-88).[113] Son of Captain Reginald Wallis (1891-1940), a noted Brethren evangelist who had worked in interdenominational settings, Arthur had taken up full-time ministry after the war, settling in the assembly at Ottery St Mary in Devon. By the late 1940s, he was developing a deep concern for revival, which was reinforced by a visit to the Isle of Lewis in 1951 to investigate the revival which had just occurred there, and he would write a classic book on the subject, *In the Day of Thy Power* (1956).[114] Wallis's thinking was to be shaped by two men, G.H. Lang and David Lillie. From the early 1940s, Wallis was in contact with Lang, and gained from him a hunger for God and a passion for holiness and radical discipleship.[115] Lillie (b.1913) had been 'baptised with the Spirit' and begun to speak in tongues shortly after leaving his assembly around 1940 in search of the fullness of the Spirit, and commenced an independent house church near Exeter. Described, along with Wallis, as 'the theological architect of modern Restorationist ecclesiology',[116] he testified that 'It was particularly Lang's personal commitment to biblical Christianity and ecclesiology which stimulated my desire to see the recovery of some semblance of authentic New Testament church life in my lifetime.'[117] So Lang's influence on modern Restorationism was seminal, if indirect. Restorationists shared his passion for personal holiness; they sought to remain faithful to what they understood Scripture to teach, even when that entailed departing from the received tradition; they conceived the church in organic rather than bureaucratic terms, insisting that the New Testament provided sufficient guidance for the establishment of an apostolic church order.[118]

---

[112] To qualify this, it should be noted that during the post-war period many, perhaps most, Pentecostals would have been dispensationalists; the relationship between dispensationalism and cessationism is too complex to be analysed fully here. But the point remains true of Brethren, since their understanding of the purpose of charismatic gifts was conditioned by their commitment to a dispensationalist hermeneutic which related such gifts to God's dealings with Israel.

[113] On Wallis, see *BDE*; Jonathan Wallis, *Arthur Wallis: Radical Christian* (Eastbourne: Kingsway, 1991).

[114] See also Arthur Wallis, 'The '59 Revival in Ulster', *W* 89 (1959), 239-41.

[115] Peter Hocken, *Streams of Renewal: The Origins and Early Development of the Charismatic Movement in Great Britain* (revised ed.; Exeter: Paternoster, 1997), 13; cf. the letters between them during the mid-1950s (CBA Box 76).

[116] Andrew Walker, *Restoring the Kingdom: The Radical Christianity of the House Church Movement* (revised ed.; Guildford: Eagle, 1998), 21-2.

[117] David Lillie, *Restoration: Is this still on God's programme?* (Exton, Devon: the author, [1994]), 11; cf. Hocken, *Streams of Renewal*, 12-13. Lillie had been introduced to Lang and his writings in the late 1930s by the Pentecostal missionary W.F.P. Burton (David Lillie, 'Thanks for the Memory: G.H. Lang', *A*, November 1991, 25-6; Lillie to P.H. Stunt, 19 June 1968, CBA Box 7).

[118] From a very different stream of Brethren, Andrew Borland also testified to the impact Lang had on him as a young man; he may have been one of the sources of Borland's burden for revival and concern for holy living ('They Pass On', *BM* 69 (1959), 14).

Wallis and Lillie came into contact in the early 1950s, and from 1958-65 organised a series of residential conferences in which desire for revival was coupled with ecclesiological radicalism and exploration of the charismatic dimension of spiritual experience. Wallis's departure from Brethren was a very gradual affair, and he was writing and speaking in Brethren circles until the early 1960s, a final article during 1964 arguing for acceptance of what was going on in the Charismatic movement. In it, he asserted that God's strategy in history was '*to bring back His people to the purity, power and principles of the New Testament Church, through successive movements of the Spirit*'. Surveying such movements throughout history, he argued that Pentecostalism demonstrated that supernatural gifts had not been withdrawn. 'We cannot afford to ignore a movement that has remained fundamental and evangelistic, and that has been manifestly blessed of God, despite its blemishes – what movement has not had these?' His belief was that God was preparing many for something which would eclipse anything previously seen. Many Brethren, he claimed, had entered into a new experience of the Spirit.[119] Well before that, however, he had withdrawn from his assembly and commenced a church in his house. His influence led to the secession from Chapelfield Hall, Whipton, near Exeter, of Jack Hardwidge, a son of Brethren missionaries, who was to become the founder of Isca Christian Fellowship, a house church in Exeter which grew to 800 members by the early 1980s.[120]

A number of other Restorationist leaders had roots in Open Brethren: one who gave his reasons for leaving Brethren in some detail was Hugh Thompson, from Cwmbran in Wales. Thompson served with Counties Evangelistic Work as an evangelist in Wiltshire from 1959 until 1964, when he resigned.[121] Among his reasons were rejection of one-man evangelistic ministry arising from a belief that team work in church planting was the apostolic pattern of outreach, and an unease with the concept of brief tent missions as widely practised at that time; apprehension at what he saw as centralised control and funding was another factor. He had also come to reject traditional Brethren eschatology in favour of an expectation of widespread revival preceding the Lord's return; he saw this as already beginning, in the form of the Charismatic movement.[122] Counties regarded his views as amounting to departure from generally-accepted Brethren doctrine and practice (nowadays many of its evangelists are sympathetic to the Charismatic movement), but he had a point: if Brethren rejected one-man ministry on the basis that no one person could have all the gifts, it was logical to reject one-man evangelism on the same basis. If Counties had followed the practice of working in pairs, common in Northern Ireland, such objections would have had less force. Thompson later linked up with another Welshman, Bryn Jones, becoming a leading figure in the Harvestime movement. David Matthew, who also joined Harvestime, had been an elder, and had led his assembly into merger with two local house churches to form a larger congregation based in the centre of Bradford. The trends which led his assembly away from Brethren were the adoption of planned ministry before the Breaking of Bread and a wish to accept those who exercised charismatic gifts.[123] Others to move to Restorationist churches and groups included Graham Perrins of

---

[119] Arthur Wallis, 'God's Spirit is Working Today', *H* 43 (1964), 85, 84.

[120] Roger Forster (ed.), *Ten New Churches* (n.pl.: MARC Europe, 1986), 117-19; Jonathan Wallis, *Arthur Wallis*, 93.

[121] For Thompson's commendation, see 'TLWW', *BM*, 70 (1960), 191.

[122] See the papers preserved in Counties Evangelism's Executive Oversight Minutes.

[123] *W* 107 (1977), 314-15; cf. Walker, *Restoring the Kingdom*, 111.

Cardiff (who had been a full-time worker among assemblies), David Mansell of North London, David Tomlinson, and Gerald Coates of Cobham, Surrey, founder of what became the Pioneer network of churches.[124]

A man who influenced a number of early Restorationist leaders, though never identifying completely with the movement, was Campbell McAlpine, whose father had been a Brethren evangelist in Scotland.[125] Similarly, Roger Forster, whilst not a thoroughgoing Restorationist, worked closely with Restorationist leaders from the 1980s onwards.[126] During the late 1950s he had belonged to the Belvedere assembly in South-East London as a young man who was developing an evangelistic ministry, and spoke at the first of the Wallis/Lillie conferences.[127] Although he founded Ichthus Christian Fellowship in Forest Hill, London, in 1974, he seems to have continued to think of himself as Brethren in some sense. He was one of the signatories inviting people to assist in gathering data for a 1978 survey of Open Brethren,[128] and referred (significantly) to Ichthus as 'our own local assembly' in a *Harvester* article in 1980.[129]

The extent to which Restorationism was indebted to Brethren thinking and practice is debated. Lillie has been inclined to minimise it, not least because in his experience Brethren did not share the vision of a restoration of New Testament church life; he argued instead that Restorationism rediscovered from the New Testament such Brethren distinctives as plural leadership.[130] Nevertheless, his fullest ecclesiological work, *Beyond Charisma* (1981), strikes many familiar notes. Peter Hocken, who has investigated the origins of the British Charismatic movement exhaustively, notes a number of Brethren characteristics evident in Lillie, Wallis, and the conferences which they organised: dismissal of existing churches as irrelevant to what God was doing, the unrenewability of denominations, plural lay leadership, the according of a prominent place to the Breaking of Bread,[131] and denial that they were creating a new

---

[124] See Coates, *Intelligent Fire*; Hocken, *Streams of Renewal*, 12, 264; Nigel Scotland, *Charismatics and the New Millennium: The impact of Charismatic Christianity from 1960 into the new millennium* (revised ed.; Guildford: Eagle, 2000), 23; Jonathan Wallis, *Arthur Wallis*, 132. There was also an ex-Taylor brother, David Devenish of Bedford.

[125] Hocken, *Streams of Renewal*, 25.

[126] For Forster, see Brian Hewitt, *Doing a New Thing?* (London: Hodder & Stoughton, 1995), ch. 4; Anthony O'Sullivan, 'Roger Forster and the Ichthus Christian Fellowship: The Development of a Charismatic Missiology', *Pneuma* 16 (1994), 247-63; Shuff, *Searching*, 218-19. Forster was influenced by Lang's teaching on rewards for believers, mission, and the local church (Chilcraft, 'Groves' theory and practice of mission', 9n).

[127] Another Brethren speaker at that conference was Metcalfe Collier (Jonathan Wallis, *Arthur Wallis,* 130-1).

[128] Graham Brown and Brian Mills, *"The Brethren" Today: A Factual Survey* (Exeter: Paternoster for the Christian Brethren Research Fellowship, 1980), 54.

[129] Roger Forster, 'Nationwide Initiative in Evangelism', *H* 59 (1980), 108.

[130] Lillie, *Restoration*, 83.

[131] This was still evident in the programme of Isca Christian Fellowship during the early 1980s, as my wife recalls. She also noted the number of ex-Brethren in leadership, and the Brethren stress on knowing one's Bible and the provision of solid teaching.

denomination.[132] To these we should add the view of denominations as perpetuating division among believers, insistence on the autonomy of each local congregation (for which Wallis contended in 1961),[133] the strongly eschatological orientation of early Restorationism (if not the eschatological scheme),[134] and the Restorationist interpretation of church history, which has been described as an updated and Pentecostal version of that advanced by Broadbent.[135] This received definitive expression in David Matthew's book *Church Adrift*, which was based on a series of articles in *Restoration*, the magazine issued by Harvestime. In a remarkable review, which could be seen as undercutting the justification for the separate existence of Brethren, Rowdon criticised its underlying view of history as a series of upward steps after a long initial descent, which the current movement was bringing to a conclusion. Noting the similarities between this and early Brethren thinking, Rowdon asserted that God had a habit of bringing revival within existing structures, rather than always abandoning churches which had fallen away in favour of raising up new movements in each generation.[136] Doubtless Brethren, who had tended to see church history as in some sense a preparation for the emergence of their movement, would not have taken kindly to a version of their scheme which made Brethrenism merely a step in the run-up to Restorationism, though this is not evident in Rowdon's comments.

Negatively, Restorationism was influenced by the Brethren agenda as something to react against; thus its eschatology was formulated in reaction against Brethren expectations of ongoing decline into apostasy.[137] The triumphalist post-millennialism of Restorationist ecclesiology, in which such churches were seen as raised up to prepare the way for the coming of the King, represented a decisive rejection of Brethren 'remnant ecclesiology'. Once dispensationalism was rejected, its arguments against the continuance of charismatic gifts could be discounted, freeing individuals to seek their restoration. Related to this is Shuff's claim that 'rather than ecclesiology it was Brethren's perception of the immediacy of the activity of the Holy Spirit that represented the most fundamental link between the ethos of Brethren and a new form of Restorationism'; this was to be evident in worship, Bible study, and the expectation of revival.[138]

So how did Open Brethren respond to the emergence of Restorationism and other house churches? One article expressed concern that the tendency of those in house churches to regard their congregations as representing the New Testament pattern led to a negative attitude towards other churches and to proselytism; the author was also unhappy about claims regarding the restoration of apostleship, the separation of Christ from Scripture in

---

[132] Hocken, *Streams of Renewal*, 41, 205; cf. *H*, June 1990, 25. One wonders whether the concept of 'apostolic teams', which Restorationists derived from Watchman Nee, owes anything to Brethren insistence on leadership as plural.

[133] Lillie, *Restoration*, 15.

[134] Walker, *Restoring the Kingdom*, 70.

[135] *Ibid.*, 147.

[136] *PN* 7 (n.s.), July 1986, 15-16.

[137] It is also ironic that Lang's theology was shaped by his opposition to the Exclusive Brethrenism in which he grew up, as is evident from *The Local Assembly* and *Departure*, and yet it contributed to the emergence of some of the most highly centralised movements of modern British Evangelical history in Restorationism.

[138] Shuff, *Searching*, 204, 207.

reacting against legalism, and the practice of shepherding.[139] J.K. Howard saw the movement as a protest group, comparable to Brethren, Anabaptists and Quakers; he criticised their subjectivism, probably a result of their inward-looking approach 'with a strong martyr and remnant complex' which produced divisiveness and spiritual arrogance. Although he tempered this by pointing to Acts 5.38-9, it is hard to avoid thinking that such arguments had been equally applicable to Brethren.[140]

We now turn to examine Open Brethren attitudes to claims that the whole spectrum of charismatic gifts was being restored. There is some slight evidence of interest in charismatic phenomena throughout the twentieth century, demonstrating that the movement's commitment to dispensationalist cessationism was never total. In 1950, a questioner asked Harold St John whether there was any evidence that spiritual gifts had been withdrawn. His reply was that they had undoubtedly appeared among the second-century Montanists, the Wesleyans, and more recently in China. Sign gifts might still be given occasionally, by the sovereign decision of God, although miracles were not a permanent feature of the church's life. Believers should be grateful if these appeared now, and 'there is no evidence that the gifts of 1 Cor. 12 have been withdrawn'.[141] The normal view, however, continued to be that such gifts appeared only 'while God's relation with His earthly people still existed, and while the Scriptures were not completed'.[142] One writer even called tongues 'a Satanic parody of an early church gift, which gift, having fulfilled its purpose, lapsed long ago'.[143] Moreover, attitudes towards the Pentecostal movement remained largely negative.[144] By the early 1960s, leaders were becoming concerned about the possible impact on assemblies of charismatic practices. Early in 1962, Howley invited Wallis, Lillie, and other charismatics to meet with Brethren including Stephen Short, A.G. Nute, and Douglas Brealey to discuss the issues. Wallis impressed them as a godly man, although they were not convinced by charismatic theology.[145]

An indicator of changing thinking among Open Brethren regarding charismatic issues is provided by two issues of the *Journal of the Christian Brethren Research Fellowship*. In 1965, a special issue, made available to the public, considered the topic in depth.[146] Coad noted the ecclesiological affinity of Open Brethren with Pentecostalism, but balanced this with the assertion that

It is in just those tendencies which they share with Pentecostal churches, that so many of the weaknesses which have caused distress within the ranks of Brethren have arisen. There is the

---

[139] Stanley Linton, 'The Church in the house - A cause for concern?', *W* 107 (1977), 162-3.

[140] 'QA', *W* 107 (1977), 167. Leakage of Brethren to house churches has continued; I understand that in Ulster, many young people, even from 'tight' assemblies, have made such a move.

[141] 'QA', *W* 80 (1950), 27. Cf. J.W. Prior, 'QA', *W* 74 (1944), 72: 'There appears to be sound evidence that in recent times such gifts have been given at the beginning of Gospel testimony in heathen lands.'

[142] W.E. Vine, 'Notes on I Corinthians', *BM* 57 (1947), 270; cf. J.M. Davies, 'The Gift of Tongues', *PS* 6 (1954-5), 200-1.

[143] P. Parsons, 'BQB', *BM* 76 (1966), 8.

[144] See, for example, E.W. Rogers, 'The Modern Tongues Movement', *H* 36 (1957), 67-8.

[145] Peter Lineham, 'Tongues must Cease: The Brethren and the Charismatic Movement in New Zealand', *CBR* 34 (November 1983), 29, citing G.C.D. Howley to R. Coope, 29 August 1962.

[146] *JCBRF* 9 (August 1965).

excessive individualism and its tendency to division: there is also the too glib profession of acquaintance with divine things, and of the guidance of the Spirit. There is therefore another school of thought, not obscurantist in the face of new light, but nevertheless fearful whether this may not be an advance at all, but a strengthening of all too regrettable tendencies from which many have been struggling to break free.[147]

In another article, Coad argued that Pentecostal teaching rested on distorted and selective exegesis, New Testament terms were used wrongly (such as baptism and filling with the Spirit), the Pentecostal doctrine of the Spirit was too supernaturalistic, and that many tongues and healings were the product of natural psychosomatic mechanisms.[148] On the other hand, a former missionary, George Patterson, expressed the conviction that many Brethren meetings were dependent on the exercise of human intellect rather than the activity of the Spirit, and that frequently acceptance of the message was likewise merely intellectual.[149] As Don Tinder wryly noted in the correspondence which ensued: 'that Brethren oppose charismatics with much the same arguments that we were once facing ourselves ... indicates how far we've evolved!' Among them he instanced the division of Christians into two classes, divisiveness, and the call to cease fettering the Spirit in old forms of worship.[150]

The articles, along with the strong opposition to charismatic practices among Open Brethren in New Zealand (where Arthur Wallis had ministered during 1963-4) elicited a response from David Lillie in the form of *Tongues Under Fire*, published by a charismatic body, the Fountain Trust. This included eight testimonies of (former) Brethren who had received the gift of tongues, and a detailed examination of Brethren exegesis of the biblical passages at issue. In Lillie's opinion, 'the evidence strongly suggests that the real aversion is on experimental rather than on Scriptural grounds'.[151] Brethren, he alleged, were afraid: of the supernatural, of spiritual deception, of the impact on their cherished traditions, and of the reproach and material loss which they would suffer through adopting charismatic views. Underlying their understanding of the issues was the conception of spiritual life as essentially a rational matter.

By 1977, a shift in attitude was becoming evident in the contents of an issue of the *Journal* entitled 'New Directions – Papers on Neo-Pentecostalism and on Urban Evangelism'.[152] Donald Bridge, who moved between Brethren and Baptists as a pastor, advised that space be created for gifts to be exercised, but that individuals should be asked not to exercise them in the main meetings of the church, in order to avoid distress and dissension.[153] Peter Cousins, asking why the Charismatic movement had had so little impact on Brethren, put it down to the prevalence of dispensationalist theology and an

---

[147] F.R. Coad, 'Preface', *JCBRF* 9 (August 1965), 3.

[148] F.R. Coad, 'Introduction: the Divine Encounter', *JCBRF* 9 (August 1965), 5-15.

[149] George N. Patterson, 'Pentecostalism, East and West' *JCBRF* 9 (August 1965), 35-6.

[150] *JCBRF* 11 (February 1966), 25.

[151] D.G. Lillie, *Tongues under Fire* (London: Fountain Trust, 1966), 26. Cf. Peter Lineham's comment on events in New Zealand: 'There is reason to believe that Brethren views were in fact based less on their reading of I Corinthians than on their fear of anything irrational in their midst, or anything which would distract young people from their loyalty to the assemblies.' ('Tongues Must Cease', 46)

[152] *JCBRF* 29 (1977).

[153] Donald Bridge, 'Pastoral Problems in the Local Church', *JCBRF* 29 (1977), 24-5.

emphasis on the 'once for all' nature of salvation which left little room for post-conversion experiences.[154]

It is worth returning for a moment to the point made by Lillie and Patterson about the rationalistic nature of Brethren spirituality. In the 1930s, one reason for the attractiveness of Brethren to many in the denominations was that they presented a coherent doctrinal system in the form of dispensationalism, being less afraid than many other Evangelicals to use their minds. However, in the existential climate of the 1960s, charismatic spirituality flourished and Brethren struggled to relate to those influenced by it, in part because of its non-rational nature. One writer set the Charismatic movement in what he saw as its cultural context: 'One can discern a definite connection with this revival of demonism with hypnotism, hippyism, psychiatry, brain-washing and what in the western world is becoming popular: the mystical meditations of Hinduism.' He condemned it as interference in forbidden parts of the human personality.[155] Whilst his views might have been expressed in a somewhat exaggerated form, he was by no means the only Evangelical to make the connection between the spirit of the age and the popularity of speaking in tongues.

A more nuanced approach was taken by J.H. Large of the outward-looking Cholmeley Hall in North London. Writing in *Precious Seed* in 1965, he rejected the idea that tongues were either from God or the devil: 'it is quite possible for the Spirit of God to be acting upon a man's spirit whilst his reactions are complicated by the interference of human emotionalism in the soul'. He upheld the dispensationalist argument that 'the gifts mentioned in the context of "tongues" were to serve a temporary purpose until the more perfect order was established'. Contemporary tongues were usually 'nothing more than gibberish uttered under intense excitement', but when individuals let themselves go and surrendered control of their faculties, they could be laying themselves open to demonic influence.[156]

Even today, there continues to be a rationalistic strain within conservative Brethrenism, evident in the 'cut and dried' feel to some magazine articles on spiritual issues.[157] Believers are exhorted to establish what Scripture teaches, a process which involves extensive use of the mind, and then to put it into practice, in a manner which savours on occasion of legalism; although lip-service is paid to the Holy Spirit, there is, as a result, not the same sense of dependence on him which might be expected from those who assert the Spirit's pre-eminence in the worship meeting. Such rationalism is also evident in the discussion of the creation–evolution debate and the frequent focus on this by conservative assemblies in their outreach.[158]

Anti-charismatic views continued to be expressed, and probably remain the majority outlook among Brethren. Stephen Short reported on a convention of the Full Gospel Businessmen's Fellowship International (FGBMFI) in London which he attended. He noted the tendency to assume that if a person spoke in tongues, they were a Christian; the stress on healing; the movement's claim to be an instrument of Christian unity (in which

---

[154] P. Cousins, 'Gospel and Spirit: The Anglican Joint Statement', *JCBRF* 29 (1977), 69.

[155] Robert McClurkin, 'The Gift of Tongues; What Saith the Scriptures', *BM* 83 (1973), 333.

[156] J.H. Large, 'Revival and "Tongues"', *PS* 16 (1965), 40, 44, 45.

[157] This would be true of Protestant fundamentalism in general; for a fuller examination of this point, and of the philosophical basis for the movement, see Harriet A. Harris, *Fundamentalism and Evangelicals* (Oxford: Clarendon, 1998).

[158] Cf. the long series on this topic in *BM* 104 (1994).

Roman Catholics were included – their participation in the Charismatic movement was a frequent stumbling-block for Brethren); and the apparent doctrinal vacuum (doubtless exacerbated by the FGBMFI's policy of banning teaching in favour of testimony at its meetings).[159]

A missionary in Brazil, A.E. Horton, who admitted to having spoken in tongues as a young man, expounded a fairly traditional Brethren understanding of tongues, but admitted that he could not prove from Scripture that the sign-gifts had ceased completely.[160] His article provoked a lengthy correspondence, including 'An open letter on tongues' from three New Zealand brethren, R.A. Laidlaw, W.T. Miller, and W.H. Pettit.[161] They wished they had met the appearance of tongues with firm opposition a few years back (when Wallis was ministering in the country), rather than Horton's 'extreme caution'. But what really provoked a storm was their statement that one assembly had been put outside the fellowship of assemblies by representative Brethren. This struck at the heart of Open Brethren ecclesiology, and a number of respondents condemned this action as contradicting belief in independency.[162] A further letter from the New Zealand trio extolled the healthy and aggressive outlook of their assemblies. They claimed that when tongues-speaking was introduced, it caused havoc and disruption, hence their action, and they could not imagine those who produced a UK assembly list including one which had adopted such views as the New Zealand assembly in question did.[163] F.F. Stunt suggested that many correspondents were missing the point, which was not whether these things should be practised, but whether those who did so should be excluded from the Lord's Table. There were two subsidiary issues: whether local churches should band together over such an issue; and the need for elders to face up to their responsibility to deal with false doctrine when it appeared, rather than taking the easy way out and 'debarring Christians from the Lord's Table because they fear the doctrines those Christians will bring with them'.[164]

Charismatic influence has also been a major factor in the increasing polarisation between conservatives and progressives. In 1981, one observer commented on the considerable move to the 'extreme right' since the Charismatic movement began affecting assembles in Northern England; he expressed the conviction that the pockets where 'Needed Truth' ideas were held were no longer so small.[165] Clearly, there were those who were growing more conservative in reaction against the spread of charismatic thinking. Some assemblies attracted Evangelicals from elsewhere precisely because they took a clear anti-charismatic line. As one brother who wanted things to stay that way wrote:

---

[159] Stephen S. Short, '"Full Gospel" Convention', *W* 96 (1966), 25-7.

[160] A.E. Horton, 'The sign of Tongues', *W* 95 (1965), 203-6, cf. 429-30. Cf. *idem*, 'What is "that which is perfect"?' (*W* 96 (1976), 333-4), which refused to interpret 1 Corinthians 13.10 as referring to the completion of the canon of Scripture, though Horton believed on other grounds that sign-gifts were gradually withdrawn.

[161] *W* 95 (1965), 384-6.

[162] *W* 95 (1965), 465-7. Among them were G.J. Polkinghorne, Metcalfe Collier, Derek Warren, and Jack Hardwidge.

[163] *W* 96 (1966), 110-11.

[164] *W* 96 (1966), 148.

[165] Kingsley Melling to Roy Coad, 6 June 1981 (CBA Box 4).

> I joined an assembly many years ago because the brethren adhered to the scriptures faithfully and because the movement was non-ecumenical, non-charismatic and inflexible in upholding truth. Since then assemblies have been infiltrated by charismatics causing divisions. If people wish to be charismatic, ecumenical or contrary to brethren truths why don't they join churches who are of these persuasions and leave the assemblies alone.[166]

It is also true that some assemblies have experienced serious problems as a result of charismatic practices. In 1981, two-thirds of Birkbeck Chapel, Sidcup, left in a charismatic split;[167] the weakened assembly closed five years later. In 1986, a majority of the Harpenden assembly left to join a Restorationist church, leaving just two children and five adults, but in this case the story had a happier ending, as the assembly grew again through outreach to particular sections of the community.[168] Even churches which eventually adopted an explicitly pro-charismatic viewpoint experienced some difficulties along the way. Greenford, for instance, lost a number of converts as the result of tensions during the 1970s and 1980s over charismatic issues; even in the late 1990s, successful use of the Alpha Course brought in a number of converts who were not interested in what they saw as Brethren traditions, with the result that further tension ensued. This was only resolved when the entire eldership stood down and a new trust deed was adopted.[169]

Even missionaries were drawn into the conflict over charismatic issues; thus Mr and Mrs Ian McCulloch, serving in Paraguay, had their commendation withdrawn by their home assembly because of their association with neo-Pentecostal practices.[170] They subsequently became leaders of a charismatic fellowship at Emsworth, Hampshire.[171] One Scottish assembly withdrew its commendation of a missionary because he had been practising Pentecostalism for some years; it was claimed that there were others abroad who had changed their views similarly. Such assemblies considered it dishonest to take money from assemblies and conduct work which, by its acceptance of charismatic practices, disrupted them or built up something else.[172] At home, several Counties evangelists left the movement over this issue during the 1970s.[173]

Yet charismatic practice remained relatively uncommon among Brethren until the 1990s. Of the churches responding to the 1988 survey (a sample probably weighted towards the progressive end of the movement), 4% saw speaking in tongues as a part of their meetings, 8% had prophecy, and 7% healing; the corresponding figures for 1998 were just 5%, 13%, and 12% respectively.[174] Only a small minority of assemblies could therefore be described as charismatic; one estimate in the mid-1990s put the number

---

[166] *H*, December 1985, 23.

[167] *H*, December 1982, 16. The split came in spite of the adoption by the church of a mediating statement on charismatic issues, neither cessationist nor advocating a 'second blessing'; this was reprinted in 'Readers Forum', *H* 58 (1979), 90-1.

[168] *H*, February 1990, 25.

[169] Rowdon (ed.), *Ten Changing Churches*, 20-1, 25-6.

[170] *EOS* 97 (1968), 122. For a similar notice, see *EOS* 99 (1970), 97.

[171] Eileen Wheeler, *The God who Speaks* ([Bexhill]: the author, 2000), 45, 62-3, 108.

[172] *BM* 89 (1979), 190.

[173] Mills, *Story*, 47.

[174] Peter Brierley et al., *The Christian Brethren as the Nineties Began* (Carlisle: Paternoster for Partnership in association with MARC Europe, 1993), 110; Graham Brown, *Whatever Happened to the Brethren? A survey of local churches in 1998-1999* (Carlisle: Paternoster for Partnership, 2003), 82.

below twenty, although acknowledging that many more permitted a wider range of spiritual gifts to be exercised than had traditionally been the case, and more still used the worship songs emerging from the Charismatic movement.[175] Thus a series in *The Harvester* during 1976-7 asked 'Can We Learn from the Pentecostals?' The answer was positive, especially in the areas of body life and demonstrative worship (which was contrasted with Brethren intellectualism). The charismatic style of worship proved attractive to many assemblies, such as that commenced during the 1970s on the Hartcliffe council estate in Bristol. The evangelist Graham Loader, who was involved with this assembly, pointed out the inadequacy of the cerebral Brethren pattern of worship in such a context: 'The converts themselves would not be acclimatized to meetings that were an academic exercise. They needed provision for the release of the Spirit in worship and praise.'[176] In line with much of the rest of British Evangelicalism, therefore, progressive Brethren have adopted the ethos of the Charismatic movement without necessarily making the exercise of gifts such as tongues and prophecy a regular feature of their worship. It is perhaps a misnomer to call such churches 'charismatic'.

Many individuals within non-charismatic assemblies testified to a new experience of the Holy Spirit. As early as 1968, many young people in the Beacon Heath assembly in Exeter had received the baptism in the Holy Spirit.[177] A few years later, *The Harvester* printed an anonymous testimony to the blessing of the gift of tongues.[178] By the late 1970s, John Ward (a convenor of the London Missionary Meetings) and his wife could claim that many Brethren had found a fresh experience of the Spirit, and argued that many in assemblies were longing for a deeper spiritual reality.[179] This is borne out by the obituary of a well-known leading brother, K.G. Hyland of Poole. Hyland had had a landmark experience of the Spirit about which he said little because it did not conform to assembly norms of spirituality. However, during the last few years of his life he was involved in promoting renewal conferences in Devon; the last before his death, in 1978, was fully booked, indicating continuing interest and spiritual hunger.[180]

19.2.4 Changing Thinking on Ecumenism

Thinking among some Open Brethren on the practice of ecumenism developed in parallel with that among some more open Evangelicals during the 1960s. This, along with a concern to distance the movement from the Taylor Brethren, who were then receiving considerable and unfavourable media coverage, and the desire to clarify the nature of Brethren identity, influenced the approach taken by the histories of the movement by Coad and Rowdon which appeared in the late 1960s: Coad presented Open Brethren assemblies as an example of the independent congregations which provided a necessary counterbalance throughout church history to the tendency of mainstream churches to

---

[175] Alan Batchelor (intro.), *Don't Muzzle the Ox: Full-time Ministry in Local Churches* (Carlisle: Paternoster for Partnership, 1997), 79, 90. For the story of how one assembly 'went charismatic', see John Cavanagh and Frank Wilding, 'Spiritual Gifts in a time of change at Brook Chapel, Runcorn', *PP* 4 (January 1997), 18-21.

[176] Graham Loader, 'Birth and Growth in Bristol', *H* 57 (1978), 18.

[177] Jonathan Wallis, *Arthur Wallis*, 195.

[178] Anon., 'Family Forum: Tongues – a Testimony', *H* 53 (1974), 152.

[179] John and Evelyn Ward, 'Spiritual renewal', *W* 109 (1979), 72-3.

[180] *H* 58 (1979), 60, 162.

become too institutionalised; Rowdon included an appendix exploring the 'ecumenical' views of early Brethren leaders.

Much Brethren opposition to ecumenism was rooted in an eschatology which foretold a 'coming great church' from which believers must separate.[181] However well-intentioned, the ecumenical movement was a preparation for the final doctrinal landslide which would precede the Second Advent.[182] Here too, less widespread adherence to traditional eschatological views, with their inbuilt separatist dynamic, made it possible for broader sympathies to gain a wider hearing in a minority of assemblies than would otherwise have been the case. A letter from T.C.F. Stunt expressed the hope that 'Christians among us will not fail to recognise the evident spiritual renewal current in the Roman Catholic Church, because they are too attached to a scheme of prophecy that has already doomed these people to apostasy.'[183] Other factors, more significant now than they were during the 1960s, include an increased appreciation of the Christian tradition as a whole, growing awareness of the importance of the visible church, and a tendency to emphasise shared experience as opposed to precise agreement in doctrinal definition. Perhaps the most important, though, is the recognition that Britain is an increasingly pluralist and post-Christian society, and that from such a viewpoint what unites the churches is greater than what divides them. On the other hand, Brethren wariness of ecumenism has to be understood in the light of the fact that occasional instances of opposition from other churches (often Anglican) have continued to occur.[184]

But we must return to the 1960s, which were in many respects the 'ecumenical decade' of British church history, replete with hopes and schemes for organisational union. In 1964, delegates to the BCC assembly at Nottingham committed themselves to seek visible union by Easter 1980. F.F. Bruce was asked whether Evangelicals should take a more positive view of the WCC now that it had strengthened its doctrinal basis. Bruce replied that he was not keen on another layer of bureaucracy, but 'let the evangelical contribution to the World council consist one hundred per cent of undiluted evangelical witness, and the outcome need not be feared'. Brethren were independent, so there was no question of association with the WCC through any denominational structure, but local councils of churches could include assemblies; it was up to each to decide whether or not to join.[185] A less positive view of such co-operation came from Tatford, who contended that it was inconsistent for an undenominational collection of Christians to be represented on an interdenominational body, probably under Anglican control and allowing Roman Catholic co-operation.[186] Another writer saw the aim of ecumenical activity as institutional union of the churches involved, rather than more powerful gospel preaching to the world. The WCC basis of faith was meaningless because every shade of doctrinal opinion was tolerated, and few Evangelicals were involved. The Ecumenical

[181] The only survey of Open Brethren attitudes to ecumenism remains F.R. Coad, 'The Ecumenical Movement: Evangelical Apprehensions', in Anon. (ed.), *Christian Unity: Papers given at a conference of Brethren at Swanwick, Derbyshire, in June, 1964* (Bristol: Evangelical Christian Literature, [1964]), 22-39.

[182] 'WW', *W* 84 (1954), 179.

[183] *W* 97 (1967), 468.

[184] E.g. 'LF', *BM* 92 (1982), 48 (Weald, Kent); 93 (1983), 251 (Wickhambrook, Suffolk); 113 (2003), 94 (Plymouth).

[185] 'QA', *H* 41 (1962), 74.

[186] *H* 42 (1963), 65.

movement was 'the great apostasy of our time', and true unity was spiritual.[187] In 1968, Tatford printed a letter from the Rev. John G. Weller of the BCC, correcting the idea (persistent in Evangelical circles) that the WCC's aim was reunion with Rome:[188] reunion could only be between churches themselves; the WCC's task was to bring them into contact with each other and to promote the study and discussion of unity issues. Tatford was unmoved, citing in his editorial examples of statements implying that the Ecumenical movement's goal was one world church.[189] He spoke from an acquaintance with WCC thinking which was evident in the frequent comments in *The Harvester* on ecumenical gatherings and publications since the WCC's first assembly in 1948.[190]

It is important to note that during the 1960s, progressive Brethren laid considerable stress on what they saw as the open approach to fellowship practiced by A.N. Groves. Apart from the fact that this misrepresented his views to some degree, since he regarded all existing church bodies as destined for destruction and sought to call believers out of them, it appears to have been something of a search by ecumenically-minded Brethren for a precedent to support their own ecumenical involvement. Thus in 1980 Roger Forster, urging assemblies to get involved in the ecumenical Nationwide Initiative in Evangelism, appealed to Groves' practice of bearing with evil for the sake of what was good.[191]

A significant degree of openness to ecumenical contact was shown in some of the papers presented at the 1964 Swanwick Conference on the theme of Christian unity. Rowdon's paper on denominationalism surveyed early Brethren ecclesiology and then drew a number of lessons for contemporary church life: among them were the argument that whilst Brethren could not strictly accept existing forms of the church as valid, they must not judge believers who could remain in them with good conscience; believers should be free to exercise their gifts wherever opportunity was given and, conversely, assemblies should be free to use the gifts of others regardless of their denominational affiliation. He concluded: 'We may well live to see widespread secessions of evangelical christians from Protestant denominations. Are we ready to receive them?'[192] Coad's survey of the Ecumenical movement shrewdly claimed that 'many evangelical criticisms are directed not at what the Council [the WCC] is, as [sic] at what it is feared it might become',[193] and asserted that what matters was how Brethren acted locally, not how they should respond to such imaginary fears.[194] Ellison explored the practical side of ecumenism, and argued that although Brethren could not join the BCC because that would entail their becoming a multi-church denomination in order to become the kind of body the BCC could recognise; assemblies could co-operate with other churches at a local level.

---

[187] A.G. Newell, 'What is Christian Unity?', *H* 43 (1964), 113-14.

[188] For a statement of this view, see Harold P. Thorp, 'The Ecumenical movement: what is meant by the term? and: to what will it lead?', *AT* 93 (January-February 1968), 9-12.

[189] *H* 47 (1968), 103, 93.

[190] Before Tatford's views are dismissed as extreme, it should be noted that Orthodox ecumenists such as Georges Florovsky made a similar criticism of the WCC's ecclesiological pretensions; during this period its leaders were not speaking with one voice, since some sought such a 'super-church' while others saw the WCC as a non-ecclesial fellowship of churches.

[191] Roger Forster, 'Nationwide Initiative in Evangelism', *H* 59 (1980), 108-10.

[192] Harold H. Rowdon, 'Disunity, Denominationalism and the Brethren', in Anon. (ed.), *Christian Unity*, 12-21.

[193] Coad, 'Ecumenical Movement', 28.

[194] *Ibid.*, 39.

He himself served on committees within the International Missionary Council and the WCC Department of Evangelism and World Mission, and had also served in the BCC, as well as undertaking other WCC work; at no point did he feel he had been asked to compromise his beliefs.[195]

Such arguments cut no ice with most Brethren, however. Reviewing the conference report, A.M.S. Gooding was aghast that born-again believers could contemplate recognising the WCC, since the Ecumenical movement was a preparation for the final apostasy. Brethren who did so were 'extremists', not representative of assemblies as a whole. He considered Coad's address by far the best of the conference, but warned against confusing the unity envisaged by ecumenists with that of true believers as practised by early Brethren.[196] In a later article, he responded to the argument that the relevance of Brethren history lay in the concern of Groves and others for visible unity. He feared that many Evangelicals were being deceived by the calls for this, and that most who wanted it had never been born again.[197]

Although the nature of the Open Brethren movement meant that any kind of affiliation to national bodies as a 'denomination' was impossible, given their lack of such structures, some assemblies have been involved in local councils of churches from the early 1960s. Changing patterns of ecumenical relationship generally, including a greater emphasis on 'grass roots' ecumenism, have facilitated such involvement. By the late 1980s, a few Open Brethren were even contributing to the Inter-Church Process initiated by the then BCC. Alan Bamford was Principal of the ecumenical Westhill College in Birmingham during the late 1970s, but the most important Brethren ecumenist was John Boyes, Executive Director of Partnership from 1982-91. Boyes was something of a maverick on ecumenical matters, serving on the BCC's Evangelism Committee and its Theological working party, and chairing its Youth Evangelism steering group. There was consternation when it appeared that some Brethren, Boyes among them, had signed the 'Swanwick Declaration' committing British churches to the Inter-Church Process. In a letter to *Harvester*, Boyes explained that the only thing the Brethren attenders at the conference had signed was a visitors' list, and that the declaration itself was accepted by acclamation.[198] Because their commitment to local autonomy precluded formal membership as a body, Brethren only had observer status in the new ecumenical instruments (Churches Together in Britain and Ireland and its national counterparts), but could send a delegation to their gatherings; the Swanwick Conference felt that they should, although local autonomy meant that official observers representing assemblies could not be appointed.[199] However, ecumenically-minded progressives remain a minority within the movement as a whole, and many assemblies who are ecumenically involved may not have thought through the issues in any sustained manner so much as gone along with the flow of local events. In the 1988 survey, 18% of assemblies were affiliated to

---

[195] H.L. Ellison, 'Some Practical Aspects', in Anon. (ed.), *Christian Unity*, 42-4.

[196] A.M.S. Gooding, 'Christian Unity', *BM* 75 (1965), 217-19, 245-6.

[197] A.M.S. Gooding, 'The Last Days', *AT* 95 (May-June 1968), 55, 57.

[198] *H*, July 1988, 22.

[199] Swanwick Conference, convenors' minutes, 17 April 1989 (CBA Box 109); Gerald T. West to Colin Davey, 19 April 1989 (Partnership Archive).

their local council of churches or equivalent, and 18% were members of the EA; ten years later, the figures were 32% and 38% respectively.[200]

But if most Brethren were not enthusiastic for institutional ecumenism, neither were they thoroughgoing separatists (at least, not in Southern England): Howley, in a review of some British Evangelical Council addresses on ecumenism, agreed with much of the content but rejected separatism if it meant separation from other Evangelicals; 'God's principle of unity is the common life of the Body of Christ'.[201] It seems likely, therefore, that there was a touch of anti-Exclusivism in Open Brethren thinking about ecumenism. In the next chapter we explore the changes taking place within the movement, which set progressive assemblies on a course which converged with that of many other Evangelical churches and thus reinforced their tendency to reject separatism and exclusivism of all types.

---

[200] Brierley et al., *Brethren*, 110; Brown, *Whatever Happened*, 86. Brown puts the increase in EA membership down to the success of that body's recruitment policy, but it still represented a small proportion of assemblies as a whole (earlier we quoted a figure of 123 assemblies in membership in 1998).

[201] 'Touchstone', 'Paperbacks and booklets of interest', *W* 102 (1972), 458; cf. *idem*, 'Freedom from Sectarianism', *W* 106 (1976), 465, where he emphasised the need to relate to each local congregation on an individual basis, and rejected the popular Reformed concept of 'guilt by association' as falling into the trap of exclusivism because it ran counter to belief in assembly autonomy.

CHAPTER 20

Re-inventing Open Brethren Identity

A major theme of the post-war history of Brethren in Britain and Ireland has been that of identity: assemblies have frequently struggled to articulate what it is which makes them distinctive, and some have lost a sense of 'Brethren' identity. This has had serious consequences for the institutions and agencies which had previously helped to bind the movement together. In this chapter we shall explore this theme with reference to publishers, periodicals, and conferences, and in later chapters we shall consider evangelistic and missionary agencies.

20.1 Open Brethren Agencies

20.1.1 Publishers and Periodicals

Even official denominational publishers have struggled to survive during recent decades, so it is not surprising that, with no central resources to draw on, some major Brethren publishers have disappeared. Those which have survived in reasonably good shape are those from the conservative end of the movement. Pickering & Inglis, like *The Witness*, which they published, occupied the middle ground of Open Brethrenism, and so were 'squeezed from both sides', losing out to both separatists and progressives. The company merged with another Evangelical publisher, Marshall, Morgan and Scott, in 1981 to form Marshall Pickering; this was bought out by an American Evangelical firm, Zondervan, in 1983, who were in turn bought by HarperCollins. Pickering & Inglis' distinct identity thus disappeared, as did most of the titles which they had published; for example, the last issue of their list of assemblies appeared in 1983. As for the bookshops which they owned, the last (in Glasgow) was sold to Send The Light (STL) in 1999.[1]

The changing fortunes of Paternoster epitomise those of the movement itself. After the war it enjoyed several decades of expansion, in which its publications became highly regarded by many well beyond Brethren circles. Probably the best-known were the *Jungle Doctor* series for older children by the Australian missionary Paul White, and Bruce's works of biblical scholarship. Throughout this period it remained a family company, run by Howard Mudditt and his son Jeremy. However, after a period of slowly worsening fortunes, disaster struck on 16 August 1990 when fire destroyed the warehouse at Carlisle in which Paternoster's stock was stored. Of about 240 titles on their list, 170 had to be deleted.[2] The others were reprinted, but strict financial controls imposed in the wake of the fire meant that the company was no longer able to subsidise *The Harvester*. Shortly afterwards, the booklist was taken over by STL, although the Paternoster imprint has been retained. Paternoster has now moved into specialist academic publishing from a more broadly Evangelical perspective, and few of its titles could be described as 'Brethren'.

---

[1] Nicholas Gray to the author, 28 July 2004. STL was originally set up as the publishing arm of OM, on which see section 23.3.

[2] Anon., 'Newswatch: Blaze Destroys Christian Books', *H*, October 1990, 27.

By contrast, John Ritchie have succeeded in maintaining their traditional market and output, though one writer hinted at obstacles having been placed in their way:

> A number of attempts have been made over the years to buy the business, shut it down or separate the magazine from it – all, I judge with a view to getting control of the magazine and changing the teaching. It has only been though the help of God and the determination of leading members of staff that the magazine has continued until the present.[3]

Their catalogue continues to list a wide range of publications from a traditional standpoint, both reprints and works by new writers. In addition, several new conservative publishers have emerged, such as Gospel Tract Publications of Glasgow (1977)[4] and Penfold Book and Bible House of Bicester. A businessman in the Bath area, Roy Hill, has commenced Christian Year Publications, which reprints certain Brethren hymnbooks and publishes other works, the best known being *The Assemblies Address Book*. In 1989, Hill was encouraged by David Restall of Echoes of Service to take over the production of such a list; as an individual, he is able to publish it without its acquiring any kind of official character, an advantage not enjoyed by Pickering & Inglis.[5] The moderate Exclusive publisher Chapter Two also advertise in Open Brethren magazines, following in the tradition of such publishers as C.A. Hammond and the Central Bible Truth Depot.

Heightened concern with issues relating to Open Brethren identity was a major stimulus to the appearance of two new magazines, *Precious Seed* and *Assembly Testimony*. *Precious Seed* first appeared in September 1945, as a result of dissatisfaction with the perceived failure of existing magazines to provide a positive exposition of assembly principles and extensive news coverage of evangelistic work throughout the British Isles. Its initiators sought to avoid creating an identifiable subgroup within Open Brethren, and to a considerable extent have succeeded as a result of the clear yet eirenically-expressed tone of its pages and the willingness evident in recent years to include reports of the doings of Brethren evangelists of varying standpoints. One who gave considerable time to the new magazine was Charles Gahan (1895-1976), a full-time Bible teacher and church planter who had pastored New Park Hall, Barking.[6]

Its ethos and purpose were made clear in a memorandum of a conference at Taunton on 9 January 1945; forty questionnaires had been sent out to full-time workers, and the replies indicated unanimous dissatisfaction with the editorial policy of *The Harvester*. They felt that it had changed since it began with the intent to promote gospel work. The Llanfairfechan and Bristol home workers' conferences had long made representations, but to no avail. Accordingly, it was decided to start a new magazine, although this was not in competition with or opposition to *The Harvester*. It would have a regional focus, covering gospel work in South-West England, and providing Scriptural ministry and an evangelistic appeal. No charge would be made (a policy which would in time affect the circulation of other magazines), and no advertisements allowed except for sound and

---

[3] A.M.S. Gooding, 'Reminiscences', *BM* 101 (1991), 132.

[4] 'LF', *BM* 88 (1978), 208.

[5] Roy Hill to the author, 3 December 2002, 14 October 2004; cf. idem, 'Christian Year Publications', *PS* 60.2 (May 2005), 14-15..

[6] Anderson, *They Finished their Course*, 73.

helpful literature.[7] Crucial to the thinking of those who gathered was the conviction that the war had accentuated a decline in teaching concerning assembly truth, and that such teaching needed to be set before believers in a way which was not happening currently:

> It was the considered opinion ... that the need could best be met by publishing an attractive magazine containing sound exposition of New Testament principles of worship and service, together with reliable information of Gospel work in connection with the above assemblies. These brethren did not overlook the fact that there were already a number of magazines in circulation among these assemblies, but they felt that from an assembly point of view these magazines left much to be desired; instruction in New Testament church teaching was scanty in the extreme, and in these magazines there was a lack of information about the activities of the assemblies and the labours of God's servants in the work of the Gospel.[8]

The Harvester (the only established magazine to take much notice of the newcomer) was not convinced by the explanation offered for its appearance. Tatford questioned the justification for commencing a new magazine, claiming that its objects were almost identical with those of his own, and that the secretary of the committee responsible had written to him denying any intent to start a new magazine.[9] However, the difference between the two publications is immediately evident, and this appears to have been one of those occasions where Tatford's irritation got the better of his editorial judgment.

Precious Seed rapidly established itself far beyond South-West England, broadening its coverage accordingly, and the number distributed rose steadily, reaching 20,500 by 1980.[10] Circulation remains fairly high, about 15,000 in 2004, almost 40% of this being sent to eighty-six countries overseas; interestingly, 'a large number' of Baptists are among the readers.[11] For many years published bi-monthly, it now appears quarterly. It continues to offer thoughtful and positive exposition of traditional Brethren principles (at present somewhat less conservative, especially in practical matters, than *The Believer's Magazine*), combining this with an awareness of the need of assemblies to respond to the changing context in which they minister. Thus recent issues have seen articles on such practical matters as the implications of new legislation concerning child protection, food safety, and disability discrimination.[12] It also continues to provide reports of assembly outreach, although these appear to take up less space than they did for many years, perhaps because less is happening. Nevertheless, they indicate that traditional assemblies are by no means all dying, and that some have a vigorous programme of outreach and are seeing conversions. Since the late 1990s an increasing proportion of devotional and expository articles have come from North American writers

---

[7] Anon., 'MEMORANDUM of a Conference of some home workers convened to consider the present unsatisfactory character of "The Harvester", and the possibility of a new Magazine more in keeping with God's way of things among assemblies gathered to the Lord's name' (typescript, 1945; CBA Box 68).

[8] C. Gahan, '"Precious Seed" 1945-1970', *PS* 21 (1970), 131; cf. Anon., 'Introducing the New Magazine', *PS* 1.1 (September 1945), 1.

[9] [F.A, Tatford]?, 'A New Magazine', *H* 22 (1945), 119.

[10] *PS* 31 (1980), 4.

[11] Anon., 'Situation in 2002', memorandum; Roy Hill to the author, 14 October 2004.

[12] However, the editors had to defend an article on trusteeship against criticisms that such a topic was 'unedifying' (*PS* 59 (2004), 27).

(for many years there were none), reflecting the international nature of the magazine's current readership.[13]

Assembly Testimony was founded in 1952, and expresses the strongly separatist theology of Ulster Open Brethren, in reaction to the openness of some, especially in Southern England, to interdenominational co-operation. Like *Precious Seed*, it was distributed free of charge, and sought to stress assembly truth. The first issue opened with an article by William Bunting, its editor until 1966, entitled 'God's Pleasure in His Assembly', in which Bunting averred that 'There can be no sight upon earth so delightful to our blessed Lord as this corporate testimony to His Name.'[14] In his opinion it was a shame to support any Christian activity which fell short of or contradicted this, especially if doing so weakened the local assembly's testimony. Such Brethren 'high churchmanship' reflected (and was necessary in order to counter) the strong churchmanship evident in various expressions of Ulster religion. The magazine affirmed the importance of vigorous and forthright evangelism, but not at the price of commitment to upholding assembly principles.

The Harvester was no happier about its appearance than it had been about that of *Precious Seed*. Tatford scored a spectacular own goal when he described the new arrival as 'the production of some obscure sect in Northern Ireland' and claimed that 'We are acquainted with many Christians in Ulster and can assure readers that this curious production is not the mouthpiece of accredited brethren nor of the assemblies in that country.'[15] He was deluged by letters, including one from Bunting, who pointed out that 138 out of 155 Ulster assemblies received parcels, and individuals in the others also received it; the magazine was indeed a Brethren production, expressing the views of those who refused to hobnob with clerics who opposed New Testament principles.[16] Grudgingly, Tatford admitted that it was produced by Brethren, but 'In view of the sectarian viewpoint adopted, we regret that this is so.'[17] Nevertheless, support for it may not have been as uniform as Bunting had implied: 'Simple Believer' claimed that many copies were destroyed unread, and another correspondent that some assemblies had returned parcels addressed to them (which implies that they were sent unsolicited). Another writer asserted that the great majority of members did not like it; the fact that 138 assemblies received it did not mean they supported the views expressed.[18] All the same, the practice of many Ulster assemblies does appear to be fairly close to the separatism advocated in its pages. Circulation appears to have peaked at around 16,000 in 1988,[19] and now hovers around the 14,000 mark; only 24% of copies now go to readers in the province, with 19% going to England, 9% to Scotland, and 3% to Wales.[20] Perhaps the most influential of its editors has been A.M. Salway Gooding (editor from 1967-91), who

---

[13] Roy Hill to the author, 14 October 2004.

[14] *AT* 1 [1952], unpaginated.

[15] [F.A. Tatford], 'The Bookshelf', *H* 35 (1956), 93.

[16] *H* 35 (1956), 100; cf. [W. Bunting?], '"The Harvester" Review', *AT* 24 (July-August 1956), 14-15.

[17] 'FEC', *H* 35 (1956), 99.

[18] *H* 35 (1956), 130.

[19] *AT* 219 (January-February 1989), 28.

[20] Brian Currie to the author, 6 January 2003; William Neill to the author, 9 January 2003.

had become known in the 1950s as a critic of the progressive High Leigh conferences (see below) and a defender of the traditional understanding of 'living by faith'.[21]

It is noteworthy that both these periodicals have always been issued on a donation basis, donations often being sent by assemblies rather than by individual readers, and that no external advertising is accepted by either. Their circulation soon climbed vastly higher than that of the established magazines (which had to be paid for), and the latter struggled as a result, although *The Believer's Magazine* (now *Believer's Magazine*) has continued to appear. A factor in its survival, at the time when the free magazines were establishing themselves, was the quality of editorship provided from 1938-77 by Andrew Borland, which imparted theological weight to the magazine without making it obscure or minority interest. His intention was to steer a middle course on such contentious issues as reception to fellowship, contact with non-Brethren Evangelicals, and the need for change.[22] However, the range of topics covered during the 1950s was limited: there were few articles on contemporary issues, Borland preferring to include contributions on devotional, exegetical, or 'Brethren' themes. After he retired, the magazine seemed to lose its way for some years, partly because of the appointment of an editorial team of whom no one member played a leading role. Since 1999, it has reverted to one-man editorship under John Grant, and the quality of articles is improving. Its circulation, primarily in Scotland and Ulster, is just over 5,000.[23]

A.M. Salway Gooding (1915-99)   Andrew Borland

A landmark in the development of the Open Brethren identity crisis was the demise of *The Witness* in 1980, after 110 years, ostensibly for financial reasons.[24] Gradually it had come to share the same ethos as *The Harvester*, and in a steadily-contracting market there was simply no need for two such magazines. It was nominally amalgamated with *The Harvester*, although the biblical features which were initially continued all disappeared within a few years. Under the editorship of the Bible teacher G.C.D. Howley (1907-80)

---

[21] On Gooding, see Plant, *They Finished their Course in the 90s*, 131-41. He was known in Scotland as Arthur Gooding, but to avoid confusion with a Suffolk-based assembly teacher of the same name I have referred to him by the name which he often used when signing articles.

[22] Andrew Borland, 'The Editor's Epilogue', *BM* 84 (1974), 356-7.

[23] Edwin Taylor to the author, 7 November 2002.

[24] *W* 110 (1980), 354. *BM* suggested that departure from the original basis lost it a lot of friends (J. A[nderson]., 'Editorial Searchlight', *BM* 91 (1981), 65).

from 1955-77, it had broadened its scope to include articles on church history (not merely Brethren history) and contemporary issues. Howley, whose articles under the pseudonym 'Touchstone' earned him a reputation as a perceptive observer of the Christian scene, could have given a strong and well-grounded lead to moderate and progressive Brethren, but for his sensitivity to criticism.[25]

The changing face of *The Harvester*: covers from 1923, 1973, and 1993

---

[25] Harold Rowdon, 'Brethren in Britain, 1945-2000: A Personal Sketch', paper delivered at the BAHN Conference, Gloucester, 11 July 2003. On Howley, see Anderson, *They Finished their Course in the 80's*, 83-5.

The Harvester experienced a long and painful decline. Even in the years immediately after the war, it carried little news or notices from Scotland or Northern Ireland, evidence that its readership was drawn mainly from less conservative assemblies in England. During the 1960s, it carried more articles by American authors than its two main competitors, which may have lessened its apparent relevance to British readers. Unlike *The Witness*, it failed to modernise its appearance, which must have lost it readers. It also appeared somewhat out of touch, including too many articles by dead authors, too many on abstruse subjects such as philosophy, and too few on practical matters. Perhaps the content reflected Tatford's own interests – a risk with strong one-man editorship. His tenure of the editorial chair came to an end in 1972, and his successor (1973-83) was Roy Coad. Unlike Tatford, Coad did not see the magazine's role in terms of upholding traditional Brethren principles, neither did he see any point in duplicating the teaching provision of local churches; rather, he wanted to broaden his readers' horizons and to challenge them to fresh thought.[26] In an interview published in 1974, he acknowledged that some older readers had been disillusioned by his approach, but claimed that there was much interest from younger folk who had been beginning to give up hope on the Brethren movement, and from former Brethren. He regarded magazines as having an especially important role to play among assemblies, because (in the absence of any denominational structures and agencies) they offered Open Brethren the only way to sense and express their unity.[27] Coad brought a new emphasis on Christian lifestyle and on Christian thinking about the issues of the day, reflecting the growth of interest in such matters among Evangelicals of many shades. On the other hand, certain traditional emphases were neglected, as is demonstrated by the lack of reviews of Brethren books.

Paternoster were concerned about the financial viability of *The Harvester* and had contingency plans to cease publishing it in 1981 or 1982. Circulation had begun to fall in the 1960s, and by 1980 had dropped below 1,700; incorporation of *The Witness* brought it back up to almost 3,500 and staved this off, but the circulation of 5,000 needed to secure its future was never reached, and by 1991 it had slumped to less than 2,000.[28] A late 1980s rescue attempt failed to secure adequate financial backing or new subscribers.[29] The 1990 fire meant that *Harvester* could no longer be subsidised by the profits from Paternoster's book publishing, as had happened for many years.[30] Changing its name to *Aware*, it tried to reinvent itself under STL ownership as no longer a specifically Brethren magazine. When the final editor, John Allan, set out what it stood for in 1993, he did not include any distinctively Brethren doctrines or principles.[31] However, it failed to secure an adequate niche in the publishing market; after several years of uncertainty, and a reduction in frequency to bi-monthly from 1994, it eventually ceased publication early in 1995. One reason for this is that from the early 1970s under Tatford it had been perceived

[26] Roy Coad, "'To Set Up a Workshop'", *H* 52 (1973), 270-1.

[27] Kathleen White (ed.), 'Family Forum', *H* 53 (1974), 178-9.

[28] *H*, November 1981, 20; Jeremy Mudditt to Neil Summerton, 19 August 1991 (CBA Box 139); Neil Summerton, 'Goodbye Harvester?', *A* September 1990, 2.

[29] For papers relating to this, see CBA Box 139.

[30] Jeremy Mudditt to Roy Coad, 31 July 1991 (CBA Box 139). This may also explain the cessation of Paternoster's evangelistic monthly, *Emergency Post*; this had been issued since October 1939 and its circulation in the 1960s reached 160,000, but a radical revamp under John Allan's editorship appears to have resulted in a serious decline.

[31] *A*, August 1993, 1.

as increasingly unsympathetic to Brethren teaching, which led to the loss of many readers.[32] The progressive constituency among assemblies was not yet large enough to sustain a monthly magazine, and the hope of some that it could serve as 'a mechanism for establishing a new identity for a certain substantial corpus of Brethren churches'[33] was thus disappointed. It was not Brethren enough for some, and too Brethren for others, but its disappearance may have exacerbated the identity crisis among progressive Brethren, as well as being a fruit of it.

It must be noted that Coad and G.J. Polkinghorne (the final editor of *The Witness*) both worshipped during the late 1970s in the same progressive assembly (Chiltern Chapel, Carshalton Beeches);[34] the risk was therefore that both would be perceived as offering a southern suburban perspective. Whilst suburbia was a context in which Open Brethren were relatively strong, suburban assemblies were frequently progressive in their outlook. Allan was also in fellowship with a progressive assembly (Belmont Chapel, Exeter), as were some of the main writers for *Aware*. Many members of such churches would have preferred to read interdenominational monthlies such as *Today*, *Renewal*, or (for younger members) *Buzz*. To some extent, then, the editors may have been developing in their thinking too fast for their more conservative readers. Unfortunately, this coincided with a more general decline in reading habits among Evangelicals, and in society at large.

The nearest to a progressive Brethren periodical is now *Partnership Perspectives*, which was conceived in an attempt to fill the gap left by the demise of *Harvester/Aware*.[35] It has established itself as a thoughtful production dealing with a wide range of issues pertinent to local church leaders, but since it is read primarily by subscribers to Partnership, it cannot play the kind of role which was played by *The Witness* and *The Harvester* in giving Open Brethren at large a sense of cohesion and identity, although the agency which publishes it may be able to do so for progressive assemblies. Whilst a new periodical aimed at ordinary church members might be desirable, it is doubtful that such a venture would be economically viable in the current Christian publishing climate.

20.1.2 *Conferences*

The period since 1945 has been marked by two somewhat contrasting developments. The first is the widespread decline of the Saturday and annual conferences convened by local assemblies (after initial post-war popularity, which probably owed something to the easing of travel restrictions), outside Scotland and Northern Ireland. The second is the appearance of residential conferences which have played a significant role in the shaping of progressive Brethren thinking. Although coverage of the latter may seem fuller than is warranted by their size, they are important because they, and reactions to them, shed a great deal of light on the process of questioning and reformulating a sense of Open Brethren identity which has been going on since the war, and on the serious tensions within the movement.

[32] Tatford was a trenchant critic of 'exclusive' tendencies among Open Brethren, alienating a number of people as a result.
[33] Neil Summerton to Jeremy Mudditt, 13 February 1986 (CBA Box 139).
[34] *H* 57 (1978), 30.
[35] Neil Summerton to the author, 29 December 2004.

Local and regional conferences were both widespread and well-attended for the first part of the post-war period. Ulster has probably seen less decline in the popularity of conferences than other parts of the United Kingdom. The Belfast Easter Conference has continued to attract large congregations. On Easter Monday 1949, an estimated 4,000 were present, and whilst attendances declined, they remained relatively high: over 2,000 in 1983 and 1,600 in 1994, for example.[36] Elsewhere, though, large-scale regional events, such as the twice-yearly series of ministry meetings at Bloomsbury in London, have tended to die out; the Bloomsbury meetings themselves succumbed in 1985, the convenors feeling that such gatherings could no longer cater for the diverse needs of contemporary believers.[37] For the most part, they no longer attract the younger generation, and the price of reinventing them in order to do so (the loss of many existing supporters) would be too high. Such larger conferences as continue are often mission-orientated.

For the most part, Saturday and Bank Holiday conferences still follow a fairly traditional format. Some even maintain an open platform, to which 'Exercised ministering brethren [are] expected.'[38] Those at Newport and Treorchy in South Wales, as well as Parsons Street in Bristol, remain open.[39] Doubtless there are others which do likewise; certainly such conferences remained common in Devon into the 1950s.[40] But almost all the intimations of Scottish conferences advertised in *Believer's Magazine* now include details of the invited speakers.

There has been decline in the frequency, popularity, and perhaps also quality of assembly conferences, due to such factors as the falling membership of assemblies likely to hold them, the perceived irrelevance of their format and content to many younger believers, the increasing popularity of alternative ways of spending free time at weekends, the loss of a sense of cohesion among assemblies and of commitment to anything outside one's local congregation, and the relative lack of speakers of a calibre sufficient to ensure good attendances. Saturday evening ministry meetings became quite common in Scotland during the 1970s and 1980s, whereas they were not in the 1950s.[41] They have become a feature of conservative assembly life elsewhere in Britain, a number of assemblies arranging such meetings on a monthly basis and circulating an annual programme to neighbouring meetings. Some local churches now organise residential weekends, but many are attracted by interdenominational events such as Spring Harvest, another factor which has contributed to the decline of a sense of distinctive Brethren identity.

Residential conferences enjoyed a measure of popularity among less conservative assemblies, although they too have tended to die out in recent years with the loss of cohesion within the movement. In the post-war years, there were a number of residential Bible readings and conferences, often taking place during the 'inside' of a week, and usually in seaside resorts (such as Bournemouth, Eastbourne and Ayr) during the weeks at the beginning and end of the season. These survived until the 1980s, but now are virtually extinct outside Scotland and Northern Ireland. Loss of venues may have been a factor in

---

[36] *BM* 93 (1983), 158; 104 (1994), 187; 'TLWW', *BM* 59 (1949), 143.

[37] *H*, February 1985, 27.

[38] *BM* 63 (1953), 15 (announcement for a conference at Plantation Gospel Hall, Glasgow).

[39] Roy Hill to the author, 14 October 2004.

[40] Plant, *They Finished their Course in the 90s*, 72.

[41] *Ibid.*, 100.

this; for example, Netherhall, Largs, closed in 1988.[42] However, loss of interest is probably more significant, since those wishing to hold such conferences have often been able to find new venues.

As noted in the previous chapter, longing for revival was a stimulus to the commencement of what became a series of residential conferences at High Leigh, moving to Swanwick in 1957 to attract more attenders from the Midlands and the North. 'High Leigh' never set out to be a continuing movement, but conference proceedings were published from the start (a traditional Brethren practice for conferences deemed significant). The first was initiated by T.I. Wilson, an elderly brother whose Strict Baptist background sensitised him to the fact that Brethren who did not accept Darby's eschatological views risked being silenced. Wilson approached Harold St John as to whether opposing views might be aired by senior brethren. St John responded positively, and chaired a two-day conference at a London hotel in January 1953. Its convenors were so moved by the ability of those present to handle disagreement in a gracious way that they decided to repeat the exercise, holding a conference that autumn on *The Holy Spirit and the Assemblies* which analysed the reasons for the perceived lack of spiritual vitality among Open Brethren.[43]

At a time when many were concerned at the inroads being made by partial rapture teaching and other views which diverged from traditional Brethren eschatology, conservative brethren had misgivings from the start. Tatford commented on the report of the first conference, entitled *Christ's Second Coming "At Any Moment" or "Certain Events First"*: 'We opened it, expecting to find help and clarification, but were disappointed. We fear that this report will only confuse the young and cause dissension among those who are older. It seems a pity that it has been published.'[44] Significantly, he appears to have kept aloof from these conferences.

The 1954 conference, which considered *The New Testament Church in the Present Day*, generated further suspicion because of its readiness to challenge traditional views on women's silence, co-operation with non-Brethren churches, and supporting full-time teachers: although the report of its proceedings was warmly commended in *The Believer's Magazine*,[45] an *Assembly Testimony* article questioned the convenors' authority to call the conference, and claimed that since they had no biblical authority for so doing, its results could not be from God.[46] A particular target for critics was Montague Goodman's justification of preaching among the denominations.[47] Goodman often came in for conservative criticism, primarily because what he *said* was unacceptable, but also, one suspects, because of what he *was* – to many conservatives, he would have epitomised Southern, middle-class, interdenominationally-minded, 'liberal' Brethrenism. Certainly many Scottish Brethren regarded these conferences as representing an English middle-class denominationalising tendency.[48]

[42] Dickson, *Brethren in Scotland*, 302.

[43] G.W. Robson to N. Dickson, 6 January 1990 (CBA Box 61).

[44] *H* 32 (1953), 108; a similar, but more nuanced, review appeared in *BM* 63 (1953), 167, offering the opinion that 'confusion has been worse confounded'.

[45] *BM* 64 (1954), 177.

[46] E.A. Toll, 'A Conference and Questions arising out of it', *AT* 16 (January-March 1955), 5-9.

[47] E.g. Anon., 'A Challenge to Witness', *BM* 65 (1955), 85-6.

[48] Dickson, *Brethren in Scotland*, 241-2.

Things were made worse by the next conference, on the theme of *A New Testament Church in 1955*. High Leigh 1955 can perhaps be seen as a defining moment in Open Brethren history. Looking at the report now, it may be hard to understand why it should have provoked so much reaction, but from this point the cracks within the movement were increasingly visible. The opposition was all the more vehement because this was an *internal* division. In an address on 'The Church and its Members', which Coad later described as a watershed for Open Brethren because it helped them re-establish a sense of identity and self-confidence,[49] Howley warned against a current of narrow legalistic teaching which he saw in some assemblies, and condemned 'the bitter spirit and behaviour that such doctrines produce'.[50] He contended that the denominations showed much more spiritual life now than they had done in the days when the movement began; assemblies should not on that account cease to exist, but they must reform themselves, and their distinctive testimony should not be one of separation from fellow Christians. Goodman addressed the shortage of workers in his address on 'The Church and its Mandate'. Claiming that assemblies were doing nothing to train young men for evangelism or for ministry, he asserted that promising men often sought other spheres of service outside Brethren. In his view, the movement was failing to support workers properly; it was anomalous that there should be a large fund for the support of Brethren working abroad, but nothing for their counterparts at home (this, of course, was somewhat of an exaggeration), in spite of the fact that the movement was largely dependent on them for the upbuilding of assemblies. He suggested that suitable young men be supported at an institution such as LBC (in his view, there was no need for Brethren training centres). Harold St John's remarkable closing address (on 'Spiritual Pride in the Church') urged Brethren to learn humility. They owed much to other Christian traditions (he instanced Catholicism, Anglicanism, the Salvation Army, and the Quakers) and should hesitate before criticising them.

Borland wrote an extended review of the conference report for *The Believer's Magazine*.[51] The strong wording which he used at times shows how deeply he felt about the issues, but it is noticeable that some aspects of the conference received equally strong commendation. Methodologically, he alleged that the proceedings were marked by loose thinking and a misuse of Scripture to support particular points. He also queried the report's quasi-official tone and predicted that a succession of conferences would promote the tendency to look to them for guidance (a tendency which would have been regarded as running contrary to assertions of assembly autonomy). His overall impression was 'that the Conference met to pass censure on those assemblies whose conduct does not have the approval of brethren with a very liberal attitude towards church teaching'.[52] There was wholesale condemnation of assemblies, yet a lack of condemnation of other unscriptural religious communities. The class factor, which so often complicated relationships between Open Brethren of different outlooks, surfaced again in his comment that 'the Laodicean spirit ... is more likely to be prevalent in a "Brethren assembly" (so-called) where men of worldly competence are in evidence than in one composed mainly of godly

---

[49] *H* 59 (1980), 266.

[50] Anon. (ed.), *A New Testament Church in 1955*, 21.

[51] Andrew Borland, 'High Leigh: Whither', *BM* 66 (1956), 208-10, 216-19, 240-3, 265-6; 67 (1957), 1-3, 25-6.

[52] *Ibid.*, 209.

brethren drawn from the working classes'.[53] He feared that the ultimate aim was 'to bow
the assemblies politely out of existence, destroy their distinctive testimony, and
gradually merge them into some other religious body'.[54] As for Goodman's suggestion
that the lack of well-taught preachers be remedied by supporting men to study at LBC, he
considered this the germ of clerisy.

Salway Gooding's review proceeded along similar lines to Borland's.[55] Referring to
Howley's assertion that the denominations were less sectarian now than when Brethren
began, and that their leading principle had been the unity of God's people at a time when
the denominations generally were spiritually dead, he argued that if so, 'we ought to go
out of existence, the reason for our being created is now non-existent; surely it would be
far more honest to become extinct than to hunt around for a reason to continue!'[56]
Gooding built up an ideal type of a High Leigh church, served by men trained at
interdenominational institutions and supported by a central fund; he also wondered where
such 'paid ministers who have never been taught church truth' would lead the movement.

In line with its emphasis on positive exposition, *Precious Seed* offered only implicit
criticism. An anonymous article spoke of pressure to abandon Brethren convictions for
unscriptural practices, and asserted that God was calling the movement to self-
examination and renewed conviction about its distinctives. The author believed that if
Brethren could demonstrate that their views were Scriptural and workable, many would be
open to learn from them.[57]

A caveat appeared in the reports from 1956 that 'This volume is issued and should be
read solely as a Report. It is not an expression of the views of the conveners, nor of the
conference, but of the individual speakers who expressed them. If this is borne in mind it
will obviate much well-meant but ill-directed criticism.'[58] However, this did not deter
critics from giving considerable attention to the more controversial conferences. Strong
criticism was again occasioned by the 1964 report on *Christian Unity*.[59] Although
conferences continued to be held each year, no reports were published after 1966 until
1978.

Like High Leigh 1955, the 1978 Swanwick Conference, the report of which was
published under the title *Where do we go from here?*, could be seen as something of a
defining moment. Evangelical press coverage headlined the idea of Open Brethren as a
movement in crisis and declining rapidly. An anonymous reviewer in *The Witness*
pointed out that the four biggest topics – church life and witness, leadership, worship,

---

[53] *Ibid.*, 210. Borland saw the report as coming from a Southern perspective and as ignorant of the
prevailing outlook in Scotland.

[54] *Ibid.*

[55] [A.M.S. Gooding], *The Editor of the* Christian Worker *reviews 'A New Testament Church in
1955' [Report of High Leigh Conference of Brethren]* (Kilmarnock: John Ritchie, [1956]). Gooding's
review first appeared in *CWo*, July 1956, 135-43, and August 1956, 159-65, forming a rare exception to
that magazine's policy of carrying only expository articles and Sunday School lesson outlines – an
indication of how seriously Gooding regarded the report.

[56] *Ibid.*, 3.

[57] Anon., 'A Situation we must face', *PS* 7.8 (May-June 1956), 236-9.

[58] Anon. (ed.), *A Return to Simplicity: Conference of brethren held at "High Leigh," Hoddesdon
from September 28th to October 1st, 1956* ([Stanmore: T.I. Wilson], n.d.), 6.

[59] See section 19.2.4.

and women – were the same as those dominating the 1954-5 discussions.[60] For all the talking, many were evidently no nearer solving the problems raised by these topics than they had been a generation earlier.

Assembly Testimony carried a lengthy series of articles by Salway Gooding, who had asked readers to provide him with information, reviews, and other relevant material. He criticised the appearance of authority given to a conference whose participants had no official standing or representative authority, an appearance which was strengthened by the publication of proceedings. In his view, 'the vast majority of those in assembly fellowship do not want and will not have this "New Brethrenism."'[61] He criticised Coad's contribution on 'Unity' as potentially divisive because of its concern for unity with the world and the denominations at the expense of unity among assemblies, and claimed that the conference's proposals were 'more likely to cause dis-unity in local assemblies than anything that has taken place in the last 50 years'.[62] Noting that the strategy advocated at Swanwick was not to change the movement but to start with one's own assembly, Gooding warned elders to watch out for those seeking to introduce Swanwick-type thinking on such matters as the role of women, the appointment of trained pastors to serve local congregations, the introduction of a salaried ministry, and interdenominationalism.[63] His opinion was summed up in a warning which appeared in a prominent position on the back cover of a later issue, 'BEWARE OF THE LEAVEN OF SWANWICK'.[64]

By the 1980s, the conferences were focusing more on practical issues such as the relationship between the church and the world (1984); relationships in the church (1993); evangelism (1992, 1995); moral and ethical problems (1988, 1990); and charismatic issues ('The Kingdom and the Power and the Glory', 1987; how God speaks today, 1991). Fundamental questions of identity and ecclesiological principle appear to have been shelved. A memorandum to the conference committee from its chairman, Nigel Lee, in 1991 commented that the state of the conference reflected that of the movement: 'The Brethren have little sense of being a "movement" that is going somewhere, with distinctives that are worth proclaiming. Many of the characteristics of Brethren churches over the last 150 years have been "discovered" by other churches, and the assemblies in consequence have lost the prophetic dimension they perhaps once had.' Lee called for the conference to be aimed at independent local churches.[65] On his copy of the memorandum, one committee member, G.W. Robson, had noted: 'the only raison d'etre [sic] of this conference is the health of the body corporate of the Brethren. If it ceased to serve that purpose, it might as well cease.' In 1996, it did. Perhaps, as with *Aware*, the Brethren identity had been so diluted as to be no longer a factor in attracting interest; it may be, too, that some of the convenors were less than positive about their own identity as Brethren.

---

[60] *W* 109 (1979), 119.

[61] A.M.S. Gooding, 'The Brethren facing a crisis', *AT* 162 (July-August 1979), 75-6.

[62] A.M.S. Gooding, 'Swanwick Conference of Brethren: "Where is Here" and "Unity"', *AT* 163 (September-October 1979), 99-101.

[63] A.M.S. Gooding, 'Two more addresses – "Leadership" and "Maturity"', *AT* 164 (November-December 1979), 128.

[64] *AT* 166 (March-April 1980), 48.

[65] Nigel Lee, 'The Future of the Swanwick Conference in the 1990's' (typescript, 11 January 1991; CBA Box 108).

Another influential series of conferences was the Young Men's Bible Teaching Conferences (YMBTC) held from 1956 at Oxford, moving to Winchester in 1969.[66] A letter from twenty-five leading figures, mostly from Southern England, commending the first conference, stated that it had been arranged 'as the result of a growing concern among some brethren regarding the quality of biblical exposition and gospel witness in the assemblies to-day, as compared with former times'. They noted the loss of many gifted young men to other churches, and the widespread lack of a grasp of fundamental biblical themes and of basic homiletical guidance. The conference was intended to remedy those deficiencies.[67] To that end, the programme featured solid teaching and instruction in practical topics such as sermon construction. A prominent figure in these conferences was James Houston (b.1922), a former Glanton brother who had joined Open Brethren while at Oxford after the war.[68]

These conferences proved a stimulus, not only to individuals seeking to serve God in their own assemblies, but also to the formation of the CBRF. It was also at a session of this conference in 1960 that Coad presented a paper on the movement's history which was the germ of his later *History of the Brethren Movement*.[69] From 1971 the conference was opened to ladies because, the convenors explained, (i) women needed an understanding of their husband's ministry to be effective partners, and (ii) an increasing number of women were exercising teaching ministries outside churches alongside men, and serving in many spheres within assemblies in Bible ministry.[70] All the same, attendance gradually declined, and the last was held in 1979; in 1981 the committee invited CBRF to take on board the original vision of providing relevant Bible teaching and practical training.[71] These conferences never provoked the opposition which the Swanwick conferences did, perhaps because although many of the speakers were drawn from the movement's progressive wing, the convenors appear to have avoided controversial topics, and offered no hostages to fortune by publishing detailed reports.

A number of other annual residential conferences were created, some of which continue. A 'hive-off' from the Oxford conference was held at Durham from 1968.[72] The Wessex area, which had seen its first such gatherings in 1945, was by the 1960s able to boast conferences for young people, teaching conferences for men, and 'Christian home' conferences for young married couples.[73] The first Women's Bible Study Conference was held in 1959, the idea of women who had been present at the Oxford conferences to serve

---

[66] The first conference actually took place at Weston-super-Mare. For one participant's view of these and the Swanwick conferences, see Bruce, *In Retrospect*, 158-61.

[67] *W* 86 (1956), 143.

[68] Houston became a tutor in Geography at Hertford College, Oxford, but his first love was Christian spirituality. When he moved to Regent College, Vancouver, in 1968, he had opportunity to explore this in depth and to develop an Evangelical approach to spiritual direction. In Oxford, he shared a flat for seven years with the Russian Orthodox theologian Nicholas Zernov, and was part of a theological study group which included C.S. Lewis, whose example as a lay theologian appealed to him (on Houston, see *BDE*; Arthur Dicken Thomas, Jr, 'James M. Houston, Pioneering Spiritual Director to Evangelicals: Part One', *Crux* 29.3 (September 1993), 2-10).

[69] Jeremy Mudditt to Roy Coad, 20 March 1968 (CBA Box 165; paper in Box 13(2)).

[70] *H* 50 (1971), 75.

[71] Circular from the committee, 5 June 1981 (CBA Boxes 7, 147(1)).

[72] YMBTC minutes, 20 April 1967, CBA Box 110.

[73] K.G. Hyland, 'The Wessex residential conferences', *H* 52 (1973), 45.

refreshments; its aim was 'to train young women to take their full share in assembly life'.[74] A similar conference in Wales from 2000 relieved some of the pressure on space at the main conference, whose constituency tended to be drawn from South-West England. In East Anglia, another conference for women began in 1963, to complement that for men which had been running since 1957. It too proved highly successful; like the other women's conferences, it was open to attenders from all denominations, and it gave birth to a daughter conference for Essex in 1984. Finally, the Swanwick Conference for Ladies began in 1966.[75]

In recent decades, occasional conferences of conference convenors or leading brothers have been called, to discuss matters of mutual interest and deliberate on the way ahead for the movement. The first took place in January 1965, and the invitation reflected

> ... the concern that is felt by many brethren on account of the attitudes prevalent in some Brethren circles – for instance the unreasoning adherence, in a purely negative way, to an attitude and outlook that has no relevance to the circumstances and conditions of today. It is believed to be this that begets the disloyalty that is the subject of frequent comment and is causing a drift away from the Brethren assemblies.[76]

Such issues were to be aired frequently at these gatherings and in the conferences represented.

The most important, in terms of practical results, was a residential conference for representatives of Brethren agencies at LBC in 1981. It considered a range of issues including identifying, training, and deploying gifted individuals, commendation and support of workers at home and abroad, the development of means of communication within the movement to replace conferences and itinerant preachers as means of disseminating new thinking, and the effective use of different types of conference.[77] A continuation committee was formed; although not allowed to commence new initiatives it could act as a stimulus to existing bodies in their work. Project groups were also set up to work on specific areas such as evangelism, world mission, full-time workers, training, information and resource provision, and student work; Partnership would later be active in most of these areas.

During the 1980s, Partnership considered closing down, but 'decided to make one last effort by convening key leaders'.[78] Broader representation was thus evident at a landmark consultation convened at Nantwich by Partnership in 1991. Its theme, *The Strengthening, Growth and Planting of Local Churches*, was close to the heart of many, and drew representatives from almost a hundred congregations. Presentations alerted attenders to both the critical condition of assemblies in many parts of Britain and the possibility of a brighter future under God. Churches were urged to strengthen relationships with other churches, rather than attempting to be self-sufficient, and it does seem that many became more open to inter-church co-operation from this point. For

---

[74] *H* 39 (1960), 25.

[75] *W* 96 (1966), 311. For details of many of these conferences, see the submissions for the 2002 consultation of Brethren agencies (CBA Box 146 (19)).

[76] Circular from W.M. Capper and F.N. Martin to conference committee members, October 1964 (CBA Box 9(13)).

[77] For papers relating to this conference, see CBA Box 148(1).

[78] Neil Summerton to the author, 29 December 2004.

many present, this was when they hit rock bottom and began to look up. Much of Partnership's subsequent activity was the result of the mandate given it at Nantwich.[79] However, the conviction expressed on the cover of the report that it would be 'bound to arouse intense debate amongst Brethren' and 'of great interest to members of all denominations' does not appear to have been justified. Conservative publications did not take notice of it in the way that they had done of earlier reports, an indication of how far apart the two streams were now flowing. Further such consultations were convened at Warwick in 1993, on the theme of *Churches in Partnership for Strengthening and Growth,* and Swanwick in 1998, on the theme of *Revival in our churches?*

Partnership has also convened conferences dealing with topics of pressing concern to local leaders, such as ethical issues or new thinking concerning various aspects of church life. These regional gatherings appear to fulfil similar functions to the meetings for elder brethren which flourished for so long in centres such as Cardiff, Glasgow, and Manchester, although they do not function as a 'joint oversight': their aim is not co-ordination but resourcing and networking. Apart from the consultations mentioned above, Partnership has also convened residential conferences which have filled some of the gap left by the demise of the Swanwick Conferences.

20.2 The Various Strands of Contemporary Open Brethren

Dickson has summarised Open Brethren ecclesiological distinctives as the autonomy of local congregations, believer's baptism, weekly observance of the Breaking of Bread with open worship, and the absence of an ordained ministry.[80] Some of these have come under question in more progressive parts of the movement, which has resulted in serious internal tensions. In fact, the sheer variety within contemporary Open Brethrenism is one of its most noticeable features, coupled with the lack of contact – even suspicion – between assemblies of different outlooks. Whether such diversity, which Exclusives as well as some conservative Open Brethren have criticised as evidence of weakness, can be overcome is highly debatable, but this section attempts to analyse the two main groupings as a basis for improved mutual understanding.

20.2.1 Increasing Polarisation

At the beginning of this period, there was fairly widespread concern that assemblies might inadvertently have fallen into a sectarian position which was little better than that of the churches from which they had separated, and which thus made them less attractive to potential new recruits such as returning ex-servicemen. Lang had expressed apprehension at what he saw as increasing exclusivism among Open Brethren.[81] Montague Goodman claimed that they had become sectarian instead of witnessing to the unity of Christ's body; the result of the latter had been that other Christians found the 'rightness' of the Brethren way of meeting a feature which attracted them to the movement, but departure from the original ground had resulted from a concern with what separated Brethren from other bodies, as well as the notion that fellowship with others

---

[79] *Ibid.*; Gerald West, *Update* 5 (Summer 1997).
[80] Dickson, *Brethren in Scotland,* 6.
[81] See the letters in CBA Box 76.

entailed a commitment to all that they taught.[82] In spite of such concern, a more separatist outlook continued to gain ground among assemblies, possibly deriving vitality from its reaction to the progressive outlook, which was also becoming more vocal. A succession of issues acted as catalysts for post-war controversy. One of the first was reception to fellowship, to which magazines devoted considerable space during the late 1940s and 1950s; this issue had never really gone away since the debates of the 1880s. From the mid-1950s there was debate about involvement in interdenominational evangelistic activities, and then concerning the High Leigh/Swanwick conferences. The inevitable result was polarisation. In 1956, a letter from W.I. Mallen to *The Harvester* lamented the growing divergence between 'the High Leigh liberalists and the inflexible members of the rigid school', both of whom seemed in his view to advocate some kind of centralisation.[83] Tension was evident within, as well as between, assemblies. The Lancashire brother Kingsley Melling claimed that it was present in nearly all the assemblies he visited;[84] his article generated a considerable correspondence, some of it anonymous for fear of comeback.[85] Such tension could have painful consequences: a letter in *Harvester* during 1990 challenged the way progressives had often introduced change, silencing and sidelining conservative dissenters, and welcoming their departure. It was alleged that this movement had been 'so very often cruel and political in its behaviour', especially to older believers.[86] If similar sentiments were not more often voiced by progressives, it was probably because some left assembly circles altogether or ceased to regard themselves as 'Brethren'. In 1997 Summerton suggested that as many of 250 out of 900 English assemblies saw themselves as no longer Brethren,[87] and it was claimed that many such churches had experienced a period of being cold-shouldered by more traditional assemblies.[88]

In 1985 Salway Gooding gave vivid expression to conservative suspicions of the progressive programme:

> Determined efforts are being made all over the mainland of the British Isles to change the shape of the assemblies, to make them more like the denominations around, to remove the distinctive feature of obedience to the word of God, and to speed up a deliberate departure from the word of God. ... There are those who circulate literature, hold seminars and seek to lead astray young men by personal contacts – Beware![89]

The previous year, even Tatford had expressed his low opinion of contemporary progressive developments, though during the immediate post-war period he had done much to set them in motion. 'The distinctive witness of assemblies is being obliterated and there is a marked inclination to adopt the pattern and practices of churches of "other denominations".' He discerned 'a growing tendency to jettison personal responsibilities, if possible, and to centralise administration and ministry in one local "pastor"'. Other

---

[82] Montague Goodman, 'Where have we drifted?', *H* 24 (1947), 103-4.
[83] *H* 35 (1956), 184-5.
[84] Kingsley Melling, 'Sham "Open" Assemblies', *H* 41 (1962), 88.
[85] *H* 41 (1962), 136-7.
[86] Keith Sherwood, letter in *H*, March 1990, 25.
[87] Partnership Council of Management awayday minutes, 6 December 1997 (CBA Box 132).
[88] *PIN* 8 (August 1997), 32.
[89] A.M.S. Gooding, 'Editor's Message', *AT* 195 (January-February 1985), 3.

symptoms of decline included growing acceptance of divorce and remarriage; acceptance of charismatic gifts at home and on the mission field; a change in attitude to Scripture, visible in the *Bible Commentary for Today*, in which some views 'show a liberal tendency and provide interpretations which would once have been rejected out of hand by assemblies'; and the loss of consensus of opinion on eschatology (this seems to have hurt him most).[90]

Polarisation and suspicion were worsened by the increasing tendency to commute in order to find an assembly whose ethos in worship was acceptable, whose teaching on issues such as prophecy, charismatic gifts, or the role of women was deemed scriptural, or whose provision for young people was sufficiently extensive; probably an element of social class was also at work. Conservatives also justified commuting: a *Believer's Magazine* editorial during 2002 argued that 'sisters speaking publicly and gathering without headcoverings' were grounds for exception to the usual rule of worshipping with one's nearest assembly.[91] In some areas, the result of commuting was that large assemblies grew larger, and small ones grew smaller.

Although the *de facto* schism between conservative and progressive assemblies had bedevilled the movement for most of its history, it could be argued that the higher profile given to contentious issues (and the increasing frequency with which these seem to have arisen) has made the problem worse during the last fifty years than at any previous point. When Peter Cousins wrote an introduction to *The Brethren* in 1982, designed for use in school Religious Education classes, he had to picture not one imaginary assembly but two, one conservative and one progressive. Yet even the strongly conservative William Bunting asserted that another assembly should not be disowned unless it had been proved guilty of condoning immorality or fundamental error, or was begun in schism, or its lampstand had been removed.[92] However, the last of these reasons was perhaps capable of wider definition than might at first be realised. When one of Bunting's successors as editor of *Assembly Testimony*, Brian Currie, addressed this topic, he argued that the removal of an assembly's lampstand (which he understood as losing its character as a faithful testimony to God of those who uphold his truth) might occur long before it ceased to exist. The process began with disobedience to the Scriptures on such matters as interdenominational co-operation, charismatic manifestations, or the public participation of women. In his opinion, 'when an assembly loses "its place", instead of becoming weaker numerically and eventually fading away, a lot of innovations are introduced in an attempt to camouflage the fact that the Lord is absent'. So a seemingly prosperous and growing company might not be a true assembly any longer; the

---

[90] Fred[eric]k A Tatford, 'Progression or Retrogression', *BM* 94 (1984), 320-1. He commented that during his forty years as a magazine editor, he had followed early Brethren teaching, but the magazine which he had edited now treated prophetic understanding as an unimportant matter on which believers might differ. A few months earlier, he had written to *The Harvester* protesting at two 'Answers to Questions' which had deemed all details of prophecy except the fact of the Second Coming to be speculative and unimportant, a view which he saw as writing off large parts of Scripture (*H*, July 1984, 24). Such a dismissal of a theme on which he had majored in his spoken and written ministry was probably the last straw for him.

[91] [John Grant], 'The Local Assembly', *BM* 112 (2002), 98.

[92] William Bunting, *Spiritual Balance: or the perils of unscriptural extremes* (Kilmarnock: John Ritchie, 1968), 73. Brethren affirmed the eternal security of the believer, but there was evidently no corresponding doctrine of the eternal security of the assembly.

introduction of innovations might attract many unsaved, but the result would be a mixed multitude whose desire was for more entertainment. If the gathering in question persisted in rejecting correction, then 'it becomes obvious to the spiritual mind that since almost every semblance of a New Testament assembly has been obliterated it is manifest that it has lost "its place"'.[93] In this way, conservative Brethren sidestep the challenge presented by the growth of many progressive assemblies; one person's evidence of blessing is another person's worldly innovation. Nevertheless, some 'tight' Brethren have cast longing glances at the apparent blessing in 'looser' gatherings. One questioner in *The Believer's Magazine* asked, 'Why is it that in many assemblies where there appears to be departure from the NT pattern of scripture [*sic*] there are crowded meetings and frequent baptisms, yet where there is faithfulness there is often little or no blessing?' The answer was that blessing may be granted in spite of an assembly's disobedience; that crowds were not necessarily evidence of blessing; that believers should humble themselves regarding their lack of zeal and effort; and that there was a danger of pride in one's rightness hindering blessing.[94] With such depth of mutual mistrust, it will be hard for progressive assemblies to win over those in the middle who feel some force in conservative arguments.

To some extent, the division between conservatives and progressives, which reflects that between sect-type and denomination-type outlooks,[95] can be viewed along class lines. Tension between those of different social classes has recurred ever since Newton's days at Plymouth, although it has not always been acknowledged and no in-depth work has been done on it. There is some evidence that a measure of class discrimination was evident in such matters as the choice of leadership and church officers, attitudes towards those of a different social class, and the unspoken appeal to the better-educated in the music, style of worship, and relatively high abstract content of the preaching.[96] Although the CBRF was aware of such problems from the start, it was largely ineffective in overcoming them. The Open Brethren 'man in the street' did not contribute to its *Journal*, and would have been intimidated by its fairly highly intellectual tone. Brethren from a more working-class background would probably have belonged to assemblies which disapproved of CBRF, or regarded some of its preoccupations as, quite literally, 'academic', and therefore irrelevant. As a result, the *Journal*'s comments sometimes seem to be *about* ordinary people rather than *from* them, and CBRF did not really help them to have a voice in the movement. Indeed, its existence (and even its title and activities) served only to demonstrate the fundamentally middle-class nature of much Southern English Brethrenism. As an agency designed for churches rather than individuals to belong to, Partnership has tried to take a less strongly cerebral approach, but since it started with a largely middle-class membership, it has some way to go. Some progressive assemblies have succeeded in integrating people from different social classes, but I suspect that there is a measure of correlation between class and outlook: the more conservative an assembly, the lower down the class ladder the bulk of its membership is

---

[93] Brian Currie, 'A Consideration of Lampstand Removal', *AT* 237 (January-February 1992), 17-20.

[94] J.R. Baker, 'QB', *BM* 102 (1992), 59.

[95] Dickson, *Brethren in Scotland*, 365.

[96] Cf. H.L. Ellison, 'The Gospel and the Man in the Street (1)', *JCBRF* 2 (August 1963), 8-9. Ellison had urban English assemblies primarily in mind.

likely to be. Further work needs to be done on this, against the backdrop of an examination of similar themes in Evangelicalism at large.

20.2.2 *Conservatives*

The growth of what has been described as the 'tight' stream of Open Brethren came about through the need to socialise new converts into the movement and ensure that they did not erode its distinctive characteristics, and has been reinforced more recently by the perceived threat to those distinctives which is presented by progressive thinking.[97] Such assemblies tend to regard the New Testament as providing a pattern for church life to be followed in detail, rather than as offering illustrations drawn from particular cultural contexts of how fundamental principles were worked out.

One conservative writer listed what he saw as the distinguishing features of a New Testament assembly. They included the weekly Lord's Supper ('it is this weekly feast that has preserved the assemblies from the apostasy [*sic*] of the religious world, for in it the Spirit of God interprets the meaning of the Cross every Lord's day'); the church as the repository of all God's truth ('Interdenominationalism exposes God's people to the errors of all. The safety of the assemblies lies in their separation'); the freedom of the Spirit, contrasted with domination by paid pastors; government by scriptural oversight ('We are convinced that the Devil is setting up machinery in many companies of the Lord's people that will make it easy for their return to Babylon and be swallowed up in the ecumenical spirit of our age [*sic*]'); faithful presentation of the gospel, including repentance; and local autonomy, contrasted with the centralisation implicit in the existence of Bible schools, central oversights, or missionary societies.[98]

Certain aspects of the perceived New Testament pattern have received particular stress in the last six decades, often in reaction to their being questioned by others:

1. *Separation.* Conservative assemblies have tended to maintain a fairly thorough-going separation from other churches, not merely because their ecclesiology is different, or because they disapprove of the inroads made by liberal doctrine, but also because they believe that such bodies will form part of 'Babylon', the apostate Christendom whose ultimate downfall and judgment was predicted in the New Testament. Such an outlook has certain practical consequences: care is exercised in the reception of believers from elsewhere, and those from other assemblies are expected to present a letter of commendation from their assembly or its oversight. Advertisements and websites often state 'Letter of commendation appreciated' (or even 'required'). Furthermore, there is a disapproval of co-operation with non-Brethren congregations; as one writer put it, 'If it is believed that God was behind the coming-out, it is hardly likely that He will support a going-back.'[99]

Some conservatives make a fine distinction between separation and separatism:

> ... our reluctance to associate with outside groups is based on the desire to maintain the unity of believers and is therefore not schismatic. Our fervent desire is that all born again believers would join with us.

---

[97] Dickson, *Brethren in Scotland*, 369.

[98] Robert McClurkin, 'New Testament Assemblies: A plea for divine simplicity', *AT* 165 (January-February 1980), 5-9.

[99] F.E. Stallan, 'Lessons From the Past', *BM* 97 (1987), 206-7 (quotation from page 207).

... we understand scriptural separation to be from the world and from those who are wilfully disobedient to the Lord and His word. Separatism, on the other hand, is schism from other believers and a refusal to believe that He can bless outside the immediate local company or other identical groups. ...[100]

Such an approach rests on the questionable assumption that those who do not meet as they do are 'wilfully disobedient', and has roots in Darby's stress on separation from evil as the divine principle of unity. In its defence, however, it could be argued that during the 1950s and 1960s, most Evangelicals had a lifestyle and priorities which paralleled those of conservative Brethren, but whereas such Brethren have maintained these largely unchanged, most Evangelicals have drifted away from them, so creating a significant gap between the two constituencies. The greater the perceived gap, the easier it is to justify maintaining it; conservative assemblies would see themselves as having less in common with other Evangelicals and so see less need for, or value in, co-operation with them.

Traditional polemic against the denominations continues, focusing on such features as liberal theology, alleged centralisation, and 'one man ministry'.[101] The accuracy of the last two charges is increasingly debatable, and conservative thinking on such matters needs to be better informed and more carefully expressed if it is to carry weight with outsiders rather than merely reinforcing the existing convictions of those in assemblies.

2. *Conservatism.* The very strength of some traditional assemblies could be a weakness. Reflecting on the fortunes of twenty-eight churches surveyed in both 1966 and 1978, Brown concluded,

One is led to speculate that what changes are eventually adopted will be too little and too late, and that the innate conservatism which keeps these churches functioning so sturdily will, in the end, prevent them adapting to their environment so that they will no longer be able to maintain themselves, let alone give a valid, relevant testimony to their Lord.[102]

The risk is that separation may breed introversion, unthinking refusal to change, and an inability to relate to a culture which is losing touch with Christianity. Gospel Halls (and conservatives usually retain this designation for their buildings, as we shall see) may hold evangelistic meetings in which the gospel is faithfully, but not relevantly, preached; they may also distribute tracts of a similar nature. The challenge for conservatives is thus to adapt to a changing cultural context without compromise.

3. *Dispensationalism.* Traditional Brethren eschatology is maintained, and defended because it offers both a coherent interpretative framework for Scripture and a defence against the possible incursion of liberal ideas. Arising from this, such assemblies uphold the sharp distinction between the heavenly and earthly spheres which we saw in Darby's thought, and on the basis of this often refuse to vote or participate in government, believers being citizens of heaven and strangers on earth.

4. *Women.* The silence of women in assembly gatherings continues to be enjoined. Furthermore, the wearing of head coverings is *de rigueur*, advertisements and websites often requesting 'sisters to have heads covered'. Some teach that women's hair should not be cut short, one writer considering this 'as much an ordinance of God as Baptism and the

[100] Tom Wilson, 'Separation and Separatism', *PS* 40 (1989), 133.
[101] E.g. A. Sinclair, 'Does it matter where I go for fellowship?', *BM* 109 (1999), 13-14.
[102] Graham Brown, 'Decline and Fall?', *H*, September 1981, 5, 7.

Lord's Supper'.[103] Married women are often encouraged to fulfil traditional Victorian home-based roles rather than working outside the home full-time. Silence and headcovering are increasingly stressed by some conservative assemblies, in reaction against progressive trends, and sometimes appear as fundamental truths alongside such things as the person and work of Christ, salvation by faith, observance of baptism and the Lord's Supper, and the obligation to evangelise.

20.2.3 Progressives

In 1956, a letter from Randle Manwaring predicted that in twenty-five years many assemblies would die out if they did nothing; he urged them to reorientate themselves as free churches, perhaps with paid evangelists or pastors.[104] To a degree, this is exactly what happened, although over a rather longer timescale. A major factor in that process has been the work of CBRF. This body was founded in 1963, arising out of the Young Men's Bible Teaching Conferences, although a precursor, the Study Group on Church Principles, had been quietly active since about 1956, discussing papers and gathering historically-significant printed material.[105] Originally, CBRF's primary purpose was the study of Brethren history and principles; there were no restrictions on membership, although applications were to be countersigned by an existing member to assure the committee of the applicant's *bona fides*.[106] Early issues of its journal were marked 'for private circulation only'. This perceived secrecy, which may have been a defensive reaction to conservative criticism of the 1955 High Leigh conference, gave rise to the allegation that it was some kind of secret society, which had on occasion to be rebutted, as in a 1972 article by Rowdon which sought to dispel a number of misconceptions. He explained that the caution regarding accepting new members and circulating its publications was intended to create a climate in which members felt free to engage in frank debate. The fellowship was fully committed to Brethren ideals, among which Rowdon included welcoming non-Brethren and commitment to the authority of Scripture. It was not committed to a particular ecumenical line, nor did it have a particular prophetic axe to grind. Finally, it was not exclusively 'intellectual'. Rowdon pointed out that respected figures such as Tatford were happy to be identified with CBRF.[107]

CBRF never achieved the wider membership it hoped for. It probably fell foul of the polarisation between conservatives and progressives; one *Assembly Testimony* described it as an interdenominational fellowship, nothing to do with Brethren in any official sense, which was marked by an ecclesiastical latitudinarianism bordering on ecumenism, a rejection of typological teaching and acceptance of a liberal (i.e. not pretribulational, premillennial) view of prophecy, and intellectual snobbery.[108] The lack of members led to financial stringency, thus hindering the flow of publications, which in turn meant that the movement was less likely to attract new members. Minutes indicate an ongoing self-analysis, paralleling that among assemblies at large. Membership had been almost 1,500 during the late 1960s, but was down to about 500 by 1980; five years later, it was half

---

[103] H. Winfield Graham, 'Symbolic Declarations', *AT* 80 (November-December 1965), 89.
[104] *H* 35 (1956), 184-5.
[105] Cf. Coad's appeal for material on early Brethren in 'TLWW', *BM* 66 (1956), 287.
[106] Roy Coad, 'QA', *W* 96 (1966), 88.
[107] Harold H. Rowdon, 'A fellowship of minds', *W* 102 (1972), 369-71.
[108] [A.M.S. Gooding], Editorial review of 'The Brethren', *AT* 101 (May-June 1969), 64-5.

that figure, and most of those had joined in the early days.[109] So serious had things become that CBRF (renamed Partnership from 1987) was on the verge of disbanding, but after prayer it was decided to make one last effort (at the Nantwich consultation) to rally Brethren and former Brethren who were seeking renewal.[110]

Within a few years, a new focus was mooted, on contemporary church life rather than research. The intent was to provide a network for churches to support one another (thus filling a gap left by the decline of old-style conferences and periodicals), as well as offering assistance to local church leaders. This represented a fairly radical change from the CBRF's research-orientated beginnings, and the concern was to retain contact with churches which had themselves changed radically and lost their Brethren links in the process.[111] It was founded on the conviction that the lack of a thought-out approach to leadership had been a key factor in the Brethren movement's decline since 1960, and that fostering good leadership was vital for future success. During the early 1980s, and with some initial advice from the FIEC, a linking service had been introduced for matching up churches with full-time workers. This became known as the Partnership Link-Up Service, and was co-ordinated initially by Brian Mills and then for a number of years by Alan Batchelor, an elder at King's Road Evangelical Church, Berkhamsted. The historical side of CBRF was taken over by the Brethren Archivists' and Historians' Network, founded in 1992 as a result of the conference on Brethren history and heritage which took place at Regent's College, Vancouver, in 1990.[112]

Following the Nantwich consultation of 1991, which confirmed the new focus, Partnership began to work at bringing leaders together and resourcing them.[113] To that end, a steady stream of periodicals and books has appeared. As well as arranging consultations and regional conferences, it makes available the services of several experienced workers to advise churches on such matters as the introduction of change. In addition, membership was opened to churches and corporate bodies in Britain from 1991, and overseas from 1993. By the end of 2003, it comprised 154 churches, ten organisations and 244 individuals in Britain, and twenty-four churches, thirty-four organisations (mostly libraries) and sixty-eight individuals abroad.[114] If we break down the number of British churches listed in the 2003 directory, we find that seventeen are in Scotland (about 8% of assemblies), where a body with similar concerns (Interface) was active from 1988 until its absorption by Partnership in 2001, four in Wales (5%), three in Northern Ireland (under 2%), and the rest in England, where they make up approximately

---

[109] Anon., 'Five Years of C.B.R.F.' (typescript, c.1968; CBA Box 4); Neil Summerton to Jonathan Lamb, 1 November 1985 (CBA Box 139).

[110] Neil Summerton, 'Introduction', in Harold H. Rowdon (ed.), *Churches in Partnership for Strengthening and Growth: Papers from the Partnership Consultation held at the University of Warwick, 10-12 July 1993* (Carlisle: Paternoster for Partnership, 1994), 7.

[111] Harold Rowdon, 'Open Brethren since World War II'. Some had their stories told in *Ten Changing Churches*, but there are others, such as Preston Chapel, Yeovil, which is now an avowedly charismatic fellowship, and International Gospel Church (formerly Woodcroft Hall), Burnt Oak, which has adopted the 'cell church' model. Strathaven Gospel Hall, Lanarkshire, re-formed as a broader-based Evangelical church including almost all the former members (David Shields, 'How we started again', *A*, March 1992, 23-4).

[112] Neil Dickson, 'Editorial', *BAHNR* 1.1 (Autumn 1997), 1.

[113] Neil Summerton, in Rowdon (ed.), *Churches in Partnership*, 5.

[114] *PP* 25 (January 2004), 8.

18% of the total number of assemblies, although regionally there would be considerable variation.[115] Many other churches are sympathetic to what Partnership is doing, but uneasy about corporate membership of anything because they fear that their autonomy would be compromised thereby.[116]

We have noted that some progressive assemblies were reluctant to identify themselves as Brethren any longer; reasons included the fear of being confused with Taylor (often misleadingly known as Exclusive) Brethren by outsiders, and antagonism shown by conservative assemblies. In addition, some felt more at home among one of the new charismatic networks of churches. The half-humorous description of many progressive churches as the 'Were Brethren' denomination indicates the unease they feel with their origins.[117] Even Partnership has seen a few churches drop out because they no longer wish to be identified as Brethren. However, this unease is markedly less in Scotland, where Brethren identity has held up rather better, partly because of the stronger inter-church links which have always existed as the result of a higher concentration of assemblies in urban and suburban Scotland than in most of the rest of Britain.

In a series of articles on Brethren identity,[118] Beth Dickson, a former associate editor of *Aware*, captured the ambivalence about identity felt by many changing congregations:

> Those who changed no longer wanted to call themselves 'Brethren' because that title linked them to all the hardening of the arteries within the parent movement they wanted to forget. It was also often a source of emotional pain because the tradition, in which people had grown up and first heard the call of God, had rejected them for following the very voice it had enabled them to hear in the first place. The name-calling, the refusal to recognise a God-given desire, the contempt – some of which occurred between different generations of the same family – which these people suffered should never be underestimated. As an antidote to this rejection, however, churches, which embarked on a programme of change, began to rediscover their common heritage with other Evangelicals. This reinforced the uncertainty about whether there was any necessity at all in being ecclesiologically distinctive....
>
> And yet the distinctives of plural eldership, weekly communion, every-member ministry and a strong emphasis on mission and church planting in that particular combination were so strongly imprinted that it would hardly have crossed our minds to give them up.[119]

She argued that such fellowships needed each other, not least because other churches would not understand the particular problems which they faced. Progressives had forgotten (deliberately, because of the pain involved) the good things about the old churches, including the spiritual power which was present. Having lived through the

---

[115] *Ibid.*; cf. [Harold Rowdon], *Partnership Directory No.3* (Carlisle: Partnership, 2003).

[116] Neil Summerton, 'Administrative News', *PN*, n.s. 5 (October 1994), 31. In 1991, Rowdon suggested that almost 20% of Open Brethren congregations in Britain were being 'reborn' (Harold H. Rowdon, 'Is the Brethren Movement Actually Being Reborn? Progress report on local churches. 2', *A*, March 1991, 21-2).

[117] Neil Summerton, *Local churches for a new century: A strategic challenge* (London: Partnership, 1996), 12.

[118] Beth Dickson, '"Who are the Brethren and does it matter?" revisited', *PP* 21 (October 2002), 21-3, 26-8, 31-3.

[119] *Ibid.*, 22.

worst of the polarisation and identity crisis, it was time to move on, drawing on the best of the past.

Rowdon has argued consistently for the need of local Open Brethren congregations to network together, as those which share a common heritage and thus face similar issues and problems. His arguments deserve fuller consideration, not least because they try to overcome isolationism without committing churches to any kind of formal denominational allegiance. Contending that inter-church co-operation was both biblical and necessary, he claimed in 1980 that there were 'an indeterminate number of churches which are linked together by ties of history and general outlook on a number of biblical and theological issues, and that this sense of belonging together finds expression in numerous tangible ways, such as magazines, conferences, ministering brethren who circulate mainly (or entirely) among the churches in question'.[120]

The growth of 'Were Brethren' attitudes was evident when in 1987 he asked, 'Is the Brethren Movement being reborn?' Welcoming evidence of a new sense of realism and a recognition that the world has changed, as well as a return to the absolute authority of Scripture, he was nevertheless driven to express regret that many changing assemblies regarded themselves as no longer Brethren. In part, they were responding to the judgement passed on them by traditionalist assemblies, and seeking to get away from what the term implied. But 'perhaps the feeling that reborn Brethren churches are no longer Brethren stems most from not realizing how radical the original Brethren were. ... You don't cease to be Brethren when you introduce innovations that are scripturally warranted and culturally relevant: you show that you *are* Brethren!' Stay with us, he pleaded; we need your help.[121]

Any denomination would say that inter-church fellowship provides encouragement and strength, fosters expansion, and safeguards the maintenance of its distinctives. Rowdon interpreted Brethren acquisition of a corporate identity as something which occurred spontaneously: 'as soon as they developed distinctives, they began to gravitate towards those who shared them, to make common cause with them, and to work together to further their common interests'. His judgment was that 'one reason for the present dilemma amongst Brethren is that we have lost our distinctives'. In his view, there remained differences of ethos, emphasis, and style (and especially history) between Brethren churches and others which possessed similar features. There was diversity among assemblies, it was true, but this also was a vital element of Brethren identity. Brethren developed a common identity through the creation of publishing houses, conferences, evangelistic agencies, and other such means. So, such churches could join in these today – and others could be created as needed.[122]

The evidence is that progressive churches have yet to be convinced by his case, since many prefer to regard themselves as 'non-denominational' fellowships knowing no allegiance apart from those to the universal church of all true believers and the local congregation. Many agencies which provided opportunities of fellowship for supporting assemblies have declined or disappeared, and those which remain do not always enjoy much progressive support. On the other hand, the development of Partnership indicates that attempts are being made to fashion new ways of giving expression to a sense of

---

[120] Harold H. Rowdon, 'Co-operate – or Perish', *H* 59 (1980), 195-9 (cf. his 1979 paper to London assemblies).

[121] Harold Rowdon, 'Is the Brethren Movement being reborn?', *H*, March 1987, 1-2.

[122] Harold Rowdon, 'Towards a New Identity', *H*, January 1988, 1-2.

common identity and vision. Perhaps, too, churches are relating to each other at the level of leadership rather than membership; one progressive congregation (Northwood Hills Evangelical Church, Middlesex, which Rowdon himself had attended until his retirement from LBC in 1991) observed that a sense of obligation to relate to other assemblies had been replaced by contact with local denominational churches, as well as between full-time workers in progressive Brethren churches. However, such contacts did not excite the same degree of congregational interest.[123]

But what did Rowdon see as Open Brethren distinctives? In a series of articles for *Harvester*, he attempted to isolate these and then to evaluate progressives and conservatives in the light of them. He listed them as the supreme authority of Scripture, '*the* distinguishing characteristic of being "Brethren"', devotion to Christ, a particular view of the church (believers gathered together, each gifted by God, and using those gifts in open worship), and Christian devotedness.[124] He then evaluated the outlook and practice of traditional assemblies under these four headings. Their main weakness, he considered, was that they read Scripture in the light of an interpretative tradition. Their devotion to Christ was beyond question, but their Breaking of Bread services showed a restricted concept of worship; furthermore, their study of Scripture tended to focus on the details of biblical prophecy and was marked by an unbalanced stress on Christological typology. In their ecclesiology, he saw differences from other Open Brethren on the matters of leadership and reception to fellowship, some of which represented significant deviations from Scripture. They were committed disciples, although often well off; what they gave was probably more than compensated for by what they did not spend on worldly entertainments.[125] Turning to the progressives, he praised their performance in all four areas. Rowdon concluded that a substantial degree of family likeness remained between the two streams, and that mutual recrimination should be avoided. He urged them to recognise each other, even if differences were too great to permit much common action.[126]

Far from insisting that Open Brethren manifested characteristics which were seen nowhere else in the Christian world (apart from what he saw as their unique submission to the authority of Scripture coupled with a refusal to codify its teaching in credal or systematic form), Rowdon rejoiced in their apparent lack of distinctiveness. 'Once "Brethren" imagined that the time would come when all Evangelicals would come and join them. Perhaps the time is coming when there will be no need for this: they will be "Brethren" without knowing it!'[127] This means that some alternative way of justifying continued separate existence has to be found, and his writings appear to indicate that this is based on a shared heritage which has given rise to certain common challenges and problems: in responding to these, he sees value in churches taking counsel together and pooling experience and expertise. In his view, churches have much to gain from this, as

[123] Rowdon (ed.), *Ten Changing Churches*, 76.
[124] Harold H. Rowdon, 'Have the Brethren grown away from their Roots? 1. Brethren Roots', *H*, July 1988, 7.
[125] Harold H. Rowdon, 'Have the Brethren grown away from their Roots? Traditional Brethren Shoots', *H*, August 1988, 12-13.
[126] Harold H. Rowdon, 'Have the Brethren grown away from their Roots? Non-traditional Brethren Shoots', *H*, September 1988, 13-14.
[127] Harold Rowdon, 'Reflections on Lausanne II in Manila', *H*, October 1989, 7.

well as certain responsibilities towards weaker fellowships.[128] However, to focus on a shared past and the problems which it has bequeathed could seem rather a backward-looking approach. Rowdon does seek to balance this with a positive appreciation of aspects of that heritage, and his hope that other independent churches would align themselves with reborn assemblies indicates that the past is not being allowed to function in a restrictive way. This is clearly visible in an article based on a paper which Rowdon gave to a gathering of Brethren leaders in Manila, in which he wondered whether a new 'Brethren' movement would emerge, with a charismatic flavour and including independent non-Brethren churches.[129]

In a paper given to the Swanwick consultation in 1998, Rowdon advanced the thesis that the modern denomination is an entity comparable with the groups of churches in the New Testament period which enjoyed a special relationship with each other because they came from the same ethnic group or geographical area. He sees these as subgroups of the church universal.[130] Extending his thinking about inter-church co-operation to the international level, he called for improved communication and stronger links between Brethren in different countries. This was not to be undertaken in any narrowly denominational sense, however; since Brethren were only part of Christ's church, such activity should be balanced by involvement in bodies such as the EA and the World Evangelical Fellowship. His paper appears to have been a catalyst for the appearance of *International Partnership Perspectives*, an annual bulletin containing reports from Open Brethren in countries all over the world, which was a development of the previous *Partnership International Newsletter*. Such a publication has a significant potential, given an understanding of the church in which different countries are seen as partners rather than some as 'senders' and others as 'receivers'.

20.2.4 What's in a Name?

One way of distinguishing various types of assembly is to look at the names by which they are known. Brethren were reluctant for much of their history to call their gatherings 'churches'. Initially, 'meeting' seems to have been the preferred title; it is still used by many Exclusive Brethren. Open Brethren tended to use the designation 'assembly'; some Pentecostals have followed them in this, notably the 'Assemblies of God', in whose shaping the former Open brother John Nelson Parr had a major role. The rejection of 'church' was because of the tendency of many to use it of a building rather than a group of people, and the desire of Brethren to distinguish between the universal body of believers – the church – and its local manifestation – the assembly.[131] Some, even among Open Brethren, were also influenced by Darby's idea that the church on earth had been irreparably ruined, and that it was a mistake to try to set up 'churches' now.

---

[128] E.g. Harold Rowdon, 'Local Churches', *IPP* 4 (2002), 3-7. Some of his ideas were anticipated in David J.A. Clines, 'The Churches next door', in an untitled pamphlet containing papers to be read at the CBRF annual meeting, 28 October 1967.

[129] Harold H. Rowdon, 'The Brethren Movement Worldwide', *A*, October 1990, 12-14.

[130] Harold Rowdon (ed.), *Revival in our churches? Report of the Partnership consultation held at The Hayes, Swanwick, 25-28 September 1998* ([n.pl.: Partnership, 1998]), 38-42; for an earlier statement of this, see his *Who are the Brethren and does it matter?* (Exeter: Paternoster on behalf of Christian Brethren Research Fellowship, 1986), 23-6.

[131] H.L. Ellison, *The Household Church* (Exeter: Paternoster, 1979[2]), 19.

As for the designations given to the premises in which they met, the 1851 Census returns show that many called their premises 'Room' or 'Meeting Room', and many Exclusive (and a decreasing number of Open) congregations have continued to do so. It was in the wake of the 1859 Revival and late-nineteenth-century revivalist activity that the designation 'Gospel Hall' or 'Hall' rapidly became the most popular. So characteristic did it become that a correspondent to *The Harvester* during 1951 expressed the opinion that this was becoming a recognised name and that there was a danger of tending towards sectarianism.[132] However, it became very clear in many parts of post-war Britain that what had begun as an evangelistic device became fossilised as a tradition which ended up hindering the very evangelistic effectiveness which it had been designed to facilitate. Concern to recover that effectiveness was therefore one stimulus to change. Analysis of assembly lists indicates that in 1959 96% of assemblies in England and Wales used the designation 'Hall', 'Gospel Hall', or 'Mission Hall'.[133] Since then, there has been rapid change in parts of Britain, and the names used currently are set out in Table 20.1.

It is not surprising that almost all Ulster assemblies keep the traditional nomenclature, since they remain highly traditional in their outlook and practice. Neither is it unexpected that 'Chapel' should be popular in England (especially the South and Midlands) and Wales, but not further north, where it often designates a Roman Catholic building. 'Chapel' and 'Church' have often been adopted in order to make the building's purpose clear to outsiders, to identify them as belonging to mainstream Christianity, and probably also as an expression of upward social mobility, but some traditional assemblies have reverted to the title 'Gospel Hall'.

Table 20.1: Most frequent current designations of assemblies (all figures are percentages)

	England	Wales	Scotland	Northern Ireland	Republic of Ireland
Hall/Gospel Hall etc	47	71	76	94	53
Church/Evangelical Church etc	24	14	20.5	1	20
Chapel	21	5	0.5	0	0
Fellowship	5	4	1	1	10
Assembly	2	3	2	3	10
Other	1	3	0	1	7

Sources: my databases of assemblies, the latest information for most being that in the 2002 assembly list and the 2003 Partnership directory; where more than one title is used by an assembly, the one used for the congregation takes precedence over that for the building; Scottish figures supplied by Dr Neil Dickson.

The legitimacy of the use of the designation 'Evangelical Church' (which began to appear after the war) has been a recurring topic of debate, however. In *The Believer's Magazine*, F.C. Scott argued that such a title seemed sectarian, as well as being a

[132] *H* 30 (1951), 1.

[133] Brierley et al., *Brethren*, 67n.

tautology: if there was no evangel the gathering could not be called a church.[134] Peter Cousins asserted in *The Harvester* that 'Gospel Hall' was used partly to indicate that the gathering was not simply another church, and that it differed from the denominations; such designations as 'Evangelical Church' or 'Chapel' indicated a congregation's desire to identify with, rather than differentiate itself from, other churches.[135] Some imputed unworthy motives to those who advocated such a change of name, Bunting seeing it as arising from pride and a desire to be more in step with other religious bodies.[136] In similar vein, these lines equated titles with theological soundness (or unsoundness):

> In days of movements Ecumenical,
> Some call their Churches Evangelical:
> Making their standing an enigma;
> Losing their separation's stigma.
>
> ...
>
> Could we but capture in declension
> That honoured title, sweet to mention:
> The 'Gospel Hall,' where Christians muster,
> The Lord is there, in undimmed lustre![137]

But Etloe Evangelical Church in Bristol explained that they had changed from 'Gospel Hall' to 'Evangelical Church' to reflect the fact that the work going on there was much more than evangelistic proclamation.[138] They were not alone, and this trend mirrored a broadening understanding of the nature and implications of the gospel.

As for the collective title of assemblies as a whole, there was a tendency during the 1960s and 1970s to prefer the designation 'Christian Brethren', partly in order to distinguish themselves from other groups; one Essex local paper reported that a mission was 'supported by the Christian Brethren movement, nothing to do with the Plymouth Brethren movement'.[139] 'Plymouth Brethren' is often used by the authorities to refer to Taylor meetings; conversely, Taylor Brethren themselves often use the unqualified designation 'Brethren'; confusion is thus inevitable.

The quest for a name (and thus a corporate identity) was attacked by more conservative writers. Vine had expressed his disapproval of any distinctive designation, as it implied that assemblies constituted a denomination. Where a description was required by the authorities, he advocated the use of something like 'Those who are known as "The Brethren"'.[140] He repeated his views in a 1949 pamphlet *The mistaken Term "The Brethren"*. There he insisted that 'Brethren' (the use of which began with the designation 'Plymouth Brethren') was a term which comprehended all believers, not simply those in

---

[134] 'BQB', *BM* 78 (1968), 187.

[135] 'Question and Answer with Peter Cousins', *H*, August 1981, 11.

[136] *AT* 8 (June-August 1953), 2.

[137] John Campbell, 'Heterodoxy and Orthodoxy', *AT* 162 (July-August 1979), 74.

[138] Linton and Linton, '*I Will Build my Church*', 104.

[139] Counties Evangelistic Work 1961 report, 6. A lengthy correspondence in *The Witness* during 1962 appears to have been sparked off by a desire to avoid being confused with the Taylor Brethren.

[140] *W* 76 (1946), 71.

assemblies; its use with reference to assemblies began with others, and was not a designation chosen by those who formed part of the movement. Similarly, in 1955 a writer in *Assembly Testimony* claimed that the distinctiveness of assemblies 'lies in the very fact (among other things) that no "distinctive" name is employed to label them'.[141] As one assembly website puts it, 'We believe that all who trust Christ are without exception members of God's family and of the one body of Christ. To make this Christian unity true in practice, we prefer not to give ourselves a denominational name that seems to divide us from others, but simply to be known as Christians.'[142] Borland claimed support from Bruce for his contention that the title 'Brethren' belonged to all, and its use to refer to assemblies in particular savoured of denominationalism.[143] However, Bruce himself considered it futile to protest against such a firmly-established usage; it was no more exclusive in its connotations than the use of the title 'Friends' (derived from John 15.15) by early Quakers, but simply the use of a biblical designation for fellow believers.[144] Some, such as E.W. Rogers, accepted the title grudgingly: 'Since others call us "Plymouth Brethren" (and abbreviations thereof) and since we should more strongly resent being placed in any other category, ... I suppose we must submit. You will never be able to stop the worldling putting labels on the saints.' Authorities insisted on classifying assemblies because they failed to appreciate the movement's true position.[145]

However, local communities were often suspicious of religious groups which disclaimed any distinctive designation, and liable to confuse them with other groups, a factor which contributed to the pressure to find a suitable name for assemblies as a constituency, and for the buildings in which they met. Brethren 'Halls' could be confused with Jehovah's Witnesses' 'Kingdom Halls' or British Legion Halls. Howley pleaded for some designation to be used on notice boards outside assembly premises so that people would know who the group were which met there. In his opinion, there was a danger of being too obscure and so losing credibility with outsiders. Putting a name on the notice board (and so implicitly accepting some kind of 'denominational' identity) was better than the sectarian appropriation of Matthew 18.20 (as uniquely applicable to Brethren gatherings), and was also useful in local lists of places of worship. He reminded readers that the name 'Christian' was first given to believers by others, implying that the fact that assemblies had not chosen the name 'Brethren' did not make its use illegitimate.[146]

More recently, the itinerant evangelist and teacher Michael Browne interpreted the search for a name as indicative of a desire to be socially acceptable. In his opinion, 'Christian Brethren' was a sectarian title; its use erected a barrier between those in the movement so designated and those outside it.

To the question, what then should we call ourselves? we reply: We are an independent, autonomous, local congregation or assembly of Christians who meet at such and such a place, or in such and such a building or street. Let that suffice! Any questions or difficulties arising from

---

[141] E.A. Toll, 'A Conference and Questions arising out of it', *AT* 18 (June-July 1955), 7.

[142] Anon., 'Cromwell Hall Christian Centre', <www.cromwellhall.co.uk>, accessed 3 April 2005.

[143] A. Borland, *Woman's place in the Assemblies* (Kilmarnock: John Ritchie, [c.1970]), 5-7.

[144] Bruce, *In Retrospect*, 286.

[145] *PS* 1.3 (April 1946), 21.

[146] 'Touchstone', 'The Notice Board', *W* 86 (1956), 164.

such an explanation are not of our making, but lie in the minds of those who have departed from the divine pattern of the NT.[147]

For those holding such views, any capitalised use of 'We', 'Brethren', or 'Assemblies' bore implicit testimony to a sectarian outlook.

A problem with refusal to accept any distinctive designation was, as a letter to *The Harvester* pointed out in 1975, that refusal to acknowledge a name implied hypocrisy (such people might call themselves Christians but everyone else would call them Plymouth Brethren), and that assemblies had something to hide; in any case, if they did not give themselves a name, the world would. So, the name 'Christian Brethren' should be accepted precisely because it was a name for all believers.[148] More recently, however, many progressive assemblies have rejected it, often because of its associations with particular attitudes and practices (e.g. dispensationalism, or the insistence that women should have their heads covered in worship). Thus Rowdon called for it to be dropped as 'tarnished beyond recovery'.[149] The most 'narrow' assemblies have rejected any distinctive title because of their conviction that their way of being church marks them out from all other Christian traditions, and the most progressive congregations have rejected the designation 'Brethren'. In between are those who are ready to acknowledge the ecclesial status of non-Brethren congregations but also to accept their own roots in (and continuing identification with) the Brethren movement, and to see that movement in quasi-denominational terms.

Underlying the question of what name to accept was that of whether Open Brethren constituted a denomination. The issues involved were summed up by Peter Cousins in 1979:

In many respects, it is apparent that the 'Brethren' do not constitute a denomination. They have no central organisation, no basis of faith or credal statement, 'their' local churches are not structurally linked. There is more diversity of practice than is sometimes realised. But against these considerations we must set others. There is a 'list of assemblies' on sale. There is a 'circuit' or 'network' within which certain preachers, magazines and even hymnbooks are current. Even the tendency to disclaim the title of denomination is a further distinctive. And there is certainly a tradition which is highly regarded although variously interpreted and which passes through (for example) Plymouth, Bristol and Dublin. In fact, of course, some local churches are so careful not to invite speakers from outside this 'non-denomination' that they make their own sectarian or denominational tendencies appallingly clear. ...[150]

He might have added the existence of a distinct dialect of the language of Zion; one writer claimed that the use of the phrase 'gathered to the name of the Lord Jesus' had done more than any other phrase to make the movement a denomination.[151] Similar realism was

---

[147] Michael Browne, 'Who are the Christian Brethren?', *BM* 96 (1986), 216.

[148] *H* 54 (1975), 75. The letter was signed 'I.M. Sutton', apparently a pseudonym for the editor, Roy Coad.

[149] In H.H. Rowdon (ed.), *The Strengthening, Growth and Planting of Local Churches* (Carlisle: Paternoster for Partnership, 1993), 110.

[150] 'QA', *H* 58 (1979), 12.

[151] Kingsley G. Rendell, 'The principle of unity among the early brethren', *W* 93 (1963), 323-6.

shown by Bruce, who argued that assemblies shared a common historical identity and
constituted a 'sociological entity'.[152]

Assembly noticeboards are often recognisable by their distinctive wording or the
distinctive activities advertised, as in this example

I would argue that we can discern in Open Brethren a tension between two concepts of
denominationalism which was also evident among Baptists and Congregationalists, who
likewise affirmed the autonomy of local churches. There was an older, less rigid
understanding of a denomination as constituted primarily by shared ecclesiological
identity (in other words, a common pattern of church life and order which led local
congregations to gravitate to one another), and a newer nineteenth-century view which
gave prominence to denominational structures and societies and regarded support of these
as a moral obligation. Brethren emerged during the 1820s, just when the newer
understanding was coming to the fore: the Baptist Union was founded in 1813 and
refounded in 1832, and the Congregational Union was founded in 1831. The founding of
assemblies could be seen as a protest against it, as could the emergence of the non-
denominational churches which owed much to Brethren practice but retained a recognised
pastoral ministry; in practice, though, Brethren have often preferred to support 'our'
missionaries and evangelistic agencies, to read 'our' magazines and books, and to attend
conferences held by like-minded assemblies, all of which indicate a similarly
'denominational' outlook. Some (notably the Churches of God) sought to erect
'denominational' structures, but it is not necessary to have a central headquarters or an
official statement of faith in order to function as a denomination.

If we look at the issue from a sociological viewpoint, we find evidence of both
'sectarian' and 'denominational' attitudes. A 'sect' does not accept the ecclesial status of
other religious organisations, just as many Brethren have been reluctant to allow that
other bodies of believers constitute 'churches'. A denomination, however, 'accepts the
validity of other similar religious organisations'.[153] When Goodman expressed his
concern about exclusive attitudes in 1946, implicit in his words was the idea that the
Brethren way was the right way, and the one which other believers would do well to
follow; that is no longer the view of most progressives. The shift to a more
'denominational' outlook has made it possible for many assemblies to co-operate with

other churches in evangelism, although it has also meant that there is less reason for individuals to continue worshipping with an assembly as opposed to joining some other type of church.

In 1963, Ellison argued for a more open approach to churches of other denominations in *The Household Church*. Based on a series of articles for *The Witness* and addressed primarily to the English urban context, it argued that the closest New Testament parallel to the modern assembly was in fact 'the church in the house', of which there might be several in a city such as Corinth or Rome. From this, he drew the conclusion that no assembly could see itself as self-sufficient, possessing all the gifts and resources needed to build itself up. Neither could it meet all the needs in its locality, or undertake all the work which could be done. Such an outlook enabled him to adopt a more open attitude towards local churches of other denominations and special meetings for groups within the church, both being expressions of the household principle.[154] This type of approach has become quite widespread in suburban England, but it has helped to precipitate a crisis of identity.

20.3 The Open Brethren Identity Crisis

It has become commonplace during recent decades to speak of an Open Brethren identity crisis, but this is compounded by the fact that in practice assemblies do not constitute a homogenous movement. Indeed, they probably never did, but the fragmentation has become more pronounced and more visible since the 1950s. Rowdon divides British assemblies into four roughly equal groups: the first comprises those which have closed in the last decade or two, or which are in serious danger of doing so very soon; the second comprises those which are not about to close but which are struggling to remain effective; the third group are maintaining their numerical strength without experiencing significant change (mainly in Northern Ireland, with some in Scotland); the fourth are those which are changing or actively contemplating change. Weakening of traditional inter-assembly links means that all except traditional assemblies are in danger of losing a sense of collective identity.[155] But for each group, that sense takes a somewhat different shape.

In this connection, it is worth noting that a whole succession of magazines were founded to counter a perceived neglect of assembly truth and so contribute to establishing a clear sense of identity: *Needed Truth*, *The Believer's Magazine*, *Precious Seed*, and *Assembly Testimony*. The existence of the Study Group on Church Principles was further evidence of such a concern. However, it was probably the 1978 Swanwick Conference which made the wider Evangelical constituency aware that more progressive Brethren were undergoing a crisis of identity. Conservative Brethren have not been affected in the same way or to the same extent.

Just as early Brethren may have thought that they were the only ones rediscovering New Testament church life, so their descendants may see themselves as the only ones wrestling with certain problems. Yet, however painful the identity crisis has been, Brethren are not the only ones who have been experiencing it: the lessening in some quarters of a distinctive sense of identity parallels what is happening in other Evangelical constituencies and denominations. Evangelical Anglicans and Baptists, and

---

[154] Ellison anticipated today's 'youth churches' by a long way in arguing that even the Lord's Supper could be celebrated by young people's groups (*Household Church*, 53).

[155] *IPP* 1 (July 1999), 30.

denominations as diverse as Strict Baptists and classical Pentecostals, have all felt compelled to revisit the question of their own identity and the reasons for their separate existence. Even para-church bodies such as the EA had to reinvent themselves during the 1980s.

In part, this is a response to the increasingly visible homogenisation of Evangelicalism, which is especially apparent in areas such as worship style: assemblies are now more likely to sing the same hymns and songs as other Evangelicals, and the concept of open worship which was so dear to Brethren has been widely accepted, although there are signs of a reversion to more structured worship, which are also apparent in some progressive assemblies. A similar process is evident in the field of leadership, many churches now encouraging the development of plural lay leadership, but Brethren setting individuals apart as pastors or full-time workers of other types. However, Open Brethren have probably felt the pain more sharply than other constituencies because of their lack of a denominational structure; none of the agencies which have fostered a sense of common identity have as permanent a feel about them as a denominational headquarters. The result of the homogenising process is that it is increasingly difficult to distinguish a progressive assembly from a progressive independent Evangelical church (or any other type of progressive Evangelical church). Assemblies move out of the Brethren orbit, but others move in, such as some of the recently-formed independent fellowships in Ireland, or some of the member churches of Partnership. Similarly, individuals rarely have the same sense of denominational loyalty nowadays, and on moving to a different area are often happy to settle in a church with a different label from their previous home. This leads to a dilution of any distinctive Brethren identity in many assemblies located where there is a high level of population mobility. The phenomenon is accentuated when the same thing happens with regard to leadership, as leaders are appointed who have little or no Brethren background, and no interest in maintaining a Brethren ethos.

So far, all attempts to provide an adequate *raison d'être* for Open Brethren have failed.[156] They seem to be sectarian (as when Brethren defined themselves negatively, in terms of what they were not), vague, or simply not distinctive. A typical explanation for Brethren allegiance was provided by Tatford in *The Harvester*: he associated with them because 'they adhere to the plain teachings of the New Testament, they submit to the guidance of the Holy Spirit, they recognise all believers as members of the Body of Christ and they acknowledge the Headship of Christ'.[157] But other Evangelicals could say precisely the same; as it stood, there was nothing distinctive about it. Furthermore, there is little evidence that Open Brethren remain *doctrinally* distinctive; as Bruce observed, 'It is practice rather than doctrine that marks them out.'[158] In connection with the work of Christ, the concept of imputed righteousness is still rejected by some,[159] but this would now be paralleled by questioning among some English Evangelicals of such concepts as

[156] Rowdon acknowledged that few if any Open Brethren distinctives could be seen as essential (Harold H. Rowdon, *Who are the Brethren and does it matter?* (Exeter: Paternoster on behalf of Christian Brethren Research Fellowship, 1986), 30).

[157] F.A. Tatford, 'Why are you a "P.B."?', *H* 31 (1952), 86; cf. *idem*, 'Why meet with Brethren?', *H* 47 (1968), 112.

[158] F.F. Bruce, *Who are the Brethren?* (Glasgow: Pickering & Inglis, [1962]), 7.

[159] G.C.D. Howley, *H* 30 (1951), 32; Ian Jackson, 'Called according to His purpose (Rom 8.28-32)', *BM* 113 (2003), 168-9.

substitutionary atonement. As for distinctive teaching concerning sanctification, Rowdon suggests that this has been articulated more through contributions at the Breaking of Bread than through specific sermons or writings on the subject. It is noteworthy that George Harpur's contribution to *The Faith* on sanctification did not reject the Reformed idea that the Law of God is the believer's rule of life.[160] The traditional emphasis on the believer's being positionally sanctified as one who is seated in heavenly places in Christ has been echoed elsewhere, for example by the ex-Anglican charismatic leader Colin Urquhart.[161] Most interestingly, traditional repudiation of annihilationism is no longer universal. The November 1993 issue of *Aware* included a number of articles on this topic, offering a notably even-handed coverage. Furthermore, not only did Paternoster publish *The Fire that Consumes* by the American writer E.W. Fudge around this time, but Rowdon described it as presenting a 'persuasive case' in a review for the *Partnership Newsletter*.[162] Here, too, Open Brethren have not proved immune to theological change within wider Evangelicalism. Even ecclesiologically, plural leadership, rejection of the necessity of ordination, and belief in every-member ministry have spread far beyond assemblies.

Some might see lack of distinctiveness as a problem to be overcome, but it can be seen as in some ways a positive thing, because it demonstrates that many Open Brethren really are what they profess to be – assemblies of 'mere Christians', whose circle of fellowship is no narrower than that of the whole body of Christ. Perhaps, therefore, we may view them as a movement with a centre rather than one with a boundary (as provided by address lists and other such devices). Since Brethren insist that the centre of their gathering is Christ alone, they are free to associate with all other Christ-centred local congregations. We are back to Groves, who held that he was free to share fellowship with any gathering where Christ was present to bless. As for assemblies as a movement, perhaps the grain of wheat must fall into the ground and die if it is to bring forth fruit (John 12.24). It could therefore be asked whether the demise of Open Brethren really matters. Lang considered that the ruin of Christendom did not present a problem for those seeking to follow the apostolic pattern of gathering, because local churches could still be formed, and the same argument could be applied to the movement. I am not aware, however, that anyone has explored what this might mean in practical terms, and how local churches might relate to each other in a 'post-Brethren' world, although Summerton foresees the possibility of progressive Brethren and some independent charismatic congregations merging as the latter mature.[163] But I do not think we are about to see the demise of Brethrenism: apart from the spiritual vitality and burden for renewal which is evident in some quarters, it could be argued that just as during the 1950s denominations which Brethren had written off experienced a remarkable measure of renewing and reviving, so too we should not rush to write off the Brethren or to speak of them in the past tense, because they too may experience such a reviving.

Whilst it may be difficult to isolate a distinctive *raison d'être* for Brethren, it is possible to see assembly life as representing a distinctive combination of ideas: none of those mentioned by Dickson (and referred to above) are distinctive when taken individually, but the combination of them is, and that other congregations which practise

---

[160] Harold H. Rowdon, 'The Brethren Concept of Sainthood', *VE* 20 (1990), 99.

[161] See Colin Urquhart, *In Christ Jesus* (London: Hodder & Stoughton, 1981).

[162] *PN* n.s. 5 (October 1994), 40.

[163] Summerton, *Local churches for a new century*, 22.

them have usually derived them from Brethren. So it could be said that assemblies which continue to practice these represent a distinctive way of being church, but share a common purpose with other churches. Such a view would be consonant with the understanding of the movement as in some sense a denomination, rather than a sect. Of course, not all Brethren would see things that way, and it would be futile for those of different outlooks to attempt to reach an agreed understanding of their identity.

In the end, too much navel-gazing may be misplaced, since the message of Brethren decline may be not so much that they faced unique problems as that they were not immune to wider social and theological trends. Discussions about Brethren identity sometimes have a touch of spiritual hypochondria about them. Furthermore, Brethren in many other parts of the world are noticeably free from such preoccupations. It may be more appropriate to spend less time looking for symptoms of malaise, and getting on with living, confident that as God has blessed their spiritual forebears who sought to live close to him, so he can bless them and their successors.

20.4 Exclusive Brethren and the Churches of God since 1914

20.4.1 Exclusive Developments[164]

As Shuff has pointed out, what Exclusive Brethren of all types, as well as the Churches of God, opposed was primarily independency rather than the 'open table' *per se*.[165] They therefore shared a connexional approach to matters of polity, although this worked somewhat differently in various groups: some appear to have been more centralised (e.g. the Taylor Brethren, among whom the current leader or 'man of God' acts in practice as a visible focus of unity, and his teaching is carefully followed by each meeting throughout the world), whereas others sought merely to ensure that local assemblies always acted in concert, recognising one another's decisions and maintaining a circle of fellowship which excluded those who were not sound in faith, godly in life, and separate from ecclesiastical 'evil' (e.g. the Kelly Brethren). There were differences of ethos, too: Glanton Brethren were often the most outward-looking and evangelistically-active Exclusive stream (especially in their home territory of Northumberland), while the Kelly Brethren probably possessed the most theologically astute leadership. Several Open Brethren Bible teachers were former Kelly Brethren,[166] one of the best-known being Fereday.

Until recently, it was hard to see what separated the Kelly-Lowe-Glanton (or Reunited) Brethren from 'tight' Open Brethren, unless it was that the former had a more connexional ecclesiology; each group read and commended the other's writings. However, in the last few years, the former group have split, a major issue being the reception of ex-Taylor Brethren, the issue being whether an explicit disavowal of the denial of Christ's eternal

---

[164] On twentieth-century Exclusive history and thinking, see B.W. Burton, *A Further Review of Recovery to the Truth and its Maintenance (1827-1997)* (Lancing, Sussex: Kingston Bible Trust, 1997); Dronsfield, *'Brethren' since 1870*; A.J. Gardiner, *The Recovery and Maintenance of the Truth* (Kingston-on-Thames: Stow Hill Bible and Tract Depot, [1951, revised ed. 1963]); Shuff, *Searching*; Bryan R. Wilson, *"The Brethren": a current sociological appraisal* ([Oxford]: n.p., [2000]²); *idem* (ed.), *Patterns of Sectarianism*, ch. 9. I have paid particular attention to the Taylor Brethren, because they form the largest Exclusive group in Britain, and the one best-known to outsiders.

[165] Shuff, *Searching*, 60.

[166] 'Touchstone', 'William Kelly, Christian Scholar', *W* 86 (1956), 12.

Sonship should be required for fellowship. Disavowal of the distinctive Christological views of F.E. Raven had earlier been seen as essential by many Kelly-Lowe Brethren, and made them somewhat suspicious of Glanton Brethren when reunion was first mooted.[167] The approach taken then, and insisted on by some now, has its roots in the insistence on the need to 'judge the question' which first surfaced in the 1840s, and which complicated subsequent attempts at reconciliation; where error has been taught or condoned, those guilty must retrace their steps and renounce the error.

Estimates of membership of the various Exclusive groups are hard to come by, and their reliability is uncertain. However, the 1990 edition of the *UK Christian Handbook* gave figures of 390 Taylor meetings with 12,018 members, and eighty-one meetings and 2,175 members for all other Exclusive groups.[168] The figures for 2002 are tabulated below. From these, it is clear that Taylor Brethren are by far the most significant Exclusive group, an impression reinforced by the number of new halls which they have erected in the last fifteen years.

Table 20.2: UK Exclusive Brethren statistics, 2002

Group	Membership	Number of assemblies
Plymouth Brethren No. 4	12,700	405
Kelly	27	2
Reunited (Kelly-Lowe-Glanton)	1,053	76
Tunbridge Wells	115	17
Total	14,895	500

Source: Peter Brierley (ed.), *UK Christian Handbook Religious Trends No.4, 2003/2004* (London: Christian Research, 2003).

A Taylor Brethren hall at Horley, Surrey. Note the lack of windows, a standard practice for this group's meeting places

The history of the Taylor Brethren deserves particular comment. They have been led by a succession of 'men of God', the best-known of whom were James Taylor (1870-1953)

---

[167] Shuff, *Searching*, 109-11.

[168] Figures as quoted in Brierley et al., *Brethren*, 9.

and his son, also named James (1899-1970). Darby, Raven, and the elder Taylor are
looked upon as the 'three great ministries' through which much truth has been
recovered.[169] The movement's developing introversion during the twentieth century was
due in part to the belief that the assembly was the sphere in which God was uniquely
active. Members believe that a fuller understanding of divine truth is gradually being
unfolded as a result of the Holy Spirit's work within their movement, especially through
the teaching of the 'man of God'. Questioning new teachings is therefore very difficult,
and secessions have occurred each time a major development has taken place.[170] The most
significant of these were in 1960-1, over the issues of membership of professional
associations and eating with non-members, and 1970, over divergent accounts and
interpretations of James Taylor Junior's behaviour while ministering at Aberdeen.[171]
Possibly a third of British Taylor Brethren left as a result of the latter, and at least half the
withdrawals were in Scotland, where the meetings were 'decimated'. It appears that the
closer the meeting to Aberdeen, or the more in contact it was with events, the higher the
proportion of withdrawals. In the Aberdeen meeting itself, initially only one household
remained. The seceders (sometimes known as 'Outs') have often continued to meet
separately,[172] although some groups have disintegrated, and a few have aligned
themselves with Open Brethren. Examples include a group, possibly at Amersham, which
invited a Counties evangelist to hold meetings in their new hall in the early 1960s,[173] and
the Christian Meeting Room, Haywards Heath, which withdrew from Taylor circles around
1970. As in 1906-7, some prefer to regard themselves as 'independent', neither Open nor
Exclusive. 'Out' meetings appear to have a better chance of continuing where they are a
viable size and are bound together by something other than, or additional to, their 'Out'
status, such as a clear focus on evangelism, or on the activities of Acts 2.42.
Psychologically, it may be that this also enables them to come to terms with past
experiences and to 'move on'.

    Taylor Brethren have been the object of considerable media attention since the early
1960s, culminating in a television documentary broadcast by the BBC as part of its
'Everyman' series early in 2003, in which a number of members and ex-members were
interviewed. The movement's belief in the need to remain separate from the world, its
perceived secretiveness, and the stories told by former members, have done much to
stimulate this curiosity. To complicate things, much that has been written about the
Taylor Brethren is open to question in its selection, presentation, and interpretation of
evidence, rather than being researched and written to rigorous standards (exceptions are
the writings of Shuff and Wilson). On several occasions, therefore, they have taken legal
advice and even initiated legal action in order to get authors to withdraw assertions

---

[169] J.T[aylor] Jr, *Notes of Readings in New York 1956 1957 1958, Volume Three* (Kingston-on-
Thames: Bible and Gospel Trust, [1974]), 41.

[170] In this way, those who might undermine the movement's separatist ethos were removed (Shuff,
Searching, 129).

[171] For accounts from both sides, see Shuff, *Searching*, 252-3, 266-8. The Taylor Brethren
interpretation of events is rooted in the conviction that God had a vessel whom he would not allow to
fail; Taylor spoke and acted as he did in order to bring out what was in others by provoking reaction,
being willing to draw reproach on himself in order to do so.

[172] They are not agreed on the extent to which the Taylors' teaching should be followed; for
instance, should all of it as far as 1970 be accepted, or merely as far as 1959?

[173] Counties Evangelistic Work report for 1962, 11.

deemed unacceptable. However, there is some evidence that the leaders' avoidance of publicity is beginning to lessen, as they recognise that too much reserve could be counter-productive. Their current policy may be summed up as 'nothing to hide, nothing to parade'.[174]

BRETHREN'S MEETING ROOM
PLACE OF PUBLIC RELIGIOUS WORSHIP
registered pursuant to Places of Worship Registration Act 1855 & Local Government Finance Act 1988

Information about meetings may be obtained by contacting the trustees by telephone
0306 876448 or 0293 772341

This noticeboard is typical of those outside Taylor Brethren halls. Visitors to services are not encouraged

The generally unfavourable attitude of the media has caused certain problems for Open Brethren. They have felt that at times they were being confused with Taylor Brethren, with negative consequences for their own outreach and relationships with the community. This has been complicated by the Taylorites' consistent use of 'Brethren' to refer to themselves. In the early 1960s, the editors of *The Witness* and *The Harvester* sent a letter to the national press explaining the differences between Open and Taylor Brethren, but no paper published it.[175] Bruce, in his pamphlet *Who are the Brethren?*, felt it necessary to do something similar.[176] Asked how Open Brethren might best dissociate themselves from Taylor Brethren in the public eye, Bruce advised behaving so as to make clear that Open Brethren did not share their principles or practice, but avoiding censorious or sarcastic comments regarding the group.[177]

Around 1960 there was some wariness about the possibility of ex-Taylor Brethren influencing Open assemblies towards certain Taylorite views. An Ulster writer, Albert McShane, asserted that those who deny Christ's eternal Sonship should not be allowed to remain in fellowship.[178] Andrew Stenhouse, a missionary in Chile, saw the movement's basic error as the recognition of a corporate body composed of assemblies, and claimed that it was unsound on such matters as infant baptism, conversion, and regeneration, resulting in many members having a false confidence regarding their spiritual state.[179] However, most Open Brethren appear to have neglected such issues in scrutinising ex-Taylorite applicants for fellowship. Tatford, commenting on the controversy about

---

[174] These words were used by the Taylors' successor, J.H. Symington, in an interview during 1977.

[175] *H* 43 (1964), 145.

[176] Bruce, *Who are the Brethren?*, 3; the pamphlet was reprinted (slightly revised) as Appendix 1 of *In Retrospect*.

[177] 'AQ', *H* 42 (1963), 107; cf. 'AQ', *H* (43) 1964, 154.

[178] A. McShane, 'The Eternal Sonship of Christ', *AT* 29 (May-June 1957), 14.

[179] Andrew Stenhouse, 'The Evils of Exclusivism', *AT* 82 (March-April 1966), 18-21.

association with non-members, urged that the opportunity be taken to repair the breach which occurred in the mid-nineteenth century by welcoming excommunicated Taylor Brethren, rather than regarding them with suspicion because their admission might lead to introduction of exclusive ideas.[180]

One consideration often overlooked is that Taylor Brethren preach a gospel which is recognisably Evangelical; it is not uncommon in towns where they have a meeting to see them engaging in open-air work and tract distribution at lunchtimes and on Saturdays. Therefore, however much one might disapprove of aspects of their belief and practice, it should be recognised that there are many fellow believers among them, even though each movement will wish to avoid being confused with the other.

An issue which has brought the Taylorites further publicity is education. They are known for withdrawing children from Religious Education lessons, and for refusing to allow them to use computers. In recent years, many families with secondary-age children have taken them out of school and educated them privately. This has now been formalised with the setting up of schools under the umbrella of Focus Learning Trust. A report prepared for the Department for Education and Skills indicated that at the beginning of 2005 there were thirty-seven such schools in England, and two each in Wales, Scotland, and Northern Ireland, with a total of around 2,000 pupils aged 11-17. The reasons given for this development include disapproval of the teaching and moral atmosphere in state schools. Because members have not been allowed to engage in post-school education since the early 1960s, qualified teachers are drawn from outside the movement, although members assist in other ways.[181] The report stresses that they receive no Government support, and they have begun to appeal to local schools and businesses for financial sponsorship, a development which may be seen as 'spoiling the Egyptians'.

20.4.2 The Churches of God

A summary of the movement's development to the mid-1960s was provided by Charles Oxley, himself a former member. He gave a total of sixty or seventy Churches of God in Britain, and another dozen overseas. The movement's executive body was the annual conference, led by about a dozen 'Leading Brethren'. Conference reports and *Needed Truth* provided an authoritative guide for biblical interpretation, assembly business, procedure in meetings and policy on such matters as recognition of overseers and reception into fellowship. Brethren agreed not to minister on subjects or passages which were under consideration with a view to developing an agreed interpretation. Oxley noted that the recent troubles among Taylor Brethren had prompted Churches of God leaders to attempt to propagate their views among all types of Brethren.[182] It seems possible that, as with Taylor Brethren, negative media coverage of the separatist outlook of the Churches of God, and some sad events precipitated by this, may have been a factor in the reaction by some Scottish Open Brethren against 'Brethren' as a title during the 1960s.

The most fruitful period of the twentieth century for the Churches of God in Britain was the decade from 1945, although occasional new assemblies have been commenced throughout the century. Advertising has proved a fruitful means of making contacts, and a

---

[180] *H* 40 (1961), 17, cf. 177.

[181] Anon., 'Focus Learning Affiliated Schools: an overview' (typescript, 2005).

[182] C.A. Oxley, 'The "NEEDED TRUTH" Assemblies: A Summary of their Origin, Distinctive Tenets, Organisation and Practices', *JCBRF* 4 (April 1964), 21-32.

mailing centre was set up in 1977 to deal with the requests for literature.[183] Whilst making full use of modern technology and methods of communication, especially in their missionary work, the Churches of God have maintained nineteenth-century Brethren attitudes towards involvement in politics or the armed forces, although their strict separation from other religious bodies is being challenged by the involvement of student members in Christian Unions, and the willingness of some to attend meetings in other churches. A more serious problem, however, was the issue of divorce, which caused controversy in 1979-80; some Scottish assemblies were halved in size as members seceded who objected to the reception of anyone who had remarried after divorce (the official view today is that such people could be received if they confessed their sin in remarrying; before this, reception of remarried divorcees was only possible for innocent parties whose previous spouses had been guilty of fornication).[184] A number of the seceders joined Open assemblies, where they would have reinforced 'tight' tendencies.[185] This leakage has continued: since 1960, there have been considerable losses, including many members' children, often to Open Brethren, and in the decade to 1992, it is said that nearly 20% of the Scottish membership joined Open Brethren.[186] By 2004, numbers of Churches of God were down to twenty-six in England, eighteen in Scotland, five in Wales, and five in Northern Ireland.[187] Remarkably, Macdonald as a member of the movement called for a review of the continuing separation from Open Brethren and the development of co-operative links, but there is no evidence that this is imminent.

For the foreseeable future, the various groups of Brethren look likely to continue pursuing their separate courses; they have a difficult enough task maintaining internal unity, without attempting to deal with broader issues. In the next chapter we examine some changes which have resulted in Open Brethren becoming marked by ever-increasing diversity of practice.

---

[183] [Park], *Churches of God*, 61-2.

[184] Clarke, 'Churches of God', 32, 34, 72; Doodson, *Search*, 27; Macdonald, 'One Hundred Years', 46-8.

[185] 'LF', *BM* 91 (1981), 80.

[186] Macdonald, 'One Hundred Years', 54, 67.

[187] See the list on their website, <www.churchesofgod.org>.

CHAPTER 21

Internal Change

For a significant proportion of assemblies, the pattern of activities has remained largely unchanged throughout the post-1945 period. Sunday morning Breaking of Bread and Sunday evening Gospel service (11 and 6.30 still appear to be the most popular times for these), a midweek meeting for prayer and ministry (perhaps one for each, in assemblies which can sustain this and are of a traditional cast of mind), and outreach activity which focuses on a Sunday School (though many also run a midweek children's work) and a Women's Meeting. Monthly ministry meetings on a Saturday evening still take place in a number of areas, especially where a congregation drawn from surrounding assemblies is assured. The table below demonstrates the persistence of a traditional pattern of assembly life.

Table 21.1: Patterns of Sunday worship, 2002

Pattern	England	Wales	Scotland	Ireland	Total
Morning + evening/ morning + afternoon (purpose unspecified)	9	1	1	-	11 (9%)
Morning Breaking of Bread + afternoon/ evening Gospel	51	5	6	12	74 (60%)
Morning Breaking of Bread and/or Family (weekly/monthly)/Gospel Service + evening Service/ Teaching	8	-	8	-	16 (12.5%)
Morning Family Service + evening Breaking of Bread	3	-	-	-	3 (2.5%)
Morning Breaking of Bread and/or morning Family/Gospel Service	6	-	-	-	6 (5%)
Other	7	1	5	1	14 (11%)
Total	84	7	20	13	124 (100%)

Source: advertisements in [Roy Hill], *The Assemblies Address Book: useful addresses and other information for Christians* ([Stanton Drew,] Bristol: Christian Year Publications, 2002[5]).

Some assemblies continued their round of activities without seriously thinking about either introducing change or about why change should not be introduced. Bureaucratic, introverted, and hung up on details, many failed to plan for the longer-term future until they were irreversibly weakened. Today, many are being forced by declining numbers to give up their range of activities one by one.

Others, often reluctant to identify themselves as Brethren, have a pattern of activities which is virtually indistinguishable from that of many other Evangelical churches of various denominations. Thus a somewhat different pattern appears from the surveys conducted by the CBRF and Partnership. It should be noted that assemblies responding to these surveys would often have been among those more open to change, and therefore that the movement as a whole will have changed less than the table below might imply.

Table 21.2: Results of 1978/1988/1998 assembly surveys

Year	1978	1988	1998
Number of replies	249	308	322
Breaking of Bread (%)	100	100	99
Prayer meeting (%)	95	96	90
Gospel meeting (%)	93	77	<50
Family service (%)	43	64	75
Sunday School (%)	91	82	73
Ministry meeting (%)	87	91 Bible teaching	85 Bible teaching
Women's meeting (%)	81	73	67
Full-time/part-time leader/worker (%)	9	20	33
Average assembly size	50 including children	52	58

Sources: Brierley et al., *Brethren*; Brown, *Whatever Happened*; Brown and Mills, *"Brethren" Today*.

In this chapter we explore some of the changes which have been introduced in assembly life, focusing on Bible teaching, worship, leadership, the roles played by women, and outreach.

21.1 The Growth of Systematic Bible Teaching

During the war years, a widely-felt need was the provision of systematic Bible teaching. It was asserted that even where some attempts were made in this respect, speakers seldom took more than a month of weekly meetings, thus limiting the depth or scope of the topics which they could tackle.[1] One attempt to remedy the lack was that of local Bible schools, meeting weekly for a limited period of the year. For example, a report of the Haymarket Bible School in Central London, which began immediately after the war, noted its aim to improve the Bible knowledge of youth in assemblies. The sessions looked at the origins, setting, problems, and interpretation of the biblical writings, and at suitable study methods. Note-taking was expected, and there was an examination.[2]

The Glasgow Bible School commenced in 1955, aimed at new converts and young Christians. Coinciding with the need to provide follow-up teaching for converts of Billy Graham's 1955 Kelvin Hall crusade (a weekly meeting providing basic teaching for them was its immediate predecessor), it was an immediate success. George Harpur, who conducted it from 1956-86, had given himself to full-time Bible teaching as a result of becoming aware during the war that Brethren no longer had the degree of Bible knowledge which had marked them previously. The school ran annually, two nights a week for a month, and each session included individual and group work as well as input from Harpur, the aim being to teach students the *how* as well as the *what* of Bible study. As late as 1986, up to 400 attended, 90% of them under twenty-five, and including a significant proportion from outside assemblies.[3] From 1965 Harpur ran a similar venture in Wimbledon.[4] Other ventures were the result of co-operation by regional clusters of assemblies, as in south-west Essex from 1949 and in the Bexleyheath area from the early 1950s.[5] More recently, since 2002 GLO has offered a 'Mini-Bible School' package which can be mounted wherever requested.[6] However, the fashion for Bible schools has passed, in part because they were too cerebral in their approach. Concepts such as 'school' and 'lecture' do not appeal to many, and much of the movement is struggling to develop alternative approaches to the provision of learning opportunities. Attempts are being made by a minority of assemblies, however, to package teaching in a culturally-familiar format, usually in the context of youth work. For instance, the assembly at Maesteg reported a young people's sleep-over and teaching session.[7]

Another attempt to meet the need for solid teaching was the commencement in Britain of Emmaus Bible School in 1951. Now based at Eastham in the Wirral, this offers a wide range of distance-learning courses for young people and adults, all from a traditional Open Brethren perspective (the movement originated in North America). It has attracted many Christian students from outside Brethren, and also offers evangelistic courses. By 1973, enrolments were running at a thousand a week, 85% of whom were linked together in local church study groups.[8] Schools and prisons have also used the material.

The Bible reading, which has been seen as more characteristic of Brethren than even the Breaking of Bread,[9] has continued to decline in popularity, and many found the

---

[1] E.g. 'WW', *W* 75 (1945), 8.

[2] *H* 23 (1946), 69-70.

[3] Anderson, *They Finished their Course in the 80's*, 60; Ian Ford, 'Glasgow Summer Bible School', *H*, July 1986, 18; George Harpur, 'An adventure in teaching Bible-study', *W* 92 (1962), 216-18; W.G. Stephen, 'How Things are Done: Some Glasgow Activities', *W* 87 (1957), 31.

[4] *H*, September 1987, 26.

[5] 'FEC', *H* 26 (1949), 97; *H* 32 (1953), 72; *W* 86 (1956), 127.

[6] *Spearhead*, Summer 2003, 11.

[7] *PS* 55 (2000), 78.

[8] Harold Catlow, 'by the way [*sic*] … The Emmaus Bible School Story', *H* 52 (1973), 222-3.

[9] Rowdon, *Who are the Brethren?*, 33.

ministry meeting more helpful. In time, continuing decline in midweek attendance, which had resulted in the frequent combination of prayer and ministry meetings in the 1940s and 1950s, led many assemblies to introduce ministry at the Breaking of Bread (though this has now been dropped by many churches).[10] However, an alternative was provided in some measure by the increasing popularity of discussion groups and then house groups. In 1956, Howley claimed that 'The modern discussion group is simply (when dealing with things Biblical) the Bible reading of older times.'[11] He saw the causes of decline of the Bible reading as being that it was no longer conducted by well-taught leaders, those who took part were often guilty of a lack of preparation, and it had become a place for unedifying controversy on knotty points. It needed a leader who could blend contributions into a unity. Some conservative Brethren have resisted the trend toward small groups, claiming that the practice of splitting into home groups, with all free to speak, is deplorable, denies the diversities of gifts bestowed by the Spirit and 'inevitably gives rise to the spread of false teaching'.[12] It has even been alleged that such things violate 'body truth',[13] presumably because it is believed that the character of the assembly is obscured and its discipline undermined when it splits into small groups. Such gatherings would be more difficult to 'police' than meetings in the hall which are intended for the assembly as a whole.

In some circles, Bible readings can still attract: *Believer's Magazine* continues to carry advertisements for residential Bible readings (though far fewer than formerly), and *Precious Seed* reported in 1980 that a small Suffolk assembly held a three-day reading over the New Year which attracted eighty to one hundred people, including a large number of under-twenty-fives.[14] Among Kelly-Lowe-Glanton (sometimes known as Reunited) Brethren, the annual Easter conference at Plumstead (now moved to Canterbury) attracts around 300 of all ages from Britain and Europe to participate in a traditional-style Bible reading.

Other remedies which have been tried include the attempt to introduce more of a 'teaching' component to the gospel service. Ellison argued that 'Wherever there is marked blessing on young people's work, it is almost always due to consecutive and consistent teaching. This is the element that is normally missing in the conventional Gospel meeting.'[15] Although this had the potential for introducing believers as well as the unsaved to something of the richness of the gospel, it has foundered upon the increasing non-viability in most parts of Britain of any outreach activity timed for Sunday evenings. I suspect that assemblies which did this have now moved on to replace the gospel service with an all-age family service. This has sometimes been seen as militating against the provision of solid teaching, because of the need to cater for all ages. Whilst they have often made their evening service into a time of Bible teaching and (in England) communion,[16] the tendency to come to church once instead of twice on a

---

[10] Brown, *Whatever Happened*, 33.

[11] 'Touchstone', 'The Bible Reading', *W* 86 (1956), 122.

[12] A.W. Foster, 'Steadfast in the Faith (3)', *BM* 109 (1999), 72.

[13] *BM* 110 (2000), 135.

[14] *PS* 31 (1980), 45.

[15] *H* 55 (1976), 86.

[16] Progressive Scottish assemblies hold a morning family service in addition to, rather than instead of, the Breaking of Bread.

Sunday means that such expedients face the same problem as the midweek meetings have done.

Some assemblies have become known as centres for good teaching. In 2005 Moorlands Evangelical Church in Lancaster appointed a pastor in conjunction with an interdenominational body, the North-West Partnership, with the objective of establishing a culturally-relevant conservative Evangelical teaching ministry for students in this university town.[17] During the 1960s, the teaching at the assembly in Warwick attracted numbers of Christians from Exclusive meetings and from churches of other denominations, although this resulted in a dilution of the congregation's Brethren ethos, a problem which has occurred elsewhere.[18] Sadly, the more frequent pattern is for individuals to leave Open Brethren because of the perceived lack of Bible teaching. It may be that expectations have risen, fuelled by the impact of Evangelical expository preachers such as Martyn Lloyd-Jones and John Stott, and of Brethren itinerant teachers such as Harpur, Alan Nute, and Stephen Short. Lay preachers, with limited time for preparation, could rarely hope to provide expository ministry of such depth; but it is not clear that full-time workers are always able to do better. Perhaps any malaise affecting Brethren preaching is one shared with other branches of the Evangelical movement.

21.2 Styles of Worship

In 1967, a contributor to the *Journal of the Christian Brethren Research Fellowship* asserted,

> If I walk into an assembly where I have never been before, I can be morally certain that the following will occur: There will first of all be a hymn, followed by a prayer. The alternation of hymn and prayer will continue for about three-quarters of an hour (not necessarily in the 'hymn-sandwich' form, for there may be two or more prayers in a row, but never more than one hymn; and there will perhaps also be a 'little word'). At about 11.50 (if the meeting began at 11), the bread is broken, and the collection and notices will certainly come after that, and usually in that order. There will be a sermon of some sort, and the closing item will be a prayer. My guess is that no more than 10 per cent of assemblies in this country fail to conform to this pattern.[19]

Whilst this pattern is still widespread, change is occurring, and in this section we shall outline something of its impact on hymnody and on the Breaking of Bread. In the field of hymnody, there has been a slow but steady assimilation of the Open Brethren repertoire to that of other Evangelical churches, as they have discovered hymns which have been well-known everywhere else. On the one hand, such Open Brethren books as have appeared have contained an increasing proportion of 'standard' hymns found in the books of all Protestant denominations. On the other, many assemblies have adopted non-Brethren books instead of (or alongside) those produced within the movement, partly because it was easier and cheaper to have one book which could be used for all services, and have been affected by wider Evangelical trends in the area of corporate worship, such

---

[17] 'The North West Partnership of Local Churches', <www.northwestpartnership. com>, accessed 15 April 2005.

[18] Franks, *Saltisford*, 25, 37.

[19] David J.A. Clines, 'Liturgy without Prayerbook', *JCBRF* 15 (April 1967), 11-12.

as the proliferation of musical instruments used to accompany the singing and the decline in congregational four-part harmony.

A typical example of change in the area of music is provided by the Hoylake assembly in the Wirral. By 1967, it had decided to use the organ for accompanying singing at the Breaking of Bread. In 1983, it replaced *Hymns of Light and Love* and *Golden Bells* with *Hymns of Faith*, including the Mitchley Supplement (see below). The following year saw the introduction of *Mission Praise*, followed by *Junior Praise*. By the end of the 1980s, the singing was led by a music group.[20] In some assemblies, books have been rendered obsolete by new projection methods, a feature which will make it even less likely that distinctively Brethren hymns will remain in use, since few if any are included in the selections available in electronic form for projection.

The last significant Open Brethren hymnal was *Christian Worship*, compiled by B. Howard Mudditt, which appeared in 1976 after a lengthy gestation process – though I do not think this was why its compiler supplied an article entitled '"I should like to die, said Willie" Musings on the Making of a Hymnbook'.[21] The popularity among assemblies of interdenominational books such as *Mission Praise* and *Songs of Fellowship*, coupled with the shrinking number of assemblies, means that it is increasingly unlikely that a new hymnal for Open Brethren would be an economic proposition, although in the 1990s Christian Year Publications issued *Hymns for Remembrance and Worship*, compiled because many of the new books available were felt to be unsound.[22] The same publisher has reprinted older books such as *Hymns for Christian Worship and Service* and *Hymns of Light and Love,* as well as two interdenominational books widely used by assemblies, *Golden Bells* and *Hymns of Faith* (Mitchley Hill Chapel, Sanderstead, had produced supplements to *Golden Bells* in 1959 and *Hymns of Faith* in 1967, in order to avoid the need for separate books for morning and evening services[23]). In 1999, John Ritchie secured the copyright of the *Believer's Hymn Book*; the company has since reprinted it.[24] That there is a market for older books is evident from the fact that, as late as 1980, *Hymns of Light and Love* was continuing to sell 2,500-3,500 copies a year.[25] The *Believer's Hymn Book*, which first appeared in 1884 (although it has been expanded since, notably with a 1959 supplement which added a large number of standard 'non-Brethren' hymns, an early indication of the assimilation of Open Brethren worship to that of wider Evangelicalism), receive its first staff music edition in 1981.[26] In some quarters lingering Exclusive influence persisted through the hymnals used; thus the assembly at Horsham, which had moved from Lowe to Open circles in the early 1920s, did not switch from *Hymns for the Little Flock* to *Hymns of Light and Love* until 1960, and when it did the reason was not theological but the need to replace books which were falling apart.[27]

Many Open Brethren have been influenced by the trend towards greater informality in worship, but not all, even among more progressive members, found the new ethos

---

[20] [R.A.S.], *Hoylake Chapel*, 72-3.

[21] *H* 54 (1975), 217-22.

[22] A letter from its compiler, Allan Cundick, appeared in *BM* 101 (1991), 176.

[23] *W* 97 (1967), 162. *Golden Bells* was used by most Southern England assemblies for 'public' services ([G.C.D. Howley], 'Editorial survey', *W* 91 (1961), 121)

[24] *BM* 109 (1999), 359.

[25] Andrews, 'Brethren Hymnology', 6.

[26] *Ibid.*, 1, 5.

[27] *Denne Road Gospel Hall, Horsham, News Letter,* 2 (July-September 1960), 3.

congenial. Peter Cousins, lamenting the aesthetic poverty of Brethren worship, described the widely-used *Songs of Fellowship* as 'late twentieth century garbage'. He had been taught that beauty in worship was suspect; as the Suffering Servant had no form or comeliness, so neither should our worship. Now, even the Authorised Version of the Bible, the one beautiful element which conveyed a real sense of the numinous, was gone.

> In one sense nothing has changed. When engaged in worship I never have expected to enjoy the words or the music or the architecture. Because I value all sorts of other things about the fellowship to which I am committed, I am reconciled to leaving two thousand years of European culture outside the chapel door every Sunday. All the same, I still find myself wondering whether it is really necessary that our worship should be either banal or reminiscent of a TV games show.[28]

Yet the trend to informality often met stern resistance at the Breaking of Bread: assemblies which were able to introduce change in all other meetings found it impossible to do so here. One woman referred to the schizophrenia of such assemblies, and offered a vivid evocation of the traditional Morning Meeting:

> ... as we went in we sensed a whispery hush. As I looked around I saw a sea of velvet pleated hats and fur collars, amongst which the elders were instantly recognizable by their dark suits and grave expressions, as they crept around doing the preliminaries before the service began. It proceeded in a completely predictable fashion. We had three or four short homilies from elderly gentlemen, all on different topics, interspersed with three or four hymns, and one or two prayers. The ladies were silent, heads bowed beneath the velvet. A faint grey mist seemed to hang in the air. At 11.50 precisely we broke bread.

> After the meeting was over, an extraordinary change came over the gathering. People stood up, crossed the room to see their friends and a gentle hubbub of chatter and conversation broke out. People laughed and embraced, shook hands and greeted each other ...[29]

In her view, such worship alienated a proportion of the members. It was attended largely by the elderly and the committed, most of whom could not bear the thought of change in the Brethren's distinctive meeting: others felt unable to reach the standard of language and length in prayer, and perhaps also felt socially out of place. Domination of proceedings by the elders indicated that they were unconsciously assuming a priestly role.[30]

In similar vein were the depressing observations of a Hertfordshire elder who had a wide acquaintance with both Brethren and interdenominational Evangelicalism, Derek Warren:

> ... many young people do not appear to value the unstructured nature of the traditional Breaking of Bread Service: while older people as well are now questioning its validity for the times in which we live. The Service itself has in many assemblies fallen into a rut and is often slow moving and uninspiring. There is an atmosphere that discourages innovation or anything not in

---

[28] Peter Cousins, 'Threadbare worship?', *A*, April 1992, 10.
[29] Sheila Westbury, 'The Morning Meeting: a woman's view', *H*, April 1990, 22.
[30] *Ibid.*, 23.

accord with the traditional line. The hymn book used was compiled 100 or more years ago and the singing is unaccompanied. The same people take part week in and week out and their turns of phrase have almost become a liturgy. Of course, this is an exaggeration, but it is too near the truth, in far too many assemblies.[31]

Resistance to change was deep-rooted: in 1959, a correspondent in *The Harvester* asserted that over half a century earlier there had been many private discussions among leading brethren regarding the desirability of having two Sunday morning meetings, but that whilst almost all agreed on this, they felt unable to say so publicly for fear that it would provoke division.[32] In recent years, though, difficulties surrounding the introduction of change at the Breaking of Bread have been a factor in the beginnings of a move away from it as the central service, although the 1998 survey indicated that 73% of assemblies held a traditional or near-traditional Breaking of Bread as their main worship gathering.[33] Summerton argued that 'the key change that most traditional "Brethren" churches need to make in order to see growth is to move the Breaking of Bread service away from Sunday morning, so as to be able to use that time-period differently'.[34] In his view, the Breaking of Bread was the most difficult aspect of worship to change; it might require creating a new meeting, or making decisive changes to its structure.[35] It should also be noted that the cerebralism of the Breaking of Bread runs counter to the prevailing cultural mood: Keith Barnard, a full-time worker from Cambridge, suggested that the reluctance of young Christians to attend the Breaking of Bread was because it is culturally alien because of its word-orientated nature; he argued that the open, contributory style of worship summed up by 1 Corinthians 14.26 could be practised in home groups instead (a more appropriate setting for breaking bread in any case, given the first-century context) and that contributions on Sundays could be pre-arranged to reflect various styles.[36]

One reason for the difficulties associated with introducing change at the Breaking of Bread has been the continuing insistence that it must follow a certain pattern believed to have been prescribed in the New Testament. During the late 1940s and early 1950s, there was a recrudescence of extreme patternism in relation to the Breaking of Bread, led by men such as I.Y. Ewan of Abernethy in Perthshire. A letter from W.R. Lewis and E.W. Rogers condemned certain patternist teachings disturbing assemblies as 'ritualism'. Among them were the idea that the brother giving thanks represented the Lord and then the assembly, which amounted to clerisy, putting a man between us and God. There was also the attempt to imitate all Christ's actions at the Last Supper, as in breaking the loaf. They claimed that insistence on the use of unleavened bread and unfermented wine had split assemblies. Vine and Lewis also criticised the idea of forbidding the offering of thanksgiving to Christ, and the rewriting of hymns to fit this notion, as well as the use of Leviticus rather than the New Testament to regulate the conduct of the Remembrance meeting. All told, they claimed, the ritualists went beyond Scripture, and produced something which was no

---

[31] P. Derek Warren, 'An Elder Looks On. The "Morning Meeting"', *H* 59 (1980), 225.

[32] J.F. Bergin, letter in *H* 38 (1959), 75.

[33] Brown, *Whatever Happened*, 36. Interestingly, this shift is paralleled in the Evangelical Anglican move away from the centrality of Parish Communion, which enjoyed a brief vogue in the two decades after the Keele Conference of 1967.

[34] Neil Summerton, 'The practice of worship: biblical and historical', *CBR* 39 (1988), 40.

[35] Neil Summerton, 'The practice of worship: desirable reforms', *CBR* 39 (1988), 41, 47.

[36] Keith Barnard, 'Open Worship or Open Word-ship?', *PP* 4 (January 1997), 22-5.

better than an ordered denominational service.³⁷ Although a group of Scottish assemblies
adopted Ewan's ideas, attachment to the idea of the autonomy of assemblies was such that
no attempt was made to institute some kind of centralised body linking them, and no
formal schism occurred such as had produced the Churches of God.³⁸ It is worth noting at
this point that during the early 1950s Taylor Brethren were also clarifying what they
believed to be the prescribed pattern for this service, although with rather different
results. However, I have not found any evidence to suggest that their pattern was
introduced to Open Brethren by individuals moving from one group to the other.

21.3 New Patterns of Leadership

The basic thesis of Neil Summerton's work on eldership, *A Noble Task* (first published in
1987), was that the present state of assemblies was due to deficiencies in the areas of
government, leadership and ministry; he argued that what was distinctive about Brethren
thinking was not the mere plurality of leaders, but their collective responsibility for
governing and leading the congregation.³⁹ The deficiencies had long been the subject of
discussion and prayer, and attempts had been going on since the war years to put things
on a better footing, although it is significant that Watson's 1949 symposium on *The
Church* contained no discussion of full-time workers as one possible way forward.

The 1950s were marked by increasing openness to the idea of formally-recognised
elders, which represented a step away from Darby's influence (this was nothing new for
Open Brethren in Scotland, who may have been influenced by Presbyterian thinking), and
then too by the introduction of a diaconate, usually charged with assisting the elders by
taking on the 'practical' aspects of assembly activity. Such appointments were motivated
in part by a desire to conform to what was perceived as the New Testament pattern for
church government. However, with a move away from this perspective to a more
pragmatic approach, diaconates have now fallen out of favour. During the 1990s, many
progressive assemblies moved towards a more functional approach to leadership; since
they no longer regarded Scripture as setting out a prescribed pattern for church life, they
saw themselves as free to adopt whatever leadership models were consistent with biblical
principles and helpful in their situation. Under the influence of contemporary
management thinking, task-orientated teams, assignment of specific areas of

---

³⁷ *W* 82 (1952), 120-1; also in *H* 29 (1952), 106. Cf. Harry Lacey, 'Legality and the Lord's
Supper', *PS* 3.3 (March-April 1950), 66-73.

³⁸ Dickson, *Brethren in Scotland*, 234-7, 251.

³⁹ Neil Summerton, *A Noble Task: Eldership and Ministry in the Local Church* (Exeter: Paternoster,
1987), 15. Cf. Peter Lowman, 'A Plea for a Radical Brethrenism', paper given at the Summer School
on the Christian Brethren movement, Regent College, Vancouver, 2-7 July 1990 (typescript, [1990];
CBA Box 32/43), fos. 331-2, 338, which argued that the movement's lack of creative and strategic
thinking may have been due to the need to stress faithfulness rather than innovation during the earlier
decades of the twentieth century when few other groups were maintaining the faith, and that the
aversion to one-man ministry may have begotten a fear of appearing to dominate by exercising
leadership gifts and a focus on maintenance.

responsibility to deacons, and appointment of part-time or full-time workers with specific job descriptions all became part of church life.[40]

21.3.1 Reinventing the Full-time Worker

Full-time workers, in their modern guise, first appeared during the 1960s, at the point where denominational ordinations began to fall rapidly. In 1962, *The Witness* announced the commendation of Peter Milford as a full-time worker, who was moving to Sedbury (near Chepstow) at the invitation of the assembly to help in evangelism and pastoral work in the area.[41] J.H. Large spent twelve years as an elder with Cholmeley Hall during the 1960s, it being understood that he would devote a sizeable proportion of each year to ministry there, and that when at home he would be available for pastoral work.[42] In 1969, Peter Morris, who had trained at LBC, began a twenty-year ministry at Greenford.[43] By 2003, there were an estimated 170 full-time workers, fifty full-time evangelists and twenty full-time itinerant Bible teachers.[44]

Historical precedent for this step was provided when Rowdon demonstrated the existence from the beginning of full-time (though not salaried or formally employed) workers attached to particular assemblies or groups of assemblies.[45] A few full-time workers had continued to serve local assemblies throughout the movement's history, such as M'Vicker at Clapton, or Charles Gahan at Barking from 1931-42. As the number of men of independent means declined, there was a shift from viewing full-time ministry as an itinerant and freelance activity towards an emphasis on settled and supported ministry, partly because the workers themselves faced increasing practical pressures on their family life and finances.

It is important to note that whilst many recent apologists for this development have appealed to the nineteenth-century practice of gifted individuals settling in an assembly and giving themselves to a pastoral and teaching ministry in it, they have not always reflected on the different ways in which this was practised: whereas contemporary workers are often employed by the church on a contractual basis, and paid a salary (often with housing provision, as is the case for most denominational ministers), their nineteenth-century counterparts regarded themselves as responsible directly to God who had called and gifted them, and did not enter into any kind of contractual arrangement with the assembly where they served. In addition, the earlier cultural belief that gentlemen had a duty to serve society by exercising leadership was no longer a factor in Brethren thinking.

---

[40] For a number of case studies, see *PP* 12 (October 1999). John Boyes had been a management lecturer and consultant, and doubtless had a significant influence in this; others associated with Partnership are also 'management professionals'.

[41] *W* 92 (1962), 115.

[42] Pauline Summerton, 'Cholmeley Evangelical Church, Highgate, London, 1884-1994: A History from a Personal Perspective', *BAHNR* 2.1 (Winter 2000), 11.

[43] Rowdon (ed.), *Ten Changing Churches*, 20-1.

[44] Harold Rowdon (ed.), *Country Reports on the Work of Brethren Churches … For the International Brethren Conference on Mission 3, held at Selimbar, Romania, 2-7 July 2003* (n.pl.: n.p., [2003]), 61.

[45] Harold H. Rowdon, 'The Early Brethren and the Ministry of the Word', *JCBRF* 14 (January 1967), 11-24.

There were several reasons for the trend towards full-time workers: the need to avoid the loss of promising young men to denominational ministry (especially once increasing numbers began to undertake theological training and naturally wanted to put it to good use after graduating),[46] a desire to improve the quality of care and teaching in assemblies, the influence of a trend towards professionalisation in many areas of life, perhaps an increasing convergence with mainstream Evangelicalism, the spread of a more long-term and strategically thought-out approach to assembly life, increasing recognition of the nature and scope of certain spiritual gifts (especially that of pastoring) which entailed making space for their exercise, and increasing openness to the principle that what is acceptable overseas must also be acceptable at home (a reversal of Brethren missiology, which in earlier years had not infrequently assumed that the pattern of assembly life at home could be exported lock, stock, and barrel to the mission field).

The impact of missionary practice on the home scene deserves further comment. Jonathan Lamb has suggested that Brethren missionary practice '*relativised and called into question many of the cardinal "principles" of the Brethren Movement*' in areas such as church government, the introduction of 'diocesan' structures, the practice of co-operation with other groups, the roles allowed to women, acceptance of the legitimacy of institutional work (e.g. in education and health care) as opposed to itinerant preaching and teaching, and methods of finance.[47] Readiness to adapt for the sake of the gospel thus replaced a rigid commitment to a particular pattern of church life. A missionary in Peru, Ray Cawston, drew attention to the variety of Brethren patterns of working which existed abroad: 'some missionaries have formed teams centred on a locality for medical or educational work, others have formed country-wide associations, others have become pastors of their local churches, others have travelled widely with no firm links anywhere, and some have been fiercely independent'.[48] Some missionaries who returned home brought such flexibility with them, and others on deputation must have sowed seeds of alternative ways of thinking in the minds of their hearers. However, we should not overestimate the importance of this, as trends within British Evangelicalism would have been more significant in shaping assembly thinking.

Larsen thinks that the appearance of full-time salaried workers struck a blow at the traditional understanding of 'living by faith'.[49] This may be true of North America, but I think that in Britain things happened the other way round: challenges to the traditional understanding of 'living by faith' made it easier for assemblies to contemplate appointing full-time workers on a formal basis. Some rethinking of 'living by faith' took place from the 1950s, stimulated by contributions to *The Witness* from Dennis Clark, a missionary in New Delhi. He called for a sense of personal involvement in financing God's work, and suggested that assemblies produce an annual budget, reporting periodically on progress, on the basis that systematic giving was a biblical principle.[50] A second article examined biblical teaching concerning 'living by faith'. Clark insisted that all believers lived by faith. Some, he acknowledged, had a special gift of faith: this

---

[46] Mills recalled visiting an Anglican theological college during the late 1950s and discovering that 50% of the students were from assemblies ('Local Church Full-Time Workers', *H*, July 1982, 9).

[47] Jonathan Lamb, 'Home and Away', *PP* 8 (April 1998), 12-14.

[48] Ray Cawston, 'Accountability', *CBR* 36 (September 1985), 47.

[49] Larsen, '"Living by Faith"', 92-5.

[50] Dennis E. Clark, 'Assembly Finance: Some Biblical Principles', *W* 88 (1958), 6-8; cf. *idem*, 'The assembly budget', *W* 90 (1960), 210-12.

was especially evident in the early church, as were other gifts not now to be expected. The remarkable provision of the needs of Müller and Groves may have been divine testimony to what God was doing at that time, which has now declined just as tongues did in the early church; contemporary believers should adjust to more 'normal' circumstances. The result of our idea of faith as connoting service without guaranteed support was a reluctance to budget or to assume financial responsibility, and disapproval of salaried brethren. In Clark's opinion,

> ...the migration of gifted men to various denominations and mission groups, is to some extent at least, due to their dissatisfaction with the financial circumstances at present prevalent in assembly circles. A number of Christian workers, otherwise convinced in regard to the assembly position, are deeply concerned at the seeming indifference to the subject of the support of the ministry. ...

> Has [our tradition] evolved from a mistaken premise based on the dealings of God with George Muller [*sic*], or is it based on a sound and consistent exposition of the Word of God?[51]

Clark's article touched a raw nerve, and there was extensive debate in the correspondence columns of *The Witness*. Coad summed it up, saying that Clark's main points were that 'faith lines' were not the only valid way of supporting workers, and that greater responsibility needed to be shown in giving. Since respondents had agreed that support comes through others, the question was how this should occur. Scripture was largely silent, and Müller's reasons for deciding to forego guaranteed income in 1830 were not universally applicable. Clark was not contravening assembly principles by allowing a 'salaried' approach. Coad also dismissed the contention that salary necessarily implied control.[52] Other periodicals, however, condemned Clark's proposals. A letter from 'Ex-Baptist' in *The Believer's Magazine* claimed that they would require a degree of organisation which would conflict with belief in the autonomy of assemblies and workers.[53] Borland considered that they undercut the basis on which workers were supported and lacked biblical justification; the apparent obsession with money created the suspicion of materialism.[54] A.M.S. Gooding paralleled this debate with that occasioned by the 1955 High Leigh conference's proposals for full-time salaried workers at home, and regarded it as a landmark issue in what he saw as the progressive drift away from biblical principles.[55]

As so often, progressive thinking was expressed in the pages of the *Journal of the Christian Brethren Research Fellowship*, which devoted an issue to 'Leadership in the Churches' in 1980. Summerton defended the appointment of full-time workers. Apart from the facts that they were neither commanded nor prohibited by the New Testament, and that it was not always possible to distinguish sharply between itinerant and settled ministries,

[51] Dennis E. Clark, 'Faith Lines', *W* 89 (1959), 123.
[52] F.R. Coad, 'Faith Lines: – A Summing Up', *W* 89 (1959), 204-5.
[53] 'Ex-Baptist', '"Faith Lines"', *BM* 69 (1959), 163-4.
[54] [Andrew Borland], 'Editorial', *BM* 69 (1959), 217, 219.
[55] A.M.S. Gooding, 'Lest Haply We Drift', *CW*, July 1959, inside front cover; *idem*, 'Lest Haply We Drift', *AT* 42 (July-August 1959), 5-6; *idem*, 'Faith Lines', *CW*, August 1959, ii-iii.

There are in fact good practical reasons in favour of supporting full-time workers. In the past, Brethren assemblies have often relied for leadership and pastoral work on commercial and professional men who could organize their lives in order to give much time to the needs of the local church. Social organization makes that much more difficult now: the well-to-do are no longer a leisured class; professional men and civil servants customarily work much longer hours than was the case even before the second world war; there are in some parts of the country many fewer small businessmen in the assemblies who can put their resources, for example, their secretaries, at the disposal of the church. ... At the same time, rising expectations have affected the church as much as other spheres: Christians read the New Testament and they see a dynamic mission, a quality of pastoral care and a common life which many Brethren churches seem to lack; and they ask why their elders are not delivering the goods. Many elders feel the answer is that there is too little time and their gifts are spread too thinly over too many responsibilities.[56]

The worker's task was to draw out the gifts of all so that the body functioned as it should. 'Whether full-time workers in local churches would be a benefit to Brethren churches would in the final analysis depend on the attitude and personal commitment of the congregations as a whole.'[57]

In the same issue, Brian Mills explored the reasons for the current Open Brethren leadership crisis, and affirmed the variety of leadership patterns to be found in the New Testament. In assemblies, it was also possible to find a variety of patterns: no leadership, leadership by a brothers' meeting or church meeting, leadership by one man, settled workers as part of a plural leadership; (majority) recognised oversight, usually self-perpetuating, often supervisory rather than pastoral, leadership by elders and deacons, and area leadership (i.e. regional oversight meetings).[58]

However, residual suspicion of the concept of making appointments to office, derived ultimately from Darby, has meant that Open Brethren have struggled with the question of what to call those whom they have appointed to work as pastors, teachers or evangelists. They have been concerned to avoid the appearance of 'one-man ministry' (something which is on the way out in the denominations, although conservative Brethren polemic has often failed to acknowledge this, just as it has failed to acknowledge that the appointment of a full-time worker does not necessarily lead to 'one-man ministry' in an assembly). It appears that they have attempted to sidestep some of the theological issues by developing their own terminology: such terms as 'Residential Full-Time Workers', 'Fully-Supported Workers', and 'Full-Time Workers' have all entered the vocabulary and abbreviations lists of progressive Brethren. But the term 'pastor' is now used fairly frequently, another indicator of the way that progressive assemblies are shedding certain distinctive aspects of their Brethren identity and converging with wider Evangelicalism.

Progressive churches are still in the early stages of working out their understanding of leadership. Sometimes appointments are made on an *ad hoc* basis, as a church responds to a crisis in its ministry. That at Greenford experienced a growth spurt in 1992 which led to the introduction of leadership teams as a way of lightening the workload of the elders.[59] For the most part, they are quite clear that they wish to avoid the 'one man ministry' which Brethren have always condemned, but they appear less sure about what they would

[56] Neil Summerton, 'Leadership and ministry in the Church', *JCBRF* 30 (1980). 42-3.

[57] *Ibid.*, 43.

[58] Brian Mills, 'Leadership in the Churches', *JCBRF* 30 (1980), 45-52.

[59] Rowdon (ed.), *Ten Changing Churches*, 23.

put in its place. Such issues as terminology, relationship to other (voluntary) leaders such as elders, areas of responsibility, and relationship of gift and office are all being explored. More traditional assemblies, however, are often content with their understanding of leadership, but in many cases have to face the problem of its seeming ineffectiveness.

Writing in 1982, Mills said that he knew of seventy to eighty assemblies in England and Wales with full-time workers. In 1979, he had commenced what became known as the 'Partnership Link-Up Service'.[60] It experienced some teething problems related to the quality of workers on offer, the way that churches handled the discussions, and its own response to problems when these were identified.[61] But these have largely been overcome, and by now full-time workers can be found throughout the British Isles, although there are very few in Northern Ireland. The Partnership directory for 2003 lists eighty-two workers, including four couples, who spend all or most of their time working with subscribing churches (of which approximately 150 are listed); there are many more working with other assemblies. They may be youth workers, pastoral visitors, administrators, teachers, visionary leaders, or evangelists; one great advantage for Open Brethren is that they are relatively free of the kind of tradition which has encumbered other churches, in which the pastor has been seen as a jack of all trades; such a perspective has often made it difficult for many denominational church members (and churches) to conceive of any other kind of worker.

The decision to appoint a full-time worker is a big one for an assembly to take, because it involves a radical reassessment of accepted traditions and interpretations of Scripture. Bearwood, Birmingham, was not unusual in taking five years to consider the issues before appointing its first full-time worker in 1994.[62] Not surprisingly, therefore, the quest for full-time workers has not been without its problems. In the 1950s, Lloyd-Jones believed that if large numbers of assemblies were ready to call ministers, there were many Evangelicals who would jump at the opportunity and leave the denominations in which they were serving.[63] Some from other backgrounds have been called to Brethren congregations, but the result has sometimes been to lessen a congregation's sense of its Brethren identity, and such workers have sometimes not always been sensitive to accepted ways of doing things. In some cases, there was a mismatch of expectations between the congregation (or its leaders) and the worker, a failure to define areas of responsibility sufficiently clearly, or a lack of attention to the worker's practical needs. Inevitably, in a tradition which has not been used to having full-time workers in local congregations, some appointments were unsuccessful. For example, in the late 1950s one assembly appointed one of its elders to take a third of the Sunday evening services and half the Thursday Bible readings, at a fixed salary. Initially this proved successful but attendance gradually decreased because, it was felt, his language was over the heads of some; he died, a disappointed man, in 1968. A member candidly acknowledged that 'our first experiment with a paid pastor was a failure because we failed to give him the necessary support'.[64]

---

[60] Brian Mills, 'Local Church Full-Time Workers', *H*, July 1982, 9-11.

[61] Partnership Council of Management minutes, 12 September 1996 (CBA Box 132).

[62] Anon., *Bearwood Chapel Centenary 1896-1996* (n.pl.: n.p., 1996), unpaginated.

[63] Lloyd-Jones to Fred Catherwood, 30 August 1955, in Iain H. Murray (ed.), *D. Martyn Lloyd-Jones: Letters 1919-1981* (Edinburgh: Banner of Truth, 1994), 141-2.

[64] Venables, *Meeting Room*, 11.

21.3.2 Attitudes towards Training

Linked with the changing attitude toward full-time workers was a new appreciation in some quarters of the value of Bible colleges and professional training. Both sides of the debate about such training were aired in *Echoes Quarterly Review* during 1953. One writer questioned the motivation behind the post-war Bible college boom. In his view, it was mostly due to the fact that ex-servicemen could obtain government funding for training, and the growth of the belief that any specialised job needed training. He considered that the better way was for young men to study alongside an older one: this could include university or correspondence courses where appropriate.[65] In response, Montague Goodman, who could be said to have a vested interest in the subject because of his involvement with LBC, warned against lumping all colleges together. Faults were due to the type of training, not to the fact of having been trained. In his view, there was a need for a more intellectual approach in evangelism than had been the case fifty years earlier. As he put it, 'Why is it that men of culture and intellectual training are in so small a minority among us? Is it not that the quality of the ministry is often so deplorably poor that thoughtful people are discouraged from attending?'[66]

Conservatives have continued to be suspicious of training (and of trained men). For example, when a questioner asked *The Believer's Magazine* in 1985 whether Bible schools were scriptural, the reply reiterated that the assembly was the sphere for training, and that in Bible colleges dispensational and assembly truth were not taught.[67] Other reasons advanced have often included a fear that liberalism would infect assemblies through men trained at Bible colleges, and that a kind of clerical caste of the trained would emerge.

In more recent years, new opportunities and patterns for training have arisen, which offer a more equally balanced combination of theoretical input with practical experience. Gospel Literature Outreach (GLO), which was set up in Australia during the 1960s, commenced operations in the UK in 1974. A training centre was opened at Motherwell in that year, which is now known as Tilsley College.[68] Here students spend a year living in community, following a course of biblical and theological study, and engaging in outreach. During the 1980s Counties set up a training programme whereby potential evangelists could spend a year or two working alongside a more experienced partner, and now also run Year Out Teams as part of this, working alongside local churches. In south-west England, the initiators and managers of South West Youth Ministries are closely linked with Brethren. This agency offers three kinds of training: a 'gap year' placement for school-leavers, a post-first degree placement, and a part-time master's degree in Mission, validated by the University of Wales.[69]

An increasing amount and variety of training has also been made available for local leaders. The increasing variety of ministry options, the complexity of pastoral issues, the new emphasis on pastoral counselling, and the felt need to engage with contemporary culture in order to make the church's witness more effective, have ensured that training

---

[65] Metcalfe Collier, 'Training for Christian Service', *EQR* 5.2 (April-June 1953), 34, 37-9.

[66] Montague Goodman, 'Training for Christian Service', *EQR* 5.3 (July-September 1953), 69-71; cf. *idem.*, 'Where are the Sons of the Prophets?', *H* 31 (1952), 26-7.

[67] J.R. Baker, 'QB', *BM* 95 (1985), 244.

[68] Anon., 'Preparation for Service', *EOS* 121 (1992), 59.

[69] [Neil Summerton], 'Meeting of Representatives of Key Bodies held on 13 October 2004: summary of discussion and conclusions' (typescript, 2004).

events for local church leaders often secured enthusiastic responses both nationally and locally from the 1980s onwards. From 1995 this has been backed up, for those linked with Partnership, by *Partnership Perspectives*, each issue of which focuses on a particular aspect of church life. However, it must be said that the majority of such training is provided by the more progressive agencies, and that conservative assemblies are less well served.

21.4 The Roles of Women

It has been asserted that 'few groups have more rigorously excluded women from ministry and leadership in the local church than the Brethren – at least so far as the home churches were concerned'.[70] Such an attitude may have hindered the movement's expansion, as Ellison claimed: 'The objection to active participation by women is the reason why they [Brethren] have never been very successful in areas where Methodism is or has been strong.'[71] More recently, it has contributed to the loss of members to other denominations.[72] One woman argued that post-war contact between Brethren girls and others, through such avenues as the increased opportunities for higher educational study, showed them that other churches were far more liberated in this respect. As a result, many Brethren women had joined churches in the denominations or taken up work with para-church bodies. Noting the unprecedented openings for women in society, she pointed out that many now had to work, a contrast with the original assembly model of family life.[73]

However, since the war a considerable proportion of Open assemblies have been rethinking their understanding of biblical teaching concerning the role of women within the church, sometimes quite radically. The result is that, as with other denominations, there is now a wide variety of views on the topic, and considerable tension between those of differing perspectives. (There has been less debate about women's roles in society, although it is clear that some continue to consider her place to be in the home.) The magazines have seen a steady flow of correspondence on the topic, usually focusing on the interpretation of specific passages such as 1 Corinthians 11.2-16, 14.33-37, and 1 Timothy 2.8-15, at the expense of extended reflection on the fundamental theological principles involved. The issue causes deep pain to convinced individuals on both sides, which means that change in assemblies is usually protracted and often partial; even then, it is not uncommon for individuals who disagree with such change (or the lack of it) to secede. Traditional interpretations continue to exercise a strong hold over many; the 1994 edition of Summerton's *A Noble Task* added an appendix on the ministry of women, in which his own struggles to reconcile affirmation of this with the scriptural evidence are apparent.

The traditional viewpoint continues to be upheld in many quarters. In 1949, Watson affirmed the traditional prohibitions on women's participation in assembly gatherings,

---

[70] Neil Summerton, *A Noble Task* (2nd ed.), 134. He suggests that the greater latitude allowed to women on the mission field may have been the unintended fruit of regarding the 'natives' as children; thus what women were doing would be regarded in a similar light to Sunday School teaching (*ibid.*, 146n).

[71] Ellison, 'The Gospel and the Man in the Street', 6. Methodism, he argued, was the only religious movement in England which really made any impact on the masses (*ibid.*, 5).

[72] See Dickson, *Brethren in Scotland*, 350, 357-8, and the sources there cited.

[73] Sheila Westbury, 'Women in the Church', *A*, March 1992, 18.

whilst recognising the likelihood that women did participate audibly on other occasions.[74] In 1969, A.M.S. Gooding claimed that over 90% of assemblies still forbade women to pray audibly in their meetings.[75] Elsewhere he expressed the view that allowing women to pray would be the thin end of the wedge, leading to their participation in other aspects of worship, and ultimately ruling the assembly.[76] Around 1970, a thoughtful restatement of the traditional viewpoint came from Andrew Borland, whose booklet *Women's Place in the Assemblies: an assessment of Bible teaching*, drew extensively on the arguments of earlier writers such as Hoste, Hogg, Vine, and Lewis. In 1979, an editor of *The Believer's Magazine* asserted that at the Swanwick Conferences, 'our own folk are trying to undermine the New Testament teaching to which we thought we were all committed'; responding to the claim that over half the membership of assemblies were denied a public voice, he claimed to know several hundred assemblies and was not aware of strong calls in many of them for sisters to take part; in any case, he argued, public meetings were not the most important part of the assembly's life.[77] More recently, a series by J. Grant on 'The Role of Sisters in the Assembly' in *Assembly Testimony* during 2000 presented the traditional view, but included a whole article on the teaching roles played by women, which in his view were varied, if always informal and outside the context of assembly gatherings. He even referred with approval to a well-taught woman who was known to instruct men on the way home from the assembly Bible Reading. Not all traditionalists have offered such an affirmation of the contribution to be made by women.

On the other side, a number of women have produced detailed re-examinations of the Bible passages usually taken to preclude the audible participation of women in meetings. The former Exclusive sister Joyce Harper's *Women and the Gospel* appeared as a CBRF Occasional Paper in 1974, while Olive Rogers, daughter of E.W. Rogers and formerly a missionary in India, made a major contribution to a 1996 Partnership booklet entitled *Does God Expect Less of Women*.[78] Both writers focused on exegesis, and carefully avoided making specific practical suggestions concerning how their views would work out in assembly life.

The Lord's Supper was often the last meeting to be opened up to women; in 1965, Clifford Wadey claimed that although he knew of some assemblies where women were allowed to pray, he knew of none where they did so at the Breaking of Bread.[79] So, when 180 women gathered for a conference at Swanwick in 1967, for example, four husbands had to join them for the worship meeting.[80] In more recent decades, though, surveys have indicated gradual change in a substantial proportion of assemblies. In 1978, 20% of assemblies responding allowed women to take part audibly at the Breaking of Bread, and 36% allowed them to pray at the Prayer Meeting. In 1988, only 4% allowed women to teach, but by 1998 the figure was 13%; in the latter year, 53% of assemblies allowed

[74] In Watson (ed.), *The Church*, 214.

[75] [A.M.S. Gooding], 'Editorial review, "The Brethren"', *AT* 100 (March-April 1969), 41.

[76] [A.M.S. Gooding], 'A New Testament Commentary', *AT* 109 (September-October 1970), 113.

[77] J. A[nderson]., 'Editorial Searchlight', *BM* 89 (1979), 65.

[78] See also Olive Rogers, 'The Role of Women in the Church', *JCBRF* 26 (September 1974), 6-12; reprinted in Ellis and Gasque (eds.), *In God's Community*, and (slightly updated) in *JCBRF* 33 (1983), 57-68.

[79] *JCBRF* 7 (February 1965), 25.

[80] Joyce K. Stunt, 'A Little Space', *H* 46 (1967), 185.

women to participate audibly in the main meetings, but only 16% to give thanks for the bread and wine. In all cases, the larger an assembly, the more likely it was to allow greater freedom for women to participate. As for the positions held by women, in 1988, 1% allowed them to serve as elders, 13% as deacons, and 30% on church committees; by 1998 the figures were 1%, 22%, and 48% respectively, with 21% allowing them to serve on leadership committees.[81] An early example of a woman in full-time work was Anne Russell, commended from a Scottish assembly to work at Newtownards in Ulster in what amounted to the role of a deaconess.[82] The first woman to be appointed in her own right as a Counties evangelist joined their ranks in the 1990s.[83] It is possible that the new, more pragmatic, approach to leadership appointments may have made it easier for some who would object on biblical grounds to the appointment of women as elders, to accept their involvement in leadership. Some congregations could therefore open a wide range of roles and offices to women, but under overall male eldership.[84]

21.5 Changing Patterns of Evangelism

The foreword to the 1952 annual report for Counties Evangelistic Work commented on the far-reaching social change occurring in the villages which had been its traditional focus of activity:

> The widespread expansion of bus services and all forms of transport has brought the town and village much closer together, the wireless is found in nearly every home, and now the television is fast becoming commonplace where electricity is available – the Travelling Library, the visiting Welfare Unit, the Mobile Cinema, all these have contributed to an entirely new outlook, a sophistication unknown to previous generations of country folk, and a corresponding disinclination to want anything to do with either the Evangelist or his message.[85]

Such factors, along with the exponential rise in car ownership, have provided competing attractions and made it harder for the evangelist to gain an audience. Partly in response to this, the post-war decades have seen radical change in the way much evangelism relates to the community around the assembly, manifest in the introduction of different types of activity. The desire for change was fuelled by the frustration of many returning servicemen, who had been used to exercising responsibility and engaging in vigorous evangelism, as is evident from several articles in *The Harvester* during the late 1940s.[86] Overall, for all but the most traditional assemblies, outreach has become less aggressive and confrontational, with evangelism being seen as a longer-term process which includes the patient building of contacts in the community through such means as contact groups for parents and toddlers. Such activities, along with expressions of social concern such as lunch clubs for the elderly, are now somewhat more likely to be seen as

---

[81] Brierley et al., *Brethren*, 36, 45; Brown, *Whatever Happened*, 63, 69-71.

[82] Anne Russell, 'A Woman in the Work', *H* 55 (1976), 268-70; another such worker (unidentified) was referred to in Graham D. Brown, 'How Can We Improve Our Evangelism? – Deductions from a survey of assemblies', *JCBRF* 21 (May 1971), 52.

[83] Mills, *Story*, 8, 50.

[84] E.g. (in 1994) Cholmeley Evangelical Church (Pauline Summerton, 'Cholmeley', 11).

[85] Counties Evangelistic Work Annual Report, 1952, 4.

[86] E.g. Wing-Commander R.G. Mainwaring, 'Facing the Problems of 1946', *H* 23 (1946), 3-4.

having a value in themselves, quite apart from any potential for evangelistic conversations. Concern to spread the gospel by whatever means possible has helped to reconcile some to the adoption of innovative methods, as we shall see.

The gospel march, here under way in a 1950s Scottish village, was as radical once as other methods are now

21.5.1 What Happened to the Gospel Service?

In examining Open Brethren evangelism, we must begin by exploring what has happened to the Gospel service. The early 1940s debate about this meeting continued, although there was a surprising degree of resistance to suggestions for change. It was acknowledged that improvements were needed; Tatford pointed to the need for consideration of such matters as the preacher, the venue, the furniture, the lack of effort to get folk along, and the lack of action by many members.[87] One English assembly (whose identity will not be revealed) acknowledged that 'It was possible that as this meeting had been conducted on similar lines for the last century the time had come for certain changes to be made.' But relatively few questioned the rationale of the concept itself. Even recent surveys have indicated that while many assemblies acknowledge that the Family service is far more effective than the Gospel service, they are slow to abandon the latter, an indication of the hold exercised by assembly tradition. Some assemblies, though, have repackaged the evening Gospel service as a Family service, and a larger number have begun to serve tea beforehand.

However, from the 1960s many assemblies also introduced Family services. In some respects this paralleled changes in Anglican and Free Church patterns of worship, but in the 1950s and 1960s Open Brethren were also inspired by the example of North American assemblies, a proportion of which had replaced their Gospel services with a highly-successful Sunday Morning 'Family Bible Hour'. One example was Mitchley Hill Chapel, located in the dormitory suburb of Sanderstead in Surrey. Founded in 1957, they were able to start from scratch rather than inheriting a pattern of activities. Enquiry established 11 a.m. as the time for maximum church attendance locally, so they arranged a Family Service then, holding the Breaking of Bread before or after. Topics for the services were planned in advance, as were most of those for the evening Bible teaching sessions (which

---

[87] F.A. Tatford, 'What is Wrong with our Gospel Meetings?', *H* 31 (1952), 27.

were aimed mainly at Christians).[88] A few years earlier, the small assembly at Starcross in Devon had found that a new focus on reaching families helped to increase their Gospel meeting attendance from eight to ten believers to around seventy, over half of whom were unsaved.[89] By the mid-1990s, with the widespread breakdown in family life and the consequent negative image of 'family' held by a number of people, as well as the increasing proportion of single people in the population, a few congregations were beginning to move away from the stress on Family services.[90] A very small number have been attracted by such concepts as the 'Seeker Service' developed by Willow Creek in the United States.

Other experiments were also tried. In 1947, Albert Hall, Shawlands, in Glasgow, introduced radical alterations to the format of their Gospel services. Invitation cards were given out in the road outside, and conversations struck up. The meeting (at 7.30 p.m, which itself would be a radical enough change for many!) was in two parts, the first being devoted to singing, and the second to a twenty-minute gospel message, with refreshments in the interval. By such means they succeeded in attracting about forty outsiders each week, mostly aged seventeen to twenty-five, a contrast with their previous lack of success.[91] Similar approaches were tried elsewhere, almost always on a Sunday evening, and often following, rather than replacing, the regular Gospel service. However, the focus was still on bringing people in rather than going out to them, and the spread of television and car ownership was to bring a fairly speedy end to many such ventures.

Even *The Believer's Magazine* was willing to print articles advocating change. During 1964, an Ayrshire headteacher, W.K. Morrison, acknowledged the value of some of the new approaches, such as introducing radical changes in the format and timing of the Gospel meeting. 'Our message is unchanged and unchangeable, but if the methods appropriate to past decades no longer touch the people, we must think vigorously and be prepared to make new approaches.'[92] More strikingly, he pointed out that according to 1 Corinthians 14, unsaved people were present at the Breaking of Bread; he suggested inviting them to witness it, arguing that missionary experience had shown it to be a powerful witness.[93] In 1986 another Scottish writer made a similar point, arguing that the early church had but one meeting, at which many unsaved would have been present, and which included breaking bread, in his view a wonderful explanation of the gospel.[94]

21.5.2 Developments in Work among Children and Young People

During years after the war, Sunday Schools continued to be highly popular, and it was not unknown for an assembly to be founded as a result of such an outreach.[95] Children's work

---

[88] F.G. Timmins, 'New lamps for old', *W* 90 (1960), 14-15; cf. *PS* 9 (1957-8), 157.

[89] *H* 28 (1951), 110.

[90] Batchelor (ed.), *Don't Muzzle the Ox*, 91.

[91] David Kaye, 'New Tactics for Sunday Evening', *H* 25 (1948), 5, 7.

[92] W.K. Morrison, 'Christians of the Sixties. 2. Bringing the Gospel to the people', *BM* 74 (1964), 121.

[93] W.K. Morrison, 'Christians of the Sixties. 3. The Life of a local church', *BM* 74 (1964), 147-50, 132.

[94] Ken H. Matier, 'The Breaking of Bread', *PS* 37 (1986), 133.

[95] E.g. Headington, Oxford (1949); Harryville, Ballymena (1950); Hamworthy, Dorset (1953); Beacon Hall, Loughborough (1954); Goodwood Hall, Leicester, and Pheasey, Birmingham (both 1955);

has continued to be the main focus of the outreach of many assemblies, although it was no longer so easy to reach the adults through the children. One report of outreach commented that 'As in so many places, work amongst the adults was as disappointing as that among the children was encouraging.'[96] Not only was it easier; it also appeared to be more fruitful: Tom Rees, whose campaigns were widely supported by Open Brethren, found that 75% of believers in Britain had been converted before the age of fourteen, and that only 5% were converted after reaching twenty-one.[97] As late as 1960, an estimated 18,000 children attended Open Brethren Sunday Schools in the London area.[98]

Other assemblies have linked their youth work with organisations such as Campaigners and Covenanters; the latter in particular has proved quite popular, even among traditional assemblies, with Covenanter groups in 29% of those responding to the 1978 survey.[99] The first Every Boys' Rally (an import from New Zealand, where they were widely adopted) in Britain was commenced at Victoria Hall, Belfast, in 1958. By 1978, there were twenty-seven Every Boys' or Girls' Rallies in Northern Ireland,[100] where their use of uniform and evangelistic orientation has proved highly attractive. The work's aims are twofold: to lead children to a personal faith in Christ and help them grow spiritually; and 'To teach them how to develop a strong Christian character through a balanced spiritual, educational, physical and social programme which will cater for the well-being of the whole person.'[101] The movement never really took root elsewhere, however, and only a handful appeared in England. It earned some local criticism, the editor of *Assembly Testimony* referring to what he saw as the temptation to resort to new methods in an attempt to remedy evangelistic ineffectiveness rather than engaging in confession and repentance.[102]

More recently, the introduction of legislation relating to health and safety and child protection has complicated things considerably. Articles on these topics have introduced assemblies to the issues and the advisable courses of action.[103] However, a proportion of parents are likely to be reluctant to allow their children to participate in activities where they are not present, which hastens the decline in attendances at children's activities. Since the 1970s, there has also been a noticeable shift in emphasis towards schools work, with a number of full-time evangelists and local believers taking regular lessons and assemblies.

During this period, youth work was probably the source of the greatest proportion of converts in Open Brethren assemblies. Summer youth camps have played a particular role in this, harvesting from the seed sown during the year in assembly Bible classes. Such camps had begun before the war, but mushroomed in popularity in England and Scotland during the late 1940s; during 1946, several articles appeared in *The Harvester* on youth

---

Bethany, Cheltenham (1957); Llanrumney, Cardiff; Newbold, Chesterfield; and Cloughfern, Newtownabbey (all 1958).

[96] *PS* 5 (1952-3), 64.

[97] 'WW', *W* 82 (1952), 138.

[98] Anon., 'Sunday School Teachers' Convention', *W* 90 (1960), 445.

[99] Brown and Mills, *"Brethren" Today*, 16.

[100] *H* 45 (1966), 141; *W* 108 (1978), 382.

[101] Anon., 'Ministires [*sic*], Woodford Gospel Assembly', <www.woodfordgospelassembly.org>, accessed 27 March 2005.

[102] W. Bunting, 'Modern Methods', *AT* 43 (September-October 1959), 2, 4.

[103] E.g. Steve Buckeridge, 'Safe from Harm', *PS* 58 (2003), 10-11.

camps, outlining the methods of work and reporting blessing seen.[104] They have usually been organised on a regional or county basis, and some assemblies have held their own camps. A number of camps have purchased their own grounds and property.

Some assemblies also opened youth clubs on similar lines to those run by local education authorities, a development which had its roots in government thinking during the war years. Since 1970, a number of assemblies have appointed full-time or part-time youth workers. Many were apprehensive about going down the youth club road, however; apart from the possibility of damage to property and concerns that the gospel would not be soundly proclaimed, there were apprehensions about ceding assembly autonomy to government control.

In connection with youth work, some assemblies have experimented with methods of communication which were a long way from traditional gospel preaching, but which were seen as more suited to the younger generation. In 1965 Cholmeley Hall reported holding a 'Beat Service', including songs, testimonies and short messages, which saw some conversions. The reporter, evidently not one of the 'beat generation', commented,

> It is appreciated that this type of approach is naturally unacceptable to many friends who normally attend a Sunday evening service, but it should be borne in mind that this is an idiom which has appeal to the modern teenager. They listen attentively to plain speaking when up-to-date word forms are used and are able to absorb the message from the loud cacophony, which by some is called music.[105]

The same assembly's innovative approach was evident again in the 1980s, with multi-media presentations including such things as drama and rap music, 'all just about consistent with the spirit of the nineteenth-century gospel meeting',[106] a verdict which the more conservative would have challenged! But youth events had been held for most of the century, and continued to take place in new guises. In 1966, workers in Bristol found that existing Saturday evening united ministry meetings could not cater for teenagers and commenced evangelistic rallies as well as celebration meetings; the latter were to prove a means whereby young people from assemblies were exposed to a more charismatic style of worship.[107]

It is interesting to note that some of those with a vision for youth work have themselves been elderly. The chapter on the topic in *The Church* was contributed by Rendle Short, who was by then approaching seventy but still deeply interested in student work; likewise W.T. Stunt (1909-78), one of the Editors at Echoes of Service, appears to have been in his sixties when he persuaded fellow-trustees of the Western Counties and South Wales Evangelization Trust 'to conduct gospel work at pop festivals such as Twerton and Shepton Mallet. He participated personally and was seen until the early hours of the mornings serving tea and talking about the Saviour to drug addicts and drop-outs.'[108]

---

[104] For an account of one such camp, see David Porter, *So much more: the story of over forty years camping with the Merseyside Christian Youth Camps* ([Kirkby]: Merseyside Assemblies Youth Camps Trust, [1986]).

[105] *W* 95 (1965), 430.

[106] Pauline Summerton, 'Cholmeley', 10.

[107] Linton and Linton, '*I Will Build my Church*', 259-60.

[108] Anderson, *They Finished their Course*, 151.

21.5.3 New Methods of Outreach

With the decline of the traditional tent campaign evangelists have adopted different methods. Tents became frequent targets for vandals and arsonists; several were lost in 1968-9, followed by others at Lancing (Sussex) in 1973 and Cardiff the following year.[109] The Ayrshire Gospel Outreach wooden tent was likewise destroyed by vandals in 1976.[110] The Lancashire tent report for 1980-1 recorded that during the Moss Side riots in Manchester, a hostile crowd gathered round the tent at Oldham, intending to burn it down, but that a strong police presence prevented this.[111] These problems, coupled with the cost of insurance and the red tape involved in securing local authority approval, have been another factor in the move away from tent campaigns. Portable wooden halls continued to be used (and new ones constructed) in northern areas, but a sign of the times was provided by a reference to a 'Gospel Portakabin' in Scotland.[112] By the 1960s, many evangelists were using other methods such as films and squashes. Door-to-door work has continued (since people are no longer so willing to come to meetings), and even increased in popularity between 1978 and 1988.[113] Working in pairs, whilst still the norm in Northern Ireland and frequent in Scotland, has thrown up a new problem: two evangelists working in Northamptonshire were surprised to discover in 2001 that people on the estate thought that they must be a homosexual couple.[114]

From the 1960s, Open Brethren had realised and exploited the potential of agricultural shows in England and the Irish Republic; these offered a convenient means of contacting families who lived in isolated settings, and provided a shop-window for Postal Sunday School courses. As part of this outreach, exhibitions were devised, which could also be used in other contexts.[115] Some were intended for use by assemblies in a particular area, such as that devised by Brethren in Ayrshire. Counties maintained a travelling Bible exhibition from 1985-2001, which has been retired. In its place is 'GSUS Live', a mobile classroom (now joined by a second) which tours schools, introducing students to the Christian faith through the exploration of such themes as forgiveness, fear, and loneliness. This is quite a change, when one realises that horse-drawn caravans were being used in West Sussex and Kent as late as 1951.[116]

Whilst many Brethren have remained disapproving of the cinema, films have been widely used in outreach. The 'Fact and Faith' films, produced by Moody Bible Institute in Chicago, appeared in Britain during the late 1940s and continued to be used for several decades.[117] Soon after, Counties was encouraged by John Laing to take its first halting steps in the use of films shot on location during evangelistic campaigns for deputation meetings. By the late 1950s, films were being heavily used for evangelistic and deputation purposes, and nowadays many evangelists use films or film clips in their work. American evangelistic films such as 'Thief in the Night' and 'The Sound of the

---

[109] *W* 103 (1973), 282; 104 (1974), 383.

[110] Anon., 'Ayrshire Gospel Outreach', <ayrshiregospeloutreach.org.uk>, accessed 3 April 2005

[111] CBA Box 25.

[112] 'LF', *BM* 91 (1981), 271.

[113] Brierley et al., *Brethren*, 38.

[114] *BM* 111 (2001), 285.

[115] E.g. in the Irish Republic (*PS* 23 (1972), 95, 128).

[116] Executive Oversight minutes, 27 February 1951; although not part of Counties, the Yorkshire assemblies did not stop using a horse-drawn caravan until 1957 (Beaumont, *Telling Yorkshire*, 8).

[117] Tatford welcomed them warmly in 'FEC', *H* 27 (1948), 13.

Trumpet' presented a form of Brethren eschatology to quite considerable audiences during the 1970s and 1980s, a technologically up-to-date counterpart to gospel sermons which pandered to the fear of being left behind at the rapture. However, some expressed second thoughts about the medium: Tom Rees showed the first gospel film in Britain in 1947, but came to the opinion that they pandered to the appetite for entertainment. In his opinion, films could lead people into cinema addiction and would damage the assembly's midweek meetings.[118]

GSUS Live, a mobile classroom used by Counties evangelists in schools work

Evangelistic Mobile Units were introduced immediately after the war: these were vans equipped with amplification equipment, which could transport groups of workers to venues for open-air meetings. The first was introduced by assemblies in south-west London, and went on the road in 1947. Other areas in and around London followed suit in subsequent years. As late as 1975, the south-west London unit was operating six nights a week, and twice a year evangelistic rallies were held in Trafalgar Square followed by report meetings in a local church. However, by the 1970s, the operators were struggling to find sufficient people to man it, and a letter from a veteran worker, William Baigent, described it as 'the Cinderella of assembly witness'.[119] Nevertheless, the Bristol unit was still functioning in 1982.[120] Elsewhere, village work continued until at least 1980 around Manchester and in Devon.[121]

Brethren services began to be heard on the BBC's regional and national radio networks after the war, the fruit of some years' persistent lobbying by W.H. Clare; in 1967 he informed *The Witness* that nearly sixty services had so far been broadcast.[122] Usually a Gospel Service or selection of hymns was broadcast, but on occasion listeners were able to tune into the Breaking of Bread. Evangelists such as Murphy, Hutchings, and Saunders could not use the BBC for their programmes, so they turned to offshore or overseas

[118] T.B. Rees, 'Go Steady on those Films!', *H* 34 (1955), 164.

[119] Robert D. Griffiths, 'Up-to-Date Evangelism', *H* 23 (1946), 75; Leslie James, 'The South West Mobile Unit', *H* 54 (1975), 8-11; letter in *H* 54 (1975), 105.

[120] Linton and Linton, *'I Will Build My Church'*, 102.

[121] Cf. *PS* 31 (1980), 92; *PS* 32 (1981), 166 respectively.

[122] *W* 97 (1967), 149.

stations such as Manx Radio and Trans-World Radio. Some local groups also constructed their own recording studios. For example, in the mid-1960s one was built at Ebenezer, Filton Avenue, Bristol, to record programmes for missionary stations; it was run by Don Feltham, who later moved to Eastbourne and set up ECHO Recordings.[123]

Open-air work using a Mobile Unit, Douglas, Lanarkshire, 1965

Brethren were also reaching out to those on the margins of society. In 1976, *The Believer's Magazine* reported a number of Scottish prisons and detention centres where Brethren were holding Bible studies and evangelistic meetings.[124] A more recent report on work in Barlinnie Prison states that this began over eighty years ago as an outreach of the Bible Training Institute in Glasgow; weekly Bible classes were conducted with the support of successive governors and chaplains, and although attendance was now much smaller due to the provision of other leisure activities, quite a number have been converted.[125]

Edwin Lewis preaching during a radio broadcast from Victory Gospel Hall, Kingstanding, Birmingham, in 1950

---

[123] *H* 43 (1964), 17.

[124] 'LF', *BM* 86 (1976), 367.

[125] Gordon Haxton, 'Into All The World: Barlinnie Prison, Glasgow – Bible Class', *BM* 113 (2003), 150.

21.5.4 Growth and Change in Regional Work

Counties Evangelistic Work has played an increasingly significant role during this period, training and resourcing assemblies for outreach as well as channelling support for a team of evangelists. Yet just after the war there were proposals to wind up the work.[126] This outcome was averted, and in 1947 it was agreed to amalgamate the oversights of South-Eastern Counties, Eastern Counties, and Counties into one.[127] Gradually other areas were incorporated: Northamptonshire and Wiltshire by 1961, the Western Counties in 1963, and Gloucestershire and Monmouthshire by the end of the decade. However, securing adequate backing from assemblies continued to be a headache. In 1955, a circular was sent to overseeing brethren throughout the area served by Counties seeking more systematic financial support, which indicated that each year about 35-40% of assemblies in this area were sending gifts. Interest did rise during succeeding years: attendance at the annual meetings jumped from about 1,100 in the early 1950s to 3,000 in 1958 with their move to Westminster Central Hall, a level which was maintained into the mid-1960s. Even as late as 1981, about 2,000 were present at the annual meeting, which by this point included seminars as well as report meetings.[128] Regional fellowships have brought churches together in support of their local evangelist, and in some areas serve as bearers of a sense of common identity for Brethren churches. However, there are indications that more recently support has been affected by the identity crisis which has led to many progressive churches being reluctant to identify themselves any longer as Brethren, and therefore ceasing to support Counties (even though not all its evangelists are Brethren). Furthermore, although Counties itself is flourishing, its support base among assemblies is declining as the Open Brethren community shrinks. Other problems noted in 1978 included controversies in assemblies hindering effective outreach and resulting in evangelists being left to work on their own, and the lack of assembly interest in some areas in nurturing new converts which resulted in their settling in other churches.[129] In compensation, there has been a widening of both the support base and the scope of the work: most Counties evangelists have been willing to engage in interdenominational work; during Billy Graham's visits in 1984-5, fourteen staff and evangelists worked with Mission England; such activity has contributed to their securing a higher profile among non-Brethren Evangelical churches.[130]

The number of workers listed in Counties publicity has increased steadily: in 1944 there were eight, eleven in 1949, seventeen in 1959, twenty-one in 1968, and in 2002 there were twenty-six couples and two single people, as well as retired and associate evangelists. The age profile appears to have changed as well; in 1947, one worker was to be informed that 'present conditions called for younger brethren',[131] and a significant proportion of workers now appear to belong to the under-forty age group. The days of long service such as that given by S.K. Glen, who evangelised Essex from 1905-60, are gone.

---

[126] Coad, *Laing*, 193.

[127] Counties Evangelistic Work, General Oversight minutes, 1 April 1947.

[128] 'LF', *BM* 91 (1981), 368; *H*, December 1981, 19.

[129] Report on Counties for a consultation of Brethren agencies, 17 June 1978 (CBA Box 148(1)).

[130] Mills, *Story*, 9; assemblies provided a relatively high proportion of the full-time evangelists on which Mission England could draw.

[131] Counties Evangelistic Work, Executive Oversight minutes, 11 November 1947.

The continuing emergence of new evangelists has been paralleled elsewhere: in 1975, *The Believer's Magazine* reported that during the previous twelve years about two dozen younger men had been commended from Scottish assemblies to full-time service at home, which at that point would usually have been evangelistic work.[132] Similar agencies have also emerged, and a more co-ordinated approach to the work became widespread. The Yorkshire work experienced a new lease of life from 1960, when it began a five-year programme to reach every part of the county. This included using students during the summer vacations under direction of a younger evangelist, and postal work with Postal Sunday School and Emmaus courses.[133] The Lancashire Gospel Tent work began in 1948, and Northern Counties Outreach in 1973. North of the Border, about 170 elders met in February 1965 to consider whether to establish a work on the Counties pattern.[134] The result was the founding of the Scottish Counties Evangelistic Movement, building on activity which had been going on in the Borders since the early 1960s, in an attempt to reach rural Scotland and help small assemblies.[135] More recently, the Gospel Outreach Trust was founded to reach areas in Scotland without assemblies.[136]

In recent years, an awareness of the inadequacy of short-term campaigns has meant that Counties evangelists have been encouraged to spend a proportion of their time working alongside (or planting) a local church; a number of new fellowships have been planted as a result, usually in small towns or suburbs. Whereas earlier evangelists had frequently lived elsewhere and only come to their area for the summer season, now workers were asked to settle in their 'patch' and develop links with churches and other bodies. The changing strategy was outlined by its General Secretary, Brian Mills, in 1979. It focused on church planting in spiritually-deprived areas. By living in an area, an evangelist could develop a long-term strategy based on a sound understanding of the local situation and build relationships with Christian and non-Christian bodies. He instanced the work of Victor Jack, who had been the evangelist in Suffolk for fifteen years, which included missions, but also the writing of suitable literature, and the provision of relevant teaching and training. As a result, a dozen people from Suffolk had gone overseas as missionaries and three were working with Counties, from an area which had seen nobody becoming a full-time worker for many years.[137] Similarly, a number of evangelists put down roots in new housing areas around Bristol during the 1970s, identifying with the community and making a long-term commitment to it.[138]

Other spin-off activities have been developed as adjuncts to the work of evangelism. In 1975 Victor Jack took over Sizewell Hall in Suffolk as a conference centre, and in 1979 David Iliffe founded the Sussex-based organisation Children Worldwide, which resources children's and youth workers as well as running camps and conferences. However, Counties still operates on the same principles of not exercising control over evangelists' movements or guaranteeing them an income.

---

[132] J. A[nderson]., 'Editorial', *BM* 85 (1975), 65.

[133] Beaumont, *Telling Yorkshire*, 10-12.

[134] Counties Evangelistic Work, Executive Oversight minutes, 2 February 1965.

[135] See Dickson, *Brethren in Scotland*, 335-6.

[136] J. Paterson, Jr, 'Gospel Work Nearer Home', *BM* 110 (2000), 182-4.

[137] Brian Mills, 'Evangelizing Rural Parts', *H* 58 (1979), 145-8; cf. *idem, Story*, 32-3.

[138] Robert Scott-Cook, 'Evangelism by the Local Church', *H* 58 (1979), 21-3, 20.

21.5.5 Attitudes to Mass Evangelism

A number of mass evangelists continued to be active among Open Brethren. With the ending of the war, city-wide tent missions recommenced in Cardiff and elsewhere. The former boxer and socialist Stan Ford (1920-91) conducted such missions from the end of the war until the early 1980s; he also found a response among students at Cambridge during the 1960s.[139] Hedley Murphy (1928-85) from Belfast conducted large-scale missions in Northern Ireland and Scotland, as well as producing a radio programme, the 'Irish Gospel Hour'; some of his methods, and the interdenominational support which he attracted, earned him criticism from more separatist brethren.[140] Better-known was Eric Hutchings (1910-82), a Manchester lawyer who, as a worker with British Youth For Christ, was responsible for Billy Graham's first visit to Britain in 1946; in 1952, he founded his own organisation, the 'Hour of Revival Association', specialising in large-scale crusades (emphasising the need for careful spiritual preparation) and radio broadcasts.[141] But the best-known was probably Dick Saunders; he joined Counties Evangelistic Work in 1960 from the Open-Air Mission, and in the late 1960s was recognised as its first national evangelist. His 'Way to Life' campaigns attracted support from all types of Evangelical church. In 1967, Peter Brandon left Counties amicably because he felt called to city and town crusades, but Saunders, seeking their approval of his wider vision (his work had been subject to questioning), asked whether they should change their focus to include this type of activity. He was approved as an evangelist with a roving commission, not restricted to one area, although it was recognised that some delicate issues might arise when he conducted missions in areas where other Counties evangelists were active.[142]

Some tension was evident between advocates of mass evangelism in special campaigns and those who preferred to emphasise the ongoing work of individual and assembly outreach. Writing in *The Harvester* during 1947, Tom Rees, whose Royal Albert Hall campaigns attracted vast crowds, defended it, while Andrew Borland saw united assembly evangelism as much better, because converts could be taught church truth.[143] There was recurrent criticism of failure to adhere to biblical principles in such gatherings: clergy were invited to sit on the platform and to take part, women assumed public roles (singing solos and giving testimonies), and collections were taken from the unconverted. Furthermore, converts were not always directed to assemblies, and aspects of fundamental teaching such as baptism were often omitted.[144] Even Montague Goodman, who would become an outspoken supporter of Billy Graham, cautioned in 1949 against over-estimating the worth of mass evangelism, which often resulted in decisions rather than converts.[145]

---

[139] On Ford, see *BM* 101 (1991), 254; Plant, *They Finished their Course in the 90s*, 77-81.

[140] On Murphy, see Anderson, *They Finished their Course in the 80's*, 119-22; Hedley G. Murphy, *"Under His Wings"* [Belfast: author, 1969].

[141] On Hutchings, see Anderson, *They Finished their Course in the 80's*, 87-9; *H*, November 1982, 21-2; J. Erskine Tuck, *Your Master Proclaim: the story of the Eric Hutchings evangelist crusades, and the Hour of Revival Association* (London: Oliphants, 1968).

[142] Counties Evangelistic Work, General Oversight minutes, 14 August 1967.

[143] Thomas B. Rees, 'Mass Evangelism', *H* 24 (1947), 26, 28; Andrew Borland, 'Personal Evangelism', *H* 24 (1947), 90.

[144] E.g. J. A[nderson]., *BM* 87 (1977), 321.

[145] In Watson (ed.), *The Church*, 145-6.

Successful local campaigns were still being reported, principally during the 1950s, and a 'no frills' campaign by two evangelists at Prestwick in 1974, which lasted for seven weeks, saw at least forty professions, including eighteen from a local school.[146] However, in 2000 one Scottish writer drew attention to a marked decrease in special evangelistic campaigns during the last ten to fifteen years in some areas of the UK, and in their length from an average six weeks in the 1960s and early 1970s to two or three weeks.[147] It is noticeable from reports that even in Northern Ireland evangelists are commenting more frequently on the lack of interest among unsaved people, and thus their series of meetings are probably becoming shorter as well.

But what was the result of all this activity? In the following chapter, we shall examine the statistics and attempt some analysis of the movement's changing fortunes. Before doing so, however, it is worth highlighting one possible missed opportunity. The 1950s were, in religious terms, quite a conservative decade. They may be seen as the decade of 'mere Christianity', in which lay apologists for the Christian faith, such as C.S. Lewis, enjoyed considerable attention from the media and the churches. The idea of focusing on a presentation of the basic truths of the Christian faith is one which might have been expected to appeal to Open Brethren as providing a backdrop for more directly evangelistic preaching, but they do not appear to have produced many speakers of this type. This may possibly indicate a weakness in the movement's grasp of the truth and its presentation, an unduly narrow conception of the Christian message, or a preoccupation with internal concerns. Perhaps this sheds some light on complaints about the lack of teaching in Gospel Meetings which were voiced during the 1950s and 1960s. In recent years, however, many more have become aware that it is no longer possible to assume even the most basic knowledge of the facts of Christianity, and some have responded to this in their outreach. Such sensitivity will become increasingly necessary in a pluralist setting which tends to question any claim to absolute truth.

---

[146] *PS* 25 (1974), 93-5.
[147] Stephen Grant, 'Whatever happened to the Gospel Campaign (1)', *BM* 110 (2000), 232-3.

CHAPTER 22

Decline – and Growth?

In an article sparked off by the work of revising the list of Open Brethren assemblies which he publishes, Roy Hill asks 'What is happening to UK Assemblies?'[1] By the end of 2003, he says, the number had declined to 705 in England, 195 in Scotland, 173 in Northern Ireland, and 75 in Wales, with an estimated 40,000 members. Provisional figures for 2005 indicate a further fall, to 682, 204, 171, and 74 respectively.[2] In this chapter we attempt to answer the question which Hill poses, basing the discussion as far as possible on database analysis.

22.1 The Overall Picture

Immediately after the war, the movement appeared prosperous, growing, and focused on outreach. Freedom from the restrictions of wartime, along with the enthusiasm of returning ex-servicemen, meant that many assemblies were quick to mount evangelistic campaigns.[3] New halls were being opened (some replacing war-damaged premises)[4] and large-scale missions appeared to be bringing results, although they tended to result in the addition of converts to existing assemblies rather the formation of new ones, something of a contrast with the pre-war period.[5] Evangelism was in the air generally, and in 1945 the Church of England issued a report on the subject, *Towards the Conversion of England*. However, the post-war surge did not reach as high as that after the First World War,[6] and when the tide receded again, it went further out.

The figures in Appendix IV show that throughout this period there was a net loss of assemblies in Scotland, something which did not become evident in England in the 1960s and Wales in the 1980s. By contrast, most other wholly Evangelical denominations held their own or increased during the 1970s and 1980s.[7] More encouragingly, the period saw

---

[1] *BM* 114 (2004), 107-9.

[2] Roy Hill to the author, 17 April 2005.

[3] Cf. Linton and Linton, '*I Will Build my Church*', 85.

[4] From the 1930s onwards, a number were built to standard designs produced by Laing; cf. S. Greenwood, 'Church Halls', 1960[2] (CBA 146(17)). This booklet of plans (based on actual examples) and specifications was initiated by Laing. Some local histories refer to gifts received from him during the 1960s for assembly building and furnishing.

[5] I have only traced twenty-four assemblies which owe their formation primarily to special campaigns during this period, as against 151 which resulted from longer-term outreach (comparative figures for 1914-45 were 126 and 151); there were none in Northern Ireland, in spite of the popularity of such campaigns there.

[6] Harold Rowdon, in *idem* (ed.), *Strengthening, Growth and Planting*, 135.

[7] Brierley et al., *Brethren*, 71. Another group which has declined is the Strict Baptists, and it would be worth exploring possible parallels; since they tended to be concentrated in different areas from Brethren (with the exception of Suffolk and London), decline may in part be related to internal factors such as each group's strong attachment to particular cultural forms.

a net increase in the numbers of assemblies in both Northern Ireland and the Irish Republic.

Table 22.1: Total numbers of new and disappearing assemblies by decade, 1945-2004[8] (numbers of assemblies closed are shown in brackets)

	England	Scotland	Wales	N. Ireland	Republic of Ireland	Total
1945-54	99 (66)	23 (31)	7 (4)	8 (4)	3 (6)	140 (111)
1955-64	101 (92)	14 (39)	7 (7)	1 (8)	– (–)	123 (146)
1965-74	72 (82)	10 (38)	11 (4)	2 (2)	4 (4)	99 (130)
1975-84	31 (195)	10 (36)	4 (13)	8 (8)	– (1)	53 (253)
1985-94	59 (116)	9 (24)	6 (15)	5 (3)	12 (4)	91 (162)
1995-2004	25 (147)	– (31)	1 (11)	5 (4)	8 (7)	39 (200)
Total	387 (698)	66 (199)	36 (54)	29 (29)	27 (22)	545 (1002)

The high numbers of new assemblies, and even higher incidence of closures, should be seen in the light of the total number of assemblies as shown in Appendix IV. Since there was a total of 1,728 assemblies in 1951, it is evident that there is a relatively high turnover rate of Open Brethren gatherings, and detailed analysis indicates that many had a short life, perhaps appearing in only one or two address lists.

With hindsight, it seems that much of the apparent growth was related to large-scale migration from the inner cities (which saw very few new assemblies[9]) to the new suburban estates. It was transfer growth rather than conversion growth, and reflected the upward social mobility of many members; moreover, it was members transferring between churches of the same denomination rather than transferring between denominations.[10] For example, a large London overspill estate was built at Billericay, Essex, during the late 1950s, to which many children from the Sunday School at Salway Hall, Woodford, moved. The Sunday School's superintendent visited the estate, and found a small group of believers meeting for prayer and Bible study; together with the Woodford believers they began outreach which resulted in the forming of a new assembly a few years later.[11] Over three million houses were built between 1951 and 1964,[12] so it is not surprising that

---

[8] For the basis of calculation, see p. 287.

[9] The only exceptions I have traced are St Andrew's, Plaistow, London (by the early 1990s), and Viewpark, Uddingston, Glasgow (1992).

[10] Neil Summerton to the author, 29 December 2004.

[11] Anon., Sunnymede Chapel [Billericay] Opening Thanksgiving Service brochure, 27 November 1971 (CBA Box 36).

[12] Hastings, *English Christianity*, 413.

many new assemblies were planted among them, often the result of outreach by neighbouring congregations.[13] The new towns, which received large numbers of people from urban areas being cleared of slums, also saw assemblies planted,[14] although there was no co-ordinated church-planting strategy with this objective.

The importance of migration as a factor in the appearance of new assemblies is confirmed by the fact that closures in inner-city areas, as well as in the ring of older communities separating the inner cities from the suburbs, paralleled suburban plantings.[15] A review of the 1975 assembly list called attention to the great need of

---

[13] Assemblies planted in suburban areas, almost all on new estates, include Northwood Hills (1948); Chaddesden, Derby (1951); Borehamwood (1952); Paulsgrove, Portsmouth (1954); Belhus Park, South Ockendon (c.1955); West End, Fareham; Hainault; Goodwood Hall, Leicester; and Cranham, Upminster (all 1955); Queen Edith Chapel, Cambridge, and West Moors, Bournemouth (both 1956); Ballysillan and Newtownbreda, Belfast; Bethany Hall, Cheltenham; St Paul's Cray, Orpington; Mitchley Hill Chapel, Sanderstead; and Stockton Heath, Warrington (all 1957); Roseford Hall, Cambridge; Cheshunt; Ingrebourne Chapel, Hornchurch; and Kirkby, Liverpool (all 1959); Highfields, Stafford; and Walcot, Swindon (both 1960); Beacon Heath, Exeter; and Greenfinch Hall, Ipswich (both 1961); Whitleigh, Plymouth (1962); Allesley Park, Coventry; Topsham, Exeter; Tilehurst, Reading; and Wainscott, Rochester (all 1963); Oxgangs, Edinburgh; Bethany, Penarth; Thirlmere Christian Fellowship, St Albans; Ainsdale, Southport; and Sunningdale, Yeovil (all 1964); Rathmines, Dublin (c.1965); Antingham Hall, Norwich (1965); Maghull, Liverpool (1966); New Addington and Fernielea, Aberdeen (both 1967); Martlesham, Ipswich (1960s); Lancaster Hall, Bury St Edmunds (by 1970); Worting, Basingstoke (c.1970); Woodpark, Ayr; Offmore, Kidderminster; and Blenheim Chapel, Maidenhead (all 1970); Milltimber, Aberdeen (1975); North Arbury, Cambridge, and Ballyduff, Newtownabbey (both 1976); Glenwood, Cardiff (1977); Holm Evangelical Church, Inverness (1982); Thornhill, Cardiff (1985); Alderley Edge (c.1990); and Newton Farm, Hereford (1995). Noteworthy is a cluster of new assemblies planted on estates in the Bristol area, at Lawrence Weston (1956), Hanham (1957), Lockleaze (1958), Henbury (1963), and Hartcliffe (1969).

[14] Examples include Roe Green Hall, Hatfield (1951); Laindon, Basildon (by 1952); Harefield Hall, Harlow (1955); Threshold, East Kilbride (1956); Auchmuty, Glenrothes (1956); Ingaway Chapel, Basildon (1961); Oakwood Chapel, Harlow (c.1962); Broadwater Chapel, Stevenage (by 1968); Skelmersdale (c.1971); Westwoodhill, East Kilbride (1973); Netherfield, Milton Keynes (1974); Almondvale, Livingston (1981); Vale Chapel, Runcorn (1983); City Church, Runcorn (1986); and Eastfield, Cumbernauld (1990).

[15] Examples of urban closures include:

London: Higham Hill, Walthamstow (1959); Woodberry Hall, Stamford Hill (after 1959); Beresford Chapel, Denmark Hill (by 1964); Winstanley Road, Battersea (1964); Church Gate Hall, Fulham; and Hargrave Hall, Upper Holloway (both after 1968); Evelyn Hall, Deptford (1969); Kings Highway, Plumstead (after 1970; not the same assembly as that which closed in 1939); and Park House Hall, Kensington (both 1971); Springfield Hall, Tottenham (by 1974); Latimer Hall, East Ham; and Carlton Hall, Kentish Town (both after 1975); King George Street, Greenwich (1978); Church Lane, Charlton (1980); Kenmont Hall, Willesden (1982); Overstone Hall, Hammersmith (1983); Paragon Hall, Hackney; and Bethany Hall, North Kensington (both after 1983); Park Road, Crouch End (by 1986; another plant here closed in 2003); Folkestone Road, Walthamstow (1990); Clapton Hall; Lee Gospel Hall; Cumberland Road, Plaistow; and Wadham Hall, Walthamstow (all after 1991); Parkhill Chapel, Kentish Town (c.1995); and Southcroft Hall, Streatham (after 1995).

Birkenhead: Camden Hall (1961); Milner Hall (1982); Park Hall, Tranmere (1999); and Hope Hall, New Ferry (2000).

Glasgow, evidenced by the fact that there were now fewer than twenty assemblies in the city. 'It always surprises the reviewer to compare our interest in the so-called unreached counties with their population of a few thousands with the hundreds of thousands in our pagan cities where the Lord's work is so visibly declining.'[16] Migration was clearly the major factor at work: in 1978, one observer noted that since 1945, the population of Glasgow had decreased by approximately 400,000, and over a dozen assemblies had closed.[17] For example, the membership of Elim Hall reached a high point during the 1940s, with almost 400 in fellowship, but post-war migration meant that by 1982 it was down to about 100, mostly pensioners, and closure followed in 1991.[18] Likewise, the assembly at Springburn, Glasgow, declined from 343 in 1935 to thirty-six in 2001, due largely to the closure of local railway works and movement to new housing developments on the edge of the city.[19] Other cities offered similar cases. In London, two assemblies which once had 600-700 members declined and closed, King George Street, Greenwich (1978), and Folkestone Road, Walthamstow (1990). Dublin's Merrion Hall saw the assembly move out in the late 1980s, and the building was gutted by fire, but it has been restored and is now a luxury hotel.

New developments were not the only setting in which assemblies emerged. A number continued to be planted in rural areas, which had been the traditional sphere of work for Counties Evangelists.[20] Some longer-established built-up areas also saw plenty of new

---

Birmingham: Digbeth (after 1951); New John Street (after 1959); and Wenman Street (late 1960s).

Bristol: Unity, Midland Road (c.1952); Cumberland Hall, Hotwells (1970); Milton Park (1974); St Nicholas Road and Hartcliffe Road (both after 1991); and Merrywood Hall (after 1995).

Glasgow: City Temple Hall and Garngad (both 1945); Wellcroft Halls (1946); Bridgeton Gospel Hall (1951); Baltic Hall (1958); Balmore Road Gospel Hall (c.1958); Camlachie (1962); Townhead Gospel Hall (1965); Union Hall (1970); Campbellfield Halls, Gallowgate (1974); Wolseley Hall, Oatlands (1975); George Lyon Memorial Hall, Bridgeton (1976); Crosshill (1991); Parkhead Gospel Hall (1992); Clydebank Gospel Hall (1993); Victoria Hall, Clydebank (1995); and Abingdon Hall, Partick (2002).

Leeds: Flaxton Terrace (1961) and Fenton Hall (1969).

Liverpool: Knowsley Road, Bootle (1976); Oxford Hall, Waterloo (1983); and Windsor Hall, Holden Street (after 1983).

Manchester: Ford Street, Salford (1945); Ordsall Lane, Salford (1969); Hope Hall, Ardwick (1974); Bright Hall, Eccles (1984); and Warwick Hall, Hulme (1990).

Tyneside: Alfred Street, Gateshead (after 1960); Wolseley Road, Byker (1973); and Bethany Hall, Newcastle (1994).

[16] J. Anderson, *BM* 85 (1975), 373.

[17] 'LF', *BM* 85 (1978), 175.

[18] Anon., *Elim Hall*, 30; Dickson, *Brethren in Scotland*, 420.

[19] Anon., 'Springburn Gospel Hall, Glasgow 1881-2001', *PS* 59 (2001), 19.

[20] Examples in which Counties evangelists were involved include Gamlingay (1951); Charlton, near Andover (1954); Ely (1968); Staplehurst (1969); Bodmin (1971); Halesworth (1976); Shipdham, near Thetford (1977); and Petworth (late 1970s). Other new rural assemblies include East Yell, Shetland (1946); Kirk Michael, Isle of Man; Torrington; and Witley, Surrey (all 1948); Silverton, Exeter (1950); Sedbury (c.1951); Bramley, Surrey; Papa Stour; and Scalloway, Shetland (all 1951); Clawton (1951, to Holsworthy 1955, then Bridgerule 1960); Sanquhar and Welney (both 1952); Ashbourne (1953); Crowborough (1963); Peebles (1968); Dereham and Gretna (both 1969); Kingussie

assemblies appearing: this was especially evident in counties such as Glamorgan, Hampshire, Lancashire, Staffordshire, and Yorkshire, as well as the areas around Birmingham and Manchester.

Hollingbury Hall, Brighton, closed in the early 1990s and is now semi-derelict

Old-style secessions still occurred on occasion: at Dunchurch in Northamptonshire, 'a group of believers from various denominations were meeting each Thursday evening to break bread. They were concerned about being gathered round our Lord in New Testament simplicity and were also praying for revival. Sectarianism and traditionalism bored them.'[21] A secession from the Methodists at Heywood in Lancashire during 1967, however, was never fully accepted by local assemblies, mainly because women continued to be allowed to speak and pray in meetings,[22] and it eventually associated with the Fellowship of Independent Evangelical Churches (FIEC), in whose lists it appeared from 1969. In Scotland, an evangelistic campaign at Luthermuir in the mid-1970s resulted in the secession from the local Church of Scotland of eight members and the commencement of an assembly amid much local attention, not all of it friendly.[23]

On the other hand, closures were particularly evident, not only in inner cities, but also in industrialised counties which were experiencing economic decline, such as Ayrshire, Glamorgan (in spite of the numbers of new assemblies commenced),[24] Lanarkshire, and Midlothian. A 1985 survey had indicated that 58% of assemblies in Wales had fewer than twenty-five members, half of whom were aged over sixty, a situation which had arisen

---

(1971); Hitcham (1972); Luthermuir, Angus (1975); New Quay, near Aberystwyth (1978); and Kelso (1990). Not all have survived.

[21] *Counties Evangelistic Work Report for 1963*, 13.

[22] Brady and Evans, *Brethren*, 69-70. Acceptance was dependent on the favourable verdict of the Manchester area overseeing brethren meeting together, which was not forthcoming.

[23] *BM* 85 (1975), 271.

[24] Closures in Glamorgan included Pengam, Cardiff (Breaking of Bread ceased 1945); Windsor Hall, Cardiff (after 1946); Barry Docks; Olivet, Neath; Porth; and Clydach, Swansea (all after 1959); Buttrills, Barry; Thornhill and Penyrheol, Caerphilly (all after 1975); Morriston; Pwllgwaun, Pontypridd; Dowlais; Pantyffordd, Neath; Skewen; Ebenezer, Swansea (all after 1983); St Mellons, Cardiff (after 1987); Merthyr Tydfil (1989); Gorseinon (1990); Briton Ferry; Hazel Road, Swansea; Ystradgynlais (all after 1990); Abertridwr and Tonypandy (both 1991); Thornhill, Cardiff (1992); and Bethany, Penlan, Swansea (1995).

largely because of the catastrophic decline of the coal and steel industries. The resulting high proportion of elderly members made many assemblies reluctant to cater for the needs of young families, and many individuals and churches were drifting away from Brethren circles.[25] However, reports in *Precious Seed* from the 1990s onwards indicate that a number of smaller assemblies have been making real efforts to cater for this missing generation, and seeing some success in their outreach.

Quite apart from the migration of members, life in an urban setting could prove very difficult for assemblies. Several noted persistent problems with vandalism, a factor which led in a few cases to complete closure,[26] while one at Cheetham in Manchester had to relocate in 1998 after violent neighbours threatened the safety of female members.[27] Yet it is clear that many have maintained a witness in tough areas; for example, Brook Street, Tottenham, maintained an outreach work for some years on the Broadwater Farm estate, scene of the riots of 1980-1 in which a policeman was killed.[28] Some have even managed to grow in such unpromising soil: that at Greenford doubled in size during the 1990s as it adopted a more charismatic ethos.[29] I am not sure that other Evangelical denominations have done as well in this respect, although it must be conceded that many such assemblies rely on workers commuting from more salubrious locations, a factor which limits their ability to make meaningful contacts in the area around their premises.

Unique challenges were faced by assemblies in Northern Ireland. The obituary columns of *The Witness* and *The Believer's Magazine* recorded several members of assemblies, some of them civilians, who lost their lives in terrorist attacks. Premises were also liable to attack. A member of one Belfast city centre assembly explained that the only meetings at the hall were on Sundays: prayer meetings took place in members' homes, and youth work in suburban premises until it was judged safe for it to return to the centre.[30] The hall in Belfast's Ormeau Road was petrol bombed, vandalised, and bombed again; fear led to declining attendance and a move to a quieter part of the city in 1987.[31] The hall at Drumreagh was twice destroyed by terrorist activity.[32] As late as 1996, the hall at Drumaness was burnt down during a period of heightened sectarian tension.[33] Conferences were sometimes moved from large public venues to Gospel Halls, or were cancelled altogether. However, the province's assemblies had always had a deep commitment to outreach (in the post-war period, it had been claimed that almost all assemblies mounted at least one gospel effort each year[34]), and this continued. Tent work was maintained, even in Belfast, after violence broke out again in the late 1960s; indeed, Hedley Murphy reckoned that Ulster was unusually responsive to the gospel and claimed that, outside

---

[25] Gill Capper, in Rowdon (ed.), *Strengthening, Growth and Planting*, 111-14.

[26] E.g. Drumchapel, Glasgow (1960s); Fishwick Street, Rochdale (1978); and Auchmuty, Glenrothes (2001).

[27] *PS* 53 (1998), 25.

[28] Cf. the reports in *BM* 96 (1986), 89; *PS* 31 (1980), 70.

[29] Rowdon (ed.), *Ten Changing Churches*, 19.

[30] Anon., 'The Women's Page. A Christian and her problem No.6. Teaching in Ulster', *H* 50 (1971), 185.

[31] *BM* 97 (1987), 312.

[32] *BM* 98 (1988), 94.

[33] *BM* 106 (1996), 281.

[34] *PS* 4 (1951-2), 255.

Belfast, attendances at his crusades were not affected by 'the troubles'.[35] And if open-air
meetings were prohibited, Brethren found another way to take the message where people
were by paying for texts to be displayed on buses from the mid-1970s.[36] Even terrorist
prisoners in The Maze, from both sides of the divide, were visited, as were hospitalised
members of the security forces and the Royal Ulster Constabulary, reports of such activity
appearing in *Precious Seed* throughout the 1980s.

The unrest in Ulster has had an unexpected consequence for assemblies. Young people
in the province have become known for devoting themselves to their studies, in part as a
way of escaping psychologically, and perhaps ultimately physically, from events around
them. Their higher educational achievement has meant that many have been exposed to
'liberalising' influences at university and college, and in particular to contact with
believers from other Evangelical traditions. From the concerns expressed in articles on
higher education in periodicals such as *Assembly Testimony*, it may be inferred that some
are not content with their parents' choice of religious allegiance, and are choosing to
move away from assemblies to other churches where there is a greater perceived openness
to the benefits of higher education and an increased sense of cultural relevance. Some have
joined the new charismatic churches, while others have found homes in Baptist
congregations. Bound up with the educational gap opening up between young people and
their parents is the fact that many assemblies in the province were working-class in
origin and so faced an attendant risk of anti-intellectualism. Such a problem is not unique
to Ulster, but is more clearly evident there because of the greater homogeneity and clearer
separatism of the province's assemblies, which so far have remained immune to the
decline affecting the rest of the United Kingdom. This disparity between generations may
be the most serious problem confronting Ulster assemblies, but it does not yet appear to
have been widely recognised. Whether they will adapt in response, or whether they will
see a growing leakage of younger members as has happened elsewhere in the United
Kingdom, is not yet clear.

Elsewhere, assemblies in rural areas have shared in the continuing trend for younger
people to move away in search of employment and be replaced by retirees, although some
must have resulted from, or been sustained by, this influx. By 1995, about a dozen of the
twenty Dorset assemblies had fewer than twenty members.[37] In Devon, the number of
assemblies, which peaked at 108 in 1933, was down to fifty-eight by 2002; the number of
Suffolk assemblies had declined from thirty-nine in 1927 to twenty-two by the same date.
Town assemblies appear to flourish, while nearby village ones struggle because of their
inability to offer an attractive range of activities and the consequent choice of many
young couples and families to commute to a larger church.

Most of the regional portraits provided for the Partnership consultation at Nantwich in
1991 painted a picture of traditional, ageing, and declining assemblies, although with
some growth as the result of youth work. Such was the gloom of the picture that
participants were driven to an extended time of prayer. However, the Irish Republic
presents a very different picture from any of the Nantwich reports. It has seen remarkable
changes since becoming independent. There has been a decline in the influence exercised
in the public arena by the Roman Catholic Church, with a consequent decline in the moral
consensus, and that church has also become more open in its attitude towards other

---

[35] *H* 52 (1973), 37.
[36] *PS* 56 (2001), 44.
[37] *PS* 50 (1995), 127.

churches since the Second Vatican Council (1962-5). The nation's economic resurgence during the 1990s caused it to become known as 'the Celtic Tiger', and resulted in a rapid rise in living standards. Membership of the European Union has strengthened continental links and broadened horizons, yet at the same time the nation has shown an increasingly confident sense of national identity: no longer does this need to be expressed defensively, in the form of a reaction against attempts at domination by English culture. New congregations have appeared with an identity which is significantly different from that of earlier assemblies.

The greatly-weakened state of Irish assemblies during the early 1950s (whose numbers had declined from forty-four in 1904 to twenty-six by 1951) may well have been one reason for the decision of the Editors of *Echoes of Service* to treat it as a receiving country from 1951, and from 1953 its workers were listed in the *Daily Remembrancer*. Another reason was put forward by a worker in the country, Fred Pontin of Cork. He drew attention to the fact that Eire had only three or four full-time workers from assemblies, compared with over forty-five in Northern Ireland. For all practical purposes, he wrote, the Republic should be recognised as a foreign mission field; appropriate methods of reaching Roman Catholics should be developed, and British believers must pray for the country as for other foreign fields. His vision was for at least one worker per county.[38] This was largely realised: by 1979, there were nineteen couples and two single workers, as well as occasional help from Ulster, and significant numbers have remained ever since.[39] By 1998, there were twenty-six assemblies, forty-three missionaries and six other full-time workers.[40]

In 1955, Pontin outlined his strategy for work in the Republic in the *Echoes Quarterly Review*. Eire was the base for an army of Roman Catholic missionaries who went all over the world, yet the Catholic community was largely unreached. What he longed for was not just the salvation of individual souls, but to see saved Catholics linked together and a corporate testimony established.[41] This was a remarkable vision, given that as late as 1966, no assembly in the country had many former Catholics among its members.[42] Evangelists had tended to concentrate on contacting Protestant homes, partly because a preacher who visited Catholic homes would experience intense opposition from Protestant clergy and lose Protestant support.[43]

In 1957, Pontin's vision began to become a reality with the commencement of a Postal Sunday School work, based in Cork before moving to Dublin in 1966 and later to Mountmellick.[44] This was led by Bert Gray, an Englishman who spent many years

---

[38] *W* 82 (1952), 25; cf. F.L. Pontin, 'Why Eire?', *H* 30 (1951), 141.

[39] 'LF', *BM* 89 (1979), 111.

[40] Anon., 'The Essential Facts: Republic of Ireland', *EOS* 127 (1998), 309.

[41] F.L. Pontin, 'Eire: A Strategic Mission Field', *EQR* 7.3 (July-September 1955), 19-23. Brethren in Ireland have never been open to the kind of ecumenical co-operation practised by some progressive English assemblies.

[42] Anon., *Opportunity and Responsibility in Ireland* (Dublin: Look and Live, 1966), unpaginated.

[43] *PS* 6.6 (September-October 1954), 191; 13 (1962), 91. Some Protestant clergy were almost as unsympathetic to an evangelist's visiting Protestant homes.

[44] This appears to have been intended initially to reach isolated children of Protestant families (*EOS* 86 (1957), 180. However, the work was renamed Postal Bible School, as 'Sunday School' was seen as having Protestant connotations. By 1967 there was a special course designed for Catholic children.

working in Ireland. Initially lessons used in New Zealand were adapted, but they are now written locally. The Lessons were extensively used in Catholic schools, and Bible Educational Services was set up in 1971 to provide educational resources, engage in outreach, and arrange activities to build up believers. By 2002, there were over 4,000 students in twenty-five counties of the Republic (the rest of the island being catered for by five other centres), and over seventy schools were using the lessons.[45] Another agency was the Dublin-based Gospel Literature Distribution, which commenced in the 1960s and owed something of its vision to the model provided by OM, an international non-denominational agency run along 'faith lines' in which Brethren have always been strongly represented. Also inspired by OM was Look and Live, which was commenced in 1963 by a returned missionary, George Macdonald, sending literature by post to most homes in Ireland (it should be noted that before the Second Vatican Council, personal contact with Catholics was sometimes hazardous). Summer teams organised by GLD engaged in colportage work from the late 1960s. Many young people took part in these teams, and a number are now serving overseas as missionaries. Other groups, such as the Dublin-based Ireland Outreach, also set about the task of reaching people: this agency was founded in 1972 by North American workers, in association with Irish assemblies, and has engaged in literature distribution, church-planting in the Dublin area, the provision of religious education material for schools (under the name Aids for Bible Education), and the distribution of Emmaus Bible School courses.[46]

Partly as a result of the influx of workers and the activities in which they engaged, decline among older assemblies has been more than compensated for by the appearance of a number of new independent fellowships, often comprising former Roman Catholics. Only a minority of these have aligned themselves with assemblies, although others had their origins as a result of assembly outreach; insistence by some Brethren on the observance of such traditions as a particular dress code for meetings has meant that a number of converts have moved to other types of church. In 2002, workers in one south-eastern town, Enniscorthy, identified a need for a church fellowship which would not be seen as 'Protestant';[47] the origins of many of these new groups have enabled them to avoid a label which is fraught with unhelpful connotations in the Irish context because of the traditional links between Protestantism and British rule. However, such groups, often meeting in homes, are liable to domination by one person (a problem experienced by some of the earlier assemblies founded by gentry); they may close, split, or become charismatic. It is difficult to treat them as a homogeneous entity since they are almost as varied as independent congregations in England or Scotland. Yet it is with them that the future of assembly-type congregations lies, since they are culturally Irish in a way that existing assemblies tend not to be. In disconnecting themselves from a Protestantism which is regarded as politically-based, they are following in the steps of the earliest Brethren, including Darby himself.

A prominent role in this development appears to have been played by the assembly at Mallow Street, Limerick. From the early 1970s it experienced an influx of dozens of new converts, including a considerable number of ex-Catholic young people. The average age

---

[45] A. Gray, 'Postal Sunday Schools', *PS* 18 (1967), 77-9; *EOS* 102 (1973), 74-5; Noel McMeekin, 'Reaching the Young People', *EOS* 130 (2002), 540; *idem*, 'Postal Bible School in the Republic of Ireland', *PS* 58 (2003), 76-7.

[46] See Ireland Outreach's promotional material, and some papers in CBA Box 24.

[47] John Stanfield, 'Church Planting in Enniscorthy', *EOS* 130 (2002), 550.

of the assembly halved from fifty to twenty-five, and attendance tripled by the mid-1980s; some began to form fellowships in outlying towns. By 1996 there were fellowships in Ennis, Shannon, Tipperary, and Thurles, comprised mostly of former Roman Catholics. Other new churches were appearing in Nenagh, Charleville, Newcastle West, and Listowel.[48] As a result, assemblies and newer fellowships are beginning to dot the map in areas hitherto unrepresented.[49]

22.2 Why did People Leave?

In the early 1960s, Open Brethren expected that large-scale Evangelical secessions from mainstream churches would soon occur, and that they would benefit thereby. *The Harvester* reported such secessions and other expressions of concern by Evangelicals in mixed denominations. However, it is remarkable how few of the seceders settled with assemblies. For example, a steady trickle of individuals, ministers, and churches left the Baptist Union in England during the 1960s and 1970s, over the issues of ecumenical involvement and then liberal theology. Yet very few joined the Brethren, and no churches did so; many allied themselves with the FIEC and the new Reformed Baptist movement, and a number provided a nucleus for the 'house-church' movement (joined by a number of former Brethren, as we saw earlier). Indeed, for much of this period, the movement has been in the opposite direction, and in some eyes the number of committed individuals who have left assemblies for other churches has assumed serious proportions. The Baptist minister Ian Coffey, in the preface to a major work from Partnership, the *Church Leaders' Handbook*, wondered how one branch of the church could produce so many gifted people and not retain them; he suggested that it might in fact be God's purpose for the movement to meet wider needs.[50] We should remember, too, that denominational mobility has been a prominent feature of British church life in recent decades; people are more likely to be committed to particular priorities (such as Bible teaching or youth provision) than to remaining in a particular denomination. What must be a concern to Brethren leaders, however, is that gains from other denominations, important as they are in the growth of some congregations, do not appear to have balanced the overall losses.

In 1965, the *Journal of the Christian Brethren Research Fellowship* devoted an issue to testimonies about 'Why I left the Brethren'. A dozen stories appeared, including those of David Lillie (who had left twenty-five years earlier) and Andrew Anderson (who had become a FIEC minister). Reasons given for departure included receiving a call to a settled ministry (which was contrasted with the perceived ineffectiveness of, and exhaustion arising from, itinerant ministry), rigidity, legalism, narrowness and bigotry, a professed withdrawal from society which was coupled with pride in possessions and social standing, lack of teaching, misunderstanding of the young by the old, leavers' changing views concerning the work of the Holy Spirit, disparity between Brethren practice and principle in assembly life, frustration (the reasons given may often have been just the last straws precipitating withdrawal), isolationism (and self-delusion on the part of assemblies concerning their freedom from sectarianism), lack of order in worship, the nature of the

[48] David and Kay Stevens, 'Limerick', *EOS* 125 (1996), 441; *idem*, 'Outreach in the West', *EOS* 130 (2002), 537; Tatford, *That the World May Know*, 8.219; personal information.

[49] Similarly, there are still virtually no Welsh-speaking assemblies (the only one listed in 2002 was at Penygroes, near Ammanford in Carmarthenshire) and no Gaelic-speaking assemblies in Scotland.

[50] Harold Rowdon (ed.), *Church Leaders Handbook* (Carlisle: Paternoster for Partnership, 2002), x.

oversight (which was seen as self-perpetuating or open to domination by one man), the lack of scope for women to use their gifts, and questioning whether the Brethren pattern of assembly life was really the only scriptural one.[51]

A counterbalance was provided by a later issue 'On Being with the Brethren'. An article entitled 'Why I have stayed with the Brethren' included contributions from Bruce, S.S. Short and Francis Stunt.[52] Contributors expressed appreciation of the facility for sharing fellowship with all believers, the atmosphere of spiritual and intellectual freedom, and theological reasons such as the authority of the New Testament for church order, the gathered nature of the church, the reception of all believers, the autonomy of the local church, the priesthood of all Christians, and the freedom for gifted men to minister (no women contributed to this issue). Others were invited to write about 'Why I joined the Brethren'.[53] Their reasons included a search for spiritual vitality, soundness in doctrine and practice, a desire to give practical expression to their view of unity, the movement's evangelistic zeal, and its freedom from clericalism and traditional accretions. The same things which some found in assemblies led others to look beyond assemblies, and much depended on the particular setting where people found themselves: their decisions to join or leave may often represent responses to particular situations rather than as necessarily indicating their opinion of the movement as a whole.

Many seem to have moved for negative rather than positive reasons: Dickson found that dissatisfaction was the primary cause of such movement in Scotland during the 1970s and 1980s.[54] Rowdon has suggested that in a number of assemblies, a measure of change occurred during the 1960s, but that they failed to continue changing and became set in the pattern adopted then, leading to the possible loss of some whose hopes had been raised by the initial changes.[55] The dissatisfaction would have been made worse by the widespread rediscovery outside Brethren of principles which the movement had always considered distinguished its church order from all others. Although Brethren traditionally stood for every-member ministry, the new stress on discovering and deploying the spiritual gifts of each member of the congregation, expounded by the American church growth theorist Peter Wagner and others, found a far more enthusiastic response among churches in the denominations than it did among Brethren. Possibly the fear of replacing the Spirit's leading by human organisation rendered elderships apprehensive about undertaking such an exercise. However, it is likely that a number of members may have become frustrated at their inability to find a sphere of service and may have left for other churches where they felt there was more freedom to practice the very things which their Brethren upbringing had led them to see as desirable.

Worship, which came to the fore with the explosive growth of the charismatic movement from the 1960s, was another factor which led many to move. Some felt that certain spiritual gifts were not recognised among assemblies; others felt that the worship was dominated by particular individuals, stale, or unduly restricted in its focus on Calvary. It was even alleged that 'A well known evangelist said not so long ago that the morning meeting was doing more to kill off the assemblies than any other single factor.'[56] As a

---

[51] Anon., 'Why I Left the Brethren', *JCBRF* 8 (June 1965), 5-22.

[52] *JCBRF* 10 (December 1965), 5-12.

[53] *Ibid.*, 12-17.

[54] Dickson, 'Brethren and Baptists', 372-87.

[55] Rowdon, 'Brethren in Britain, 1945-2000'.

[56] Stanley Linton, 'Readers' Forum: Where do we go from here?', *H* 59 (1980), 92.

result, many have joined charismatic churches, but probably just as many (some of them from Exclusive meetings) have found homes in Anglicanism or other communions with a more ordered style of worship; the post-war trend towards a weekly celebration of the Eucharist (which Anglican Evangelicals followed from 1967 for a couple of decades) would have been attractive to Brethren nourished on the weekly Breaking of Bread. A number have been ordained; although I know of no British ex-Brethren bishops, a former Echoes of Service Editor, Donald Boak, did become an Anglican cleric.[57] CBRF's first Secretary, John Somerville-Meikle, became a Roman Catholic,[58] and a few Brethren have become Orthodox.

The perceived lack of solid and systematic Bible teaching (in itself a remarkable phenomenon when we recall that the movement had traditionally been renowned for its Bible teachers) was another factor precipitating many departures. A number of former Brethren now minister in the FIEC, whose emphasis on local autonomy and clear Evangelical stance must prove attractive to them; a few FIEC churches began as secessions from assemblies because of a perceived lack of expository preaching, while other assemblies have joined the FIEC as churches.[59] One congregation in Inverness joined the Baptist Union of Scotland in 1991,[60] and many individuals have joined Baptist churches of various types throughout Britain, of whom a number have become ministers.

Other factors leading to decline and departures included a lack of visionary leadership (many busy elders did not have sufficient time for reflection and reading), unwillingness to change or risk using younger members, and spiritual lukewarmness allied to an improvement in living standards. To these Neil Summerton adds spiritual pride, opposition to the charismatic movement, failure to adapt accepted patterns of activity for the sake of reaching outsiders, over-emphasis on the independence of local congregations, restrictions on the roles open to women, and a lack of pastoral care.[61] To some, it must have seemed that the movement was getting everything wrong, in spite of its high ideals.

22.3 Responses to Decline

In spite of the problems identified above, Open Brethren were not always as ineffective as some thought they were, especially when compared with other denominations. The focus on assemblies as a group, which was apparent in much post-war heart-searching, was subject to criticism: in 1948, a *Precious Seed* article responded to recent criticism of the condition of assemblies by asking 'Are things ready to die? And if so, what then?' It argued that decline did not justify departure from scriptural principles, and that, since Scripture recognised not denominations but individual assemblies, the question should be 'Is your assembly dying?' If so, then the remedy was to strengthen it, action which would

---

[57] *A*, March 1991, 30.

[58] *PP* 5 (October 1997), 1.

[59] Brian H. Edwards (former FIEC President) to the author, 4 February 2003. Assemblies which have joined the FIEC during the 1980s and 1990s (there had been a handful in earlier decades) include New Park Hall, Barking; Glenbrook, Higher Blackley; Oakwood Chapel, Harlow; Kingsbridge; Llandudno; Blenheim Chapel, Maidenhead; Selsey; and Wareham.

[60] Dickson, *Brethren in Scotland*, 361.

[61] Summerton, *Local churches for a new century*, 7-9.

be of greater value than involvement in para-church efforts which duplicated assembly functions.[62]

It is important to recognise that the issue goes deeper than the contrast sometimes drawn of traditionalist decline and progressive growth. Progressive assemblies may be attracting people for cultural rather than spiritual reasons, as seems to have happened in the late nineteenth century. On the other hand, traditional assemblies may still see growth through conversions, especially where there is a vigorous youth work. However, there is undeniably a measure of introversion on the part of some traditionalists, often coupled with a nostalgic looking back to a supposed golden age, whether in the assembly's own earlier history or the New Testament. Some tried to keep their assemblies alive by artificial means. From the 1970s, advertisements appeared for men to help maintain the testimony (presumably with the Breaking of Bread and the midweek meeting in view), sometimes offering accommodation to those who responded.[63] Others were dependent on men commuting from elsewhere. A common fruit of introversion was a narrow outlook, which justified the assembly's continuing existence by pointing to the unfaithfulness of other assemblies, as well as denominational congregations.

On the other hand, some assemblies responded to decline by adaptation and accommodation, which could at its worst (though by no means as often as traditionalist critics alleged) become a frantic search for expedients to stem the losses. Where such adaptation has been the result of sustained reflection on the application of biblical principles, some strong congregations have been built up, but the resources to engage in this are often lacking in small assemblies, and the emphasis on autonomy of local congregations makes it difficult for them to draw on teaching input from elsewhere: it is one thing to invite an itinerant teacher to give a series of addresses on a prophetic or typological subject, but quite another to invite the same person to meet with local leaders to review an assembly's spiritual state and suggest ways of responding to it. However, the movement's history furnishes enough examples of this happening, as visiting teachers had long been consulted by local brethren on knotty points, for contemporary leaders to have precedent for calling in outside help.

Greater co-ordination of activity (or calls for it) was another response to decline. Some London assemblies north of the Thames began meeting in 1979 after an appeal from Rossmore Hall, Marylebone, for consideration of problems faced by the small struggling assemblies in the area. A discussion paper produced for them by Harold Rowdon suggested that north London assemblies were clustered in small groups, reflecting their origins from a mother church, and that Brethren were weakest at the level between local and national – that involving regional co-operation.[64] Rowdon defended inter-church co-operation as scriptural, and as something often practised by assemblies in such matters as providing speakers, letters of commendation, and even the circulation of appeals for money. But, he said, Brethren had been reluctant to *consult* together, or to think or act in 'denominational' ways. However, there *was* an Open Brethren tradition: a specific number of churches who together formed a recognisable group, served by particular individuals, reading certain magazines, supporting what amounted to a denominational missionary

---

[62] *PS* 1.14 (January-February 1948), 167-8.

[63] Before this, magazine editors might bring particular situations to readers' attention, and very occasionally a rota of visiting brethren might be organised, but advertising by assemblies was rare.

[64] Harold Rowdon, 'Assemblies in North London – A Call to Action' (typescript, n.d.; CBA Box 147(2)).

society, and attending conferences convened for their benefit. As a result, a Counties regional fellowship was formed in 1980, and there is some evidence of groups of assemblies co-operating, but assemblies in London are mostly small and struggling. This was just one example of concern to re-establish a presence in inner-city areas. In 1974, the East London full-time worker Patrick Sookhdeo, reviewing the Anglican bishop David Sheppard's book on urban needs and challenges, *Built as a City*, expressed the conviction that the Open Brethren model of church life had great potential in such a setting.

> In many ways, the Brethren have a considerable amount to offer to the inner city. Our unstructured and informal service allows for greater participation by all those who love the Lord; the fact that we do not have a paid ministry means that we can afford to keep an assembly going when other churches have to close, and local leadership is not stifled because of the greater sharing of responsibility. Our emphasis on evangelism means that people are reached with the Gospel in a continuous way, and our emphasis on small meetings allows for a greater degree of fellowship and concern for one another.

However, he went on to point out the downside of this model as then being practised:

> Our emphasis on the independence of each local assembly has resulted in the neglect of areas in which there are no assemblies. We need to learn how to think strategically and to develop some form of corporate responsibility. Our emphasis against paid ministers has resulted in many assemblies closing in these areas because of lack of leadership and teaching, and in few starting because we have no policy for church planting. Our emphasis on contemplation and meditation during the morning worship has resulted in the attraction of those with good intellectual ability such as professional and business persons. But we have neglected the ordinary man who cannot rise to such heights and who may require greater informality. Our emphasis on evangelism and 'preaching the word' has resulted in the neglect of those around us who are in need of practical demonstrations of Christian love and justice.
>
> Our emphasis on non-political involvement has led us inadvertently to support the status quo, in that it suits our purposes better. Our wealth and riches, which have been the means of the Gospel spreading to the uttermost parts of the earth, now tie us to salubrious suburbia, and away from the need and depression of the inner city. Our emphasis on missions overseas has resulted in the neglect of the vast mission-field in Britain, which in some ways has more need that [sic] many parts of Africa. To our credit we have engaged in considerable evangelism in rural areas, yet we have failed to apply a similar concern to the inner city, apart from the occasional 'soup kitchen'.[65]

When *Faith in the City*, the controversial Church of England report, appeared in 1985, Sookhdeo welcomed it as prophetic, and challenged Brethren to support workers in the newly-designated Urban Priority Areas and to co-operate with other Christian traditions.[66]

There has been some encouragement in such work. For example, a GLO team working on the large council estate of Viewpark in Glasgow saw a church planted successfully, the

[65] Patrick Sookhdeo, 'The Inner City: Lost to the Gospel?', *H* 53 (1974), 144-5.
[66] Patrick Sookhdeo, 'Faith in the City', *H*, April 1986, 4-5.

result of an initial three-year commitment and extensive community involvement on an estate with 25% unemployment.[67] More recently, Counties, GLO, and the UK Evangelization Trust (formerly the East of England Evangelization Trust and now Stewardship) have joined to commence the 'Church Planting Initiative', being joined later by Partnership. This began with the aim of recycling funds from the sale of Brethren properties to support individuals or teams in key church-planting locations.[68] Whilst there was an initial willingness to come alongside dying churches, it has been decided that it is better to start from scratch after an assembly has closed.

A recurrent response to decline was the conducting of surveys, reflecting both the popularity of such a method of information-gathering in the 1960s and the incidence of businessmen, who were attempting to quantify the movement's progress, among its leadership.[69] The first took place in 1966, and focused on evangelism, covering seventy-five selected assemblies of all sizes and types in England and Wales.[70] Its verdict was damning: 'Virtually no assembly claimed success in evangelising adults'.[71] This was put down to lack of contact with outsiders and inability to communicate with them in an understandable way; churches were 'too "production-orientated" and not sufficiently "consumer-orientated"', thinking in terms of what they could do rather than the needs of those whom they were seeking to reach.[72]

During the 1970s, several meetings of leaders considered the way ahead for the movement, and decided to begin by surveying assemblies. The CBRF agreed to sponsor the work and publish the results, which appeared in 1980 as *"The Brethren" Today: A Factual Survey*, edited by Graham Brown (a market researcher) and Brian Mills.[73] Again, the overall picture which emerged was not encouraging. Over the previous five years, 43% of assemblies had grown and 37% declined. Small assemblies were overstretching themselves, maintaining numbers of activities which were not achieving their goals.[74] Missions were frequent but led to few conversions.[75] Yet 75% of churches responding indicated evangelism as one of their top three priorities; the others commanding wide support were spiritual growth (37%), praise and worship (30%), preaching the Word (28%), fellowship (24%), and being a centre of witness (21%).[76]

A problem with these surveys was that of obtaining a sufficiently high proportion of responses for the results to be representative. Conservatives were not only suspicious of the organisation sponsoring the work; many disapproved of this method of assessing the movement's condition. An editorial paragraph in *Assembly Testimony* headed 'Warning – Researchers!' instructed assemblies not to fill in survey forms; such surveys were 'unscriptural and completely unnecessary', whether undertaken by Brethren or others.[77] In

---

[67] Graham Poland, 'Bridging the Gap', *H*, November 1988, 6-7. An assembly had existed here during the 1960s, but had closed.
[68] *PU* 6 (Winter 1997-8); 8 (Winter-Spring 1999).
[69] Brierley et al., *Brethren*, 1.
[70] Brown, 'How can we improve', 44-57.
[71] *Ibid.*, 47.
[72] *Ibid.*, 52, cf. 45.
[73] Brown and Mills, *"Brethren" Today*, 7.
[74] *Ibid.*, 13, 32.
[75] *Ibid.*, 12.
[76] *Ibid.*, 52.
[77] *AT* (May-June 1981), 94.

1988, a postal survey sent to assemblies on the 1983 address list achieved an overall response rate of just 20%.[78] It indicated that over the previous five years 39% of assemblies had grown, but 45% had declined. Large assemblies were getting larger, and small ones smaller.[79] The average assembly size varied from thirty-nine in Wales to seventy-eight in Northern Ireland (though the latter figure was based on a total response of just thirteen assemblies), with an overall size of fifty-two; Open Brethren therefore had the smallest average congregational size of the denominations.[80]

The English Church Census of 1989 (some data from which was integrated into the report of the 1988 servey, *The Christian Brethren as the Nineties Began*) attracted a somewhat higher response rate from Brethren (perhaps because it was not perceived as associated with any one stream within the movement), as the figures below indicate:

Table 22.2: Brethren data from the English Church Census, 1989

	Response rate	Adult churchgoers 1979	Adult churchgoers 1985	Adult churchgoers 1989
Open	38%	44,000	41,300	43,500
Closed	35%	7,000	7,300	7,600

Source: Peter Brierley, *'Christian' England: What the 1989 English Church Census reveals* (London: MARC Europe, 1991), 44-5, cf. 42.[81]

By now, the age profile of Brethren congregations was giving cause for concern: 23% of attenders were over sixty-five (as against 15% in the population as a whole), but only 11% were in their twenties (16% of the population) and 16% aged thirty to forty-four (20% in the population).[82] This indicated that assemblies were likely to be short on manpower. In addition, it was clear that the main strength of the movement now lay in suburbia: 52% of Brethren adults belonged to suburban assemblies, 27% to town assemblies, 13% to rural assemblies, and 8% to city centre and inner city assemblies.[83]

The most recent survey was conducted in 1998-9, and involved contacting all English, Welsh, and Scottish churches in the 1997 address list. (Northern Ireland was excluded because of the previous extremely low response rate there.) 29% responded, though regional percentages varied from 21% in Yorkshire to 41% in East Anglia.[84] The author thought it likely that even where churches were growing, transfers rather than conversions accounted for a significant proportion of new members.[85] What was

---

[78] Brierley et al., *Brethren*, 5.

[79] *Ibid.*, 14, 19.

[80] *Ibid.*, 12, 72.

[81] Brierley referred to 'Closed Brethren', whom he equated with 'Plymouth Brethren No. 4' (from the US Census Bureau classifications), better known in Britain as the Taylor Brethren. For an explanation of the US classifications, see Arthur C. Piepkorn, 'Plymouth Brethren (Christian Brethren)', *JCBRF* 25 (September 1973), 45-8.

[82] Brierley et al., *Brethren*, 63.

[83] Brierley, *'Christian' England*, 59.

[84] Brown, *Whatever Happened*, 1-2.

[85] *Ibid.*, 24-5.

worrying was that the age profile was becoming increasingly weighted towards the elderly. In the average assembly, 43% of the members were aged sixty or over (rising to 58% in churches of less than forty members, and compared with 28% of the population as a whole) and under-forties accounted for just 30% (as against 48%).[86]

More recent research by Brierley has found that estimated Sunday attendance at Open assemblies in England has declined commensurately with the decline in numbers of assemblies, from 70,500 in 1989 to 49,900 in 1998, but appears to have held up much better in Scotland, falling only from 18,880 (Open and Exclusive combined) in 1990 to 18,200 in 2002. English 'Closed Brethren' attendance has apparently increased, from 12,300 in 1989 to 14,400 in 1998.[87] Since it is the small, elderly assemblies which are closing, continuing rapid decline looks likely for the next few years, and it will take time for any widespread change in outlook and evangelistic effectiveness to be reflected in the numbers of assemblies.

[86] *Ibid.*, 22.

[87] Peter Brierley, 'The Christian Brethren in the 1998 English Church Attendance Survey', <www.partnershipuk.org/pdf/ECASBrethren.pdf>, *idem*, 'The Christian Brethren in Scotland', <www.partnershipuk.org/pdf/SCCBrethren%2004.04.pdf>, both accessed 14 January 2005.

CHAPTER 23

The Open Brethren:
Still a Missionary Movement

23.1 The Globalisation of Assembly Mission

Overseas mission is one aspect of Open Brethren identity which remains significant, and which is embraced by all sections of the movement. However, even here there has been considerable change. Traditionally, British Brethren saw themselves as belonging to a sending country, and relations with Brethren communities overseas as mediated primarily through missionaries; the last significant expression of this attitude to international relationships was Frederick Tatford's ten-volume series *That the World may Know*, published by Echoes of Service from 1982-6. This charted the work of missionaries country by country throughout the world, rather than presenting the history of national assemblies. However, more recently globalisation and the disappearance of the British Empire (with the associated colonialist attitudes) have had an impact on relationships, and more progressive or internationally-aware British Brethren usually see themselves as part (and by no means the strongest part) of a movement which has outgrown its British origins to become potentially a truly international expression of Evangelical Christianity.[1] There is a shift from viewing relationships in terms of senders and receivers to viewing them as co-operative partnerships. This is given visible manifestation in occasional international leaders' conferences. The first-ever such event took place in Switzerland in 1985, for European leaders, with a follow-up three years later, but global conferences have since been held in Singapore (1993), Rome (1996), and Romania (2003). Furthermore, it is not unknown for missionaries to be sent by assemblies abroad to work with assemblies in Britain, which can thus be seen as a receiving country.

23.2 Fluctuating Interest

There were encouraging post-war signs of a revival of interest in mission. In 1947, it was reported that 105 new workers for overseas had been commended in twenty months, and new missionary conferences and rallies were being convened.[2] *Echoes of Service* reported an increase of 1,200 subscribers since the end of the war.[3] However, like the confidence of assemblies in their future prospects, this soon began to falter: in 1950, it was reported that the number of MSCs had declined greatly in the past twenty or thirty years, partly due to a lack of suitable literature.[4] The classes gradually died out in Britain, and the last MSC study conference took place in 1986; the mission component of these had declined, other sources of information were increasingly easy to access, and missionary support needs

---

[1] See, for example, Rowdon (ed.), *Country Reports*, and the reports appearing in *IPP*.
[2] A. Pulleng, 'The Sound of a going', *H* 24 (1947), 101.
[3] *EOS* 76 (1947), 61.
[4] *EQR* 2.2 (April-June 1950), 33.

were becoming highly specialised and thus beyond what the classes could provide. One of the Editors of *Echoes of Service*, writing that year, expressed the opinion that the movement's impact lessened after *Links of Help* was absorbed by *The Harvester*, and that nothing had quite replaced it.[5]

Part of the congregation at the London Missionary Meetings, 1966

The decision to launch *Echoes Quarterly Review* was taken in January 1948, and owed much to W.E. Vine's advocacy of the project.[6] The Editors had wanted to increase the size of *Echoes of Service*, but paper control regulations prevented it; however, there was no hindrance to their starting a new magazine. As we have noted, it was a time of revived interest in mission, and soundings indicated that the time was right for such a venture.[7] According to a flyer which appeared in *The Harvester*, the new periodical aimed to foster mission interest among the young, to supply material for missionary study groups and young people's meetings, to stimulate missionary interest generally, and so stir up prayer. To some extent, it was thus filling the gap left by the disappearance of *Links of Help*. In spite of the high quality of the material, it never quite fulfilled its progenitors' hopes; circulation remained static at around 4,000, and in 1978 it was decided that *Echoes of Service* could henceforth incorporate longer articles without the need to prune the extracts from missionary letters which formed the bulk of its content. There was thus no more need for a second title.[8]

Attendance at missionary meetings has often been used as an index of missionary interest among assemblies. During the 1950s, the London Missionary Meetings drew congregations of up to 3,500, and it was not unknown for a hundred missionaries to be present. As late as 1965, it was being suggested that a larger venue needed to be found.[9]

However, decline set in shortly afterwards. A letter to *The Witness* on the subject in 1978 suggested that tight assemblies banded together for fellowship and co-operation, as did open ones, with the result that those in the middle lost out; the writer saw these

[5] S.F. Warren, 'Missionary Study Class Movement', *EOS* 115 (1986), 361-2.
[6] *EQR* 2.1 (January-March 1950), 1.
[7] Anon., 'These Twenty Years', *EQR* 20.4 (October-December 1968), 4.
[8] *EQR* 30.4 (October-December 1978), 3.
[9] *W* 95 (1965), 464.

meetings as a case in point, and offered a plausible assessment of the state of the movement. 'The situation at Westminster ... may be a reflection of what is happening locally. And I venture to predict that if things continue as they are, two distinct groups of "open brethren" could develop by the end of the century, if not before.'[10] The London meetings ceased in 1989, to be replaced by an annual 'Echoes Day' which moved round the regions.[11] One of the convenors explained that the meetings were ceasing because of declining attendance, the cost and danger of travel to central London, the decline in number and size of London assemblies, a decline in missionary interest in some churches, and a decline in prayer support as evidenced by the end of the monthly London prayer meeting in 1986.[12] Nevertheless, some areas continue to hold annual missionary conferences, the largest probably being that in Lancashire, which has traditionally been a strongly mission-minded area.

As for *Echoes of Service* itself (now simply *Echoes*), from 1950 extracts from missionaries' letters were printed in the order in which missionaries' names appeared in the daily prayer guide, making it easier to use. Accordingly, circulation rose from 11,700 in 1950 to 15,300 in 1964.[13] However, by 2002 it had dropped to around 8,000.[14] As with the publications of most long-established Evangelical missions, most of the present readers are older people, often with deep-rooted and longstanding loyalty to supporting assembly missionary work.

So, although the high proportion of members serving as missionaries can be demonstrated, is it accurate to say that assemblies are, in general, mission-minded? One Editor, W.T. Stunt, challenged this as far back as 1955. He calculated that there was one missionary to every 108 assembly members, apart from those serving with various societies. Turning his attention to missionary giving, he reckoned that assemblies sending gifts via Bath included about three-quarters of the total membership in England, Ireland and Wales, which he estimated at 60,000 – i.e. 45,000 potential donors. Gifts apart from legacies for 1953 amounted to £75,000, but £51,000 came from 648 individuals. So, in his opinion, most members were not mission-minded.[15] His analysis may be questioned, since it omits giving through other channels and direct giving to missionaries,[16] but the main thrust of his argument still needs to be taken seriously. (Similarly, the 2003 accounts of Echoes of Service indicate that of a total income of £3,597,000, £1,194,000 came from charitable trusts, £895,000 from legacies, £858,000 from individuals and just £444,000 from assemblies.) It is corroborated by examination of the nature of assembly mission interest. Open Brethren have continued to provide a disproportionately large number of the total British Protestant missionary force; in 1976, for example, of 5,862 such missionaries, 565 were listed by Echoes of Service.[17]

---

[10] *W* 108 (1978), 278-9.

[11] The one I attended, at Guildford in 2001, had a maximum congregation of only 300, in spite of the large number of missionary reports and the extensive exhibitions by assembly mission agencies.

[12] Anon., 'The London Missionary Meetings – End of an Era', *H*, December 1989, 17.

[13] *EOS* 93 (1964), 163.

[14] Papers for the 2002 consultation of Brethren agencies (CBA Box 146 (19)).

[15] W.T. Stunt, 'Are We Really Missionary-Minded?', *EQR* 7.1 (January-March 1955), 2-4. To some extent, such assessments are relative: other denominations, and Brethren today, would doubtless be delighted with such a level of missionary support.

[16] Neil Summerton to the author, 29 December 2004.

[17] Coad, *Laing*, 73, drawing on *The UK Protestant Missions Handbook*, 1.76, 78.

Although the proportion of missionaries to assembly members has declined from 88 per 10,000 in 1988 to 70 in 1998, it is still higher than that for any other Protestant denomination.[18] However, with reference to the home support base, a distinction can be made between being mission-minded and being missionary-minded, and the latter may more accurately describe the attitude of many older assembly members than the former (here too they reflect the outlook of many other Evangelical congregations). Missionary interest seems to be related more to the missionary than to the field, and assemblies tend not to maintain strong links with overseas areas once their workers return home. It also appears that assemblies are not always fully abreast of changes in the way that a missionary's role is perceived 'on the field', and perhaps have a more traditional image than is appropriate to an era of global fellowship. Educating believers in the changed realities of today's world is a difficult task, made more so by the demise of some of the periodicals which could have carried articles on the subject, and the lack of articles on such matters (as opposed to reports of actual work done) in most which remain.

However, during the 1960s new methods of fostering interest were adopted with some degree of success. In 1960, an exhibition and conference were held at Elim Hall, Glasgow, arranged by a committee called together by the Home and Foreign Missionary Fund (the Scottish counterpart to Echoes). The interest shown indicated that a large exhibition would be welcomed. This took place in Glasgow's Palace of Arts from 27-30 September 1961, and the stands adopted a variety of up-to-date approaches such as push-button displays and a room heated to tropical temperature. Such devices earned some criticism from more conservative brethren who considered them pandering to a craving for entertainment. The total attendance was estimated at over 14,000; 3,000 were at the closing rally in St Andrew's Hall, over 1,000 were turned away. James Caldwell, a missionary in Zambia, was even interviewed on television.[19] Other exhibitions were held during the 1960s and 1970s, but none were as high-profile as this one. A striking local initiative was the Hamilton Missionary Fellowship, which ran from 1960-88 and aimed to provide support for missionaries and to educate young people about mission. It held weekly meetings and acquired a building as a centre for its spiritual and practical activities in support of mission. Over forty went into full-time service at home or abroad as a result of its work.[20] Such innovative presentation of the Great Commission is needed for each generation.

23.3 Changing Patterns of Support and Service

As with many other UK-based mission agencies, Echoes of Service has seen extensive change in thinking regarding almost every aspect of mission theory and practice. Some resisted such change; Lang continued to blame the Editors for what he saw as the widespread departure from God's principles: 'our brethren at Bath have taken the lead and are mostly responsible'.[21] A minority of assemblies, mostly in Scotland, Ulster and

---

[18] Ian Burness, 'Present Trends & Emphasis', paper produced for the 2002 consultation of Brethren agencies (CBA Box 146(19)), unpaginated.

[19] Anon., 'Operation Overseas. The Glasgow Missionary Exhibition', *EQR* 14.1 (January-March 1962), 25-8; Dickson, *Brethren in Scotland*, 210; T.J. Smith, '"Operation Overseas"', *BM* 71 (1961), 324-6; 'Ex-Baptist', letter in *BM* 71 (1961), 374.

[20] S.F. Warren, 'The end of an Era', *EOS* 117 (1988), 292-3.

[21] G.H. Lang to E. Tipson, 1 January 1953 (CBA Box 68).

Northern England, still prefer to stand apart from Echoes of Service and other such agencies, in the belief that these attempt to 'control' the work and movements of those on their lists in a way which contravenes the direct responsibility of workers to the Lord who called them.

During the post-war years, there may have been some justification for Lang's attitude. W.T. Stunt recalled that a number of difficulties had arisen among those who went out from 1947-51, many of whom came home prematurely. In response, it was suggested at a meeting of 'elder brethren' in 1949 that local assemblies, who might not be fully conversant with the nature and requirements of work overseas, should communicate with the Editors before commending members. The following year, at a similar meeting, the Editors made suggestions to help assembly elders when commending members for overseas service, which were incorporated in a pamphlet entitled *Workers Together*. The increased care which followed resulted in a smaller proportion of casualties.[22] However, one later Editor felt that the 1940s and 1950s had been marked by a more autocratic and 'hands on' approach, and expressed approval of a more recent retreat from it.[23] It was another Editor, Arnold Pickering (1908-84), who helped restore the emphasis on commendation as being primarily the responsibility of local assemblies.[24] Nowadays, it is made clear that the Editors do not control the work of missionaries, nor do they commend them for service, but act as sources of advice and channels of fellowship between missionaries and assemblies in the form of information, gifts, prayer, and pastoral care.[25]

Changing patterns of service have also been evident, with the growth of short-term mission, especially by young people and the newly-retired. The former tend to express their mission interest by participating in such ventures as summer teams, short-term placements, and relief work. Since 1984, those spending at least three months abroad have been listed in *Echoes of Service*. Although an estimated 20% return as long-term missionaries, there has been concern at the decline in a sense of lifetime commitment to missionary service, and at the drop-out rate among long-term workers.[26] Other aspects of change emerge from analysis of the lists of workers issued by Echoes of Service.

[22] S.F. Warren, 'The Westminster Missionary Meetings 1967', *EQR* 20.1 (January-March 1968), 5; cf. Annual Reports for 1949 and 1950.

[23] E.E. Costello, 'Tested by Time', *EOS* 113 (1984), 70. Similar concerns were evident in the field of home mission; the secretary of Counties Evangelistic Work until 1953, E.H. Grant, functioned like a director of a missionary society, drawing up the programme of work for each summer season. Some supporters wanted a more 'hands–on' approach to the work; from 1948 an Executive Oversight composed mainly of business and professional men met regularly, although tensions surfaced at times between this body and the General Oversight, which was supposed to be drawn from interested assemblies and which had the nominal oversight of the work. Some wanted a similar executive body for Echoes of Service, but this was deemed unacceptable.

[24] *EOS* 113 (1984), 546.

[25] For example, in Ian Burness, 'Echoes of Service', *PS* 57 (2002), 18-19.

[26] Burness, 'Present Trends'.

Table 23.1: Number of workers listed and annual income: Echoes of Service, 1945-2002

Year	'45	'49	'54	'59	'64	'68	'77[27]	'83	'90	'96	'02
NoW	circa 1000	1134	1148	1154	1168	1132	559	402	374	385	374
GB&I	?	716	680	639	642	590	479	350	326	347	347
NwW	16	71	44	65	29	37	n/a	n/a	n/a	n/a	n/a
GB&I	1	44	17	16	17	20	17	10	13	17	18
Inc.	74	99	111	157	204	232	569	1108	2917	2386	3440

Key:
NoW = Number of workers GB&I = From Britain and Ireland
NwW = New workers Inc = Income (£000s)

Sources: Stunt et al., *Turning the World Upside Down*, announcements in *Echoes of Service*, and the Daily Prayer Guide.

Echoes income 1913 – 2002 at constant prices

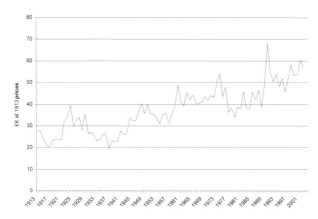

Source: Echoes of Service annual reports, photocopied into two volumes, 'ECHOES Receipts and allocations 1885-1986' and '1987–'.

The increase in the total number of workers during the period to 1964 hides a decline in the number of workers from Britain. Even while assemblies at home were growing in the 1940s and 1950s, their missionary zeal appears to have been declining. The apparent dramatic decline between 1968 and 1977 is largely due to the decision to cease listing workers commended from North America and Australasia from 1972, except where married to somebody from Britain.[28] From that point, the great majority of workers listed would

---

[27] For the year to 31 July 1977.
[28] *EOS* 100 (1971), 195.

have been commended from British assemblies.[29] Numbers of missionaries from Britain appear to have stabilised from the mid-1980s, although this may be due in part to decisions to include in the *Daily Prayer Guide* workers with GLO from 1990 and 'tentmakers' (missionaries who support themselves by working in some 'secular' capacity) who have the commendation of their home assembly from 1996.[30]

Numbers of new missionaries increased dramatically for a few years after the war, a maximum of fifty-eight commendations from Britain being reported for 1948 (out of a total of eighty-nine that year). Until 1970, almost every year saw fifteen to thirty commended from Britain, but since then figures have fluctuated between four and twenty-seven, with one year (1991) seeing thirty-six new workers. The ratio of men to women has changed surprisingly little, averaging about 41:59 over the period from 1944-2003 (although for the decade 1964-73, it was 37:63, and for 1984-93, it was 45:55). Rowdon suggested in 1985 that increasing use of full-time workers at home was likely to affect the numbers going abroad,[31] but this has not, apparently, been the case. However, it may have affected their financial support; the graph below indicates that in real terms, Echoes income has doubled since 1914, but during the same period average personal income has increased fourfold. Whereas formerly there were relatively few workers at home to support, now there are increasing numbers of evangelists, pastors, teachers, and others. In addition, the membership of assemblies has shrunk, perhaps by a third, and it is probable that in recent decades a greater proportion of missionary giving goes to non-Brethren agencies.[32]

Although numbers of workers on the Echoes list have fallen, a range of new agencies have begun work, such as GLO. Other service agencies include Harvest Fields, which began in 1960 in the Belfast area. In 2001, its newsletter had a circulation of about 4,800, and the agency was helping to support sixty-two couples and sixteen single or widowed workers and retired workers, all of whom had some kind of link with Ireland.[33] Very few of these missionaries would appear on the Echoes list. In Scotland, missionary support is often channelled through the Home and Foreign Missions Funds (known as Interlink since 1994), which began in 1880. In 2000, eighty-two missionaries appeared on its lists; they would also be included on the Echoes list. It has a council of elder brethren, who interview and approve candidates for service, although the responsibility for commendation rests with the local assembly; the agency also seeks to stimulate assembly missionary interest.[34] The Lord's Work Trust, which was founded by John Ritchie in order to channel gifts received in response to reports of missionary work appearing in *The Believer's Magazine*, also acts as a channel for gifts and information. It is in touch with 'hundreds' of workers commended from assemblies, a proportion of whom would appear on other agencies' lists, some of them working with interdenominational societies, and issues a regular bulletin of news and prayer items, *Look on the Fields*. Its income in 2003-4 was approximately £3.5 million, about the same as that of Echoes of

---

[29] For example, in the 2003 *Daily Prayer Guide*, only thirty workers out of 374 had been commended from countries outside the British Isles.

[30] Peter Grosvenor, 'Tentmakers', *EOS* 125 (1996), 445.

[31] Harold H. Rowdon, 'World Mission – the Way Ahead', *CBR* 36 (September 1985), 61.

[32] Neil Summerton to the author, 8 February 2005.

[33] George Hall, 'Harvest Fields – a brief history', *PS* 56 (2001), 91.

[34] Dickson, *Brethren in Scotland*, 144-5; Interlink home page, <www.interlink.org.uk/about_us.htm>, accessed 16 June 2004.

Service; 98% was earmarked for specific individuals or needs. Funds for workers at home and overseas also continue to be transmitted through the SKI; during the year 2003-4, this amounted to £1,056,000.[35] Other channels of finance include organisations such as Stewardship Services, and a proportion of support is also sent directly by assemblies and individuals to workers.

Specific aspects of missionary work have been supported by a range of small organisations. During the 1950s and 1960s the Missionary Technical Fellowship was active in supplying missionaries with specialist information and on occasion materials or even machinery. Brass Tacks began in 1986 in order to provide short-term practical assistance on such projects as constructing or refurbishing buildings.[36] Medical Missionary News began when a group of Brethren doctors met at the London Missionary Meetings around 1922; from 1934 a magazine was issued, whose circulation was approaching 8,000 by 1997. For many years annual report meetings were held in conjunction with the London Missionary Meetings. Initially, the agency served as a source of information, but has now extended its remit to include the provision of equipment, medicines and other materials for medical work. By 1997, its annual income had exceeded £400,000, although missionaries pay half the cost of the items they need. Non-Brethren missionaries also use its services.[37]

The personal needs of missionaries are also met by a variety of bodies. Muriel Hogg, daughter-in-law of C.F. Hogg, began the Womens' Missionary Fellowship in 1952; this is based at a former Baptist chapel in Kilburn, where parcels are made up for sending to missionaries and a clothing store maintained.[38] What became the Retired Missionaries' Aid Fund was founded in 1914, and had 220 workers on its books by 1994.[39] The needs of children are met from the Missionaries' Children's Fund, which draws on the money released by the closure and sale of the children's home in Bury St Edmunds in 1966.[40]

Looking back over the movement's history, we can see how the lack of any formal denominational structure for Open Brethren has resulted in the emergence of a plethora of organisations, each set up to meet a specific need. Nevertheless, there has been relatively little duplication of effort, each group having a clear focus which is often distinct from that of other bodies. During the last few years, in order to foster good working relationships between these groups (and others serving Open assemblies), Partnership has sponsored occasional consultations bringing together leaders from a variety of different agencies, including those connected with overseas mission.

One change during this period, which complicates an attempt to assess how mission-minded assemblies are, has been a greater openness to serving with or supporting interdenominational or even denominational societies. The work of the Bible Societies and other such agencies continued to occupy an honoured place in assembly missionary vision because of their focus on circulating the Scriptures. In 1950, W.T. Stunt noted that the Bible Societies had circulated tens of thousands of Darby's Elberfeld translation of the Bible into German, and listed the translations published by them for which Brethren had been responsible to some degree. He also noted that the British and Foreign Bible Society

---

[35] *The George Müller Foundation: Report on the Work 2003-2004*, 53.

[36] Colin Breeze, 'Brass Tacks', *EOS* 126 (1997), 345-7; Bresnen, *Assemblies in the Wirral*, 144.

[37] David Hickish, 'Medical Missionary News', *EOS* 126 (1997), 340-4; cf. *LOH* 12 (1923), 14-15.

[38] Joy Riley, 'The Women's Missionary Fellowship', *EOS* 126 (1997), 351-2.

[39] P.C. Smart, 'Serving Tables', *PS* 55 (2000), 48.

[40] Brian Davies, 'Missionaries' Children's Fund', *EOS* 126 (1997), 348-50.

(BFBS) supplied missionaries with cheap Scriptures. Among Brethren who had contributed to its work were Broadbent, who used to spend hours at Bible House in London reporting on his visits to Europe, and Laing, who succeeded George Goodman on the General Committee. The conclusion drawn by Stunt was that assemblies were closely linked with the BFBS, and so had an obligation to support it.[41] Nevertheless, occasional criticisms were voiced concerning its readiness to involve Roman Catholics and liberal Protestants in translation projects.

Although there had always been a number of Open Brethren serving with interdenominational faith missions, attitudes towards missionary societies tended to be rather negative, partly because some Brethren had seceded from such bodies. The 1959 annual report of Echoes of Service commented, 'we understand that one society has lost such a large proportion after training and a period of service, longer or shorter, that the Directors consider it inadvisable now to accept, as missionaries, those who have been in assembly fellowship. They take the view that such are never really happy in a missionary society.'[42] However, there has been a widespread change of thinking; numbers serving with such societies have increased steadily, both in real terms and as a proportion of the Open Brethren missionary force. In 1986, a list of British Brethren serving with OM ran to no less than forty-four names,[43] and the following year it was reported that twenty-nine out of 113 British missionaries with the New Tribes Mission came from assemblies.[44] Of the assemblies participating in the 1988 survey, 44% had commended individuals as missionaries, and 13% had members serving as short-term workers. But of 324 missionaries, only 150 had gone out in fellowship with Echoes of Service; 146 were serving with missionary societies, and almost all the rest were independent of all agencies.[45] The high proportion of members serving with missionary societies (possibly as much as a half of Open Brethren missionaries from Britain, although the assemblies participating in this survey would have been more likely than others to commend their members to such agencies) is a remarkable development, especially when we remember that complaints about the diversion of assembly interest and funds to such bodies had appeared throughout this period. Given the centrality of mission to Brethren identity, it is surely one of the most significant factors to take into account when exploring how Open Brethren see themselves in relation to 'the denominations'. One reason for this shift must be the adoption by many societies of a far more 'church-based' approach to mission from the 1970s, involving the transfer of a significant degree of responsibility for workers from the society to the home church, and a greater emphasis on working alongside, and as part of, local churches on the field. This has meant that there is now much less difference between the policy of such bodies and that of Brethren agencies, and

---

[41] W.T. Stunt, 'The Bible Society and Missionaries from Assemblies', *EQR* 2.2 (April-June 1950), 41-2, 57.

[42] *EOS* 88 (1959), 66.

[43] *H*, June 1986, 16. OM has often had key Brethren in leadership positions, maintains a clear focus on evangelism and Bible teaching, and is run on 'faith lines' with a pronounced lay ethos. Notes produced for a conference of Brethren agencies in June 1978 described Brethren as 'by far the largest denomination represented in OM' (CBA Box 148(1)).

[44] *H*, March 1987, 16.

[45] Brierley et al, *Brethren*, 110-11. Interestingly, the 20% of assemblies responding to the survey accounted for almost half of the missionaries in fellowship with Echoes of Service (Brierley et al, *Brethren*, 112).

so Brethren find it easier than before to work with them. Whilst progressive assemblies are the most willing to commend their members for service with such bodies, Echoes of Service still enjoys a measure of support from progressive churches, an indication of its role as a unifying agency among assemblies. Indeed, it is the only agency which has links with a majority of British assemblies, and an example of how Brethren are much readier to co-operate for evangelism than for other purposes.

As for changing thinking about missiology, Brethren were slower than many Evangelicals to adopt a more holistic approach to mission. Many continued to emphasise the traditional priorities of evangelism and church planting. For example, Bruce, in an address at the 1953 London Missionary Meetings, called for mission to focus on church planting; he regarded schools and hospitals as auxiliaries to this which could be taken over by hostile governments for other purposes, whereas independent local churches could not.[46] His address was undoubtedly influenced by awareness of the Communist threat, which was kept at the forefront of Brethren thinking by frequent comment in *The Harvester* and *The Witness*, and by awareness of the experiences of Geoffrey Bull and George Patterson in Tibet during the early 1950s.[47] Yet even after the collapse of East European Communism in the late 1980s, traditional Brethren still retained the same understanding of mission because it was rooted in their overall worldview, which gave little place to anything which could be categorised as mere 'world improvement', such as political lobbying or seeking structural change. Even the *Lausanne Covenant* received little attention in Brethren circles, apart from the series of articles in *The Harvester* during 1976-7. Nevertheless, extensive media coverage of the disastrous famine in Ethiopia, and the massive popular response which this generated, were factors leading the Editors at Echoes of Service to set up an Overseas Disaster Fund from 1984, as well as other funds for channelling relief giving. Medical work continues to be highly regarded; in 1959, 250 out of approximately 1,150 names on the Echoes list indicated that they had some kind of medical qualification.[48] Overall, it is probably fair to say that Brethren missiology is essentially an application to overseas contexts of the same principles which guide evangelistic and church-planting work at home, although with a considerable measure of adaptation to differing socio-cultural contexts.

23.4 Mission at Home

With the increasing presence of overseas nationals in Britain since the end of the war, a number of Brethren have sought to reach particular ethnic groups. An early example of this was the Gospel to Britain's Guests. This outreach was commenced around 1940 by Ransome W. Cooper (1881-1979) in order to reach 'displaced persons' later known as 'European voluntary workers'. By the early 1950s, there were well over 250,000 refugees from Iron Curtain countries in Britain, three-quarters of them nominally Roman Catholic. The government offered guaranteed work for two years in mining, hospitals, textiles, or

---

[46] F.F. Bruce, 'The Apostolic Witness', *W* 83 (1953), 209, 212.

[47] See Geoffrey Bull, *God Holds the Key* (London: Hodder & Stoughton, [1959]); *idem, When Iron Gates Yield* (London: Hodder & Stoughton, [1955]); George Patterson, *God's Fool* (London: Faber & Faber, [1956]); *idem, Tibetan Journey* (London: Faber & Faber, [1954]). On Bull (1921-99), who after his release from imprisonment spoke to large audiences about his experiences, see Plant, *They Finished their Course in the 90s*, 37-44.

[48] Anon., 'Medical Work', *EOS* 88 (1959), 18.

agriculture. Cooper stated in 1952 that Slav assemblies existed in Nottingham, Derby, Bradford, Bolton, and Halifax, in fellowship with local English assemblies, and listed eleven Brethren who were working among these communities.[49] Among them were well-known names such as James Lees (1879-1958)[50] and Stuart Hine (1899-1989), translator of the hymn 'How Great Thou Art' from Russian into English.[51] All were fluent in the relevant languages, many having served in Central and Eastern Europe as missionaries before the war. Prisoners of war were also the subject of outreach efforts, and some assemblies with camps nearby arranged services in German or Italian to which these men were invited; successful work was done among them by men such as J.H. Hughes of Nutley, Sussex, one of a number of Counties evangelists who proved adept at switching his field of work during and after the war. Contact with German believers in this way stimulated expressions of practical concern, such as the 'Inasmuch' Relief Fund, based in the Wirral, which sent thousands of parcels of food and other basic necessities to believers in Germany, Austria, and elsewhere. Beginning in the late 1940s, it functioned for about twenty years.[52]

The next wave of immigration was primarily from the West Indies: between 1955 and 1962, 260,000 Caribbeans came to Britain.[53] In 1950s, decline in the Lewisham assembly was arrested by the accession of a number of Jamaicans, and in 1960 it began a monthly International Rally to reach such immigrants.[54] Other assemblies in areas of high immigration from the Caribbean started similar ventures. Attempts were also made to reach immigrants from India and Pakistan, often by missionaries who had returned from the field. In 1958, it was reported that one such, a Dr Zingers, had become a General Practitioner in Walsall and with her husband hoped to start outreach among her many Indian and Pakistani patients.[55] A few years later, the assembly at Southall began similar work.[56] Several assemblies found this a fruitful area of activity; in 1992 that at Kenton, Middlesex, reported that a children's mission had attracted fifty-nine Asian children and only one 'English' child.[57] A few years later, Totterdown Gospel Hall in Bristol reported that, in spite of opposition, a number of baptisms had resulted from a regular Sunday afternoon gospel meeting for the Asian community.[58]

---

[49] Ransome W. Cooper, 'European Voluntary Workers', *EQR* 4.1 (January-March 1952), 3-6. Frequent reports of this work appeared in *BM* and *W* from the late 1940s. The only other denominations to work among these groups that I know of were the Roman Catholic and the Orthodox, another indication that Open Brethren were considerably more mission-minded than other Protestant communities.

[50] See Ransome W. Cooper, *James Lees: Shepherd of Lonely Sheep in Europe* (London: Pickering & Inglis, 1959).

[51] See Anderson, *They Finished their Course in the 80's*, 67-74; Stuart K. Hine, *Not you, but God* (3 parts in 1 vol.; Burnham-on-Sea: the author, 1973-[82]).

[52] For details, see Bresnen, *Assemblies in the Wirral*, 139-44.

[53] Hastings, *English Christianity*, 510.

[54] A.J. Fagg, *Lewisham assembly 1868-1968: a centre of Christian witness* (London: n.p., 1968), unpaginated.

[55] *EOS* 87 (1958), 134.

[56] *PS* 17 (1966), 31-2; 20 (1969), 188.

[57] *PS* 43 (1992), 155.

[58] *PS* 50 (1995), 91.

More recently, a few assemblies have engaged in evangelistic and relief work among asylum seekers and refugees; one Tyneside assembly reported that several had been baptised and brought into fellowship as a result, but noted that it took care to offer assistance to all in need in its locality, not just to asylum seekers (whose presence, and perceived preferential treatment by the authorities, have sometimes provoked violent local opposition).[59]

Some ethnic congregations have been formed in association with assemblies. We have already noted that during the 1940s and 1950s there were several Slav congregations. More recently, ethnic Chinese assemblies have emerged. For example, one was active in Chorlton-cum-Hardy, Manchester, during the early 1990s, which owed its origins to an offshoot of Open Brethren in Hong Kong. Another in Heaton Moor, near Stockport, began life as a congregation associated with Witness Lee, a successor of Watchman Nee whose 'Local Church' movement caused considerable controversy by claiming that its assembly was 'the local church' in a particular place (a claim similar to that made by some Brethren in earlier generations); this particular congregation seceded from Lee's movement in 1988 and adopted a more open attitude to other Evangelical believers and churches.[60]

With the increased racial diversity evident in most British cities, Brethren, like other Evangelicals, have given considerable thought to the issue of reaching adherents of other faiths. An early example of this was provided by William Walker, who had been a missionary in India, in 1968. In an article for *Echoes Quarterly Review*, he outlined the different Indo-Pakistani groups and challenged assemblies to reach out to them.[61] Another pioneer in this field was Maurice Hobbs, who had been brought up among the Stuart Brethren but joined Open Brethren before becoming a colonial administrator. Returning to Britain in 1967, he settled in a multi-ethnic part of Birmingham and was active in the Evangelical Race Relations Group, although he left Brethren during the early 1970s.[62] Perhaps the most venturesome assembly activity in this field was a missionary conference at Preston as long ago as 1969. The customary rally included parallel presentations of Christianity and Islam by Robbie Orr (a missionary from Pakistan) and the leader of the local Muslim community.[63] Such openness has undoubtedly been practised in individual contacts but is rare in the public setting. Evangelicalism is indebted to Brethren, however, because of the ground-breaking work done from the 1970s by Patrick Sookhdeo on the topic of Christian relations with Asian ethnic communities. Commended to this work by Cholmeley Hall, he founded In Contact, authored *Asians in Britain* and edited *Jesus Christ the Only Way* (both published by Paternoster during the 1970s), saw several fellowships planted in the London boroughs of Newham and Tower Hamlets, and has since become widely known through his work with the Barnabas Fund, which seeks to support believers (especially in Islamic countries) persecuted for their faith through prayer and giving. A substantial proportion of its initial support came from Brethren.[64]

---

[59] *PS* 56 (2001), 73; 57 (2002), 25-6.

[60] Brady and Evans, *Brethren*, 128, 156, 158-9.

[61] William Walker, 'The Stranger Within our Gates', *EQR* 20.4 (October-December 1968), 17-24.

[62] See Maurice E.J. Hobbs, *This is My Story* (n.pl.: the author, 2003).

[63] S.F. Warren, 'Another Missionary Conference', *EQR* 21.3 (July-September 1969), 28-31.

[64] Neil Summerton to the author, 29 December 2004.

The existence of ethnic assemblies, and Britain's changing religious complexion, are just two indicators of the vast difference between the context in which Brethren first appeared and those in which many assemblies now exist. With these changes have come changes in the outlook and ethos of the churches, and of the Evangelical constituency. The pace and extent of change have been difficult for many to keep up with, and it is small wonder that Brethren, like many other Evangelicals, have been revisiting the question of what constitutes their distinctive identity. Nevertheless, their story is not yet complete and their usefulness not yet ended. In the final chapter I shall offer some reasons for this view.

PART 5

Conclusion

CHAPTER 24

Conclusion:
Open Brethren Today – and Tomorrow?

In a book review, Neil Summerton drew on his experience as a civil servant to offer a piece of advice: 'I have always found that a very useful step in policy making is to establish how we got to where we are.'[1] Having established how Open Brethren got to where they are, this chapter offers some thoughts from an outsider's perspective which might contribute to their 'policy making' today, and some suggestions for further research.

24.1 What has Happened to the Original Principles?

Rowdon argued that the characteristic activity of early Brethren was not the Breaking of Bread but the Bible reading, and that the main distinguishing feature of Brethren is the absolute priority given to the Scriptures. In support of his claim, he noted that much nineteenth-century Brethren literature consisted of expository works.[2] I would suggest that as a result, six hallmarks of Open Brethren life and thought have emerged:

    i. Rejection of the clergy-laity distinction in favour of a radical application of the priesthood of all believers.

    ii. The practice of believer's baptism (with the exception of a few who advocated household baptism), although it should be noted that not all assemblies have made this a requirement for membership.

    iii. The centrality of the Lord's Supper, set in the context of open worship, to the life of the church.

    iv. The sole (rather than supreme) authority of Scripture in determining belief and practice.

    v. The autonomy of each local assembly (the main characteristic distinguishing Open from Exclusive Brethren).

    vi. A commitment to mission at home and overseas.

Separation from all other 'systems', which is claimed by some as a fundamental principle, has never been universally taught or practised, and thus cannot be seen as a distinctive of the movement as a whole, although it is a distinctive of *some* Brethren, especially in Northern Ireland and Scotland. Conversely, openness of fellowship to sound and godly believers of all denominations and none, whilst treated by some as fundamental, was practised more by southern assemblies and remains a minority viewpoint in Scotland and Northern Ireland.

Eschatology, while important in the thinking of the great majority of Brethren, was not a subject on which the earliest leaders were ever completely agreed, and was arguably less significant as an underlying motivation for post-1859 Brethren. As Coad has pointed

---

[1] *PP* 11 (April 1999), 26.

[2] Rowdon, *Who are the Brethren?*, 33.

out, the infamous conclusion to Neatby's history of the movement was modified in its second edition to say only that Brethren took shape *in part* 'under the influence of a delusion' (that of the immediate Second Coming), which 'left its traces, more or less deeply', on the system's distinctives.[3] One thread running through the post-war story, which I had not expected to prove so important, concerns the decline in popularity of traditional Brethren eschatology. This should not be overstated, since the majority of Open Brethren still hold such views, but it is significant, in that it has cleared the way for rethinking on issues as diverse as ecumenism, charismatic renewal, and the legitimacy of social and political involvement. If this eschatology was not in any case a fundamental principle of earliest Brethren thinking, then it would seem possible that its waning may make it easier to recapture the original vision for unity and to engage in some rethinking on the issue of separation.[4] Lang has claimed that there is no necessary connection between a particular eschatological system and Open Brethren ecclesiology,[5] although he appeared to make such a connection himself! More significantly, it was some years before *Precious Seed* and *Assembly Testimony*, both founded to provide expositions of assembly truth, began to devote much space to articles on eschatological topics.

If openness to all believers alive today is right, then it surely follows that Brethren should recognise, and benefit from the gifts of, believers throughout previous generations.[6] This involves reflecting on their attitude towards 'tradition', which may be more culturally-conditioned than biblical. I am not advocating that Brethren throw away what some have seen as their sole distinctive. Rather, I would say that it needs modifying to reflect both the reality of Brethren history and the teaching of Scripture itself concerning the handing on of the faith. It would be possible to show that the first generation of Brethren often owed more to the tradition of the universal church than they acknowledged (e.g. in their expositions of the Trinity or the Person of Christ). Later on, a robust interpretative tradition developed, which guided individuals in their understanding of Scripture and which was used on occasion as a justification for excluding from the platform teachers whose ministry departed from it. That tradition was handed down principally by means of the magazines, especially their 'Question and Answer' pages, and by ministry of recognised ('accredited') itinerant teachers at conferences. If we examine the New Testament, we see that the apostle Paul exhorted his co-workers and churches to stand by the traditions which they had received and approved of them for doing so (1 Corinthians 11.2, 15.1; 2 Timothy 2.2). Whilst churches today will not wish to hand on their traditions unaltered in the way that Paul expected, they could still follow him in acknowledging the value of the handing-on process. Rather than claiming that we have no place for tradition, it would be better to open our eyes to the reality of its presence, and to consider how far it may be employed in a positive way. Assemblies stand as part of a

---

[3] *H* 58 (1979), 240.

[4] Among related questions worth exploring, we may ask whether Brethren preoccupation with eschatological and typological detail represented a retreat of spirituality from engagement with the world, and whether the decline of interest in such things is evidence of increasing engagement with the world or of worldliness. Of course, some Brethren would equate these, but a significant number would not.

[5] Lang, *Groves*, 290.

[6] Failure to do this was a factor in the later appearance among Open as well as Exclusive Brethren of some aberrant understandings of the Person of Christ; cf. F.F. Bruce, 'The Humanity of Jesus Christ', *JCBRF* 24 (September 1973), 5-15.

two millennia-old tradition which could shed valuable light on some of the problems they now face. For example, discussions about local autonomy and the need for inter-church relations could be informed by an awareness of how such issues have been faced in earlier centuries, notably by seventeenth-century Baptists in formulating their theology of association.

There is another issue which arises from consideration of tradition. If a discriminating openness to other Christ-centred traditions is desirable, how much more is a willingness to relate to other streams within the Open Brethren tradition? In 1944, Watson lamented the tendency to find fault with the shortcomings of assemblies, and suggested that rather than adding to the burdens of those trying to maintain a testimony under difficult conditions, it would be better to offer encouragement.[7] How, without compromising their convictions, could assemblies of different outlooks begin to encourage one another in that which they approve? Some practical steps in this direction, such as the development of mutual prayer support, could boost the morale both of struggling conservative assemblies and of progressive churches who have felt the pain of rejection by their brethren. Brethren need to find a way of containing the divisions among them, which offer sad confirmation of the allegation that Protestantism has an inbuilt tendency to fragment, otherwise they will begin to lose members to traditions which emphasise their visible unity and historical continuity with the church of past generations. If Rowdon's vision of a network of congregations is to be fully realised, it must be recognised that most Open Brethren structures and networks were in some way evangelism-orientated; Counties and Echoes of Service are but two of the most prominent examples of this. Yet it is also true that the legitimacy and extent of evangelistic co-operation has long been a bone of contention between separatists and more open Brethren. Many of the concerns in this area arose from experiences which cannot simply be dismissed by the other side. Related to this is the tension evident since the 1830s between the evangelistic and ecclesiological impulses within the movement. Those seeking to establish a network of congregations must either find a way in which differing approaches to evangelistic co-operation can be allowed for, or accept that there may develop several parallel informal networks, each reflecting differing approaches to this topic, which need to establish relationships marked by mutual respect.

We can look at this openness to others from another perspective, in the light of the final item on my list: although recent decades have seen a radical change in our understanding of the Christian world, in which the idea of sending and receiving nations has been challenged by that of national Christian communities as global partners, the implicit expectation that every believer will have a world vision remains. A sense of oneness with all believers worldwide, and an openness to receive from them, should be a powerful stimulus to develop co-operative links between assemblies in Britain and elsewhere. As W.E. Vine long ago observed, 'The degree of unity and harmony which has prevailed among [assemblies] is due in considerable measure to the missionary spirit which has characterised them. Indeed, speaking of individual assemblies, it may be said that their spiritual prosperity has been in direct proportion to their missionary zeal.'[8]

It is the way in which the Brethren give expression to the third item in my list which remains most distinctive; however, that appears to be in serious danger of being let slip by progressive assemblies. Aided by the patternism of many later nineteenth-century

---

[7] 'WW', *W* 74 (1944), 64.

[8] W.E. Vine, Preface to [Short], *Principles*, iii.

leaders, in some assemblies communion may be observed without theological justification being given for its format; hence it is frequently under-appreciated. In the words of David Clines, 'Both the Scripture and the preaching of the Word are neglected in our morning services, and the result is that the rich significance of the Lord's Supper is only dimly recognised by most of the members of our churches.' Such an outcome, he contended, was the result of too narrow a concept of worship, which restricted it to adoration.[9] This may be a factor in (i) the neglect of the Lord's Supper among some contemporary Open assemblies, and (ii) the allegedly fossilised nature of the observance, and of the open worship in which it is set, in some quarters. Open Brethren today face the challenge of developing an inclusive style, as well as an inclusive theology, for their conduct of this service, so that families, for example, are able to attend. The sober contemplative nature of this service as traditionally conducted is not 'family-friendly' and runs counter to the emphasis of much contemporary outreach on reaching families. This may be one of the main reasons why the service is declining, and thus may be a significant factor contributing to the movement's crisis of identity. Any change needs to be undergirded by a sound theological, and not merely pragmatic, justification, which includes a rich understanding of the nature of worship and of what the Christian community is doing when it celebrates what Anglicans call 'this memorial of our redemption'.

If it is felt that the truths listed above are biblical, and that God blessed the testimony to them, it would be tragic to let go of them. Their practical expression may change in line with changing circumstances and cultural contexts, but it would be unwise to jettison old ways of doing things without ensuring that we have adequate and appropriate alternatives to express those truths. The choice offered by James Houston in 1962 remains today:

> Today we face three alternatives: we can maintain the status quo in our assemblies, not seeing and not desiring any reforms; or we may allow ourselves to become so discouraged that we leave the Brethren Movement to serve in other spheres that we think will be more effective; or we can be determined by God's help to remain where we are and seek by personal realism and truly sacrificial service to help in reviving and establishing local churches that they may be effective in witness and worship.[10]

24.2 The Scope for Further Research

Lengthy as this book has turned out to be, several topics deserve fuller attention than it has been possible to give them. Firstly, it would seem worth making a full-scale investigation of the nature, role, and functions of leaders among Open Brethren. In the first generation, many were aristocrats, landed gentry, or former clergy; the late nineteenth century saw the baton passed to the evangelists, and for most of the twentieth century leadership was frequently in the hands of businessmen (one could extend this further to assert that they in turn were succeeded by solicitors); nowadays, the progressive constituency is led by full-time workers of various types. The ways in which the nature of

---

[9] Clines, 'Liturgy without Prayerbook', 11.

[10] J.M. Houston, 'Needed - a Third Force', *JCBRF* 1 (May 1963), unpaginated. This issue comprised papers originally delivered at the 1962 Young Men's Bible Teaching Conference.

the movement's leadership has affected its vision would be worth exploring. There is a view that at the heart of the Open Brethren identity crisis is a leadership crisis, which has been a key factor in the post-1960 decline, affecting progressive and traditional assemblies.[11] It arises from the fact that the movement has never produced an adequate formulation of the relationship between divine and human leadership. Granted that many assemblies have been marked in recent years by a mentality which focuses on maintenance rather than mission, in what ways is this related to their understanding of the nature of local and national leadership?

There may also be a cautionary tale here. We have seen the importance of personalities and print in a movement with no denominational structures to hold it together. Even in the connexional approach adopted by Exclusive Brethren, personalities seem to have played crucial roles, and most sections were known by the names of their leaders (Kelly, Grant, Stuart, Lowe, Raven, Taylor). It is only a matter of time before individual initiative becomes the cult of personality, reinforced by the aura conveyed by the use of initials to refer to the movement's best-known writers. A study of the extent to which this cult of personality has influenced the attitudes of both ordinary members and the personalities in question would be highly instructive.

Secondly, further research is urgently needed on Open Brethren mission and missiology. Perceptive analyses have been offered of individual missionaries, notably A.N. Groves, and of topics, such as 'living by faith', but no overall survey of Brethren mission to compare with Fiedler's survey of faith missions has yet appeared. As for actual missionary work, Tatford's exhaustive accounts focus primarily on the doings of missionaries and provide little analysis of either what they achieved or the nature of the indigenous works which ensued; neither is there much consideration of movements which emerged apart from missionary input. As part of such research, there is room for regional and national surveys, looking at assembly mission and the developing shape of local churches in Eastern Europe, the heart of Africa, or the Islamic world, for example.

Thirdly, I have been unable to do more than throw out a few hints concerning the theme of social class and its relevance for an understanding of the development and fragmentation of Open Brethren. Whilst the availability of data is patchy, it would be possible to utilise church registers to investigate how an assembly's social class changed over time, as well as data provided by the 1851 census returns. Perhaps such work needs to be done at a local or regional level first. It would then be easier to explore such matters as the relationship between social class and theological outlook.

Fourthly, it would be worth exploring the implications of changes in eschatological belief for the form and content of gospel preaching and personal testimony. The lengthy series of articles on 'My Conversion and Call' in *Assembly Testimony* (approximately ninety to the end of 2004) would furnish a valuable collection of evidence for this, and it is interesting to note the frequency with which the fear of being left behind at the rapture featured in these accounts. As part of this, research could explore whether preaching shaped or responded to the form which conversion accounts were expected to take, and the way in which conversion socialised individuals into a group with certain defined eschatological beliefs.

Finally, there are other areas of research relating to the movement as a whole, such as the extent of continuity between pre- and post-1859 thinking: to what extent did later assemblies take over the ecclesiology of the 1830s and 1840s, and did revivalism lead to

---

[11] Neil Summerton to the author, 29 December 2004.

significant modifications of it? Related to this is the question of the movement's early vision: it can be argued that presentations of the early decades often say as much about the outlook of modern writers as they do about that of early Brethren, and that an idealised vision of that period both underlay the work of CBRF's early leaders and provided something for its opponents to react against. Once this has been adequately explored, it is possible to consider in more detail the extent to which later leaders developed or betrayed such a vision.

In looking at the extent of continuity between early and later Brethren, it would be worth examining those regions where Open Brethren put down strong roots before 1859: Devon, Herefordshire, and Suffolk, to name three. In historical research, there is a level between the local history, covering the story of a particular assembly, and a history of this type which attempts to outline the movement's development in national terms. The former risks being so specific that it is inadequately related to wider developments; the latter risks taking refuge in unsubstantiated and vague generalisations. There is thus ample scope for a regional-based approach to Brethren history. This would involve detailed investigation of patterns of growth and decline within particular regions of Britain, against the background of regional cultural, demographic, and socio-economic change. Little of this nature has so far been done, and it would have been impossible for me to undertake such a task. This represents a significant gap in Brethren historiography, especially when compared to that of denominations such as the Baptists or the Congregationalists. Such work would provide a much firmer basis for a successor to this book.

Linked with this is the investigation of the part played by Brethren in the wider local church scene; for example, it would be immensely interesting if someone were to research the earlier history of Bethesda, Bristol, as part of a wider investigation of nineteenth-century Nonconformity in the city. This would highlight the web of connections, as well as the parallel developments, between Brethren and other churches, thus showing that the movement was not *sui generis*. The same is probably demonstrable for Plymouth. To some extent, this has been done with reference to Dublin, and the results have illuminated the first section of this book. At the national level, it would be worthwhile to examine the relation between later growth of the Brethren movement and the fluctuating fortunes of pan-denominational organisations such as the EA; I suspect that there may be a degree of inverse correlation between them, and it would be useful to establish the reasons for this.

24.3 Afterword: An Unfinished Story

Reports of the imminent demise of Open Brethren are, I believe, exaggerated. In my opinion, the last word has not been said. The story is thus unfinished in the sense that it has not yet ended. As a historian, it is beyond my remit to offer predictions as to the likely future of Open Brethren. However, the concept of an autonomous congregation, with a minimum of organisation and a maximum of flexibility to respond to changing and possibly hostile circumstances, is one which has proved resilient under trial, as in Eastern Europe, and capable of adaptation to a wide variety of cultural contexts around the world. It has been said that if Brethren did not exist, someone would have to invent them. Brethren ideals have an assured future because they have a past: Lang and Broadbent were correct in seeing them as representing perennial tendencies within Christian theology, proven in a variety of contexts, and which need to be kept within the church catholic.

Coad has also highlighted the value of such congregations as a perennial corrective to the tendency of mainstream churches towards institutionalisation.

We may also speak of the story as unfinished because the wider church still has much to learn from Brethren experience and reflection. Brethren have drawn attention to aspects of corporate Christian experience which have been neglected by the churches of the Reformation, notably in the central place which they have given to the Lord's Table.

From another angle, the story is unfinished in the sense of being incomplete. So much can never be known about the history of individual assemblies because of the lack of evidence, or if it can be known there is not space to include it here.

Finally, and soberingly, the story is unfinished in the sense of being provisional. Further research is needed, as indicated above; it has not been possible to investigate all the questions thrown up by this study, or follow up all the leads to further evidence. But even that will not make the story significantly less provisional; the definitive account will one day be revealed and we shall know as we are known, and it is right that all of us, whether historians, church leaders, or members, undertake our service with that long-term perspective.

APPENDIX 1

Early Conferences

Date	Venue	Identification	Dates	Other known accounts/references
1830	PHEI	Powerscourt House, Enniskerry, Ireland	Mon-Wed, Sept.	
1831	PHEI	Powerscourt House, Enniskerry, Ireland	Mon Oct 3 – Fri 7	*CH* 2 (1831), 287.
1832	PHEI	Powerscourt House, Enniskerry, Ireland	Mon Sept 24 – Fri 28	*CE* n.s. 1 (1832), 790-1; Darby, *Letters*, 1.5-7n (from *CH* 3 (1832), 290-2).
1833	PHEI	Powerscourt House, Enniskerry, Ireland	Mon Sept 23 – Fri 27	Anon., *Interesting Reminiscences*, 20-1; 'Small Notebook 4', 116; Tayler, *Craik*, 168-9.
1834	EPDI	Ely Place, Dublin, Ireland	Mon Sept 15 – Fri 19	
1835	EPDI	Ely Place, Dublin, Ireland	Mon Sept 7 – Fri 11	
1836	SGDI	Sandymount Green, Dublin, Ireland	Mon Sept 5 – Fri 9	Stunt, *Awakening*, 303.
1838	GHCE	Gloucester Hotel, Clifton, England	Mon June 4 – Fri 8	Darby, *Letters*, 3.232-4; Rowdon, *Origins*, 232, 234-5.
1839	RHLE	R[egent?] Hotel, Leamington, England	Mon June 3 – Fri 7	Darby et al., *Collectanea; I* 2 (1839), 363.
1840		Taunton	January	Tayler, *Craik*, 206.
1840		Exeter		

1841	RHLE	R[egent?] Hotel, Leamington, England	Fri July 16– Tues 20	
1841		Freemasons' Tavern, London	July	
1842		Liverpool		
1843	LE	Liverpool, England	Thurs Nov 2 – Weds 8	Anon., 'Notes in unknown hand'; Darby, *Letters*, 1.66.
1845		London		William Kelly, *John Nelson Darby as I knew him* (Belfast: Words of Truth, 1986), 8.

Main source: Anon., *Questions for Eight Weeks' Consideration* (1838), and the continuation sheets, *Ninth Week* (1839) and *Questions* (1841), in a volume of tracts once owned by William Trotter, in the Chapter Two archive.

APPENDIX 2

A Brethren Family Tree

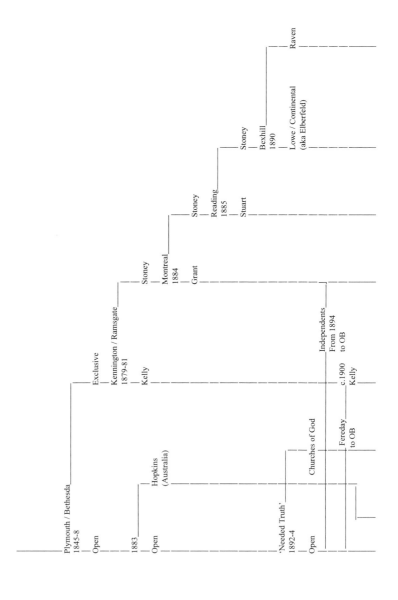

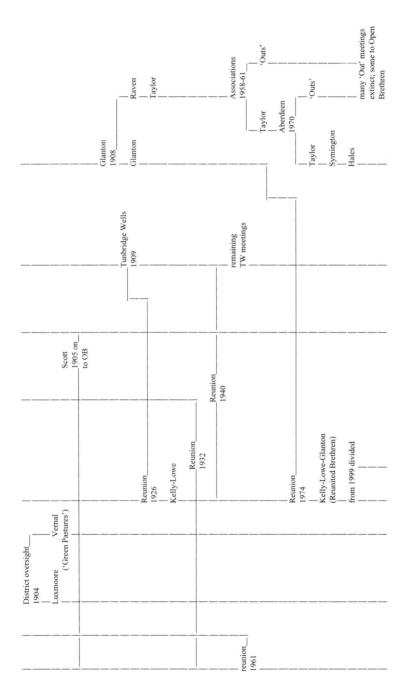

NB: This chart is somewhat simplified, and does not show minor Exclusive divisions, nor most small movements from one stream to another.

Relative Strength of Different Types of Brethren by Region and County, 1892–1901

England	Open	NT	Kelly	Lowe	Raven
South-East	**266**	**11**	**98**	**89**	**199**
Bedfordshire	4	-	1	1	5
Berkshire	8	-	1	2	11
Buckinghamshire	21	-	2	-	7
Channel Islands	2	-	5	1	2
Essex	18	1	9	9	19
Hampshire	27	1	9	11	24
Hertfordshire	16	1	1	1	10
Isle of Wight	5	-	7	1	7
Kent	37	-	17	16	26
London	74	3	27	27	35
Middlesex	12	-	6	4	5
Oxfordshire	2	-	1	1	7
Surrey	23	2	5	6	21
Sussex	17	2	7	9	20
East Anglia	**50**	**1**	**11**	**10**	**23**
Cambridge	3	-	3	-	3
Norfolk	21	1	-	2	9
Suffolk	26	-	8	8	11
South-West	**191**	**-**	**35**	**30**	**97**
Cornwall	8	-	-	6	8
Devon	88	-	11	4	23
Dorset	19	-	6	9	11

Gloucestershire	28	-	6	5	27
Somerset	37	-	7	4	12
Wiltshire	11	-	5	2	16
East Midlands	**18**	**9**	**9**	**9**	**54**
Derbyshire	4	6	1	1	5
Huntingdonshire	2	-	-	-	5
Leicestershire	1	2	-	1	4
Lincolnshire	6	-	2	4	23
Northamptonshire	3	-	1	-	7
Nottinghamshire	2	1	5	3	7
Rutland	-	-	-	-	3
West Midlands	**64**	**8**	**15**	**4**	**53**
Herefordshire	15	-	1	-	4
Shropshire	8	3	-	-	4
Staffordshire	11	3	6	1	13
Warwickshire	20	2	5	1	16
Worcestershire	10	-	3	2	16
North-East	**50**	**11**	**20**	**14**	**87**
Durham	12	4	3	2	17
Northumberland	9	2	-	1	23
Yorkshire	29	5	17	11	47
North-West	**84**	**18**	**12**	**5**	**54**
Cheshire	13	4	1	-	10
Cumberland	11	2	4	-	9
Isle of Man	1	1	1	2	1
Lancashire	53	10	6	3	32
Westmorland	6	1	-	-	2
Total	**723**	**58**	**200**	**161**	**567**

Wales

North Wales	1	1	2	-	8
Anglesey	-	-	-	-	-
Caernarvonshire	-	-	1	-	2
Denbighshire	-	1	1	-	1
Flintshire	1	-	-	-	3
Merioneth	-	-	-	-	-
Montgomeryshire	-	-	-	-	2
South Wales	31	3	6	2	8
Brecon	-	-	-	-	-
Cardiganshire	-	-	-	-	1
Carmarthenshire	1	-	-	-	-
Glamorgan	18	3	4	2	3
Monmouth	10	-	2	-	2
Pembroke	2	-	1	-	2
Radnor	-	-	-	-	-
Total	32	4	8	2	16

Scotland

South	28	7	-	4	18
Berwick	1	-	-	-	2
Dumfries	6	2	-	2	4
Kirkcudbright	5	-	-	1	2
Peebles	2	2	-	-	2
Roxburgh	1	1	-	1	6
Selkirk	2	2	-	-	1
Wigtown	11	-	-	-	1
Lowlands	177	54	8	2	64
Ayr	46	11	-	-	10

Bute	2	1	-	-	-
Clackmannan	2	-	-	-	1
Dunbarton	7	3	-	-	1
Fife	13	5	1	-	9
Kinross	-	-	-	-	-
Lanark	69	19	4	2	18
East Lothian	2	-	-	-	3
Midlothian	5	4	2	-	11
West Lothian	6	3	-	-	3
Renfrew	16	5	1	-	4
Stirling	9	3	-	-	4
Highlands	**69**	**9**	**5**	**-**	**44**
Aberdeen	28	3	1	-	7
Angus	7	1	1	-	2
Argyll	3	-	-	-	2
Banff	8	-	-	-	5
Caithness	1	-	-	-	1
Inverness	-	1	-	-	1
Kincardine	3	-	-	-	1
Moray	4	3	-	-	1
Nairn	1	-	-	-	1
Orkney	8	-	-	-	3
Perth	1	-	2	-	9
Ross & Cromarty	1	-	-	-	-
Shetland	4	1	1	-	9
Sutherland	-	-	-	-	2
Total	**274**	**70**	**13**	**6**	**126**

Ireland

Ulster	126	2	6	6	21
Antrim	27	-	3	2	2
Armagh	17	1	-	1	1
Down	37	1	2	3	9
Fermanagh	4	-	-	-	1
Londonderry	10	-	1	-	4
Tyrone	18	-	-	-	2
Cavan	4	-	-	-	-
Donegal	4	-	-	-	1
Monaghan	5	-	-	-	1
Connacht	**3**	**-**	**-**	**-**	**9**
Galway	-	-	-	-	1
Leitrim	1	-	-	-	1
Mayo	-	-	-	-	2
Roscommon	2	-	-	-	2
Sligo	-	-	-	-	3
Leinster	**15**	**-**	**1**	**2**	**13**
Carlow	-	-	-	-	-
Dublin	7	-	1	1	3
Kildare	1	-	-	-	1
Kilkenny	1	-	-	-	-
Kings = Offaly	1	-	-	1	1
Longford	-	-	-	-	2
Louth	-	-	-	-	1
Meath	-	-	-	-	1
Queens = Leix	-	-	-	-	3
Westmeath	1	-	-	-	-
Wexford	2	-	-	-	-

Wicklow	2	-	-	-	1
Munster	**13**	**-**	**-**	**1**	**4**
Clare	-	-	-	-	-
Cork	5	-	-	-	3
Kerry	4	-	-	-	-
Limerick	1	-	-	-	-
Tipperary	2	-	-	1	1
Waterford	1	-	-	-	-
Total	**157**	**2**	**7**	**9**	**47**

For details of sources, see **Table 6.1**.

Number of Open Brethren Assemblies, 1887–2005

	1887	1897	1904	1922	1927	1933	1951	1959	1968	1970	1975	1983	1991	1995	1997	2002	2005
England	575	723	816	940	1031	1113	1103	1134	1111	1104	1092	1025	918	862	818	748	685
Wales		32	41	59	83	99	99	104	105	107	107	108	94	88	84	79	74
Scotland[1]	184	274	313	357	367	379	344	322	305	289	288	265	254	238	230	213	204
N. Ireland	79	113	123	138	137	145	158	164	168	167	168	173	169	171	172	172	171
Rep. of Ireland[2]		43	44	40	37	39	26	23	25	22	24	22	31	30	27	31	31
Total	838	1185	1337	1534	1655	1775	1728	1747	1714	1689	1679	1593	1466	1389	1331	1243	1165

Sources: Open Brethren assembly address lists, supplemented by information from magazine announcements and other sources recorded on my databases of assemblies. 1887 figures are the totals from G.A. Sprague's list as given in 'List of Assemblies', *EH* 2 (February 1887), 4. The 2005 figures were kindly supplied by the compiler, Roy Hill.

[1] Opening and closing dates for Scottish assemblies have been derived primarily from Dickson, *Brethren in Scotland*, Appendix 3.

[2] Although this designation does not apply to the years before independence, for the sake of consistency I have given separate figures for the whole period for Northern Ireland and the Republic.

Clerical Seceders in Britain

This list draws upon and supplements the appendix in Carter, *Anglican Evangelicals*. Those who seceded overseas, while training, or as a result of training but before ordination, are not included.

Date	Name	Denomination	Location	Notes
1831	Lancelot C.L. Brenton	Anglican	Stadhampton, Oxon	
1831	W.M. Caldecott	Anglican	East Devon	
1831	Henry Craik	Baptist	Shaldon	
1831	W.G. Lambert	Anglican	Devizes?	
1831	George Müller	Baptist	Teignmouth	
1831	G.V. Wigram	Anglican	Plymouth	Unclear whether he took up a curacy
1832	Henry Borlase	Anglican	St Keyne, Cornwall	
1832	R.C. Chapman	Strict Baptist	Barnstaple	
1832	J.L. Harris	Anglican	Plymstock	
1832	J. Methuen	Anglican	Corsham	
1832	William Morshead	Anglican	Bath	
1833	Richard Hill	Anglican	South Milton, Devon	
c.1833	Thomas Tweedy	Anglican	Cork	

1828-34	J.N. Darby	Anglican	Calary, Co. Wicklow	
1834	John Vivian	Anglican	Torquay	
1835	C.F. Hargrove	Anglican	Westport	
1836	J.M .Code	Anglican	Westport	
1837	R. Burdon Sanderson	Anglican		Unclear whether he was actually a clergyman
1838	W.H. Dorman	Independent (i.e. Congregational)	Islington	
1838	Alexander Stewart	Presbyterian	Stafford	
1839	J. Markham	Anglican	Stafford	
1839	John Bowes	Methodist, then non-denominational	Liverpool	
c.1839	George Jeckell	Anglican	Wymondham	
1830s	George Carr	Anglican		
1830s	? Moseley	Baptist or Anglican	South Devon	
1830s	? Robinson	Anglican		
1840	John Offord	Baptist	Exeter	
c.1840	William Morris	Congregational	Plymouth	
1843	Obadiah Atkins	Congregational	Wymondham	
1844	Andrew J. Jukes	Anglican	St John's, Hull	later returned
c.1848	T.H. Reynolds	Anglican		
By 1850?	W.H. Darby	Anglican		

Mid 19th c.	? Peters	Anglican	Quenington, Gloucestershire	
Mid 19th c.	James Mellis	Baptist		
Mid 19th c.	Edward Crowley	Anglican	Leamington?	joined Exclusives
1855	C.H. Coles	Baptist	Brentford	
1855	C.H. Marston	Strict Baptist	Bedfordshire	
1858	?	Anglican	NW England	joined Exclusives
c.1860	J. Denham Smith	Congregational	Kingstown, Dublin	
Early 1860s	J.G. M'Vicker	Presbyterian, then Baptist	nr. Ballymena	
By 1862	Richard Holden	Anglican		joined Exclusives
1862	William Lincoln	Anglican	Walworth, London	
c.1862	Samuel Dodds	Presbyterian	Dalry	a missioner
1865	T. Shuldham Henry	Anglican	Dublin?	
By 1866	Frederick Newman	Anglican	Bedfordshire	
1866	W.T. Turpin	Anglican	St Silas, Glasgow	joined Exclusives; later returned to Anglicans
1872	John Rae	Baptist	Helensburgh	
1872	Charles Bird	Anglican	West Fordington, Dorset	
1873	Theophilus Lessey	Congregational	Islington	
1874-85	William Gudgeon	Baptist	Melksham	

1875	Edward Dennett	Baptist	Lewisham	joined Exclusives
c.1875	F. Bannister	Anglican	Hereford	
c.1878	Mark Harrison	Anglican	Sheffield	possibly not ordained
1880	W.J. Grant	Baptist	Kilmarnock	previously a Free Church of Scotland ministry candidate
1881	H. D'Arcy Champney	Anglican	Cambridge	joined Exclusives
c.1883	Henry A. Hammond	Anglican		
1893/4	Alphaeus Wilkes	Anglican	Whitton, Ipswich	
Late 19th c.	R.M. Henry	Baptist	Belfast	
n.d.	A.C. Ord	Anglican	Bournemouth	joined Exclusives
c.1900	W.D. Dunning	Baptist	Ilminster	
By 1901	T.R. Coleman	Presbyterian		
By 1901	J. Coleman	Presbyterian/ Congregational	Oswestry	
By 1902	W.H. Turner	Wesleyan Methodist	Folkestone	
By 1906	Arthur Fryer	Anglican		
By 1907	? Riseborough	Baptist		
By 1908	R. Lecomte	RC	Jersey	
By 1908	Michael Grant	Baptist	Northern Scotland	
By 1908	E.H. Grant	Baptist	Shankhill, Belfast	

After 1908	Barnes Lawrence	Anglican		
Early 20th c.	W. Fuller Gooch	Baptist	West Norwood	
Early 20th c?	John McKnight	Baptist	Belfast?	
Early 20th c.	A. Tobitt	Anglican	East Sussex	
c.1910	William Hagan	Baptist	Carrickfergus	
1920	R.A. Foster	Baptist	Liverpool	also with Railway Mission
1921	?	Presbyterian	Leeds	
1922	Norman A. Brown	Baptist	Tuebrook, Liverpool	
1922	E.P. Luce	Anglican	Oldham	
1935	William Wilson	Baptist	Belfast	
1938	P.W.H. Lessey	Baptist	Cardiff	had pastored in South Shields
1939	H.L. Ellison	Anglican	Romania	returned to England
1940	Alexander Cooke	Baptist	Belfast?	
1940	Frederick Stradling	Baptist	Scottish Borders	
1944	T.W. Ball	?	Belfast	
c.1945	John Norris	Pentecostal	Ballymena?	
1946	Samuel Jardine	Baptist	Mountpottinger Belfast	
1954	Alex Lyttle	Baptist	Co. Antrim	
1955	Frank Holmes	Anglican	Crowborough	

Late 20th c.	Peter Donald	Baptist		
Late 20th c.	Tom Glover	Baptist		
Late 20th c.	Donald Bridge	Baptist/ Independent Evangelical	Frinton	moved between these and Brethren

APPENDIX 6

Writing your Assembly's History

As a glance at the Bibliography will show, histories of local assemblies, whether in hard copy or on the Internet, have been an invaluable source for this work. However, producing a history of your assembly can be a daunting prospect, especially if you have never done anything of that nature before. The following suggestions are offered to assist in making local histories as useful as possible. Some other denominations have also produced helpful introductions to writing congregational histories; one example is 'Writing your Church or Chapel History' (<www. strictbaptisthistory.org.uk>).

The first thing to consider is your intended audience. If you are writing for present and former members of your assembly, you will need to adopt a different approach from that which would be needed in a work designed for non-members. For the latter, many additional things may need explaining, such as the significance of the Breaking of Bread, or some of the theological terminology in use among Brethren. You may also wish to avoid making too many references to individuals and details of assembly activities which will not be of interest to non-members. Either way, remember that you are writing a history rather than preaching a sermon; your task is to record what *did happen*, before you venture any opinions as to what *should have happened*. If you know anybody who would be willing and competent to read and comment on what you have written, it would be wise to ask for their assistance in order to make your work the best possible.

Secondly, what material is available to you? For background information, books on Brethren history and biographies of individuals connected with your assembly are vital. But it also helps to make the story come to life if you can consult works on the wider religious and general history of the period, and on local history; for example, directories such as *Kelly's Directory* or the *Post Office Directory* were produced for many towns on an annual basis, and listed businesses and places of worship. As for unpublished material, see whether there are minute books, account books, membership registers, or other records relating to your assembly. There may be photographs of assembly activities, such as Sunday School treats, or of individuals associated with it.

Where can you find all these? Probably individuals in your assembly can help with loans of material. But you could also ask at your local library whether they have any books which might help. Also, each county has a Record Office which holds vast quantities of unpublished and published material relating to local history. It is well worth contacting it, but try to make your inquiries as specific as possible. The manuscript catalogues of many such libraries may be accessed through the Access to Archives website, at <www.a2a.org.uk>.

There are two Brethren archives of national significance. The first is the Christian Brethren Archive, which was founded in Manchester in 1980.[1] I have found it a marvellous resource, and I hope that others will be stimulated to explore its riches. There is an online catalogue at <http://rylibweb.man.ac.uk/data2/spcoll/cba/>. Another

---

[1] Contact the archivist at The Christian Brethren Archive, The John Rylands University Library, The University of Manchester, Oxford Road, Manchester M13 9PP; tel: 0161 275 8723).

valuable archive is that held at Chapter Two in London.[2] This specialises in material relating to Exclusive Brethren, but also has a considerable number of nineteenth-century Open Brethren works.

'A picture is worth a thousand words'. Photographs like these, of Glenbuck Gospel Hall, Ayrshire, in 1955 (external above, internal below), bring a story to life and stir up memories. If you can find photographs of your building at various points in its history, you can illustrate how aspects of its life and work have changed over time

Another thing to consider is whether you wish to include illustrations. This will influence what method of production you choose. Of course, desktop publishing makes it possible to design and produce good-quality works yourself, although you will not wish to make multiple copies on a home computer! It is worth taking care over the design and layout of your work, so that its appearance does justice to the care taken in researching it. There are helpful guides available on such topics.

---

[2] For details, contact Edwin Cross, Chapter Two, Fountain House, 1A Conduit Road, London, SE18 3AJ (E-mail: <chapter2uk@aol.com>; Tel: 0208 854 5522).

Other historians are often interested to know about the sources you have used. It is helpful, therefore, to include at the end of your work a Bibliography, listing all the sources you have consulted. This should include newspaper and magazine articles as well as books. If you have used unpublished material details of this will be of particular interest. It is also helpful to indicate where such material is located (if it is held by somebody who will not wish to receive inquiries from other researchers, you could put something like 'in private hands' for the location). Also, remember to make sure that you observe legislation relating to the use of copyright material. Libraries will be able to tell you where to obtain helpful advice on these matters; it is important to get them right, especially as a Christian.

Finally, if you are producing a publication intended for sale, make sure that people find out about it! Consider sending free copies for review to Brethren magazines such as *Believer's Magazine*, *BAHN Review*, or *Precious Seed*, your local newspaper, or (if they accept books for review) to periodicals dealing with the history of your county. You may also wish to advertise it, although this can be expensive. Try to arrange for the book to be available through suitable local bookshops or museums (you will need to offer them a reasonable discount for it to be worth their while), and consider donating a copy to your local library. You could also send information to former members and other people likely to be interested, and to local history societies and other such bodies.

If you are bitten by the history bug, you could also consider joining the Brethren Archivists' and Historians' Network. This publishes *BAHN Review*, an occasional journal on Brethren history, and organises conferences at which participants can offer papers sharing the fruits of their researches, as well as hearing well-known speakers.[3]

---

[3] For details of BAHN, contact, see the Partnership website, <www.partnershipuk.org>.

Bibliography

1. PRIMARY

1.1. Unpublished

1.1.1. ASSEMBLY RECORDS (ALL IN THE CBA)
Smethwick, Bearwood Gospel Hall (Boxes 166-167)
Blackley, Gospel Hall (Box 97)
Bramhall (Box 1)
Carlisle, Hebron Hall (Box 144)
Clapton (Boxes 45-51)

Eccles, Bright Hall (Box 3)
Hackney, Paragon Hall (Box 54)
Hereford (5625)
Ross-on-Wye (5626)
Leominster, Waterloo Rooms (5627)
Streatham, Southcroft Hall (Box 100-101)
Stretford, Gospel Hall (5633, Box 13(18))
Woolpit (Boxes 102-103)
Various assemblies in Lancashire (Box 25)

1.1.2. OTHER MANUSCRIPT MATERIAL
Anon., 'Barnstaple and District Plan and Prayer list', [1982], CBA 5642.
Anon., 'Focus Learning Affiliated Schools: an overview', typescript, 2005.
Anon., 'Greenock leads the way', typescript, n.d., CBA Box 140(10).
Anon., 'The Lord's Work in Italy', manuscript book containing copies of *Letters of Interest*, CBA 7341.
Anon., Mass Observation report of a visit to the Breaking of Bread service at Hebron Hall, Bolton, 17 April 1938, CBA, uncatalogued.
Anon., 'Notes in unknown hand of Bible Readings Nov. 2nd-8th. 1843 & Meetings at Freemasons Hall April 7-9. 1846 re:- Plymouth Division', CBA Box 161(2).
Anon., 'Overtown Gospel Hall: Past to Present', typescript, n.d., CBA Box 146(3).
Anon., 'Situation in 2002', memorandum, 2002, personal collection.
Anon., Sunnymede Chapel [Billericay] Opening Thanksgiving Service brochure, 27 November 1971, CBA Box 36.
Anon., 'Trustees of Church Lane Meeting Room, Stafford, 1839-1920', typescript, n.d., CBA 5635 (1).
Beverley, R.M., letters to the Howard family, LMA 1017/1523-36.
[Bond, Norman M.], [List of Devon and Cornwall assemblies], typescript, 1951.
Bruce, F.F., letter to J.R. Casswell, 5 February 1968, CBA Box 9 (13).
Caldwell, John R., copy of letter dated 14 September 1892, CBA Box 9 (9).
Certificates relating to the Dowglass family, Devon Record Office, 57/4/2.
[Chamings, Arthur], 'Some Papers and Letters in Connection with the Separation of the 1880's and 1890's', typescript, [1987], CBA 15029.
Coad, Roy, 'Study Group on Church Principles. Bulletin No. 3 – February 1958', CBA Box 146 (16).
Craik, Henry, diary for 1863-5, Müller's Homes, Bristol.
Darby, J.N., letters, CBA 5540.
Darby, J.N., translations of letters (originals in *Le Messager Evangelique*), typescript, n.d., Bible & Gospel Trust, Hounslow.
Echoes of Service, 1885-2003 annual reports, photocopied into 2 vols, 'ECHOES Receipts and allocations 1885-1986' and '1987-'.
Elven, Cornelius, letter dated 18 July 1839, West Suffolk Record Office 739/92, photocopy.
'Fry Collection', notebooks of the recollections of B.W. Newton: 'Reminiscences' 1-2 (CBA 7067-8), 'Small Notebooks' 1, 3, 4, 6-12 (CBA 7057-66); also photocopies of some pages of missing 'Small Notebooks' 2 and 5 (CBA Box 13 (30)).
'Fry MS Book', transcribed and ed. A.C. Fry and F.W. Wyatt, manuscript, n.d., CBA 7049.
Greenwood, S., 'Church Halls', 1960^2, CBA Box 146(17).

Harris, A.N., 'The Plymouth Brethren: reminiscences of over Fifty years ago', typescript (from original manuscript of 1911), CBA Box 13 (29).

'Diary of the Rev. John Hill', St Edmund Hall MS 67, Bodleian Library.

Howard, Robert, letter to Captain Wellesley, 25 March 1866, LMA 1270/067.

Kelly, William, transcripts of letters and will, 1849-1906, Chapter Two.

Lang, G.H., letters and papers, CBA 241-273, Boxes 11, 26, 63-76.

Lang, G.H., letter to Mr. [E.H.] Broadbent, 30 March 1926, CBA 5629.

Letters and circulars relating to the Devonshire House Conferences of 1906-7, CBA 2247-2414 and Chapter Two.

Letters and papers in the archive of Echoes of Service, Bath.

Letters and papers in the archive of the George Müller Foundation, Bristol.

Letters and papers in the archive of Partnership (formerly Christian Brethren Research Fellowship), London (now deposited with the CBA).

Letters by and relating to the Taylor Brethren, Chapter Two.

London Annual Conference, minutes 1951-4, CBA Box 13 (23).

Luce, E.P., 'Why I Left the Church', typescript, [1927], personal collection.

Minute books, annual reports, and other papers in the archive of Counties Evangelistic Work, Westbury.

Papers relating to 2002 consultation of Brethren agencies, CBA Box 146 (19).

Papers relating to the Christology of Constantine Metallinos, CBA Box 9 (22).

Papers relating to the Christian Brethren Research Fellowship, later Partnership (UK), CBA Boxes 4-7, 132, 148 (1).

Papers relating to *Harvester/Aware* rescue attempt, CBA Box 139.

Papers relating to the High Leigh and Swanwick conferences, CBA boxes 106, 108-112.

Papers relating to the Home Workers' Fund, CBA Box 27.

Papers relating to Ireland Outreach, CBA Box 24.

Papers relating to meetings of London assemblies north of the Thames, CBA Box 147 (2).

Papers relating to the Young Men's Bible Teaching Conferences, CBA Boxes 13(2), 138, 147 (1).

Sibthorpe Papers, scrapbook of personal documents relating to the life of J.N. Darby, CBA Box 154.

[Summerton, Neil], 'Meeting of Representatives of Key Bodies held on 13 October 2004. Summary of discussion and Conclusions', typescript, 2004.

Summerton, Neil, 'Partnership's Vision and Strategy', paper delivered at the Partnership People Consultation, Loughborough, 2-3 July 2004.

Tregelles, S.P., letters to B.W. Newton, CBA 7181 (7) and (61).

Watson, J.B., letters and papers, CBA Boxes 229-255.

1.2. Published

1.2.1. BRETHREN PERIODICALS

Assembly Testimony
Basketfuls of Fragments
Brethren Archivists' and Historians' Network Review
The Believer's Magazine (*Believer's Magazine* from 1992)
The Believer's Pathway
The Bible Treasury

Report of the Scriptural Knowledge Society/Brief Narrative of Facts relative to the (New)
    Orphan Houses ... and the other objects of the Scriptural Knowledge Institution for
    Home and Abroad
CBRF Broadsheet
CBRF Newsletter (Partnership Newsletter from 1986; Partnership Perspectives from
    1995)
The Christian Witness
The Christian Worker
Conscientious Objectors' News
Counties Evangelistic Work. Annual reports
Counties Evangelization. The Herts and Middlesex District
Counties Quarterly
Denne Road Gospel Hall, Horsham, News Letter
The Disciple
Echoes of Service (The Missionary Echo until 1885)
Echoes Quarterly Review
The Eleventh Hour
Evangelization of Eastern Counties
The George Müller Foundation: Report on the Work
The Golden Lamp
The Gospel Graphic (The Christian Graphic from November 1921)
The Harvester (Harvester from 1985; Aware from August 1990)
The Inquirer
International Newsletter (International Partnership Perspectives from 1999)
The Journal of the Christian Brethren Research Fellowship (Christian Brethren Review
    from issue 31 (1982))
Links of Help (absorbed into The Harvester 1936)
The Missionary Reporter
Needed Truth
News
The Northern Assemblies (The Assemblies from March 1874)
Onward
Precious Seed
The South-Eastern Counties Evangelization
Spearhead
Trent Vale Times
The Truth Promoter
Update
Wholesome Words
The Witness (The Northern Evangelistic Intelligencer until 1872; The Northern
    Intelligencer 1873-4; The Northern Witness 1875-86; incorporated into The
    Harvester 1980)

1.2.2. NON-BRETHREN PERIODICALS
Christian Brethren's Journal and Investigator
Christian Examiner
Christian Herald
Christian Investigator, and Evangelical Reformer
Christian Observer

Footsteps of Truth
The Gospel Standard
The Latter Rain
The Revival
Sword and Trowel
Words of Life

1.2.3. ASSEMBLY ADDRESS LISTS (LISTED IN DATE ORDER)
1.2.3.1. Open
[Jordan, J.W.], *List of Some Meetings in the British Isles and Regions Beyond Where Believers professedly gather in the Name of the Lord Jesus for Worship and Breaking of Bread in remembrance of HIM, upon the first day of the week*, London: the author, [1897].
[Jordan, J.W.], *List of Some Meetings in the British Isles and Regions Beyond Where Believers professedly gather in the Name of the Lord Jesus for Worship and Breaking of Bread in remembrance of HIM, upon the first day of the week*, London: Dawe, [1904].
[Grant, Ernest H.], *List of some Assemblies in the Home and Eastern Counties. 1921*, London: the author and Pickering & Inglis, [1921].
Anon., *List of Some Assemblies in the British Isles, Where Believers professedly gather in the Name of the Lord Jesus for Worship and Breaking of Bread in Remembrance of Him upon the first Day of the Week*, London and Glasgow: Pickering & Inglis for the compiler, [1922].
Anon., *List of Some Assemblies in the British Isles, Where Believers professedly gather in the Name of the Lord Jesus for Worship and Breaking of Bread in Remembrance of Him upon the First Day of the Week*, London and Glasgow: Pickering & Inglis for the compiler, 1927.
[Pickering, Henry], *Directory of Some Assemblies in the British Isles and elsewhere Where Believers professedly gather in the Name of the Lord Jesus for Worship and Breaking of Bread in Remembrance of Him upon on the First Day of the Week*, London: Pickering & Inglis, 1933.
[Rowe, A.J.], *List of South Wales Assemblies with Correspondents*, [Barry: A.J. Rowe, 1946].
Anon., *Assemblies in Britain and other parts, Where Believers gather in the Name of the Lord Jesus on the First Day of the Week for Breaking of Bread*, London: Pickering & Inglis, 1951.
Anon., *Assemblies in Britain and other parts, Where Believers gather in the Name of the Lord Jesus on the First Day of the Week for Breaking of Bread*, London: Pickering & Inglis, 1959.
Anon., *(Birmingham and district) list of assembly correspondents and Sunday School superintendents*, [Birmingham: H.J. Taylor, 1962].
Anon., *A list of Assemblies in Britain and other parts*, London: Pickering & Inglis, 1968.
Anon., *A List of Assemblies in Britain and other parts*, London: Pickering & Inglis, 1970.
Anon., *Birmingham & district list of assembly secretaries, Sunday School superintendents, Women's Meeting leaders*, [Birmingham: P. Chamings], 1973.
Anon., *A list of assemblies in Britain and other parts*, London: Pickering & Inglis, 1975.

Anon., *Birmingham & district list of assembly secretaries, Sunday School superintendents, Women's Meeting leaders*, [Birmingham: P.B. Swain], 1978.

Anon., *Christian Brethren assemblies round the world*, Basingstoke: Pickering & Inglis, 1983.

[Hill, Roy], *The Assemblies Address Book: useful addresses for Christians*, Stanton Drew, Bristol: Christian Year Publications, 1990.

[Hill, Roy], *The Assemblies Address Book: useful addresses for Christians*, Stanton Drew, Bristol: Christian Year Publications, 1991[2].

[Hill, Roy], *The Assemblies Address Book: useful addresses and other information for Christians*, Corston, Bath: Christian Year Publications, 1995[3].

[Hill, Roy], *The Assemblies Address Book: useful addresses and other information for Christians*, Corston, Bath: Christian Year Publications, 1997[4].

[Rowdon, Harold], *Partnership Directory No. 2*, Carlisle: Partnership, 2000.

[Hill, Roy], *The Assemblies Address Book: useful addresses and other information for Christians*, [Stanton Drew,] Bristol: Christian Year Publications, 2002[5].

[Rowdon, Harold], *Partnership Directory No. 3*, Carlisle: Partnership, 2003.

1.2.3.2. Exclusive

(The Exclusive group covered is indicated in brackets; the designations 'Stoney', 'Raven', and 'Taylor' each refer to those in fellowship with Darby in the 'Ramsgate' division.)

Z., Y., *List of Meetings*, [London: n.p., 1873].

Z., Y., *List of Meetings*, [London: n.p., 1877].

Anon., *List of Meetings, June 15, 1882*, London: n.p., 1882. {Stoney}

Anon., *References. [July, 1884]*, n.pl.: n.p., [1884]. {Stoney}

Anon., *References. [January, 1885]*, n.pl.: n.p., [1885]. {Stoney}

[Race, F.E. and W.J. Hocking], *List of Meetings of saints gathered to the Lord's Name in Great Britain and Ireland*, London: T. Cheverton, 1892. {Kelly}

Dix, Thos. R., *List of Meetings*, [London: n.p., 1901]. {Lowe}

Besley, John J., *List of Meetings*, n.pl.: n.p., [1901]. {Raven}

Besley, John J., *List of Meetings*, n.pl.: n.p., [1903]. {Raven}

Besley, John J., *List of Meetings*, n.pl.: n.p., [1906]. {Raven}

[Wolston, W.T.P.], *List of Meetings. Scotland*, Edinburgh: 'Gospel Messenger' Office, 1907. {Raven}

Besley, John J., List of Meetings, n.pl.: n.p., [1911]. {Raven}

Anon., *List of Assemblies of God*, n.pl.: n.p., [c.1922]. {Vernal}

[Smith, Hamilton], *List of Meetings. Great Britain and Ireland, July 1925*, [Sutton: the author, 1925]. {Glanton}

Anon., *List of Gatherings*, n.pl.: n.p., [c.1930]. {Kelly-Lowe}

Anon., 'UK & Ireland', typescript, [2002]. {Taylor}

1.2.4. CENSUSES OF RELIGIOUS WORSHIP

Aitken, John (ed.), *Census of Religious Worship 1851: The Returns for Worcestershire*, Worcestershire Historical Society n.s. 17, Worcester: Worcestershire Historical Society, 2000.

Ambler, R.W. (ed.), *Lincolnshire Returns of the Census of Religious Worship 1851*, Lincoln Record Society 72, Lincoln: Lincoln Record Society, 1979.

Anon., *The Independent's Religious Census of Sheffield, Rotherham, Chesterfield, Barnsley, Worksop, and Retford, Taken on Sunday, November 20ᵗʰ, 1881*, Sheffield: Leader and Sons, 1881.

Anon., *The Religious Census of London*, London: Hodder and Stoughton, 1888.

Anon., *Results of the Census of 1851, with respect to the religious and educational establishments of Scotland*, Edinburgh: Adam & Charles Black, [1854].

Brierley, Peter, *'Christian' England: What the 1989 English Church Census reveals*, London: MARC Europe, 1991.

Burg, Judith (ed.), *Religion in Hertfordshire 1847 to 1851*, Hertfordshire Record Society 11, [Ware]: Hertfordshire Record Society Publications, 1995.

Bushby, D.W. (ed.), *Bedfordshire Ecclesiastical Census 1851*, Publications of the Bedfordshire Historical Record Society 54, [Ampthill]: Bedfordshire Historical Record Society, 1975.

Ede, J. and N. Virgoe (eds.), *Religious Worship in Norfolk: The 1851 Census of Accommodation and Attendance at Worship*, Norfolk Record Society 62, n.pl.: Norfolk Record Society, 1998.

Field, Clive D. (ed.), *Church and Chapel in Early Victorian Shropshire: Returns from the 1851 Census of Religious Worship*, Shropshire Record Society 8, Keele: Centre for Local History, 2004.

Legg, Edward (ed.), *Buckinghamshire Returns of the Census of Religious Worship 1851*, Buckinghamshire Record Society 27, [Aylesbury]: Buckinghamshire Record Society, 1991.

Mann, Horace, *Census of Great Britain, 1851. Religious Worship in England and Wales [abridged]*, revised ed., London: George Routledge, [1854]

Mann, Horace, *Religious Worship and Education: Report and Tables*, London: George E. Eyre and William Spottiswoode, 1854.

Milburn, G.E., *Religion in Sunderland in the mid-Nineteenth Century*, Occasional Paper No. 3, Sunderland: Department of Geography and History, Sunderland Polytechnic, 1982.

Mudie-Smith, Richard, *The Religious Life of London*, London: Hodder and Stoughton, 1904.

Roake, Margaret (ed.), *Religious Worship in Kent: The Census of 1851*, Maidstone: Kent Archaeological Society, 1999.

Tiller, Kate (ed.), *Church and Chapel in Oxfordshire 1851*, Oxfordshire Record Society 55, [Oxford]: Oxfordshire Record Society, 1987.

Timmins, T.C.B. (ed.), *Suffolk Returns from the Census of Religious Worship of 1851*, Suffolk Records Society 39, Woodbridge, Suffolk: Boydell Press, 1997.

Tranter, Margery, David A. Barton and Paul S. Ell (eds.), *The Derbyshire Returns to the 1851 Religious Census*, Derbyshire Record Society 23, Chesterfield: Derbyshire Record Society, 1995.

Vickers, John A. (ed.), *The Religious Census of Hampshire 1851*, Hampshire Record Series, Winchester: Hampshire County Council, 1993.

Vickers, John A. (ed.), *The Religious Census of Sussex 1851*, Sussex Record Society 75, Lewes: Sussex Record Society, 1989.

Watts, M. (ed.), *Religion in Victorian Nottinghamshire: The Religious Census of 1851*, University of Nottingham Centre for Local History Record Series 7, Nottingham: University of Nottingham Department of Adult Education, 1988.

Webb, Cliff and David Robinson (eds.), *The 1851 Religious Census: Surrey*, Surrey Record Society 35, Guildford: Surrey Record Society, 1997.

Wickes, Michael J.L. (ed.), *Devon in the Religious Census of 1851: A Transcript of the Devon section of the 1851 Church Census*, [Appledore]: the author, 1990.
Wolffe, John (ed.), *Yorkshire Returns of the 1851 census of religious worship. Vol.1, Introduction, City of York and East Riding* (York: Borthwick Institute of Historical Research, 2000).

1.2.5. BIOGRAPHIES AND AUTOBIOGRAPHIES OF BRETHREN AND FORMER BRETHREN
1.2.5.1. Collective
Anderson, James, *They Finished their Course*, Kilmarnock: John Ritchie, 1980.
Anderson, James, *They Finished their Course in the 80's*, Kilmarnock: John Ritchie, 1990.
Hutchinson, J.G., *Missionaries from Ireland now with the Lord*, Glasgow: Gospel Tract Publications, 1988.
Hutchinson, J.G., *Whose Praise is in the Gospel: a record of one hundred and nine Irish evangelists*, Glasgow: Gospel Tract Publications, 2002.
Hutchinson, James G., *Sowers, Reapers, Builders: A record of over ninety Irish evangelists*, Glasgow: Gospel Tract Publications, 1984.
McDowell, Ian, *Chief Women Among the Brethren*, Chadstone, Victoria: Chadstone Computing, 1992[2].
Pickering, H[enr]y (ed.), *Chief Men among the Brethren*, London: Pickering & Inglis, [1931][2].
Plant, Robert, *They Finished their Course in the 90s*, Kilmarnock: John Ritchie, 2000.

1.2.5.2. Individual
Allen, Cecil J., *Two Million Miles of Train Travel*, Shepperton: Ian Allan, 1965.
Anderson, James, *Willie Scott: 55+ Years of Service*, Glasgow: Gospel Tract Publications, 1986.
Anderson, John A., *Autobiography of John A. Anderson, M.D. China Inland Mission*, Braemar: the author, 1950[2].
Anon., *A Brief Account of the life and Labours of the late W.J. Lowe*, London: C.A. Hammond, [1927].
Anon., *A brief record of the last days of Robert Howard*, London: printed for private circulation, 1871.
Arnott, Anne, *Wife to the Archbishop*, London and Oxford: Mowbrays, 1976.
Beer, Patricia, *Mrs Beer's House,* London: Macmillan, 1968.
Bennet, W.H., *Robert Cleaver Chapman of Barnstaple*, Glasgow: Pickering & Inglis, [1902].
Blow, Samuel, *Reminiscences of thirty years' Gospel Work and Revival Times*, Glasgow: Gospel Tract Publications, 1988.
Bowes, John, *The Autobiography or History of the Life of John Bowes*, Glasgow: G. Gallie, 1872.
Bowyer [Honey], William, *Brought out in Evidence: an autobiographical summing-up*, London: Faber and Faber, 1941.
Brealey, W.J.H., *'Always Abounding;' or, Recollections of the Life and Labours of the late George Brealey, the Evangelist of the Blackdown Hills*, London: W.G. Wheeler, [1897[3]].
Bready, J. Wesley, *Doctor Barnardo: Physician, Pioneer, Prophet*, London: George Allen & Unwin, 1930.

Bridge, Donald, *God has resources: from the Pilgrim Preachers to the Ernest Luff homes*, Exeter, Paternoster Press, [1982].

[Broadbent, E.H.], *Life and Times of Thomas Newberry, Editor of* The Englishman's Bible, Glasgow: Pickering & Inglis, n.d.

Brown, Horatio F., *John Addington Symonds: a biography compiled from his papers and correspondence*, 2 vols; London: John C. Nimmo, 1895.

Bruce, F.F., *In Retrospect: Remembrance of things past*, revised ed., London: Marshall Pickering, 1993.

Burnham, Jonathan D., *A Story of Conflict: The Controversial Relationship between Benjamin Wills Newton and John Nelson Darby*, Carlisle: Paternoster, 2004.

Capper, W. Melville and Douglas Johnson, *Arthur Rendle Short, Surgeon & Christian*, London: Inter-Varsity Fellowship, 1954.

Capper, W.M. and D. Johnson (eds.), *The Faith of a Surgeon: Belief and Experience in the Life of Arthur Rendle Short*, Exeter: Paternoster, 1976.

Chapman, R.C. (ed.), *Seventy Years of Pilgrimage: being a Memorial of William Hake*, Glasgow and London: Publishing Office & Christian Literature Depot and James E. Hawkins, n.d.

Clare, W.H., *Pioneer Preaching or Work Well Done*, London: Pickering & Inglis, n.d.

Coad, Roy, *Laing: The Biography of Sir John W. Laing, C.B.E. (1879-1978)*, London: Hodder and Stoughton, 1979.

C[oates]., C.A., *Frederick John William, eighth Earl of Cavan: a life-sketch*, [n.pl.: n.p, c.1890].

Coates, Gerald, *An Intelligent Fire*, Eastbourne: Kingsway, 1991.

Cooke-Trench, Thomas Richard Frederick, *A Memoir of the Trench Family*, n.pl.: privately printed, 1897.

Cooper, Ransome W., *James Lees: Shepherd of Lonely Sheep in Europe*, London: Pickering & Inglis, 1959.

Croft, L.R., *Gosse: The Life of Philip Henry Gosse*, Walton-le-Dale, Preston: Elmwood Books, 2000.

Cross, E.N., *The Irish Saint and Scholar: A Biography of William Kelly 1821-1906*, London: Chapter Two, 2004.

Dann, Robert Bernard, *Father of Faith Missions: The Life and Times of Anthony Norris Groves (1795-1853)*, Waynesboro, GA: Authentic Media, 2004.

Denny, H.L.L., *History of the Denny Family of Tralee*, Tralee: "Star" and "People," n.d.

Dickson, John Trew, *William J. McClure: "A Beloved Brother and Faithful Minister"*, Grand Rapids, MI: Gospel Folio Publications for the author, n.d.

Dobbie, Sybil, *Faith and Fortitude: The Life and Work of General Sir William Dobbie*, Gillingham, Kent: P.E. Johnston, 1979.

Fenn, Mrs, *Albert R. Fenn: Reminiscences of Life and Work in England and Spain*, London: Echoes of Service, [1902].

Fromow, George H., *B.W. Newton and Dr. S.P. Tregelles: Teachers of the Faith and the Future*, London: Sovereign Grace Advent Testimony, 1969[2].

Gopsill, F.P., *Centenary of Archie Henry Boulton 1884-1984*, n.pl.: n.p., [1984].

Gosse, Edmund (ed. Peter Abbs), *Father and Son: A study of two temperaments*, Harmondsworth, Middlesex: Penguin, 1983.

Gosse, Edmund, *The Life of Philip Henry Gosse, F.R.S.*, London: Kegan, Paul, Trench, Trübner, 1890.

Gribble, Robert, *Recollections of an Evangelist: or, incidents connected with village ministry*, London: William Yapp, 1858[2].

Groves, A.N. [ed. A.J. Scott], *Journal of Mr. Anthony N. Groves, missionary, during a journey from London to Bagdad, through Russia, Georgia, and Persia. Also, a journal of some months' residence at Bagdad*, London: James Nisbet, 1831.

Groves, A.N. [ed. A.J. Scott], *Journal of a Residence at Bagdad, during the years 1830 and 1831, by Mr. Anthony N. Groves, Missionary*, London: James Nisbet, 1832.

Groves, Edward Kennaway, *George Müller and his successors*, Bristol: the author, 1906.

Groves, H., *"Not of the World": Memoir of Lord Congleton*, London: John F. Shaw, 1884.

Groves, Mrs. Anthony Norris, *Memoir of Anthony Norris Groves (containing extracts from his letters and journals)*, London: J. Nisbet, 1856 (reprinted, with *Christian Devotedness*, Sumneytown, PA: Sentinel, 2002^2).

[Habershon, E.M.], *Ada R. Habershon: a gatherer of fresh spoil. An autobiography and memoir compiled by her sister*, London: Morgan & Scott, n.d.

Hake, J.H. (ed.), *Letters of the late Robert Cleaver Chapman*, London and Glasgow: Echoes of Service and Pickering & Inglis, [1903].

Harrison, Godfrey, *Life and Belief in the Experience of John W. Laing, C.B.E.*, London: Hodder and Stoughton, 1954.

Hawthorn, John, *Alexander Marshall: Evangelist, Author and Pioneer*, London: Pickering & Inglis, n.d.

Hambleton, John, *Buds, Blossoms and Fruits of the Revival; a testimony to the great work of God in these last days*, London: Morgan & Chase, n.d.

Hine, Stuart K., *Not You, but God*, 3 parts in 1 vol.; Burnham-on-Sea: the author, 1973-[82].

Hobbs, Maurice E.J., *This is My Story*, n.pl.: the author, 2003.

Holmes, Frank, *Brother Indeed: The Life of Robert Cleaver Chapman, "Barnstaple Patriarch"*, reprint of 2nd ed.; Kilmarnock: John Ritchie, 1988.

Hooper, William, *"These Many Years": A Retrospect of fifty-six years of the Lord's leading, and a brief survey of the early days of the Open Brethren Movement in Swindon and District*, Swindon: the author, 1939.

[Howard, Maria], *Memorials of John Eliot Howard of Lord's Meade, Tottenham*, n.p.: n.pl., 1885.

Inchfawn, Fay, *Those Remembered Days: A Personal Recording*, London: Lutterworth, 1963.

[Isbell, J.B.], *'Faithful unto Death'. A Memoir of William Graeme Rhind, R.N., who fell asleep in Jesus, March 17, 1863*, London: William Yapp, [1863].

Jacks, L.P., *From Authority to Freedom: the Spiritual Pilgrimage of Charles Hargrove*, London: Williams & Norgate, 1920.

Jeaffreson, Herbert H. (ed.), *Letters of Andrew Jukes*, London: Longmans, Green, 1903.

Kelling, Fred, *Fisherman of Faroe: William Gibson Sloan*, Göta, Faroe Islands: Leirkeria, 1993.

Kelly, William, *John Nelson Darby as I knew him*, reprinted Belfast: Words of Truth, 1986.

Kirkwood, Janet Howard and Crewdson Howard Lloyd (eds.), *John Eliot Howard, F.R.S., 1807-1883: A budget of papers on his life and work*, Oxford: n.p., 1995.

Laird, John M., *No Mere Chance*, London: Hodder & Stoughton and Scripture Union, 1981.

Lang, G.H., *Anthony Norris Groves: Saint and Pioneer: A Combined Study of a Man of God and of the Original Principles and Practices of the Brethren with Application to Present Conditions*, London: Paternoster, 1949^2.

Lang, G.H., *Edmund Hamer Broadbent: Saint and Pioneer*, London: Paternoster, 1946.

Lang, G.H., *An Ordered Life: An autobiography*, London: Paternoster, 1959.

Latimer, Robert Sloan, *Dr. Baedeker: and his apostolic work in Russia*, London: Morgan & Scott, 1908².

Linnell, David, *Blake, Palmer, Linnell and Co.: The Life of John Linnell*, Lewes: The Book Guild, 1994.

McAlpine, John, *Forty Years Evangelising in Britain*, London: Pickering & Inglis, 1947.

Macnicol, John, *Twentieth Century Prophet*, Eastbourne: Prophetic Witness, 1971.

Macpherson, John, *Henry Moorhouse: The English Evangelist*, London: Morgan and Scott, n.d.

Mawhinney, Brian, *In the Firing Line*, London: HarperCollins, 1999.

Millard, Maurice, *The Time of Their Life*, n.pl.: the author, 2003.

Moore-Anderson, A.P., *Sir Robert Anderson, K.C.B.*, and *Lady Anderson*, London: Marshall, Morgan & Scott, 1947.

Morgan, G.E., *"A Veteran in Revival". R.C. Morgan: his Life and Times*, London: Morgan & Scott, 1909.

Morton, Grace and Mary, *Gleanings from the Life of Charles Morton, A Servant of Jesus Christ*, Kilmarnock: John Ritchie, n.d.

Müller, George (ed. G. Fred. Bergin), *Autobiography of George Müller, or a million and a half in answer to prayer*, London and Bristol: J. Nisbet and The Bible and Tract Warehouse, 1906².

[Murdoch, Alexander], *Life among the Close Brethren*, London: Hodder and Stoughton, 1890.

Murphy, Hedley G., *"Under His Wings"*, [Belfast: the author, 1969].

Neatby, Mrs, *The Life and Ministry of Thomas Neatby*, Glasgow and London: Pickering & Inglis and Alfred Holness, n.d.

Needham, G.C., *Recollections of Henry Moorhouse, Evangelist*, Chicago: F.H. Revell, 1881.

Newman, F.W., *Phases of Faith; or, passages from the history of my creed*, London: John Chapman, 1850.

O'Sullivan, Anthony, 'Roger Forster and the Ichthus Christian Fellowship: The Development of a Charismatic Missiology', *Pneuma* 16 (1994), 247-63.

Owles, J. Allden, *Recollections of Medical Missionary Work*, Glasgow: Pickering & Inglis, [1909].

Parr, John Nelson, *"Incredible"*, Fleetwood: the author, [1972].

Paterson, James, *Richard Weaver's Life Story*, London: Morgan and Scott, n.d.

Peterson, Robert L., *Robert Chapman: A Biography*, Neptune, NJ: Loizeaux, 1995.

Pierson, Arthur T., *James Wright of Bristol: a memorial of a fragrant life*, London: James Nisbet, 1906.

Pierson, Arthur T., *George Müller of Bristol*, London: Pickering & Inglis, 1972.

Pitt, F.W., *Windows on the World: A record of the life of Alfred H. Burton B.A., M.D.*, London: Pickering & Inglis, n.d.

Porter, David, *The man who was Q: the true story of Charles Fraser-Smith, the 'Q' wizard of World War II*, Exeter: Paternoster, 1986.

Raynor, David, *The Standard Bearer: A biography of Charles Oxley*, Weston Rhyn, Oswestry: Quinta Press, 2001.

Rea, Tom, *The Life and Labours of David Rea*, Kilmarnock: John Ritchie, [1917]; reprinted as *David Rea*, Glasgow: Gospel Tract Publications, 1987.

[Reich, Max I.] (ed.), *Selected Letters with brief memoir of J.G. M'Vicker*, London: Echoes of Service, [1902].

Reid, John, *F.W. Grant: His Life, Ministry and Legacy*, Plainfield, NJ: John Reid Book Fund, 1995.

Rendall, Robert, *J.B. Watson: A Memoir and Selected Writings*, London: Pickering & Inglis, 1957.

[Ritchie, John], *Donald Munro, A Servant of Jesus Christ*, Kilmarnock: John Ritchie, n.d.

[Ritchie, John], *James Campbell, A Servant of Jesus Christ*, Kilmarnock: John Ritchie, n.d.

R[oss]., C.W. (ed.), *Donald Ross, pioneer evangelist of the North of Scotland and the United States of America*, Kilmarnock: John Ritchie, n.d.

Ruoff, Percy O., *The Spiritual Legacy of George Goodman*, London: Pickering & Inglis, 1949.

Ruoff, Percy O., *W.E. Vine: His Life and Ministry*, London and Edinburgh: Oliphants, 1951.

Ryland, J.E., *Memoirs of John Kitto, D.D., F.S.A.*, Edinburgh: William Oliphant, 1856.

[S., E.], *Recollections of a visit to Robert C. Chapman, of Barnstaple*, Glasgow: Pickering & Inglis, [1902].

St John, Patricia, *Harold St. John: A Portrait*, London: Pickering & Inglis, 1961.

St John, Patricia, *Patricia St John Tells Her Own Story*, Carlisle: OM, 1995.

Salwey, Ruth, *The Beloved Commander*, London: Marshall, Morgan & Scott, 1962.

'Septima' [Grace Hurditch], *Peculiar People*, London: Heath Cranton, 1935.

Sieveking, I. Giberne, *Memoir and Letters of Francis W. Newman*, London: Kegan, Paul, Trench, Trübner, 1909.

Snook, Roger K., *A Friend of God: The Life and Service of Albert Fallaize*, Bath: Echoes of Service, 1986.

Soros, Susan Weber and Catherine Arbuthnott, *Thomas Jeckyll: architect and designer*, New Haven and London: Yale University Press for the Bard Center for Studies in the Decorative Arts, Design, and Culture, 2003.

Spring, Howard, *And another Thing* ..., New York and London: Harper and Brothers, 1946.

S[tanley], C., *Incidents of Gospel Work: shewing, how the Lord hath led me*, London: G. Morrish, n.d.

Stokes, G.T., 'John Nelson Darby', *Contemporary Review* 48 (1885), 537-52.

Stoney, A.M., *An account of early days*, London: Chapter Two, 1995.

Tayler, W. Elfe, *Passages from the Diary and Letters of Henry Craik, of Bristol*, London: J.F. Shaw, [1866].

Thomas, Arthur Dicken, Jr, 'James M. Houston, Pioneering Spiritual Director to Evangelicals: Part One', *Crux* 29.3 (September 1993), 2-10.

Thwaite, Ann, *Glimpses of the Wonderful: The Life of Philip Henry Gosse 1810-1888*, London: Faber and Faber, 2002.

Tregelles, George Fox, 'The Life of a Scholar', *Friends' Quarterly Examiner* 31 (1897), 449-60.

Trotter, Mrs. Edward, *Lord Radstock: an interpretation and a record*, London: Hodder and Stoughton, n.d.

Tuck, J. Erskine, *Your Master Proclaim: the story of the Eric Hutchings evangelist crusades, and the Hour of Revival Association*, London: Oliphants, 1968.

Turner, W.G., *William Kelly as I knew him*, London: C.A. Hammond, n.d.

Wagner, Gillian, *Barnardo*, London: Eyre & Spottiswoode, 1980.

Wallis, Jonathan, *Arthur Wallis: Radical Christian*, Eastbourne: Kingsway, 1991.

Webster, Nesta H., *Spacious Days: An Autobiography*, London: Hutchinson, [1949].

Weremchuk, Max S., *John Nelson Darby*, Neptune, NJ: Loizeaux, 1992.

Winter, George, *With Tent and Caravan: the story of thirty-seven years' evangelizing in North-West England*, Penrith: Reeds, 1950.

Wreford, Heyman, *Memories of the Life and Last Days of William Kelly*, London: F.E. Race, n.d.

Wright, Max, *Told in Gath*, Belfast: Blackstaff, 1990.

1.2.6. WORKS BY CRITICS

Anon., 'Darbyism', *QJP* 11 (1859), 371-4.

Anon., *The New Opinions of the Brethren, examined by a spectator*, London: Benjamin L. Green, [1849].

Anon., 'The Plymouth Brethren', *CO* 62 (1866), 896-913.

Anon., 'Plymouth Brethrenism: its spirit, principles, and practical consequences', *CO* 62 (1866), 598-616.

Anon., *A Retrospect of Events that Have Taken Place Among the Brethren*, London: B.L. Green, 1849.

Anon., [review of Brethren works], *ER* 5 (January-June 1839), 571-90.

Bailie, H., *Who are They? The Brethren*, Belfast: Northern Publishing Office, [c.1950].

Black, James, *New Forms of the Old Faith: Being the Baird Lecture [sic] delivered in 1946-47 under the title EXTRA-CHURCH SYSTEMS*, London: Thomas Nelson, 1948.

Black, James, 'The Plymouth Brethren: How They Arose and What They Believe', [Edinburgh: n.p., ?1925].

[Brownlie, W.R.], *The Gifts of the Spirit and the Ministries of the Lord: Letters to a Member of "the Brethren"*, Glasgow: D. Hobbs, 1877[2].

Carson, James C.L., *The Heresies of the Plymouth Brethren*, London: Houlston, 1877.

Cox, John, *Test before you Trust; or, the new doctrine and the old divinity compared*, London: Nisbet, [1862].

[Cox, John, Jr], *An Earnest Expostulation. A Letter addressed to the Author of "High Church Claims of the Exclusive Brethren"*, London: Houlston & Wright, [1869].

[Cox, John, Jr], *A Refutation of Certain Charges made by the Brethren*, London: Houlston & Wright, 1867.

Cox, R., *Secession Considered: in a Letter to the Rev. J.L. Harris, M.A., late fellow of Exeter College, Oxford, and Perpetual Curate of Plymstock; in Reply to an address to his parishioners, on seceding from the Church of England*, London: Hatchard, 1832.

Croskery, Thomas, *A Catechism on the Doctrines of the Plymouth Brethren*, London: James Nisbet, 1868[6].

[Croskery, Thomas], *Plymouth Brethrenism: its Ecclesiastical and Doctrinal Teachings; with a Sketch of its History*, London: Hodder & Stoughton, 1874[2].

Croskery, Thomas, *Plymouth-Brethrenism: A Refutation of its Principles and Doctrines*, London and Belfast: William Mullen, 1879.

Dennett, Edward, *The Plymouth Brethren: their rise, divisions, practice, and doctrines*, London: Elliot Stock, 1870[2].

Dobree, Osmond, *Separation from Evil: not God's Principle of Unity*, London: Wertheim, Macintosh & Hunt, n.d.

Garbett, C., *Reply to Captain Hall's pamphlet, entitled "An Address to the Christians,"* &c., Hereford: W.H. Vale & J. Parker, 1839.

[Govett, R.], *Address to the Christians commonly called Plymouth Brethren, on Liberty of Ministry and Gift*, Norwich: Josiah Fletcher, 1847.

Gregory, J. Robinson, *The Gospel of Separation: A Brief Examination of the History and Teachings of Plymouth Brethrenism*, London: Charles H. Kelly, 1894.

Guinness, H. Grattan, *A Letter to the "Plymouth Brethren" on the Recognition of Pastors*, London: James Nisbet, 1863.

[Haldane, A.], *Errors of the Darby and Plymouth Sect. Reprinted and revised from the "Record" newspaper; with additions*, London: James Nisbet, 1862[2].

Houston, Thomas, *Plymouthism & Revivalism: or, the Duty of contending for the Faith in opposition to prevailing errors and corruptions*, Belfast: C. Aitchison, [1874][2].

'Investigator', *Who are They? The Brethren*, [Belfast]: Committee on the State of Religion in conjunction with the Publication Board of the Presbyterian Church in Ireland, [c.1950].

Latimer, W.T., *A Lecture on the Doctrines of Plymouth Brethren*, Belfast: James Cleeland, [1890][3].

Myland, C., *Plymouth Brethrenism (so called) tested by the Word of God, with remarks on Mr. Guinness' approaching End of the Age, The Irrelevancy of his Mathematics*, Reading: J. Read, [1881].

Macintosh, Duncan, *Brethrenism; or the Special Teachings, ecclesiastical and doctrinal, of the Exclusive Brethren, or Plymouth Brethren; compiled from their own writings. With Strictures. Also, a reply to the ex-editor of the British Evangelist*, London: Houlston, [1875][4].

McIntosh, Hugh, *The New Prophets: Being an account of the operations of The Northern Evangelistic Society*, Aberdeen: A. & R. Milne, 1871.

Maclaren, Ian [signed 'John Watson'], 'A Mysterious Order', *British Weekly*, 5 December 1901, 193-4.

Mearns, Peter, *Christian Truth viewed in relation to Plymouthism*, Edinburgh: William Oliphant, 1875[2].

'Minister (of the Diocese of Ardfert), A', *Must I separate from the Church of England? A Letter to the Rev. Charles Hargrove, upon his pamphlet, entitled Reasons for Retiring from the Church of England*, Tralee: J.D. Goggin, [1836].

'Minister of the Established Church, A', *The Perpetuity of the Moral Law; being a Reply to Mr. Groves's book; entitled, The New Testament in the Blood of Jesus, the sole Rule of Morals and Discipline to the Christian Church*, Madras: J.B. Pharoah, 1838.

Porteous, J. Moir, *Brethren in the Keelhowes; or, Brethrenism tested by the Word of God*, London: Simpkin, Marshall, 1876[6].

Reid, William, *Plymouth Brethrenism unveiled and refuted*, Edinburgh: William Oliphant, 1876[2].

Rees, A.A., *Four Letters to the Christians called "Brethren," on the subject of Ministry and Worship*, London: Passmore and Alabaster, n.d.[2].

Rust, Cyprian Thomas, *The "Brethren." An examination of the Opinions and Practices of the new sect usually denominated "Plymouth Brethren"*, Colchester: I. Brackett, 1844.

Rust, Cyprian Thomas, *'"The Old Paths." A few brotherly hints to "The Brethren:" more particularly addressed to Mr. W.H. Dorman, Late of Islington*, London: Simpkin, Marshall, 1842.

Sirr, Joseph D'Arcy, *A Memoir of the Honorable and Most Reverend Power le Poer Trench, last Archbishop of Tuam*, Dublin: William Curry, Jun., 1845.

Sirr, Joseph D'Arcy, *Reasons for Abiding in the Established Church: a letter to the Rev. Charles Hargrove, A.B.*, Dublin: R.M. Tims, 1836.

Sirr, Joseph D'Arcy, *Westport Darbyism Exposed*, Dublin: Wm. Curry, Jun., 1843.

Smith, J. Harmar, *The Link Broken: a letter explanatory of his retirement from "Brethren's" meetings*, London: Houlston & Wright, [1867].

[Synge, John], *Observations on "A Call to the Converted," as it relates to Members of the Church of England, addressed to Capt. P. Hall, R.N.*, [London: Seeley, 1831].

Teulon, J.S., *The History and Teaching of the Plymouth Brethren*, London: SPCK, 1883.

Torry, James, *Baptism, its Subjects and Mode, viewed in connection with the heresy of the Plymouth Brethren*, Kirkwall: William Peace, [1870][2].

Townsend, William, *Church & Dissent: being reflections and reasonings that have induced the author, after eighteen years' communion among the Plymouth Brethren, to leave them, and enter the communion of the Church of England*, Lewes: Sussex Express, [1872].

Tregelles, S.P., *Five Letters to the Editor of "The Record," on recent Denials of our Lord's vicarious Life*, London and Aylesbury: Hunt, Barnard, 1910 (reprint of 1864[2]).

Tregelles, S.P., *Three Letters to the Author of 'A Retrospect of Events that have taken place amongst the Brethren'*, London: Houlston, 1894[2].

Whately, E.J., *Plymouth Brethrenism*, London: Hatchards, 1877[2].

1.2.7. CONFERENCE REPORTS

Anon. (ed.), *The Apostolic Faith in a Pagan Society: Addresses given at a Conference of Brethren at Swanwick*, [n.pl.: n.p., 1960].

Anon. (ed.), *Christian Unity: Papers given at a conference of Brethren at Swanwick, Derbyshire, in June, 1964*, Bristol: Evangelical Christian Literature, [1964].

Anon. (ed.), *Demonstration of the Spirit and Power: Addresses given at a Conference of Brethren at Swanwick, October 1966*. Bristol: Evangelical Christian Literature, n.d.

Anon., *Freemason's Hall, May 30th, 31st, and June 1st, 1865. Meetings for Prayer and for Addresses on the subject of the Lord's Coming*, [London?]: n.p., [1865].

Anon. (ed.), *The Growth and Progress of the Church of God. Conference of brethren at Swanwick. September 1958*, [Stanmore: T.I. Wilson], n.d.

Anon. (ed.), *"Holiness unto the Lord". Report of a Conference of brethren at Swanwick. September 1957*, n.pl: n.p., n.d.

Anon. (ed.), *The Holy Spirit and the Assemblies: Report of a Conference held in London on September 12th & 13th, 1953*, [Finchley: T.I. Wilson, 1954].

Anon. (ed.), *A New Testament Church in 1955: High Leigh Conference of Brethren*, Stanmore: T.I. Wilson, [1955].

Anon. (ed.), *The New Testament Church in the Present Day: A Report of a Conference held at High Leigh, Hoddesdon*, n.p: n.pl., [1954].

Anon., *Notes of Conference held at Devonshire House, London, May 9-11th, 1907*, London: S.W. Partridge, [1907].

Anon. (ed.), [Pamphlet (untitled) containing papers to be read at the CBRF annual meeting, 28 October 1967].

Anon. (ed.), *The Personal Knowledge of God. Addresses given at a Conference of Brethren at Swanwick. September, 1963*, [London: G.W. Robson], n.d.

Anon. (ed.), *Personal Life and Behaviour in a Pagan Society: Addresses given at a Conference of Brethren at Swanwick*, [n.pl.: n.p., 1961].

Anon., *Questions for Eight Weeks' Consideration, Addressed to the Church of God,* London: Central Tract Depot, 1838 (also continuation leaflets for 1839, *Ninth Week,* and 1841, *Questions*).

Anon., *Report of Three Days' Meetings for Prayer and for Addresses on the subject of the Lord's Coming, held in Freemasons' Hall, May 30th, 31st, & June 1st, 1865,* London: William Yapp, 1865.

Anon. (ed.), *A Return to Simplicity: Conference of brethren held at "High Leigh," Hoddesdon from September 28th to October 1st, 1956,* [Stanmore: T.I. Wilson], n.d.

Anon. (ed.), *The Rule of God in The Life of Man. Addresses given at a Conference of Brethren at Swanwick. September, 1962,* [London: G.W. Robson], n.d.

Anon. (ed.), *Second Thoughts on the New Morality.* Bristol: Evangelical Christian Literature, n.d.

Anon., *A short report of the Devonshire House Conference Meetings,* Sidcup: W.T., [1906].

Bamford, Alan G. (ed.), *Where do we go from Here? The future of the Brethren: Report of Addresses and Discussions at the Swanwick Conference of Brethren, September 1978,* Worthing: H.E. Walter, 1979.

Catherwood, H.F.R., W.W. Vellacott, and J.B. Watson, *Revival in our time: A Call to Christians (Notes of a special meeting held by Representatives of the Assemblies of London in the Lecture Hall at the Westminster Central Hall on November 21st 1947),* London: Conveners of Revival in our Time, [1947].

[Darby, J.N. et al.], *Collectanea: being some of the subjects considered at Leamington, on the 3d of June and four following days in the year 1839,* Edinburgh: J.S. Robertson, 1882.

[Ellison, H.L. and K.G. Hyland], *Report on International Conference at the Ecumenical Institute, Chateau de Bossey Switzerland July 22nd to 26th 1968,* Pinner, Middlesex: Christian Brethren Research Fellowship, [1968].

[Newton, B.W. and H. Borlase], *Answers to the questions considered at a meeting held at Plymouth on September 15, 1834, and the following Days; chiefly compiled from Notes taken at the Meeting,* Plymouth: Tract Depot, 1847^{2}.

Rowdon, Harold H. (ed.), *The Brethren Contribution to the Worldwide Mission of the Church: International Brethren Conference on Missions held at the Anglo-Chinese School, Singapore, 9-15 June 1993,* Carlisle: Paternoster for Partnership, 1994.

Rowdon, Harold H. (ed.), *Churches in Partnership for Strengthening and Growth: Papers from the Partnership Consultation held at the University of Warwick, 10-12 July 1993,* Carlisle: Paternoster for Partnership, 1994.

Rowdon, Harold (ed.), *Revival in our churches? Report of the Partnership consultation held at The Hayes, Swanwick, 25-28 September 1998,* [n.pl.: Partnership, 1998].

Rowdon, Harold H. (ed.), *The Strengthening, Growth and Planting of Local Churches,* Carlisle: Paternoster for Partnership, 1993.

[Ruoff, Percy O.] (ed.), *Christ's Second Coming" At any moment" or "Certain events first": A Report of a Conference in London, January 3rd and 4th, 1953,* n.pl.: n.p., [1953].

1.2.8. OTHER WORKS BY BRETHREN WRITERS

Alexander, L.W.G., *Discerning the Body: An Examination and a Refutation of Needed Truth Doctrines,* Glasgow: Pickering & Inglis, n.d.

Allen, Leslie C., *The Books of Joel, Obadiah, Jonah and Micah,* New International Commentary on the Old Testament, Grand Rapids: William B. Eerdmans, 1976.

Anderson, Robert, *The Gospel and its Ministry: A Handbook of Evangelical Truths*, London: James Nisbet, 1907[13]; Grand Rapids, MI: Kregel, 1956[17] (all references are to the earlier edition).

Anderson, Robert, *Spirit Manifestations and "the Gift of Tongues"*, Glasgow: Pickering & Inglis, n.d.[5].

Anderson, Teresa L., *A Sister's Letter to Sisters*, Surbiton: Counties Evangelistic Work, [c.1943].

Anon., *The Bethesda Question*, London: G. Morrish, n.d.

Anon., *Clerisy: its Origin, Character, Progress, and End*, Kilmarnock: John Ritchie, n.d.

Anon., *Copy of a Letter from ***** to the Rev. ***, [Worcester: E.B. Rouse, n.d].

Anon., *Eldership*, Bath: Echoes of Service, n.d.

Anon., *Index to the Bible Treasury: A Monthly Magazine of Papers on Scriptural Subjects edited by William Kelly, June 1856–July 1920*, London: Chapter Two, 1995[4].

Anon., *Interesting Reminiscences of the Early History of "Brethren:" with Letter from J.G. Bellett to J.N. Darby*, Weston-super-Mare and London: Walter Scott and Alfred Holness, [c.1884].

Anon., *The Midland Evangelization Trust. 1916*, Birmingham: H. Ernest Marsom, [1916].

Anon., *Opportunity and Responsibility in Ireland*, Dublin: Look and Live, 1966.

Anon. (ed.), *Private correspondence between New York, London, and Shanghai, 14th October, 1933 to May 4th, 1934*, n.pl.: n.p., [1934].

Anon., *Some Remarks upon the circular letter issued, on the subject of a meeting of humiliation and prayer*, [Plymouth: Rowe, 1846].

Anon., *Some Teachings of the Salvation Army, contrasted with the Word of God*, Glasgow: The Witness Office, n.d.

Anon., *A Statement from Christians assembling in the name of the Lord, in Ebrington Street, Plymouth*, [Plymouth]: n.p., [1848].

Anon., *A Statement of the position of Bethesda, 1906*, [Bristol: John Wright, 1906].

Anon., *The Types of the Tabernacle and what they teach*, London: Gospel Tract Depot, n.d.

Anon., *A Word to all True Believers in the Lord Jesus Christ, with reference to the great Industrial Exhibition For 1851*, London: J.K. Campbell, 1851.

Anon. (ed.), *Words of Truth for the Saints of God*, 4 series, London: 1 Warwick Square, n.d.[2].

Anon., *Working Together*, Bath: Echoes of Service, n.d.

Baigent, John, *Teaching in the Local Church*, Exeter: Christian Brethren Research Fellowship, 1986.

Banks, F.A., *Spiritual Growth and Other Writings of the late Frederick Arthur Banks. Volume 1*, n.pl.: Needed Truth Publishing Office, 1898.

Barker, Harold P., *Why I Abandoned Exclusivism*, London: Pickering & Inglis, n.d.

Batchelor, Alan (intro.), *Don't Muzzle the Ox: Full-time Ministry in Local Churches*, Carlisle: Paternoster for Partnership, 1997.

[Batten, J.E.], *A Letter to the saints meeting in Ebrington Street, Plymouth*, Plymouth: J.B. Rowe, [1847].

Beattie, Hunter, *The Christian and War*, Glasgow: the author, n.d.

Bell, G.W., *Building to Divine Pattern Or, "Jerry-Building" – Which?*, Kilmarnock: John Ritchie, [1936].

[Bellett, J.G.]?, *A Few words on the Present Revival*, London: G. Morrish, n.d.

[Bellett, J.G.], *A Letter on Neutrality as to Christ, or Bethesda*, n.pl.: n.p., n.d.

Bellett, J.H., *The Faith and Practice of the Non-Exclusive Brethren; with remarks on Elders, and Pastors and Teachers, in answer to letters to the Brethren by Messrs. R.M. Beverley, H. Grattan Guinness, & A.A. Rees, and to "The Church of Old"*, London: Yapp & Hawkins, [1869?].

Bennet, W.H., *A Return to God and His Word: Remarks on Mr. W. BLAIR NEATBY'S 'History of the Plymouth Brethren'*, Glasgow: Pickering & Inglis, [1914].

[Beverley, R.M.], *Analysis, by a Student of Prophecy, of "Thoughts on the Apocalypse" by B.W. Newton, of Plymouth*, London: Longmans, Brown, Green, and Longmans, 1845.

Beverley, R.M., *The Church of England Examined by Scripture and tradition: in an answer to lectures by the Rev. John Venn, of Hereford, on the Christian ministry*, London: R. Groombridge, 1843.

Blackwell, Caroline S., *A Living Epistle; or, Gathered Fragments from the correspondence of the late Caroline S. Blackwell*, Kilmarnock: John Ritchie, [1898³].

Borland, Andrew, *The Ecumenical Movement and Assemblies*, Kilmarnock: John Ritchie, n.d.

Borland, Andrew, *Old Paths & Good Ways in personal, family, and church life*, Kilmarnock: John Ritchie, [1938].

Borland, A., *Woman's place in the Assemblies: an assessment of Bible teaching*, Kilmarnock: John Ritchie, [c.1970].

Borlase, H., *Papers by the late Henry Borlase connected with the Present State of the Church*, London: Hamilton, Adams, 1836.

Bowes, John, *The Purity of the Church*, Cheltenham: the author, n.d.

B[renton], L.C.L., *A Fragment on Church Government*, Ryde: Hartnall, 1845.

Brenton, L.C.L., *Sectarianism and the Lord's Table. An appeal to the Christians in Ryde*, Ryde: Hartnall, 1845.

[Brewer, Charles], *My Book of Remembrance*, Leominster: Charles Brewer, [1909]².

Brierley, Peter et al., *The Christian Brethren as the Nineties Began*, Carlisle: Paternoster for Partnership in association with MARC Europe, 1993.

Brown, Graham, *Whatever Happened to the Brethren? A survey of local churches in 1998-1999*, Carlisle: Paternoster for Partnership, 2003.

Brown, Graham and Brian Mills, *"The Brethren" Today: A Factual Survey*, Exeter: Paternoster for the Christian Brethren Research Fellowship, 1980.

Bruce, F.F., *Who are the Brethren?*, Glasgow: Pickering & Inglis, [1962].

[Budd, J.W.], [Notes concerning the excommunication of W.W. Fereday,] East Dulwich Green: J.W. Budd, 1900.

Bunting, William, *Spiritual Balance: or the perils of unscriptural extremes*, Kilmarnock: John Ritchie, 1968.

Burridge, J.H., *Christian Unity: A Treatise on "Brethren," the Church of God, and Ministry*, London: Alfred Holness, [c.1892].

Burridge, J.H., *George Müller and the Great Tribulation*, Birmingham: the author, n.d.

Burton, Alfred H., *What is Exclusivism? A review of Mr Alex. Marshall's "Holding Fast the Faithful Word"*, London: James Carter, 1908.

Caldwell, John R., *Epitome of Christian Experience in Psalm xxxii; with the Development of Christian life*, Glasgow: Pickering & Inglis, [1917].

Caldwell, John R., *A Revision of Certain Teachings Regarding The Gathering and Receiving of the Children of God*, London: Pickering & Inglis, n.d.

Caldwell, John R., *Separation from the World, Jehoshaphat, and other papers*, Glasgow: Pickering & Inglis, n.d.

Coates, C.A. [ed. W.M.B.], *Letters of C.A. Coates*, Kingston-on-Thames: Stow Hill Bible and Tract Depot, n.d.

[Congleton, Lord], *The Bath Case; or, who made the division at Bath?*, Brighton: n.p., 1849.

[Congleton, Lord], *The Bristol Case; and divisions in other places connected therewith*, [London: J.K. Campbell, 1849].

Congleton, Lord, *Lord Congleton's First Letter to Mr. G—.*, [Brighton: J.F. Eyles, 1862].

[Congleton, Lord], *Reasons for Leaving Rawstorne-Street Meeting*, London, [Brighton: J.F. Eyles, 1847].

[Congleton, Lord], *The Tottenham Case; with an introduction by A.N. Groves*, [Brighton: n.p.], 1849.

Cooper, Ransome W., *The Gospel to Britain's Guests*, Stirling: Stirling Tract Enterprise, n.d.

Cooper, Ransome W., *The Gospel to Britain's Guests: The story of the first year*, Stirling: Stirling Tract Enterprise, n.d.

Cousins, Peter, *The Brethren*, Exeter: Religious Education Press, 1982.

Craik, Henry, *New Testament Church Order. Five Lectures*, Bristol: W. Mack, 1862.

Crawley, H.C., *A Plea for Unity Among the People Called Brethren: with a resumé of the Devonshire House Conference*, Glasgow: Pickering & Inglis, [1907].

Crawford, Dan, *"Touching the Coming of the Lord"*, Aylesbury: Hunt, Barnard & Co., n.d.

Culverhouse, J., *Observations on the Discipline, amongst "The Brethren"*, London: n.p., [1860].

Darby, J.N. (ed. W. Kelly), *Collected Writings*, 34 vols; Kingston-on-Thames, Stow Hill Bible and Tract Depot, n.d.

D[arby]., J.N. [ed. J. A. Trench], *Letters of J.N.D.*, 3 vols; Kingston-on-Thames, Stow Hill Bible and Tract Depot, n.d.

D[arby]., J.N., *Miscellaneous Writings of J.N.D.*, Oak Park, IL: Bible Truth Publishers, n.d.

Darby, J.N., *Synopsis of the Books of the Bible*, 5 vols; Kingston-on-Thames, Stow Hill Bible and Tract Depot, 1943-9.

[Darby, W.H.], *The Union of Believers*, [Dublin]: the author, 1873.

Davis, C.J., *Aids to Believers*, London: Pickering & Inglis, n.d.

Davis, C.J., *"A Few Counsels regarding some Prevalent Errors. By an Elder." A Lecture, having special reference to the above, delivered in the Ball-Room, Aberdeen*, Aberdeen: Tract Depot, [1869].

D[enny?]., E., *On Swearing, addressed to those who desire to maintain the Lord's honour*, Plymouth, n.p., n.d.

Dickson, Neil (ed.), *An Island Shore: Selected Writings of Robert Rendall*, Kirkwall: The Orkney Press, 1990.

Dobbie, W.G.S., *Christianity and Military Service*, London: Pickering & Inglis (for the Officers' Christian Union), [1936].

Dorman, W.H., *The High-Church Claims of the Exclusive Brethren. A Series of Letters to Mr. J.L. Harris*, 6 parts; London: Morgan and Chase, [1868-9].

Dorman, W.H., *Principles of Truth; or, Reasons for Retiring from The Independent or Congregational Body, and from Islington Chapel*, London: W.H. Broom and Rouse, n.d.[3] (first published 1838).

Dorman, W.H., *A Review of Certain Evils & Questions that have arisen amongst Brethren*, London: J.K. Campbell, 1849[2].

Dorman, W.H., *Truth for the Times: A Letter to the Dissenters*, London: Simpkin, 1842.
Dyer, Kevin, *Must Brethren Churches Die?*, Exeter: Partnership, 1991.
Dyer, W.B., *A Confession of Doctrinal and Practical Errors*, [Bristol]: n.p., [1848].
E[lliott]., R[ussell]., *Some Plain Words to Brethren*, Ealing: the author, [1930].
E[lliott]., R[ussell]., *The Spiritual Revival of the Nineteenth Century and Our Relation to it To-Day*, Wimbledon: the author, n.d.².
Elliott, Russell, *What is the Real Fellowship of the Church of God? A Letter*, n.pl: n.p., [1910].
Ellis, David J. and W. Ward Gasque (eds.), *In God's Community: Essays on the Church and Its Ministry*, Wheaton, IL: Harold Shaw, 1979.
Ellison, H.L., *The Household Church*, Exeter: Paternoster, 1963, 1979².
Ellison, H.L., 'Some Thoughts on Inspiration', *EQ* 26 (1954), 210-17.
'An ex-Baptist Pastor' [M.H. Grant], *Twice Delivered*, Kilmarnock: John Ritchie, n.d.²·
'An Ex Member of the Society of Friends' [S.P. Tregelles?], *Open Communion, with Liberty of Ministry, the only practicable ground for real union amongst Christians*, Central Tract Depot, 1840⁴.
Fereday, W.W., *Fellowship in Closing Days*, Littlehampton: W. Hignett, [c.1900]³.
F[ereday]., W.W., *A Letter by W.W. Fereday regarding the so called "Open Brethren"*, London: Chapter Two, 1997 (first published 1893).
[Gooding, A.M. Salway], *The Editor of the* Christian Worker *reviews 'A New Testament Church in 1955' [Report of High Leigh Conference of Brethren]*, Kilmarnock: John Ritchie, [1956].
Goodman, George, *God's Principles of Gathering*, London: Pickering & Inglis, [c.1922]².
Goodman, Montague, *An Urgent Call to Christian Unity*, London: Paternoster, 1948.
Groves, A.N. (ed. G.P.), *Catholic Christianity; and Party Communion, delineated in Two Letters by the late A.N. Groves*, London: Morgan & Chase, n.d.
Groves, A.N., *On the Liberty of Ministry in the Church of Christ*, Sidmouth: J. Harvey, 1835.
Groves, A.N., *On the Nature of Christian Influence*, Bombay: American Mission Press, 1833.
Groves, A.N., *The Present State of the Tinnevelly Mission. With an historical preface, and reply to Mr. Strachan's criticisms; and Mr. Rhenius's letter to the Church Missionary Society*, London: James Nisbet, 1836².
Groves, A.N., *Remarks on a Pamphlet, entitled "The Perpetuity of the Moral Law"*, Madras: J.B. Pharoah, 1840.
Groves, E.K., *Conversations on 'Bethesda' Family Matters*, London: W.B. Horner, [1885].
Groves, H., *Darbyism: Its Rise, Progress, and Development, and a review of 'the Bethesda question'*, London: James E. Hawkins, n.d.⁴.
Hall, P.F., *Discipleship: or, reasons for resigning his naval rank and pay*, London: J.K. Campbell, [1848].
H[all]., P.F., *Grief upon Grief: A Dialogue*, London: Houlston & Wright, 1866².
H[all]., P.F., *Unity: a fragment and a dialogue*, London: J.K. Campbell, 1851.
Hargrove, Charles, *Reasons for Retiring from the Established Church*, London: Tract Depot, 1838².
Hargrove, Joseph (ed), *Notes on the Book of Genesis, with some Essays and Addresses by the late Rev. Charles Hargrove, Volume III. Essays and Addresses*, London: John F. Shaw, 1870.

Harley, J.E., *My Reasons for Giving up Exclusivism*, [London: Fevez, 1891][2].

H[arley]., T.E., *Sectarianism*, n. pl:, n. p., [1908].

Harper, Joyce, *Women and the Gospel*, CBRF Occasional Paper No. 5, Pinner, Middlesex: Christian Brethren Research Fellowship, 1974.

Harris, J.L., *Address to the Parishioners of Plymstock*, Plymouth: Rowe, 1832.

Harris, J.L., *A Letter to the Christians meeting in Mr. Hingston's Loft, Kingsbridge*, London: Campbell, [1847].

Harris, J.L., *What is a Church? Or, reasons for withdrawing from the ministry of the Establishment*, Plymouth: Rowe, 1832.

Hitchman, Henry, *Some Scriptural Principles of the Christian Assembly*, Kilmarnock: John Ritchie, [c.1930][2].

Hocking, W.J., *A Few Papers relating to Assembly Affairs in Germany (1937)*, London: C.A. Hammond, [1937].

Hole, F.B., *Modern Mystical Teachings and the Word of God*, London: Central Bible Truth Depot, n.d.

Holiday, A.J., *The Character of the Last Days*, Glasgow: Pickering & Inglis, n.d.

Holmes, Frank (ed.), *Spiritual Renewal: The Charismatic Question*, South Molton: Quest (Western), 1977.

H[opkins], R.T., *Fellowship among Saints: what saith the Scriptures?*, Glasgow: Publishing Office, 1884.

Hoste, William, *Rejudging the Question: being consideration of a pamphlet by H.S. entitled: "Open Brethren"*, London: Pickering & Inglis, [1930].

Hoste, William, and W.E. Vine (eds.), *Light for Dark Days: a plea for adherence to the Holy Scriptures*, London: Morgan & Scott, 1928.

Howard, J.E., *A Caution against the Darbyites, with a word to the authors of two recent pamphlets*, London: G.J. Stevenson, 1866.

Howard, J.E., *Eight Lectures on the Scriptural Truths most opposed to Puseyism*, London: Longmans, Brown, Green, and Longmans, 1845.

Howard, Robert, *Church Principles*, London: James E. Hawkins, n.d.

Howley, G.C.D. (ed.), *A Bible Commentary for Today*, Glasgow: Pickering & Inglis, 1979.

Huebner, R.A., *J.N. Darby's Teaching regarding Dispensations, Ages, Administrations and the Two Parentheses*, Morganville, NJ: Present Truth, 1993.

Huebner, R.A., *The Truth of the Pre-Tribulation Rapture Recovered*, Morganville, NJ: Present Truth, 1982.

H[urditch]., C.R. (ed.), *Dublin Addresses, as delivered at several of the Half-Yearly believers' Meetings in Dublin, From 1862 to 1872. With an Outline of their History*, London: J.F. Shaw, 1873.

Jukes, Andrew, *The Way which some call Heresy. A letter to the clergy and laity of the Church of England, on clerical subscription*, London: James Nisbet, 1862[2].

Kelly, W., 'The Doctrine of Christ and Bethesdaism', in *Pamphlets*, Sunbury, PA: Believers Bookshelf, 1971.

Kelly, W., *Lectures on the Church of God*, London: C.A. Hammond, n.d.

Kent, C.S., *Whither are we Drifting?*, [Sutton: the author, 1933][2].

L., E., *Some Reflections of [sic] 1928 Conferences and other matters*, [Charmouth, Dorset: n.p., [1928][2].

Lamb, Jonathan, *Making Progress in Church Life: How to handle change positively*, Carlisle: Paternoster for Partnership, 1997.

[Lambert, W.G.], *A Call to the Converted*, abridged ed., Hereford: County Press Office, 1837.

Lang, G.H., *The Christian Relation to the State and to War*, Walsham-le-Willows: the author, 1937[2].

Lang, G.H., *Church federation: A Study in Church Life and Order, with special reference to Denominational Federating*, Walsham-le-Willows, Suffolk: the author, 1942[3].

Lang, G.H., *The Churches of God: a Treatise for the Times*, London: Paternoster, 1959[2].

Lang, G.H., *Departure: a warning and an appeal addressed by one of themselves mainly to Christians known as Open Brethren Including discussions upon the Constitution, Government, Discipline and Ministry of the Church of God and of the Principles and Practice of Service in the Gospel*, Miami Springs, FL: Conley & Schoettle, 1986[3].

Lang, G.H., *Firstborn Sons, their rights and risks*, London: S.E. Roberts, 1936.

Lang, G.H., *The Local Assembly: Some Essential Differences between Open and Exclusive Brethren considered Scripturally and Historically*, Wimborne: the author, 1955[5].

Lang, G.H., *The Modern Gift of Tongues: whence is it? A testimony and an examination*, London: Marshall Brothers, [c.1911].

Lang, G.H., *Past, Present, and Future: Guidance and Warning for Followers of the Lamb*, Walsham-le-Willows, Suffolk: the author, [1943].

Lincoln, William, *Address of the Rev. W. Lincoln to the Congregation of Beresford Episcopal Chapel, Walworth, On Sunday Evening, November 23rd, 1862, upon the occasion of his Quitting the Communion of the Established Church*, London: James Paul, [1862].

[Line, John and George Taplin], *A Letter to all Christians*, [Reading: George Taplin, 1906].

[Line, John and George Taplin], *A Statement regarding the Fellowship of Saints*, [Reading: George Taplin, 1906].

Macdonald, Jas, *The Real Issue in the Present Crisis. Letter to a brother*, [Manchester: W. Mauchan, 1960].

M[ackintosh]., C.H., *The Assembly of God: or, the All-Sufficiency of the Name of Jesus*, Addison, IL: Bible Truth Publishers, 1982.

[Mackintosh, C.H.], *The Great Exhibition*, London: J.K. Campbell, [1851].

Mackintosh, C.H., *Notes on Deuteronomy*, Kilmarnock: John Ritchie, 1946.

[Mackintosh, C.H.], *Practical Reflections on the Life and Times of Elijah, the Tishbite*, Bath: Isaac Bryant, 1850.

[Mackintosh, C.H.] *Sanctification: what is it?*, London: George Morrish, [c.1861][2].

[Mackintosh, C.H.], *Unity: what is it? And am I confessing it?*, London: W.H. Broom and Rouse, n.d.

Marshall, Alexander, *"Holding Fast the Faithful Word." Or, Whither are we Drifting?*, Glasgow: Pickering & Inglis, [c.1910].

Marston, C.H., *The Spirit of God grieved, and the Church of God sleeping*, London: William Yapp, 1855.

Marston, C.H., *Grieving the Spirit; a sermon, preached in Clifton Chapel, Beds, September 14, 1856*, London: Houlston and Stoneman, [1856].

M[aunsell]., T., *"What was I that I could withstand God?" Acts xi.17*, Hereford: W. Yapp, 1852.

Miller, A.B., *What is God's Path for His People?*, Glasgow: Pickering & Inglis, [1912].

Neatby, T., *Two Letters on important subjects relating to Fellowship*, [London: the author, c.1882].

Bibliography 551

[Nelson, Robert], *To Certain Brethren meeting in the name of the Lord Jesus, who have been excommunicating others on account of errors in doctrine*, n.pl.: n.p., [1849].

Nelson, Robert, *Protest against the Proceedings of Mr. John N. Darby*, Tunbridge Wells: n.p., [1852].

Newberry, T., *Jesus in the Midst; or, The Centre of Gathering, and the first principles of the Church of God, as given in Matthew XVI. & XVIII.*, London: W.H. Broom, 1865[2].

Newton, B.W., *Letter to a Friend*, Plymouth: Tract Depot, n.d.

Newton, B.W., *A Remonstrance to the Society of Friends*, London: Nisbet, 1835.

O[liphant]., J.S., *A Letter on Bethesda Fellowship; with an appendix on the true basis of communion*, London: G. Morrish, [1871][2].

O[liphant]., J.S., *The Bethesda Fellowship, 1907*, Southampton: n.p., [1907].

Page, W., *Evangelists and Assemblies*, [London: H.A. Raymond, c.1904].

P[almer]., J.S., *Bethesda: are its Principles and Practice those of Truth and Holiness? A Few Words by an Eye and Ear Witness*, London: James Carter, [1893].

Petter, P.W., *Assembly Service*, London and Edinburgh: Marshall, Morgan & Scott, [1930].

Pickering, H[enr]y, *The Believer's Blue Book*, London: Pickering & Inglis, [1929].

Pickering, H[enr]y, *Which is the Correct Christian Baptism?*, London and Glasgow: Pickering & Inglis, n.d.

von P[oseck]., J.A., *The Word of God, or Private Revelations: Which?*, [Lewisham: the author, 1881].

Powerscourt, Lady, *The Letters & Papers of Lady Powerscourt*, London: Chapter Two, 2004 (first published 1838).

Raven, F.E., *Letters of F.E. Raven and Fragments from his Ministry*, Kingston-on-Thames: Stow Hill Bible and Tract Depot, [1963].

[Reid, William], *The Literature and Mission of the Plymouth Brethren*, London: James Nisbet, 1875 (facsimile reprint London: Chapter Two, n.d.).

Ritchie, John, *In Defence of the Truth: replies to some recent strictures on church subjects. I. The church, (its calling, position, and destiny.) II. The old paths; (or, the things which remain.) III. "The way which they call heresy": (remarks on Mr. W. Blair Neatby's book, "A history of the Plymouth Brethren.")*, Kilmarnock: John Ritchie, n.d.

Ritchie, John, *"The Way which they call Heresy." Remarks on Mr. W. Blair Neatby's book, "A History of the Plymouth Brethren"*, [Kilmarnock: John Ritchie, n.d.].

[Rogers, E.W.], *The Christian Believer and Military Service*, Kilmarnock: John Ritchie, [1937].

Rogers, Olive, et al., *Does God expect less of Women?*, Carlisle: Paternoster for Partnership, 1996.

Rowdon, Harold (ed.), *Church Leaders Handbook*, Carlisle: Paternoster for Partnership, 2002.

Rowdon, Harold (ed.), *Country Reports on the Work of Brethren Churches ... For the International Brethren Conference on Mission 3, held at Selimbar, Romania, 2-7 July 2003*, n.pl.: n.p., [2003].

Rowdon, Harold (ed.), *Declare His Glory: Congregational Worship Today*, Carlisle: Paternoster for Partnership, 1998.

Rowdon, Harold H., *London Bible College: the first 25 years*, Worthing: Henry E. Walter, 1968.

Rowdon, Harold H., *Who are the Brethren and does it matter?*, Exeter: Paternoster on behalf of Christian Brethren Research Fellowship, 1986.

[Savage, John Alfred], *The Epochs and Dispensations of Scripture*, London: Chapter Two, n.d. (first published 1893).

Schofield, A.T., *Christian Sanity*, new ed., London: Marshall Brothers, 1926.

Scott, Walter, *Is the Sword to Devour for Ever?*, Carlton, Nottinghamshire: the author, n.d.[3].

Short, A. Rendle, *A Modern Experiment in Apostolic Missions*, Bristol: W.B. Harris, n.d.

Short, Stephen S., *The Ministry of the Word*, CBRF Occasional Paper No. 1, Bristol: Christian Brethren Research Fellowship, 1965.

Sibthorpe, W.M., *A Defence of the Truth: called for by Neatby's "History of the Plymouth Brethren"*, London: James Carter, 1903[2].

Smith, Hamilton, *The Facts Restated: A Criticism of recent pamphlets defending the principles of Open Brethren*, Weston-super-Mare: the author, 1930.

Smith, Hamilton, *Open Brethren: Their Origin, Principles and Practice*, Weston-super-Mare: the author, 1930.

S[mith]., H[amilton]., *Open Brethren: their Principles and Practice*, Sutton: the author, 1921.

Smith, J. Denham, *Winnowed Grain; or, Selections from the Addresses of the Rev. J. Denham Smith*, London: S.W. Partridge, 1863[3].

Smith, Nathan Delynn, *Roots, Renewal and the Brethren*, Pasadena, CA and Exeter: Hope Publishing and Paternoster, 1987.

Soltau, Henry W., *An Exposition of the Tabernacle, the Priestly Garments, and the Priesthood*, London: Morgan & Chase and W. Yapp, n.d.

Soltau, H.W., *They Found it Written; or, those called by some "the Brethren": Who are they? What are their doctrines?*, Glasgow: Pickering & Inglis, n.d.

S[tanley]., C., *Justification in the Risen Christ; or, "The Faith which was once delivered to the saints"*, London: G. Morrish, n.d.

Stewart, Alex, *Is Christ divided? Or What is Schism. Stewart's Appeal to the Brethren*, London: Pewtress, [c.1860].

Stoney, J.B., *Letters from J.B. Stoney. Second Series*, 3 vols; Kingston-on-Thames: Stow Hill Bible and Tract Depot, n.d.

Stoney, J.B., *A Message to the Quemerford Meeting*, n.pl.: n.p., [1896].

Summerton, Neil, *Local churches for a new century: A strategic challenge*, London: Partnership, 1996.

Summerton, Neil, *A Noble Task: Eldership and Ministry in the Local Church*, Exeter: Paternoster, 1987, 1994[2].

Swan, Charles A., *The Slavery of To-Day or, The Present Position of the Open Sore of Africa*, Glasgow, London and New York: Pickering & Inglis, Alfred Holness and D.T. Bass, n.d.

Tatford, Frederick A. (ed.), *Revival in our Time*, London: Paternoster, 1947.

Tatford, Fred[eric]k A. (ed.), *The Faith: a symposium*, London: Pickering & Inglis, 1952.

T[aylor]., J., Jr, *Notes of Readings in New York 1956 1957 1958, Volume Three*, Kingston-on-Thames: Bible and Gospel Trust, [1974].

[Tregelles, S.P.], *The Blood of the Lamb and the Union of Saints*, London: Central Tract Depôt, n.d.

Trench, G.F., *The Church and its Ministry*, London: James E. Hawkins, n.d.[2].

Trench, George F., *God in Government; or, The Christian's Relation to the State*, London: John F. Shaw, n.d.

Trotter, W., *Bethesda in September 1857; or, An answer to the Question, why do you still stand apart from Bethesda?*, London: George Morrish, [1857].

Trotter, W., *Five Letters on Worship and Ministry in the Spirit*, London: G. Morrish, n.d.

[Turner, W.G. and W.R. Kelsey], *Why not Open Brethrenism?*, n.pl.: n.p., n.d.

Vine, W.E., *The Church and the Churches*, Kilmarnock: John Ritchie, 1964[3] (first published c.1931).

Vine, W.E., *The Divine Plan of Missions*, Waynesboro, GA: Christian Missions Press, n.d. (first published c.1927).

Vine, W.E., *A Guide to Missionary Service*, London: Pickering & Inglis, 1946.

Vine, W.E., *The mistaken Term "The Brethren"*, Bath: Echoes of Service, [1949].

Vine, W.E., *Spiritual Gifts: With special reference to "Tongues" and "Healings"*, Bath: Echoes of Service, n.d.

Walker, Robert, *The Christian and War: An Examination of the Pacifist Position*, Chryston: the author, 1942.

[Wallis, Arthur], *Revival and the Reformation of the Church*, Eastbourne: St Anthony's Hall, [1962].

Wallis, R., *The New Life*, London: Pickering & Inglis, n.d.

Watson, J.B. (ed.), *The Church: a symposium*, London: Pickering & Inglis, 1949.

Watson, J.B., *Devotion to Christ the Need of the Hour*, London: Pickering & Inglis, [1945].

[Wigram, G.V.], *An Appeal to saints that remain still in Bethesda and Salem, as to certain bad doctrine*, London: J.K. Campbell, 1848.

Wigram, George V., *The Englishman's Greek Concordance of the New Testament*, Grand Rapids, MI: Zondervan, 1970 (reprint of 1903[9]).

Wigram, George V., *The Englishman's Hebrew and Chaldee Concordance of the Old Testament*, Grand Rapids, MI: Zondervan, 1970 (reprint of n.d.[5]).

Wigram, G.V., *Hymns for the Poor of the Flock*, London: Central Tract Depôt, 1838.

[Wigram, G.V.], *On Ministry in the Word*, London: Tract Depot, [c.1844].

Wigram, G.V., *The Present Question; 1848-1849*, London: J.K. Campbell, [1849].

W[igram]., G.V., *Remarks on a Paper entitled "A Statement from Christians assembling in the name of the Lord in Ebrington Street, Plymouth"*, [Plymouth: Rowe, 1848].

W[igram, G.V.?]., *Some Remarks on a Recent Letter from Plymouth*, London: n.p., 1846.

Y[oung]., H., *A Plea for the Honour of Christ*, London: J.K. Campbell, n.d.

'Younger Brother, A' [A. Rendle Short], *The Principles of Christians called "Open Brethren"*, Glasgow: Pickering & Inglis, [1913].

1.3. Websites

1.3.1. GENERAL

NB: Almost all Brethren agencies and magazines now have their own websites; I have not listed these unless accessed for this book, as addresses are liable to change.

mikevinson.home.mindspring.com/fellowshipletter.html, Andrew Jukes, 'Second Letter to the Gatherings of Brethren at Leeds and Otley, in reference to a Circular lately put forth by them', accessed 22 July 2003.

www.assemblytestimony.org, *Assembly Testimony*, accessed 7 April 2005.

www.churchesofgod.org, Churches of God website, accessed on various occasions.

www.gospelhall.org.uk/assemblies/list/, Andrew R. Abel, assembly list, 2 January 2001), accessed November 2002; 16 July 2003, accessed 8 March 2005.

www.interlink.org.uk/about_us.htm, Interlink website, accessed 16 June 2004.

www.lordsmeade.freeserve.co.uk/howard.htm, 'The Howard Family', accessed 10 July 2002; Howard Lloyd, 'Reminiscences', 1903/4, accessed 10 July 2002.

www.qhpress.org/quakerpages/qwhp/mirobit.htm, obituaries of Max I. Reich, accessed 10 July 2002.

www.spurgeon.org/s_and_t/pb.htm, Anon., 'The Darby Brethren', *Sword and Trowel*, July 1869, accessed 8 March 2005; C.H. Spurgeon, 'Plymouth Brethren', *Sword and Trowel*, March 1867, accessed 22 May 2001.

1.3.2. LOCAL ASSEMBLIES

NB: only those from which information has been derived for this book (or the associated database) are listed below. Many others may be found by accessing the sites at www.gospelhall.org.uk/assemblies/list and www.partnershipuk.org.

www.allanderchurch.org.uk, Allander Church, Milngavie, accessed 3 April 2005.

www.almachurch.org, Alma Church, Clifton, Bristol, accessed 27 March 2005.

www.bermondsey-gospel-hall.org.uk, Hope Gospel Hall, Bermondsey, accessed 27 March 2005.

www.chilternchurch.org.uk, Chiltern Church, Sutton (Surrey), accessed 3 April 2005.

www.cromwellhall.co.uk, Cromwell Hall, Manchester, accessed 3 April 2005.

www.devachurch.org, Deva Church, Prestatyn, accessed 3 April 2005.

www.elmfield.org, Elmfield Chapel, Harrow, accessed 3 April 2005.

www.fordslane.org.uk, Fords Lane Evangelical Church, Bramhall, accessed 27 March 2005.

www.gospelhallstandrews.org, Gospel Hall, St Andrews, accessed 3 April 2005.

www.grosvenorchurch.org.uk, Grosvenor Church, Barnstaple, accessed 27 March 2005.

www.hasbury.org, Hasbury Christian Fellowship, Halesowen, accessed 27 March 2005.

www.hebronchurch.org.uk, Hebron Church, Aberdeen, accessed 27 March 2005.

www.hebrongospelhall, Hebron Gospel Hall, Bicester, accessed 27 March 2005.

www.helionsgospelhall.co.uk, Gospel Hall, Helions Bumpstead, accessed 7 April 2005.

www.horebchapel.co.uk, Rhosneigr Evangelical Church, accessed 3 April 2005.

www.kingsroadchurch.org, Kings Road Church, Berkhamsted, accessed 27 March 2005.

www.moorlands.org.uk, Moorlands Evangelical Church, Lancaster, accessed 3, 15 April 2005.

www.meadow-way.org.uk, Meadow Way Chapel, Hellesdon, Norwich, accessed 3 April 2005.

www.newcraigs.co.uk, Newcraigs Evangelical Church, Kirkcaldy, accessed 3 April 2005.

www.Portswood.org, Portswood Church, Southampton, accessed 3 April 2005.

www.queenswaychapel.co.uk, Queensway Chapel, Melksham, accessed 3 April 2005.

www.rathminesgospelhall.com, Rathmines Gospel Hall, Dublin, accessed 27 March 2005.

www.scotthall.org.uk, Scott Hall Christian Fellowship, Leeds, accessed 3 April 2005.

www.upperhillstreet.org, Gospel Hall, Upper Hill Street, Coventry, accessed 27 March 2005.

www.woodfordgospelassembly.org, Woodford Gospel Assembly, Armagh, accessed 27 March 2005.

www.woodvale.org.uk, Woodvale Chapel, Ainsdale, accessed 27 March 2005.

2. SECONDARY

2.1. Unpublished

2.1.1. MANUSCRIPT MATERIAL

Andrews, John S., 'Brethren Hymnology', typescript, [1990], personal collection.

Coad, Roy, papers relating to *A History of the Brethren Movement*, CBA Boxes 163-5.

Copinger, H.B., 'Annals: The Lord's Work in the Nineteenth and Twentieth Centuries', transcribed and ed. S. Newman-Norton, typescript, [c.1971], British Orthodox Church Library, London.

Cross, Edwin N., 'Charles Henry Mackintosh 1820-1906', typescript, 2001, Chapter Two archive.

[Cross, Edwin N.], biography of Edward Dennett, typescript, n.d., Chapter Two archive.

[Cross, E.N.], 'Irish Saint and Scholar: A biography of William Kelly', typescript, [c.1985], Chapter Two archive.

Dempster, John A.H., 'Aspects of Brethren Publishing Enterprise in Late Nineteenth-Century Scotland', typescript, 1983, CBA Box 145(1).

Dickson, Neil, 'Ecumenism or Separatism: Brethren Orkney Origins [sic] in the 1860s', paper delivered at the BAHN Conference, Gloucester, 11 July 2003.

Dinnes, Eric, letter to David Brady, 19 December 1983, CBA 7343.

Elwood, Thomas, 'Origin of some assemblies in Belfast', manuscript and typescript transcription, n.d., CBA Box 11(25).

Gribben, Crawford, 'The Worst Sect that a Man can Meet', typescript, n.d. (published as '"The worst sect a Christian man can meet": opposition to the Plymouth Brethren in Ireland and Scotland, 1859-1900', *Scottish Studies Review* 3 (2002), 34-53).

Holthaus, Stephen, 'George Müller in Germany', paper delivered at the BAHN Conference, Wiedenest, Germany, 3 July 2005.

Howard, Michael and Raymond Lloyd, 'Howard and other family connections in 19th century Tottenham', typescript, 1989, CBA Box 212.

L., R., 'Notes on the rise and progress of the work at Hale St., Staines', manuscript, 1921, CBA Box 9 (16).

Johnson, Jean, 'Brethren in Bearwood: the earliest days', paper presented at the BAHN Conference, Gloucester, 11 July 2003.

Macdonald, Norman, 'One Hundred Years of Needed Truth Brethren: A Historical Analysis', typescript, 1993, Chapter Two archive.

Miller, John, Arthur T. Doodson and Rice Thomas Hopkins Horne, 'R.T. Hopkins', typescript, n.d., CBA 13784.

Papers given at the Summer School on the Christian Brethren movement, Regent College, Vancouver, 2-7 July 1990, typescript, [1990], CBA Boxes 30-32.

Roberts, Don, 'A History of the Cardiff Assemblies', typescript, 1992, private collection.

Rowdon, Harold, 'Brethren in Britain, 1945-2000: A Personal Sketch', paper delivered at the BAHN Conference, Gloucester, 11 July 2003.

Rowdon, Harold, [notes on twentieth-century Brethren history], now deposited with the CBA.

Rule, W.M., 'All Ye Are Brethren', typescript, [1931], CBA Box 12/18.

Sayer, David, address on early Brethren in Suffolk, typescript, [1954], personal collection.

Schnieder, Michael, '"The extravagant side of Brethrenism": Studies in the life of Percy Francis Hall (1801-84)', paper delivered at the BAHN Conference, Wiedenest, Germany, 4 July 2005.

Short, S.S., typescript obituary of A.R. Short, private collection.
Stunt, Timothy C.F., 'Some Centralizing Tendencies among open Brethren before the Second World War', typescript, 1999, personal collection.
Thomson, James Ewing, 'Memorandum on the Plymouth Brethren Group, commonly known as the Vernalites', typescript, [2000], CBA Box 140(10).
Trimen, R, 'The Rise and Progress of the Work of the Lord', typescript, [1904], personal collection.
West, Gerald T., '1851 Religious Census: Returns from admitted Brethren', typescript, 2003.
West, Gerald T., 'From Friend to Brother: The spiritual migration of Luke Howard & his family, and the meetings of Friends and Brethren at Tottenham', typescript, July 2003.
West, Gerald T., 'London Assemblies in the 1851 Census', typescript, 2003.

2.1.2. THESES AND DISSERTATIONS
Acheson, Alan R., 'The Evangelicals in the Church of Ireland, 1784-1859', PhD thesis, Queen's University, Belfast, 1967.
Bass, Clarence B., 'The Doctrine of the Church in the Theology of J.N. Darby with special reference to its contribution to the Plymouth Brethren movement', PhD thesis, University of Edinburgh, 1952.
Botton, Kenneth V., 'Regent College: an experiment in theological education', PhD thesis, Trinity International University, 2004.
Buchanan, Andrew D., 'Brethren Revivals 1859-70', BA dissertation, University of Stirling, 1990.
Burnham, Jonathan David, 'The Controversial Relationship Between Benjamin Wills Newton and John Nelson Darby', DPhil thesis, Oxford University, 1999.
Carter, Grayson, 'Evangelical Seceders from the Church of England, c.1800-1850', DPhil thesis, Oxford University, 1990.
Cartmell, John, 'Friends and Brethren in Kendal: A Critical analysis of the Emergence of the Brethren Church in Kendal from the Quaker Meeting Between 1835 and 1858', Honours dissertation, International Christian College, Glasgow, 1999.
Chilcraft, Stephen John, 'Anthony Norris Groves' theory and practice of mission', MA dissertation, Birmingham Christian College, 2003.
Clarke, Julian N., 'The Origins, Development, and Doctrine of the Church of God: a study in Brethren history and hermeneutics', BA (Hons) dissertation, Manchester University, 1984.
Dann, Robert Bernard, 'Anthony Norris Groves (1795-1853): a radical influence on nineteenth-century Protestant church and mission', forthcoming PhD thesis, Liverpool University.
Deng, Shih-An, 'Ideas of the Church in an Age of Reform: The Ecclesiological Thoughts of John Nelson Darby and John Henry Newman, 1824-1850', PhD thesis, University of Minnesota, 1994.
Dickson, Neil T.R., 'The History of The Open Brethren in Scotland 1838-1999', PhD thesis, University of Stirling, 2000.
Dixon, Larry Edward, 'The Pneumatology of John Nelson Darby (1800-1882)', PhD thesis, Drew University, 1985.
Elmore, Floyd Saunders, 'A critical examination of the doctrine of the two peoples of God in John Nelson Darby', ThD dissertation, Dallas Theological Seminary, 1991.

Embley, P.L., 'The Origins and Early Development of the Plymouth Brethren', PhD thesis, St Paul's College, Cheltenham, 1966.

Grass, Timothy George, 'The Church's Ruin and Restoration: The Development of Ecclesiology in the Plymouth Brethren and the Catholic Apostolic Church, c.1825-c.1866', PhD thesis, King's College, London, 1997.

Gray, Clifton Daggett, Jr, 'The Meaning of Membership as Perceived by Plymouth Brethren', PhD dissertation, Boston University Graduate School, 1963.

Johnson, Jean M., 'Early Brethren in Barnstaple and Bearwood: a comparison with Edmund Gosse's *Father and Son*', [Open University] A425 project, n.d.

Krapohl, Robert Henry, 'A search for purity: The controversial life of John Nelson Darby', PhD dissertation, Baylor University, 1988.

McLaren, Ross Howlett, 'The Triple Tradition: The Origin and Development of the Open Brethren in North America', MA thesis, Vanderbilt University, 1982.

Nebeker, Gary Lynn, 'The Hope of Heavenly Glory in John Nelson Darby (1800-1882)', PhD dissertation, Dallas Theological Seminary, 1997.

Orchard, Stephen C., 'English Evangelical Eschatology 1790-1850', PhD thesis, Cambridge University, 1969.

Owen, Carol A., 'Brethren in Warrington', teacher's certificate dissertation, Padgate College, 1973.

Patterson, Mark Rayburn, 'Designing the Last Days: Edward Irving, The Albury Circle, and the Theology of *The Morning Watch*', PhD thesis, King's College, London, 2001.

Shinn, Roger W., 'The Plymouth Brethren and Ecumenical Protestantism', ThD dissertation, Union Theological Seminary, 1968.

Shuff, Roger N., 'From Open to Closed: A Study of the Development of Exclusivism within the Brethren movement in Britain 1828-1953', BD dissertation, Spurgeon's College, 1996.

Shuff, Roger Norman, 'Searching for the True Church: Brethren and Evangelicals in mid-Twentieth-Century England', PhD thesis, University of Wales (Spurgeon's College), 2003.

Smith, A. Christopher, 'British non-Conformists and the Swiss "Ancienne dissidence". The Role of Foreign Evangelicals and J.N. Darby in The Rise and Fall of the "Ancienne Dissidence" in French-Speaking Switzerland: 1810-1850', BD treatise, Baptist Theological Seminary, Rüschlikon, 1979.

Stewart, Kenneth J., 'Restoring the Reformation: British Evangelicalism and the 'Réveil' at Geneva 1816-1849', PhD thesis, New College, Edinburgh, 1992.

Taylor, Malcolm Leonard, '"Born for the Universe": William Kelly and the Brethren Mind in Victorian England (Aspects of the Relationship between Science and Theology)', MPhil thesis, University of Teesside, 1993.

Ward, John Percy, 'The Eschatology of John Nelson Darby', PhD thesis, University of London, 1976.

Wilson, Elizabeth Kay, 'Brethren Attitudes to Authority and Government: with particular reference to pacifism', Master of Humanities dissertation, University of Tasmania, 1994.

2.1.3. CORRESPONDENCE

All letters were to the author.

Rosamunde Codling, 3 January and 30 April 2005.

Brian Currie, 6 January 2003.

Rob Dann, 23 July 2003.
Kenneth Dix, 6 September 2005.
Brian H. Edwards, 4 February 2003.
Nicholas Gray, 28 July 2004.
Roy Hill, 3 December 2002, 14 October 2004, 17 April 2005.
William Neill, 9 January 2003.
Harold Rowdon, 12 February 2004.
T.C.F. Stunt, 28 November 2003, 3 March 2004.
Neil Summerton, 29 December 2004, 8 February 2005.
Edwin Taylor, 7 November 2002.
J.D. Terrell, 21 June 2005.
Max Weremchuk, 11 March 2003.

2.2. Published

2.2.1. LOCAL AND REGIONAL ASSEMBLY HISTORIES

Andrews, Penelope, *The Moorlands Testimony 1897-1980*, Lancaster: n.p., 1980.
Anon., *The 120ᵗʰ Anniversary of the Bath Assembly of Christian Brethren And The 70ᵗʰ Anniversary of Manvers Hall*, n.pl.: n.p., [1957].
Anon., *1900. Bethesda Handbook, for the use of those in Fellowship*, [Bristol], n.p., [1900].
Anon., *Ahorey Gospel Hall Centenary Meetings*, n.pl.: n.p., 1981.
Anon., *Bankfoot Gospel Hall, Wibsey Bank, Bradford 7*, [Bradford: Bankfoot Gospel Hall], n.d.
Anon., *Bearwood Chapel Centenary 1896-1996*, n.pl.: n.p., 1996.
Anon., *Bethesda Hall, Tyn-y-Parc Road, Whitchurch, 50ᵗʰ Anniversary 1932-1982*, Rhiwbina: S.K. Bateman, 1982.
Anon., *Brook Street Chapel, N.17, A Little of our History*, London: n.p., 1963.
Anon., *Castleton Chapel [Mumbles] 1881-1981*, n.pl.: n.p., [1981].
Anon., *A century of witness 1885 to 1985: Ebenezer Hall, Navy Lane Lerwick, Shetland*, Lerwick: n.p., 1985.
Anon., *A Century of Gospel Work and Witness*, [Belfast]: Wright Graphics, 1994.
Anon., *Denne Road Gospel Hall, Horsham, Sussex, Centenary Year 1963*, n.pl.: n.p., [1963].
Anon., *Elim Hall, centenary 1882-1982*, [Glasgow]: n.p., 1982.
Anon., *The Gospel Hall, Neath ... A Brief History (1934-1999)*, n.pl.: n.p., [1999].
Anon., *Gospel Hall, Station Road, Chesham, The Hundred Years 1876-1976*, n.pl.: n.p., n.d.
Anon., *Jubilee Year. Brief History of Merrion Hall, Dublin, 1863-1913*, [Dublin]: n.p, [1913].
Anon., *Mackintosh Evangelical Church. 100 Years of Worship and Witness*, n.pl.: n.p., [1997].
Anon., *Merrion Hall Dublin: One Hundred Years of Witness 1863-1963*, [Dublin: n.p., 1963].
Anon., *Minster Hall, Cardiff 1927-1967*, n.pl.: n.p., n.d.
Anon., *Queen Edith Chapel, Cambridge*, [Cambridge]: n.p., [c.1956].
Anon., *A record of the Lord's work at the Hall, King George Street, Greenwich (1875-1935)*, [London]: n.p., 1935.
Anon., *Roman Road Hall, Motherwell: Centenary 1875-1975*, [Lanark]: n.p., n.d.

Anon., *Seventy-Five Years of Christian Witness 1902-1977*, [London]: Victoria Hall Evangelical Church, [1977].

Anon., *Westcliffe Road Chapel Shipley Centenary 1875-1975*, [Shipley: Westcliffe Road Chapel, 1975].

Anon., *The Work of the Lord in a Surrey Village: a testimony carried out at Lingfield, with a short biographical sketch of Sydney Charles Austin*, London: Pickering & Inglis, n.d. [1925].

[Baigent, John], *The West Side Story: One Hundred Years of Christian Witness 1902-2002*, London: West Side Church, [2002].

Baker, G.C., *Clapton Hall, Alkham Rd, Cazenove Rd, Stoke Newington N16. 1867-1967*, London, n.p., 1967.

Barber, John, *Coleman Street's Children: a history of Colman Street Gospel Hall (Coleman Street Chapel) 1900-1999 and of the Brethren in South-East Essex*, Southend: the author, 2000[2].

Barton, Leonard G., *Bearwood Chapel: One Hundred Years of Witness 1879-1979*, [Halesowen]: n.p., [1979].

Bergin, G. Fred[erick]., *Ten Years After: a sequel to The Autobiography of George Müller*, London: J. Nisbet, 1911[2].

Borland, John S., *History of the Brethren movement in Galston. On the occasion of the jubilee of the opening of the Evangelistic Hall On November 26, 1898*, Kilmarnock: n.p., 1948.

Brady, David and Fred J. Evans, *Christian Brethren in Manchester and District: A History*, London: Heritage Publications, 1997.

Brealey, Douglas, *The Sixty-Sixth Record of the Lords Work on the Blackdown Hills (Devon and Somerset)*, n.pl.: n.p., [1953].

Bresnen, Fred, *Assemblies of Christians in the Wirral*, Leeswood, Flint: Fred and Audrey Bresnen, 2002.

B[rewer]., C., *Early Days in Herefordshire*, n.pl.: n.p., 1893.

[Brown, Matthew S.R. et al.], *Aberdeen Christian Conference Centenary 1874-1973*, Aberdeen: Alex P. Reid, 1972.

Bull, Christopher, *(A short history of) Shrewsbury Chapel, (Redhill: issued to mark the centenary on 3rd December 1988 of the opening of the Chapel)*, [Redhill]: n.p., 1988.

Chapman, Robert, *The Story of Hebron Hall Assembly, Larkhall, 1866-1928. A Short History of the Inception, Progress and Personalities of the Assembly*, Kilmarnock: John Ritchie, 1929.

[Clifford, David], *The centenary of Gerston Chapel, Paignton 1888-1988*, Paignton: n.p., 1988.

Cordiner, F., *Fragments from the Past: An account of people and events in the Assemblies of Northern Scotland*, London: Pickering & Inglis, 1961.

[Crabb, E.W.], *50 Years of Glebe 1935/1985*, [Harrow]: n.p., [1985].

Cracknell, Theo, *From Tent Campaign to Town Chapel*, [Newent, Gloucestershire]: Glebe Gospel Chapel, n.d.

[Currie, David], *"Till the Work on Earth is Done"*, [Belfast]: n.p., [1987].

[Davies, E.T. and D.D. Chrystal], *Bethesda Church, Great George Street, Bristol. A brief account of its formation, history and practice, particularly in relation to pastoral oversight*, [Bristol: Bible & Tract Depôt, 1917].

[Evans, Fred], *A Christian Witness in Stockport 1910-1985*, n.pl.: n.p., [1985].

Fagg, A.J., *Lewisham assembly 1868-1968: a centre of Christian witness*, London: n.p., 1968.

[Farguson, Roy], *Leckwith Anniversary. 40ᵗʰ Anniversary Souvenir*, n.pl: n.p., 1978.

Fergusson, Andrew, *He Sent them Out*, Bromley: Bermondsey and Brook Lane Medical Mission, 1988.

Franks, Don, *The Saltisford Story*, [Warwick]: n.p., [1999].

Fulton, R., *Bethany Hall, Troon: A Hundred Years of Christian Witness*, [Troon]: n.p., 1970.

Glenny, E.B., *New Park Hall, E.H. Glenny memorial, Axe Street, Barking: centenary year 1846-1946: a century of Christian witness*, n.pl: n.p., 1946.

Johns, Stephen, *The Gospel Hall, Tillicoultry: a short history*, Tillicoultry: Gospel Hall, 1990.

Langford, A.W., *An Account of Brethren in Hereford*, [Hereford]: n.p., [1958].

Leonard, Archibald, *A brief history of Christian witness in Betchworth, Surrey, for over 100 years, including some personal recollections of the writer*, Leatherhead: n.p., 1960.

Linton, K. and A.H. Linton, '*I Will Build my Church'. 150 Years of local church work in Bristol*, Bristol: the authors, 1982.

[Pickering, C.J.], *1865-1965: The Half-Yearly Meetings of Christians, Glasgow*, n.pl.: n.p., n.d.

[Pratt, Colin], *West Street Chapel 1888-1988: The History of West Street Chapel, Carshalton*, n.pl.: n.p., [1988].

[Priestley, Eric], *1876-1976*, [London: Endlesham Hall, 1976].

P[robert]., E.C., *Sesquicentenary of Gospel Work and Witness. Adamsdown Gospel Hall, Clyde Street, Cardiff. 1852-2002*, n.pl: n.p., 2002.

[S., R.A.], *Hoylake Chapel: the first 90 years*, Hoylake: n.p., [1989].

Savage, K., *Steadfast in the Faith*, Oxford: Rewley Press, n.d.

Short, E.R., *The Story of "Bristol Bethesda"*, [n.pl.: n.p., 1932].

Short, Stephen Somerset, *Waterloo Hall, Weston-super-Mare: centenary booklet*, [Weston-super-Mare]: n.p., 1977.

Strang, Alex, *Centenary of Hebron Hall Assembly Larkhall 1866-1966*, n.pl.: n.p., [1966].

Surridge, F.W., *The Finest of the Wheat*, Bridford Mills, Devon: n.p., 1950.

Taylor, Josiah E., *Fifty Years of gospel Testimony and witness in Smethwick*, n.pl.: n.p., [1963].

Venables, George J., *The Meeting Room, Church Lane, Stafford*, [Stafford]: n.p., [c.1984].

Venables, George J., *Down Memory Lane with the Christian Brethren of Church Lane Meeting Room, Stafford 1838-1982*, [Stafford]: n.p., [1982].

Walker, Joseph L.G., *Centenary of the Pollokshaws Assembly, 1873-1973*, [Glasgow]: n.p., 1973.

Walker, Stuart and Megan Walker, *The Origins and History of West Road Church, Bury St. Edmunds, from 1847 to the present day*, [Bury St Edmunds: the authors, 2003].

Walkley, Victor G., *A Church set on a Hill: the story of Edgmond Hall, Eastbourne 1872-1972*, Eastbourne: Upperton Press, 1972.

[Warren, Stan], *Lancashire Missionary Conference Centenary 1895-1994: 20ᵗʰ Century Challenge*, n.pl.: n.p., [1994].

White, R.H., *Strength of the Hills: The Story of the Blackdown Hills Mission*, Exeter: Paternoster, 1964.

Woollams, Betty, *Stones of Thanksgiving: High Street Chapel, Hopton, 1854-2000*, n.pl.: Oxfootstone, [2000].

2.2.2. BIOGRAPHIES AND AUTOBIOGRAPHIES OF NON-BRETHREN INDIVIDUALS

Anderson, James, *An Outline of my Life; or selections from a fifty years' religious experience*, Birmingham: Publishing Committee of Churches of Christ, 1912.

Anon., *Brief Memorials of the Rev. B.W. Mathias, late chaplain of Bethesda Chapel*, Dublin: William Curry, Jun., 1842.

[Bellett, Miss L.M.], *Memoir of the Rev. George Bellett, M.A., formerly incumbent of S. Leonard's, Bridgnorth, and late rector of Whitbourne, Herefordshire*, London: J. Masters, 1889.

Braithwaite, Robert, *The Life and Letters of Rev. William Pennefather, B.A.*, London: John F. Shaw, n.d.

Brockie, William, *Memoirs of Arthur Augustus Rees, Minister of the Gospel at Sunderland*, London: Simpkin, Marshall, 1884.

Broomhall, Marshall, *Hudson Taylor: The Man who believed God*, London: China Inland Mission, 1954[17].

Carpenter, Andrew (ed.), *My Uncle John: Edward Stephens's Life of J.M. Synge*, London: Oxford University Press, 1974.

Drummond, Andrew Landale, *Edward Irving and his Circle*, London: James Clarke, [1937].

English, E. Schuyler, *H.A. Ironside: Ordained of the Lord*, Oakland, CA: Western Book and Tract Co., 1946.

Evans, James Joyce, *Memoir and Remains of the Rev. James Harington Evans, late minister of John-Street Chapel*, London: James Nisbet, 1852.

Freer, Frederick Ash, *Edward White: His Life and Work*, London: Elliot Stock, 1902.

Gilbert, Josiah (ed.), *Autobiography and other Memorials of Mrs Gilbert, (formerly Ann Taylor)*, 2 vols; London: Henry S. King, 1874.

Haldane, Alexander, *The Lives of Robert Haldane of Airthrey, and of his Brother, James Alexander Haldane*, London: Hamilton, Adams, 1852[2].

Hewitt, Brian, *Doing a New Thing?*, London: Hodder & Stoughton, 1995.

McGrath, Alister E., *To Know and Serve God: A Biography of James I. Packer*, London: Hodder & Stoughton, 1997.

Madden, Mrs. Hamilton, *Memoir of the late Right Reverend Robert Daly, D.D., Lord Bishop of Cashel*, London: James Nisbet, 1875.

Mozley, T., *Reminiscences: Chiefly of Oriel College and the Oxford Movement*, London: Longmans, Green, 1882.

Murray, Iain H., *David Martyn Lloyd-Jones: The Fight of Faith 1939-1981*, Edinburgh: Banner of Truth, 1990.

Oliphant, Mrs. M.O.W., *The Life of Edward Irving*, London: Hurst & Blackett, [c.1870][5].

Porter, David, *The Man who was 'Q': the true story of Charles Fraser-Smith, the 'Q' wizard of World War II*, Exeter: Paternoster, 1986.

Quinn, James (ed.), *The Religious Belief of James Buchanan*, [Omagh: n.p., 1955].

Radcliffe, Mrs., *Recollections of Reginald Radcliffe*, London: Morgan and Scott, [1895?].

Railton, Nicholas M., *Transnational Evangelicalism: the case of Friedrich Bialloblotzky (1799-1869)*, Arbeiten zur Geschichte des Pietismus, Band 41, Göttingen: Vandenhoeck & Ruprecht, 2002.

Reade, H. Musgrave, *Christ or Socialism? A Human autobiography*, London: Pickering & Inglis, n.d.

Samuel, Leith, *A Man Under Authority: The Autobiography of Leith Samuel*, Fearn, Ross-shire: Christian Focus, 1993.

562 Bibliography

Story, Robert Herbert, *Memoir of the Life of the Rev. Robert Story*, Cambridge: Macmillan, 1862.

Strachan, Gordon, *The Pentecostal Theology of Edward Irving*, London: Darton, Longman & Todd, 1973

Wheeler, Eileen, *The God who Speaks*, [Bexhill]: the author, 2000.

Whittaker, Colin, *Seven Pentecostal Pioneers*, Basingstoke: Marshall Pickering, 1983.

2.2.3. GENERAL WORKS ON BRETHREN HISTORY

Airhart, Phyllis D., '"What Must I Do To Be Saved?" Two Paths to Evangelical Conversion in Late Victorian Canada', *CH* 59 (1990), 372-85.

Bass, Clarence B., *Backgrounds to Dispensationalism: its historical genesis and ecclesiastical implications*, Grand Rapids, MI: Baker Book House, 1977.

Baylis, Robert H., *My People: The Story of Those Christians Sometimes Called Plymouth Brethren*, Wheaton, IL: Harold Shaw, 1995.

Beattie, David J., *Brethren: the story of a great recovery*, Kilmarnock: John Ritchie, 1940.

Beaumont, H., *Seventy Five Years of Telling Yorkshire: a history of the Yorkshire Tent and Bible Carriage Work*, [Wyke, Bradford: the author, c.1974].

Broadbent, E.H., *The Pilgrim Church*, Basingstoke: Pickering & Inglis, 1985 (first published 1931).

Brock, Peter, 'The Peace Testimony of the early Plymouth Brethren', *CH* 53 (1984), 30-45.

Bromley, E.B., *They Were Men Sent from God: A Centenary Record (1836-1936) of Gospel Work in India amongst Telugus in the Godavari Delta and neighbouring parts*, Bangalore: Scripture Literature Press, 1937.

Burton, B.W., *A Further Review of Recovery to the Truth and its Maintenance (1827-1997)*, Lancing, Sussex: Kingston Bible Trust, 1997.

Callahan, James Patrick, *Primitivist Piety: The Ecclesiology of the Early Plymouth Brethren*, Lanham, MD: Scarecrow Press, 1996.

Carron, T.W., *The Christian Testimony through the Ages*, London: Pickering & Inglis, 1955.

Coad, F. Roy, 'Brethren Businessmen and Social Responsibility', in Anon. (ed.), *Christians in the Business World*, Leicester: UCCF Associates for the Historians' Study Group, 1982, 19-25.

Coad, F. Roy, *A History of the Brethren Movement*, Exeter: Paternoster, 1976².

Coad, F. Roy, *Prophetic Developments: with Particular Reference to the Early Brethren Movement*, CBRF Occasional Paper No. 2, Pinner, Middlesex: Christian Brethren Research Fellowship, 1966.

Collingwood, W., *'The Brethren': A Historical Sketch*, Glasgow: Pickering & Inglis, [1899].

Crutchfield, Larry V., *The Origins of Dispensationalism: The Darby Factor*, Lanham, MD: University Press of America, 1992.

C[uendet]., F., *Souvenez-vous de vos Conducteurs*, Vevey: Editions Bibles et Traités Chrétiens, 1966.

Dempster, John A.H., 'Aspects of Brethren Publishing Enterprise in Late Nineteenth-Century Scotland', *Publishing History* 20 (1986), 61-101, extracted from PCI FullText, published by ProQuest Information and Learning Company, 2001.

Dickson, Neil, 'Brethren and Baptists in Scotland', *BQ* 33 (1990), 372-87.

Dickson, Neil, *Brethren in Scotland 1838-2000: A Social Study of an Evangelical Movement*, Carlisle: Paternoster, 2002.

Dickson, Neil, *Modern Prophetesses: Women Preachers in the nineteenth-century Scottish Brethren*, n.pl.: Partnership Publications, n.d. (first published 1993).

Dickson, Neil, 'Open and Closed: Brethren and Their Origins in the North East', in James Porter (ed.), *After Columba - After Calvin: Community and Identity in the religious traditions of North East Scotland*, Aberdeen: Elphinstone Institute, 1999, 151-70.

Dickson, Neil, 'Shut in with Thee': The morning meeting among Scottish Brethren, 1830s-1960s', in R.N. Swanson (ed.), *Studies in Church History* 35, Woodbridge: Boydell & Brewer, 1999, 275-88.

Doodson, A.T. (ed.), *The Search for the Truth of God*, Bradford: Needed Truth Publishing Office, 1947.

Dronsfield, W.R., *The 'Brethren' since 1870*, revised ed.; Ramsgate: Aijeleth Shahar, 1993.

Eaton, Kent, 'Beware the Trumpet of Judgment!: John Nelson Darby and the nineteenth-century Brethren', in Fiona Bowie and Christopher Deacy (eds.), *The Coming Deliverer: Millennial Themes in World Religions*, Cardiff: University of Wales Press, 1997, 119-62.

E[vans]., A[nne]., *The Brethren: As I knew them from 1840 to 1902*, Stroud: n.p., n.d.

Gardiner, A.J., *The Recovery and Maintenance of the Truth*, Kingston-on-Thames: Stow Hill Bible and Tract Depot, [1951, revised ed. 1963].

Giorgi, Lorenzo and Massimo Rubboli (eds.), *Piero Guicciardini 1808-1886. Un Riformatore Religioso nell'europa dell'ottocento. Atti del Convegno di Studie, Firenze, 11-12 Aprile 1986*, Firenze: Leo S. Olschki, 1988.

Gilmore, William, *These Seventy Years*, Kilmarnock: John Ritchie, [1954].

Huebner, R.A., *Precious Truths Revived and Defended through J.N. Darby. Volume One: Revival of Truth, 1826-1845*, Morganville, NJ: Present Truth, 1991.

Huebner, R.A., *Precious Truths Revived and Defended through J.N. Darby. Volume Two: Defense of Truth, 1845-1850*, Morganville, NJ: Present Truth, 1994.

Huebner, R.A., *Precious Truths Revived and Defended through J.N. Darby. Volume Three, Defense of Truth, 1858-1867*, Morganville, NJ: Present Truth, 1995.

Ironside, H.A., *A Historical Sketch of the Brethren Movement*, Grand Rapids, MI: Zondervan, 1942.

Lang, G.H., *God at work on his own lines: as seen in various lands in centuries nineteen and twenty*, Wimborne: the author, 1952.

Lineham, Peter J., *There We Found Brethren: A History of Assemblies of Brethren in New Zealand*, Palmerston North: G.P.H. Society, 1977.

McDowell, Ian, *A Brief History of the "Brethren"*, Epping, NSW: Victory Books, [1968].

McDowell, Ian, 'The Influence of Plymouth Brethren upon Victorian Society and Religion', *EQ* 55 (1983), 211-22.

Miller, Andrew, *The Brethren: a brief sketch of their Origin, Progress and Testimony*, London: G. Morrish, [c.1879].

Miller, Andrew (revised by G.C. Willis), *"The Brethren" (commonly so-called): a brief sketch*, Kowloon, HK: Christian Book Room, [1963].

Miller, Andrew, *Short Papers on Church History*, 3 vols; London: W.G. Wheeler, [1873-8].

Mills, Brian, *A Story to Tell: Evangelism in the Twentieth Century*, Carlisle: OM, 1999.

[Mills, B.R.], *Yesterday Today: Counties Evangelistic Work 75th anniversary*, Reading: Counties Evangelistic Work, [1974].

[Moede, G.F.], 'Assemblies of Brethren', *Ecumenical Review* 24 (1972), 130-44.

Monkhouse, Patrick, *The Brethren [Reprinted from] "The London Evening Standard"* ... *19th April, 1937*, Cardiff: Big Tent Missions, 1945.

Neatby, William Blair, *A History of the Plymouth Brethren*, London: Hodder & Stoughton, 1901, 1902[2] (all references are to the earlier edition).

Nebeker, Gary L., 'John Nelson Darby and Trinity College Dublin: A Study in Eschatological Contrasts', *Fides et Historia* 34 (2002), 87-109.

Newton, John W., *The Story of the Pilgrim Preachers and their 24 Tours throughout Great Britain: With many Stirring Scenes, Genuine Conversions, Peculiar Positions, and Soul-stirring Experiences*, London: Pickering & Inglis, [1938].

Newton, K.J., *Brethren Missionary Work in Mysore State*, CBRF Occasional Paper No. 6, Pinner, Middlesex: CBRF, 1975.

Noel, Napoleon (ed. William F. Knapp), *A History of the Brethren*, 2 vols; London: Chapter Two, 1993 [1936].

[Park, J.J.], *The Churches of God: their Origin and Development in the 20th Century*, Leicester: Hayes Press, [1987].

Petter, P.W., *The Story of The Pilgrim Preachers and their Message*, London and Edinburgh: Marshall, n.d.

Porter, David, *So much more: the story of over forty years camping with the Merseyside Christian Youth Camps*, [Kirkby]: Merseyside Assemblies Youth Camps Trust, [1986].

Rennie, Ian S., 'Aspects of Christian Brethren Spirituality', in Loren Wilkinson (ed.), *Alive to God: Studies in Christian Spirituality presented to J.I. Packer*, Downers Grove, IL: IVP, 1992, 190-208.

'Roborough' [Florence Philp], *"Everyday Saints." Sketches from Life of some of my Friends among the "Open Brethren"*, n.pl.: n.p., [1919].

Ronco, Daisy D., *Risorgimento and the Free Italian Churches, now Churches of the Brethren*, Bangor, Wales: privately printed, 1996.

Rowdon, Harold H., 'The Brethren Concept of Sainthood', *VE* 20 (1990), 91-107.

Rowdon, Harold H., 'The Concept of Living by Faith', in Anthony Billington, Tony Lane and Max Turner (eds.), *Mission and Meaning: Essays Presented to Peter Cotterell*, Carlisle: Paternoster, 1995, 339-56.

Rowdon, Harold H., 'The Early Brethren and Baptism', *VE* 11 (1979), 55-64.

Rowdon, Harold H., *The Origins of the Brethren 1825-1850*, London: Pickering & Inglis, 1967.

Rowdon, Harold H., 'A Nineteenth-Century Nestorius', *VE* 1 (1962), 60-75.

Rowdon, Harold H., 'Secession from the Established Church in the Early Nineteenth Century', *VE* 3 (1964), 76-88.

Rowdon, Harold (ed.), *Ten Changing Churches*, Carlisle: Paternoster for Partnership, 1999.

Shuff, Roger, *Searching for the True Church: Brethren and Evangelicals in mid-Twentieth-Century England*, Carlisle: Paternoster, 2005.

[Stokes, G.T.], [review of a number of Brethren writings], *London Quarterly Review* 27 (1866), 1-37.

Stunt, T.C.F., *Early Brethren and the Society of Friends*, CBRF Occasional Paper No. 3, Pinner, Middlesex: Christian Brethren Research Fellowship, 1970.

Stunt, T.C.F., 'Two Nineteenth-Century Movements', *EQ* 37 (1965), 221-31.

Stunt, W.T. et al., *Turning the World Upside Down*, Bath: Echoes of Service, 1972[2].

Tatford, Fred[eric]k A., *That the World may Know: Volume 8. West European Evangel*, Bath: Echoes of Service, 1985.

[Terrell, J.D. and J.M. Gault], *The Search for the Truth of God: The New Testament answer in Churches of God*, Leicester: Hayes Press, 1992[2].

Trotter, W., *The Origin of (so-called) Open-Brethrenism. A Letter by W. Trotter giving the Whole Case of Plymouth and Bethesda*, Lancing, Sussex: Kingston Bible Trust, [1987].

Veitch, Thomas Stewart, *The Story of the Brethren Movement*, London: Pickering & Inglis, [1933].

Ware, George W., *A Review of Certain Contentions for the Faith (Jude 3)*, [London: L.W. Haverly, n.d.].

Welch, C.E., 'The First Plymouth Brethren Chapel', *Devon and Cornwall Notes & Queries* 29 (1962-4), 9.

Wertheimer, Douglas, 'The Identification of some characters and incidents in Gosse's "Father and Son"', *Notes and Queries* n.s. 23 (1976), 4-11.

Wilson, Bryan R. *"The Brethren": a current sociological appraisal*, Sheffield: Duplicopy, 1981 ([Oxford]: n.p., [2000][2]).

Wilson, Bryan R. (ed.), *Patterns of Sectarianism: Organisation and Ideology in Social and Religious Movements*, London: Heinemann, 1967.

2.2.4. OTHER BACKGROUND WORKS

Acheson, Alan R., *A History of the Church of Ireland, 1691-1996*, Blackrock and Dublin: Columba Press and APCK, 1997.

Akenson, Donald Harman, *The Church of Ireland: Ecclesiastical Reform and Revolution, 1800-1885*, New Haven and London: Yale University Press, 1971.

Anon., *Letters concerning their Principles and Order from Assemblies of Believers in 1818-1820*, Glasgow: Pickering & Inglis, 1889.

Barclay, Oliver, *Evangelicalism in Britain 1935-1995: a personal sketch*, Leicester: IVP, 1997.

Barclay, Oliver (ed.), *Pacifism and War*, Leicester: IVP, 1984.

Barclay, Oliver R., *Whatever happened to the Jesus Lane lot?*, Leicester: IVP, 1977.

Baxter, Robert, *A Narrative of Facts, Characterizing the Supernatural Manifestations, in Mr. Irving's Congregation, and Other Individuals, in England and Scotland and Formerly in the Writer Himself*, London: James Nisbet, 1833.

Baxter, Robert, *Irvingism, in its Rise, Progress, and Present State*, London: James Nisbet, 1836.

Bebbington, D.W., *Evangelicalism in Modern Britain: A History from the 1730s to the 1980s*, London: Unwin Hyman, 1989.

Bebbington, D.W. (ed.), *The Baptists in Scotland: A History*, Glasgow: Baptist Union of Scotland, 1988.

Bebbington, David, *Holiness in Nineteenth-Century England: The 1998 Didsbury Lectures*, Carlisle: Paternoster, 2000.

Best, G.F.A., 'The Evangelicals and the Established Church in the Early Nineteenth Century', *Journal of Theological Studies* 10 (1959), 63-78.

Best, Geoffrey, *Mid-Victorian Britain 1851-75*, London: Fontana, 1979.

Bicknell, Richard, 'In memory of Christ's Sacrifice: Roots and Shoots of Elim's Eucharistic Expression', *Journal of the European Pentecostal Theological Association* 17 (1997), 59-89.

Billington, Louis, 'The Churches of Christ in Britain: A Study in nineteenth-Century Sectarianism', *Journal of Religious History* 8 (1974), 21-48.

Bloxham, V. Ben, James R. Moss and Larry C. Porter (eds.), *Truth Will Prevail: The Rise of the Church of Jesus Christ of Latter-day Saints in the British Isles 1837-1987*, Cambridge: Church of Jesus Christ of Latter-day Saints, 1987.

Bosch, David J., *Transforming Mission: Paradigm Shifts in Theology of Mission*, Maryknoll, NY: Orbis, 1991.

Bowen, Desmond, *The Protestant Crusade in Ireland 1800-70*, Dublin: Gill & Macmillan, 1978.

Bowman, John Wick, 'The Bible and Modern Religions: II. Dispensationalism', *Interpretation* 10 (1956), 170-87.

Bradley, Ian, *The Call to Seriousness: The Evangelical Impact on the Victorians*, London: Jonathan Cape, 1976.

Briggs, Asa, *The Age of Improvement 1783-1867*, London: Longmans, 2000[2].

Brockett, Allan, *Nonconformity in Exeter 1650-1875*, Manchester: Manchester University Press for the University of Exeter, 1962.

Brooke, Richard Sinclair, *Recollections of the Irish Church*, London: Macmillan, 1877.

Brown, Roger L., *The Welsh Evangelicals*, Tongwynlais, Cardiff: Tair Eglwys Press, 1986.

Brown, Stewart J., *The National Churches of England, Ireland, and Scotland 1801-1846*, Oxford: Oxford University Press, 2001.

Bulteel, H.B., *A Sermon on I Corinthians II.12 Preached before the University of Oxford, at St. Mary's on Sunday, February 6, 1831*, Oxford, W. Baxter, 1831.

Burleigh, J.H.S., *A Church History of Scotland*, London: Oxford University Press, 1960.

Cardale, J.B., 'On the Extraordinary Manifestations at Port Glasgow', *Morning Watch* 2 (1830), 869-73.

Carter, Grayson, *Anglican Evangelicals: Protestant Secessions from the Via Media, c.1800-1850*, Oxford: Oxford University Press, 2001.

Cashdollar, Charles D., *A Spiritual Home: Life in British and American Reformed Congregations, 1830-1915*, University Park, PA: Pennsylvania State University Press, 2000.

Chadwick, Owen, *The Victorian Church. Part I: 1829-1859*, London: SCM, 1971[3].

Chadwick, Owen, *The Victorian Church. Part II: 1860-1901*, London: A. & C. Black, 1972[2].

Cobbett, William (ed. George Woodcock), *Rural Rides*, Harmondsworth, Middlesex: Penguin, 1967.

Cottle, Joseph, *Strictures on the Plymouth Antinomians*, London: T. Cadell, 1823.

Cunningham, Valentine, *Everywhere Spoken Against: Dissent in the Victorian Novel*, Oxford: Clarendon Press, 1975.

Davies, C. Maurice, *Unorthodox London: or, phases of religious life in the metropolis*, London: Tinsley Brothers, 1876[2].

Davies, E.T., *A New History of Wales: Religion and Society in the Nineteenth Century*, Llandybie, Dyfed: Christopher Davies, 1981.

Dix, Kenneth, *Strict and Particular: English Strict and Particular Baptists in the nineteenth century*, Didcot: Baptist Historical Society, 2001.

Dobbie, Ian, *Sovereign Service: The Story of SASRA 1838-1988*, Aldershot: SASRA, 1988.

[Dowglass, T.], *Man's Responsibility for the gift of a Saviour, and the responsibility of the church for the gift of the Holy Ghost*, Totnes: S. Hannaford, 1835.

Drummond, A.L. and James Bulloch, *The Church in Victorian Scotland 1843-1874*, Edinburgh: St Andrew Press, 1975.
Edwards, David L., *Christian England*, revised ed., London: Fount, 1989.
Fiedler, Klaus, *The Story of Faith Missions*, Oxford: Regnum Lynx, 1994.
Fielder, Geraint, *Lord of the Years*, Leicester: IVP, 1988.
Flegg, Columba Graham, *Gathered Under Apostles: A Study of the Catholic Apostolic Church*, Oxford: Clarendon, 1992.
Forster, Roger (ed.), *Ten New Churches*, n.pl.: MARC Europe, 1986.
Freeman-Attwood, Marigold, *Leap Castle: a place and its people*, Wilby, Norwich: Michael Russell, 2001.
Froom, L.E., *The Prophetic Faith of our Fathers*, 4 vols; Washington, D.C.: Review & Herald, [1946].
Gilley, Sheridan and W.J. Sheils (eds.), *A History of Religion in Britain: Practice and Belief from Pre-Roman Times to the Present*, Oxford: Blackwell, 1994.
Gorsky, Martin, *Patterns of Philanthropy: Charity and Society in nineteenth-Century Bristol*, Woodbridge: Royal Historical Society / Boydell Press, 1999
Grass, Tim, '"The Restoration of a Congregation of Baptists": Baptists and Irvingism in Oxfordshire', *BQ* 37 (1998), 283-97.
Gribben, Crawford and Timothy C.F. Stunt (eds.), *Prisoners of Hope? Aspects of Evangelical Millennialism in Britain and Ireland, 1800-1880*, Carlisle: Paternoster, 2005.
Griffin, Stanley C., *A Forgotten Revival: East Anglia and NE Scotland – 1921*, Bromley: Day One, [1992].
Harris, Harriet A., *Fundamentalism and Evangelicals*, Oxford: Clarendon, 1998.
Harrison, J.F.C., *Early Victorian Britain, 1832-51*, Glasgow: Fontana, 1988.
Harrison, J.F.C., *Late Victorian Britain, 1870-1901*, Glasgow: Fontana, 1990.
Hastings, Adrian, *A History of English Christianity 1920-1990*, London and Philadelphia: SCM and Trinity Press International, 1991.
Heasman, Kathleen, *Evangelicals in Action: An Appraisal of their Social Work in the Victorian Era*, London: Geoffrey Bles, 1962.
Hempton, David and Myrtle Hill, *Evangelical Protestantism in Ulster Society 1740-1890*, London and New York: Routledge, 1992.
Hempton, David N., 'Evangelicalism and Eschatology', *JEH* 31 (1980), 179-94.
Hilton, Boyd, *The Age of Atonement: The Influence of Evangelicalism on Social and Economic Thought, 1785-1865*, Oxford: Clarendon, 1988.
Hocken, Peter, *Streams of Renewal: The Origins and Early Development of the Charismatic Movement in Great Britain*, revised ed., Exeter: Paternoster, 1997.
Holmes, Janice, *Religious Revivals in Britain and Ireland 1859-1905*, Dublin: Irish Academic Press, 2000.
Hoppen, K. Theodore, *The Mid-Victorian Generation 1846-1886*, New Oxford History of England, Oxford: Oxford University Press, 1998.
Hylson-Smith, Kenneth, *The Churches in England from Elizabeth I to Elizabeth II. Volume III: 1833-1998*, London: SCM, 1998.
Inglis, K.S., *Churches and the Working Classes in Victorian England*, London and Toronto: Routledge & Kegan Paul and Toronto University Press, 1963.
Irving, Edward, *For Missionaries after the Apostolical School: A Series of Orations*, London: Hamilton, Adams, 1825.
Irving, Edward, *Narrative of Facts connected with recent manifestations of Spiritual Gifts*, reprinted from *Fraser's Magazine*, London: James Fraser, 1832.

Isichei, Elizabeth, *Victorian Quakers*, Oxford: Oxford University Press, 1970.

Jeffrey, Kenneth S., *When the Lord Walked the Land: The 1858-62 Revival in the North East of Scotland*, Carlisle: Paternoster, 2002.

Jeremy, David J., *Capitalists and Christians: Business Leaders and the Churches in Britain, 1900-1960*, Oxford: Clarendon, 1990.

Johnson, Douglas, *Contending for the Faith: A History of the Evangelical Movement in the Universities and Colleges*, Leicester: IVP, 1979.

Kay, William K., *Inside Story: A History of British Assemblies of God*, Mattersey: Mattersey Hall Publishing, 1990.

Kay, William K., *Pentecostals in Britain*, Carlisle: Paternoster, 2000.

Kent, John, *Holding the Fort: Studies in Victorian Revivalism*, London: Epworth, 1978.

Lillie, David, *Beyond Charisma*, Exeter: Paternoster, 1981.

Lillie, David, *Restoration: Is this still on God's programme?*, Exton, Devon: the author, [1994].

Lillie, D.G., *Tongues under Fire*, London: Fountain Trust, 1966.

Lovegrove, Deryck W. (ed.), *The Rise of the Laity in Evangelical Protestantism*, London: Routledge, 2002.

McDowell, R.B. and D.A. Webb, *Trinity College Dublin 1592-1952: An Academic History*, Cambridge: Cambridge University Press, 1982.

McLeod, Hugh, *Class and Religion in the Late Victorian City*, London: Croom Helm, 1974.

Macpherson, D., *The Great Rapture Hoax*, Fletcher, NC: New Puritan Library, 1983.

Macpherson, D., *The Unbelievable Pre-Trib Origin*, Kansas City: Heart of America Bible Society, 1973.

Magee, W., *A Charge Delivered at His Triennial and Metropolitan Visitation in St. Patrick's Cathedral, on Tuesday the 10th of October 1826*, Dublin: R. Graisberry, 1827.

Murray, Iain H. (ed.), *D. Martyn Lloyd-Jones: Letters 1919-1981*, Edinburgh: Banner of Truth, 1994.

Murray, Iain H., *The Puritan Hope: A study in Revival and the interpretation of Prophecy*, London: Banner of Truth, 1971.

Neatby, W. Blair, *The Christian and War*, London: Friends' Tract Association for Friends' Home Mission and Extension Committee, 1915.

Nee, Watchman, *The Normal Christian Church Life*, Kowloon: Hong Kong Church Book Room, 1962.

Newton, B.W., *Ancient Truths Respecting the Deity and True Humanity of the Lord Jesus. Christ, Our Suffering Surety. Note on 1 Peter ii. 24*, London: Sovereign Grace Advent Testimony, 1893[2].

Newton, Benjamin Wills, *Catholicity, in a dispensation of failure, a sure token of apostasy*, London and Ryde: Houlston and Arthur Andrews, 1892[3].

Newton, B.W., *Occasional Papers on Scriptural Subjects*, vol. 4, London: Houlston & Wright, 1866.

Newton, Benjamin Wills, *Remarks on a Tract entitled "Justification in the Risen Christ"*, London: Houlston, 1896[2].

Notman, Alison, *Faith & Vision: The Moorlands Story*, Sopley, Dorset: Moorlands College, [1997].

Nott, Louis P., *Gideon 1810 to 1910: The Vicissitudes of a City Chapel*, Bristol: n.p., 1909.

Orr, J. Edwin, *The Second Evangelical Awakening in Britain*, London and Edinburgh: Marshall, Morgan & Scott, 1949.

Patterson, Mark and Andrew Walker, '"Our Unspeakable Comfort": Irving, Albury and the origins of the pre-tribulation rapture', in Stephen Hunt (ed.), *Christian Millenarianism from the Early Church to Waco*, London: Hurst, 2001, 98-115.

Piggin, Stuart and John Roxborogh, *The St. Andrews Seven*, Edinburgh: Banner of Truth, 1985.

Price, Charles and Ian Randall, *Transforming Keswick*, Carlisle: OM, 2000.

Rae, John, *Conscience and Politics: The British Government and Conscientious Objection to Military Service 1916-1919*, London: Oxford University Press, 1970.

Randall, Ian, *Educating Evangelicalism: The origins, development and impact of London Bible College*, Carlisle: Paternoster, 2000.

Randall, Ian M., *Evangelical Experiences: A Study in the Spirituality of English Evangelicalism 1918-1939*, Carlisle: Paternoster, 1999.

Randall, Ian and David Hilborn, *One Body in Christ: The History and Significance of the Evangelical Alliance*, Carlisle: Paternoster, 2001.

Read, Gordon and David Jebson, *A Voice in the City*, Liverpool: Liverpool City Mission, [1979].

Reynolds, J.S., *The Evangelicals at Oxford 1735-1871: a record of an unchronicled movement, with the record extended to 1905*, Appleford, Oxfordshire: Marcham Manor Press, 1975.

Robinson, William, *The History and Antiquities of the Parish of Tottenham*, 2 vols; London: Nicholls, 1840[2].

Rosman, Doreen M., *Evangelicals and Culture*, London and Canberra: Croom Helm, 1984.

Rosman, Doreen, *The Evolution of the English Churches 1500-2000*, Cambridge: Cambridge University Press, 2003.

Rouse, Ruth and Stephen Charles Neill (eds.), *A History of the Ecumenical Movement 1517-1948*, London: SPCK, 1954.

Rowell, Geoffrey, *Hell and the Victorians: A study of the nineteenth-century theological controversies concerning eternal punishment and the future life*, Oxford: Clarendon, 1974.

Russell, G.W.E., *The Household of Faith: Portraits and Essays*, London and Oxford: A.R. Mowbray, 1906[3].

Sandeen, E.R., *The Roots of Fundamentalism: British and American Millenarianism 1800-1930*, Chicago: University of Chicago Press, 1970.

Scotland, Nigel, *Charismatics and the New Millennium: The impact of Charismatic Christianity from 1960 into the new millennium*, revised ed., Guildford: Eagle, 2000.

Scott, P.G., 'Richard Cope Morgan, Religious Periodicals, and the Pontifex Factor', *Victorian Periodicals Newsletter*, 16 (June 1972), 1-14.

Sell, Alan P.F., *Church Planting: A Study of Westmorland Nonconformity*, Worthing: H.E. Walter, 1986.

Smith, Ian, *Tin Tabernacles: Corrugated Iron Mission Halls, Churches & Chapels of Britain*, [Pembroke]: Camrose Organisation, 2004.

Smout, T.C., *A History of the Scottish People 1560-1830*, London: Fontana, 1985.

Snell, K.D.M. and Paul S. Ell, *Rival Jerusalems: The Geography of Victorian Religion*, Cambridge: Cambridge University Press, 2000.

Stewart, James Haldane, *Thoughts on the Importance of Special Prayer for the General Outpouring of the Holy Spirit*, London: Hatchard, 1821.

Strachan, Gordon, *The Pentecostal Theology of Edward Irving*, London: Darton, Longman & Todd, 1973.

Stanley, Brian, *The Bible and the Flag: Protestant missions and British imperialism in the nineteenth and twentieth centuries*, Leicester: Apollos, 1990.

Stunt, Timothy C.F., *From Awakening to Secession: Radical Evangelicals in Switzerland and Britain 1815-35*, Edinburgh: T. & T. Clark, 2000.

Stunt, Timothy C.F., 'Geneva and British Evangelicals in the early nineteenth century', *JEH* 32 (1981), 32-46.

Tanner, Marcus, *Ireland's Holy Wars: The Struggle for a Nation's Soul, 1500-2000*, New Haven and London: Yale University Press, 2001.

Tidball, Derek J., *Who are the Evangelicals? Tracing the roots of the modern movements*, London: Marshall Pickering, 1994.

Toon, Peter, *Evangelical Theology 1833-1856: A Response to Tractarianism*, Marshall, Morgan & Scott, 1979.

Townsend, W.J., H.B. Workman and George Eayrs (eds.), *A New History of Methodism*, London: Hodder and Stoughton, 1909.

Tregelles, S.P., *The Hope of Christ's Second Coming: How is it Taught in Scripture? And Why?*, London: Samuel Bagster, 1886².

Trotter, W., *The Justice and Forbearance of the Methodist New Connexion Conference as they were illustrated in the case of W. Trotter, giving a complete account of his trial before the Halifax Conference, containing a full answer to sundry tracts or pamphlets published by J.H. Robinson and T. Allin, etc*, London: R. Groombridge, 1841.

Vidler, Alec R., *The Church in an Age of Revolution: 1789 to the present day*, The Pelican History of the Church 5, Harmondsworth, Middlesex: Pelican, 1974.

Walker, Andrew, *Restoring the Kingdom: The Radical Christianity of the House Church Movement*, revised ed., Guildford: Eagle, 1998.

Walker, John (ed. William Burton), *Essays and Correspondence, chiefly on Scriptural Subjects*, London: Longman, Orme, Brown, Green & Longman's, 1838.

Wellings, Martin, *Evangelicals Embattled: Responses of Evangelicals in the Church of England to Ritualism, Darwinism and Theological Liberalism, 1890-1930*, Carlisle: Paternoster, 2003.

Wilson, Bryan, *Religious Sects: a sociological study*, London: Weidenfeld and Nicolson, 1970.

Wolffe, John (ed.), *Evangelical Faith and Public Zeal: Evangelicals and Society in Britain 1780-1980*, London: SPCK, 1995.

Wright, N.T., *Evangelical Anglican Identity: the connection between Bible, Gospel and Church*, Oxford: Latimer House, 1980.

2.2.5. REFERENCE WORKS

Anderson, Gerald H. (ed.), *Biographical Dictionary of Christian Missions*, Grand Rapids, MI: William B. Eerdmans, 1999.

Anon., *Who's Who 2003: An annual biographical dictionary*, London: A. & C. Black, 2003.

Anon., *Who Was Who 1971-1980*, London: A. & C. Black, 1989².

Anon., *Who Was Who 1991-1995*, London: A. & C. Black, 1996.

Brierley, Peter (ed.), *UK Christian Handbook Religious Trends No. 4, 2003/2004*, London: Christian Research, 2003.

Burgess, Stanley M., Gary B. McGee, and Patrick H. Alexander (eds.), *Dictionary of Pentecostal and Charismatic Movements*, Grand Rapids, MI: Zondervan, 1989.

Cameron, Nigel M. de S. (ed.), *Dictionary of Scottish Church History and Theology*, Edinburgh: T. & T. Clark, 1993.

Cook, Chris and John Stevenson, *The Longman Handbook of Modern British History 1714-1987*, Harlow: Longman, 1988[2].

Cross, F.L. and E.A. Livingstone (eds.), *The Oxford Dictionary of the Christian Church*, Oxford: Oxford University Press, 1997[3].

Douglas, J.D. (ed.), *The New International Dictionary of the Christian Church*, Exeter: Paternoster, 1978[2].

Ehlert, Arnold D., *Brethren Writers: A Checklist with an Introductory Essay and Additional Lists*, Grand Rapids, MI: Baker Book House, 1969.

Jeremy, David J. (ed.), *Dictionary of Business Biography: a biographical dictionary of business leaders active in Britain in the period 1860-1980*, 6 vols, London: Butterworths, 1984-6.

Larsen, Timothy (ed.), *Biographical Dictionary of Evangelicals*, Leicester: IVP, 2003.

Lewis, Donald M. (ed.), *The Blackwell Dictionary of Evangelical Biography 1730-1860*, 2 vols, Oxford: Blackwell, 1995.

Stephen, Sir Leslie and Sir Sidney Lee (eds.), *Dictionary of National Biography*, 63 vols, London: Oxford University Press, 1885-1901.

Wraight, Heather (ed.), *UK Christian Handbook 2004/5*, Eltham, London: Christian Research, 2004.

2.3. Websites

bristolinformation.co.uk/srch/srchit.asp?list=list&gdoc=rs&howmany=200, 'Bristol Information', accessed 16 January 2005.

rylibweb/man.ac.uk/data2/spcoll/cba/, Christian Brethren Archive, accessed on various occasions.

www.ayrshiregospeloutreach.org.uk/, Ayrshire Gospel Outreach, accessed 3 April 2005.

www.bibles-direct.com, R.L. Allan & Son Publishers, accessed 20 April 2005.

www.british-history.ac.uk/, 'British History Online: The Victoria History of the Counties of England' (various pages), accessed 16-17 January 2005.

www.globalserve.net/~mybrethren/history/hy12stow.htm, G.A. Rainbow, 'The Stow Hill Depot – A Historical Sketch', accessed 15 February 2003.

www.gospelcom.net/lcwe/statements/covenant.html, 'The Lausanne Covenant', accessed 8 December 2004.

www.northwestpartnership.com, 'The North West Partnership of Local Churches', accessed 15 April 2005.

www.ntsayrshire.org.uk/AyrshireStats/Ch16Sectn04.php, 'The Third Statistical Account of Scotland: Ayrshire', accessed 16 January 2005.

www.partnershipuk.org/pdf/SCCBrethren%2004.04.pdf, Peter Brierley, 'The Christian Brethren in Scotland', accessed 14 January 2005.

www.partnershipuk.org/pdf/ECASBrethren.pdf, Peter Brierley, 'The Christian Brethren in the 1998 English Church Attendance Survey', accessed 14 January 2005.

www.preciousseed.org/assemblyhistories, brief histories of a number of assemblies, accessed 6 November 2002.

www.smr.herefordshire.gov.uk/post-medieval/chapels/religious_census2.htm, untitled summary table of 1851 Religious Census returns, accessed 16 January 2005.

www.statistics.gov.uk/articles/economic_trends/ET604CPI1750.pdf, Jim O'Donoghue, Louise Goulding, and Grahame Allen, 'Consumer Price Inflation since 1750' (from *Economic Trends* 604 (March 2004), 38-46), accessed 20 January 2005.

2.4. Electronic Resources

Matthew, H.C.G. and Brian Harrison (eds.), *The Oxford Dictionary of National Biography*, Oxford: Oxford University Press, 2004.

General Index